PENGUIN BOOKS

# THE MERITOCRACY TRAP

Daniel Markovits is the Guido Calabresi Professor of
Law at Yale Law School and the founding director
of the Center for the Study of Private Law.

---

## Praise for *The Meritocracy Trap*

"Ambitious and disturbing . . . Markovits forcefully interrupts the comfortable
bath of self-flattery in which our well-graduated professionals pass their hours."
     —*The New York Times Book Review*

"An imaginative new book that will prompt endless debate in the faculty lounge,
the country-club tap room, and the family dinner table . . . a book that will jolt
and provoke the reading public . . . Markovits produces shocking figures about
the yawning wealth gap on leafy campuses." —*The Boston Globe*

"*The Meritocracy Trap* is a work in the line of Thorstein Veblen's *The Theory of
the Leisure Class* (1899), John Kenneth Galbraith's *The Affluent Society* (1958)
and Michael Harrington's *The Other America* (1962)."
     —*The Wall Street Journal*

"*The Meritocracy Trap* defines a central issue of our age: the rise of new elites
who, unlike their aristocratic forebears, seem to have the moral high ground.
The system is rigged in a different way, but it's still rigged all right.
     —*The Sunday Times*

"We've been waiting for the Big Book that explains America's wrong turn. Daniel
Markovits has supplied it. *The Meritocracy Trap* is a sociological masterpiece—a
damning indictment of parenting and schools, an unflattering portrait of a ruling
class and the economy it invented. Far too many readers will recognize themselves
in his brilliant critique, and they will feel a rush of anger, a pang of regret, and a
burning desire to remake the system."
     —Franklin Foer, author of *World Without Mind*

"Provocatively weighing in on growing inequality, Daniel Markovits weaves a disturbing tale of merit and social division. Pulling no punches, he warns us that meritocracy is a trap, fetishizing certain skills and endless assessments. Markovitz shows—in exquisite detail—the perverse link between an upper-class education and elite jobs and how together they enrich the few, while devaluing and demoralizing the rest." —Jerry Brown, former governor of California

"At once wide-ranging and rigorous, subtle and penetrating, Markovits's book is revelatory both in its particulars and in its big picture. Anyone who wants to argue about the merits of meritocracy must take account of this book."
—Kwame Anthony Appiah, professor of philosophy and law, New York University; author of *The Lies That Bind: Rethinking Identity*

"Daniel Markovits has written a bold, brave critique of the meritocracy-backed version of inequality that prevails today. He argues persuasively that meritocracy is destructive and demoralizing for winners and losers alike. Challenging conventional wisdom, Markovits shows that technological change is not a fact of nature that happens to increase the value of highly credentialed workers; instead, the prevalence of credentialed elites calls forth technologies that bias the labor market in their favor and hollow out the middle class. This is a splendid book that should prompt soul-searching among meritocrats."
—Michael J. Sandel, author of *What Money Can't Buy: The Moral Limits of Markets*

"The system is rigged. And the culprit, Daniel Markovits argues, is meritocracy—the same ideal that was supposed to promote fairness. Brilliant, lucid, and urgent, *The Meritocracy Trap* exposes a national catastrophe."
—James Forman Jr., Pulitzer Prize–winning author of *Locking Up Our Own*

# THE
# MERITOCRACY
# TRAP

*How America's Foundational Myth*
*Feeds Inequality, Dismantles the Middle Class,*
*and Devours the Elite*

## DANIEL MARKOVITS

PENGUIN BOOKS

PENGUIN BOOKS
An imprint of Penguin Random House LLC
penguinrandomhouse.com

First published in the United States of America by Penguin Press,
an imprint of Penguin Random House LLC, 2019
Published in Penguin Books 2020

Figure 6 from Reardon, Sean F. 2011. Figures 5.7 and 5.8. "The Widening Academic
Achievement Gap Between the Rich and the Poor: New Evidence and Possible
Explanations," from *Whither Opportunity,* edited by Duncan, Greg, and Murnane,
Richard. © Russell Sage Foundation. Reprinted with permission of Russell Sage
Foundation, 112 East 64 Street, New York, NY 10065.

ISBN 9780735222014 (paperback)

THE LIBRARY OF CONGRESS HAS CATALOGED THE HARDCOVER EDITION AS
FOLLOWS:
Names: Markovits, Daniel, 1969– author.
Title: The meritocracy trap : how America's foundational myth feeds inequality,
dismantles the middle class, and devours the elite / Daniel Markovits.
Description: New York : Penguin Press, 2019. | Includes bibliographical
references and index.
Identifiers: LCCN 2019007519 (print) | LCCN 2019017772 (ebook) |
ISBN 9780735222007 (ebook) | ISBN 9780735221994 (hardcover)
Subjects: LCSH: Middle class—United States. | Intellectuals—United States. |
Equality—United States.
Classification: LCC HT684 (ebook) | LCC HT684 .M33 2019 (print) |
DDC 305.5/50973—dc23
LC record available at https://lccn.loc.gov/2019007519

Printed in the United States of America


*Designed by Amanda Dewey*

*For Sarah*
*and*
*our children*

# CONTENTS

*Part Three*

# A New Aristocracy

# INTRODUCTION

**M**erit is a sham.

An entire civilization resists this conclusion. Every decent person agrees that advantage should be earned through ability and effort rather than inherited alongside caste. The meritocratic ideal—that social and economic rewards should track achievement rather than breeding—anchors the self-image of the age. Aristocracy has had its day, and meritocracy is now a basic tenet of civil religion in all advanced societies.

Meritocracy promises to promote equality and opportunity by opening a previously hereditary elite to outsiders, armed with nothing save their own talents and ambitions. It further promises to harmonize private advantage and public interest, by insisting that wealth and status must be earned through accomplishment. Together, these ideals aspire to unite all of society behind a shared vision of hard work, skill, and deserved reward.

But meritocracy no longer operates as promised. Today, middle-class children lose out to rich children at school, and middle-class adults lose out to elite graduates at work. Meritocracy blocks the middle class from opportunity. Then it blames those who lose a competition for income and status that, even when everyone plays by the rules, only the rich can win.

Meritocracy harms the elite as well. Meritocratic schooling requires rich parents to invest thousands of hours and millions of dollars to get elite educations for their children. And meritocratic jobs require elite adults to work with grinding intensity, ruthlessly exploiting their educations in order to extract a return from these investments. Meritocracy entices an anxious and inauthentic elite into a pitiless, lifelong contest to secure income and status through its own excessive industry.

Finally, meritocracy now divides the elite from the middle class. It drives the middle class to resent the establishment and seduces the elite to cling to the corrupt prerogatives of caste. Meritocracy ensnares the society that both classes must share in a maelstrom of recrimination, disrespect, and dysfunction.

Meritocracy's charisma disguises all these harms, making it difficult to accept—indeed, seriously to consider—that meritocracy itself lies behind them. Even the angriest critics of the age embrace the meritocratic ideal. They charge that corrupt elites only pretend to reward achievement but actually favor their own. By indicting individual bad actors for failing to honor a meritocratic ideal in practice, they reaffirm meritocracy in principle.

But in fact, social and economic structures, rather than personal vices, cause the disaffection and discord that increasingly overwhelm American life. Whatever its original purposes and early triumphs, meritocracy now concentrates advantage and sustains toxic inequalities. And the taproot of all these troubles is not too little but rather too much meritocracy.

Merit itself has become a counterfeit virtue, a false idol. And meritocracy—formerly benevolent and just—has become what it was invented to combat. A mechanism for the concentration and dynastic transmission of wealth and privilege across generations. A caste order that breeds rancor and division. A new aristocracy, even.

## MERITOCRACY'S FALSE PROMISES

I am a meritocrat: a product and now an agent of the constellation of forces that these pages lay bare.

In the summer of 1987, as meritocracy gathered steam, I graduated from a public high school in Austin, Texas, and headed northeast, to attend Yale College. I then spent nearly fifteen years studying at various universities—the

London School of Economics, the University of Oxford, Harvard University, and finally Yale Law School—picking up a string of degrees along the way.

Today, I teach at Yale Law School, where my students unnervingly resemble my younger self: they are, overwhelmingly, products of professional parents and high-class universities. I pass on to them the advantages that my own teachers earlier bestowed on me. In all these ways, I owe my prosperity and my caste to elite institutions and to the training and employment that they confer.

Now at full flourish, meritocracy flies its flag conspicuously over the institutions that collectively ordain the elite. Harvard University, for example, calls itself "a haven for the world's most ambitious scholars," and Harvard's mission statement adds that its purpose is not simply academic excellence but also to "educate the citizens and citizen-leaders for our society," so that they might learn "how they can best serve the world." The firms that dominate employment among graduates of Harvard and other top schools carry the same arguments into the elite's adult life. Goldman Sachs has been called "probably the most elite work-society ever to be assembled on the globe," and the firm's website advertises the "progress" that it promotes far outside the elite, for example by brokering investments that spark a "renaissance" in Newark, New Jersey, and a "resurgence" in New Orleans. This familiar script—repeated again and again—simultaneously trumpets the elite's exceptional talents and reconciles hierarchy to the moral imperatives of democratic life, by connecting elites to the common interest as midwives to general prosperity.

These promises mark a revolution. Once, aristocrats got status by birthright, based on race or breeding, and abused undeserved privilege to hoard unjust advantage. Today, meritocrats claim to win their status through talent and effort—to get ahead fair and square, using means open to anyone. Once, lazy aristocrats produced little or nothing at all. They lived lavishly by exploiting other people's labor. Today, hardworking meritocrats claim to pull their weight, insisting that their enormous accomplishments contribute fair value to the societies they lead.

Earlier hierarchies were malign and offensive. But meritocracy claims to be wholesome—both just and benevolent. True to its Latin etymology, meritocracy glorifies only *earned* advantage and promises to transform the elite to suit a democratic age—to redeem the very idea of hierarchy.

Meritocracy's rituals reinforce these ideals by making them concrete and accessible, bringing the idea of deserved advantage to life. The graduation ceremonies that have become part of the rhythm of the American summer show how this works. At Yale Law School, commencement spans two splendid days. Luminaries, including Bill Clinton and Joe Biden, Ruth Bader Ginsburg and Sonia Sotomayor, exhort graduates to follow their passions and to deploy their talents for the greater good. Professors dress in brightly colored caps and gowns made of wool, silk, and even fur. University officers wear bejeweled collars and carry ceremonial maces. A former dean dons the sumptuous costume of an honorary doctor of laws awarded at Bologna, the oldest continuously operating university in Europe.

These celebrations are neither wanton nor casual. Instead (like weddings), they promote serious purposes and carry profound meanings, both political and personal. The speeches reaffirm the meritocratic elite's service to the common good. The medieval pageantry invests meritocracy with the remaining, inherited allure of the aristocratic hierarchies that it displaces—looking back in order to reach forward, repurposing old bottles to carry new wine. In a Gothic quad, as shadows lengthen across the summer afternoon, history feels present and alive. The university appears as a smooth band, stretching unbroken across the generations. Commencements connect a timeless past seamlessly to an inevitable future, absorbing the strains of transition and reassuring graduates who stand at the threshold of adulthood. Rituals render the future familiar, even before it arrives. They entrench meritocracy into the master narrative of modern life.

Meritocracy speaks in terms and settings so consistent that they fashion a distinctive language, repeated across contexts, again and again—a form of life, familiar to every citizen of the age. This gives meritocracy an enormously powerful charisma. Meritocracy's luster captivates the imagination and arrests the gaze, to suppress critical judgment and stifle reform. By identifying itself with basic decency and insinuating itself into the assumed background of everyday experience, meritocracy conceals the harms that it now imposes on all who encounter it. Indeed, it makes alternative ways of awarding advantage seem absurd: unfair or corrupt, as when privilege is apportioned through prejudice or nepotism; or simply foolish, as if high positions might be assigned by lot.

But as meritocracy advances, its achievements impose a new and oppressive hierarchy, unrecognizable even a generation ago. An unprecedented and distinctively meritocratic inequality tarnishes a new gilded age. Elites increasingly monopolize not just income, wealth, and power, but also industry, public honor, and private esteem. Meritocracy comprehensively excludes the middle class from social and economic advantage, and at the same time conscripts its elite into a ruinous contest to preserve caste. Meritocratic inequality—the growing gap between the rich and the rest—bends America to an ominous arc.

As meritocratic inequality grows, and meritocracy's burdens increase, its moral claims falter and its rituals lose their power. The meritocratic code's grip over the imagination wears off, and resistance to its dogmas builds. Familiar bromides about earning advantage by promoting the general interest become unconvincing, and the rhythms of the past no longer soothe.

Instead, discontent over meritocratic inequality provides fertile ground for critical ideas. The most important is the idea that the afflictions that dominate American life arise not because meritocracy is imperfectly realized, but rather on account of meritocracy itself.

## HOW MERITOCRACY OPPRESSES THE MIDDLE CLASS AND EXPLOITS THE ELITE

Meritocratic competition expels middle-class Americans from the charismatic center of economic and social life and estranges them from the touchstones by which society measures and awards distinction, honor, and wealth. Although meritocratic energy, ambition, and innovation have transformed the mainstream of human history, meritocracy concentrates these vibrant wellsprings of creativity in a narrower and narrower elite, farther and farther beyond the practical and even the imaginative horizons of the broad middle class.

Meritocracy makes the Ivy League, Silicon Valley, and Wall Street into arenas for elite ambition. Innovators in these places can remake the life-world, transforming the internet (at Stanford and Google), social media (at Harvard and Facebook), finance (at Princeton and Wall Street generally), and a thousand other smaller domains. But a middle-class child, consigned to the backwaters of the meritocratic order, will more likely be buffeted by the next great invention than build it. Meritocracy banishes the majority of citizens to the margins of their own society, consigning middle-class children to lackluster schools and middle-class adults to dead-end jobs.

Common usage often conflates meritocracy with equality of opportunity. But although meritocracy was embraced as the handmaiden of equality of opportunity, and did open up the elite in its early years, it now more nearly stifles than fosters social mobility. The avenues that once carried people from modest circumstances into the American elite are narrowing dramatically. Middle-class families cannot afford the elaborate schooling that rich families buy, and ordinary schools lag farther and farther behind elite ones, commanding fewer resources and delivering inferior educations. Even as top universities emphasize achievement rather than breeding, they run admissions competitions that students from middle-class backgrounds cannot win, and their student bodies skew dramatically toward wealth. Meritocratic education now predominantly serves an elite caste rather than the general public.

Meritocracy similarly transforms jobs to favor the super-educated graduates that elite universities produce, so that work extends and compounds inequalities produced in school. Competence and an honest work ethic no longer assure a good job. Middle-class workers, without elite degrees, face discrimination all across a labor market that increasingly privileges elaborate education and extravagant training.

Meritocratic exclusion reaches opportunities as well as outcomes, and meritocratic values add a moral insult to these material injuries. Even as it denies the middle class real opportunities for excellent schooling and meaningful work, meritocracy makes achievement in school and at work into the soul of honor. Meritocracy therefore frustrates efforts to satisfy the very standards that it announces, ensuring that most people will not measure up. Americans outside the elite know all this, and the dynamism in the elite only emphasizes listless weariness among the middle class. Even where material conditions remain tolerable, meritocratic inequality consigns the spiritual life of the middle class to an unbeatable, slow, devastating decline.

Meritocracy also no longer truly serves even the elite that it appears to privilege. It concentrates training and work that were once spread evenly across society onto an elite that is literally too narrow to carry their weight. The same forces that deplete the middle class overburden the elite.

Aristocrats were born; but meritocrats must be made. The old, hereditary elite bequeathed its caste effortlessly to its children, by birthright. Each new generation of aristocrats assumed its titles and great houses automatically on the death of the old. Meritocracy, by contrast, requires families who wish to transmit caste down through their generations continually to build and re-build privilege, as each generation must reestablish its eliteness afresh, by its own accomplishments. Meritocrats achieve this by raising children in a distinctive way. Whereas aristocrats lacked both the inclination and the capacity to train their children, meritocrats—especially women who sacrifice their own careers to do the work of meritocratic motherhood—increasingly devote their wealth and also their skills and energies to educating their children.

Rich children devote their days to absorbing this education. For fully a third of their lives—beginning at birth and extending deep into adulthood—children of rich parents benefit from and suffer through a training regimen whose planned intensity and ruthless demands would be unrecognizable to their middle-class counterparts today, or indeed to their own grandparents a half century ago. The framers of the U.S. Constitution required presidents to be at least thirty-five years old in order to ensure that only experienced adults would hold the office. Today, a thirty-five-year-old meritocrat can easily still be in school.

Elites grow more vividly strained as meritocracy matures, and today, even those at the top are beginning to turn against the intense, competitive training that makes them. The millennial generation—the first to have lived entirely inside the mature meritocracy—appreciates these burdens most keenly. Elite millennials can be precious and fragile, but not in the manner of the special snowflakes that derisive polemics describe. They do not melt or wilt at every challenge to their privilege, so much as shatter under the intense competitive pressures to achieve that dominate their lives. They are neither dissolute nor decadent, but rather tense and exhausted.

They are also increasingly self-aware. My students at Yale—the poster children for meritocracy—are more nearly overwhelmed and confounded by their apparent blessings than complacent or even just self-assured. They seek meaning that eludes their accomplishments and regard the intense education that constitutes their elevated caste with a diffidence that approaches despair. The vast majority hail from privileged families, and they recognize their overrepresentation and instinctually doubt that they deserve the advantages they enjoy. (Privilege so dominates the culture of elite universities that the small minority of elite students who come from modest backgrounds form support groups of "first-generation professionals" in order to ease their entry into an alien society.) These students have been nurtured, but also cultivated, coached, drilled, shaped, and packaged—all in an unrelenting quest to succeed at school and preserve their caste—and they scorn all this maneuvering for advantage and deride their own complicity in it. They are consumed by what a recent survey calls a "collective frenzy" to advance in the "prestige economy" that allocates income and status.

My students, like their peers all across the meritocracy, are caught in a "collective anxiety" driven by fear of not measuring up. They doubt their past achievements and worry that the future will merely repeat a gauntlet that they have just run, only exchanging intensely competitive schools for equally competitive jobs. Even the meritocratic elite fears—inarticulately, but with good reason—that meritocracy does not promote its true flourishing, so that it will be wealthy but not well.

## HOW MERITOCRACY DIVIDES SOCIETY

Meritocracy imposes these burdens jointly and in interlocking battalions, as variations on a shared theme, two faces of a single calamity. An integrated mechanism literally concentrates income and status, as meritocratic competition simultaneously excludes the middle class from credible opportunities for real advantage and press-gangs elites into an excessively intense pursuit of fruitless gain. Meritocracy thereby draws the elite and the middle class—the rich and the rest—into a close but hostile embrace. Meritocratic inequality inspires the hostility, entwining the classes in misunderstandings, friction, discord, and even open warfare. Meritocracy, that is, nourishes a systematic class conflict that deforms social and political life.

The middle class experiences the elite as commandeering opportunities and advantages (education and work, income and status) that once rightfully belonged to it—as imposing a shameful and therefore unpardonable exclusion. The exclusion naturally breeds resentment and mistrust, directed against the ideals and institutions that meritocracy valorizes. The middle class increasingly regards elite schools, universities, and professional firms as alien places that at best indulge eccentric values and at worst impose those values on everyone else—as clubs, dominated by worthless book learning, political correctness, and arrogant self-dealing. Ironically (although following a profound inner logic), these resentments, borne of exclusion, often focus on the forms of inclusion that meritocracy exalts, including in particular—as in complaints about political correctness—the meritocratic embrace of a multicultural elite.

The resentments, moreover, have direct and powerful—even world-changing—consequences. They enabled Donald Trump to become president of a wealthy, powerful, and famously optimistic nation by relentlessly attacking the status quo, repudiating what he calls "the Establishment," and blaming the state of the country on a corrupt alliance of meritocratic elites and cultural outsiders. Trump's dark vision replaces the American dream with what his apocalyptic inaugural address—painting a nation in deep decline, overrun by poverty, crime, and economic decay—called "this American carnage." His imaginative world and express language ("America First") evoke the frustration and anger of the Great Depression at home and, abroad, of nations devastated by economic crisis and humiliating defeat in total war. A powerful and prosperous society does not typically behave like one laid low by defeat and humiliation. Meritocratic inequality, and the resentments that it produces, explain why America did.

The resentments in which Trumpism traffics, and the repudiationism that it pursues, express the spiritual burden of life at the bottom of the meritocratic caste order, among what Trump's inaugural address called "the forgotten men and women of our country [who] will be forgotten no longer." These groups most thrill to Trumpism's endeavor to replace the narrative of progress that dominates conventional American politics with one of rescue— to the prospect that Trump might "Make America Great Again." Nearly two-thirds of whites without a BA reported that Trump's similarly dark and angry speech at the Republican National Convention reflected their feelings about the country. And nearly three-fifths of Trump's Republican Party believes that colleges and universities are bad for America.

Meritocratic inequality and class conflict also corrupt elites, including (again ironically) in ways that enable the Trumpist politics that the same elites despise. The fact that middle-class children are effectively excluded from advantage does not guarantee inclusion for rich children. And as meritocratic inequality sharpens hierarchy to a spiky-fine point, even the privileged confront a precarious existence. Elites desperately fear losing caste, and their anxiety naturally isolates them and breeds condescension toward the middle class. Moreover, elites know that meritocracy favors their caste and they suspect that, although they cannot explain how, the same forces that burnish the gloss on the elite spread a pall of gloom over the middle class. No matter how pure their motives and how scrupulous their victories, meritocratic elites are implicated, including through achievements that they admire, in inequalities that they deplore.

Familiar maxims about privilege and its responsibilities still propose to align meritocratic inequality with the common interest, suggesting that if only the elite would behave well then all would be well. But as meritocracy's burdens mount and meritocratic inequality increases, these platitudes lose their power. The magnanimous triumphalism that suffused elite life in meritocracy's early years has given way to frightened and brittle arrogance.

Fragile elites disdain middle-class habits and values as a defense mechanism to ward off self-doubt. Meritocrats lionize achievement, or even just distinction, and disparage ordinariness as a bulwark against rising insecurity. They cling to any attitudes and practices—ranging from the absurd (food snobbery) to the callous (corporate rightsizing)—that might confirm their merit and validate their advantage, to others and, above all, to themselves. These crimped and confused attitudes further aggravate middle-class resentments, and at the same time debilitate elites politically. To this day, elites remain too disenchanted to reimpose a sanguine vision on American politics, or even to sustain it among themselves. Meritocratic discontent empowers Trump's dark populism to dominate the political imagination even among the elites who scorn it.

## THE PARADOX OF MERITOCRACY

Meritocracy's sparkle captures the imagination and distracts analytical attention. It dominates the self-image of the age, disabling criticism and corrupting critics. But scratch the surface to remove the sheen, and a deep well of discontent opens up below. Meritocracy's discontents present a dramatic irony so deep that it looks, from inside the meritocratic order, like a paradox.

Middle-class resentment against the elite appears misguided. Today, in principle, anyone can succeed. Education has never been as extravagantly funded or widely available as it is today, and even the most exclusive schools and colleges—which once admitted only white, Christian men and even within this group selected students for breeding—today base admissions on academic achievement. Jobs and careers have similarly dismantled outmoded chauvinisms and are now overwhelmingly open to effort and talent. Institutions that once confronted large classes of citizens with a wall of categorical exclusion now expressly admit anyone who can make it.

The anxiety felt within the elite astounds especially. The training that goes into an elite degree has never before been as excellent, and graduates have never been as accomplished. The social and economic advantages conferred by education have also never been greater. Elite graduates should be proud of their past and confident about their future status and income.

Nevertheless, the complaints persist, multiply, and grow ever louder. As meritocratic inequality increases and meritocracy loses its charisma, rising elite anxieties join an older, more mature dissatisfaction, already well known to the American middle class. The grievances build because they connect lived experience to an important truth, fashioning a master key for diagnosing the troubles that dominate economic and social life today, both existentially in the individual person and politically in public life. Meritocratic inequality makes an otherwise bizarre picture of America credible and politically potent.

Meritocracy's discontents invite a structural attack on the incumbent regime, grounded in a criticism of meritocracy itself. Although they appear independent and even opposed, the oppression of the middle class and the exploitation of the elite share a common root. Through diverse means and following divergent pathways, the American elite, the American middle class, and America itself are all caught in the meritocracy trap.

Like all really big things, meritocracy is difficult to comprehend from up close. After five decades of rising economic inequality, the elite and the middle class appear—unreflectively, at first blush—to inhabit separate worlds. According to the common view, there are now two Americas, one for the rich and the other for the rest. The loudest voices, on the left as well as the right, insist that the country—in economics, in politics, and even in social life—is coming apart.

A step back opens a wider perspective and reveals that the common view is mistaken. The elite and the middle class are not coming apart at all. Instead, the rich and the rest are entangled in a single, shared, and mutually destructive economic and social logic. Their seemingly opposite burdens are in fact two symptoms of a shared meritocratic disease. Meritocratic elites acquire their caste through processes that ruthlessly exclude most Americans and, at the same time, mercilessly assault those who do go through them. The powerfully felt but unexplained frustrations that mar both classes—unprecedented resentment among the middle class and inscrutable anxiety among the elite—are eddies in a shared stream, drawing their energies from a single current.

*The Meritocracy Trap* begins, in the manner of a doctor encountering a new disease, simply by setting out the symptoms of advanced meritocracy. Part One therefore chronicles meritocracy's discontents and reports on the human costs of a caste hierarchy that simultaneously excludes most people and damages the few that it admits. The account aspires empathetically to describe the facts of life under meritocratic inequality, and the sentiments that these facts unleash, so that people, across the meritocratic divide, will recognize their lived experience and respond: "Yes. This is how things are for us." Because meritocracy's charisma disguises its evils, and thereby bewilders those who suffer its frustrations, recognition begins to bring release. The release provides relief even when newfound wisdom recommends uncomfortable self-examination and poignant self-reproach.

Next, Part Two describes in detail how meritocracy works. This effort explains the social and economic arrangements—concerning income, education, and work—that meritocracy puts in place. It chronicles the means by which meritocratic developments have produced a vastly unequal distribution of advantage and exposes the mechanisms by which the ensuing inequality harms both the middle class and the elite. The argument shows, at each step, that these inequalities and burdens arise not on account of deviations or retreats from meritocracy but rather directly because of meritocracy's successes, on account of its consummation. The inner movements of the meritocratic machine reveal the construction of the meritocracy trap.

Finally, Part Three unmasks meritocracy—to expose a new form of aristocracy, purpose-built for a world in which the greatest source of income and wealth is not land but labor. Meritocracy claims to be fair and benevolent, to align private interest and the common good, and to promote freedom and opportunity for all. In fact, however, meritocratic social and economic inequality betrays the values that meritocracy's stated principles endorse and that its rituals extol. Like aristocracy once did, meritocratic inequality now comprehensively organizes the lives of people caught inside it. And like aristocracy, meritocratic inequality establishes a durable, self-sustaining hierarchy, supported by feedback loops between meritocracy's moving parts. Merit itself is not a genuine excellence but rather—like the false virtues that aristocrats trumpeted in the ancien régime—a pretense, constructed to rationalize an unjust distribution of advantage.

## ESCAPING THE MERITOCRACY TRAP

*The Meritocracy Trap* was conceived inside meritocracy's institutional machinery—indeed, in one of the rituals that shore up meritocracy's charisma—and it is steeped in all the complexities and ironies that meritocracy invites.

In May 2015—one month before Donald Trump descended into his lobby to announce that he would run for president—the graduating class at Yale Law School asked me to deliver its commencement address. Like many others, I had been thinking about economic inequality, and so I determined to contrast the bloated opulence that elite graduates inherit with the diminished and devalued portion allotted to the rest of America. I had in mind to confront the graduates with a conventional morality tale—a stern warning against temptations to exploit their degrees for narrowly private gain, combined with a pious invocation to serve the public good.

But as I sat down to write and imagined actually speaking to students I knew—whose undoubted privileges produced afflictions alongside advantages—the righteous impulse deserted me, to be replaced by something stranger: a curious amalgam of powerful empathy and sinister foreboding. Although I could not then see through meritocracy's paradoxes to resolve them, a new emotional posture and organizing frame for my remarks emerged. People are more benign than the common view supposes, but circumstances are much more malignant.

The pieties embraced by meritocracy's champions and the sanctimonious anger wielded by inequality's critics both misjudge the challenges that we face. Our anxieties concerning meritocracy and economic inequality are warranted, but they cannot be resolved by identifying villains or even righting clear wrongs. Rather, they reflect a deep and pervasive dysfunction in how we structure and reward training and work—how, in a basic and immediate way, we live our lives. This diagnosis attacks no one, but it should discomfit everybody.

The diagnosis, although uncomfortable, also kindles hope for a cure. We are trained to think of economic inequality as presenting a zero-sum game: to suppose that redistribution to benefit the bottom must burden the top. But this is not such a case. Meritocratic inequality does not in fact serve anyone well, and escaping the meritocracy trap would therefore benefit virtually everyone. Emancipation from meritocracy would restore middle-class Americans, now cut off from dignity and prosperity, to full participation in social and economic life. Emancipation would invite the elite, now entangled in strained self-exploitation, to trade a diminution in wealth and status that it can easily afford in exchange for a precious increase in leisure and liberty, a reclaiming of an authentic self. And emancipation would heal a society that meritocracy has made oppressive and mistrustful.

The problem remains how practically to escape the meritocracy trap: how to broker the politics and design the policies required to reestablish a democratic social and economic order. This is no easy task. If the book's diagnosis is correct, then meritocratic inequality stems from economic and social forces whose depth and power resemble those at play as industrial capitalism displaced feudal agriculture two centuries ago. And if a time traveler could explain to a well-meaning English king or prime minister in 1800 that, by 1860, the forces of industrialization would so disrupt the social order and generate such inequality as to drive the life expectancy of a child born in urban Manchester down to levels not seen since the Black Death, there would quite possibly have been no way to stop the decline.

Nevertheless, we are more self-aware and more effectual than past generations. If we come to understand that meritocratic inequality produces near-universal harm, then we can muster the political will to cure it. And if we can muster the political will, we enjoy more degrees of policymaking freedom and a greater capacity to influence events. The book proceeds from the faith that political understanding—concerning structural forces rather than just moralistic recriminations—is a necessary condition for intelligent and effective action. It aspires to leverage understanding into a politically potent force for change and also to propose concrete policies that will reclaim a more equal, democratic economic and social order.

These hopes invoke virtues—clarity of mind and the capacity to convert understanding into effective action—that are themselves commonly associated with meritocracy. And there is no contradiction in thinking that meritocracy might solve its own problem, unlock its own trap, to recover its original, democratic promise and refashion an open, fair society whose elite does well by promoting the public good.

On the other hand, a hope is not a plan. To escape the meritocracy trap, politics must overcome all the vulnerabilities and bad incentives that meritocracy enshrines in public life. Both the rich and the rest must learn to see through the anxieties—from populist and nativist resentment through small-minded competitiveness and arrogant condescension—that currently divide them. Both classes must recognize that their distresses, and even their antagonisms, share in meritocracy a single source. And both classes must join in a coalition in which each eases its own afflictions by empathizing with, and even shouldering, the meritocratic burdens that now afflict the other.

Even where everyone would benefit from democratic renewal, achieving this coalition requires self-disciplined imagination. But meritocracy's discontents leave the virtues that this generous and redemptive politics demands in short supply. Moreover, anxiety and bitterness block both the rich and the rest from recognizing that more immediately alluring alternatives merely seed a gathering storm. A very different coalition of manipulative oligarchs and resentful populists now threatens to repudiate meritocracy wholesale and to erect something considerably darker in its stead.

Blindness to this risk—on display when an uncomprehending America enabled Donald Trump's rise—would constitute meritocracy's final irony.

# THE MERITOCRACY TRAP

*Part One*

# Meritocracy and Its Discontents

# ONE

# THE MERITOCRATIC
# REVOLUTION

For virtually all of human history, income and industry have charted opposite courses.

The poor worked immensely long and intensely hard. In 1800, the average English laborer worked sixty-four hours a week; in 1900, a typical American still worked sixty hours; and as late as the 1920s, blue-collar workweeks exceeded fifty hours. Virtually all these hours were drudgery and toil. The rising middle class would eventually temper both facets of working-class labor and assimilate many workers, but it abandoned neither. The manufacturing jobs that once built a flourishing middle class absorbed and exhausted the workers who did them.

The rich, by contrast, customarily led lives of extravagant and conspicuous leisure. High society, for centuries and even millennia, embraced elegant recreation, and the elite despised industry.

Low wages consigned workers inescapably to modest incomes. No amount of industry could make a nineteenth-century laborer even comfortably well-off. And while the post–World War II boom allowed mid-twentieth-century workers to earn their way into middle-class comfort, elite wealth remained flatly inaccessible.

The rich, for their part, paid for leisure using incomes derived from land, factories, or other capital, which they generally inherited. Both the rich and the rest owed their circumstances to accidents of birth rather than choices or accomplishments. Long after formal titles of nobility had passed into neglect or even been abolished, society remained in effect a hereditary aristocracy. You could learn how poor people were simply by asking how hard they worked.

Today, unprecedented social and economic arrangements reverse these age-old associations. Middle-class jobs are disappearing, and the workers who for centuries pulled the economy's laboring oar work progressively less hard. The middle class is not idle—reluctant to work. Rather it is increasingly idled—denied opportunities to work. A profound technological transformation eliminates middle-class jobs and renders mid-skilled labor surplus to economic requirements. The total work hours lost through these trends approach the difference between the hours worked by men and by women at midcentury. The new order, that is, suppresses working- and middle-class employment today by about as much as sex discrimination suppressed women's employment two generations ago. This deprives the middle class of the income and status that industry confers.

The new technologies do not eliminate work altogether. To the contrary, they actually increase the demand for super-skilled, elite labor. The once-leisured rich, in a stark contrast to the middle class, work harder than they ever have before, harder than the rest of society, and absolutely very hard. Prime-aged adults (men and women combined) with a BA or more education are less than half as likely to have abandoned the workforce than their counterparts with a high school degree or less. Moreover, when they are employed, elites work substantially longer hours than their middle-class counterparts, and they enjoy less leisure. Indeed, despite pervasive use of labor-saving household appliances, elites actually enjoy less leisure today than they did at midcentury.

Elite values and customs have adapted to suit these new facts. High society has reversed course. Now it valorizes industry and despises leisure. As every rich person knows, when an acquaintance asks "How are you?" the correct answer is "So busy." The old leisure class would have thought this a humiliating admission. The working rich boast that they are in demand.

A revolution in wages completes the new work order. Middle-class jobs still cannot make a person rich. But the elite's intense industry now generates colossal incomes. Top jobs commonly pay annual wages of $500,000, $1 million, or even $5 million, and a few pay $10 million, $100 million, or even $1 billion. Indeed, rich people today owe the bulk of their incomes to their labor, and work has become the dominant path to wealth. Moreover, elites get these high-paying jobs based on immense skill, won through rigorous training, and they keep their jobs through intense, competitive, and enormously productive industry. Today, asking how long people have studied and how hard they work reveals not how poor they are, but how rich.

This new regime radically transforms who gets and stays ahead. The new order rejects the aristocratic hierarchy that dominated the old. Instead, it embraces the meritocratic idea that economic and social advantages should track not breeding but rather ability, effort, and output, and that all three must be proved by success in ongoing competition, first in school and then at work.

Once, a leisured elite dominated and exploited a subordinate working class. Labor, moreover, constituted subordination—for slaves, for serfs, for indentured servants, and even for industrial workers (whose "labor" movement reclaimed an indignity as a marker of pride). Now the industrious rich dominate the rest. The leisured aristocracy that for millennia monopolized income and status has ceded the field to a new elite constituted through industry—not a sub-, but a *super*ordinate working class.

The meritocratic elite that this regime establishes is composed of a core that captures the incomes just described (perhaps 1 percent of households) and a larger penumbra that works in the social and economic orbit of these incomes (perhaps another 5 or 10 percent). Meritocracy constructs this elite through two movements. Each involves a contest or tournament. Together, they build and then set the meritocracy trap.

First, meritocracy transforms education into a rigorous and intense contest to join the elite. It concentrates training in the narrow, super-educated caste that wins the competition for places and grades at the top schools and universities. Second, meritocracy transforms work to create the immensely demanding and enormously lucrative jobs that sustain the elite. It fetishizes skill, centering both industry and pay around a narrow caste of superordinate workers.

Both faces of meritocracy—elite education's intense and competitive training and elite work's immense industry and outsized rewards—have become so ingrained that they seem natural and even inevitable. It is difficult to imagine life without them. But both faces in fact are strikingly new. The story of their rise opens a window into the meritocratic machine, and a close study of their reign exposes meritocracy's discontents.

## MERITOCRATIC TRAINING

Elite education used to be anything but intense. For much of the twentieth century, through the late 1950s, elite universities overwhelmingly awarded places based on breeding rather than merit. The Ivy League did not admit nor even pursue the "best and the brightest" so much as sustain and burnish the social patina of America's leading families. Even graduate and professional schools selected their students by astonishingly casual means. A midcentury graduate of Yale Law School, for example, recently told an oral historian that he came to Yale after Jack Tate, then dean of admissions, told him at a college fair—straight away, and on the basis of a single conversation—"You'll get in if you apply."

Things began to change in the middle of the twentieth century. Presidents James Bryant Conant at Harvard and (slightly later) Kingman Brewster at Yale, seeking to open up, expand, and energize the American elite, expressly rejected aristocratic exclusion and rebuilt college admissions to emphasize achievement rather than breeding. By 1970, the cordial alliances among established families, schools, and colleges that long sustained a genteel elite had all been broken. A fierce rivalry now determines who attends America's best universities. The change, moreover, rang in a revolution—a difference of kind rather than just degree—that has transformed the basic character of elite education.

Admissions officers have exchanged casual assessments of social suitability for intensive and rigorous talent screening, and applicants have exchanged family traditions favoring one or another college for a coldblooded pursuit of status, as measured by university rankings.

The earlier example illustrates the transformation. Over fifty thousand candidates a year now apply to American law schools, and perhaps three thousand of these apply to Yale, the top-ranked school. Yale Law School now takes admissions anything but casually—three faculty members independently evaluate each file—and following this process, Yale admits about 8 percent of applicants (making the admissions competition four times as intense today as it was at midcentury). The median admitted student received an A average in college and scored above the 99th percentile on the Law School Admission Test (LSAT). Finally, applicants almost slavishly esteem status and enroll in the highest-ranked school that admits them. Roughly 80 percent of those whom Yale admits eventually enroll.

Yale Law School may present an extreme case, but it is not distinctive. Broadening the field leaves the pattern intact, indeed unaltered. The top five law schools—Yale, Stanford, Harvard, Chicago, and Columbia—collectively admit about 15 percent of applicants. The median students at all five had A averages in college and LSAT scores in the top 3 percent. And although precise and definitive data are not available, a reasonable estimate suggests that of the roughly two thousand people admitted to these schools each year, no more than five—which is to say effectively none—attend a school outside the top ten.

The law school admissions competition does not represent an aberration or isolated moment in an elite student's life. Rather, a top law school adds the final link in a long chain of rigorous schooling. Students at elite professional schools overwhelmingly earned their A grades at highly selective colleges: the admissions competition for places at Harvard, Yale, Princeton, and Stanford is three times as intense today as it was just twenty years ago. Moreover, students at these elite colleges disproportionately attended highly competitive high schools and indeed highly selective elementary schools and even preschools. In other words, to secure a really elite education, a student must rank among the top fraction of a percent in a massive, multistage meritocratic tournament, one in which the competitors at every stage conspicuously agree about which schools constitute the biggest prize.

Every one of these schools, all along the chain, offers intensive training commensurate to its elite status. Top schools, that is, all make immense investments in their students' educations: elite private schools spend as much as $75,000 per student per year (more than six times the national public school average), and elite colleges and graduate schools spend over $90,000 per student per year. The total excess investment that an elite education represents, over and above the investments made in middle-class schooling, amounts to millions of dollars.

Education works, and these enormous investments pay off. Study and testing foster diligence and ambition, and training builds skills. Harvard Law School's dean welcomes incoming students with the promise that "no law school better prepares lawyers, public servants, and leaders for a changing world," and at Yale Law School, a recent dean told each graduating class that they were "quite simply, the finest new law graduates on the planet." These claims might appear boastful and even narcissistic. But, astonishingly, the claims assert concrete, determinate, and determinable facts, which are proved in the two-sided admissions competition for places and students. Demonstrating these facts has dominated elite students' entire lives. For nearly three decades, Yale Law School graduates—and indeed graduates of every top college and professional school, in every field—have studied, worked, practiced, and drilled. They have been continually inspected. And finally, they have been selected. This, after all, is what it means to join the meritocratic elite.

The lifelong education that culminates in an elite advanced degree, and also the competition to get the training and obtain the degree, have never been as intense as they are today. Finishing schools that certified breeding and polished manners have transformed into rigorous training centers that select for accomplishment and build skills. An elite degree therefore represents relentlessly demanding, ambitious, and successful training. And no prior elite has ever been as capable or as industrious as the meritocratic elite that such training produces. None comes close.

## MERITOCRATIC WORK

Meritocratic work extends the patterns of meritocratic education through adult life. Elite jobs mirror the intensity and competitiveness of elite schools and fetishize the skills that these schools provide. At the same time, the income and status that the top jobs bestow on superordinate workers match the labor effort these jobs require. Both the demands and the rewards of elite work are greater today than they have ever been before.

The elite's work habits—the rhythms of a rich person's day—were once as relaxed as elite schooling. This was no accident. The aristocrats possessed few special abilities and no taste for industry. They therefore lacked both the means and the motive to take over work. And so the midcentury economic order naturally and even necessarily put middle-class workers at the charismatic center of making and selling things and also of financing and managing the firms that made and sold them. Mid-skilled, middle-class labor dominated virtually all sectors of the midcentury economy. Mid-skilled industrial workers famously dominated manufacturing; mid-skilled local, independent merchants dominated retail; mid-skilled community bankers, loan officers, and stockbrokers dominated finance; and mid-skilled middle and line managers dominated the administration of virtually all American firms. The old aristocracy instinctively ceded the labor market to the middle class; a leisured elite invited middle-class industry.

No longer.

While aristocrats naturally gave work over to the middle class, meritocracy's superordinate workers possess both the skills and the inclination to work industriously. They unsurprisingly attract economic attention. Over the past forty years, computers, robots, and other new technologies have changed how goods are made and services delivered. These disruptive technologies (invented by interested innovators and tailored to suit skills that meritocratic education makes newly available) shift the center of production away from mid-skilled and toward super-skilled labor.

Automated industrial robots, for example, replace mid-skilled manufacturing workers with super-skilled workers who design and program the robots. Innovations in distribution, warehousing, and e-commerce displace middle-class independent merchants with subordinate Walmart greeters and Amazon warehouse workers at the bottom, and super-rich owners of megastores—including the world's richest family (the Waltons of Walmart) and the world's richest person (Jeff Bezos of Amazon)—at the very top. Derivatives and other new financial technologies allow elite workers on Wall Street to dispense with middle-class community bankers, loan officers, and stockbrokers. And new management techniques allow top executives and CEOs to discard middle and line managers and to exert immense powers directly to organize and control production workers. These and countless other parallel innovations simultaneously exclude middle-class workers, whose skills they render superfluous, and elevate elite workers, whose skills they make economically essential. Collectively, they displace work away from the middle class and onto the elite, to create the superordinate working class.

Today's lawyers illustrate and document these patterns. In 1962 (when elite lawyers earned a third of what they do today), the American Bar Association could confidently declare that "there are . . . approximately 1300 fee-earning hours per year" available to the normal lawyer. Today, by contrast, a major law firm pronounces with equal confidence that a quota of 2,400 billable hours "if properly managed" is "not unreasonable," which is a euphemism for "necessary for having a hope of making partner." Billing 2,400 hours requires working from 8 a.m. until 8 p.m., six days a week, without vacation or sick days, every week of the year. Graduates of elite law schools join law firms that commonly require associates and even partners to work sixty-, eighty-, and even hundred-hour weeks.

Lawyers, because they must track billable hours in six-minute intervals, record an experience that all top workers share. Elite finance workers once kept "bankers' hours"—originally named for the ten-to-three business day fixed by banks from the nineteenth century through the mid-twentieth and later used to refer more generally to any light work. Elite managers, for their part, worked as "organization men," cocooned by lifelong employment in a corporate hierarchy that rewarded seniority above performance. Today, investment bankers work "17 hours a day . . . seven days a week," in the words of one, "until midnight or one a.m. every night, including weekends, full-day weekends, and then probably pulling an all-nighter every week or every other week," in the words of another. Similarly, the organization man has given way to what the *Harvard Business Review* calls the *extreme job:* a job that involves "physical presence at [the] workplace [for] at least ten hours a day," a "large amount of travel," "availability to clients 24/7," "work-related events outside [of] regular work hours," and an "inordinate scope of responsibility that amounts to more than one job."

The work histories of law, finance, and management all reflect a broader trend—they do not report exceptions but rather illustrate a new rule governing elite work. More than half of the richest 1 percent of households now include someone who works over fifty hours per week (which is over fifteen times the rate among the poorest fifth of households). Overall, prime-aged men from the top 1 percent of the income distribution work nearly 50 percent longer hours, on average, than their counterparts from the bottom half.

Elite jobs of all sorts nowadays demand hours—routinely, as a matter of course—that would have been thought unimaginable, because degrading, by an earlier, more genteel American elite. For centuries, the old order imposed a social taint on those who worked not from passion—for honor and exploit, or as a calling—but industriously, for wages. But that stigma, which remained at midcentury, has today been entirely erased and even reversed. Elite workers across all fields now valorize long hours and conspicuously and almost compulsively publicize their immense industry—including through their habits of speech—as a way of asserting their status. Meritocracy makes effortful and industrious work—busyness—into a sign of being valued and needed, the badge of honor.

Elite training, skill, and industry yield income as well as status. First-year associates at top law firms in New York and other big cities today earn about $200,000 per year (and effectively every Yale Law graduate who seriously seeks such a job gets one). Moreover, elite lawyers' incomes grow markedly greater still as their careers mature. A law firm now exists that generates profits per partner exceeding $5 million annually, and more than seventy firms now generate more than $1 million of profits per partner every year. The partnerships at these firms are overwhelmingly dominated by graduates of elite law schools. Over half of partners at the five most profitable firms are graduates of law schools conventionally ranked in the "top ten," and four-fifths of the partners at the $5-million-per-partner firm graduated from law schools conventionally ranked in the "top five."

Specialist doctors, professional finance-sector workers, management consultants, and elite managers all also require elite degrees and again generally make several hundred thousand dollars a year. Incomes exceeding $1 million are startlingly common in all these fields. And the really top earners—managing directors at investment banks, C-suite executives at large corporations, and the highest-paid hedge fund managers—take home tens or hundreds of millions of dollars a year. As in law, the top employers overwhelmingly hire graduates of the very top schools—sometimes literally just Harvard, Princeton, Stanford, Yale, and perhaps MIT and Williams. Often, they do not even recruit new workers anywhere else. The economic returns to schooling have consequently skyrocketed in recent decades, and—especially at elite schools and colleges—double or even triple the returns to investments in stocks or bonds. This produces an astonishing segmentation of income by education.

In industry after industry, the labor market now fetishizes the skills that meritocratic education produces, so that super-skilled workers dominate production. At the same time, mid-skilled workers become redundant. In some cases, middle-class employment never recovers: mid-skilled manufacturing, retail, and middle-management jobs have notoriously disappeared. In other cases, a new work order segregates subordinate and superordinate workers: mid-skilled community bankers have been replaced by subordinate clerks on Main Street and superordinate speculators on Wall Street. Some of the newly subordinate workers even supply the booming market for personal services provided to rich households, whose members now work such long hours and command such high wages as to make it almost unreasonable for them to do their own chores.

Either way, innovation increasingly divides work into what might be called gloomy and glossy jobs: gloomy because they offer neither immediate reward nor hope for promotion, and glossy because their shine comes from income and status rather than meaningful work. (As meritocracy advances, and more middling jobs give way to gloomy and glossy ones, the lion's share become gloomy.) Meritocracy's shadow, cast over mid-skilled work, accounts for the darkness that engulfs gloomy jobs today, and its brassy light gives glossy jobs a false sheen. The meritocratic culture of industry helps to prop up the intense work effort required when a society concentrates economic production on a narrow elite.

## AN UNPRECEDENTED INEQUALITY

Meritocracy's two components, having developed together, now interact as expressions of a single, integrated whole. Elaborate elite education produces superordinate workers, who possess a powerful work ethic and exceptional skills. These workers then induce a transformation in the labor market that favors their own elite skills, and at the same time dominate the lucrative new jobs that the transformation creates. Together these two transformations idle mid-skilled workers and engage the new elite, making it both enormously productive and extravagantly paid. The spoils of victory grow in tandem with the intensity of meritocratic competition. Indeed, the top 1 percent of earners, and even the top one-tenth of 1 percent, today owe perhaps two-thirds or even three-quarters of their total incomes to their labor and therefore substantially to their education. The new elite then invests its income in yet more elaborate education for its children. And the cycle continues.

The sum total of elite training and industry, and of the elite labor income that meritocracy sustains, is absolutely immense. Meritocracy makes economic inequality overall dramatically worse today than in the past and shockingly worse in America than in other rich countries.

The top 1 percent of households now captures about a fifth of total income and the top one-tenth of 1 percent captures about a tenth of total income. This means that the richest household out of every hundred captures as much income as twenty average earners combined and the richest out of every thousand captures as much income as a hundred average earners combined. Compared to the period between 1950 and 1970, this roughly doubles the share owned by the top 1 percent and triples the share owned by the top one-tenth of 1 percent. Moreover, in spite of common complaints that capital increasingly dominates economic life, between two-thirds and three-quarters of these increases in fact come from growing elite labor incomes—from the massive paydays to superordinate workers just described. Rising economic inequality, that is, principally comes not from a shift of income away from labor and toward capital but rather from a shift of income away from middle-class labor and toward superordinate labor.

When they get big enough, differences in degree become differences in kind. At the middle of the last century, the economic distribution in the United States broadly resembled that in other rich democracies, including Canada, Japan, and Norway. Today, income inequality in the United States exceeds that in India, Morocco, Indonesia, Iran, Ukraine, and Vietnam. These national data cumulate local conditions, and narrowing the focus renders general statistics distressingly tangible: Fairfield County, Connecticut, for example, suffers greater economic inequality than Bangkok, Thailand.

America has become an economy and a society constituted by meritocracy, implemented through an unprecedented complex of competition, assessment, achievement, and reward, all centered around training and labor. This state of affairs—an immensely unequal economic order in which the richest person out of every thousand nevertheless overwhelmingly works for a living—has no precedent anywhere or anytime across all of human experience.

## SEDUCED BY MERIT

A powerful instinct nevertheless defends these inequalities. Early moral victories against birthright privilege, combined with the new elite's raw skills and vast energies, make it hard to quarrel with the idea that advantage should track effort and talent. Certainly this is better than the aristocratic worship of bloodlines that meritocracy displaced. Even in the face of rising discontent over the society that it has built, meritocracy itself retains an excellent reputation.

Meritocracy's champions develop these intuitions. They insist that grades and test scores measure students' academic achievements, that wages track workers' output, and that both processes align private advantage and the public interest. Meritocratic practices reinforce these associations. Entire professions—educational testing, compensation consulting—work to improve and to ratify the connections. In these ways, meritocracy makes industry—effort and skill, converted into economic and social product—into the measure of advantage.

These connections enabled the meritocratic revolution to push aside dull, sluggish, and inert aristocrats, to open the elite to anyone who is ambitious and talented, and to arouse the superordinate workers whose vigor and dynamism now light up the culture and drive the economy forward. Meritocracy, according to this view, promotes widespread prosperity. The enormous productivity of the meritocratic elite ensures that even if the rich do better under meritocratic inequality, the rest still do well. Moreover, meritocracy further ensures that advantage tracks desert. Superordinate workers owe their huge incomes to their immense industry. Indeed, the triumphalist view proposes, meritocracy transforms inequality itself, to reconstitute its moral character. Meritocratic inequality therefore arises without either deprivation or abuse. Whereas aristocratic inequality was both wasteful and unjust, meritocratic inequality declares itself at once efficient and just.

Until the financial crisis of 2007–8 unsettled meritocratic self-regard, one or another version of this triumphalism ruled the ideological field, effectively unopposed by any substantial critics or even skeptics. Even today, critical voices remain muted, or at least distorted and defanged, by meritocratic triumphalism's enduring power.

Meritocracy disguises its external effects and inner logics, and its institutions and rituals (universities, graduations) consolidate the disguise. Meritocratic practice projects meritocratic ideas onto everyday existence, to build the settings in which people live and narrate their lives and the fixed points around which their life stories revolve. Meritocracy lives through experience and not just logic, capturing the imaginations and limiting the critical faculties of those embedded in it. Indeed, meritocratic ideology and meritocratic inequality rise in tandem and drive each other forward, much as an immune system might select for more and more resistant parasites, which in turn render it increasingly indispensable. The disguise makes meritocracy—which is in fact contingent, recent, and novel—seem necessary, natural, and inevitable. Meritocracy wrong-foots critics of inequality by making itself appear inescapable—assuming all the powers of a tyranny of no alternatives.

Even critics of the rising economic inequality that meritocracy produces refrain from attacking meritocracy itself. One common complaint, which figures prominently in popular politics on both the left and the right, alleges that the rich do not in fact owe their incomes to merit at all but rather to nepotism and opportunism—to legacies of old-fashioned aristocracy. According to this view, elite schools and universities admit students based on cultural capital, class background, or legacy status rather than intelligence or academic ability, elite employers hire based on social networks and pedigree rather than skill or talent, and superordinate workers command their immense incomes through rent seeking or outright fraud. A second familiar criticism, developed in great detail by Thomas Piketty, attributes increasing economic inequality to a shift of income away from labor and in favor of capital and, in the extreme, to a rising oligarchy. According to this view, economic and political forces are reconcentrating wealth, redistributing income to become both more capital-intensive and more concentrated at the top, and by these means rebuilding an old-fashioned rentier elite as the economically and politically dominant caste in a twenty-first-century version of patrimonial capitalism.

Both arguments attack the current elite's meritocratic bona fides. They reproach inequality for departing from meritocracy, and they implicitly cast more and better meritocracy as the solution to economic injustice. The most prominent critics of economic inequality—no less than those who celebrate current economic arrangements—therefore capitulate to meritocracy's charisma, expressing rather than rejecting meritocratic commitments. Meritocracy has become the shared frame in which conventional disagreements about economic inequality play out, the dominant dogma of the age. Meritocracy, that is, has become the present era's literal common sense.

This state of affairs arises directly out of meritocracy's nature. To begin with, economic inequality in itself—inequality without deprivation—is hard to condemn without seeming a scold. As long as the middle class has enough, what is wrong with the elite's having more, especially if it owes its great fortune to equally great industry? To complain smacks of envy. Charges of fraud, nepotism, and patrimonial capitalism give the case against inequality a more seemly face. They name clear wrongs and confer an aura of moral seriousness on economic inequality's critics. Moral outrage then acquires a life of its own, and this makes accounts that emphasize economic inequality's meritocratic roots (in elite training, effort, and skill) appear unduly sympathetic to the rich, unduly complacent about the world, and even quietist.

The commonplace objections to rising inequality also conveniently absolve their principal constituencies of primary responsibility for it. The intellectuals and other professional elites who advance these objections may belong to the 1 percent, but they can take comfort in telling themselves that they are neither fraudsters nor aristocratic rentiers. Complaints about gratuitous self-dealing and resurgent patrimonial capitalism allow superordinate workers to condemn economic inequalities from which they benefit without really questioning either their own income and status or the meritocratic system that secures both. Elites can say that the problem lies not with them but with others, and they can cast themselves as innocent bystanders to inequalities that they sincerely regret. They may shout their condemnations from the rooftops without ever admitting complicity, or accepting responsibility, or abandoning any commitments essential to their own survival. Indeed, focusing attention on the private vices of bad actors, and conspicuously distancing itself from these vices, only burnishes the broader elite's meritocratic luster.

Nevertheless, the common view romanticizes much and conceals more. Although the moral wrongs that conventional complaints emphasize are real, these corruptions operate on the margins of the meritocratic regime. Fraud, rent seeking, and the resurgence of capital make real contributions to rising inequality, and diatribes against them denounce real targets. But the dominant causes of inequality lie elsewhere, inside meritocracy itself, and therefore on ground that inequality's main critics find less congenial.

The selection processes for elite schools and jobs do include nepotism, but they remain overwhelmingly driven by achievement and skill, which is to say by good-faith judgments of merit. The intensive training that rich parents give their children produces massive achievement gaps, so that meritocratic admissions themselves skew student bodies dramatically toward wealth, and the meritocratic elite can produce dynasties even without nepotism. Indeed, this effect is so powerful that the students at the top schools can become wealthier even as the admissions process becomes more meritocratic and the size of the legacy preference declines. Universities, rightly condemned for the legacy preferences they deploy, make it difficult precisely to quantify nepotism's effects on their student bodies. But an example illustrates how powerfully merit can dominate nepotism in producing a skew to wealth among elite students. Yale Law School, facing meritocratic pressures, including to maintain the sky-high LSAT scores on which the school's ranking depends, has ended its practice of giving children of alumni an extra "point" in the scoring system that it uses to rank applicants. Nevertheless, the student body includes as many and in some years even more students from households in the top 1 percent of the income distribution than from the entire bottom half.

Similarly, although elite incomes do swell on account of self-dealing, they remain overwhelmingly driven by elite industry. A bank might gain millions of dollars in fees from sharp or misleading practices—as when Goldman Sachs, in a deal called ABACUS that the Securities and Exchange Commission declared fraudulent, received $15 million for marketing asset-backed securities without disclosing that one of the portfolio's principal architects (the hedge fund manager John Paulson) was betting against them. But these gains pale before Goldman's total earnings, which amount to billions of dollars. More generally, while fraud accounts for billions of dollars of elite income, rising top income shares amount to trillions of dollars. Overall, the elite's income growth remains principally driven by massive increases in performance-related pay.

Finally, although capital is seizing income share away from labor, perhaps three-quarters of the increase in the 1 percent's income share comes from shifts of income within labor, as stagnant median wages coevolve with exploding wages for superordinate workers. Some specific instances of this pattern—for example, that large-firm CEOs were paid about twenty times a typical production worker's income in the mid-1960s but are paid three hundred times as much today—are well known. But incomes across industries have followed the same trend. A cardiologist earned perhaps four times a nurse's salary in the mid-1960s and more than seven times as much in 2017. Profits per partner at elite law firms have grown from less than five times a secretary's salary in the mid-1960s to over forty times as much today.

The change is perhaps most dramatic in finance. David Rockefeller received a salary of about $1.6 million (in 2015 dollars) when he became chairman of Chase Manhattan Bank in 1969, which amounted to roughly fifty times a typical bank teller's income. Last year Jamie Dimon, who runs JPMorgan Chase today, received a total compensation of $29.5 million, which is over a thousand times as much as today's banks pay typical tellers.

All told, nearly a million workers do the superordinate jobs described earlier and capture the enormous wages that these jobs pay. And rising economic inequality mostly stems not from capital's increasing dominance over labor, but rather from these superordinate workers' increasing dominance over middle-class workers.

Rising inequality is not driven principally by villains, and moralistic attacks on bad actors neglect morally complex but massively more consequential structural wrongs. Indeed, the commonplace objections to rising economic inequality undermine themselves. When critics embrace meritocracy in principle, they ensure their own impotence and in fact buttress the inequality they purport to condemn. The moralists are the real trivializers. And only arguments that underline rising inequality's meritocratic bona fides confront the true depth and breadth of the problem.

Meritocracy is not the solution to rising inequality but rather its root. Meritocracy's inner logic has become undemocratic and opposed to economic equality. Even when meritocracy operates precisely as advertised, it promotes the dynastic succession of status and wealth and turns a ratchet that increases economic inequality. Ordinarily decent people, responding reasonably to economic and social forces that they do not control and cannot escape, produce outcomes from which very few people benefit and that still fewer celebrate.

The central tragedy of the age reflects meritocracy's triumph. Meritocracy—not by betraying its ideals but rather by realizing them—imposes a caste order that equality's champions should condemn. And combating inequality requires resisting the meritocratic ideal itself.

# TWO

# THE HARMS OF
# MERITOCRACY

Middle-class children born at the close of the Second World War, before meritocracy's rise, received a warm welcome from an open-hearted, rapidly expanding world. Median incomes nearly doubled between the mid-1940s and the mid-1960s, so that even children who never joined the elite were virtually certain to grow richer than their parents. Good fortune, widely shared, spreads beyond individual households and families to wash over a culture. At midcentury, thriving middle-class communities deployed their new wealth to invent an entirely new way of life.

Middle-class prosperity even put a physical stamp on the world. Cities transformed, as car ownership reduced distances and construction raced to keep up with the middle class's exploding demand to own houses. Villages and rural communities became suburbs, and suburban life assumed a previously unimaginable affluence. Over the 1950s, a previously sleepy resort town like St. Clair Shores, Michigan, transformed into a thriving suburb of prosperous Detroit. A local bowling alley owner remembers that in those days, his pinboys would leave their childhood jobs on their eighteenth birthdays and present themselves at one of the Big Three automakers, to be hired at $100 per week, the equivalent of perhaps $40,000 a year today. Their union jobs, moreover, effectively guaranteed lifelong employment, and if the young men proved good workers, they would be trained into tool- and diemakers or other skilled tradesmen and eventually paid the equivalent of nearly $100,000 per year, with benefits. Midcentury workers could achieve all this, moreover, without any formal education beyond high school.

This "privileged working class," as the business owner still calls it, made St. Clair Shores rich enough to sustain the twenty-seven-story Shore Club Highrise Apartments and Marina, which was built starting in 1962 overlooking Lake St. Clair. Similar new developments blanketed the country, connected by new roads, and a new social as well as physical world was born. Midcentury American workers succeeded so profoundly that they remade the American class structure, rising up to give themselves a new name and building a broad middle class that could represent and dominate society writ large. John Kenneth Galbraith would make middle-class prosperity into the theme of his classic midcentury book *The Affluent Society*.

Today, meritocracy again transforms middle-class life, only now for the worse. The middle class has not become poor; indeed, economic growth probably makes it richer today than it was at midcentury. But the contemporary middle class is nevertheless much worse off on meritocracy's account. Where the midcentury middle class thrived and grew, meritocracy now bequeaths it a stagnant, depleted, and shrinking world. And where the midcentury middle class dominated the national imagination, meritocracy now exiles it from the heart of economic and social life and confines it to economic hinterlands and cultural backwaters.

St. Clair Shores illustrates the new world also, in all its tangled and conflicted complexity. The town faces no acute deprivation and suffers no obvious injustice or oppression: median family income in St. Clair Shores, at just under $70,000, almost precisely matches the national median, which nearly triples the poverty threshold, while poverty, at about 9 percent, falls below the nationwide rate. Children play in well-tended yards on tree-lined streets of modest—three-bedroom, eleven hundred square feet—but well-built and immaculately maintained one-story houses, which become slightly larger (and often acquire a second story) nearer the lake that gives the town its name. St. Clair Shores encourages good husbandry, giving awards for beautification and issuing citations for even minor neglect, such as flaking paint or feeding birds in the front yard. Residents embrace this vision of civic life: a councilman proudly reports that the town sustains over thirty volunteer municipal boards, commissions, and committees. Summer in St. Clair Shores begins with what people claim is the largest Memorial Day parade in Michigan, headlined in 2018 by Olympic figure skater Nancy Kerrigan and also featuring Al Sobotka, who drives the Zamboni for the Detroit Red Wings. Summer ends with a classic- and hot-rod-car cruise down Harper Avenue. Residents, reflecting on this portrait, say that the middle-class values of the 1960s still dominate the town.

This way of life, for all its apparent controlled steadiness, leaves St. Clair Shores with little to look forward to and much to fear. Meritocracy is slowly dismantling what the midcentury economy built.

The town's southern neighbor and former cultural and economic engine, Detroit, has suffered decades of relentless deterioration, culminating in the largest municipal bankruptcy in American history. It will never recapture midcentury affluence: the manufacturing jobs that made the midcentury middle class are largely gone, and no one in St. Clair Shores thinks that they are coming back. The wellsprings of midcentury wealth have dried up.

The present-day economy, moreover, neither attracts firms established elsewhere to move to St. Clair Shores nor stimulates start-ups, so that the town enjoys very little new economic investment. St. Clair Shores sustains few glamorous or otherwise truly elite jobs, and workers there lack opportunities to advance into management or the professions. Fewer than a quarter of the adults in St. Clair Shores hold a bachelor's degree and fewer than one in ten hold a graduate or professional degree. There are therefore virtually no really rich people in St. Clair Shores, at least by national standards. A local businesswoman and civic leader uses annual incomes of $300,000 to $400,000 to illustrate the very richest few people in town—a tidy sum, to be sure, but outside the top 1 percent.

The economic energy and social dynamism that suffused St. Clair Shores at midcentury have dissipated, and the town's commercial culture now stagnates. Its architecture—Arts & Crafts cottages and midcentury modern ranches—has worn well, but there are no stylish new buildings to complement the older ones. There are no fashionable or trendy shops, restaurants, or clubs in town, and there is nothing really expensive, extravagant, exciting, or novel to do. Instead, residents seeking a night out go to places like Gilbert's

Lodge, where hamburgers (served since 1955) cost $12 and deep-dish pizza a little more. (These prices, a local schoolteacher says, mean that "people going to Gilbert's are probably more of the top" of the town's society.)

St. Clair Shores feels preserved rather than blossoming. (When Gilbert's burned down a few years ago, the owners rebuilt a copy, down to the model train running in the rafters and the trophy animal heads on the walls.) Preservation, moreover, chiefly depends on the accumulated income that older (and now-retired) workers gained and saved in the midcentury economy. The forces that preserve the town are losing ground. The St. Clair Shores Public Library, which plays a central role in the town's cultural life, has roughly a third fewer staff members than it used to, and tight budgets have reduced the library to relying on part-time and inevitably short-term workers. The library increasingly depends on private charity to meet its basic needs, and a staff member reports that the reading room still uses tables bought in 1971 (although the desk chairs were finally reupholstered a few years ago).

Even if St. Clair Shores just about sustains its current residents decorously in their established habits, its fragile condition does not allow them to grow more prosperous or to experiment or evolve, and it is not a place that people move to or even visit much. The town's population peaked in 1970, and it has lost nearly a third of its residents since then. The now-fading Shore Club—with unrenovated apartments and ramshackle common spaces— remains to this day by far the tallest building in town. And the Shore Pointe Motor Lodge, which opened in the boom years to serve the holidaymakers and other visitors who once flocked to Lake St. Clair, is still the only hotel in town.

Meritocracy consigns middle-class communities throughout the country to the same fate as St. Clair Shores. The job losses in Detroit's auto industry— which account for stagnation in St. Clair Shores—have equivalents all across American manufacturing, and these have cost the country nearly ten million middle-class jobs. More generally, super-skilled, superordinate workers have displaced mid-skilled, middle-class workers from the center of economic production. Across all economic sectors, innovations cause middle-class jobs to give way to a few glossy and many gloomy ones, so dramatically that the immense incomes paid in the glossy jobs account for the bulk of the rebalancing of income in favor of the elite and against the middle class, and therefore also for the bulk of elite income growth and middle-class income stagnation. As the incomes of the top 1 percent have tripled, the median real income has increased by only about a tenth since 1975, and median incomes have effectively not increased at all since 2000.

Meritocracy's champions insist that its hierarchies are benevolent and just: that inequality without deprivation is harmless, and that inequality that tracks industry is innocent. But the lived experience of the middle class tells a different story. Meritocracy debases an increasingly idled middle class, which it shuts off from income, power, and prestige. Moreover, even as the meritocracy trap locks an idled middle class out of the income and status conferred by work, meritocracy itself makes industry essential for status. Meritocracy therefore also subjects middle-class Americans to powerful imaginative burdens. By declaring its inequalities just, meritocracy adds a moral insult to the economic injury of middle-class stagnation. This insult carries enormous additional costs.

## THE EROSION OF OPPORTUNITY

Meritocratic inequality damages opportunities as well as outcomes.

A middle-class child in St. Clair Shores will attend passable but unremarkable public high schools and achieve undistinguished SAT scores—almost precisely tracking national averages—in a world that increasingly concentrates the returns to education in a narrow cadre of exceptional students. Graduates mostly go on to attend local colleges—Macomb Community College (which runs radio and television advertisements that still encourage high school students to enter skilled trades), Wayne State, and Michigan State. Some students, online message boards reveal, aspire to the University of Michigan. But there is no culture of high academic or professional ambition in the town, virtually no St. Clair Shores students even apply to the Ivy League or to other really elite colleges, and (residents say) actually attending such a college is so rare that a student who did so might make the local paper.

Once again, these patterns repeat throughout the country. Middle-class children today generally share their parents' diminished prospects and are barely better represented at elite colleges than are poor children. At highly competitive colleges, students from households in the top quarter of the income distribution now outnumber those from each of the middle two quarters by nearly six to one. The skew toward wealth at the most elite universities is almost inconceivably greater still. At Harvard and Yale, more students come from households in the top 1 percent of the income distribution than from the entire bottom half. Since only about one in ten Americans holds an advanced (post-BA) degree, the middle class remains locked out of just about all graduate and professional schools.

Meritocratic inequality demotes the middle class—diminishing not just outcomes but also opportunities—specifically because of meritocracy itself. Meritocrats, more than any elite that has come before, know how to train; indeed, they know training better than they know virtually anything. Meritocrats therefore cannot resist investing their massive incomes in giving their children elite educations unlike anything that middle-class parents can possibly afford. Meritocracy's inner logic makes it inevitable that intense education, provided to children while their parents are still alive, becomes the essential mechanism for the dynastic transmission of caste.

Nevertheless, the size and scope of elite investments in education astonish. Top public schools, located in rich districts and funded by real estate taxes on expensive houses, spend two or three times as much per student per year as middle-class schools do, including in St. Clair Shores. These investments buy literally extraordinary educations. Where St. Clair Shores middle school students might share a music teacher, who travels from school to school to teach 750 students a week, from a cart and without a music room, rich schools boast facilities that ordinary schools would not even dream about: a high-tech weather station in Newton, Massachusetts, for example, and, in Coronado, California, a digital media academy equipped with 3-D printers. More broadly, and probably more consequentially, the extra money available to rich schools pays for more and better teachers. A careful study of one large county revealed that principals of schools with richer students possess a full year's more experience on average than those of schools with poorer students, teachers possess nearly two years' more experience on average and 25 percent more master's degrees, and first-year teachers (who commonly struggle as they learn their craft) are less than half as common.

Elite private schools, which typically draw 80 percent of their students from the top 4 percent of the income distribution (like a gated community, a teacher in St. Clair Shores observes), invest still more extravagantly, spending as much as six times the national public school average per student. These schools possess truly astonishing facilities, with campuses that look, feel, and function like universities rather than schools. Elite private schools also employ more than twice as many teachers per student as public schools do. These teachers are themselves elite and extensively educated: fully three-quarters of the teachers at the prep schools that *Forbes* ranks as the twenty best in America hold advanced, which is to say post-BA, degrees.

The elite's massive investments in education succeed. The academic gap between rich and poor students now exceeds the gap between white and black students in 1954, the year in which the Supreme Court decided *Brown v. Board of Education*. Economic inequality today produces greater educational inequality than American apartheid once did. Educational inequality separates the rich not just from the poor but also, increasingly, from the middle class. The academic achievement gap between rich and middle-class schoolchildren, for example, is now markedly greater than the achievement gap between middle-class and poor children. By the time children apply to college, the differences are greater still and focus more specifically on the exceptional performance of elites. Rich children now outscore middle-class children on the SAT by twice as much as middle-class children outscore children raised in poverty. The elite out-train the middle class by so much that depressingly few children from non-elite households overcome caste to perform at elite levels. Only about one in two hundred children from the poorest third of households achieves SAT scores at Yale's median.

These unequal patterns arise inexorably through meritocracy's inner logic. Meritocracy's promise of equality—the theory that anyone can succeed simply by excelling, because meritocratic universities admit students based on academic achievement and employers hire workers based on skill—proves false in practice. The emphasis on excellence, whatever its motivation in principle, in fact produces admissions competitions and labor markets in which people from modest and even middle-class backgrounds cannot succeed. Exceptional cases always exist, but in general, children from poor or even middle-class households simply cannot compete in the battle for places at elite universities with rich children who have imbibed massive, sustained, planned, and practiced investment from birth or even in the womb. Workers with ordinary training, in turn, cannot compete with the immensely skilled and enormously industrious workers produced by the elite training.

These patterns, taken together, dramatically confine social mobility. Only one out of every hundred children born into the poorest fifth of households, and fewer than one out of every fifty children born into the middle fifth, will ever become rich enough to join the top 5 percent. A poor or middle-class child therefore faces longer odds against climbing the income ladder in the United States than in France, Germany, Sweden, Canada, Finland, Norway, and Denmark (and mobility in the last four of these countries more than doubles, and in some instances triples, that in the United States). Absolute economic mobility is also dwindling. The odds that a middle-class child will out-earn his parents have fallen by more than half since midcentury—and the decline is greater among the middle class than among the poor.

A cycle of exclusion ensues. Elite graduates monopolize the best jobs and at the same time invent new technologies that privilege super-skilled workers, making the best jobs better and all other jobs worse. Meritocratic labor incomes, in turn, enable elite parents further to monopolize elite education for each successive generation of children. Meritocracy therefore creates feedback loops between education and work, in which inequality in each realm amplifies inequality in the other. The rising gap between elite and middle-class wages measures the scale of meritocratic outcome inequality. The gap between elite and middle-class investments in education cashes out the scale of the dynastic transfer and of meritocratic inequality of opportunity. Together, these sums fix the strength of the meritocracy trap's exclusion.

Middle-class stagnation, elite prosperity, and rising economic and social divisions all fit together, as meritocracy transfers wealth and privilege dynastically down through the generations. Each turn of the meritocratic ratchet drives inequality inexorably forward, and these effects, taken together, dominate rising economic inequality overall. The early meritocrats harbored false hopes. Meritocracy has become the single greatest obstacle to equal opportunity in America today.

# THE END OF "STEADY GOOD"

A bartender at a popular marina restaurant in St. Clair Shores weaves all these threads together into a fabric of lived experience. After growing up in St. Clair Shores, he left for the West Coast, where he lived and worked in Seattle. Eventually, he returned—retreated—home, for a mix of reasons. Although he had earned more in Seattle, everything there was expensive, so that he was not sure that he could actually buy more, and (what is different) there were certainly many things on display in Seattle that he could *not* buy. Housing costs mattered especially, and in Seattle, prices were so high that he was entirely excluded from homeownership, not just at present but in any imaginable future. In St. Clair Shores, by contrast, virtually everything for sale is affordable for a middle-class family. The bartender can afford to shop in all the local stores and can eat out in all the local restaurants, including at Gilbert's and, for that matter, at his own restaurant. He could buy a condo for perhaps $50,000 and then live effectively rent-free, while (a local real estate agent observes) a unionized autoworker married to a schoolteacher, or a nurse married to a physician's assistant, might if they saved buy a house on the water, in the town's most expensive neighborhood. Nothing in the town is out of reach.

A society tracks its economy, so that St. Clair Shores is also more culturally democratic than Seattle, and this social structure creates a veneer that covers up failure and exclusion. Seattle, like other large coastal cities, revolves around a national (even global) elite—the superordinate workers brought there by Amazon, Microsoft, and Boeing. The bartender found himself priced out not just of consumption but also of membership and status there, so that, not being rich, he felt poor—excluded from a society built for the rich. By contrast, the middle class is at the center of life in St. Clair Shores. When asked who is important and why, residents (to a person) answered that status depends on commitment to the town rather than on education and jobs, or income and wealth; that community leaders are people who get involved, not people who are rich. Town leaders expressly reject the markers of status that dominate places like Seattle. "People don't like the elite," one says, and goes on to insist that "I've never hired anybody because of where they went to school or where they didn't go to school."

This makes status more widely available inside St. Clair Shores than in the larger world: "You can live here and feel successful for way less money," a town leader observes on being told the bartender's story, but in big coastal cities, "you can't feel successful for more money." Instead, failure and exclusion haunt life: "You've either made it or not, and then you don't feel good," she goes on to say. The bowling alley owner says simply that the bartender "felt middle class" here, and he might have added that "here" in St. Clair Shores is a middle-class world. "Steady good," another prominent resident suggested, is better than "fleeting great." It feels better to be at the center of your own poorer society than on the margins of someone else's richer one.

At midcentury, St. Clair Shores could deliver on these democratic promises. Middle-class affluence meant that "steady good" in fact grew steadily better, and the dominant role that the middle class played across the country meant that being at the center of St. Clair Shores put a person in the center of American life, period, and (given American economic dominance) even credibly at the center of global society. Economic fundamentals supported middle-class culture, and the perspective from outside St. Clair Shores affirmed the perspective from inside it.

Today, meritocratic inequality steadily erodes this democratic logic, and the veneer that disguises middle-class exclusion is cracking and flaking, in St. Clair Shores as elsewhere. The economic and cultural drivers of American society lie farther and farther beyond the middle class. Every year, an innovation will spawn a new economic or cultural boomlet somewhere, and every year, it will never be in St. Clair Shores. As the larger meritocratic world moves forward, it loses respect for the town's democratic order and middle-class values. Inside the town, life grows slowly worse—not yet wretched, but worn down and precarious.

Feelings of success inside St. Clair Shores become brittle—vulnerable to being shattered by outside perspectives—and the town struggles prayerfully to sustain a culture whose economic foundations are crumbling. To be middle class in a mature meritocracy is to be not just old-fashioned but backward-looking—committed to preservation rather than growth, and to a form of life that is inexorably in retreat; it is to protect a fortress that is both shrinking and decaying and that must fall, inevitably and soon.

St. Clair Shores, like the broader American middle class, is playing defense rather than offense. The town, which was once what one town leader calls a "very safe and controlled" space for the middle class, is, she acknowledges with wry understatement, becoming steadily less safe and less controlled.

## ADDING INSULT TO INJURY

Even as it renders middle-class workers literally redundant, meritocracy also valorizes industry and despises idleness. The middle class that built midcentury America in its own image therefore becomes, under meritocracy, an underclass—deprived not just of economic value but also of virtue and social standing. In this way, meritocratic inequality attacks not just pocketbooks but also hearts and minds, hitching the moral insult of declaring middle-class workers worthless to the economic injury of stagnant middle-class wages. Meritocratic ideals express and validate the insult and, furthermore, demand that the middle class embrace its own abasement. The meritocracy trap imprisons the imagination, casting economic exclusion as an individual failure to measure up and blocking the middle class from collective consciousness of the harms that meritocracy imposes. Meritocracy remakes the middle class as a lumpenproletariat.

Stagnation harms those who are stuck, receding opportunity saps energy and optimism, and enforced idleness draws contempt, invites indolence, and nurtures frustration and anger. It does not matter much that the middle class is caught in a place that might otherwise seem satisfactory, especially when it sees elites drawing increasingly farther ahead and out of reach.

The two-pronged meritocratic assault on income and on status unravels the middle class. When communities lose middle-class manufacturing jobs, for example, not just earnings but also marriage and fertility rates fall, and mortality rates (especially among middle-aged men) rise. Families break apart: women with a high school education or less bear more than half of their children outside of marriage (compared with just 3 percent for women with a college degree or more). Children struggle in school. And adults strain simply to survive.

Mortality rates reveal the meritocracy trap's psychic harms with almost incredible starkness. For two straight years now, midlife mortality has risen in America and life expectancy has fallen, especially for middle-class whites.

This is flatly astonishing—actually unprecedented. Under ordinary conditions, only large wars, economic collapse, or epidemic disease can kill enough people to cause sudden increases in a population's mortality. The last two-year decrease in life expectancy in the United States was due to epidemic influenza in 1962–63. But today, mortality is rising apart from any of these causes, and in a middle class that consumes more and bears a smaller labor burden than any in history. Middle-class Americans are dying, in large numbers, without material reasons.

The imaginative burden of meritocracy explains the mystery. The causes of death expose this sinister burden. Middle-class American adults are dying from indirect or even direct self-harm, as they—literally—somatize the insult of their meritocratically justified exclusion. The billboards along I-94 East from Detroit to St. Clair Shores prominently include advertisements for Narcan, a medicine used to "stop opioid overdose," and Macomb County, where St. Clair Shores lies, recorded seven times as many drug-related deaths in 2016 as in 1999. The opioid epidemic extends far beyond St. Clair Shores. Suicides, overdoses, and alcohol abuse (having increased between three and five times faster among less educated than among more educated adults) now kill Americans at rates roughly equivalent to the AIDS epidemic and account for rising mortality overall. In these and myriad other ways, the idleness that the meritocracy trap imposes on an economically superfluous middle class has exacted over a million "deaths of despair" over the past decade.

The conventional belief that meritocracy promotes meaningful work and widespread opportunity is misleading. Indeed, the common view gets things almost exactly backward. Meritocracy's champions contend that meritocracy breaks the old link between inequality and poverty. But in fact, meritocratic inequality excludes everyone outside of an increasingly narrow elite from the top schools and jobs, and meritocracy deprives the middle class of social and economic opportunity. Similarly, meritocracy's champions insist that it connects advantage to desert and so makes economic inequality morally innocuous and even admirable. But in fact, meritocratic inequality's self-righteous insistence that social and economic hierarchies are justified renders them especially poisonous and cruel for those outside the chosen elite.

The burdens that meritocratic inequality imposes on the middle class may be measured by counting its dead.

# THE EXPLOITATION OF THE ELITE

The evils that meritocracy visits on the elite are less obvious, and the wealthy are anyway not natural objects of sympathy. Nevertheless, today's meritocrats live much less well than did their aristocratic predecessors. The gloss that meritocratic inequality spreads over life at the top is not deep or humane, but shallow and even merciless.

An epidemic of effort consumes the meritocratic elite. Superordinate work pervades elite life virtually from cradle to grave. Elite effort begins in early childhood, where meritocratic parenting and education self-consciously aspire to instill the skills that superordinate work will later demand. Elite schools, both private and public, make such extreme demands on their students—three hours of homework a night in middle school and five hours in high school are not unusual—that the Centers for Disease Control has warned of schoolwork-induced sleep deprivation. An endless stream of supplemental training, provided by tutors, coaches, and test preparation services, further besieges rich children outside of school.

Unremittingly intense labor also extends deep into adulthood, spanning the life cycle of a superordinate career: the mature elite do the extreme jobs. Law firms do not just demand billable hours from associates, but also obsessively track every partner's contributions to hours billed—one updates the online database through which partners can review one another's contributions (by smartphone) every twenty minutes, twenty-four hours a day. Bankers are expected to "ratchet up" their dedication as they advance through the hierarchy. Top managers, in the words of a senior executive at a Fortune 500 firm, are "the hardest working" people in their companies, getting and keeping their jobs because they "out-work the others . . . out-practice them . . . [and] out-train them."

All these workers give harder, longer, and more intensive effort than they want to. Superordinate workers overwhelmingly say they would sacrifice income to gain leisure. Those working over sixty hours per week report that they would, on average, prefer twenty-five fewer weekly hours. They say this because, systematic studies report, work interferes with their capacity to maintain their homes, to form strong relationships with their children and good relations with their spouses, and even to have a satisfying sex life. It is therefore no surprise that one commonly hears the overworked elite speak of their "time famine." The flat, unyielding length of elite work hours engulfs the lives of superordinate workers.

Moreover, the meritocratic elite yields this immense effort under conditions of intense competitive strain. Meritocratic competition now pervades elite life. Evaluations that were once quarantined to exceptional moments like college admissions season or promotion to partner or managing director now infect every step of a meritocrat's career. Every year, from preschool through retirement, includes some contest or assessment that filters, tracks, or otherwise influences his opportunities.

Elites first confront meritocratic pressures in early childhood, when they are conscripted into a competition for grades, test scores, and school places. The most competitive preschools admit fewer than one in ten applicants. Rich parents in cities like New York, Boston, and San Francisco now commonly apply to ten kindergartens, even as each application requires running a gauntlet of essays, appraisals, and interviews—all to evaluate four-year-olds. Applications to elite private elementary and high schools repeat the ordeal, and in places where meritocratic elites congregate, top public schools are equally or even more competitive. Nearly thirty thousand students take the entrance exam for Manhattan's eight elite specialized high schools, for example, competing for just over five thousand places. College simply extends the pattern. Elite universities that just a few decades ago accepted 30 percent of their applicants now accept fewer than 10 percent (and whereas the University of Chicago admitted 71 percent of its applicants as recently as 1995, Stanford admits fewer than 5 percent today).

Superordinate work renews the contest and projects it deep into adulthood. Law firms now ruthlessly separate even their partners into tiers based on contributions to firm profits (and income spreads within the partner ranks can reach twenty to one), and the firms expel even top-tier equity partners who stop generating enough business, a practice unheard of a generation ago. Banks distinguish between merely nominal managing directors and "participating managing directors" or "partners," or between ordinary directors and "group heads"; and an annual "bonus day," which allots performance-based pay, determines the success or failure of every banker's year. Large corporations distinguish between ordinary managers and the C-suite, and even CEOs get their compensation principally as performance-related pay and face an aggressive market for corporate control. Their incomes and even jobs depend as never before on beating competitors and delivering stock price growth.

At the same time, the contests themselves have become transformatively more severe. In schools, a 30 percent admissions rate establishes a strenuous competition, but one in which a responsible candidate from a supportive family enjoys a reasonable prospect of at least one success. Admissions rates below 10 percent create a competition in which nearly any misstep disqualifies a candidate, so that success demands a single-minded willingness to sacrifice in the service of ambition and requires luck even then. At work, a strenuous but manageable competition to make partner or join management has been replaced by an overwhelming competition to reach the very top, highly exclusive tiers—the management committee, the C-suite—of an ever-pointier hierarchy.

These transformations again follow meritocratic inequality's inexorable inner logic. Rising top incomes and the growing gap between the rich and the middle class produce carrots and sticks that together rationalize the severity of meritocratic competition. Elite children strain themselves in meritocratic schools and elite adults accept the relentless rigors of the meritocratic workplace because the returns to gloomy jobs are so low, the returns to glossy jobs are so high, and so few jobs are glossy. As winners more nearly take all, the battle to win intensifies. Elite opportunity is exceeded only by the competitive effort required to grasp it.

Meritocracy fundamentally remakes elite life: at home, at school, and at work, beginning in childhood, and extending through retirement. Elite training now bends rich families to its discipline, insistently demanding demonstrable achievement. Where aristocratic children once reveled in their privilege, meritocratic children now calculate their futures—they plan and they trim, through rituals of stage-managed self-presentation, in familiar rhythms of ambition, hope, and worry. Where aristocratic parents once consigned their children to benign neglect and devoted themselves to adult life, meritocratic parents arrange their households around giving their children the greatest possible chance of winning the educational tournament. Elite work similarly bends rich adults to its discipline, insistently demanding intensive production through the whole of adult life. Meritocracy traps elites in an all-encompassing, never-ending struggle. Every colleague is a competitor. At every stage, the alternative to victory is elimination.

The meritocratic tournament inverts the conventional associations between income and status on the one hand and security on the other. Meritocracy introduces ever more distinctions specifically at the top of its hierarchy, and at the same time lengthens the social and economic ladder, so that the gaps between rungs increase as a person climbs up it. Meritocratic competition therefore grows most intense within the elite. The most successful students and workers also become the least secure, as smaller differences in performance produce greater differences in rewards at the top than anywhere else. Elite insecurity begins almost at birth and never ends—especially at the meritocratic ladder's very highest rungs.

Indeed, the narrow elite has become so small, and the competition to join the elite so intense, that the tournament begins afresh in each new generation, as no one is ever comfortably "established" in the meritocracy. Class anxiety dominates life at the top—from childhood, through youth and university, to career building and parenthood—as superordinate workers and their children live under the inescapable threat of failing to measure up and being expelled from the elite. In a dark irony, meritocracy renders rank itself precarious. The contrast between the meritocrat's slippery path to extravagant wealth and the earlier aristocrat's complacent birthright security and entitlement could hardly be starker. Meritocracy enables dynastic succession, but it imposes a heavy human tax on its dynasties.

As an entire civilization centers its economic life around the immense training and enormous industry of a tiny elite of its people, the weight that each superordinate worker must carry grows. Meritocracy concentrates production in an elite that is literally too narrow to shoulder the burden. This form of production exploits those who supply overburdened and alienated labor in order to enter and remain inside the meritocratic inner sanctum.

## THE BURDEN OF HUMAN CAPITAL

None of this is an accident. Instead, the elite's effortful striving reflects an adjustment to a new economic necessity, itself occasioned by meritocracy's inner logic. The new elite simply cannot realize its income and status without devoting itself, almost single-mindedly, to competitive training and work.

The old elite held its wealth in land and (later) factories. Land and factories can produce rents, or profits, without requiring any specific labor from their owners and often without requiring the owners to work at all. An aristocratic rentier might therefore acquire income idly. Low-paid tenants or workers provided all the labor, and the leisured aristocrat kept the lion's share of the profits. Physical and financial capital liberates its owners.

By contrast, the wealth of the new meritocratic elite consists in its own training and skills. In a sense, the meritocrat remains fundamentally a rentier. She owns an asset: her embodied training and skill, or human capital. Like every rentier, the meritocrat extracts profits, or income, from her capital by mixing it with labor. The rich do not possess a secret to effort that the rest lack. Rather, an hour's superordinate work from an elite doctor, lawyer, banker, or manager produces more value than an hour's work by an unskilled laborer, holding effort constant, because each unit of the superordinate worker's effort mixes with capabilities built through massive prior investments in training. Meritocracy sustains enormous wages for superordinate workers not on account of any extraordinary effort but rather on account of the economic value of this immense stock of human capital.

The forms of capital held by meritocrats and aristocrats have nearly opposite effects on their lives, and in particular on their freedom. Unlike land or factories, human capital can produce income—at least using current technologies—only by being mixed with its owners' own contemporaneous labor. (Even where a superordinate worker leverages her skill and training by hiring others to mix their labor with her human capital—as a partner at a law firm might hire associates to elaborate her legal intuitions, or a manager might hire production workers to implement her plans—she can mix her human capital productively with other people's labor only if she herself works intensively alongside them.) The rich now work so compulsively because this is the only way to exploit their peculiar kind of wealth. Human capital more nearly enslaves than liberates its owners.

The imaginative requirements of living off of human capital further burden the meritocratic elite—in ways at once less tangible than long hours and more profoundly disturbing. As a maturing meritocracy roots both income and status comprehensively in human capital, competition becomes more immediately and inescapably personal. The meritocratic tournament dominates the culture that frames both the external environment and the inner life (the hopes and fears) of every meritocrat. People who are required to measure up from preschool through retirement become submerged in the effort. They become constituted by their achievements, so that eliteness goes from being something that a person enjoys to being everything that he is. In a mature meritocracy, schools and jobs dominate elite life so immersively that they leave no self over apart from status. An investment banker, enrolled as a two-year-old in the Episcopal School and then passed on to Dalton, Princeton, Morgan Stanley, Harvard Business School, and finally to Goldman Sachs (where he spends his income on sending his children to the schools that he once attended), becomes this résumé, in the minds of others and even in his own imagination.

Every owner who exploits an asset purely as a means to an end alienates himself from that asset's true nature and intrinsic worth. Even a traditional rentier, who administers his estate purely to gain income, betrays the feudal bonds that once tied an aristocrat to his land. As Chekhov worried in *The Cherry Orchard,* the quest for profit "devours everything in its path and so converts one kind of matter into another." The ancient orchard that gives the play its name yields its greatest rents by being cut down to make way for holiday villas—which is to say through its own absolute destruction and the destruction of the way of life that it once sustained.

But an owner of land or factories—especially a new owner, who rejects feudal values (a son of serfs, in Chekhov's play)—might reasonably absorb or even disregard these costs. Indeed, the profits that a rentier extracts free him to devote his personal energies to his authentic interests and ambitions—in the arts, for example, or statesmanship, or even just high society—without worrying about his economic income or social status. Traditional wealth, held as physical and financial capital, does not just free its owner from the need to work; it also enables him to become more fully himself.

Human capital works in almost exactly the opposite way. The very idea that a person might be capital treats the person as a means and so invites alienation: it trains the profit system's devastating appetite on the people whose human capital produces rents. Meritocracy, moreover, applies this idea most intensively to the elite. It makes the elite worker's talents, skills, and training—her own self, her very person—into her greatest economic asset, the overwhelmingly dominant source of her wealth and caste. In order to extract income and establish status based on this kind of wealth, the superordinate worker must comprehend herself in instrumental terms. To secure her eliteness, the superordinate worker must ruthlessly manage her education and labor—training to develop skills that others value, and then working intensively in jobs and at tasks again set by others. She must act, in effect, as an asset manager whose portfolio contains her own person.

Meritocracy expands the commodification that Chekhov lamented with respect to land so that it now reaches human capital also. Indeed, meritocracy's express language emphasizes that it commodifies elite training and work. The schools and universities that educate superordinate workers parcel training into standardized, measurable, and even rankable units (think of the *U.S. News & World Report* rankings)—literally degrees. And the elite labor market then bundles tasks into discrete jobs, which can themselves be ranked (think of lists of "top" banks, consultancies, and law firms, or measures of hours billed within firms) including, again most literally, by wages. (Goldman Sachs—the poster child for superordinate labor—has renamed its personnel department "Human Capital Management.") Meritocratic production "devours" meritocrats, "converting" them from "one kind of matter" (people) "into another" (human capital). Meritocracy transposes the alienation that Chekhov's aristocrat suffered from his estate onto the meritocrat's relationship to his own person. And unlike the aristocrat, the meritocrat cannot turn to an alternative form of life to assuage or even cure his alienation.

Indeed, mature meritocracy's demands to exploit the self as an instrument of caste literally overwhelm elite life. Elite parents—reluctantly but self-consciously—allow their children's educations to be dominated not by experiments and play, but by accumulating the human capital needed for getting admitted to an elite college and, eventually, securing an elite job. Elite schools structure themselves around human capital accumulation, constantly adjusting their practices to the latest teachings of education science. Even where play is allowed, it ceases to be an end in itself and instead is subordinated to work. Sometimes play becomes a tool, used for teaching teamwork, for example, or the kinds of creative thinking that superordinate jobs will eventually demand. Other times, play is manipulated more ruthlessly still. At one elite elementary school, for example, a teacher posted a "problem of the day," which the students were required to answer before going home but given no designated time to solve, with the express purpose of training fifth graders how to snatch a few extra minutes of work time by multitasking or by sacrificing recess. By these and myriad other means, meritocracy transforms childhood itself from a site of consumption into a site of production. Its product is the human capital of the future adult superordinate worker.

Meritocratic adulthood similarly approaches work not as an opportunity for self-expression or self-actualization, but rather value extraction. A person whose wealth and status depend almost entirely on her human capital simply cannot afford to consult her own interests or passions in choosing her job— far too much rides on training and work to indulge curiosity or pursue a calling or vocation. Moreover, as wages become increasingly concentrated among the very highest-paid workers, a smaller and smaller share of jobs and job types support top incomes. Someone who wants an elite income—or, critically, even just an income sufficient to buy his children the schooling on which their own eliteness depends—must do one of a narrowly restricted class of jobs, heavily concentrated in finance, management, law, and medicine. Fewer than one in one hundred jobs, and virtually none in middle-class occupations—teaching, for example, or journalism, public service, or even engineering—pays even close to elite wages. And a person whose native interests lie in any of these fields, or indeed anywhere outside of whatever maximizes the return on her human capital, can pursue her calling only at the cost of sacrificing her own, and her children's, caste.

Far better, when confronted with such knife-edged choices, to forestall frustration by avoiding passionate commitments to begin with. This is why— in a pattern whose familiarity today disguises that it has no real historical precedent—elite workplaces are filled with people who would rather be doing something else but whose human capital has become too valuable (too essential to income and status) to squander on indulging personal ambitions: bankers who studied English or history in college, for example, or corporate lawyers who were inspired to go to law school by the American Civil Liberties Union or the Center for Individual Rights. It is also why the superordinate workers who yield this alienated labor nevertheless work at their jobs single-mindedly, and for almost all of their time. Meritocratic inequality might free the rich in consumption, but it enslaves them in production.

A person who lives like this places himself, quite literally, at the disposal of others—he uses himself up. A life measured out in this way, as on a jeweler's grain scale, proceeds under a pervasive shadow. At its worst, the meritocratic elite squanders the capacity to set and pursue authentic, intrinsically valued goals, so that honor is reduced to being useful without fuss. Even at its best, meritocracy invites deep alienation. Meritocrats gain their immense labor incomes at the cost of exploiting themselves and deforming their personalities. Elite students desperately fear failure and crave the conventional markers of success, even as they see through and publicly deride mere "gold stars" and "shiny things." Elite workers, for their part, find it harder and harder to pursue or even to know genuine passions and to gain meaning through their work. Meritocracy traps entire generations inside demeaning fears and inauthentic ambitions: always hungry, never finding, or even knowing, the right food.

Meritocratic production, by making elite workers rentiers whose incomes depend on exploiting their own human capital, renders work a site of suppression rather than expression of the superordinate worker's true self. This is, in fact, the same alienation that Karl Marx diagnosed in exploited proletarian labor in the nineteenth century. Indeed, as technological developments render mid-skilled workers increasingly surplus to economic requirements, and at the same time place super-skilled labor at the very center of productive life, meritocracy shifts the classic afflictions of capitalism up the class structure. The increasingly superfluous middle classes assume the role once occupied by the lumpenproletariat, while alienated labor comes home to roost in the elite.

Marx's knife takes an added twist. The elite, acting now as rentiers of their own human capital, exploit themselves, becoming not just victims but also agents of their own alienation. Once more, the elite should not—they have no right to—expect sympathy on this account from those who remain excluded from the privileges and benefits of high caste. Yet superordinate workers suffer worse than luxury's disappointments, and the human burdens of alienation remain real and weighty, wherever they fall. Where physical and financial capital frees its owner from the pressures to satisfy others, human capital focuses and concentrates all of these pressures insistently on the person who owns it.

The contrast between the meritocrat's bright, unreal path to extravagant wealth and the earlier elite's complacent birthright security and entitlement could hardly be starker. Where the traditional wealth allowed the aristocrat to be more truly himself, new wealth—held as human capital—condemns the meritocrat to losing her authentic self entirely. Meritocracy imposes a spiritual affliction on superordinate workers, condemning them to existential anxiety and deep alienation. No quantity of income and status can relieve it.

## WHITE-COLLAR SALT MINES

Even elite accomplishments reveal suffering and strain—the self-suppression that meritocratic competition exacts from elites. A recent applicant to Yale College, seeking to signal her intellectual seriousness and devotion to study, used her college essay to boast that once while speaking to an especially admired French teacher in high school, she urinated on herself rather than break off intellectual conversation in order to go to the bathroom. The pressure to broadcast accomplishment so pervades elite college culture that students give the practice names—for example, Stanford's "Duck Syndrome," chosen on account of the contrast between a duck's smooth glide when viewed from above water and the frantically churning legs that propel the duck below. And a respondent to a recent Harvard Business School survey of elite executives proudly insisted, "The 10 minutes that I give my kids at night is one million times greater than spending that 10 minutes at work." Ten minutes!

Meritocracy's deformations of the elite self also show a starkly tragic face. Palo Alto, California, for example—where four-fifths of adults hold a BA, over half hold graduate or professional degrees, and median family income nearly triples the national median—presents a model of meritocratic schooling. The town spends nearly twice as much per student on education as St. Clair Shores; the average student at Palo Alto's public high schools, Palo Alto High (or "Paly") and Henry M. Gunn High, scores in the top 10 percent nationwide on the SAT; and over 60 percent of graduates attend elite colleges, while forty graduates a year go to Stanford alone. But children in Palo Alto tragically succumb to the tensions that they must endure to achieve these meritocratic "successes." Paly and Gunn have in recent decades produced multiple suicide clusters and suffer ten-year suicide rates four to five times the national average. The suicides sometimes throw themselves in front of trains, and one student described the Caltrain warning whistle, heard in classrooms roughly every twenty minutes, as "like the cannon that goes off in *The Hunger Games* every time a kid dies."

The suicide clusters at Palo Alto's high schools are not unusual. Students at wealthy high schools generally now show higher rates of drug and alcohol abuse than those from poor backgrounds, and they suffer clinically significant depression and anxiety at rates double or triple the national average. These trends produce enormously high absolute levels of distress. In a recent study of another Silicon Valley high school, for example, 54 percent of students displayed moderate to severe symptoms of depression and 80 percent displayed moderate to severe symptoms of anxiety. College students, similarly, are twice as likely to have been diagnosed with depression today as they were at the turn of the millennium. Colleges again confront suicide clusters, and a task force on mental health established by the University of Pennsylvania in response to a wave of suicides there recently drew a direct connection between the meritocratic pressures that students come under and "demoralization, alienation, or conditions like anxiety or depression." A broader report, produced by a consortium of elite educators (including from Harvard's Graduate School of Education) laments the "competitive frenzy" surrounding admissions and warns that competition poses a direct threat to applicants' mental health.

Adulthood brings the elite no relief. The high tension that pervades meritocratic work stretches the elite to shrill anxiety, and even to the point of snapping. Superordinate workers—in Palo Alto, in New York, and across the country—work with frenzied intensity. Indeed, the meritocratic workplace intensifies the pressures inside the meritocracy trap, even to the point of assuming a physical expression, written on the elite body. A junior banker from New York, for example, reports flying to meet a client in spite of a sinus infection, rupturing his eardrum on the flight, and then completing his meetings with a bleeding and deaf ear, before rushing to the emergency room on landing back at home. A former lawyer similarly tells of the time when an associate in his firm passed out in the middle of a conference room, and the remainder of her team called an ambulance and, after the paramedics took her away, returned straight to work. (The associate eventually made partner, and observers treat her collapse as contributing to the promotion, by conspicuously demonstrating her commitment to her job.) Bankers have in some cases worked themselves literally to death, as when an analyst at Goldman Sachs was found dead from a high fall after repeated troubles concerning overwork. These accounts—right down to the gore—betray a monomaniac commitment to using, even abusing, oneself that is more familiar among elite athletes: they are white-collar versions of the NFL player Ronnie Lott's decision to amputate a broken finger because surgery and a cast would have forced him to miss a crucial game.

Even when meritocratic work culture pampers the body, it attacks the spirit. Amazon's offices may be less brutal—less physically grinding—than its warehouse floors, but they are nevertheless pitiless and inhumane. The firm's "leadership principles" call for managers to have "relentlessly high standards" and to "deliver results." To achieve this, Amazon requires managers to challenge each other "even when doing so is uncomfortable or exhausting" and—borrowing a technique traditionally associated with cults and totalitarian states—to be "vocally self-critical, even when doing so is awkward or embarrassing." As one worker observed, in an exposé of Amazon's workplace culture, the firm's combination of striving, criticism, and competition at work combined to ensure that "nearly every person I worked with, I saw cry at their desk." Another recently reported a performance review in which his boss spent a half hour delivering an uninterrupted litany of skills not mastered and goals not attained, only to conclude, "Congratulations, you're being promoted."

Strikingly, other insider observers reacting to the exposé did not call claims about Amazon exaggerated or cast the company as an outlier. Rather, observers of elite work overwhelmingly found the account of Amazon expected, ordinary, unsurprising, and even banal. Other elite jobs—at tech companies, banks, law and consulting firms, and even large corporations and other "white-collar salt mines"—are not materially different. Burnout pervades the elite workplace.

In order to become part of the meritocratic elite, a person must be able to absorb the strains of self-exploitation gracefully, or at least grimly. The greatest successes go precisely to those who can sustain their intensity without disruption and without breaking down. Superordinate workers know this and make endurance a measure of their status, much as the leisure class once measured its caste by polish and refinement. Amazon tells managers that when they "hit the wall" on account of their work's unrelenting effort and strain, the only solution is to "climb the wall." An investment banker recently observed that "it's hard to be a middle-level vice president and not spend 90 hours a week at the firm." In the words of a Fortune 500 executive, aspiring managers who have demonstrated their skills and dedication face a "final elimination": "Some people flame out, get weird because they work all the time.... The people at the top are very smart, work like crazy, and don't flame out. They're still able to maintain a good mental set, and keep their family life together. *They* win the race."

All the material advantages that elite meritocrats enjoy cannot secure their flourishing or well-being. Even exceptional resilience cannot remove the bitter taste that victory inflicts on those who win the meritocratic tournament. An unhappy, even disconsolate affect increasingly dominates superordinate work and elite life. Roughly two-thirds of elite workers now profess that they would decline a promotion if their new job demanded yet more of their energy. And plaintive calls for work/life balance ring ever louder in elite workplaces.

Elite discontent is driving American meritocracy toward what might be called a "Vietnam moment." When the U.S. government adopted a draft lottery that effectively ended college deferments and extended the burdens of fighting in Vietnam to rich families, the elite finally turned against the war. As the meritocracy trap closes in around elites, even the rich are turning against meritocratic inequality. As a dean of Stanford Law School recently observed in a letter to graduates, elite lawyers are caught in an intensifying ratchet: higher salaries require more billable hours to support them, longer hours require higher yet salaries to justify them, and each increase generates another in a seemingly endless cycle. Whose interests does this serve? he lamented. Does anyone actually want it?

A plea is not a plan, however: when promotions are offered, superordinate workers accept them and deliver whatever additional effort their new jobs demand, and work/life balance remains a pious slogan rather than a tangible program. The elite's attempts to avoid meritocratic discontent are defeated by meritocracy's economic logic: by the fact that an owner of human capital can get income only by exploiting herself, and by the carrots of glossy jobs and the sticks of gloomy ones. All the income and wealth that meritocracy confers on superordinate workers cannot promote freedom or flourishing. To the contrary, these nominal advantages in fact confine the elite ever more tightly inside the meritocracy trap.

# THREE

# THE COMING
# CLASS WAR

Aristocratic elites typically segregated themselves from the rest of the societies over which they ruled. Aristocrats traditionally owned things, performed rituals, and even wore clothes and ate foods that distinguished them from the masses. In some cases, laws (known as sumptuary codes) even mandated the distinctions, by forbidding non-aristocrats from owning or consuming aristocratic things.

The post–World War II American order dampened these distinctions, at least where economics was concerned. Race, gender, and sexuality divided society and imposed hierarchy and subordination in midcentury America, as they have done since the founding. But income and wealth mostly did not.

Palo Alto was not materially different from St. Clair Shores in 1960. Each town had its own local flavor: Jerry Garcia settled in Palo Alto as Bob Seger played the Crow's Nest (East) in St. Clair Shores. But median incomes and house prices were similar in both towns. Both places, moreover, grew steadily: the Stanford Shopping Center opened in Palo Alto in 1955 to meet a rising demand for places to shop, just a few years before the Shore Club Highrise Apartments would be built to meet demand for places to live in St. Clair Shores.

Palo Alto and St. Clair Shores illustrated the age. Wages across regions converged between 1950 and 1970, and college graduates were "remarkably evenly distributed" across the country: between urban and rural locations, across geographic regions, and even within cities. The elite and the middle class married and parented in the same ways, ate the same foods, watched the same television and movies, and even owned the same things, right down to the brands that made them and the stores that sold them: Americans bought 90 percent of their cars from Ford, Chrysler, or General Motors (whose most expensive models cost perhaps twice the price of an average car), half of their appliances from Sears, and a third of their watches from Timex. Postwar capitalism created a society that was not just politically but also economically and socially democratic. Quite possibly for the first time in recorded history, the rich and the rest lived the same lives and even had the same stuff.

Midcentury Americans self-consciously embraced this democratic merger and celebrated their classless society, including in popular culture. Economic fundamentals produced cultural practices that reached deeply and broadly into people's lives, to influence not just how they lived but also how they thought about how they lived, establishing an imaginative field. F. Scott Fitzgerald once remarked, in a short story, that "the very rich . . . are different from you and me," and Ernest Hemingway, in a short story of his own, had a character reply, "Yes, they have more money." With respect to economic inequality at midcentury, Hemingway was right and Fitzgerald wrong. The rich merged seamlessly into the middle class, and insofar as income did insert a seam into American society, it separated the middle class from the poor. Outside of poverty, economic inequality at midcentury presented a social blur. Economic distinctions did not disappear entirely, to be sure. But they became so small that the postwar decades are commonly called the Great Compression.

Today, meritocracy reinstates aristocratic distinctions, as meritocratic inequality resolves the social blur that once blended the rich into the middle class through small differences of degree into a razor-sharp line that separates the rich from the rest by a difference in kind.

The ratio of one-percenter to median incomes is now double what it was at midcentury, even as incomes in the middle and bottom quintiles have converged. Moreover, meritocratic inequality's effects on the lives of both the rich and the rest are not limited to income, understood as an abstract dollar sum. The rich and the rest now marry separately: 25 percent of American marriages are today composed of two college graduates (compared to 3 percent in 1960). The rich and the rest parent differently and in profoundly divergent domestic circumstances: women with a high school education or less now bear more than half of their children outside of marriage, for example, which is roughly twenty times the share for women with a college degree or more. The rich and the rest enjoy different pastimes: the rich spend so much less time at passive leisure than the rest and so much (two to five times) more time exercising that whereas "prosperous" was once a euphemism for "overweight," fitness is now a status symbol. The rich and the rest worship different gods, or at least congregate in different religions: High Church Protestants, Jews, and Hindus are unusually rich and educated, Low Church Protestants are unusually poor and uneducated, and only Catholics mirror all of society. The rich and the rest also inhabit different worlds online. An exhaustive analysis recently studied Google data on searches initiated in both the most and least prosperous counties in the country (ranked according to an index that includes income and education). The study revealed that the searches most correlated with prosperity include digital cameras, baby joggers, Skype, and foreign travel. By contrast, the searches most correlated with deprivation included health problems; weight loss; guns; video games; and the Antichrist, hell, and the Rapture.

Even geography now separates the rich from the rest. Palo Alto has left St. Clair Shores behind. Median incomes in Palo Alto now almost triple those in St. Clair Shores, and median house prices are roughly twenty times as high. Palo Alto's residents are three times more likely to hold a BA and five times more likely to hold a graduate or professional degree than residents of St. Clair Shores. The next neighborhoods over extend the isolation of the elite: Palo Alto is embedded in Silicon Valley, as St. Clair Shores is embedded in Detroit.

Similar gaps are opening across the country. Regional wages generally have diverged in the most recent four decades, and a vast educational divide has opened up between town and country: by 2000, the percentage of young adults with college degrees in rural areas was half that of the average city. College graduates, moreover, converge on a few particular and distinctive places, so that nearly half of couples in which both partners are highly educated live in large metropolitan areas. The convergence is greatest at the very top: three-quarters of the participants in a recent survey of Harvard, Princeton, and Yale alumni live in zip codes that rank in the top 20 percent on an index of income and education, half live in zip codes in the top 5 percent, and a quarter live in zip codes in the top 1 percent. The elite, moreover, did most of the traveling that caused this sorting, as young college graduates are more than twice as likely to move between states as young people with high school degrees only.

This makes perfect sense: moving far from home is exciting and even life-affirming for a superordinate worker whose sense of self comes from his job, but it is only frightening and isolating for a middle-class worker, condemned to dead-end jobs, for whom self-esteem stems from communal ties. Nevertheless, the experience of moving—for work, and to certain cities—has itself become a marker of eliteness, an axis of economic segregation.

## THE MERITOCRATIC DIVIDE

Meritocracy divides society against itself. It remakes childhood and adulthood, the home and the office, in its own divisive image, and the rich and the rest now work, marry, parent, socialize, read, eat, and even worship differently and apart from each other. These differences cumulate, and the meritocratic divide becomes too wide for the imagination to bridge, so that the rich and the rest fall out of sympathy with each other.

All these developments play out meritocratic inequality's inner logics. The rich find marriage partners in the schools and especially colleges that dominate elite youth. They then structure their adult lives to support the intense parenting and education required to pass their caste on to their children. Meritocracy even influences where the elite live. Physical capital is generally immovable and necessarily dispersed, so that a rentier elite naturally scatters throughout a country. Human capital, by contrast, is mobile and, critically, most productive when superordinate workers deploy their skills together, in close proximity. Meritocracy therefore induces the highly educated families that it creates to flee certain places and flock to others. In all these ways, and myriad others besides, meritocratic inequality comprehensively divides the rich and the rest, so that they each lead lives that the other can hardly recognize.

Although Hemingway may have won the argument with Fitzgerald at midcentury, meritocratic inequality increasingly vindicates Fitzgerald's view. Whereas the midcentury economic model achieved an amazingly deep unity of interests and of ideals across the broad middle class, economic inequality now threatens to divide America against itself, as profoundly as race and gender once did.

Racism and sexism have deep roots in American history and endure today, of course. Both insert fault lines into society that class does not displace, and persistent racial inequalities of income and especially wealth demonstrate both that American racism operates independent of class and that racial subordination persists in fact even where it is forbidden by law. But class—considered in addition to rather than instead of race and gender—now provides an organizing principle for comparably powerful social and economic stratification. Indeed, class stratification today produces inequalities that resemble the inequalities that de jure racial segregation produced at midcentury. The earlier observation that the rich/poor achievement gap in school now exceeds the white/black gap under Jim Crow reports just one instance of a broader trend. Economic differences in homeownership rates and unemployment rates, for example, have also grown to resemble racial differences at midcentury. Economic inequality now organizes life even within racial groups: among black men born in the late 1960s, for example, high school dropouts have a 59 percent chance of going to prison at some point in their lives whereas college graduates have a 5 percent chance.

These comparisons should not obscure racial subordination, but they do shine a light on class. Class appears, in this light, comprehensively to organize American social and economic life under meritocracy. Borrowing from the Victorian politician and thinker Benjamin Disraeli (who described another, admittedly different caste system), one might even say that in the United States today, the rich and the rest comprise "two nations; between whom there is no intercourse and no sympathy; who are as ignorant of each other's habits, thoughts, and feelings, as if they were dwellers in different zones, or inhabitants of different planets; who are formed by a different breeding, are fed by a different food, are ordered by different manners, and are not governed by the same laws."

Comprehensive inequality poses a threat to American society that extends far beyond the distress that the meritocracy trap inflicts on individual people, on either side of the meritocratic divide. Midcentury social solidarity—the broad unities of interest and imagination that led Hemingway to believe that the rich were distinguished only by wealth—has been shattered by meritocratic inequality. Rising inequality renders the middle class vulnerable and insecure. Winner-take-all competition gives elites growing incentives to defend their position. And elite education reframes meritocracy itself as an obstacle to social mobility and middle-class opportunity. Furthermore, meritocratic inequality also undermines the midcentury unity of ideals. (This is meritocracy's most profound threat to social solidarity, and the threat that is most deeply rooted in meritocracy's peculiar structure.) Meritocracy connects income to education and, through education, to work, family, culture, and even place, giving economic differences new dimensions of quality as well as quantity. This comprehensive divide prevents the rich and the rest from even imagining an ideal of the common good that they might share across caste boundaries.

Andrew Carnegie, writing "The Gospel of Wealth" at the height of the Gilded Age, worried that "the problem of our age is the proper administration of wealth, that the ties of brotherhood may still bind together the rich and poor in harmonious relationship." Today, the meritocratic divide threatens to tear society apart, on account of its profound depth and comprehensive breadth. As the political theorist Robert Dahl observed at the close of the Great Compression, in a worry that has proved prescient, "If all the cleavages [in a society] occur along the same lines . . . then the severity of conflicts is likely to increase. The man on the other side is not just an opponent; he soon becomes an enemy."

Meritocracy undermines social solidarity in just this way. When meritocratic inequality creates comprehensively isolated social classes, it invites class warfare.

## A NEW RULING CLASS

Politics provides class warfare's natural field of battle.

To begin with, meritocratic inequality rejuvenates an old motive for the elite to dominate political competition. Large fortunes encourage political meddling. Self-interest recommends that the rich engage politics as a means for defending their wealth. Altruism also directs the rich toward politics: once a person has bought everything that he wants for himself, it is only natural for him to turn his attentions to others. Moreover, meritocracy also inaugurates a new means for asserting dominance, creating a new supply of elite power. The skills, practices, and institutions that enable superordinate workers to dominate economic life also allow the elite to dominate politics, by controlling policy and by resisting the state when they cannot set policy directly. If democracy establishes what Dahl called "the continuing responsiveness of the government to the preferences of its citizens, considered as political equals," meritocracy undermines democratic politics and constitutes superordinate workers as a new ruling class.

The rich dominate the financing of political campaigns—to an astonishing degree. The richest 1 percent of Americans contribute more to political campaigns than the bottom 75 percent combined. Really large contributions are more concentrated still, as are the early contributions that winnow credible candidates and limit the options that voters will eventually choose among. A mere 158 families provided nearly half of all campaign contributions for the initial phase of the 2016 presidential election, and by October 2015 these families had collectively contributed $176 million. The Koch brothers' network of super-rich donors would spend nearly $1 billion on promoting free-market policies.

Meanwhile, lobbyists hired by elites dominate the policymaking that elected officials do once in office. There are roughly twice as many registered lobbyists in Washington today as there were in the early 1980s, and lobbyists who work for business, and therefore wealth, rather than for unions or the public interest comprise 98 percent of the increase. Even when it is narrowly defined, lobbying dwarfs campaign finance in scale: in a typical year, expenditures on federally registered lobbyists exceed $3 billion, and large firms spend perhaps ten times as much on lobbyists as on campaign contributions and nearly 90 percent more than they spent as recently as the late 1990s. Moreover, elite influence over policymaking extends far beyond formally registered lobbying. Corporations, for example, target their philanthropy at causes associated with legislators who sit on the committees that regulate them—so that charity mimics lobbying (only leveraged with public funds in the form of the tax deduction for charitable giving). In the limit case, lobbying of public authorities merges into direct private funding and control over public functions: the Walton Foundation (connected to the Walmart fortune) has spent over $1.3 billion on K–12 education and committed to spend another billion, with a heavy focus on charter schools (and the attendant disruption of teachers' unions).

All this money is not spent in vain. Donors, both directly and through their lobbyists, dominate the time and attention of candidates and officeholders. Elections begin, in what is called the money primary, with summits at which hopefuls court favor from groups of super-rich donors, often in resort towns (for example, Rancho Mirage, California; Sea Island, Georgia; or Las Vegas). Winning, moreover, yields no relief from the need to raise money. A "model daily schedule" for congresspeople calls for more than four hours directly soliciting donors every day in office. This roughly triples the time spent discussing policy with nondonor constituents, a disparity so great that politicians are sometimes said to resemble telemarketers rather than government officials. When Mick Mulvaney, the Trump administration's director of the Office of Management and Budget and (as of this writing) acting White House chief of staff, recently told the American Bankers Association that when he was in Congress, "If you're a lobbyist who never gave us money, I didn't talk to you. If you're a lobbyist who gave us money, I might talk to you," he merely said aloud what everyone in American politics already knows. Politicians spend the overwhelming majority of their time with donors and lobbyists whose views they promote.

Law and policy unsurprisingly follow the path set by money, time, and attention. Sometimes, money openly buys policy, with hardly any disguise. The Walton Foundation's spending has transformed public education in Washington, D.C., where the foundation has "in effect . . . subsidized an entire charter school system in the nation's capital, helping to fuel enrollment growth so that close to half of all public school students in the city now attend charters." In other cases, money's influence is less obvious—because disguised—but no less real. The financial sector, seeking to relax regulations limiting certain derivatives trading adopted through the Dodd-Frank Wall Street Reform and Consumer Protection Act in the wake of the financial crisis, bypassed the relatively public House and Senate finance committees and lobbied the low-profile agriculture committees (whose jurisdiction over the derivatives stems from efforts by nineteenth-century farmers to stabilize commodity prices). Sometimes, lobbying produces results so narrowly tailored to special interests that that policy becomes almost farcical. The casino lobby, eager to draw tourists (especially to Nevada), has exempted winnings at blackjack, baccarat, craps, roulette, and Big Six wheel from the income tax withholding regime used to stop foreign visitors to the United States from committing tax fraud.

These examples, moreover, are not exceptional. They are typical, even commonplace. Systematic studies reveal that law and policy respond sensitively to elite preferences while remaining almost totally unresponsive to the preferences of everyone else. Indeed, the rich dominate even the upper middle class: when preferences at the 90th and 70th income percentiles diverge, policy continues to respond to the 90th percentile and is only minimally responsive to the 70th. Even when the middle class and the poor unite against the rich, policy adjusts to the preferences of the rich and ignores the shared preferences of the middle class and the poor. Economic inequality begets political inequality, and meritocracy undermines democracy.

## THE INCOME DEFENSE INDUSTRY AND THE RULE OF LAW

Meritocracy undermines democratic politics not only at wholesale, when laws are made, but also at retail, when they are applied to particular people. Meritocracy has created a new class of super-skilled bankers, accountants, lawyers, and other professionals who seek favorable personalized treatment from government—concerning regulatory requirements, for example, or tax shelters—on behalf of individual clients. These professional services dwarf campaign contributions, lobbying, and political philanthropy, even combined. The trusts and estates bar alone comprises over fifteen thousand lawyers. The total revenues of the hundred largest law firms in the United States reached $90 billion in 2017, the revenues of the big four accounting firms reached $134 billion, and the revenues of the ten largest investment banks totaled over $250 billion. All these professions empower the rich to resist regulation and thereby disempower the rest from subjecting wealth to law.

They are, moreover, creatures of meritocracy—of the training that meritocratic educations provide and of the enormous labor incomes that meritocratic work affords. In this way, meritocracy directly produces a new means
for undermining democratic self-government.

Ideology disguises this lever of elite power. The common view supposes
that every property owner enjoys the same rights and protections—that she
owns things in the same way—no matter what or how much property she has.
According to this view, the state's relationship to private property is scale-
blind, so that large fortunes and small holdings receive the same legal protections, and the hedge fund billionaire owns his portfolio in exactly the same
sense in which the high school teacher owns her house. But in fact, size matters for property rights, qualitatively as well as quantitatively. A middle-class
person must comply with whatever regulations the state imposes on her and
forfeit whatever taxes it assesses. When the schoolteacher's real estate taxes go
up, she simply pays. But a rich person can use his swollen fortune to hire
skilled professionals to resist regulations and taxes, meeting the state on a
level and often even a favorable pitch. A billionaire who faces a new tax can
restructure his holdings, using perfectly legal tax shelters to avoid paying
most or even all of the levy. The middle class are lawtakers, which leaves their
property immediately vulnerable to regulations and taxes; the rich, by contrast, enjoy discretion to accept or reject law, which insulates their property
from government intrusion.

Meritocracy enhances the elite's power to resist the state. Meritocratic inequality creates incentives for the most skilled workers to grow rich by devoting themselves to defending still richer people's fortunes against government
encroachment. By inventing the superordinate private-sector job, meritocracy endows a class of workers—accountants, bankers, and lawyers—with
the means and the motive to block the state's efforts to seize, or even just to
regulate, elite wealth.

These jobs are new—direct creations of meritocracy. Historically, the private sector did not value managerial and professional skills, and the state
(which required such skills) faced effectively no private competition for elite
labor. Into the early twentieth century, top civil servants were paid ten or even
twenty times the median wage. And even at midcentury, elite government
incomes remained roughly equivalent to their private-sector counterparts. In

1969, a congressperson was paid more than he might make as a lobbyist, a federal judge received perhaps half what he might have commanded at a law firm, and the secretary of the treasury was paid a salary that was smaller than but broadly comparable to what he might have made in finance. The best-educated and most skilled workers therefore naturally gravitated toward government or other public jobs (as when subsequent sons, deprived by primogeniture of inherited lands, joined the military or the clergy), simply because they had no better (or even credible) private alternatives. This kept regulators ahead of the people whom they regulated and helped the state effectively to govern even its richest subjects.

Meritocratic inequality, by contrast, sharply increases elite private-sector wages, even as democratic sensibilities keep public-sector wages stagnant or falling. Together, these developments have completely reversed the earlier order, so that superordinate workers now earn many times more in the private sector than in government jobs. A congressperson becoming a lobbyist might multiply her income by a factor of ten, from $175,000 to perhaps $2 million; the chief justice of the Supreme Court earns roughly $270,000, while the very most profitable law firms pay their average partners over $5 million annually, or roughly twenty times as much (and the *signing bonus* paid to former law clerks at the Supreme Court, who are perhaps two or three years out of law school, is now $400,000); and the secretary of the treasury earns a little more than $200,000 annually, whereas the CEOs of JPMorgan Chase, Goldman Sachs, and Morgan Stanley might average incomes of $25 million, more than a hundred times as much.

The absolute salary numbers, and even just the ratios between elite private- and public-sector salaries, are astronomical. Moreover, and critically, the qualitative break between the prices of the lives lived by the rich and the rest occurs above the salaries of elite government workers but below the wages of the elite private-sector workers—lobbyists, lawyers, accountants, and bankers—who provide private influence over public policy. (This is almost inevitable, as house prices in elite neighborhoods are determined by the salaries of the elite private-sector workers who buy the houses.) In one sense, elite government workers make a lot of money—several times the median income. But it does not take much human imagination to understand that the broad elite of public servants naturally desire the society of their private-sector peers: that they desire to live in the same neighborhoods, to send their children to the same schools, and generally to mix on roughly equal terms with the people whom they knew at college and in graduate and professional school, and whom they regulate in their daily professional lives. Elite public officials need not be venal or otherwise corrupt to grasp hold of higher incomes or to join the society of the rich when opportunities in the private sector present themselves.

The opportunities invariably do present themselves. Elite public officials possess precisely the educations and skills the meritocratic private sector most values. (Meritocracy's hostility to prejudice expands these incentives to all elite workers—the presiding partner of the hyper-elite and conservative Cravath law firm, for example, is today a daughter of Pakistani immigrants—so that there no longer exists a subset of the super-skilled that is forced by chauvinism to resist rather than to serve wealth.) Government departments have become, in the shadow of these incentives, "barely disguised employment agencies," connecting public officials to future private employers. Even elected officials have gotten in on the act. In 1970, just 3 percent of retiring members of Congress became lobbyists; today, 42 percent of representatives and 50 percent of senators become lobbyists on leaving public office. (The move is so familiar that it has become expected: when Eric Cantor recently retired from his post as House majority leader, for example, the *New York Times* editorial board predicted that he would take a job in finance. And indeed, Cantor joined a boutique investment bank, a choice that the *Wall Street Journal* thought natural, given that he "has long been seen as a liaison of sorts between the GOP and Wall Street.")

Overall, talent now flows into the private sector in numbers so great—of demographic proportions—that they transform entire cities. Washington's elite job market is today dominated not by government hiring but rather by a private-sector effort to lure away public workers that has become pervasive, even inescapable: placemat "help wanted" ads at Washington coffee shops— for private jobs that pay midlevel officials starting salaries of a quarter million dollars or more—are sold out years in advance. Indeed, Washington is now among the nation's leading cities in venture capital deals. And so much talent now flows into businesses and professions that seek to exert private influence over government policy that the D.C. metro area has recently added over twenty thousand households to the richest 1 percent—far, far more than any other city—and has added college graduates more quickly than any other major metro area. A city where once "defense contractors knew not to wear watches that outshone the admirals'" is now awash in Tesla dealerships and restaurants with prix fixe menus priced at $200 per person, before wine.

Meritocracy directs this talent overwhelmingly to serve the private side of the interface between government regulation and the rich—to promote elite economic interests against the state. An entire industry now devotes itself to defending the elite's income and wealth—to resisting, as a recent Citigroup brochure directed at the bank's high-net-worth clients said, the "ways of expropriating wealth" favored by "organized societies" confronting "plutonomy." This income defense industry overwhelms the state, sometimes literally. Donald Trump's former top economic adviser Gary Cohn observes that "only morons pay the estate tax." Cohn's language may be crass, but it reports a simple fact: a systematic elite effort—including a media strategy, campaign contributions, lobbying, and tax planning—has effectively annihilated the estate tax. A combination of high exemptions and generous opportunities for tax planning means that in 2016, even before the 2017 tax reform further weakened the tax, fewer than fifty-three hundred families across the entire country paid any estate tax at all.

The estate tax is extreme but not exceptional. The broader complex of lawyers, accountants, and bankers advising the rich on tax havens is sufficiently large to allow what the industry calls high-net-worth individuals (people with more than $30 million of investable assets) worldwide to move roughly $18 trillion of assets offshore. Overall, during the same decades in which the top 1 percent's share of national income roughly doubled, the tax rates that it faced fell by perhaps a third. When Warren Buffett decries that he pays taxes at a lower rate than his secretary, he is reporting not an outlier but rather the limit case of a pervasive development. The rich have leveraged their rising economic power to remake the American tax system so that, taken altogether, a once-progressive regime has become effectively flat. Even when the rich are caught red-handed, they rarely get punished. The Obama Justice Department, for example, prosecuted effectively none of the financiers who caused the 2008 financial crisis, in part because prosecutors who would have handled the cases left for private-sector jobs.

# THE EMPOWERED ELITE

When it created superordinate workers, meritocracy gave the elite a tool specifically built to render itself effectively ungovernable. This development, remarkably, evokes the Middle Ages. The crown and local nobles each owed their positions to commanding the personal fighting power of small numbers of heavily armed knights. Social norms, moreover, praised martial valor equally, regardless of whether it was displayed in service to a local lord or to a distant king, and praised Christian virtue entirely apart from distinctions based on secular political boundaries. These arrangements enabled private wealth to compete directly against the state for the essential determinants of power and status, not only on material but also on moral terms. The direct competition left the crown weak and local lords strong.

From medieval times through the mid-twentieth century, a series of interconnected developments directed the state and private elites onto separate tracks. The state monopolized physical force, while private elites dominated economic life, including by owning the capital—land, slaves, and industrial machines—on which top incomes depended. And the state dominated public virtue, which took on a civic or even patriotic cast, while elites emphasized private virtues grounded in an ethic of extravagant leisure. The division of labor enabled the state to achieve dominance in the public sphere, relatively free from direct private competition.

Finally, meritocracy once again places the state and private elites into direct competition for the same basic asset (now the human capital of superordinate workers) and for the same basic virtues (now skill, effort, and industry). And just as feudal kings struggled to resist the private influence of local nobles who competed directly for the asset that underwrote their power and status, so the present-day American state struggles to resist the private influence of wealth that competes directly for superordinate labor.

In all these ways, at wholesale and at retail, meritocracy empowers the elite to dominate politics. Rather than responding to citizens "considered as political equals," government dictates to the middle class and defers to the meritocratic elite. Meritocracy undermines democracy, elevating the working rich into a ruling class.

# CORRUPTED BY MERIT

In addition to distorting the political process, meritocratic inequality also corrupts political ideals and debases the citizens who practice democratic politics. The moral insult implicit in meritocratic inequality haunts political life, making the rich complacent and the rest resentful. Elites detach from a society whose political support they no longer need and become immodestly sure of their own virtues. Meanwhile, the working and middle classes embrace populist anger and nativist resentment, rejecting expertise and institutions and assailing things foreign and unfamiliar. Inequality that is recognized as unjust can chasten those who enjoy its benefits and ennoble those who bear its burdens, as when Dr. Martin Luther King Jr. answered bigotry with the lesson that "hate cannot drive out hate, only love can do that." But today, inequality that appears justified degrades both sides of the meritocratic divide.

Meritocracy most obviously corrupts elite values by encouraging the view, as Dryden wrote, "that he, who best deserves, alone may reign." Less obviously but no less consequentially, meritocracy also makes elites at once defensive and complacent: excessively sensitive to harms associated with unmeritocratic discrimination, and numb to the harms produced by meritocracy itself.

On the one hand, meritocratic elites make prejudice that has no meritocratic gloss—based on race, ethnicity, gender, or sexuality—into a cardinal and unforgivable sin that must be suppressed absolutely and without regard for the cost. Widely embraced norms that govern elite life in the everyday therefore require a degree of caution and moralism around identity politics that has no analog for the other parts of morality. Elite society forgives (and even ignores) selfishness, intemperance, cruelty, and other long-recognized vices, but bigotry and prejudice, if exposed, can end a career. Such moralism seems selective, out of sympathy with life's complexities and confusions, and sometimes out of proportion to the harms at stake. Decent people outside the elite recognize that bigotry is wrong, but they tend to regard prejudice as an ordinary vice, like greed or meanness, to be condemned but also met with an apt indulgence for human frailty. Bigotry does cause immense individual and social harm, and charges that elite institutions—especially universities—succumb to political correctness can be politically motivated and are often made in bad faith. But they capture the important truth that elite denunciations of prejudice can be excessively hard and, partly for this reason, unduly brittle.

The elite's intense concern for diversity and inclusion also carries an odor of self-dealing. Unlike other vices, prejudice attacks meritocracy's moral foundations, raising the specter that advantage more broadly follows invidious privilege rather than merit. Meritocracy demands extreme vigilance against prejudice in order to shore up the inequalities it seeks to legitimate against their increasing size and instability. The elaborate and fragile identity politics that govern elite life follow inexorably from the elite's meritocratic foundations.

On the other hand, meritocracy inclines elites to chauvinistic contempt or even cruelty regarding inequalities that cannot be cast in terms of identity politics. Political correctness does not denounce calling rural communities "backward," southerners "rednecks," Appalachians "white trash," and the bulk of the United States "flyover country." Indeed, considered elite opinion as commonly rationalizes as condemns these slurs: a widely read essay in the *National Review,* for example, recently attacked white working-class communities as "economically . . . negative assets," as "morally . . . indefensible," and as "in thrall to a vicious, selfish culture whose main products are misery and used heroin needles," before concluding that "they deserve to die"; and a columnist for the *New York Times,* after observing that immigrants outperform native-born Americans in meritocratic competitions, called native-born citizens "the stagnant pool in which our national prospects risk drowning" and proposed (now tongue-in-cheek) that only mass deportations of the native-born could save America. Even politicians—in spite of all the costs of giving offense—show open contempt for the middle and working classes: Paul Ryan divided the world into "takers" and "makers"; Mitt Romney similarly complained that Americans who "are dependent upon government" oppose "tak[ing] personal responsibility and car[ing] for their lives"; Barack Obama suggested that "bitter" working-class conservatives "cling" to guns, religion, and prejudice in order to preserve their self-respect in the face of failing to hold their own in economic (read meritocratic) competition; and Hillary Clinton branded half of Donald Trump's supporters a bigoted "basket of deplorables."

Indeed, meritocracy extends these insults even to the few middle-class

Americans whom elite institutions admit into their caste. The groups of "first-generation professionals" that middle-class students at top universities form frame themselves as "affinity groups" on the model of identity politics based on race, gender, or sexual orientation. But the middle class stands in a starkly different identity relation to the elite from any of these other groups. A genuine embrace of diversity and inclusion allows an elite institution to tell black, or female, or gay students that while its culture is not perfect, it is committed to welcoming them on their own terms and supporting their authentic selves. But top universities cannot say anything like this to their middle-class students. Rather, they say the reverse: their meritocratic ideals and their business models require elite universities to overwrite their middle-class students' original identities and make them elite. It would be offensive almost beyond belief for Yale Law School to tell its black students, "Come study with us, and we will make you white." But Yale—for structural reasons that it cannot avoid—openly proposes to erase its first-generation professional students' middle-class identities.

Meritocratic exclusion now approaches, in its statistical effects, the racial exclusion that scars American life. Yet when meritocracy declares its inequalities just, it licenses elites simultaneously to worry endlessly about identity politics and to embrace attitudes that, in myriad ways, flatly insult the idled working and middle classes.

## NATIVISM AND POPULISM IN THE MIDDLE CLASS

Meritocratic inequality also corrupts political values outside of the elite, by generating resentments whose danger matches the elite's complacency. Americans who do not enjoy the benefits that meritocracy confers on the elite nevertheless remain subject to meritocracy's charisma. They succumb to the meritocratic embrace of skill and effort and the meritocratic association between industry and honor, only now as a frontal assault on their self-worth. Every meritocratic innovation confronts the middle class as another instrument of its abandonment, and every meritocratic embrace of diversity and inclusion confronts the middle class as reconfirming its exclusion.

A wounded dignity corrupts working- and middle-class values in ways that almost perfectly mirror the moral corruption of the elite. Where elites overdo the politics of personal identity, Americans outside the elite embrace nativism. And where elites valorize the credentials and institutions that constitute meritocratic success, Americans outside the elite lash out against the establishment and embrace populism.

When it frames inequality as justified, meritocracy deprives those at the bottom of an oppressor against whom to assert high-minded claims to justice. Moreover, the meritocratic elite's admiration for identity politics, coupled with its open contempt for mid-skilled labor, inflames resentment against minority groups among disrespected whites. Malignant nativism follows inexorably from this pattern, capturing the ideological position occupied by those trapped at the bottom end of rising meritocratic inequality and made by meritocracy to feel rejected, in favor of strangers, by their own land. Nativism is, like every ressentiment, an "anesthesia" or "narcotic." It deadens the internalized shame of nominally justified social and economic exclusion.

To make matters worse, meritocracy—precisely because it justifies economic inequalities and disguises class—denies ordinary Americans any high-minded language through which to explain and articulate the harms and wrongs of their increasing exclusion (and feeds into white racial anxieties whose roots reach all the way back into the slave-owning settler society of the colonial era). They become "victims without a language of victimhood." Those who cannot succeed in meritocratic competition therefore give their complaints the only frame that meritocracy permits, by constructing an identity politics of their own. Rising nativist assertions of white, male, heterosexual, or Christian identities—and rising complaints that the elite discriminates against these identities—follow inexorably from meritocratic inequality's economic structure and ideological limitations.

Meritocracy makes the whites whom it leaves behind into nativists by allowing them literally no place else to go. A white middle-class voter in Indiana, reflecting on Donald Trump's appeal, recently explained that "the whole idea" of white privilege irritates whites outside the elite "because they've never experienced it on a level that they understand. You hear privilege and you think money and opportunity and they don't have it." The meritocratic suggestion that a white man who cannot get ahead must be in some way deficient stokes this anger (not least because meritocracy's charisma makes those who are left out *feel* deficient). And the meritocratic fixation on diversity and inclusion channels the anger into nativist, sexist identity politics. The Indiana voter continued, "And you've got people calling them stupid and deplorable. Well how long do you think you can call people stupid and deplorable before they get mad?" When pressing needs are blocked from expressing themselves as claims of justice, they express themselves as claims of injustice.

Furthermore, meritocracy naturally produces not just nativism but also populism—a deep and pervasive mistrust of expertise and institutions. Because meritocracy identifies skill and expertise with elites, it condemns middle-class workers who accept the value of knowledge and training to internalizing their own exclusion and degradation. Resistance against meritocratic inequality—and even self-respect in the face of meritocratic exclusion— requires rejecting the institutions and the expertise through which meritocracy operates.

This logic receives a concrete expression in the fact that class resentments in America aim at the professional classes rather than at the entrepreneurial or even hereditary super-rich: not at oligarchs but rather at the doctors, bankers, lawyers, and scientists that working- and middle-class Americans feel, in the words of a much-discussed essay, "are more educated" and "are often looking down on them."

This focus mystifies professionals but in fact accurately reflects meritocratic inequality's economic and social structure. The professional class, together with the institutions (schools and firms) that train and deploy professionals, administers the meritocratic system that excludes the working and middle classes from income and status. The professional class reconstructs work and production to enforce idleness on all but superordinate workers, even as it also (and in the same breath) valorizes industry. Elite education therefore does not just advantage those who get it but also harms those who do not, by making middle-class training and skills unproductive. The gloss on the glossy jobs accounts for the gloom over the gloomy ones.

Ordinary citizens stand in a very different relationship to the super-rich. The super-rich may of course become rich without desert (as when they inherit) or even through nefarious means (as by exploiting the vulnerable). But any burdens that their wealth imposes remain idiosyncratic. Oligarchs may as it happens exploit the middle class, but they do not embody the norms and practices that underwrite the systematic domination by the rich over the rest. And ordinary citizens encounter the super-rich only in the fantasy lands of lifestyle magazines and reality television. One might even say that the super-rich escape working- and middle-class resentment precisely because they approach meritocracy at a skew angle: their privilege is not justified by the meritocratic order that sustains inequality generally, so that ordinary people can object in a more dispassionate or high-minded register, or decide simply to let the matter go. The rule that meritocratic inequality generates angry and low-minded resistance precisely on account of claiming to be justified does not apply to oligarchs. Indeed, starting a business permits economic success outside of elite institutions, and without class betrayal. Small wonder, then, that the middle-class ideal of prosperity is not to become a professional but rather to own a company.

Meritocratic inequality leads to mistrust not just of particular professions or institutions, but also the general idea of the rule of law and the associated idea that both private and public life should be regulated impersonally, by institutions and their officials, rather than by the personal authority of a charismatic leader. Due process and the rule of law underwrite the scale-blind approach to property that meritocratic income and wealth defense so successfully exploit, including to frustrate democratic efforts to redistribute through generally applicable taxes and regulations. Advanced meritocratic inequality therefore makes the meritocratic elite itself a political special interest and transforms due process and the rule of law into political tools wielded by elites, effectively as instruments of class warfare. Once again, for the rest to elevate rule-of-law institutions above democratic self-government is effectively to accept the legitimacy of their own disempowerment. Populism is not a spontaneous eruption of malevolent resentment but rather a natural and even apt reaction to extreme meritocratic inequality.

Meritocracy is therefore far from innocent in the recent rise of nativism and populism. Instead, nativism and populism represent a backlash against meritocratic inequality brought on by advanced meritocracy. Nativism and populism express the same ideological and psychological forces behind the epidemic of addiction, overdose, and suicide that has lowered life expectancy in the white working and middle class. The analogy takes the measure of the present political risk. These forces will lash out no less virulently than they turn in.

## THE CLASS WAR HEATS UP

The politics of the moment puts meritocratic inequality's democratic pathologies vividly on display.

An overconfident elite and a demoralized population, in a vain effort to abate rising meritocratic inequality, embraced decades of financialized production and debt-financed consumption, culminating in the recent financial crisis and the ensuing Great Recession. Meritocracy also led President Barack Obama to address the crisis through technocratic excellence and without a political reckoning—without assigning blame through criminal prosecutions and, more important, without subduing the financial sector or suppressing meritocratic inequality. Indeed, the Obama administration's internal composition embodied the meritocratic ideal: Obama rose from modest origins, yet he is not self-made but was rather propelled to success by a series of elite institutions, including Columbia College and Harvard Law School; and his all-star first cabinet, dominated by Ivy Leaguers, included Rhodes and Marshall scholars and even a Nobel laureate. These credentials, moreover, signaled real capabilities. The administration, playing to its meritocratic strengths, steadied the economy and restored economic growth (including, although more slowly, employment growth).

President Obama won reelection, and an elite whose hubris and greed were widely blamed for the crisis appeared, by recommitting to its core principles, to have redeemed itself. The recession ended, prosperity returned, and the nation's mood rebounded, to reassert America's familiar optimism. Even the opposition against Obama, which had threatened, through Sarah Palin's place on the 2008 Republican presidential ticket and the rise of the Tea Party, to open a populist front in American politics, seemed to recommit to the meritocratic status quo. The Romney-Ryan ticket that Obama defeated to win reelection presented the country with alternatives that, familiar partisan disagreements aside, could hardly have been more congenial to the incumbent ruling class. In all these ways, Barack Obama's 2012 victory set a high-water mark for American meritocracy.

The crisis had not passed, however, and meritocracy's redemption proved illusory. Bernie Sanders and Donald Trump—openly populist candidates who campaigned aggressively against the status quo—seized the initiative in both primaries leading up to the 2016 presidential election. When defensive political insiders dismissed the populist uprisings as a "summer of silliness," they betrayed their own wrong-footed confusion. Even after Trump became the Republican nominee, the establishment that he defined himself against remained in denial over his rise. Elites insisted that Trump could not possibly assemble a winning coalition of general election voters. The director of the Princeton Election Consortium declared (in the week of the election, no less) that Trump would not win more than 240 electoral votes and vowed to "eat a bug" if he did. But political professionals proved blind to the approaching upheaval, and an inward-looking and disenchanted elite could not stop the populist wave that elected Trump president.

Trump's repudiation of the incumbent elite set the election's master narrative. He struck stridently nativist and populist chords throughout his campaign, and he concluded with a widely televised advertisement taking aim at "a failed and corrupt political establishment." Trump's repudiationism succeeded by shifting the political frame—by winning the election's argument, to create a new politics.

On the eve of Trump's victory, the U.S. military remained unmatched and effectively unchallenged; American diplomats and businesses dominated the world's legal and economic order; the poverty rate approached historic lows; the labor market neared full employment; crime remained below historic levels; and the country's standard of living neared an all-time high. Even if not booming, America remained tolerably healthy, comparing favorably to other countries in the present and also, in important ways, to its own past. Nevertheless, Trump relentlessly attacked the society that he sought to lead. He lamented the depletion of American military might and denounced undefended borders. He accused government of squandering American wealth and dissipating the nation's treasure across all the rest of the world. He portrayed a country ravaged by poverty, industrial decline, failing schools, and epidemic crime. Improprieties—subplots concerning computer hacking and foreign interference—may have swung an essentially tied election Trump's way. But this required his achieving the tie to begin with. The most remarkable thing about Trump is not that he did win but that he could have won—that he successfully imposed this dark vision on the political imagination of the most powerful and prosperous nation in the world, often against conventional wisdom, common sense, and objective facts.

In the end, Trump carried key traditionally Democratic states, drawing decisive strength from a group of voters who had supported Barack Obama. Obama's 2012 triumph seemed to belong to another era. And the "silliness" that elites mocked over the summer of 2015 matured into a winter of discontent, with no spring in sight.

The whiplash between 2012 and 2016 baffles the elite. Trump's victory leaves observers who found it unimaginable feeling as if they inhabit a different world from the one they thought they lived in. Trump's censorious inaugural address reduced the previous Republican president, George W. Bush, to a confused curse: "That was some weird shit," he reportedly said. To comfort themselves, elites focus on idiosyncrasies of Trump's person and treat him as an exception to ordinary politics.

But the whiplash deceives, and Trump reflects rather than defies the laws of politics. Presidents Obama and Trump owe their elections not to unrelated forces, drawing strength from separate worlds, but rather to a balance of interlocking and closely matched forces in a single world. Both presidencies spring from the same source—an American meritocracy that preceded Obama's arrival on the political scene and will endure long after Trump departs. Indeed, both Obama and Trump are less causes and more consequences—specifically of meritocracy. Obama—a superordinate product of elite education—embodied meritocracy's triumph. Trump—"a blue-collar billionaire" who announces "I love the poorly educated" and openly opposes the meritocratic elite—exploits meritocracy's enduring discontents.

Trump rode rather than raised the wave of anger that elected him. His repudiationist campaign unmasked meritocracy's false hopes and channeled its profound discontents. The precarious middle class that meritocratic inequality most disadvantages was also hungriest for a candidate who "under[stood] the depth of [their] disillusion with [the] country." These voters, as J. D. Vance observes, "believe that the modern American meritocracy was not built for *them*," and they resent elite meritocratic opinion—for example, Michelle Obama's parenting advice about good nutrition—"not because [they] think she's wrong but because [they] know she's right."

When these voters heard the bipartisan elite condemn Trump as boorish or unfit for office, they knew that the elite thought the same of them. Sixty-four percent of Trump voters agreed with the statement, "Over the past few years, average Americans have gotten less than they deserve." At the same time, just 12 percent of Trump voters agreed that "over the past few years, blacks have gotten less than they deserve." (Fifty-seven percent of Clinton voters agreed with both statements.) A journalist who interviewed countless Trump supporters in Ohio reports that they all shared a "profound contempt for a dysfunctional, hyper-prosperous Washington that they saw as utterly removed from their lives." Trump's political supporters, that is, distinctively feel mistreated and believe that undeserving others are treated better. They seize the chance to rescue a longed-for past—in Trump's words, to "Make America Great Again."

Trump eventually won white voters without college degrees by 39 percentage points. He also won his largest vote shares among voters of all races with some college but no degree and among voters with annual incomes between $50,000 and $100,000—precisely the precarious middle class that meritocratic inequality most disadvantages. Trump won the fifty least educated counties by nearly 31 percent (beating Romney's 2012 vote shares in these counties by 10 percent), while he lost the fifty most educated counties by a 26 percent margin (a drop of nearly 9 percent over Romney's 2012 results). Whereas educated professionals embraced Clinton as one of their own and disparaged Trump as a buffoon, the middle class found her elaborate qualifications off-putting and sympathized deeply with Trump's rejection of expertise. A Trump-supporting businesswoman in St. Clair Shores, reacting to a refutation of the common claim that he was first in his class at Wharton, said simply, "Of course he wasn't; he's so normal."

Work influenced voting as powerfully as education. Workers whose jobs required routine labor dramatically favored Trump, while those whose jobs required creativity and expert analysis equally dramatically favored Clinton: Trump won counties in which over 50 percent of jobs are routine by over

30 percent, while he lost counties in which under 40 percent of jobs are routine by roughly the same amount. When it exalts elite jobs and degrades middle-class ones, meritocracy creates a new partisan politics of work—setting elites who derive their self-worth from work against a middle class that derives its self-worth outside of (and even in opposition to) work. Clinton's professionalism plugged into one side of the politics, while Trump's unprofessionalism plugged into the other.

The outward anger that elected Trump unsurprisingly also tracked the inward anger behind rising middle-class mortality. Trump recorded many of his biggest advances over Mitt Romney's vote shares from 2012 in counties worst hit by the opioid epidemic. St. Clair Shores, which in 1960 delivered Kennedy an optimistic 25 percentage point landslide, gave Trump an angry 10 percentage point victory in 2016.

Finally, Trumpism—and Trump's own rise—exposes the incumbent elite's meritocratic contempt for ordinary citizens and its own disenchanted weakness. Although elites resolutely opposed Trumpism, they lacked the vitality needed to sustain an alternative, more sanguine vision of American politics writ large. The effort, anxiety, and conceit of meritocratic success tempt the rich to sanctimony and blind them to middle-class concerns and resentments. When Hillary Clinton called half of Trump's supporters a "basket of deplorables," she said aloud what the broad elite, regardless of party, had long thought in private. Indeed, Trump's rise not only reconfirmed but redoubled the condescension that elites feel toward the Americans whom meritocracy excludes. The *National Review* essay that called white working-class communities "economically . . . negative assets" added that "Donald Trump's speeches make them feel good. So does OxyContin." Trump won the presidency in spite of capturing the smallest share of college-educated voters of any winning candidate since 1980. Palo Alto went for Hillary Clinton by nearly 70 percentage points.

In all these ways, meritocratic inequality inverts the midcentury relationship between economics and politics—between capitalism and democracy.

At midcentury, equality in each sector reinforced equality in the other: democratic citizens, acting as political equals, insisted on government policies that promoted economic equality and the common good; and widely dispersed and roughly equal private ownership checked private power and in this way preserved democratic political equality. This was Thomas Jefferson's dream, captured in his 1776 draft for the Virginia Constitution, which combined widespread suffrage with constitutionally guaranteed land grants for all potential voters.

Today, by contrast, inequalities in each sector compound inequalities in the other. The meritocratic mechanisms that drive economic inequality forward also generate a comprehensive and politically empowered elite. Louis Brandeis, commenting on an earlier era of economic inequality, is said to have insisted that "we can have a democratic society or we can have concentrated wealth in the hands of a few. We cannot have both." Jefferson's dream is being displaced by Brandeis's nightmare, as an American past born out of the hope for combining political and economic equality rapidly converges on an American future that achieves neither.

## MERITOCRACY UNMASKED

The meritocracy trap has no single face. A genuine but unwinnable competition excludes working- and middle-class adults from the charismatic center of economic life, denies them the income and dignity that come with earning a good living, and blocks working- and middle-class children from the educations required to get the jobs that their parents are denied. A brilliant vortex of training, skill, industry, and income holds elites in thrall, bending them from earliest childhood through retirement to an unrelenting discipline of meritocratic production that alienates superordinate workers from their labor, so that they exploit rather than fulfill themselves and eventually lose authentic ambitions that they might ever fulfill. And a web of disaffection and mistrust isolates the rich from the rest and entangles both classes in a callous and vengeful politics, in which each side seeks to dominate the other and goodwill surrenders to bad faith. In all these ways, meritocratic inequality produces pervasive discontent and deep-seated anxiety.

These observations collectively recast meritocracy in a new and revelatory light. They see through meritocracy's pretenses—to promote the common good and apportion advantage according to desert—and expose a corrupt core.

A comprehensively isolated elite monopolizes not just status and income but also political power. The elite transmits its caste to its children, to create dynasties that extend across generations. Moreover, feedback loops connect elite education and superordinate labor—the mechanisms through which the meritocratic elite both sustains and justifies its advantage. Super-educated innovators restructure work and production to favor the elite skills of super-ordinate workers; these workers deploy their immense incomes to make ex-ceptional investments in their children's educations; the children become the next generation of innovators and superordinate workers; and the cycle continues without end. The feedback loops both create elite skills and sustain the conditions that make elite skills so productive and superordinate workers who possess them so highly paid.

The qualities that meritocracy designates and rewards as merit are there-fore neither natural nor necessary virtues. The skills possessed by a banker at Goldman Sachs, or an executive at Viacom, or a lawyer at Wachtell, Lipton were worth virtually nothing in an agrarian economy. They were worth much less at the middle of the last century than they are today. And they are so valuable today largely on account of developments—a financialized economy, delayered management, and an active, heavily legalized market for corporate control—that are themselves products of economic inequality (and, in some cases, were directly invented by the firms that the workers now serve). Super-ordinate labor, that is, produces economic value and qualifies as meritorious only in the shadow of a highly complex, profoundly contingent set of social and economic conditions—with prior economic inequality at their core.

American meritocracy has become precisely what it was invented to com-bat: a mechanism for the concentration and dynastic transmission of wealth, privilege, and caste across generations. A social and economic hierarchy with these comprehensive, dynastic, and self-referential qualities has a name: an aristocracy. And meritocracy does not dismantle but rather renovates aristoc-racy, fashioning a new caste order, contrived for a world in which wealth con-sists not in land or factories but rather in human capital, the free labor of skilled workers.

Industry displaces breeding as the ground of privilege, and meritocratic education displaces aristocratic inheritance as the central dynastic technol-ogy. Elite skills are hard-won in the new order, and superordinate workers' industry is real, just as breeding and manners once set aristocrats genuinely apart. Like aristocracy, moreover, meritocracy purports to construct a social order that is not simply unequal but justly unequal. And as aristocracy's ideals once did, so meritocracy's claims about virtue and desert today persuade not just the privileged elite but also—ambivalently and unhappily, to be sure— the many whom meritocracy excludes.

But merit's allure is an illusion. Because the meritocrat's skills are valuable only against a backdrop of prior economic inequality, efforts to justify inequality based on the value, or merit, of these skills succumb to the fallacy of circular reasoning. Like the aristocratic values that it replaces, merit is not a natural or universal virtue but rather the upshot of prior inequalities. Merit is an artificial construction, built to valorize the exploitation of human capital, and, in this way, to launder an otherwise offensive distribution of advantage.

# How Meritocracy Works

FOUR

# THE WORKING RICH

In the Roaring Twenties, in the aristocratic world of P. G. Wodehouse's novels, the affable gentleman Bertie Wooster is asked if he works. "What, 'work'? As in honest toil, you mean," he answers, bemused. "Hewing the wood and drawing the old wet stuff and so forth? Well, I've known a few people who've worked. Absolutely swear by it, some of them." In Wooster's and Wodehouse's world—set mostly in London (although some in New York)—it was essential to wear just the right suit, grown men devoted their greatest energies to cultivating newts or collecting porcelain cows, and nobody worked. The elite had transformed work itself into a hobby—an eccentric resort cure, taken up as recreation. Actual industry was unimaginable.

Meanwhile, ordinary people toiled without reward. Poverty—grinding, inhumane, absolute deprivation—dominated life outside the elite. In the 1920s, widespread poverty made the aspiration to put "a chicken in every pot," modest as it sounds, into a political rallying cry. The Great Depression produced breadlines, and reasonable estimates suggest that in the early 1930s, more than half and perhaps as many as three-quarters of Americans suffered absolute poverty. And although the Second World War and the postwar economic recovery improved conditions for many Americans and built mass affluence in places like St. Clair Shores, poverty remained widespread, even pervasive, at midcentury. By one estimate, the poverty rate in 1949 was 40.5 percent.

Our world differs dramatically on both counts. The rich now work harder and more industriously than ever before, and they owe most of their income (comprising the bulk of rising inequality) to their labor. Values follow facts, and the new elite self-consciously embraces industry and understands itself as hardworking. Today, it is Bertie Wooster's unapologetic unemployment that is difficult to imagine. Furthermore, economic inequality's center of gravity has moved up the income scale. At midcentury, an urgent crisis led President Lyndon Johnson to declare a War on Poverty. Today, even as inequality increases, poverty is both rarer and less severe (although it of course endures). And whereas in the past, including at midcentury, inequality centered on the wretchedness and social exclusion of the poor, it now centers on the extravagance and privilege of the elite. Today, inequality isolates the rich from everyone else, not just the poor but also the middle class. Economic inequality now distinctively concerns not poverty but wealth.

The old rich—lazy rentiers who deployed inherited wealth and power to exploit subordinate labor—gave champions of economic justice an easy target. Widespread, grinding poverty gave egalitarian sympathies a compelling focus. And meritocracy offered egalitarians a powerful and effective cure for aristocratic inequality.

But arguments against exploitation lose their power when aimed at the hundred-hour-per-week lawyer, whose industry and exhaustion inoculate her against charges of inherited and unearned advantage, and who also exploits herself. Humanitarian concern loses force when poverty is reduced and the main claims of economic justice are made on behalf of the middle class. And when progressives embraced meritocracy as a remedy for hereditary privilege, they fired the engine that now drives inequality's increase. The familiar arguments that once defeated aristocratic inequality simply do not apply to an economic system based on rewarding effort and skill.

Meritocracy's rise over the past half century has opened a new frontier in human experience, with no historical precedent. At the same time, meritocracy has pulled the rug out from under economic equality's champions. The past no longer provides a reliable guide to understanding the present, as received moral principles and new economic stocks simply do not align.

Traditional diagnoses of economic injustice misfire at every turn, and meritocracy, which was supposed to cure inequality, has itself become the source of the disease.

Indeed, it is almost as if meritocratic inequality were specifically designed to defeat the arguments and the policies that once humbled the leisure class and declared war on poverty. The meritocratic transformation entails, bluntly put, that equality's champions must justify redistribution that takes from a more industrious elite in order to give to a less industrious middle class. This makes meritocratic inequality difficult to resist.

Difficult, but not impossible. A clear-eyed understanding of meritocracy unmasks its claim to tie advantage to desert. The first steps on the path to understanding come from studying the working rich: who they are, and how they make their money.

## FROM LEISURE TO INDUSTRY

The great sociologist Thorstein Veblen puts the working rich into historical context. Veblen was born in the middle of the nineteenth century and died in the summer of 1929, literally on the eve of the Great Depression, which would eventually destroy the order he so shrewdly described. He made the old elite the subject of his acidly observed sociology of wealth from the turn of the twentieth century, *The Theory of the Leisure Class*.

Veblen emphasized that although the poor had worked from time immemorial, and the middle class had worked from the moment of its creation, matters had always been different for the elite. In fact, leisure constituted a fixed marker of social status, enduring from barbarian times through his own era. "The upper classes," Veblen wrote, "are by custom exempt or excluded from industrial occupations," by which he meant not just factory work but rather all work that amounts to "a steady application to a routine of labor."

Moreover, the rich avoided industry not casually or by default but affirmatively and on account of their self-conceit and sense of dignity. Even nonconformists or otherwise exceptional characters who embraced industry worked with a moderation that would perplex their counterparts today: Benjamin Franklin, for example, arose each morning to pose himself the question, "What good shall I do this day?," but then, according to the daily schedule that he published in 1766, devoted no more than eight hours to work and fully four hours to "music, or diversion, or conversation."

The leisure of the rich did not amount, in Veblen's words, to "indolence or quiescence." Rather, Veblen distinguished between two socially opposite employments. On one side, he said, lies *industry*, the drudgery of ordinary work, devoted to "elaborating the material means of life." On the other lies the "non-productive consumption of time," devoted to "employments to which a degree of honor attaches," pursued to mark out social status. Veblen called activity of this sort *exploit*. Any number of activities might count as exploit, he explained, including in earlier times warfare, ritual, hunting (if done socially rather than to procure sustenance), public worship, and even public merrymaking. The elite, Veblen observed, devoted its leisure to exploit—so completely that the word *leisure* became identified with elite exploit.

By Veblen's own era, the characteristic barbarian exploits—warfare and chivalric tournament—had been reduced or abandoned in the face of new social and economic forms. But, Veblen insisted, the leisure class retained an aversion to industry and an attraction to exploit as a social marker and indeed constitutive commitment. The social form remained the same, and only its content had changed. In place of barbarian ritual, the new leisure class cultivated useless erudition (in classical languages, for example), hobbies (newts and porcelain), refined and elaborate manners, and even the conspicuous archaism and difficulty of English spelling.

All these activities, Veblen observed, share with barbarian exploit that they demand immense time and attention, but produce nothing useful. By adopting them, the elite demonstrated incontrovertibly that it could afford leisure as the masses could not. And demonstrated leisure, coupled with an aversion to industry, established the elite's social status. (Mere idleness, being too easily displayed by anyone, cannot perform this differentiating function.) By this means, the elite was constituted as a leisure class.

Veblen suspected that the leisure class was shrinking even as he identified it, and that it had perhaps entered its twilight. But the connection between wealth and leisure would outlive him and extend well into midcentury.

The leisure class survived the First World War (although fighting still counted as exploit, and many of its individual members perished in battle). In the 1920s, as Veblen archly remarked, even the uniform of the Wall

Street elite—glistening top hat, patent leather shoes, and a walking cane—emphasized through its ostentatiously fragile shine that its wearers did not sully themselves with work. And whatever lessons the elite drew from the Great Crash of 1929 did not shake its open embrace of leisure. Shortly after Veblen's death, following one of many Depression-era congressional investigations into the Wall Street crash, J. P. Morgan exhorted reporters that "if you destroy the leisure class you destroy civilization."

Even the Second World War did not quite abolish the leisure class. Bankers, for example, actually kept bankers' hours well into the twentieth century. Their typical day "began at ten and ended at three with an intermission for a three-martini, two-hour lunch." As late as 1962, Martin Mayer could write in his classic *Wall Street: Men and Money* that "the banks close at three o'clock (though people can sneak in until three-thirty if they know the way), the exchanges shut down at three-thirty . . . people who work on the floors of the exchanges, members and employees, go promptly home . . . executives take a last look at the Dow Jones ticker and start heading home to the country."

At "five o'clock," Mayer continued, "the night lines are plugged into the telephone switchboard," and the rest of "Wall Street goes home, lemmings marching to the subway." At "around six-thirty the cleaning women arrive, and the lights flash on in the towers. By eight o'clock they are going off again, and by nine even the busiest of the brokerage houses has its accounts squared away and locks the doors for the night." At midcentury, the cleaners were the hardest-working people on Wall Street.

Not everyone played along, of course. In the 1950s, for example, hard-charging takeover artists targeted firms led by the idle rich—as one of them put it, the "third-generation Yale man who spends his afternoons drinking martinis at the club." But these corporate raiders who threatened the leisure class were "treated as uncouth ruffians," censured by government investigators, and threatened with legislative sanction. Even in the breach, norms reaffirmed and enforced the facts of life among the leisured elite.

Midcentury Wall Street, moreover, was not unique or even distinctive in its taste for leisure. The corporate raiders just mentioned took aim at firms run by comfortably lazy managers who, as one contemporary observer noted, behaved as if they were gentlemen of independent means. The captains of midcentury industry came to work "dressed in a suit cut for the club rather than the factory; occupied an office which looked like a drawing room, with no sign to be seen of anything so vulgar as a digital computer." They even "nourished themselves from a cocktail cabinet just like the one at home."

Elite professionals worked similarly short hours through midcentury. The American Bar Association's 1962 assumption that lawyers would bill only thirteen hundred hours per year reflected long-standing conventional wisdom. And as late as 1977, the *American Bar Association Journal* published an essay on "Financial Planning and Control for Lawyers" in which a hypothetical firm's average lawyer billed only fourteen hundred hours in a year. These are only anecdotes, of course, and systematic data on the bar were not kept at midcentury. But any number of others report similar hours. Even applying the rule of thumb that a lawyer must work about a third more hours than she bills, this amounted to slightly over thirty hours a week in the office. Not quite bankers' hours, perhaps, but hardly onerous.

These narratives of elite sinecure would be unrecognizable today. The epidemic of elite effort introduced earlier is substantiated by countless vivid narratives and reams of data.

Young investment bankers now work 80 to 120 hours a week, often arriving at work at 6 a.m. and not leaving until midnight. In a story familiar to anyone in the business, an analyst at an investment bank once reported working 155 hours in a single week, which left him with only 13 hours to devote to the rest of his life, including sleep. A standard "disciplinary joke" among young investment bankers is that they will be lucky to get any day off besides their wedding day. Nor do the hours necessarily improve with seniority. Morgan Stanley's "top dealmaker" once bragged that he had "the stamina to work 12 hours a day regularly and 20 hours at a stretch on deals, catnapping on his office couch." Bankers' hours have given way to the ironically named "banker nine-to-five," which begins at 9 a.m. on one day and runs through 5 a.m. on the next.

Elite managers, who occupy the core of the real economy, have experienced similar increases in their hours. Amazon's "purposeful Darwinism" and "unreasonably high" expectations mean, as its founder Jeffrey Bezos once explained to shareholders, that you "can work long, hard or smart, but at Amazon.com you can't choose [just] two out of three." To implement this ideal, Amazon runs "a continual performance improvement algorithm on its staff"—a kind of panopticon monitoring that aims to cull less productive workers. Amazon also imposes itself on managers at effectively all hours, for example by sending emails after midnight and following up with text messages asking why they have not been answered. The firm is not alone in this approach. Apple, for example, has required executives to check email throughout vacations and until 2 a.m. on Sunday nights.

More generally, the comfortable, clubbable "third-generation Yale men" who managed large corporations at midcentury have long since been driven out by the imperatives of efficiency and the corporate takeovers through which these efficiencies have been wrung out of American firms. Managers' hours grew steadily over the second half of the twentieth century. By 1990, managerial workloads had increased sufficiently to cross over the regulation forty-hour week, from sinecure to hard slog. The average hours of senior executives at Fortune 500 and Service 500 firms exceeded fifty-five per week, and 60 percent of CEOs worked over sixty hours per week. Moreover, 62 percent of CEOs reported that their immediate subordinates' hours had increased over the course of the 1980s.

Indeed, senior executives commonly insist that the capacity for massive work constitutes one of the selection criteria for their jobs. A senior manager at a Fortune 500 firm recently observed that "the members of the Management Committee of this company aren't the smartest people in this company, we're the hardest working. We work like dogs. We out-work the others. We out-practice them. We out-train them." The same manager applied a similar work requirement even below the top: "I don't think we can get commitment with less than fifty or sixty hours a week. That's what other corporations are doing. To be competitive, that's what we need to do. In my gut, I can't believe we can do it very differently." The *Harvard Business Review*'s survey of extreme jobs validates the manager's intuition. According to the survey, "62% of high-earning individuals work more than 50 hours a week, 35% work more than 60 hours a week, and 10% work more than 80 hours a week." Nearly a quarter of the highest earners surveyed qualified for the *Review*'s most extreme job classification and worked "even more punishing" hours: "The majority of them (56%) work 70 hours or more a week, and 9% work 100 hours or more."

Elite professionals have also ratcheted up their work hours. Medical residents now work such long hours that the Accreditation Council for Graduate Medical Education has sought, with limited success, to restrict them to eighty working hours per week, averaged across four weeks. Lawyers' hours are similarly extreme. For example, between 1984 and 1990 the percentage of lawyers working over fifty-five hours per week more than tripled, and the share working more than two hundred hours per month increased by nearly half. And by the mid-1990s, fully 70 percent of associates in a study of lawyers from a large northeastern city worked at least half a day in an average weekend, and over 99 percent worked on weekends during busy periods. Today, "work weeks of more than 60 hours are routine in many practice settings, and 40-hour weeks are considered part-time schedules."

Often, lawyers must work longer hours still. An anonymous lawyer recently described a "busy day" as running from 7 a.m. one morning to 3:45 a.m. the next, with every hour packed with in-person meetings, double-booked client telephone calls, and between fifty and one hundred new emails. A "not-busy" day begins at 9:30 a.m. and ends at 8:45 p.m., with no break save for ordering—not eating—lunch. Elite firms, moreover, expressly embrace and even insist on such single-minded devotion to work. An associate at one large firm reports receiving an email from his boss commanding, "When you wake up in the morning, you don't brush your teeth, you look at your phone." Once again, seniority buys no relief from long hours. The leader of another major firm was equally blithe about partner hours, saying that "the only quantitative requirement of partners ... was to spend between 2,500 and 3,000 hours per year either billing clients, developing business or otherwise improving the firm's practices."

The epidemic of effort has reached into even the most seemingly idiosyncratic precincts of the elite, which were once formally reserved for exploit. The greatest athlete in the world at the turn of the twentieth century—a gentleman amateur named C. B. Fry—missed the 1900 Paris Olympics because he did not know that they were happening. And as late as the 1980s, John McEnroe famously resisted practicing. Today, McEnroe's approach is unthinkable. Professional athletes train much, much harder and longer: Olympians prepare single-mindedly over many years; Rafael Nadal practices nearly seven hours a day. Nor are athletes exceptional. Top chefs, another

once-quintessentially amateur group, now answer the demands of competitive restaurant reviews by working eighty- to one-hundred-hour weeks. Celebrities today must also work intense and long hours. Supermodels, as one
recently observed, "all train like it's the ... Olympics." Even pure celebrities—
who are famous only for being famous—constantly and effortfully cultivate
their fame.

Overwhelming, systematic evidence confirms these reports and demonstrates that the past five decades have seen a revolution in elite work habits.

In what has become known as the *time divide,* workers have shifted away
from the median forty-hour workweek and toward the extremes on either
side, so that growing shares of the population now work fewer than thirty
hours or especially more than fifty hours per week. According to one measure, the share of male employees working more than forty-eight hours a week
increased by roughly half between 1970 and 1990. Another measure reports
that the share usually working more than forty-eight hours per week rose by
half again between 1980 and 2005. The trend is particularly pronounced at
the extreme of hard work. Between 1970 and 2000, the percentage of couples
(both without and with children) who jointly worked over a hundred hours
per week increased by roughly half. The same period naturally produced a
reciprocal divergence in time allocated to work's mirror image, leisure: the
gap between hours spent in leisure by those at the 90th and the 10th percentiles of the leisure distribution increased by fourteen hours per week between
1965 and 2003.

Rising income inequality coincides with rising inequality in labor and a
mirror-image trend in leisure. Moreover, income inequality and the time divide turn out to be closely correlated, and indeed intertwined, so that the
same people who capture rising incomes also provide rising labor (and enjoy
falling leisure). The increase in long work hours has been concentrated among
highly paid and highly educated workers and the increase in leisure among
low-paid, less educated workers. The match between high weekly earnings
and long weekly hours was closer in 2000–2002 than in 1983–85. The rich,
that is, disproportionately work the long hours, and the rest disproportionately work the short ones.

Studies that focus on the extremes of work effort tell a still more startling tale. For example, between 1979 and 2006, the share of workers from the top quintile of the wage distribution who averaged over fifty hours worked per week nearly doubled (from less than one in six to nearly one in three), while the share of long-hour workers from the bottom quintile of the wage distribution fell by almost a third (from a little over one in five to roughly one in seven). In 1979, a prime-aged working man whose hourly wage put him in the top quintile of the distribution was roughly two-thirds as likely to work more than fifty hours in a typical week as a prime-aged working man from the bottom quintile. By 2006, the top wage earner was over twice as likely to work long hours as the bottom wage earner. In other words, in the roughly three decades since the end of the midcentury, the relationship between high income and long hours reversed. Trends in leisure, moreover, again mirror those in labor. Between 1965 and 2003, men with less than a high school education enjoyed an increase of roughly ten hours of leisure per week, while men with at least a college education experienced no gain or even a slight loss of leisure. (Strikingly, the elite lost leisure even as new domestic devices and other gadgets considerably increased the share of time available for leisure outside market work.)

The connection tying high wages and education to long work hours and falling leisure is less pronounced although still notable for women. But working women are often second earners in two-earner households, and the connection between joint household work effort and income could hardly be more pronounced. By the early 2000s, 75 percent of households in the top quintile of the income distribution had two or more earners working outside the house, compared to only 5 percent of households in the bottom quintile. And over 80 percent of women with college degrees but only roughly 50 percent of women high school dropouts worked outside the home.

This gender dynamic creates an especially stark contrast between today's rich and Veblen's leisure class. Veblen observed that long after the elite male worker had been forced to relinquish his leisure status and was "reduced by economic circumstances to turn his hand to gaining a livelihood by occupations which often partake largely of the character of industry," economically elite women, and especially wives, continued to abjure labor outside the home and to arrange the domestic sphere in a style designed to broadcast that they, at least, retained the leisure their husbands had lost. The rich man's nonworking wife was, at midcentury, the final expression of elite exploit, the last bastion of the leisure class. Today, this pretext has been abandoned.

The association between income and industry runs right up the scale, all the way to the very top.* Workers in the bottom 60 percent of the income distribution work much shorter hours today than they did in 1940—roughly 20 percent fewer. Workers in the next 30 percent of the distribution (who lie between the 60th and the 90th percentiles) have worked effectively constant hours over this period (although their hours have fallen since the turn of the millennium). Then, moving up through the top tenth of the income distribution, increasingly elite cohorts have seen greater increases in work hours relative to the cohorts below. The top 1 percent in particular increased its work hours by more than any lower-income cohort throughout the 1980s and 1990s. Uniquely, this cohort also continued to increase its work hours even in the 2000s. The cumulative effects of this trend are large—indeed enormous. In 1940, a typical worker in the bottom 60 percent worked nearly four (or 10 percent) more weekly hours than a typical worker in the top 1 percent. By 2010, the low-income worker devoted roughly twelve (or 30 percent) fewer hours to work than the high-income worker. Taken together, these trends shift the balance of ordinary to elite labor by nearly sixteen hours—or two regulation workdays—per week. These precise numbers and ratios should be taken with a grain of salt. But the basic story that they tell is robust, including variations in how data on work hours are collected.

Data sliced sufficiently finely begin once again to tell stories. The top 1 percent of the income distribution—representing household incomes in excess of roughly $475,000—comprises only about 1.5 million households. If one adds up the numbers of vice presidents or above at S&P 1500 companies (perhaps 250,000), professionals in the finance sector, including in hedge funds, venture capital, private equity, investment banking, and mutual funds (perhaps 250,000), professionals working at the top five management consultancies (roughly 60,000), partners at law firms whose profits per partner exceed $400,000 (roughly 25,000), and specialist doctors (roughly 500,000), this yields perhaps 1 million people.

These are surely not all one-percenters, but they are all plausibly parts of

---

* A graphical representation of these trends appears in Figure 1 on page 292.

the top 1 percent, and this group might comprise half—a sizable share—of 1 percent households overall. At the very least, the people in these known and named jobs constitute a material, rather than just marginal or eccentric, part of the top 1 percent of the income distribution. They are also, of course, the people depicted in journalistic accounts of extreme jobs—the people who regularly cancel vacation plans, spend most of their time on the road, live in unfurnished luxury apartments, and generally subsume themselves in work, encountering their personal lives only occasionally, and as strangers.

## BEYOND CAPITAL VERSUS LABOR

At least since Marx developed his theory of exploitation, critics of economic inequality have cast the rich as rentiers. On this view, idle elites enjoy the excessive returns that they receive by mixing their unearned capital with other people's exploited labor. Inequality's modern critics no doubt employ a less systematic method and strike a more moderate tone, but the conventional wisdom to this day pursues a similar style of argument, a variation on Marx's rentier theme.

Critics still commonly connect economic inequality to the familiar political and economic battle between capital and labor, associating the rich with capital and inequality's increase with capital's renewed dominance. Thomas Piketty's formidable book *Capital in the Twenty-First Century* gives this view its now-canonical statement. Familiar laments about the decline of labor unions, rising market power among large employers, and outsourcing and globalization also share this general attitude.

These complaints capture something real. Unions have been systematically dismantled in recent decades. Labor's share of national income has fallen—modestly, but appreciably—since the middle of the last century. And stock prices—which roughly capture income to capital—have indeed far outstripped the wages of ordinary workers. But these and other similar effects are, it will become clear, much too small to explain the enormous increase in top incomes and top income shares. Moreover, a close examination of elite incomes, informed by an account of the distinction between labor and capital that accurately reflects meritocratic ideas of entitlement and desert, reveals that the rich increasingly, and now overwhelmingly, owe their massive incomes to selling their own labor—to long, intensive, and exceptionally re-munerative work.

No one need weep for the wealthy. But ignoring how oppressively the rich now work is equally misleading. The intensity of elite labor structures both the lived experience and the social meaning of top incomes today. The rich now dominate the rest not idly but effortfully, by exploiting their own enor-mous skill and industry. Meritocratic inequality principally arises not from the familiar conflict between capital and labor but from a new conflict—within labor—between superordinate and middle-class workers. The politics of economic inequality inevitably reflect this complex of great wealth bur-dened by great effort, and the conventional wisdom, which disregards eco-nomic inequality's meritocratic roots, disguises as much as it reveals.

Labor income now figures prominently even at the very sharpest peak of the distribution. Eight of the ten richest Americans today owe their wealth not to inheritance or to returns on inherited capital but rather to compensa-tion earned through entrepreneurial or managerial labor, paid in the form of founder's stock or partnership shares. A slightly broader view reveals that the *Forbes* list of the four hundred richest Americans has also seen its center of gravity shift away from people who owe their wealth to inherited capital and toward those whose wealth stems (originally) from their own labor. Whereas in the early 1980s, only four in ten of the Forbes 400 were predominantly "self-made," today nearly seven in ten are. And whereas in 1984, purely inher-ited fortunes outnumbered purely self-made ones in the list by a factor of ten to one, by 2014, purely self-made fortunes had come to outnumber purely inherited ones. Indeed, the share of the four hundred top incomes attribut-able specifically to salaries grew by half between 1961 and 2007, and the share going to people with no college education fell by over two-thirds between 1982 and 2011. The shift toward labor income at the very top has been suffi-ciently pronounced to change the balance of industries in which the super-rich acquire their fortunes. In the inaugural 1982 version of the *Forbes* list, 15.5 percent of the people on the list owed their wealth to capital-intensive manufacturing, and only 9 percent came from labor-intensive finance. By 2012, only 3.8 percent of the list came from manufacturing and a full 24 percent from finance.

Labor also dominates stories of elite income at the next rung down.

Although only three hedge fund managers took home over $1 billion in 2017, more than twenty-five took home $100 million or more, and $10 million incomes are so common that they do not make the papers. Even only modestly elite finance workers now receive huge paydays. According to one survey, a portfolio manager at a midsized hedge fund makes on average $2.4 million, and average Wall Street bonuses exploded from roughly $14,000 in 1985 to more than $180,000 in 2017, a year in which the average total salary for New York City's 175,000 securities industry workers reached over $420,000.

These sums reflect the fact that a typical investment bank disburses roughly half of its revenues after interest paid to its professional workers (making it a better three decades to be an elite banker than to be an owner of bank stocks). Elite managers in the real economy also do well. CEO incomes— the wages paid to top managerial labor—regularly reach seven figures; indeed, the average 2017 income of the CEO of an S&P 500 company was nearly $14 million. In a typical recent year the total compensation paid to the five highest-paid employees of each S&P 1500 firm (7,500 workers overall) might amount to 10 percent of S&P 1500 firms' collective profits. These workers do not own the assets—the portfolios or the companies—that they manage. Their incomes constitute wages paid for managerial labor rather than a return on invested capital. The enormous paydays reflect what prominent business analysts recently called a war between talent and capital—a war that talent is winning.

Labor's dominance applies more broadly still among the million jobs listed by name in the earlier discussion of elite hours—finance-sector professionals, vice presidents at S&P 1500 firms, elite management consultants, partners at highly profitable law firms, and specialist medical doctors. These specifically identified workers collectively constitute a substantial share— fully half—of the 1 percent. The terms of trade under which they work—the economic arrangements that underwrite their incomes—are well known. All these workers contribute effectively no capital to their businesses and therefore again owe their income ultimately to their own industrious work, which is to say to labor.

Comprehensive data based on tax returns corroborate that the new economic elite owes its income predominantly not to capital but rather, at root, to selling its own labor. The data themselves can be technical and even abstruse, but a clear message emerges from them nevertheless. The data confirm that the meritocratic rich (unlike their aristocratic predecessors) get their money by working.

Even guarded estimates, which defer to tax categories that treat some labor income as capital gains, show a stark increase in the labor component of top incomes. According to this method of calculating, the richest 1 percent received as much as three-quarters of their income from capital at midcentury, and the richest 0.1 percent received up to nine-tenths of their income from capital. These shares then declined steadily over four decades beginning in the early 1960s, reaching bottom in 2000. In that year, both the top 1 percent and the top 0.1 percent received only about half of their incomes from capital (roughly 49 percent and 53 percent, respectively). The capital shares of top incomes then rose again, by about 10 percent, over the first decade of the new millennium, before beginning to fall again at the start of the second decade (when the data series runs out).

A complete meritocratic accounting of earned advantage is more expansive than this and traces income through its shallow sources back to its deep roots—to reveal that some income nominally attributed to capital in fact originates in labor and therefore should be counted as earned through effort, skill, and industry. An entrepreneur who sells founder's shares in her firm, an executive who realizes appreciation after being paid in stock, and a hedge fund manager who gets paid a "carried interest" share of profits on funds she invests (but does not own) all report capital gains income on their tax returns. But all these types of income ultimately reflect returns to the founder's, the executive's, or the manager's labor and, the meritocrat insists, are on this account earned. A similar analysis applies to pensions and owner-occupied housing. All this income is earned in a way that distinguishes it from the true capital income of the hereditary rentier who lives, at leisure, from returns on an inherited patrimony. Regardless of what the tax accounts say, therefore, accurate meritocratic accounting attributes all these types of income not to capital but to labor.

These are not marginal or idiosyncratic categories of income (although the need to translate from tax categories to moral ones inevitably introduces judgment and imprecision into any accounting). Founder's shares, carried interest, and executive stock compensation give nominally capital gains a substantial component of labor income, especially among the very rich. To begin with, roughly half of the twenty-five largest American fortunes, according to *Forbes*, arise from founder's stock still held by the founders who built the firms. Moreover, the share of total capital gains income reported to the Treasury that is attributable to carried interest alone—to the labor of hedge fund managers—has grown by a factor of perhaps ten in the past two decades and now comprises a material share of all the capital gains reported by one-percenters. And over the past twenty years, roughly half of all CEO compensation across the S&P 1500 has taken the form of stock or stock options. Pensions and housing also contribute substantially to top incomes today, roughly doubling the shares that they contributed in the 1960s. Once again, the data cannot sustain precise measurements, but these forms of labor income, taken together, plausibly comprise roughly another third of top incomes, sitting atop the roughly half of top incomes attributable to labor on even the most conservative accounting.

The data therefore confirm—top-down—the narrative of labor income that bubbles up from a survey of elite jobs. Both the top 1 percent and even the top 0.1 percent today receive between two-thirds and three-quarters of their income in exchange not for land, machines, or financing but rather for deploying their own effort and skill. The richest person out of every hundred in the United States today, and indeed the richest person out of every thousand, now literally works for a living.

This explosion of elite labor income has transformed not only the internal accounts of rich households but also the balance sheet of the economy writ large. Along the way, it has reframed the balance of economic advantage between the rich and the rest.

The transformation is unexpected and as a result often overlooked. Aristocratic inequality framed economic justice in terms of the conflict between capital and labor—between those who own things and those who work—and associated capital income with inequality and labor income with equality. This framing makes it awkward, both morally and intellectually, to locate the roots of rising economic inequality in labor. It is more natural, especially for progressives, to explain rising inequality in terms of labor's (especially organized labor's) demise and capital's resurgence.

This view remains seductive, but it is rejected by the data. Although national income has shifted against labor and in favor of capital over the past half century, this shift is simply too small—*much* too small—to account for rising top income shares. The labor-to-capital shift has increased the top 1 percent's income share by at most 2.5 percent of total national income. But the 1 percent's actual income has grown by about 10 percent of national income, from a midcentury low of roughly 10 percent to roughly 20 percent today. Accordingly, only about a quarter of the increase can be attributed to rich households' participation, as capitalists, in the overall shift in income from labor to capital. The remainder of the increase in the 1 percent's total income share—fully three-quarters—must come from within the distribution of labor income.

These calculations take a rough—even a blunderbuss—approach to intricate data; they are designed to identify dominant aggregate effects in an intuitive way rather than to quantify exact income shares. More fine-grained but also less comprehensive methods reinforce the lesson that elite labor income constitutes the dominant cause of rising top income shares. For example, between 1960 and 2000, about nine-tenths of the increase in the top decile's overall income share, about four-fifths of the increase in the top 1 percent's income share, and about two-thirds of the increase in the top .01 percent's income share came specifically from elite wages—the enormous salaries paid to top lawyers, bankers, managers, and so on. Of course, labor income, particularly for narrower elites, includes much more than just wages—law firm partners receive shares of firm profits, hedge fund managers get carried interest, CEOs get stock options, and so on. These numbers therefore achieve their clarity at the cost of being incomplete and conservative. A more complete (but commensurately more controversial) accounting that builds labor income out of wages plus a share of business income and capital gains attributes over three-quarters of the increase in the top .01 percent's income share to elite labor income.

All these complexities point to the same, simple conclusion. The traditional way of thinking about the conflict between the rich and the rest—as a battle between capital and labor—no longer captures what is really going on. Instead, the dominant sources of individual top incomes lie in superordinate labor. The overwhelmingly greater part of the recent increase in the top 1 percent's aggregate income share is attributable not to a shift of overall income away from labor and in favor of capital, but rather to a shift within labor income, away from the middle class and in favor of elite workers.

The working rich have risen by fundamentally transforming class conflict and then winning the new battle between elite and middle-class labor. The claim that meritocratic inequality reflects earned advantage may ultimately be a moral error. But it rests on economic facts.

## A CULTURE OF INDUSTRY

Shortly after his first child was born, Mark Zuckerberg—whose labor income from creating Facebook (paid to him in founder's shares) has created the fifth-largest fortune in the world—wrote his new daughter an open letter. The letter, expounding on the hopes of the meritocratic elite, admired human creativity and innovation, lamented inequality, and pledged to donate 99 percent of Zuckerberg's Facebook fortune to "advance human potential and promote equality for all children in the next generation." Zuckerberg's donation immediately placed him in the top rank of American philanthropists. But the most remarkable thing about his act is not its scale, but its setting and its motives. Zuckerberg's letter drew a direct connection between the Facebook Foundation's social mission to support education, innovation, and equality of opportunity and Zuckerberg's own devotion to the newborn daughter in whose name he dedicated the enterprise and the gift.

This connection would have been literally unimaginable to an earlier elite, for whom inherited wealth and the leisure that it allowed constituted social status. The old aristocracy joined land and titles into a single social unity, establishing elaborate express formulas to govern dynastic succession. Under aristocracy, when leisure was mandatory for the elite, disinheritance ostracized the heir. If the Duke of Marlborough had divested his only daughter of Blenheim Palace (and of the inheritance required to support a rentier's leisure) this would have been intended and understood as a profound rejection—of the daughter or perhaps of the entire aristocratic order. This relegated disinheritance to an imaginative fiction, a device used to swell the progress of a plot or to symbolize an ideal. It would have been eccentric, disruptive, and even bizarre for an actual person to disinherit his child.

Meritocratic inequality gives Zuckerberg's choice an entirely different frame. He has, of course, deprived his daughter of virtually all of a massive patrimony, including the immense capital income that would otherwise have attended her inheritance. But his remaining wealth and social position more than suffice for him to give her the education and training she needs to join the ranks of her generation's elite workers. Moreover, the economics of elite labor will enable her to deploy her training to command a high income of her own, and the social economy of esteem will enable her to convert her training, work, and labor income into her own independent social status.

Zuckerberg's giving away his fortune therefore will not deprive his daughter of any essential element of caste. To the contrary, it might even promote her caste by insulating her from the temptations to idle decadence that accompany great inherited wealth and that have notoriously led other young heiresses to ridicule and social decline, especially where social and economic arrangements have eliminated the avenues for honorable exploit that earlier elites enjoyed. By disinheriting his daughter, Zuckerberg promotes her ambition and dignity and protects her against a dissolute life.

It is therefore no surprise that Zuckerberg is anything but outlandish or alone in his giving. To date, five of the ten richest people in America, and nearly 170 billionaires worldwide (representing nearly 10 percent of the world's total), have signed Warren Buffett's and Bill Gates's giving pledge to donate the majority of their fortunes to philanthropy, either within their lifetimes or upon their deaths. The economic and social transformation from a society led by a hereditary, leisured elite to one led by the working rich has transformed what would once have been bizarre into something rational and even admirable. Zuckerberg's gift embraces rather than rejects the reigning social and economic order.

The web of meritocratic ideals that support Zuckerberg's choice today is just as thick and dense as the aristocratic ideals that would once have condemned it. The new rich do not just happen to work hard or for high wages, nor do they work industriously merely because they happen to prefer owning expensive things to having free time. Instead, the rich now pursue intense and remunerative work reflectively and for its own sake, and elite society organizes and consolidates these attitudes into a distinctive worldview (which drives both the Facebook Foundation and Zuckerberg's hopes for his own daughter).

Veblen's leisure class has been displaced not just in economic fact but also in social norms—the old elite culture of leisure has been replaced by a new elite culture of industry. Just as aristocracy once did, so meritocracy now sustains economic practices and moral principles that reciprocally support each other, in equilibrium patterns. (The new norms even allow the rich to square filial loyalty and civic duty and, like Zuckerberg, to pass their caste down through the generations openly and in good faith.)

Industry has become as mandatory for the meritocratic elite as leisure once was for aristocrats. Today, elites boast, and even complain, of their business from social necessity, as a shield against any suggestion that they might be idle or unsought-after, that their labor might be in greater supply than demand. An advertisement for the *Wall Street Journal* reads, "People who don't have time make time to read the *Wall Street Journal*."

These formulations, and the attitudes behind them, have infected the ideology of the elite. When law students were recently asked to report the maximum weekly work hours that they would accept, the mean student answered 70, and some students reported being willing to work "as many [hours] as necessary" or, more concretely, 120 weekly hours. (I have not once—literally never—encountered a Yale Law student who justified or even explained poor performance on the ground that studies should not encroach unduly on leisure; and in anonymous surveys of incoming Yale freshmen, 80 percent said that academics would take priority over extracurricular activities, and none— not a single one—has said that social life would be significantly more important than studying.) The students, moreover, do not outgrow this ideology when they enter the workforce. To the contrary: over half of people surveyed who work over 60 hours per week openly self-identify as workaholics. And I have also never heard—again, not once—a partner at a major law firm complain of slacking in her office. Actually bragging about idleness, in the vein of Bertie Wooster, would be unthinkable.

Intense work is now a symbol of excellence and dynamism, of being committed, as one investment banker explained, to doing "whatever it takes to get things done." The "extreme workers" described in the *Harvard Business Review* therefore "wear their commitments like badges of honor" and advertise their extreme industry "on their sleeves." Sometimes they do so literally. Whereas financiers once wore fine and fragile clothes to signal that they did not work, an investment banker now tells an anthropologist that Wall Street professionals "shouldn't wear suspenders because it looks like you spent too much time on your appearance, and you are supposed to just work hard. You shouldn't be wasting time putting on suspenders in the morning."

Exploit has been reconstituted as industry, completely reversing Bertie Wooster's inclination to treat work as leisure. Many of today's most intensive and remunerative jobs, including pursuits as varied as management and sport, were once gentlemen's vocations or hobbies, subject to strict social norms limiting the effort and intensity with which they might be pursued. Even celebrity—fame for its own sake, the purest form of exploit—is now framed as a form of industry, with effort openly and notoriously displayed on social media for all to see. And time itself has come to be imbued directly with economic value, including among elites who (unprecedentedly) can now bill and be paid by the hour. Lawyers and consultants, especially at the toniest firms, compete for logging the most billable hours and trade fables (and even tall tales) of immensely long hours as a disciplinary tool.

The meritocratic elite clings to its industry, stoically accepting that enormous incomes entitle employers to extract almost unbounded effort, and urging that their enormous effort justifies these incomes. They pray that their industry and income might reciprocally launder otherwise intolerable exertion and inequality.

Employers, they say, have "the right to expect [top employees] to work hard," so that it would be "unreasonable" for elite workers to "insist" on a "nine-to-five, five-day-per-week work schedule." Long work hours are what one prominent commentator called "a fair trade for . . . inflated salaries." In the words of another finance worker, clients "pay us lots and lots of money to be at their disposal 24 hours a day, 7 days a week."

Conversely, extreme hours, approaching the limits of human endurance, underwrite elite claims to deserve salaries that similarly approach the limits of the economy's capacity to pay. The *Harvard Business Review*'s extreme jobbers "consider their over-the-top efforts . . . a reflection of character . . . [so that t]o them, a 70-hour workweek is about proving their worth." And prominent conservative economist (and former chair of Harvard University's economics department) Gregory Mankiw argues that superordinate workers should enjoy enormous incomes because they have earned them, as what he calls the "just deserts" of their industry.

These claims have a dark side also, as the meritocratic elite do not just re-spect and admire industry but also disrespect and even despise idleness and leisure. Investment bankers complain about the "outside [non-elite] world," in which "people leave work at five, six p.m. [and] take one hour lunch breaks" and "just are not motivated in the same way" as they are. More concretely, Lloyd Blankfein (who was paid tens of millions of dollars for serving as the CEO of Goldman Sachs) recently argued that the unnecessary idleness of premature retirement counsels raising Social Security's retirement age.

Industrious work and long hours *constitute* the eliteness of the working rich; busyness has in itself become "the badge of honor." The social order that Veblen discerned, which had been stable across a millennium, has within a century been turned on its head: aristocrats yield to meritocrats, and the lei-sured elite gives way to the superordinate working class. Zuckerberg's hopes for his daughter reflect the social order into which she has been born.

Once, leisure constituted high status; labor "was, after all[,] the name of the subordinate class." Even the left agreed, as the working class, in the labor movement, reclaimed its subordinated name as a political ideal. Alexey Gri-goryevich Stakhanov, a record-setting hardworking Soviet coal miner, be-came the poster child for the effortful productivity of the socialist worker.

Now, meritocratic habits and norms have transformed both the rich and the rest. The baton of industrious effort has been largely detached from the in-creasingly redundant middle class and passed up the income ladder. This merger of industry and honor explains why the middle class experiences its en-forced idleness as insulting and even degrading and why the working rich com-mit to epidemic industry that the pursuit of mere wealth cannot rationalize.

Today's Stakhanovites are the one-percenters.

## POVERTY AND WEALTH

Every economy may be described in terms of two kinds of inequality: high-end, which concerns the gap between the rich and the middle class; and low-end, which concerns the gap between the middle class and the poor. Economic inequality can therefore grow and shrink at the same time, as rising high-end and falling low-end inequality occur together. When this happens, the shape of maldistribution alters. For most of human history, including at the middle of the last century, inequality and injustice centered on poverty. Today, they center on wealth.

At the end of the Second World War, a "collaboration between big business, big labor, and big government" remade American society, literally creating the modern middle class. The median real income for American men, for example, rose from $25,700 in 1947 to $41,836 in 1967 (in 2018 dollars), and the number of American households that owned their home rose over 40 percent between 1940 and 1960. By the late 1950s, when Galbraith published *The Affluent Society*, the prosperity of the middle was widely felt and had penetrated the self-image of the age—in St. Clair Shores and throughout the country.

Not all Americans were well represented by big business, big labor, or big government, however. Racial minorities and women would have to wait several decades before their claims of justice received a serious hearing, and LGBTQ people would have to wait a half century. Moreover, the poor also had no stake and no say in any branch of the triumvirate that governed mid-century America and were, as Galbraith observed, a "voiceless minority," a "silent presence . . . left out of this middle-class idyll." The middle-class boom dramatically reduced high-end inequality, but low-end inequality and poverty both endured.

In 1962, as the top 1 percent's income share approached an all-time low, another book, Michael Harrington's *The Other America,* entered this scene. Harrington was a graduate of Yale Law School and a socialist, although democratic and staunchly anticommunist. Arthur Schlesinger once called him "the only responsible radical in America." Harrington had spent much of the postwar middle-class boom immersing himself in the circumstances of America's poor. *The Other America* reflected this immersion. The book described, in vivid detail, what one reviewer called "alarming . . . pockets of despair and hunger in the depressed areas of the United States." Poverty denied many citizens what Harrington said were "the minimal levels of health, housing, food, and education that our present stage of scientific knowledge specifies as necessary for life as it is now lived in the United States." The book's "angry thesis," as another reviewer said, was that "behind the glittering façade of

America's 'affluent society' lies a ghetto of loneliness and defeat populated by the poor."

Harrington claimed that the ghetto was massive, comprising between forty and fifty million citizens whom material deprivation made internal exiles, cast out from the affluent society and in this sense almost harmed by the middle-class boom. He could not be precise, because the U.S. government did not collect poverty statistics until 1963–64 (after Harrington's book became famous). But Harrington could be sure that poverty—grinding, material deprivation—overwhelmed a substantial share of Americans. And when the official statistics debuted, roughly a quarter of the population still lived in poverty.

In any event, these statistics were for Harrington a means rather than an end. "I would beg the reader," he wrote, "to forget the numbers game. Whatever the precise calibrations, it is obvious that these statistics represent an enormous, an unconscionable amount of human suffering in this land. They should be read with a sense of outrage." Harrington aspired to be "an American Dickens" and in this way "to record the smell and texture and quality" of pervasive poverty in the midst of affluence.

Other midcentury writers shared these sensibilities and corroborated the picture that *The Other America* painted. Gabriel Kolko's *Wealth and Power in America: An Analysis of Social Class and Income Distribution*, also published in 1962 and often read together with Harrington's book, provided unemotional and even clinical but intense detail: the average poor family, Kolko wrote, had "no telephone in the house, but . . . makes three pay calls a week. They buy one book a year and write one letter a week. The father buys one heavy wool suit every two years and a light wool suit every three years; the wife, one suit every ten years or one skirt every five years. . . . In 1950, the family spent a total of $80 to $90 [about $850 in 2015 dollars] on all types of home furnishings, electrical appliances, and laundry equipment. . . . The entire family consumes a total of two five-cent ice-cream cones, one five-cent candy bar, two bottles of soda, and one bottle of beer a week."

For these Americans—and there were enough to constitute a mass rather than a fringe—middle-class affluence remained out of reach, and St. Clair Shores another country.

# THE WAR ON POVERTY

*The Other America* received respectful reviews on publication, but it drew only a modest readership and appeared at first to have no broader impact. Reviewers predicted low sales, and Harrington himself—saying that he would be happy to sell twenty-five hundred copies—traveled overseas to Europe soon after publication.

But in January 1963, Dwight Macdonald featured the book in a fifty-page *New Yorker* review entitled "Our Invisible Poor." The review, the longest of its kind in the magazine's history, was "more widely read than the books it discussed" and captured the public imagination. It also captured the attention of the political elite, and in particular of President Kennedy's economic adviser, Walter Heller, who gave some combination of Harrington's book and Macdonald's review to the president himself.

Kennedy took their lessons to heart. "I believe," Schlesinger later wrote, "that *The Other America* helped crystallize [Kennedy's] determination in 1963 to accompany the tax cut by a poverty program." While it is unclear if President Kennedy actually read the book, it was "widely assumed in Washington that he had." Certainly, Kennedy's 1963 State of the Union message took a page out of the book and reported that thirty-two million Americans were living on the "outskirts of poverty." And in April 1963, Kennedy proposed to establish a National Service Corps, with a message that began, "Poverty in the midst of plenty is a paradox that must not go unchallenged in this country." He might have added that the paradox put his own government's moral authority at risk: how could a society that condemned its poor to avoidable material misery and social exclusion legitimately expect them to remain loyal to its institutions and to obey its laws?

On November 19, 1963, Heller received a commitment from Kennedy to include an antipoverty measure in the administration's 1964 legislative program. Kennedy was assassinated three days later, but the antipoverty initiative was the first economic idea that Heller raised with the newly sworn-in President Johnson. The program appealed to Johnson's New Deal sensibilities, as he put it, and his first message to Congress, on November 27, 1963, proposed to "carry on the fight against poverty and misery, and disease and ignorance, in other lands and in our own." The popular press took up the call to arms. In his first State of the Union message, on January 8, 1964, President Johnson declared his now-famous "unconditional War on Poverty in America."

The most important thing to understand about the War on Poverty is that it reduced poverty. Victory was not complete, unconditional, or even sufficient, of course, and poverty remains real and scandalous. The War on Poverty stalled in the late 1970s, and poverty has worsened in recent years, as it always does following economic downturns. But the War on Poverty's core achievements have more or less endured, including in the face of rising economic inequality.

Even in the shadow of the Great Recession, poverty is by any measure both narrower and shallower than in the past, and abject poverty remains unrecognizably less broad or deep. The downturn hit the poor hard, but there were no breadlines this time around. Indeed, poverty today remains dramatically less severe than it was even during the post–World War II boom and the midcentury Great Compression, which progressives romantically champion as the peak of economic justice in America. Rising economic inequality today is driven overwhelmingly not by poverty but by concentrated wealth.*

The official poverty rate dropped steeply through the 1960s, from 22.4 percent in 1959 to a low of 11.1 percent in 1973. The poverty rate has been fluctuating between 11 and 15 percent since then (and the most recent available data, for 2017, report a poverty rate of 12.3 percent). The actual reduction in poverty is almost certainly much greater. A Supplemental Poverty Measure, conceived in 1992 and officially sanctioned in 2011, reports that poverty has fallen by substantially more than the Official Measure. Other, unofficial metrics record still more dramatic declines. One prominent radical recently proposed that income poverty, properly calculated, has fallen to below 5 percent.

An alternative approach to poverty, which follows Harrington's injunction to look to the lived experience of the poor and measures poverty directly in terms of consumption, reports a still more dramatic reduction. Consumption poverty rates have not been tracked for as long or as reliably as income

---

* A graphical representation of these trends appears in Figure 2 on page 293.

poverty rates. But the best available data suggest that consumption poverty has fallen from about 31 percent in the 1960s to perhaps as low as 4.5 percent by 2010. Deep poverty—the share of people living at half or less than half of the poverty threshold—is also markedly less when measured in terms of consumption rather than income. Whereas the official (income-based) deep poverty rate in 2009 remained about 6 percent, deep consumption poverty had fallen to below 1 percent.

Applying Harrington's exhortation to focus on concrete details rather than abstract statistics reveals the massive improvements that these changes have made to the lived experience of the poor. The poor can afford to buy, on average, perhaps a quarter more than they could at midcentury, and their buying power for certain essentials—most notably, food—has grown more rapidly still. (A typical poor family spends half the share of its income on keeping itself nourished as it did at midcentury.) Consumer durables also dramatically improve the well-being of the poor. In 1960, the poor had effectively no access at all to air conditioners, dishwashers, or clothes dryers, and half had no access to a car. By 2009, over 80 percent of the poorest quintile of American households had air conditioners, 68 percent had clothes dryers, 40 percent had dishwashers, and three-quarters owned cars.

Moreover, even as they consume more, the poor yield less labor in exchange. American men with less than a high school education enjoyed over fifteen more hours of "leisure" per week in 2010 than they did in 1965, and American women with less than a high school education gained over ten hours of "leisure" per week during the same period. The scare quotes indicate that this is a mixed blessing, as it principally reflects involuntary unemployment and its attendant harms. But although enforced idleness imposes important burdens, rising consumption coupled with falling labor demonstrates a decline in absolute, material poverty.

These seemingly banal increases in consumption transform lives. Anyone who has washed clothes by hand knows that "wash day" really did involve a full day of hard labor, every week. And between 1960 and 2004, the spread of home air-conditioning reduced premature heat-related deaths by as much as 75 percent. Broader markers of physical health extend this trend. The mortality rate for American children under the age of five has fallen from 30.1 per thousand live births in 1960 to 6.8 per thousand in 2015. The United

Nations' Human Development Index for the United States has increased by about 10 percent. And the life expectancy of the poor has increased (although by much less than the increase enjoyed by richer Americans).

None of this shows that poverty has been eradicated or that the lives of the remaining poor have become easy. The War on Poverty is not yet won, and a final victory remains distressingly far off. But the early gains made by the Johnson administration have not been reversed. Even after the backlash against the Great Society that began in the Reagan Revolution and has continued through the present day, and even following the economic collapse of the Great Recession, poverty remains—depending on how it is measured—at between half and a sixth of its midcentury levels.

Whatever its vices, and even as it ushers in massive new economic inequality, the American economic and political system today provides for the basic material needs of a virtually unprecedented share of citizens. The pervasive, grinding, absolute deprivation that drove the quest for economic justice at midcentury no longer dominates the American scene. Legitimate outrage at the poverty that remains does not erase and should not obscure this progress.

Our America is no longer Michael Harrington's. This is a good thing.

## A NEW RUPTURE

A second and more familiar development coincides with poverty's decline. Once again, wealth has advanced even as poverty has receded: and the top 1 percent's share of national income now more than doubles its midcentury levels. High-end inequality has increased even as low-end inequality has declined. These joint developments give economic inequality a new and unprecedented face.

Income ratios introduce these effects.* In 1964, a typical middle-class household's income (the median income) was about four times the income of a typical poor household (the average income in the poorest quintile); a half century later, it is only about three times as large. And in 1964, a typical rich household's income (the average in the top 1 percent) was about thirteen times the income of a typical middle-class household; a half century later, it

---

* A graphical representation of these trends appears in Figure 3 on page 294.

has grown to about twenty-three times as large. In other words, the poor/middle-class income gap has narrowed by about a quarter since midcentury, while the middle-class/rich income gap has nearly doubled.

Put a little differently, the poor and the middle class have converged, even as the rich have left the middle class increasingly far behind. These pressures squeeze the middle class from both ends, undoing the middle-class version of affluence, in St. Clair Shores and across the country, and steadily deflating what increasingly appears, looking backward, to have been a middle-class bubble. Indeed, 2015 was the first year since Galbraith wrote in which the majority of Americans were not middle class, and the middle class that remains is no longer the richest in the world.

An overall measure of inequality—called the Gini index—drives the revolution home. The Gini represents inequality through a single number, between 0 and 1. An index of 0 reflects perfect equality, in which all households have identical incomes. An index of 1 reflects maximal inequality, in which one household captures all of the economy's income and every other household gets nothing.

The Gini index for the American economy has risen sharply over the past fifty years, from as low as 0.38 at midcentury to as high as 0.49 today. This increase captures the commonplace sense that inequality overall has shown a stark increase, from levels that resembled Norway then to levels that resemble India now.

Two other trends are less familiar but vividly display the transformation in economic inequality's center of gravity. First, the Gini index for the bottom 70 percent of the U.S. income distribution—constructed not by redistributing any income but simply by discarding all income from the top 30 percent of households—has *fallen* (by about 10 percent) since midcentury. (Indeed, the Gini for the bottom 90 percent has remained effectively flat over this period, so that there has been no dramatic increase in inequality across the bottom nine-tenths of the U.S. income distribution.) And second, the Gini for the top 5 percent of the income distribution—now constructed by discarding all the income from the bottom 95 percent—has skyrocketed, from as low as 0.33 at midcentury to as high as 0.5 today.*

---

* A graphical representation of these trends appears in Figure 4 on page 296.

Economic inequality has fallen modestly across the bottom seven-tenths of the U.S. income distribution, and inequality has risen dramatically within the top twentieth. Indeed, for some recent years, inequality within this narrow elite now exceeds inequality in the economy overall. In other words, the income gap between the merely rich and the exceptionally rich has become so large that eliminating the poor and the middle class from the distribution would actually increase inequality. (Alternatively, the relatively stable inequality across the bottom parts of the distribution now serves as a ballast against exploding inequality within the very top.)

This result would have been unimaginable at midcentury. Then, the central economic divide separated the desperate poor from the affluent middle class, and low-end inequality dominated maldistribution. Now the central economic divide separates the super-rich from everyone else, and high-end inequality dominates. Rising inequality at the top has been accompanied not just by falling poverty but also by steady or even falling inequality at the bottom.

Finally, high-end inequality has grown faster than low-end inequality has fallen, which is why the Gini for the complete distribution has risen.

## CHANGING THE SUBJECT

These developments are not just technical curiosities, confined to national accounts and distributional tables, and interesting to economists and statisticians only. Instead, the rise of the working rich transforms the lived experience and social meaning of economic inequality. Meritocracy fundamentally changes the subject of economic justice.

Once, indolent wealth alongside widespread poverty gave inequality's critics a soft target. Aristocratic wastrels were easy to condemn, and the abject poor pulled at the heartstrings. Now, the rise of the working rich and the decline in poverty have hardened meritocratic inequality against the arguments that dismantled the leisure class. Superordinate workers seem almost admirable, and the middle class (even when it struggles) neither seeks nor elicits charity. The meritocratic turn frustrates equality's champions, and this gives the meritocracy trap a moral dimension.

Superordinate workers earn their income and status industriously, by exploiting their own effort and skill. This creates a powerful impression that meritocrats are entitled to their advantages, as under Mankiw's principle of "just deserts." Moreover, while it is obvious that nobody deserves to inherit an estate or a factory, as aristocratic rentiers used to do, meritocrats can credibly claim to deserve the skills and work ethic that drive their incomes. A progressive might look at a landowner or factory owner from the old elite and, channeling Elizabeth Warren or Barack Obama, reasonably say, "You didn't build that." But it is hard to say the same to the superordinate worker from the new elite, who (whatever her initial advantages) owes her immense income to skill that she has cultivated through her own diligence and effort. To deny that meritocrats earn and deserve their incomes seems to require denying that anyone ever earns or deserves anything.

The shift from low- to high-end inequality further hardens meritocratic inequality against conventional progressive arguments. Poverty endures, of course, and relief remains a moral imperative. But the War on Poverty (even if never completed) has transformed the political landscape. The politics of equality now focus on the growing relative gap between the top and the middle rather than on absolute need at the bottom—on frustration among the middle class rather than wretchedness among the poor. (Progressive nostalgia for the midcentury economy, when the middle class thrived while the poor suffered, symbolizes this shift.)

Meritocratic inequality makes the new focus natural. Middle-class life is hard, and the contrast between middle-class stagnation and the elite's extravagant growth and conspicuous opulence makes it harder. But the middle class cannot credibly command the intense, visceral sympathy that the poor did in Harrington's day. Then, low-end inequality was a humanitarian catastrophe. Now, high-end inequality is a political injustice. Once again, the meritocratic transformation weakens the hand of equality's champions.

Received moral principles simply do not suit new economic realities. The arguments that defeated aristocratic inequality stand at a skew angle to the political battle lines of today, and they illuminate meritocratic inequality with at most a glancing light. The meritocratic ideal that income should track industry rather than birth, which gave midcentury progressives a powerful tool for fighting aristocratic inequality, is now itself the root of a new disease and, moreover, a moral hostage that redistribution must avoid harming.

## AN EMBOLDENED ADVERSARY

From the beginnings of democracy in ancient Greece through the invention of mass democracy at the American founding, political thinkers have uniformly assumed that democratic politics enables the masses to band together and plunder the wealth of outnumbered elites.

Economic inequality's recent career confounds this assumption. Even as rising inequality concentrates more and more income in a smaller and smaller elite, government has dramatically retreated from economic redistribution. The income shares of the top 1 percent, the top 0.1 percent, and the top 0.01 percent have roughly doubled, tripled, and quadrupled in recent decades. Over the same period, the top marginal tax rate has fallen by more than half, from over 90 percent throughout the 1950s and early 1960s, to 70 percent when Ronald Reagan assumed the presidency in 1981, to below 40 percent today. Even as elites get richer and richer, government takes smaller and smaller shares of their income and wealth.

The biggest losers from these developments, moreover, are not the poor, who (even in a democracy) face obstacles to concerted political action. Instead, the biggest losers—who have simultaneously suffered a declining income share and a rising share of the tax burden—have been the broad middle class. This group includes journalists, teachers and professors, middle managers, government workers, engineers, and even doctors in general practice. It is neither ill-educated nor disempowered but, to the contrary, can influence and possibly control the nation's medical and scientific establishment, its press, its universities, and even its most important bureaucracies.

The middle class possesses political skills and enjoys political access that together make it well placed to protect its interests through democratic action. Why, then, did middle-class Americans not mobilize long ago to stop economic and political transformations that so signally burden them? What enabled a narrowing elite, operating in a democracy, effectively to plunder a massive middle class and even a large near-elite?

A frustrated commentator recently observed that even as "significant advances in recent centuries on other fronts of injustice" make "slavery, racial exclusion, gender domination, or the denial of citizenship" easy to condemn, "massive personal wealth ... remain[s] ideologically constructed as unjust to correct." Why, during decades in which virtually every other marginalized group has progressed toward equality in spite of being in the minority, did the massively most populous disadvantaged group, the 99 percent, allow itself to be increasingly dispossessed? This unprecedented development defies millennia of received wisdom and embarrasses almost every familiar account of political economy in mass democracies. It is in a way an even deeper puzzle than why the middle-class eruption, when it finally came, took the nativist and populist form that it did.

Meritocracy's charisma dissolves the puzzle, by causing the middle class to accept, and even affirm, its own increasing disadvantage. When inequality was aristocratic, ideals concerning both sympathy and right sustained the social welfare state and the War on Poverty. But today, meritocracy justifies rising economic inequality. People who feel that they have worked on productive tasks claim greater entitlement to rewards than those who feel that they have not worked, and where wealth is perceived as legitimate, support for economic redistribution declines. Mankiw sums this up when he observes, "When people can see with their own eyes that a talented person made a great fortune fair and square, they tend not to resent it." The rich insist on lower top tax rates, and the rest accept them, because both groups agree that meritocratic inequality tracks desert and that redistribution would unjustly abuse industrious workers.

The meritocratic turn even emboldens equality's enemies to attack redistribution, charging that it merely serves the ressentiment that the indolent feel at the rewards that meritocracy accords to the industrious. A Cold War–era joke imagined a Russian communist who is granted one wish and asks, "My neighbor has a cow, I do not. I wish that you should kill that cow." Today, Arthur C. Brooks, the president of the American Enterprise Institute, emphasizes that many of the concrete programs that progressives champion (including Social Security, Medicare, and subsidized college loans) distribute substantial portions of their benefits not to the poor but rather to the middle class. More pointedly still, Brooks casts the programs as simple resource grabs by a numerous and hence powerful—but unsavory—interest group. He asks, as a rhetorical thrust, whether redistributive social programs should simply grow and grow until middle-class envy is exhausted. Even egalitarians worry that their sentiments, laid bare, will reveal themselves as grasping rather than magnanimous. Where inequality is meritocratic, these arguments suggest, demands for economic justice merely launder the currency of middle-class desire.

Sometimes all these sentiments come together and the working rich shout their meritocratic entitlement and their disdain for the middle class confidently from the rooftops. An email circulated widely among finance workers at the height of the Occupy Wall Street movement, as President Obama proposed a millionaire's tax, stated the case clearly.

"We are Wall Street," the email announced. "We get up at 5 a.m. and work till 10 p.m. or later. We're used to not getting up to pee when we have a position. We don't take an hour or more for a lunch break. We don't demand a union. We don't retire at 50 with a pension. We eat what we kill."

Meritocracy empowers the working rich to lay down a moral marker, which equality's champions cannot wish away or otherwise ignore.

Instead, they must challenge meritocracy head-on.

# FIVE

# THE MERITOCRATIC
# INHERITANCE

For the class of nineteenfiftysomething at the elite prep school Groton, "Getting admitted to college brought with it no element of insecurity or nervousness; the boy and his family simply decided where he wanted to go and that was that. Every member of the class got into his first-choice college except one, who was thought to be brain-damaged." Groton's graduates were not exceptional among prep school products in this respect. Yale, for example, admitted fully 90 percent of applicants in the years before World War II and still admitted 60 percent in the mid-1950s. Even into the 1940s and 1950s, elite universities retained, as quasi-official policy, the principle that the sons of alumni would be admitted as long as they were minimally able to do their schoolwork. Inherited privilege and the success rates that it gave applicants suffused the very language of college admissions, as the sons of the best families "put themselves down for" rather than "applied to" the school of their choice. Alumni, moreover, believed "that the admission of their sons was a right."

Colleges shared these attitudes toward hereditary privilege and considered other admissions criteria wrong. Yale's faculty responded to the "disorderliness" and "sloppiness" of the "ill-bred" veterans who came to the university under the GI Bill by adopting, for the first time in the school's history, a mandatory coat-and-tie dress code. And in the 1950s, Yale's president, A. Whitney Griswold, "zestfully attacked mass education" and refused to enlarge the college better to serve the coming wave of baby boomers, saying that he would not allow the Yale man to become "a beetle-browed, highly specialized intellectual." Harvard's admissions office still openly advertised to prep school counselors and high-caste applicants that it sought to fill a "happy bottom quarter" of its class with athletes, mediocre prep school graduates, and alumni sons. Undergraduates from the best families and poshest schools remained embarrassingly absent from the academic honor rolls; at Yale, these students were underrepresented in Phi Beta Kappa by a factor of more than three to one.

Midcentury reformers, with both economic and democratic motives, adopted meritocracy and its accoutrements—including especially achievement tests and competitive admissions—deliberately to break up this unproductive and complacent elite. Harvard University president James Bryant Conant initiated the use of the Scholastic Aptitude Test (SAT) in American college admissions to help screen scholarship applicants as part of a conscious effort to introduce new groups to education at the country's most prestigious university. The Nobel Prize–winning progressive economist James Tobin, who reached Harvard's class of 1939 from a modest background in Champaign, Illinois, was one of the test's first great successes. After World War II, Harvard expanded its testing strategy, with rapid and deep consequences: by the late 1940s, Harvard's class contained as many public school graduates as prep school graduates, and the SAT scores of the average Harvard freshman from 1952 would have placed him in the bottom 10 percent of the incoming class in 1960. This represented, according to Harvard's longtime dean of admissions Wilbur J. Bender, "the greatest change in Harvard admissions . . . in . . . recorded history." Princeton followed suit, so that its student body achieved parity between high school and prep school graduates by 1955.

The revolution reached Yale last. Between 1951 and 1956, Yale admitted only seven students from the Bronx High School of Science, probably the most academically competitive high school in the United States at the time, even as it took in 275 graduates from the decidedly nonmeritocratic Phillips Academy Andover. But when change came, it came with a vengeance, and in a form that expressly embraced the meritocratic ideal of an elite built on human capital and designed to yield superordinate labor.

Griswold died in 1963, and Yale acquired, in Kingman Brewster, a new and very different president. Brewster regarded the aristocratic elite as sclerotic, and, declaring that he did "not intend to preside over a finishing school on Long Island Sound," set out to reform Yale. Meritocracy gave Brewster, who called himself "an intellectual investment banker," the blueprint for reform. By choosing students based on ability and achievement, Yale would invest its educational resources wisely and maximize their return.

In 1965, Brewster appointed R. Inslee "Inky" Clark Jr. dean of admissions, with a mandate to redesign Yale's student body on a meritocratic model. Clark, whose patrician-sounding name belied a public school education and egalitarian mentality, fired nearly the entire admissions staff and built a new team committed to recruiting students aggressively based on achievement rather than breeding. The Yale Corporation, for its part, adopted need-blind admissions in 1966, becoming the first university formally to sever the right to attend from the ability to pay.

Clark's admissions team expressly rejected the hereditary elite even as it pursued the new meritocrats. Clark refocused admissions on what he called "talent searching" and understood talent as receptivity to investments in human capital, asking "who will benefit most from studying at Yale." He called prep schools that clung to the traditional hereditary model "ingrown" and turned their graduates away: in 1968, for example, Harvard still accepted 46 percent of applicants from Choate, and Princeton 57 percent, but Yale accepted only 18 percent.

Dramatic results followed at once. In its first year, Clark's admissions office drastically reduced the share of admittees who hailed from alumni families and rejected the son of Yale's biggest donor. The new admissions policy, moreover, actively sought to replace complacent insiders with talented outsiders. Yale's class of 1970 contained 50 percent more public school graduates than did the class of 1969.

The meritocratic recruits dramatically outperformed the hereditary elite that they displaced. The class of 1970 became by far the most academically distinguished in Yale's history: its median student's SATs would have been in the 90th percentile for the class of 1961 and the 75th percentile for the class of 1966, and its average grades at Yale set a school record.

Clark cast Yale's new admissions standards as "a statement, really, about what leadership was going to be in the country and where leaders were going to come from." The old elite understood this and tried to fight back. Yale's admissions officers received frosty receptions at prep schools that had once embraced them. Alumni grumbled—as in William F. Buckley's complaint that the new standards would prefer "a Mexican-American from El Paso High . . . [over] . . . Jonathan Edwards the Sixteenth from Saint Paul's School." A rump of Yale's corporation resisted: when Clark made a presentation to the corporation about constructing a new American elite based on merit rather than birth, one member interjected, "You're talking about Jews and public school graduates as leaders. Look around you at this table. These are America's leaders. There are no Jews here. There are no public school graduates here."

But this was a losing battle. The old elite's sense that admission based on birth was a right had been displaced by the meritocratic elite's proud conviction that admission earned on account of achievement was an honor. The charismatic center of the culture had shifted to the meritocrats. As Brewster observed, by 1970 need-blind admissions became a selling point even for those who could pay. Even "the privileged took pride in the feeling that they had made it on the merits rather than on the basis of something ambiguously called 'background.'"

Meritocracy's career in education has proceeded from strength to strength in the decades since 1970, as applicant pools grow and admissions rates plummet. As recently as 1990, the top ten undergraduate colleges and universities in America admitted nearly 30 percent of their applicants; today, they admit fewer than 10 percent on average, and some admit fewer than 5 percent. Elite students' academic qualifications, unsurprisingly, have improved as well. The median SAT scores among students at Harvard, Princeton, Stanford, and Yale now all lie above the 95th percentile, and perhaps a quarter of the students have SATs above the 99th percentile.

The meritocratic training revolution has achieved its immediate economic aims. Intense and competitive education produces outstanding—literally exceptional—results. A systematic survey of adult skills in developed countries reveals that the United States has the highest overall gap between its most and least skilled citizens. Moreover, the American skills gap's origins lie—once again, exceptionally—directly in formal education: in the words of the Organisation for Economic Co-operation and Development (OECD), the United States "stands out as having a particularly large gap between [adults with tertiary education and those who have not attained upper secondary education] in both literacy and numeracy proficiency."

The present American elite, unlike in the past, and more so than in virtually every other nation, possesses exceptional skills and derives these skills from extraordinary training. The meritocratic elite deploys its hard-won skills with intense industry, in the superordinate jobs whose enormous wages make today's 1 percent so rich. Meritocracy's outputs, in this narrow sense, validate its inputs. Brewster's intellectual investment banking has paid off.

But meritocracy's narrow economic successes have turned out to undermine its broader democratic ambitions. The old elite quickly succumbed to the meritocratic onslaught, as Brewster and others had expected. But the new elite, made in the crucible of meritocracy, knows better than anything how to turn competition to its children's advantage. The very same mechanisms that once destroyed aristocratic hierarchies and dynasties now erect meritocratic hierarchies and dynasties in their stead.

The Gospel of Matthew says that the teachings of Jesus build upon themselves: "Whosoever hath, to him shall be given, and he shall have more abundance: but whosoever hath not, from him shall be taken away even that he hath." A similar "Matthew Effect" applies to secular skills under mature meritocracy. The human capital that constitutes the meritocratic elite provides in education a means for its own reproduction, and meritocracy has by embracing this means launched a "revolution in family wealth transmission." Even as meritocracy abolishes the hereditary privilege that sustained aristocratic dynasties, it embraces in education a new dynastic technology of its own. The new elite receives a meritocratic inheritance that transmits privilege, and excludes the middle class from opportunity, as effectively as the old elite's birthright used to do.

Dynasties are not all created equal, however, as some exact a price from those whose caste they secure. Aristocrats, being born, could pass their status automatically, and therefore costlessly, down to their children. But meritocrats, being made, must incur enormous costs to secure their wealth and status. Exclusive and exacting education builds human capital only by dominating the lives of those who must absorb it. Meritocracy sustains dynasties by reconstructing the family on the model of the firm, the household on the model of the workplace, and the child on the model of the product.

The meritocratic inheritance comes with strings attached, which threaten now to tie the meritocratic elite in knots. The Bible lesson is too sparing in its sympathies. Scarcity is indeed burdensome, and meritocracy condemns the middle class to inattention and underinvestment. But abundance is not always a blessing, and the excessive and ruthless training through which meritocracy makes the elite does not elevate the human spirit so much as crush it.

## BEFORE CONCEPTION

An elite child's meritocratic inheritance begins even before the child is a twinkle in its parents' eyes. Rich young adults make two interconnected decisions, concerning whom to marry and whether to stay married, that increasingly give their children advantages that children born outside the elite do not enjoy. Moreover, the rich make these choices not severally but together, embedded in communities of other rich people making similar choices. Children of rich parents are conceived, borne, and born in markedly more auspicious circumstances than middle-class children enjoy.

The elite increasingly marry each other—a practice that economists have given the ugly name *assortative mating*. Assortative mating had been common during the last decades of the nineteenth century, among the aristocracy in the Gilded Age, but then declined over the first half of the twentieth century. By 1960 only 3 percent of American marriages were between partners who both possessed college degrees.

Meritocratic inequality renewed the elite's preference for elite mates, so that by 2010, fully 25 percent of couples were composed of two college graduates. (Note that since just over 30 percent of American adults possess college degrees, this leaves only a small minority of graduates over to pair with nongraduates.) Moreover, the share of marriages composed of partners who both possess post-college—graduate or professional school—educations has quintupled, growing from under 1 percent in 1960 to over 5 percent in 2005.

The proximate reasons why are natural and largely innocent: colleges and graduate schools, which were overwhelmingly male in 1960, are today almost evenly balanced by gender. Universities, both individually and as a group, provide an obvious setting for meeting husbands and wives, and the pages of contemporary alumni magazines are filled with notices of marriages celebrated and babies conceived among classmates. But even if innocently brokered, these marriages, taken all together, enormously concentrate the elite, both within a generational cohort and especially down through the generations.

Assortative mating increases economic inequality within the marrying cohort, operating literally as a multiplier for the already growing inequality produced by rising top labor incomes. If marriage pairings had been random by education in 1960, this would have had no observable effect on household income inequality. But when highly paid superordinate workers pair off, marriage ceases to be neutral. Replacing today's actual pattern of assortative mating with random pairings, or indeed with the lower level of assortative mating from 1960, would reduce overall inequality by a fifth or more.

In addition, assortative mating increases educational inequality in the next generation down. Elites do not just increasingly marry each other but also increasingly stay married and raise children within mature, stable marriages. This difference increasingly distinguishes the elite from not just the poor but also the middle class. And the distinction confers a massive advantage on children born into rich families.

To begin with, elite, educated women increasingly bear children only after marrying, as compared to their less elite, less educated counterparts. In 1970, out-of-marriage births accounted for only about 10 percent of births to women across all education levels. Today, by contrast, education overwhelmingly determines the relationship between marriage and motherhood. Among college- and post-college-educated women, only one in twenty and one in thirty children are born outside of marriage. By contrast, in the least educated two-thirds of the population, comprising women with a high school education or less, nearly 60 percent of all children are born outside of marriage. Overall, the average mother with a high school degree only or some college (but no BA) has children two years before marriage, whereas the average college-educated mother has children two years after marriage.

Elite marriages also increasingly outlast their less elite counterparts.

Between 1960 and 1980, divorce rates roughly tripled for all Americans, but since 1980, marriage has polarized along socioeconomic lines. Divorce rates remained steady, and perhaps even increased slightly, in the bottom three-quarters of the economic distribution, whereas in the top quarter, divorce has declined, indeed back to 1960 levels. Today, women without a college degree experience divorce within ten years of marriage at more than twice the rate of women college graduates: roughly 35 percent versus roughly 15 percent. More broadly, between 1960 and 2010, the share of adults who are currently married fell by twice as much for Americans without a college degree as for those who had earned a BA (and the decline among those with some college but no degree roughly equaled the decline for those with high school educations only).

In all these ways, marriage has become a rich person's affair, and children of rich, well-educated parents are now enormously more likely than other children—including not just poor but also middle-class children—to grow up in households with both parents present. Between 1970 and 2010, the share of children to grow up without both parents grew three times as quickly among households in the middle third of the income distribution as among households in the top third. The size of the differences today is astounding. For example, about 55 percent of children in households whose income is roughly $25,000 live with only a single parent, compared to about 25 percent in households whose income is roughly $60,000, and just about 10 percent in households whose income exceeds $100,000. Moreover, 90 percent of children living in the richest and best-educated 5 percent of American zip codes live with both their biological parents.

These patterns serve meritocracy's inner economic and especially dynastic logics. When the households become sites of economic production—building the human capital of the next generation—pressures arise to choose partners and structure marriages to optimize production. Elites use wealth and status to support controlled and conservative lifestyles in order to preserve their caste. Elite marriages ensure that the meritocratic inheritance they will build once their children are born will not be squandered but will instead generate exceptional returns.

# CONCEPTION THROUGH KINDERGARTEN

Children born to rich parents begin collecting their meritocratic inheritances from the moment of conception. The exceptional stability that elite mothers enjoy benefits their children even in the womb. Meritocratic inequality makes personal and economic security into markers of eliteness. Perhaps most notably, meritocratic inequality reaches not just annual incomes but also financial security. (Divorce and financial distress go hand in hand: money troubles strain marriages, and divorce is expensive, especially for women.) As elite wealth increases, it grows more durable. Middle-class incomes, by contrast, have not just stagnated on average but also become, for individual households, more volatile: the annual odds that a middle-class family will suffer a major financial reversal (an income drop of more than 50 percent) doubled between 1970 and 2000.

These reversals stress the families who suffer them, including not just parents but also children, and stress impedes children's development. Indeed, maternal stress can harm a child even before birth, through biological pathways in utero, so that a mother's prenatal stress depresses her child's educational achievement and IQ score. The effects, moreover, are large: seven-year-olds who were exposed to high levels of maternal stress hormones before birth receive 1.1 fewer years (over half a standard deviation) less schooling and achieve verbal IQ scores five points lower (nearly half a standard deviation) than their unexposed siblings. Finally, research also shows that educated mothers are much more able than uneducated mothers to compensate for the effects of prenatal stress after their babies are born, so that the harms to children from prenatal stress are by far greatest where the stress befalls non-elite mothers. Rich babies are literally better borne than their middle-class counterparts.

Elite parents do not let up advantaging their babies when they arrive. To the contrary, rich parents exploit the extravagant groundwork that they have laid by making exceptional direct investments in their children from the moment of birth. These investments continue and compound through early childhood, beginning in the home and eventually extending into the outside world.

The rich increasingly invest more of their own time than the rest in developing the human capital of their babies, infants, and toddlers (and the class gap in parental time spent with children is greatest among the youngest children). In the 1960s and 1970s, educated and uneducated parents devoted about equal amounts of time to activities that encouraged their children's development. Over the roughly four decades since, all parents have begun to invest more time in educating their children, but college-educated parents—both mothers and fathers—have increased their investments more rapidly, indeed, twice as rapidly, according to one study. Today, college-educated parents, taken together, spend more than an hour per day longer educating their children than do high-school-only parents.

For super-elite parents, and especially mothers, the trend is more dramatic still. Roughly half of female Harvard and Chicago MBAs with two or more children, for example, leave the workforce or work part-time in order to care for their children. And motherhood drives elite women lawyers out of the workforce at rates so high that top firms refer to a "flight risk." Many factors, ranging from gender discrimination in work assignments, pay, and promotions to outright sexual harassment, contribute to this pattern and especially to the fact that so many more mothers than fathers leave the workforce. But the enormous demands of elite parenting, combined with the meritocratic imperative to build human capital in the next generation, make it socially and economically rational for one parent to leave an elite job in order to help train a couple's children.

Meritocratic norms accommodate this logic: a mother who did not possess an elite education to begin with would be embarrassing to an elite family, but it is socially acceptable among meritocrats for a hypereducated wife and mother to leave her job in order to raise children. Indeed, she honors rather than abandons the inner logic of meritocratic production, by funding her children's meritocratic inheritance and investing in dynastic succession.

Rich parents, moreover, distinguish themselves through not just the quantity but also the quality of the investments that they make in their children. The meritocratic elite adopts a deliberate program of "concerted cultivation," specifically designed to promote its children's adult achievement. Elite parents bring both their vast incomes and their life experiences to developing their children's human capital, which parents build up by mimicking their own training. Parenting in this elite style deploys methods and demands skills that parents outside the elite cannot always identify, much less match.

For example, parents with a BA are more than twice as likely to read to their children every day as parents with a high school education or less (and one and a half times as likely as parents with some college but no degree). They are roughly twice as likely to take their children to art galleries, museums, and historical sites and to enroll them in arts classes.

Indeed, the rich quite generally speak to their children more, and much more interactively, than do the rest: a three-year-old child born to professional parents will have heard nearly twenty million more words than a three-year-old born to parents who hold nonprofessional jobs and over thirty million more words than a three-year-old born to parents on welfare. The rich also speak much more effectively: the words professional parents choose, the rituals and symbols with which they invest their words, and even the tone of voice that they deploy are all qualitatively more educative than their counterparts among the working class. Some of the words sink in. Three-year-old children of professional parents know 49 percent more words than children of nonprofessionals, and those children know a further 43 percent more words than children whose parents are on welfare. (A natural experiment tragically but vividly confirms the effect: when children who are born deaf have their hearing restored through cochlear implants, the rich ones learn to speak more quickly than the poor ones.)

Even the moral psychology of parenting varies with parents' educations. Parents with postgraduate degrees are about half as likely to spank their children as parents with only a BA and about a third as likely as parents with only a high school degree or less. And widespread research shows that rich, educated parents quite generally provide their children with more open affection, greater participatory engagement, and more consistent discipline than their middle-class and especially poor counterparts.

These distinctive investments increasingly give elite children emotional skills—openness, self-confidence, self-discipline, and grit—that poor and also middle-class children cannot match. Recent systematic work on noncognitive skills and life success suggests that these emotional differences between early childhoods in elite versus ordinary households likely have still greater effects on success than the cognitive ones, including even with respect to long-term academic achievement.

Similar differences separate the early years of elite and ordinary childhood outside the home—in preschools and kindergartens. Three-year-olds from households whose annual incomes exceed $100,000 attend preschool at twice the rate of three-year-olds from households whose annual incomes fall below $60,000. Systematic data reporting preschool enrollment rates for truly elite households do not exist, but every one-percenter knows from direct experience that effectively all really rich three-year-olds attend preschool. (For the rare few who do not, this is because their parents have concluded, after careful thought, that a different deliberately constructed childcare regime is better for their children.)

Moreover, ordinary and elite preschools are almost unrecognizably different. A middle-class preschool will have reading and craft corners and (if it is good) a loving and caring if overstretched staff. An elite preschool—such as the Ethical Culture Fieldston School in New York City—may have a fully staffed and stocked library, and separate art, music, foreign language, science, and social studies departments, all staffed by teachers and even assistant teachers who hold bachelor's and even master's degrees from elite colleges and universities. The school might well have one teacher for every seven students.

Elite schools' academic programs represent only a small part of the advantage that they confer on their students. Quite apart from teaching cognitive skills, elite preschools focus intensively on their students' emotional development and character. They give students individualized attention with the aim—expressly chosen and diligently pursued—of producing children who will become self-disciplined, self-motivated, and self-directed learners, able to face and surmount the challenges that school proper will inevitably bring.

All this attention costs money, of course. Pre-kindergarten tuition at Fieldston exceeds $50,000 per year, roughly 80 percent of parents pay the full price, and the highest number of financial aid packages are awarded to families that are really quite rich, with annual incomes between $100,000 and $149,000. Indeed, elite parents fight tooth and nail to pay—the most competitive preschools admit just 5 percent of applicants (making them harder to get into than Harvard and Yale). These admissions rates have created a market for "educational consultants" to help rich four-year-olds get in. The consultants are themselves not cheap (a fee might reach $6,000), and following their advice costs parents time as well as money. A typical plan of action calls for applying to ten kindergartens, writing "love letters" (over and above the required application essays) to the top three, and studying the idiosyncrasies of each school in order to impress on school visits.

The elite embrace this seemingly absurd competition for a reason. Early education pays immense dividends: dollar for dollar, the preschool years represent the most consequential investments in a person's human capital. The leading schools of psychological thought agree that early childhood development exerts a dominant influence over the personality; there exists evidence that cognitive capacity, for example, general intelligence as measured by IQ (although not, of course, education in more particular knowledge and skills), is largely fixed by age ten; and the most substantial income-based differences in school achievement already become visible in school readiness tests administered when children enter kindergarten. Elite preschools and kindergartens know and exploit these associations, including through informal or even formal links to elite middle and high schools (in the case of Ethical Culture Fieldston, there is a formal link to the Fieldston Upper School). The websites of the pre-kindergarten programs advertise the elite colleges that their alumni eventually attend.

Quantity and quality both matter for education: practice doesn't make perfect; perfect practice makes perfect. As every elite parent knows, early childhood training on the meritocratic model is immensely intensive and immersively personal. The upshot of the vastly unequal investments in the human capital of young children by the rich and the rest is equally clear: elite children enter school proper with tremendous emotional and academic advantages already in place. By the time they are five, children from the top tenth of American households by socioeconomic status outstrip children from the bottom tenth by roughly thirty-seven, twenty-five, and thirty-nine months of schooling on the PISA tests of mathematics, reading, and science skills, and the most elite tenth outstrip the median by roughly twenty-one, nineteen, and twenty-three months.

These are enormous differences. Moreover, the elite/middle-class gap exceeds the middle-class/bottom gap, a pattern that will persist and intensify deep into adulthood.

# THE SCHOOL-AGED YEARS

Elite kindergarteners enter formal schooling with an immense advantage over both poor and middle-class peers already locked in. Even if extraordinary investments in human capital ended at the schoolhouse door, the rich would massively out-educate the rest. In fact, however, the structural advantages and exceptionally effective parenting practices of the rich do not dissolve or become inert on an elite child's fifth birthday. To the contrary, rich parents continue and indeed redouble their distinctive, methodical, and disciplined pursuit of their children's educations. The school-aged years add to rich children's meritocratic inheritance.

Some elite habits are so basic that they pass beneath notice: rich parents, for example, spend three more hours per week than poor parents just talking to their school-aged children and many more hours still at active leisure. Over the course of a childhood, these choices cumulate into a massive direct investment in rich children's education. By the time she is eighteen, a rich child will have had over five thousand more hours than a poor child of being talked to, read to, attending cultural events, seeing museums, being coached in a sport, and so on. This amounts to nearly an hour in each day of the child's life, or the equivalent of the time that an adult devotes over two and a half years at a full-time job. Her poorer counterparts, needless to say, will not spend their free hours anything like as profitably: by the time they reach eighteen, middle-class children will have spent nearly five thousand more hours watching television or playing video games than rich children, and poor children will have spent nearly eight thousand more hours of screen time.

Moreover, as children grow older, elite parents increasingly supplement their extraordinary direct, personal investments in their children with equally extraordinary investments delivered by others, through enrichment classes and especially schools. These activities might occasionally descend into farce—as in the story of rich Manhattanites who responded to their thirteen-year-old son's liking to cook by hiring professional chefs to tutor him. But once again they are in the main (indeed overwhelmingly) neither casual nor frivolous, but rather reflect a purposive, resolute, and effective program of cognitive and noncognitive training. Even a farce can quickly turn into serious training and yield real returns to a child: the teenage chef won an episode of a televised cooking tournament and opened his own catering business, two achievements that help to build skills and a CV that will eventually appeal to colleges and adult employers.

Schools constitute probably the single most important site of the American elite's exceptional investment in its children. The gap between the annual sum spent on formal schooling for a typical rich child and a typical child from the middle class has exploded in recent decades, rising effectively in lockstep with the expanding gap between top and median incomes.

Economically elite private schools loom increasingly large in the educational landscape of rich families and give extraordinary investment in elite children's formal educations its most obvious and open face. Enrollment in nonsectarian private schools has nearly quadrupled, from 341,300 students in 1965 to 1.4 million today. (Even homeschooling, long anathema to the rich, has begun to develop an elite track, and there now exist businesses that construct bespoke home schools for rich parents: the average annual cost, according to the owner of one, is $50,000 per child.)

While fully a quarter of children whose parents make over $200,000 a year attend private schools, the rate is only about one in twenty for children whose parents make less than $50,000. Moreover, the students who do attend such schools are overwhelmingly rich. Overall, 76 percent come from the top quarter of the income distribution and only 7 percent from the bottom half. The very most prestigious schools in this group have richer student bodies still. According to the president of the National Association of Independent Schools, 70 percent of the students at the top private schools come from the top 4 percent of the income distribution.

These elite private schools spend spectacular sums on teaching their students. Small student/teacher ratios—7:1 compared to 16:1 in public schools—support intense and highly personalized teaching utterly unknown in public schools. A student tour guide at one such school recently explained to a visitor that when a track meet required him to miss a math class, his teacher simply retaught the class during a free hour, exclusively to him. The teachers, moreover, are not just plentiful and attentive, but also themselves elite and extensively educated: fully three-quarters of the teachers at the prep schools that *Forbes* ranks as the twenty best in America hold advanced, which is to say post-BA, degrees.

The large, well-educated faculties also deploy vast physical resources in their teaching practices. Professional-grade laboratories, theaters, arts rooms, gymnasiums and athletic fields, and libraries are common at top private schools. The library at Phillips Exeter Academy (designed by Louis Kahn) is the largest secondary school library in the world, holding 160,000 books on nine levels, with room for 90,000 more.

Louis Kahn libraries do not come cheap, and education provided on this model costs a lot of money. The enormous tuition at Fieldston is not outlandish but rather entirely normal. Average annual tuition exceeds $50,000 at top-ranked boarding schools and $40,000 at top-ranked private day schools. Moreover, elite schools spend substantially more than this per pupil per year. Private schools possess endowments that generate further income to spend, especially on infrastructure. Many of the endowments are massive: the average endowment of the boarding schools in the *Forbes* list exceeds $500 million, or $700,000 per student. Income from these huge endowments, combined with additional annual fund drives, produces a subsidy of between $15,000 and $25,000 per student. All told, then, a student at an elite private high school gets as much as $75,000 invested in every year of her education.

Moreover, expressly private schools represent only one face of the contemporary American elite's exceptional investment in its children's schooling. The national average expenditure per student per year in public schools is just over $12,000, but this average masks a great deal of variation across states and districts. State and local governments contribute 90 percent of total public school funding in the United States, and rising economic segregation therefore allows the elite to concentrate its private resources in the education of its own children, even in nominally public schools.

Unequal investments in public school students begin at the state level. Connecticut, a rich state, spends nearly $18,000 per pupil per year, while Mississippi, a poor one, spends barely $8,000. Inequality in public school expenditures continues within states, as rich cities and towns spend substantially more per student than others do. The cumulative consequences of these effects are enormous, especially at the extremes: in a recent year, the Scarsdale Union Free School District in New York (median household income, $238,000) spent nearly $27,000 per student; the Barbourville Independent School District in Kentucky (median household income, $16,607) spent only about $8,000.

Nominally public schools in elite districts, moreover, increasingly receive substantial additional funding from private sources. Poor and even middle-class parent-teacher associations are social networks and advocacy groups, with budgets that might amount to a few dollars per pupil. But in the richest districts and schools, PTAs, local school foundations, and school booster clubs are financing vehicles, with enough clout to figure prominently in school funding overall. In Hillsborough, California, for example, the Schools Foundation expressly asks all parents to contribute at least $2,300 per child, and a Chicago elementary school recently raised $400,000 in a single night. These sums, moreover, have become commonplace rather than exceptional among wealthy public schools. In New York City, the phenomenon is so common that it has been given a colloquial name: public schools that raise more than $1 million annually are known as "public privates."

The name is apt in many ways. The very richest public schools in the country now educate in the resource-intensive style of private schools, with more and better teachers (the Grattan Elementary School PTA in San Francisco paid all or part of the salaries of six school staff members in one recent year) and extravagant facilities (recall the high-tech weather station in Newton, Massachusetts, and the 3-D printers in Coronado, California).

Finally, these inequalities in public school investments, mirroring broader economic trends, increasingly reflect gaps not between the middle class and the poor but rather between the rich and the middle class. The rich/middle-class gap (between Scarsdale and the median district) is nearly four times the middle-class/poor expenditure gap (between the median district and Barbourville): roughly $15,000 versus roughly $4,000 per pupil per year.

This is no accident. While Barbourville receives 81 percent of its budget from nonlocal sources (which is why its expenditures can approach the budgets of middle-class schools), local funding accounts for much of the expenditure gap at the top. Scarsdale's schools owe 89 percent of their budgets to local taxes, raised on houses whose median value is nearly $1 million and that cost (between mortgage interest and real estate taxes) nearly $100,000 per year to own. Nonlocal funds are simply not sufficient to match the school spending that this tax base sustains. For the middle class, Scarsdale remains a distant and different world, far out of reach and almost out of sight. Its schools, like other schools in the richest parts of the country, are public only in the thinnest, most nominal sense of the word.

All in all, then, a poor child in a poor district in a poor state might receive about $8,000 worth of schooling per year, a middle-class child in a middle-income district and state might receive $12,000, a middle-class child in a rich state might receive $18,000, a rich child in a rich state might receive $27,000, and a very rich child in an elite private school might receive $75,000 worth of schooling per year.

These differences—and especially the massive meritocratic inheritance at the top—are not normal. They depart dramatically from past American practice and also from international standards. A recent survey of thirty-four advanced economies, conducted by the OECD, reveals that the United States is one of only three nations in which public schools that serve rich students spend more per pupil and have lower student/teacher ratios than public schools that serve poor students. The skew in American school expenditures toward rich—and specifically very rich—children is simply astonishing.

The American elite's extraordinary investment in its school-aged children is not limited to formal schooling, moreover. To the contrary, the rich today invest much more heavily than the rest in extracurricular enrichment activities for their school-aged children, and the difference has again grown sharply over recent decades.

Many enrichment expenditures focus directly on the core academic subjects taught at school: science and math camps, coding and robotics clubs, and so on. Rich parents also, unsurprisingly, pay for academic tutoring and test preparation programs. The test preparation business alone, which trains students to take exams that influence college admissions, including most notably the SAT and ACT, has grown from virtually nothing in 1970 to a multibillion-dollar industry today.

Once again, the families that hire tutors skew overwhelmingly toward wealth. The poor and even the middle class cannot afford extensive tutoring, while it is difficult to find a child of elite professionals who has not spent substantial time in the care of a tutor, and usually of multiple specialist tutors. At the very high tail of the income distribution—among the top 1 percent of households—the sums spent on tutors can become staggering.

Veritas Tutors Agency, run by a Princeton graduate based in Manhattan but serving clients nationwide, charges $600 an hour for tuition in basic academic subjects; a typical tutee's family spends between $5,000 and $15,000 on Veritas services, and some families have spent as much as $100,000. Amazingly, Veritas is not even the top of the market. One test preparation tutoring company that caters to students in New York City charges $1,500 for a ninety-minute Skype tutoring session, requiring a minimum of fourteen such sessions in order to enroll. Another charges $1,250 per hour. And a third recruits Ivy League professors to give individual tuition, offering to pay the professors nearly $1,000 an hour and charging the students substantially more. (Some professors, unsurprisingly, have accepted the arrangement.) Other rich families hire full-time private tutors. In addition to earning six-figure salaries, these tutors are often provided with generous benefits, including transportation, meals, accommodation, and sometimes even personal assistants.

Rich parents are eager to sign up their children. Veritas now employs over fifty tutors, and despite their price tags, these services are so popular that some parents have booked them for their children years in advance. As the Veritas founder observes, "If you've invested half a million dollars in your child's private school education," and are "going to spend another quarter of a million dollars on their four years of college . . . whether you send them to some no-name college or you send them to Yale," then "you'd be an idiot not to spend whatever additional money to get them into a better university . . . where they'll be in a great cohort and do very well." This logic explains the explosive growth of tutoring and test preparation. The industry, moreover, still has room to grow—in South Korea, for example, private tuition accounts for 12 percent of total household expenditure, and millionaire after-school tutors have become national celebrities. One study projects that the rapidly growing global market for private tutors will soon surpass $100 billion. Harvard University's annual budget, by comparison, is roughly $5 billion.

Other forms of enrichment—in the arts, or in athletics—complement rather than directly mimic the school curriculum. Children from rich families, and especially families with highly educated mothers, are again significantly more likely than their poorer peers to join these activities in the first place. Moreover, the gap between even these extracurricular investments among elite and ordinary children has again been growing steadily over the past few decades and is now enormous. The amounts by which parents from the top income quintile outspend parents from the bottom quintile roughly tripled between 1972 and 2005, to $7,500 annually.

Families at the very top of the income distribution spend much, much more than this. Ballet lessons alone can cost up to $6,000 per child per year at top-tier schools, and raising a ballerina can cost a family $100,000 through the end of high school. A rich family whose child becomes "serious" about playing an instrument can easily spend $15,000 per year in lessons alone. Instruments themselves can cost much more. One parent reported spending a half million dollars developing her son's piano skills between the ages of six and ten. And the implicit cost of providing the support, stability, and even just the quiet physical space needed in order for a child to practice regularly and well can be greatest of all.

In all these ways, rich parents spend ever-greater sums on training their children, so that no facet of consumption inequality is increasing more rapidly than expenditure on education.* These investments are not frivolous nor even just marginal—instead, they go to the core of rich children's human capital accumulation. Better-equipped schools, staffed by more plentiful, better-educated, more experienced, and better-performing teachers, and backed by more extensive and better-designed enrichment programs, produce higher-achieving students. Enrichment expenditures similarly promote achievement. Veritas provides real education rather than gimmicks or trickery: its founder emphasizes that instead of teaching "gaming the test," he makes his students "better at what the test measures—[the] ability to read and think, process numbers and use [their] head[s] effectively." And richer children—who spend summer months with tutors or in camps that include academic components—continue to learn over the summers, even as poorer children who get no enrichment halt progress or actually retreat in reading and math. (This is especially so in the United States, where children spend less time in school than do children in other rich countries—only about 180 days per

---

* A graphical representation of these trends appears in Figure 5 on page 298.

year in class, compared to as many as 240, for example, in Japan.) Other, more traditionally "extracurricular" enrichment activities—sports, for example, or music and art—also improve life chances long after they are over and therefore involve not just consumption but investment. Children consistently involved in extracurricular activities are 70 percent more likely to go to college than children who are only occasionally involved and 400 percent more likely than children who do no such activities at all.

Sober-minded, systematic, and skilled investments in human capital pay off—education and training work. When groups of high-performing students congregate in extravagantly funded schools, each individual student adds the most value to her human capital. The cumulative differences between elite and ordinary schooling conspire, across contexts and over time, to produce vast differences in students' academic performance, depending on family income, with the greatest inequalities coming at the top.

Educational inequality has therefore increased markedly alongside rising income inequality. The gap between the test scores of high- and low-income students has grown by between 40 and 50 percent over the past twenty-five years, so that by the eighth grade, students from rich families are four grade levels ahead of those from poor ones. The achievement gap between rich and poor students in the United States today exceeds the present-day white/black achievement gap, which is three grade levels, and even exceeds the white/black gap that racially segregated schools produced at midcentury. International comparisons are equally shocking: the rich/poor achievement gap within the United States is now roughly the same as the gap between average academic performance in the United States and in Tunisia (whose GDP per capita is one-twelfth as great).

Another development is no less important, and perhaps even more. From the end of the Second World War through roughly 1970, economic inequality produced education differences primarily between the middle class and the poor. Rich students at midcentury performed little differently in school from middle-class ones. This began to change in the mid-1970s, and the change has gathered steam since. Today, the rich outperform the middle class by more than the middle class outperform the poor—indeed, by significantly more. According to the most careful and systematic study, the achievement gap between rich and middle-class middle school children began rising in the early

1970s, matched the middle-class/poor gap by the mid-1990s, and is now almost 25 percent greater than the gap between the middle class and the poor.*

These differences in academic achievement—including, critically, the
difference between rich and middle-class children—further reveal themselves in the SAT, which, on account of its central role in college admissions,
is almost certainly the single most consequential test an American school student takes. The income/achievement gaps on the SAT are enormous. Students
from families earning over $200,000 per year (roughly the top 5 percent)
score 388 points higher than students from families earning less than $20,000
per year (roughly the bottom 20 percent); and students whose parents hold
graduate degrees (roughly the top 10 percent) score 395 points higher than
students whose parents have not completed high school (roughly the bottom
15 percent). In each case, these gaps in raw scores place the average elite student in roughly the top quarter of all test takers and the average disadvantaged student in the bottom quarter.

The most striking differences once again concern comparisons not directly between the extremes but rather between the middle and each extreme.
As recently as the late 1990s, the gap between the SAT scores of middle-class
and poor test takers still exceeded the gap between the rich and the middle
class. But the elite's meritocratic inheritance has now reversed this pattern.

Today, students whose families fall in the rough middle of the American
income distribution score only about 135 points more than poor students,
even as they score fully 250 points less than rich students. And students
whose parents fall in the rough middle of the American education distribution (with an associate's degree, which is to say some education past high
school but not a BA) score only about 150 points more than students whose
parents are high school dropouts, even as they score fully 250 points less than
students whose parents have completed graduate school. As with caste and
academic achievement in school, so yet again on college admissions tests the
elite are leaving the middle class rapidly behind even as the middle class and
the poor slowly converge.

The meritocratic inheritance makes these patterns inevitable: as top incomes skyrocket, rich parents out-train middle-class parents by more and

---

* A graphical representation of these trends appears in Figure 6 on page 300.

THE MERITOCRATIC INHERITANCE 133

more. The training works so well that although the figures just rehearsed report averages, shockingly few students beat the expectations associated with their family circumstances. In 2010, for example, 87 percent of students who scored over 700 in the critical reading and math sections of the test (the top 5–7 percent of scores) had a parent with a college degree, and 56 percent had a parent with a graduate degree.

All these exceptional investments—in basic cognitive and noncognitive skills, in long-running enrichment activities, in grades and test scores—combine to construct a qualitative difference between elite high school graduates and their counterparts from poor and also middle-class families. And as always, the differences cumulate and concentrate right at the very top of the income distribution, as can be seen by looking at the results achieved by identifiably super-elite schools with familiar names. An elite public school, such as Scarsdale High School, might send 97 percent of its graduates to college. Elite private schools produce more rarefied results still. The top twenty private high schools in the country, as ranked by *Forbes,* on average send 30 percent of their graduates to the Ivy League, Stanford, and MIT alone. These schools send perhaps two-thirds of their graduates to colleges and universities ranked in the top twenty-five in their categories by *U.S. News & World Report.*

The extraordinary investments that children from rich families receive beginning at birth therefore do not end at high school graduation. Instead, the meritocratic inheritance prepares and qualifies rich high school graduates to receive yet more exceptional education and training, in college and beyond. In this way, childhood extends its reach directly and deep into adult life.

## COLLEGE AND UNIVERSITY

Colleges overall are not harder to get into today than they were in 1960. Indeed, the admissions competition among the bottom 90 percent of colleges (by selectivity) has remained steady or even eased over the past half century. But elite colleges have become more competitive. The extent of the increase in admissions competition, moreover, grows in direct proportion to a college's selectivity in the early 1960s, with the very greatest increases coming at the very top schools—the Ivy League, Stanford, MIT, and a few others—where admissions are many times more competitive today than they were two generations ago. The competition that dominates the lives of elite parents and children is narrowly focused on these hyper-elite colleges and universities.

The competition is also dominated by the very top high schools. When the twenty private high schools atop the *Forbes* ranking send 30 percent of their graduates to the Ivy League, Stanford, and MIT, they claim about a tenth of all the available places at these elite colleges. These schools, moreover, are virtually indistinguishable from a small group of others, which offer equally intensive and elite educations, to very similar student bodies, with equivalent results. (Fieldston, for example, did not make the *Forbes* top twenty, at least for the year reported, and Scarsdale High will never make the list, being nominally public.)

Simply tallying the colleges attended by graduates of one hundred or perhaps two hundred well-known and named elite high schools accounts for a third of the student bodies at the most prestigious colleges in the country. These high schools, again, overwhelmingly graduate children of very rich parents—perhaps two-thirds of their graduates come from households in the top 5 percent of the income distribution. Even casual reflection, therefore, at once suggests that the richest children, from the best high schools, dominate the student bodies at elite colleges and universities. College expands the meritocratic inheritance, extending and exacerbating the inequality between the education and training received by children of rich parents and by middle-class children.

Systematic study confirms this intuition. The percentage of Americans who earn a BA of any sort by age twenty-nine has grown dramatically since the end of the Second World War—from 6 percent in 1947, to 24 percent in 1977, to 32 percent in 2011. But almost all of this increase has come from the top half of the income distribution, and the gap between the shares of rich and poor Americans to earn a BA grew by half between 1980 and 2010. Today, each additional increment in parents' income substantially increases the chances that a child will attend college, all the way up the income distribution. The effect of parental income on the odds of graduating rather than just attending college is greater still. Conditional on beginning college, the rich complete BAs at enormously and increasingly greater rates—between two and a half and four times higher—than the rest.

Taken together, these effects entail that as of 2016, 58 percent of Americans raised in households from the top quarter of the income distribution earned BAs by age twenty-four, compared with only about 41 percent from the next quarter, 20 percent from the second, and 11 percent from the bottom. These differences matter not just for being absolutely so big but also for their relative sizes. As with the distribution of educational investment through high school, so also in college graduation rates, the gap between rich and middle-class students substantially exceeds the gap between middle-class students and poor ones. The rich/middle-class gap is also nearly double what it was in 1970.

The rich enjoy a still greater relative advantage over the rest in attending and graduating from selective colleges or universities and an especially great advantage at the most highly competitive and elite schools (although the absolute shares of students to attend are of course lower across all income classes). Even when poor students make it to college, they attend schools whose average quality lies at about the 35th percentile of all colleges, middle-class students attend schools whose average quality falls just below the 50th percentile, and students from households in the richest 1 percent of the income distribution attend schools whose average quality approaches the 80th percentile. As usual, the rich/middle-class gap exceeds—it doubles—the gap between average quality of college attended by middle-class students and poor ones.

The pattern concerning colleges that are not just selective but highly selective is more extreme still. Nothing could ensure high school graduates from rich families a spot at a truly elite college—there are too many rich families and too few elite colleges for that to be possible—but selectivity effectively does ensure that high school graduates from poor and middle-class families will not attend a really elite college. From the high school class of 2004, for example, about 15 percent of high-income students but only 5 percent of middle- and 2 percent of low-income students enrolled in highly selective colleges. These are large differences, and, once again, the gap between the rich and the middle class massively exceeds—it more than triples—the gap between the middle class and the poor.

The rates at which parents in each income bracket send their children to college of course determine the shares of students in college who hail from each income bracket. Small wonder, then, that college student populations skew spectacularly toward wealth. About 37 percent of all college students now come from households in the top quarter of the income distribution, compared to about 25 percent from each of the middle two quarters and 13 percent from the bottom quarter. The skew toward wealth within college student bodies has, once again, increased over time, especially since meritocracy's early, democratic years. In addition, because graduation rates increase with household income, the skew to wealth among college graduates is greater still than among students. The shares of all bachelor's degrees awarded to students from the bottom quarter of the income distribution, for example, was just 10 percent in 2014 (having declined from 12 percent in 1970).

These inequalities, moreover, are greatest at elite colleges, and the skew toward wealth among students at the most elite colleges and universities is simply amazing. At the roughly 150 most competitive and selective—and therefore most elite—colleges, students from households in the top quarter of the income distribution outweigh students from households in the bottom quarter by a factor of fourteen to one according to one study; and at the 91 most competitive colleges, the top outweigh the bottom by twenty-four to one, according to another. These numbers entail that 72 percent of students at elite colleges come from the top quarter and only 3 percent come from the bottom quarter.

The tiny share from the bottom is distressing but perhaps not surprising. The poor have never, to be sure, figured prominently among populations of any society's most elite institutions. But the skew toward wealth appears, shockingly, even within the top part of the income distribution. Across selective colleges, students from households in the top quarter of the income distribution outweigh students from each of the middle two quarters by between eight and four to one. At elite colleges, rich students utterly dominate not just poor students but also students from the broad middle class. Once again, these imbalances have been rising over time, and especially over the course of meritocracy's career—unsurprisingly, given rising educational inequality in early childhood and in high school. According to one study, the overrepresentation of the rich at elite colleges increased by roughly half between the late 1980s and the early 2000s. The abstract numbers reflect facts about concrete walks of life. A 2004 study of the most selective private universities, for example, found more freshmen whose fathers were medical doctors alone than whose fathers were hourly workers, teachers, clergy, farmers, and soldiers combined.

The skew toward wealth becomes sharpest and most disturbing at the very top of the educational hierarchy. The administrations of the very most elite colleges and universities do not publish systematic and comprehensive data concerning the class backgrounds of their student bodies, but students at some of them have begun to collect and report data about themselves. Student reporting at both Harvard and Yale Colleges reveals that for recent classes, the share of students from households in the top quintile of the income distribution exceeds the share from the bottom two quintiles combined by a ratio of about three and a half to one. More distressingly still, across the Ivy League, the University of Chicago, Stanford, MIT, and Duke, more students come from families in the top 1 percent of the income distribution than from the entire bottom half. The scale of this skew toward wealth is simply outlandish. Even Oxford and Cambridge, long-standing symbols of the intersection between social class and elite education, today enroll student bodies with substantially greater economic diversity than Harvard and Yale.

These facts, taken together, paint a stark overall picture. Being born to rich parents is nearly a sufficient condition for getting a BA, and it is nearly a necessary (although not a sufficient) condition for getting a BA from an elite college. College dominates the post-high-school lives of rich students, and children of rich parents dominate the student bodies of elite colleges. Whatever its origins and purposes, meritocracy now makes college a rich person's affair.

College itself exacerbates the concentration of training in the elite— extending education's special focus on the rich into adulthood and further increasing the gap between the investments in human capital that middle-class and rich people receive. Whereas organized investment in the human capital of young Americans from poor and middle-class families mostly ceases at high school graduation, college initiates a new round of investment in almost all rich youth. The special investments associated with the education provided by the most competitive colleges go almost exclusively to rich youth. These investments, moreover, are massive.

The distinctive investments that colleges make in educating students from rich backgrounds have been increasing steadily over recent decades. Higher education makes up 33 percent of all public education expenditure in the United States today, and when private expenditures are added in, colleges and universities account for 45 percent of total educational expenditures in the United States. The sums are staggering, both absolutely and relative to the rest of economic life: in 2014, postsecondary institutions spent $532 billion, or 3.1 percent of GDP (compared to $142 billion, or 2.2 percent of GDP, in 1970); and total investment in education in the United States approximately equals the total investment in nonresidential physical capital. Yale University alone now spends many times more than the entire nation's 1840 investment in education. (Strikingly, compared to other OECD countries, the United States spends a smaller than average share of GDP on elementary and secondary education but nearly twice the average share on postsecondary education.) Moreover, expenditures have grown significantly more rapidly than enrollments since 1970, which entails that real expenditures per student have increased by nearly 60 percent.

Expenditures have increased most rapidly, and enrollments most slowly, at the most elite schools. Median real per-student expenditures in the Ivy League, for example, increased by 80 percent between just 2001 and 2015. Competitive colleges quite generally spend much more on training their relatively richer students than noncompetitive colleges spend on training their relatively less rich students: $92,000 on student-oriented programs per student per year at the most selective colleges compared to only about $12,000 at the least selective ones; and this is five times the expenditure gap in the 1960s.

A part of these rising expenditures is financed from the rising incomes of parents of the students who attend elite colleges. But the larger part in fact comes from subsidies paid from outside the students' families: from rich colleges' enormous endowments, and from public monies (including tax subsidies associated with colleges' charitable status). Overall, the generally rich students at the richest 10 percent of colleges pay just 20 cents for every dollar spent on their educations, whereas the generally poor and middle-class students at the poorest 10 percent of colleges pay 78 cents on the dollar. Finally, both the subsidy and especially the gap between what ordinary and elite students receive have grown dramatically over the past fifty years. In 1967, the average annual subsidy per student was about $2,500 at the least selective colleges and about $7,500 at the most selective colleges; by 2007, the average at the bottom had grown to only about $5,000, while the subsidies for schools in the 99th percentile for selectivity had ballooned to about $75,000. Once again, the skew to wealth among elite student bodies entails that the largest subsidies go to the richest students.

College, simply put, not only increasingly concentrates training in students from rich households but also increasingly subsidizes the training that the rich receive. The size of both these elements of the meritocratic inheritance is staggering.

# GRADUATE AND PROFESSIONAL SCHOOL

According to a common narrative, college graduation marks the end of youth and the commencement (hence the name of the ceremony) of the earnest of adult life. The college graduate, on this account, leaves the nurture of the schoolhouse forever behind. Whatever else she learns or becomes, she must do it in the harsher circumstances of the "real" world.

Life today defies this telling of it, however, especially among the economic elite; and the gap between imagination and reality grows steadily. At least for increasingly educated and massively trained superordinate workers, college graduation lights a path (if not at once, then foreseeably soon) not to "real" life but to further schooling. Indeed, in the minds of typical students at the most elite American universities, college serves as a conduit to postgraduate schooling in almost the same way in which high school was earlier a mere conduit to college. This additional education further focuses investments in human capital onto an increasingly skilled but also increasingly narrow elite, further expanding the gap between the investments made in the human capital of people born to rich parents and people born to everyone else. Graduate and professional school extends the meritocratic inheritance deeper still into adulthood.

Graduate and professional education is a relatively recent phenomenon, and its prominence among elite workers is new. Indeed, elaborate graduate training was, until strikingly recently, not strictly required for getting elite jobs, including in the professions. Professional schools—law schools and medical schools—generally did not become graduate schools (requiring their students to have earned a BA prior to admission) until the early twentieth century. Most important, because they are both so numerous and so well paid, elite bankers, consultants, and corporate executives long practiced their trades without any formal graduate education in business administration. As Nitin Nohria, the dean of Harvard Business School, has observed, the mid-century American managerial elite was bound together not by university degrees but rather family networks and religious ties. In 1900, fewer than one in five business leaders had completed college.

The American professional elite managed without graduate education because it received extensive on-the-job training from its employers. Doctors acquired specialized skills as they treated patients. Lawyers apprenticed to the offices and chambers of senior lawyers and judges. Most important, once again, managers, including elite executives, received systematic and substantial workplace training as they advanced through the elaborate managerial hierarchies that administered midcentury American firms.

At IBM, for example, training for new executives began at the firm's intense Armonk training center and in a sense never ceased. Management employees typically devoted two years of their early careers to a rotating practicum through staff positions at Armonk. And they subsequently received three additional weeks of training at Armonk annually throughout their entire careers with field training added on top. A career IBM man, retiring after forty years' service, might have spent more than four years, or 10 percent, of his work life being trained by his employer. At Kodak, another leading light of midcentury American business, new employees received such quantities of training that the firm effectively never recruited employees over age twenty-five. Nor were these firms outliers. The leading midcentury study of executives observed that new workers sought out workplace training and chose their firms with training in mind, and that midcentury firms answered the call: the basic executive training program at the firms that the study considered lasted fully eighteen months.

Firms today provide nothing remotely similar. When IBM abandoned its training-backed model of lifetime employment in the early 1990s, the shock was so great that local officials asked Hudson Valley gun shop owners to close their stores. And Kodak now expressly aspires to staff no more than one-third of its core management positions with internally trained workers. The transformation belongs to contemporary management lore—a collection of middle-aged insurance executives recently reminisced that while their own training a generation earlier had typically lasted a full year, none of their firms today any longer possesses any training program at all. The lore reflects reality, as measured by data: overall, the average U.S. firm today invests less than 2 percent of its payroll budget on training.

Workplace training provided the fuel for the classic midcentury career arc, which focused on mobility within a single firm—"from the mail room to the corner office," as the saying went. (A survey that *Fortune* magazine commissioned in 1952 reported that two-thirds of senior executives had worked for their current firms for over two decades.)

Today, the fuel is spent. The character of elite work has changed in ways that reduce the value of firm-specific knowledge and increase the value of general skills, and over the same period, the structure of elite labor markets has changed in ways that reduce the commitments between firms and their employees. Workplace hierarchies are organized by occupations rather than by firms or even industries. And employers have abandoned implicit promises, once standard among managers, that competent work would merit lifetime employment and steady promotions. Instead, they offer, in the words of Apple Computer's statement to its employees, "a really neat trip while you're here" during "a good opportunity for both of us that is probably finite."

These changes, critically, all conspire to make university degrees rather than on-the-job training confer occupational access and advancement. Effectively every ambitious young doctor pursues not just the one-year internship traditionally required in order to obtain a general license to practice medicine but also longer and more intensive residencies, some of which (for example, in neurosurgery) last as long as seven years. Indeed, many specialties today require further formal, full-time training beyond the residency. Young lawyers similarly require three years of post-BA university training in law schools before they may practice law, and the nation's law schools have produced on average, roughly forty thousand new JDs each year over the past two decades. And elite workers entering finance, consulting, and management today almost universally spend two post-BA years in university training at business schools, which produce over one hundred thousand new MBAs each year. Whereas a pioneering 1932 study found that 55 percent of top corporate managers had not even attended college, nine in ten have completed college today, and elite managers now overwhelmingly hold MBAs or JDs. These patterns have by now become so thoroughly established—so deeply entrenched—in the career paths of superordinate workers that they are taken for granted, as part of the assumed background of elite life. In fact, however, they represent a profound innovation—they are less than a generation or two old.

This transformation has important consequences for the distribution of training—of investments in human capital—across American society. Post-BA training has long represented a substantial additional investment in the human capital of workers, and in particular of elite workers. The midcentury American employers who provided multiple years of formal training over the course of an elite career spent substantial sums in doing so. University-based graduate and professional schools make, if anything, larger investments in their students: expenditures per student per year at Harvard Business School have exceeded $350,000.

Shifting training for elite jobs out of the workplace and into the university changes the socioeconomic composition of the people who receive the training and the investment in human capital that it imparts. Employer-provided training likely always skewed somewhat toward wealth, as the better entry-level jobs, which provided the most training, went to applicants from more elite colleges and therefore from richer families. But university-based professional training skews dramatically toward wealth, as the disproportion of rich students at elite graduate and professional schools matches and even exceeds the socioeconomic imbalance among elite college students. (The one form of workplace training that survives and indeed thrives today—the unpaid internship—similarly favors young workers from wealthy backgrounds, who are disproportionately able to afford working for free.)

This should not come as any surprise. Most immediately, graduate and professional schools are academically competitive, and the most elite schools are immensely competitive—indeed, more competitive than even the most elite colleges. The median student at Yale Law School, for example, earned effectively straight As in college (for a 3.9 GPA) and scored above the 99th percentile on the LSAT. The median student at Harvard Business School has a 3.7 college GPA and a GMAT score in the 96th percentile. And the median student at Stanford Medical School has a 3.85 GPA and an MCAT score in the 97th percentile. These students, moreover, overwhelmingly received their grades at elite colleges; and the students at the most elite graduate and professional schools overwhelmingly received their BAs at the most elite colleges. Forty percent of the Yale Law School student body attended an Ivy League college and fully 25 percent attended Harvard, Princeton, or Yale. The student bodies of these colleges, of course, themselves skew massively toward wealth. And graduate and professional schools that draw overwhelmingly from them cannot help but replicate the skew.

Moreover, graduate and professional school is once again expensive. Necessary and unavoidable direct costs—tuition and fees—at elite professional schools are quite as high as at elite colleges, and in many cases even higher: Yale Law School's annual tuition is about $60,000, and Harvard Business School charges over $70,000. These prices cover tuition only, moreover, not including room and board. Once those expenses are added in, Yale Law estimates that a single student should expect to pay more than $80,000 over just the nine-month school year, and Harvard Business School estimates the total nine-month cost at more than $105,000. (Students report that full social participation adds $20,000 to the cost of the MBA and may be forgone only at the risk of being excluded from the intellectual and networking benefits of student life.) The indirect opportunity costs of a professional degree, measured by the income forgone during the additional years in school, equal or even exceed the direct costs.

These effects, no doubt combined with unidentified others, again produce an almost inconceivable socioeconomic imbalance in the student bodies of elite graduate and professional schools. Systematic and general data remain scarce: the skew to wealth is too extreme to be picked up by public data sets, which typically combine the broad elite into a single income category and therefore frustrate efforts to draw distinctions within the top few percent of the economic distribution; and universities themselves do not advertise a skew that they properly regard as embarrassing. But unofficial sources sustain increasingly confident judgments about elite professional students' family wealth. Harvard Business School students, discussing the social participation fees mentioned earlier, characterized those costs as "only $20,000," which gives a pretty good sense of their background wealth. And a recent systematic study of family background undertaken by Yale Law students confirms a massive skew toward wealth: more Yale Law students grew up in households in the top 1 percent of the income distribution than in the entire bottom half (roughly 12 percent to roughly 9 percent); the *median* Yale Law student grew up in a family whose household income was roughly $150,000 annually (the top fifth of the overall income distribution); and less than 3 percent of Yale Law students grew up in or near poverty.

It is hard to conceive of a more socioeconomically elite student body. And although precise microdata for other elite graduate and professional schools are not public, there is no reason to think that Harvard Business School and Yale Law School are outliers. To the contrary, a broad survey of law schools reveals that nearly two-thirds of students at top-tier law schools have at least one professional parent (who holds a post-BA degree) and more than a third have two professional parents.

Workplace training once carried the democratic impulses that early meritocrats brought to education into adulthood, allowing workers to advance through a firm's hierarchy regardless of their background. Meritocracy's subsequent history, however, has betrayed these impulses, and today meritocracy displaces workplace training in favor of university-based education. Elite graduate and professional schools now both extend the massive excess investments in rich students' human capital deep into adult life and concentrate these investments on an almost unimaginably exclusive socioeconomic elite—at once increasing and narrowing the meritocratic inheritance. They draw the concentration of training and education in the United States today to a spiky-fine point.

## VALUING THE ELITE'S INHERITANCE

Meritocrats may be made rather than born, but they are not self-made.

Elite and ordinary educations differ in almost every imaginable way: concerning the personnel, settings, styles, purposes, and programs of study through which they proceed. The differences cumulate to shepherd the elaborately educated children of rich parents into a distinctive way of life—one conspicuously consonant with the way of life adopted by adults in the superordinate working class. No simple characterization can fully capture this form of life's distinguishing marks, and no single scale can measure the distance that separates elite education from its ordinary counterpart. The elite education that enfolds rich children is in this respect again no different from the superordinate work that dominates the lives of rich adults.

The connection between elite education and superordinate labor suggests, however, that a summary measure of the gap between the educations received by the rich and the rest can capture the essence of educational inequality—much as the top 1 percent's income share clarifies economic inequality among adults. The association between elite education and top labor incomes, moreover, provides a guide to building the statistic. Labor income represents a return on a worker's human capital, and education—alongside all its other faces—builds and increases a student's human capital.

To construct a summary measure of the exceptional educations received by children of rich parents, therefore, strip away all the cultural context and institutional detail that surrounds elite education and ignore the direct, personal, and in-kind investments that elite parents make in raising and training their children. Instead, treat education simply as an investment in human capital, susceptible of measurement by dollar sums. Then ask how much more is invested in educating a typical rich child than is invested in educating a typical middle-class child—how much more is invested in a typical child from a one-percenter household in Palo Alto than in a typical child from a middle-class household in St. Clair Shores. The detailed story just rehearsed supports rough (but conservative) estimates of the critical dollar sums: $10,000–$15,000 per year in preschool; $20,000–$25,000 per year in elementary school; $50,000–$60,000 per year in middle and high school; and $90,000 per year in college and professional school.

Finally, to resolve these investments, made yearly over the course of an elite childhood, into a single sum, place the present-day elite's investments in human capital into historical perspective. The old leisure class derived its income and status principally from returns to accumulated physical and financial capital. Elite parents, embedded in the old social and economic order, naturally devoted far fewer resources to educating their children (both absolutely and relative to their middle-class counterparts). Instead, the old elite promoted its children's income and status, and ensured the dynastic transmission of wealth and privilege, through gifts of physical and financial capital—of land and factories, stocks and bonds. Typically, these gifts came as testamentary bequests, given by dying parents to children as heirs. The old mode of dynastic transmission of wealth reflected the dominant form of the wealth that it transmitted.

The meritocratic elite, by contrast, is constituted not by leisure and capital income but instead through superordinate labor. Elite parents today, embedded in the new order, naturally provide their children with the social and economic bases for membership in the superordinate working class. Investments in human capital, made while parents are still alive, have replaced bequests of physical and financial capital as the dominant means for conveying elite status down through the generations. This makes it natural to sum up these investments by calculating the size of the traditional bequest that they displace.

To do this, imagine that the difference between the resources devoted to training a child from a typical one-percenter household and the resources devoted to training a typical middle-class child were taken each year and invested in a trust fund, to be given to the rich child as a bequest on the death of his or her parents. Then calculate the size of the bequest. The exact results of this exercise depend on any number of assumptions, and so the outcome should not be accorded inapt precision. Nevertheless, a reasonable estimate (robust in the face of variations in the background assumptions) can be constructed, and the results of the exercise are truly astonishing: the excess investments in human capital made in a typical rich household—over and above the educational investments made not just in poor but also in middle-class households—today are equivalent to a traditional inheritance in the neighborhood of $10 million per child.*

*Ten million dollars per child.*

This sum values an elite child's meritocratic inheritance. It is an inheritance because it runs from parents to children and promotes an elite family's dynastic ambitions. It is meritocratic in two senses. First, the education that the inheritance buys ruthlessly promotes and rewards achievement: elite parents, tutors, and teachers all engage the child with the deliberate aim of

---

* The calculations that yield this estimate appear in tables 1 and 2 on pages 310 and 311, respectively.

building skills and accomplishments; and elite schools promote hard-nosed competition for places and, once students are admitted, for grades. And second, the child's inheritance qualifies it for the ruthlessly competitive and performance-based world of meritocratic work.

The elite's enormous investment in its children's education (enormous both absolutely and relative to the educational expenditures of the middle class) represents a new and distinctively meritocratic technology of dynastic succession, truly a "revolution in family wealth transmission." Rich parents and rich children both gravitate naturally toward human capital as the preferred means for passing income and status down through the generations. This is why total education expenditure today grows more rapidly with rising income than does expenditure on any other major category of consumption, and why inequality in expenditures on education has in recent decades increased more rapidly even than income inequality. Indeed, meritocracy's imaginative hold over today's elite is so powerful that even the super-rich—who own enough physical and financial capital to secure dynastic succession through traditional bequests—nevertheless commonly give their children a meritocratic inheritance, often (as in Mark Zuckerberg's case) as their principal or exclusive bequest.

The economic and social transformation from a society led by a hereditary leisured elite to a society led by the working rich rationalizes these practices. The meritocratic inheritance—the immense excess investments that rich parents make in their children's human capital, over and above what middle-class children receive—dominates dynastic succession in a meritocratic world. Elite education brokers the dynastic transfer. Elite labor income pays out the value of the meritocratic inheritance that education builds.

## THE END OF OPPORTUNITY

Although meritocracy once opened up the elite to outsiders, the meritocratic inheritance now drives a wedge between meritocracy and opportunity.

As the family becomes a site of production rather than consumption, and children become accumulators of human capital, the differences between elite and middle-class upbringing become economic rather than merely cultural or aesthetic and, moreover, project themselves deep into adult life.

These arrangements make meritocracy an engine of dynastic privilege, excluding poor and middle-class children from the bases of future income and status. Despite the motives that led to its adoption, meritocracy no longer promotes equality of social and economic opportunity, as it was intended and expected to do. To the contrary, the social and economic inequalities that now burden America have distinctively meritocratic roots.

Meritocracy's early career fulfilled the hopes that led Brewster and other midcentury reformers to embrace it. The aristocratic elite that meritocracy was designed to unseat lacked both the motive and the capacity to train its children to thrive in a competitive world. But it was inevitable that mature meritocracy should now undermine those hopes (and only meritocracy's enduring charisma makes it surprising). The meritocrats who make up the new elite, having achieved their own status by winning competitions at their own intensive schools and superordinate jobs, possess an unprecedented taste and aptitude for training their children.

Because training and education work, rich children systematically outperform the rest—again not just the poor, but also the middle class—at each stage of their education. At every stage of childhood, extravagant investments in the human capital of rich children produce exceptional performances by these children, which then interact with meritocratic selection criteria at the next stage, in order to deepen and extend excess investments and exceptional achievements going forward, right through childhood and youth and into adulthood. The result of this mechanism is that by the end of the process, the new generation of superordinate workers is overwhelmingly composed of children from the present generation. And at every stage, elite parents secure these advantages for their children principally by deploying, rather than circumventing, meritocracy's standards and methods. Today's dynasties are built on the meritocratic inheritance.

To be sure, academically qualified students from poor and even middle-class families face social and financial obstacles to graduating from college—and especially with elite degrees—that students from rich families do not. As a result, high school graduates from middle-class and poor backgrounds sometimes do not pursue or complete the college educations that their earlier academic achievements qualify them for. But this undermatching, although real, is too small to account for the skew toward wealth among college students—especially at the most elite schools, which contribute the most to the human capital of the next generation of superordinate workers.

The unequal educations leading up to the SAT mean that there are simply not enough really high-achieving high school graduates from outside the economic elite to make much of an impact at the most selective colleges; and there are too many from within the elite for the student bodies at these colleges to skew any way except toward wealth. Even the most capable and ambitious working- and middle-class students—cobbling together an education out of the generous but ad hoc attentions of a few exceptionally devoted teachers, supplemented by their own energy and ingenuity (as when one student from South Los Angeles taught himself "about the world by watching 'Jeopardy'")—cannot reliably compete with the thousands of hours and millions of dollars invested in rich children. Indeed, even as the academic achievement of low-income high school graduates has increased in recent decades, undermatching has declined. Today even perfect matching would not materially increase the share of students at elite colleges who hail from low-income households.

The composition of the rising elite confirms this conclusion and demonstrates that meritocratic inequality draws wealth and achievement together, so that the richest and the highest-performing students are now overwhelmingly one and the same. Elite student bodies skew not just to wealth but also to academic achievement. Indeed, the best universities enroll the vast majority of the most capable students. Roughly eighty thousand students score above 700 on the SAT's Critical Reading test in a typical year. Just the top twenty colleges in the *U.S. News & World Report* rankings enroll fully a quarter of these. And the top five law schools enroll roughly two-thirds of applicants with LSAT scores in the 99th percentile.

The old aristocrats were vulnerable to meritocratic competition because they bred underachievers, but the new meritocrats raise overachievers and therefore dominate meritocratic competition. The principal source of the skew toward wealth among college students, and especially among students at the most competitive colleges, is academic rather than narrowly financial or even cultural. The skew toward wealth does not reflect a breakdown of meritocracy so much as meritocracy's triumph. Towering educational inequality reveals the inner logic of meritocratic inequality in its dark action.

Finally, the meritocratic approach to dynastic succession confers one more advantage on the elite, which distinguishes the meritocratic inheritance from its aristocratic predecessor. Whereas inherited physical and financial wealth famously breeds temptations toward profligacy and therefore its own dissolution—hence the early-twentieth-century saying that a family might go from shirtsleeves to shirtsleeves in three generations—human capital resists being wasted by those who are given it.

The studious self-discipline that a young person must develop in order to participate in building up her human capital inspires an adult inclination not to squander it. Law, moreover, backs up this inclination: an owner cannot extract rents from her human capital without mixing it with her own contemporaneous labor; and the legal regime governing work—which permits wage labor but forbids slavery—prevents owners from selling their human capital apart from and in advance of mixing it with their labor. Indeed, because children do not inherit their parents' debts, human capital is proof against the profligacy of the prior generation also. Finally, because most education is paid for while students are still children, transfers of human capital are effectively exempted from gift and inheritance taxes.

Human capital, in sharp contrast to physical and financial capital, is therefore structured—psychologically, economically, and even legally—to resist being dissipated by its owners. Finally, the structures that have grown up around the superordinate working class—the social practices and institutions of elite education described earlier—support not just the husbanding of human capital by children who have received it from their parents but also the renewed transmission of human capital to their own children in the next generation down the dynastic line.

In all these respects, the meritocratic approach to dynasty building mimics the truly hereditary birthright aristocracy that for centuries dominated elite life. Education assumes the role in meritocracy that breeding played in the aristocratic regime, and superordinate labor takes on the role once played by hereditary landedness. (The midcentury regime, in which formally equal persons were differentiated not by breeding but by contingent inheritances of physical and financial capital, is revealed by this light as an interregnum rather than a stepping-stone on the path of progress.)

The increasing monopoly that elite families exercise over pathways to income and status, and the increasing exclusion of not just poor but also middle-class children from elite training and thus also work, realize rather than retreat from meritocratic values: the dynastic character of privilege does not reflect the corruption so much as the consummation of the meritocratic regime. (Even the rare exceptions to this monopoly, which occur when unusually talented or lucky children without rich parents break into the educated elite, serve principally to legitimate meritocracy, by distinguishing this regime from one based immediately on breeding, and perhaps also by leavening the meritocratic loaf with some energy from the outside.) Indeed, meritocracy appears poised to produce a system of intergenerational privilege more enduring than the midcentury mechanisms involving inheritance of physical and financial capital that meritocracy defeated and then replaced, a dynastic structure that closely resembles an earlier hereditary aristocracy in form and perhaps longevity.

No wonder, therefore, that Kingman Brewster—attacked as a traitor by the midcentury's moneyed leisure class—is today hailed as Yale's greatest president. He is a hero to the new meritocratic elite that his reforms created and now sustain, with no end in sight.

No wonder, but an irony, as the regime that Brewster helped to inaugurate now oppresses the elite that it also powerfully favors.

## AN EXCLUSIVE ORDEAL

Hunter College High School, in Manhattan, is one of the most elite and competitive public schools in the country. Attendance at Hunter College High immensely increases a New York City public school student's chances of academic success in college admissions and economic success in life: 25 percent of the school's graduates are admitted to Ivy League colleges. Hunter High is therefore badly oversubscribed, with ten times more applicants than spaces. The school, moreover, has for decades admitted its students exclusively on account of their performance on a rigorous entrance examination—so through a pure meritocracy.

The exam system, like every meritocracy, favors prepared candidates, and a majority of admitted students now engage test preparation services to help improve their scores on the school's entrance exam. Preparation, for its part, is expensive and therefore favors the wealthy. And indeed, the student body that Hunter High composes in this way has over recent decades skewed increasingly toward children from rich families: only 10 percent of Hunter's students come from households poor enough (household income below roughly $45,000 annually) to receive subsidized school lunches, compared to 75 percent in the New York City public schools generally. In addition, the racial composition of the school changed: between 1995 and 2010, the percentages of black and Hispanic students in the entering seventh-grade class fell by factors of four and six.

As New Yorkers began to realize that meritocracy thwarted equal opportunity, Hunter High found itself at the center of a political whirlwind. Many of the school's students and teachers, as well as its sitting principal, concluded that the health of the school depended on relaxing the entrance competition, to take into account factors besides performance on the examination. The president of Hunter College, who oversees the high school, disagreed. And so just weeks before Hunter High graduate Elena Kagan's confirmation as a justice of the U.S. Supreme Court, the school's principal resigned in controversy, leaving Hunter to search for its fourth new head in five years.

The conflict at Hunter High also had a second dimension that was perhaps thornier, but no less consequential. Even the elite children whom the school's meritocratic practices seem to serve started to complain, as the school's workload, pressure, and stratification became oppressive. The school would begin in the next year to experiment with "homework holidays" in order to relieve student stress. But elite discontent inside the school had stripped the meritocrats of some of their enthusiasm and self-confidence in the conflict over admissions. And the accommodations that Hunter High made on behalf of its students undermined the meritocrats' position in principle. How could the school justify excluding outsiders simply because they do not measure up according to a principle that the school is prepared to relax when insiders need shelter from its harsh effects?

The local squabble over Hunter High played out a dark dynamic that applies to meritocratic education quite generally. "The value to me of my education," a well-known economist once observed, "depends not only on how much I have but also on how much the man ahead of me in the job line has." This remains so, moreover, regardless of how much education (absolutely) the person ahead of me and I both possess. Meritocratic education—at Hunter High and across the country—plays out the consequences of the peculiar logic, to devastating effects.

On the one hand, and in contrast to ordinary goods, when elites buy extravagant education, they directly diminish the educations that everyone else has. When the rich buy expensive chocolate, this does not make the middle class's cheap chocolate taste worse. But when the rich make exceptional investments in schooling, this does reduce the value of ordinary, middle-class training and degrees. The parents who buy test preparation for their children reduce everyone else's chance of getting into Hunter High, and the intensive education that Hunter High provides to its students reduces everyone else's chances of getting into Harvard. Every meritocratic success necessarily breeds a flip side of failure.

On the other hand, educational competition within the elite removes an important brake on consumption that restrains demand for ordinary goods in the face of rising incomes. The rich become sated on chocolate, but they do not become sated on schooling. Instead, they invest more, and more, and more in educating their children, in an effort to outdo one another. The maximum is set only by physical and psychological constraints on the children's capacity to absorb training—in the crassest limit, the fact that schools and the parents who pay for them can hire only one teacher to engage their students at a time and that children, for their part, can study only so many hours in a day. Meritocratic education inexorably engenders a wasteful and destructive educational arms race, which ultimately benefits no one, not even the victors.

Meritocratic education in America is in both respects approaching its outer limits. The most elite schools and universities serve almost only students from families rich enough to pay the cost of limit-case schooling; and they serve them, in human terms, increasingly badly.

The students at Hunter High (as at Phillips Exeter Academy, and as at Harvard and Yale) approach their schooling with a compulsive fixation on the competition that they are in and the prizes that they seek. Not just languid play and decadent amusements, but also deep reflection and an intrinsic love of learning are becoming historical curiosities—memories of life outside the meritocracy trap. The young rich today diligently study and doggedly train, with a constant eye on tests and admissions competitions, intent on acquiring and then demonstrating the human capital needed to sustain them as superordinate workers in adulthood. Their parents, moreover, organize much of adult life around the competition to preserve caste: they read, study, train, worry, and even marry and stay married alongside their children, and on account of ambitions for their children. Helicopter parenting is just superordinate labor applied to the project of reproducing status in a meritocratic regime.

The strain of all this competitive effort builds over time, to produce measurable harms. In wealthy districts of Seoul, where students work harder than anyplace else in the world, the rates of curvature of the spine have more than doubled in the last decade, and doctors have named a new malady—"turtleneck syndrome"—in which a "child's head hunches forward anxiously." At Yale Law School, 70 percent of survey respondents—students whose professional and material prospects have never been better—affirmed that they had "experienced mental health challenges" while at Yale. Their principal complaints—anxiety, depression, panic attacks, and recurrent insomnia—all involve one or another form of nervous exhaustion. If an Ivy League education was once a patina that burnished a carefree hereditary elite, it has become an open scramble to acquire or retain an elite status that must be won and may be lost.

Meritocratic education also produces harms that are less measurable, but no less important. A life subsumed by competition infects students with shallow ambitions and deep and pervasive fears of failure. The infection has grown so severe that an entire genre is now devoted to describing it. Critics variously call elite students "very smart" but "completely confused" with "no idea what to do next," "zombies," or, in perhaps the most memorable phrase in the genre, "excellent sheep." When a group of elite professional school students was recently asked who among them would be willing to spend fifteen hours per week on an intrinsically worthless task in order to gain a career advantage, all said that they would and, moreover, expressed surprise at the question.

Critics of elite education commonly cast its ills as reflecting weaknesses or even vices among the elite. Some critics frame their complaints in overtly moralizing terms, accusing self-serving, precious, and smothering parents of raising gutless, mercenary children. Others emphasize intellectual failings and charge that the rich lack perspective, self-awareness, or an appropriate concern for their own human development—because, as David Foster Wallace prominently charged, they have been taught and complacently believe "that a self is something you just have." These complaints resemble the charges, considered earlier, that attribute top incomes to rent seeking or even fraud. Both attacks succumb to meritocracy's charisma, instinctually assuming that any evil observed in meritocracy's orbit must reflect a corruption or perversion of the meritocratic order.

In fact, however, a deeper and darker logic is again at play. The flaws of elite education do not arise because rich parents and children are unusually venal, or stupid, or otherwise callow. Instead, they follow inexorably from meritocratic inequality's internal dynamics. Where schooling is so competitive and performance in school determines so much, only outliers can afford to ignore education's instrumental functions and focus on its intrinsic worth. Saints (who are indifferent to income and status) and geniuses (who win the meritocratic race even without competing) might pursue meritocratic education for its own sake. But students of only ordinary virtue and ability must keep their eyes trained steadily on the meritocratic prize.

Adulthood sets childhood's agenda, and work remakes family in its image. The mimicry by the school of the workplace that once led radical critics to charge that schooling in capitalist America aimed to train working-class children to accept domination by capital on entering the workforce is alive and well today. Only now, the pattern applies most dramatically within the elite. Elite schooling is carefully calibrated to train students to withstand the distractions of their immediate circumstances and to resist the urge to pursue their own peculiar authentic interests in favor of doggedly shaping themselves to serve ends set externally by the meritocratic system. Far from assuming that a self is something a person simply has, meritocratic education expressly frames elite childhood as a conscious effort to build a self that will warrant success on merit. Elite schooling—exquisitely calibrated to build and measure the self as human capital—trains elite workers in the meritocratic art of instrumentalizing and exploiting themselves.

Once again, the rich—who after all capture the massive rewards of their own exploitation—are in no position to issue moral complaints. But meritocratic education is nevertheless a costly mechanism for the dynastic transmission of privilege down through the generations (and its effectiveness does not defray its costs). Benign neglect for parents and free play for children have been displaced by constant supervision and intense effort. Parents whose home lives once revolved around adult society now orient their domestic affairs intently toward training their children, and children who once lived carelessly in the present now prepare anxiously to secure their futures. The rich family, long devoted to consumption, has itself become a site of investment and production, aimed at building up the human capital of the next generation.

The $10 million meritocratic inheritance measures the financial costs of the new regime. The exhausted, anxious inauthenticity that elite students suffer measures its human costs.

In both respects, the iniquities of the parents are visited upon the children, down through the generations.

# SIX

# GLOOMY AND
# GLOSSY JOBS

An article in the *Harvard Crimson* entitled "The Jobless Class of '72" casually declared that "by choice or by chance, over half of the Class of 1972 found themselves with nowhere to go and nothing to do after graduation." This came as no surprise: in 1959, only one in ten Harvard, Yale, and Princeton graduates sought jobs immediately upon finishing school, and not until 1984 did a majority of these elite graduates turn at once to seeking work.

When they finally did take up work, elite midcentury graduates typically joined firms that effectively guaranteed lifetime employment, where pay "depended more on the number of years with the corporation than individual effort." Even the "CEO [of a midcentury firm] did not have to be especially clever or even particularly bright. He did not need to be ruthless or compulsively driven to succeed." Instead, the culture of elite jobs, William Whyte wrote in his midcentury bestseller *The Organization Man,* remained dominated by collectivism, risk aversion, and a complacent insulation from adversaries. The reason was straightforward—a society and economy led by an aristocratic, leisured elite were not especially competitive: "Rivals did not impinge."

Meritocracy upended this aristocratic workplace culture. Now that industry constitutes honor, and labor dominates top incomes, workplace norms emphasize achievement and ruthless competition. Today's elite workplace fetishizes extreme skill and effort. Super-skills (and hence also the educations and degrees that provide and mark skill) become increasingly essential not just to securing high incomes and high status but also to avoiding low incomes and low status. Frenzied competition now dominates the top jobs. And the broader labor market, once characterized by a continuum of job types with a center of gravity composed by a large mass of mid-skill, middle-class jobs, has lost that center. Middle-class jobs have been displaced by low-skill jobs at the bottom and high-skill jobs at the top. At the same time, the divergence between both the productivity and the pay of the top jobs and of all the others has increased tremendously—hence the struggle to get and stay on top.

The new work order reflects a deep economic and social logic rather than just a passing adjustment in commercial habits and office customs or a mischief born of political miscalculation and elite greed. The top jobs pay so well because a raft of new technologies has fundamentally transformed work to make exceptional skills enormously more productive than they were at mid-century and ordinary skills relatively less productive. These innovations dramatically favor superordinate workers and dramatically disfavor mid-skilled workers. The path of the transformation varies from sector to sector and industry to industry. But the pattern of work and pay at the end of the technological road repeats itself again and again.

Economists conventionally call these developments *labor market polarization* and *skill-biased technological change*. The more lyrically minded have said that the labor market is increasingly divided up into "lousy" jobs that require little training, involve simple work, and pay low wages, and "lovely" jobs that require elaborate educations and provide interesting and complex work at high pay.

This lyricism, however, ignores the most important harms that the transformation of the labor market imposes. It papers over the fact that the lousy jobs are not just boring and low-paid but also—indeed, specifically on account of job polarization—carry low status and afford no realistic prospects for advancement. It also obscures the discontent that meritocracy produces even among the elite—the burdens imposed by the enormous hours and pervasive self-instrumentalization that the allegedly lovely jobs demand.

It is therefore more apt to say that the labor market has divided into gloomy and glossy jobs: gloomy because they offer neither immediate reward nor hope for promotion, and glossy because their outer shine masks inner distress.

Technology's shadow, cast over mid-skilled work, accounts for the darkness that engulfs gloomy jobs today, and technology's brassy light gives glossy jobs their shallow sheen. Finally, as technology advances, increasingly many jobs fall subject to its wage-dampening influence and increasingly few enjoy its expansive effects. As good jobs have over the decades been transformed into gloomy and glossy ones, the lion's share have become gloomy.

# A TECHNOLOGICAL REVOLUTION AT WORK

Cafés, diners, and other informal eateries have long played a prominent role in food production and social life. For most of history, these establishments were independently owned, and they employed owner-managers, short-order cooks, and other mid-skilled, middle-class workers. The fast-food chains that came into being at midcentury standardized production, but they did not fundamentally reject the middle-class model.

Ed Rensi, who ran McDonald's in the 1990s, remembers that in the 1960s, "everything we made was by hand," so that a typical franchise employed seventy to eighty workers to cook the food that it served. Moreover, and almost inconceivably to present-day observers, McDonald's at midcentury offered its workers systematic and even elaborate training—going so far as to open its own school in order better to prepare its employees to advance through the firm's managerial hierarchy. The school, which the firm called "Hamburger University," opened in 1961 in the basement of a franchise in Elk Grove Village, Illinois, and expanded through the 1960s and 1970s to enroll and train increasingly many workers to open their own restaurants. Rensi himself was a product of the midcentury model, joining the fast-food chain as a grill man in 1966 and rising through the ranks to become CEO in 1991. Few workers rose as fast or as high as Rensi did, but his story is far from exceptional. For young midcentury Americans, entry-level work at McDonald's was both a good job and a credible stepping-stone to a chain of promotions and better jobs.

Fast food is made and sold entirely differently today. At McDonald's—and, for that matter, at all similar chains—food arrives at restaurants almost entirely prepackaged and premixed, requiring only heating before being served. Franchises employ far fewer workers today than they used to—at McDonald's, the number has fallen by over half. The elaborate prefabrication entails, moreover, that even though they are fewer, the remaining workers require less skill to prepare the food they sell; and fast-food jobs today involve little more than opening packages and pressing buttons.

The restaurants also pay lower—often minimum—wages, and Rensi now warns that campaigns to raise the minimum wage to $15 an hour will simply cause McDonald's to abandon human workers altogether, in favor of robots. Furthermore, McDonald's today offers virtually no training. Although Hamburger University still exists, it now educates incumbent managers and executives rather than recruiting new franchise operators. Indeed, the school increasingly focuses its teaching overseas, opening campuses in London and Munich in 1982 and subsequently in Sydney (1989), São Paulo (1996), and Shanghai (2010). Even its U.S. campus—relocated to McDonald's corporate headquarters in Oak Brook, Illinois—now teaches in twenty-eight languages and caters more to foreign franchise owners than to U.S. workers.

Taken together, these changes have profoundly transformed work in the fast-food industry. Sophisticated new food-processing techniques and increasingly elaborate cooking machines shift production away from street-level workers, and human labor is increasingly skewed toward a new class of workers who design and manage centralized production and distribution. In Rensi's words, "More and more of the labor was pushed back up the chain."

The development has transformed the profile of McDonald's workforce. The continuum of mid-skilled jobs through which Rensi rose has been displaced by a polarized workforce, composed of subordinate and superordinate workers with virtually nothing in common.

On the one hand, street-level work in fast food has been degraded, to involve menial tasks that require few skills. Many McDonald's workers make the federal minimum wage of $7.25 an hour; the median wage for a McDonald's employee with five to eight years of experience is just $9.15 an hour; and this is, incredibly, slightly higher than the wage at Burger King and Wendy's. Flipping burgers has become the quintessential dead-end job.

On the other hand, elite work at these firms has been elevated, as super-skilled workers at the top now design and implement production processes that dispense with the need for mid-skilled workers at street level. McDonald's current CEO has a university education and postgraduate training as an accountant and has never done full-time nonmanagerial work in the restaurant business. Moreover, elite pay has exploded. In a typical year in the late 1960s, McDonald's CEO might have made $175,000 (about $1.2 million in 2018 dollars), or just under 70 times the income of a full-time minimum-wage worker; in the mid-1990s, the CEO made roughly $2.5 million (about $4 million in 2018 dollars), or more than 250 times the full-time minimum-wage income; and in the present decade, the CEO makes roughly $8 million, or more than 500 times the minimum wage.

The technology now used to cook and serve fast food explains both developments. Technology straightforwardly suppresses wages for subordinate workers—as Rensi's warning that higher wages would provoke further mechanization emphasizes. Technology also, although less obviously, elevates wages for superordinate workers, and new management technologies in particular account for the CEOs' enormous pay.

The recent history of work at McDonald's illustrates a much broader phenomenon. Over the past half century, new technologies have collectively changed how goods and services are produced and, along the way, fundamentally transfigured the nature of work and the market for workers. Innovations, large and small, collectively shape which jobs exist: what tasks production requires and how tasks are arranged into the bundles called jobs, to be performed by a single person. Technological developments also influence the number of openings available for each type of job and therefore what wages workers receive for doing these various tasks.

A pattern emerges out of the cases. The rising technological tide has not lifted all boats equally, nor even lifted all boats at all. Instead, in sector after sector, technological innovation has shifted the center of economic production away from the middle of the skill distribution and toward the distribution's tails.

On the one hand, new technologies substitute for mid-skilled human workers and eliminate the middle-class jobs that dominated the midcentury economy. On the other, new technologies complement both unskilled and especially super-skilled workers and increase the demand for both the least and especially the most skilled workers, creating the many gloomy and few glossy jobs that dominate production today. At the same time, innovation shifts the technological cut that separates elite workers from all others higher and higher up the skill distribution. (The idea that a generic BA guarantees a place among the elite has become almost quaint—a holdover from an earlier age.) This sharply increases the economic returns to super-skills born of intensive training and at the same time depresses the economic returns to mid-skilled, middle-class work. The superordinate working class owes its rise, and the middle class its fall, to technology's divergent influences.

The most familiar new technologies, including the cooking machines that McDonald's deploys, come out of the natural sciences and engineering and involve gadgets, hardware, and software. Many other innovations, less familiar but equally important, involve new institutional arrangements and even cultural developments rather than science or engineering. New administrative methods allow elite managers directly to coordinate and control legions of production workers, but only by rendering traditional middle-class white-collar jobs, from filing clerks through middle managers, obsolete. New legal techniques allow elite financiers to invest and to manage more money more precisely, but only by eliminating mid-skilled finance workers. Cultural and social innovations—including most especially meritocracy itself—also matter enormously. The immense skills and intense work ethic that meritocracy instills allow today's elite to displace middle-class workers from the center of production and itself to pull the economy's laboring oar, as earlier aristocratic elites could not possibly have done.

Taken together, these innovations deemphasize and disadvantage mid-skilled, middle-class workers and emphasize and advantage the superordinate working class. Without these developments, meritocratic inequality would be neither economically practicable nor socially sustainable. McDonald's managers need them all in order to be capable of running the company in the new way.

These changes appear pervasively, across virtually all sectors of the labor market. Further case studies, which investigate entire industries rather than individual firms, demonstrate that McDonald's is not an eccentric example and illuminate the pattern that the example introduces. Moreover, the industries that the case studies take up—finance, management, retail, and manufacturing—familiarly lie at the epicenter of rising economic inequality. Financial and managerial elites epitomize the superordinate working class, retail workers epitomize new subordinate labor, and manufacturing workers epitomize the disappearing middle class. The case studies therefore cover a substantial share of the gloomy and especially of the glossy jobs in the economy overall.

A lesson that repeats itself over and over, across different contexts, usually captures a general truth. The polarization of the labor market applies across the entire economy. Mid-skilled, middle-class workers have generally fallen victim to the technical changes that favor the elite; and innovation generally condemns these workers to newly gloomy jobs and elevates super-skilled workers to newly glossy ones. In these ways, school also remakes work in its image, and the new work order once again plays out meritocracy's inner logic.

# FINANCE

In 1963, *The Economist* magazine asked "Has Banking a Future?" and began its answer—focused on Britain but equally applicable to the United States—by observing that banks were "the world's most respectable declining industry." To an extent hard to credit today, the midcentury elite steered clear of finance: in 1941, only 1.3 percent of Harvard Business School's graduates went to work on Wall Street. The middle class filled the jobs that the elite abjured, so that from the end of the Second World War through the 1970s, finance workers were not appreciably better educated, more productive, or better paid than the rest of the private-sector workforce. Finance had become, at midcentury, boring, banal, and ordinary—a dead end.

*The Economist*'s prognosis could hardly have been more wrong. Shortly after its downbeat prediction, banking and investment firms began to enjoy a largely unbroken half-century-long boom. A host of innovations concerning new financial instruments, new information and computing technologies, new legal and regulatory regimes, and new institutions steeply increased finance's share of economic life. Today, no sector is more closely associated with glossy jobs than finance, and finance workers—with their elite degrees, demanding hours, and enormous incomes—exemplify meritocratic inequality.

The financial sector's share of the very richest Americans has grown roughly tenfold since the 1970s, and the sector now accounts for nearly a quarter of the fifty richest Americans. About a fifth of all billionaires now work in finance, as do two-fifths of the forty thousand Americans with investable assets of more than $30 million.

A still larger group of finance workers gets paid merely very large rather than astronomical incomes. The average bonus for a director at an investment bank might in a typical recent year reach $950,000, the average bonus for a vice president might reach $715,000, and the average bonus for a third-year associate might reach $425,000. In 2005, Goldman Sachs established a bonus pool of roughly $10 billion, or $500,000 per professional employee. Even Goldman's analysts—typically twenty-two-year-olds straight out of college—might make $150,000 in a good year. Small wonder, given these incomes, that finance workers command on average about 70 percent more income than other workers and that overall, the rise of elite finance workers accounts for a substantial share—as much as 15 to 25 percent—of rising wage inequality in the economy overall. (In the meantime, wages for the lowest-paid finance workers, who now do gloomy jobs, have actually fallen recently.)

Finance might deploy a wide range of technologies, used by variously skilled workers, to deliver its services. Over roughly the past half century, the principal financial technologies and the skill profiles of finance-sector workers have both changed dramatically: an industry that was once dominated by technologies that favored mid-skilled, middle-class workers is now dominated by technologies that favor super-skilled, superordinate workers. A large mass of mid-skilled jobs has been eliminated and replaced by relatively fewer jobs, with super-skilled elite professionals, in glossy jobs, dominating the industry and deprofessionalized, low-skilled support staff, in gloomy jobs, playing only subsidiary roles. The labor market for finance workers has become polarized.

Home mortgage lending illustrates the transformation. Mortgages channel capital into the housing market by allowing people to borrow money in order to own and live in dwellings that they will eventually pay for out of future earnings. Mortgage lenders must decide how much to lend to which borrowers. The methods that lenders use to make their loan decisions determine how many and what sorts of workers they employ.

Home mortgage finance at midcentury revolved around banks that both originated mortgages and held and serviced the loans they made. These mortgages were issued through the efforts of a traditional loan officer. This was a mid-skilled, middle-class worker, charged with exercising independent judgment about the economic wherewithal and reliability of particular borrowers and the value of particular houses, to ensure that each distinct loan was providently made. The traditional loan officer based his judgment not just on brute facts (a borrower's taxable income, a home's loan-to-value ratio) but also on a broader situation sense concerning the borrower's character and standing in the community.

Traditional loan officers exercised genuine discretion and carried substantial responsibility. The North Carolina Housing Finance Agency's 1977 *Loan Originator's Guide,* for example, described its "guidelines for credit underwriting" as designed "to indicate appropriate considerations in ascertaining [an] applicant's creditworthiness," adding at once that "these guidelines are not requirements or rules which apply in all cases." Even debt-payment-to-income ratios were discussed in terms of what was "normal" and "appropriate," including after "special consideration." Loan officers could apply such guidelines only by getting to know their borrowers. For example, at Marquette Savings Bank in Erie, Pennsylvania—which maintained the traditional approach through the new millennium and is only now retreating from it—a loan officer, accompanied by one of the bank's trustees, personally visited each loan applicant on the Saturday after a mortgage application was filed, to assess the viability of the individual loan.

Banks paid for prudent judgment and skillful discretion, tracking the accuracy of individual loan decisions. Loan officers' careers were made or broken depending on whether the loans that they approved were in fact repaid. Finally, traditional loan officers possessed educational and social backgrounds commensurate to their solidly middle-class status.

Home mortgage finance operates in a profoundly different fashion today. The difference has transformed work in the sector, in two ways.

On the one hand, banks have sharply reduced the numbers of home mortgage loan officers required to process a given volume of loans, and the loan officers who remain have been distinctly—indeed transformatively—deskilled. Loan officers today do little more than help potential borrowers gather information and fill in forms: they are less professional bankers than collectors of machine-scorable data; they employ virtually no expertise or imagination; and their work emphasizes mechanical rote repetition rather than independent judgment.

Contemporary banks, by "basing [mortgage loan officers'] performance bonuses solely on volume" rather than in any way connected to the accuracy of the loan decisions, typically abandon even the pretense that these street-level workers exercise professional skill and judgment or operate on anything other than the model of an assembly line. Indeed, "high-speed" loan programs, which aimed to reduce application processing time by three-quarters, made any other approach practically impossible. As one senior executive said in an interview with *Forbes*, "A loan officer at a bank or a credit union is typically just the smiling face of the institution—the officer's job is to accept an application that the borrower has filled out, and then hand it off to the underwriting department." Banks recruit loan officers from a commensurately undistinguished applicant pool. Court papers filed in a dispute arising out of the recent financial crisis reveal, for example, that Bank of America employed loan officers "previously considered unqualified even to answer borrower questions."

On the other hand, present-day home mortgage finance also involves a new and elite cadre of super-skilled workers. The banks that originate home mortgages overwhelmingly no longer hold them but instead pass the individual loans on to institutions that securitize them. The mortgage-backed securities that this process creates bundle the rights to receive mortgage payments from masses of borrowers and then divide the bundles into tranches that receive different repayment priorities and present different balances of risk and return. This enables the securities to be rated by credit agencies and then sold to investors.

The securitization process is immensely complicated, and the workers who construct, price, and trade such mortgage-backed securities are not mid- but super-skilled. Street-level mortgage loan officers nowadays have literally no idea what financial instruments are constructed from the loans that they help to close.

The roots of this transformation lie in profound changes in the financial technology that banks use to enable homeowners to mortgage-finance their houses. Developments in contractual and regulatory frameworks made it legal for mortgage-backed securities to be constructed and traded, economic developments that applied asset pricing models made it possible to value such securities, new information technologies made it practicable to trade complex varieties at scale, and new social technologies of elite labor made it both possible and practicable for financial firms to staff the institutions that administer securitization. The management of risk through securitization would be quite impossible without all these innovations.

These technological innovations have transformed the jobs that home mortgage finance sustains. Securitization requires super-skilled workers to design and trade the new securities and therefore greatly enhances job opportunities for superordinate workers who possess the required skills. At the same time, these innovations, once deployed, reduce employment for mid-skilled traditional loan officers. Errors in origination may in effect be corrected through securitization, so that securitization makes it less valuable to ensure that individual loans are providently made. The same technological innovations that upskill superordinate investment bankers therefore also, and indeed directly, downskill street-level mortgage loan officers.

The army of mid-skilled professional loan officers that once made mortgages has been eliminated, to be replaced with a polarized workforce. A rump of gloomy Main Street workers collect data to fill in boilerplate loan applications. And a small elite of glossy Wall Street workers "correct" for the inaccuracies of initial loan decisions by repackaging loans into complex derivatives that quantify, hedge, and reallocate the risks of improvident originations. Although the two types of workers formally belong to the same sector, their jobs bear almost no resemblance to each other, making home mortgage finance a poster child for technology-driven labor market polarization.

Analogous innovation-driven transformations reappear across finance. (Some jobs—for example, insurance claims adjusters—replay the pattern down to the smallest details.) Task intensity analysis using the *Dictionary of Occupational Titles* reveals that whereas midcentury production weighted complex and simple tasks roughly equally (and only modestly more heavily than the rest of the nonfarm private sector), finance today emphatically focuses on complex tasks, to the exclusion of simple ones. In particular, finance requires decidedly more intricate communication, analytic, and decision-making skills than other sectors.

The mid-skilled, middle-class workers who had dominated midcentury finance became increasingly unequal to the rising complexity of financial tasks, and the new financial methods drew super-skilled workers into financial production. Across finance, the share of total hours worked by clerks and administrative employees has fallen from nearly 60 percent in 1970 to barely 30 percent in 2005, while the share of hours worked by managerial and professional staff has risen from roughly 25 percent in 1970 to 45 percent in 2005. The educational gap between finance and other workers has grown by a factor of seven since 1980.

Throughout this process, the most rapid rise in employment share within finance has come from the most elite subgroups in the finance workforce: the labor share provided by specialists in computers and mathematics has grown by a factor of six between 1970 and 2005, and the share provided by securities and asset traders has grown by a factor of nearly thirty. The concentration of training and skill at the very top of the financial workforce is breathtaking. The most elite financial firms, which pay by far the highest incomes, draw their workers overwhelmingly from the most competitive— and most exclusive—universities.

Indeed, banks now advertise their own super-eliteness in their recruiting pitches, making claims such as "We hire only superstars," and "We are only hiring from five different schools," and telling their new employees that they are "the cream of the crop." Elite graduates reciprocate the banks' affections: roughly half of the graduating classes at Harvard, Princeton, and Yale now interview with Wall Street firms or their affiliates, and perhaps a third of graduates actually go to work in finance. At Harvard Business School, where 1.3 percent of the class of 1941 took finance-sector jobs, about 30 percent does now (more than goes to work in any other sector).

The transformation drives the sector's growth and, finally, feeds back into finance workers' incomes. At midcentury, finance effectively mirrored the broader economy—with ordinarily skilled, ordinarily productive workers making ordinary incomes—and grew slowly, by adding new workers to do familiar tasks. Then, beginning in the 1970s, finance's share of GDP grew dramatically, but the new technologies, combined with finance workers' greater skills, sufficiently increased productivity to allow the sector to employ a stable or even falling proportion of the overall workforce. When fewer workers produce more, wages rise. Today, finance workers are both much better educated and much more highly paid than other private-sector workers.* Indeed, they are paid more even than other elite workers. First-year salaries out of Harvard Business School are now higher in finance than in any other sector (by about a third). And the potential for income growth is astronomical—the top hedge fund managers make literally billions of dollars a year.

Finance writ large reprises the path taken by home mortgage finance. Financial production has been transformed from the broadly democratic, mid-skilled enterprise that *The Economist* described to the field that embodies the superordinate working class more vividly than any other.

## MANAGEMENT

Management has followed finance's lead. Whereas midcentury management was strikingly democratic, management has become meritocratic today: both managerial work and its rewards, once widely shared, are now concentrated in an increasingly narrow elite. New technologies have transformed how American firms are run, partitioning the mass of midcentury middle-class organization men into many subordinate production workers doing gloomy jobs and a few superordinate executives doing glossy ones.

Managers came surprisingly late to the American workforce. In the early years of the republic, relationships between workers and firms were too short-lived for management even to take hold of them, and as late as the early 1900s, the turnover of industrial workers in the United States remained about 100 percent per year.

Nineteenth-century steelworkers, for example, worked as contractors or even subcontractors, paid by the ton of steel that they produced, and coal miners and mine owners contracted separately for the mining of each individual rock face. Even manufacturing companies did without much management. The Durant-Dort Carriage Company (probably the leading seller of

---

* A graphical representation of these trends appears in Figure 7 on page 302.

carriages and then automobiles in the late nineteenth century and an ancestor of Buick, Chevrolet, and eventually General Motors) built virtually nothing itself and had few employees. Instead, for most of its early history, the firm mostly marketed goods that it commissioned to be manufactured by others.

For much of the nineteenth century, the American economy made do with virtually no managers at all. Although the mechanical technologies and scale of production had become industrial, the institutional model of work remained artisanal. Individual, self-employed workers engaged large industrial concerns at arm's length, through contracts for specified outputs, rather than selling their labor power as employees. And nineteenth-century executives, for their part, were not true managers but rather owners of enterprise—the equivalent of present-day venture capitalists—who focused on financing rather than administration, labor monitoring, or quality control. Without employees to coordinate and command, there could be neither management nor managers.

The state of technology explains why nineteenth-century firms included virtually no managers. The goods and services that dominated the economy remained relatively simple and therefore easy to describe in contracts and to price. Moreover, managerial coordination's core technologies—office devices such as the telephone, vertical filing cabinet, modern (often high-rise) office block, and of course computer—had not yet been invented.

This changed dramatically between 1850 and 1950, as a set of interlocking technological innovations revolutionized economic life and brought management to the American firm. By the time the revolution was completed, management would saturate the firms, so that effectively every worker would become, in functional terms, partly a manager. The midcentury economy owed much of its democratic character to these developments. Indeed, the management function's wide diffusion throughout the workforce (including into jobs commonly thought to belong not to "management" but to "labor") substantially built the midcentury middle class.

On the one hand, the increasing complexity of manufactured goods and the increased scale of industrial production raised the costs of coordination by contract and created a demand for a managerial alternative. As sewing machines became more complicated, for example, the Singer sewing machine company found itself unable to ensure sufficient quality, reliability, and uniformity in the parts that it bought on the market. The firm began to make them instead; and making parts internally naturally required Singer to establish increasingly elaborate managerial hierarchies to monitor and coordinate internal production and secure the quality, reliability, and uniformity that the firm sought. This pattern recurred across firms throughout the Industrial Revolution, as no less than Frederick Winslow Taylor observed that mass production of complex goods would "involve new and heavy burdens" for management of industrial firms.

On the other hand, innovations in managerial technology considerably increased the supply of managerial coordination, making it possible for management to track and to direct more workers, in greater detail, than ever before. Innovations in firm organization leveraged these technologies. Armies of elaborately layered middle managers coordinated production among long-term employees, who were taught through internal training to adapt their skills specifically to the firm's production processes, and made loyal and willing to accept the vulnerabilities attendant to training tailored specifically to a single employer by lifetime employment and wide-ranging opportunities for internal advancement.

Even the unions that organized and protected lifetime employees—which at their midcentury peak represented fully a third of the U.S. private-sector workforce—in their deep structure constituted a form of managerial coordination (or "industrial self-government," as the U.S. Supreme Court observed in 1960). Union leaders were themselves in function a variety of middle manager. And the unionized production worker was transformed, by lifetime employment and internal training, into the lowest level of manager. In the structural sense, the lifetime production worker—the pinboy-cum-diemaker in St. Clair Shores—was charged with developing, or managing, his own human capital in order to maximize its long-run value for his firm.

These developments ushered in the employee-based, hierarchical, intricately managed American firm, which reached its pinnacle during the middle-class boom at the middle of the twentieth century. Effectively every employee, from production personnel right through to the CEO, belonged to an unbroken managerial continuum, with each job in the firm closely resembling its nearest neighbors. Armies of middle managers, capable of independently coordinating production, shared not just the burdens and responsibilities but also the income gained from running their firms. (Strong unions extended this effect to production workers by organizing the lower rungs of a firm's hierarchy into an alternative control center.) And top managers forswore a share of that income in exchange for the comfortable ease and cultured lifestyle embraced by the leisure class to which they belonged.

The Durant-Dort Carriage Company literally became General Motors, whose enormous size and broadly middle-class workforce could enable its CEO Charles Erwin Wilson (who had himself worked his way up the firm's managerial ladder) to declare in 1953 that "what was good for the country was good for General Motors and vice versa." The Container Corporation of America even expressed this idea in art, commissioning a twenty-year series of original prints by major contemporary artists on the "Great Ideas of Western Man." As Tom Wolfe reflected in an essay on the prints, "the ads in this series convey the message: 'We really don't do what we really do (e.g., make tin cans). What we manufacture is dignity.'" Management had become strikingly democratic, compressing the distribution of income and status within the firm. Perhaps more than any other sector, management on this model built the broad middle class.

At the end of midcentury, the technological wheel took another turn. The late 1970s and especially the 1980s inaugurated a third age of American management, in which firms returned to the nineteenth-century model, but updated it in light of twenty-first-century technologies. Today, technological advances in measurement, surveillance, communication, and data analysis give top managers immense and unprecedented powers of observation and command.

An elite executive, working from the headquarters of even the largest firm, can almost without delay construct a detailed picture of the work done by nearly every unit of the firm, no matter how small, and even of individual workers. Uber's algorithms, for example, allow a small cadre of top managers (although Uber is worth over $50 billion, it has only about sixteen thousand employees) directly to coordinate the work of hundreds of thousands of drivers who have literally never met middle management. Walmart executives can know how many cans of tennis balls a branch in suburban Albuquerque has in stock, and how many it has sold in the prior week. Amazon's management can know how many toy music boxes its Breinigsville, Pennsylvania, fulfillment center has shipped per week for the prior six months. And GE's bosses can call up the productivity of every assembly line.

Moreover, elite executives do not just monitor but can also direct production workers, often reaching into the finest details of their work. Amazon's warehouse administration—in which top-down policies regulate production workers' movements down to the individual step—is just an especially vivid example of a general practice.

These innovations strip the management function from mid-skilled jobs and deprive middle-class workers of the status and income that their managerial responsibilities once sustained. Firms no longer require middle management to mediate between business strategies set by top leadership and the implementation of these strategies among production workers. And production processes that once required all workers to exercise some managerial discretion may now be broken into constituent parts that might be performed mechanically by disempowered workers and coordinated from on high.

As the middle-management function becomes superfluous, firm hierarchies lose their middle rungs. Beginning in the 1980s, an unprecedented wave of corporate restructurings streamlined American firms. It is almost impossible to find any case of corporate downsizing before the mid-1980s, and some large companies even adopted express "no layoff" policies. But now the reorganizations expressly sought to eliminate what the corporate raider Carl Icahn once called "incompetent" and "inbred" middle managers, "layers of bureaucrats reporting to bureaucrats."

The cull was dramatic: AT&T, for example, restructured one of its units with the express aim of reducing the ratio of managers to nonmanagers from 1:5 to 1:30. Across restructurings in the 1980s and 1990s, middle managers were downsized at nearly twice the rate of nonmanagerial workers. And the share of all managers aged forty-five to sixty-four whose job tenure exceeded fifteen years has collapsed (falling by more than a quarter in just the two decades between 1987 and 2006). The process, moreover, continues today. Algorithmic management consulting firms now expressly seek "not [to] automat[e] [line workers'] jobs per se, but [rather to] automat[e] the [middle] manager's job."

All this downsizing is driven by structural considerations rather than by firm-specific economic distress: it hits profitable as well as unprofitable firms, continues during economic booms as well as busts, and peaked during the epochal economic boom in the 1990s. This massive, consciously planned corporate housecleaning of middle managers arose because new managerial technologies rendered the culled workers surplus to requirements—literally redundant.

Over the same period, American companies have also stripped the residual management function from nominally production workers. As unions collapsed—the share of private-sector workers who belong to a union has fallen from about one-third in 1960 to under one-sixteenth today—lifetime and even just full-time jobs were displaced by short-term and part-time ones. The logistics firm United Parcel Service, for example, long famous for using no part-time workers and instead emphasizing internal promotion up an elaborate corporate hierarchy, shifted systematically toward part-time workers in 1993. The firm faced a powerful and popular strike in 1997, fought by the Teamsters Union under the slogan "Part Time America Won't Work." Nevertheless, UPS has since 1993 hired over half a million part-time workers, only thirteen thousand of whom have advanced inside the company. At midcentury, unionized production labor also managed its own development within the firm. Today, short-term and part-time workers, hired under ever more tightly controlled contracts, manage nothing at all. Instead, they sell particular skills or even specified outputs.

Often, the very same employees who have been downsized return as subcontractors, in a direct and literal displacement of management by contract as a coordinating method. After IBM's massive layoffs in the 1990s, for example, as many as one in five laid-off employees returned to work for the firm as consultants.

Other firms were built from scratch on the subcontractor model. Uber drivers are paid not for their effort or even their time but rather for each ride that they complete. The clothing retailer United Colors of Benetton has only fifteen hundred employees but uses subcontractors who employ twenty-five thousand. There exist wineries that contract for grapes with some firms, winemaking with others, bottling with others still, and distribution with yet others, and so have literally no employees at all. And Volkswagen has recently built an automobile plant that is staffed almost exclusively not by its own employees but by workers of its subcontractors.

In the extreme case, new technologies erase the distinction between employees and subcontractors, so that people who are nominally hired to provide their labor in effect sell their output. Amazon's fulfillment technologies now approach this state of affairs. An algorithmically optimized pattern (called "chaotic storage" because it looks random to the human eye) arranges goods in warehouses. And a precisely mapped (to the foot, using tracking equipment and sensors) set of movements tells workers just how to take goods off of shelves and put them into boxes. In this way, Amazon replaces the middle-class workers who would traditionally have been tasked with managing warehouse administration with a highly centralized administrative regime, which breaks the production process into its constituent parts and then in effect buys each part individually. Amazon aspires to use technology to eliminate human warehouse management entirely, and the firm has to this end spent nearly $1 billion to buy the robotics company Kiva Systems. Meanwhile, the Chinese firm JD.com (which has entered a strategic partnership with Google) has already built a warehouse outside Shanghai at which hundreds of robots pack and ship roughly two hundred thousand boxes per day, attended by only four human workers.

The management function has not disappeared, of course. Instead, the managerial control stripped away from production workers and middle managers has been concentrated in a narrow cadre of elite executives, who are separated from production workers by differences of kind rather than degree. The technologies that underwrite such concentrated managerial power— not just the information systems that monitor organizations and gather and manipulate data but also the ideas and analytic frameworks employed to make sense of the data—are enormously complex. Only intensively trained managers can possibly acquire the sophistication needed effectively to implement the technologies of command that can coordinate production without relying on the many layers of middle management that administered the midcentury firm.

The new managerial elite therefore possesses elaborate educations. Executives at midcentury might (like Ed Rensi) have worked their way up a firm's hierarchy instead of attending university. But today's top managers (like McDonald's current CEO) come from elite backgrounds and typically hold MBAs or have equivalent postgraduate training. And when top executives need managerial assistance today, they look not to middle managers but rather to management consultants: external advisers who enable firms to contract out management functions once performed internally. Consultants are again intensively educated and hyper-elite: the leading firm, McKinsey & Company, brags of its "university-like capabilities," and illustrates this by observing that its proprietary research enables the firm "with the push of a button, [to] identify the top 50 cities in the world where diapers will likely be sold over the next ten years."

Finally, the technological advances that concentrate management in a narrow executive elite also inflate that elite's economic value. As top executives monopolize the management function, and firms come to depend on them for internal coordination, they capture virtually all of management's economic returns. Income streams that were at midcentury shared widely across all of a firm's middle-class middle managers become concentrated in elite executives. The status and income that CEOs and other elite managers—including at McDonald's—now command places them right next to financiers in meritocratic inequality's pantheon.

In typical recent years, the single highest-paid American CEO has taken home almost $100 million, and the mean incomes of the two hundred highest-paid CEOs have been roughly $20 million. The three-hundred-times-median work incomes that large-firm CEOs capture today is about fifteen times the CEO-to-worker income ratio from 1965. A slightly broader managerial elite, which includes the rungs just below the top, also captures massive incomes: as when the five highest-paid officers of S&P 1500 firms—seventy-five hundred workers overall—collectively receive income equal to 10 percent of the entire S&P 1500's profits.

The corporate reorganizations that decimated the middle class therefore did not simply improve American business, encouraging management to shape up, becoming lean and fit. Instead, they reconstituted firms, inserting new forms of hierarchy that have made American management, in a memorable phrase, fat and mean.

This third age of American management reverts, in important ways, to the artisanal model of work embraced by the first. Both production workers and managers understand themselves as tied not to a particular employer but rather to a set of tasks and skills. And a renovated guild system—constructed out of the schools and universities that dominate elite education and training today—provides the skills that pair workers with tasks and determine status and pay.

Management, which played a central role in building the midcentury middle class, eviscerates the middle class today. Many workers, often not even employees, do gloomy production jobs at the bottom; while at the top, a few superordinate executives, operating in delayered organizational hierarchies, exercise vast powers of command in jobs that the new technologies have polished to a bright and glossy sheen.

## THE HOLLOW MIDDLE

Finance and management are not the only industries to succumb to these new divisions at work. Other sectors of the economy have also shed mid-skilled jobs and polarized their workforces.

Midcentury retail, for example, was dominated by small, independent stores. In 1967, single-store firms still made 60.2 percent of all sales (and large chains accounted for only 18.6 percent). These stores, in turn, employed mid-skilled workers. As the *New York Times* observed, in 1962, "In the small independent establishment where the store owner doubles as sales clerk as well as buyer, he often will produce a high rate of selling productivity." Alternative models, the *Times* also noted, found it hard to compete: "In the larger establishments, retailers often find themselves in trouble because of a general low quality of personnel."

Today, retail is dominated by massive chains of enormous stores with names familiar to anyone who shops: Dollar General, Family Dollar, Walgreens, CVS, 7-Eleven, Kroger, and of course Walmart and Amazon. The large chains deploy new technologies for selling that eliminate mid-skilled workers and replace them with a gloomy mass and a glossy elite. Street-level, subordinate retail workers now perform narrow and overwhelmingly menial tasks: as shelvers, checkout operators, janitors, or even as greeters (at Walmart), and as effectively mechanized warehouse workers (at Amazon). They are paid commensurately poorly: Walmart (now the nation's largest employer) pays a median wage of just $17,500 according to one estimate, and $19,177 according to another; and the firm unsurprisingly has full-time employees who fall below the poverty line and rely on public assistance, including through holiday food drives hosted, ironically, by Walmart's stores. An Oklahoma store, for example, collected cans of food in a bin labeled "let's succeed/by donating to associates in need." Meanwhile, in 2017 Walmart's CEO made 1,118 times as much as the firm's median worker.

Superordinate retail workers deploy new technologies to centralize the tasks that successful selling requires—ranging from big-data-driven analyses of shopper behavior now provided by firms like Percolata of Silicon Valley, to price optimization programs that give discounts where consumers notice them and hike prices where they do not, to branding techniques that help customers identify goods without in-store assistance. The elite workers who develop and administer these innovations are, unsurprisingly, intensively educated and enormously skilled. Jeff Bezos, who is the founder and CEO of Amazon and the richest person in modern history, graduated summa cum laude and Phi Beta Kappa from Princeton and in the firm's early days recruited employees from among American Rhodes Scholars studying at Oxford.

Mid-skilled clerical jobs—for example, telephone operators, typists and word processors, travel agents, and bookkeepers—have also been disappearing, as elites use computers to do some clerical tasks themselves and farm others out to now-subordinate data entry workers. Law firms have over the past fifteen years shed over one hundred thousand support jobs for workers with less than two years of college even as they have added the same number of jobs for workers with JDs and BAs. And computer-assisted design programs displace mid-skilled draftsmen and empower super-skilled architects and engineers to produce more intricate and inventive designs.

No sector is immune. Even in the arts and entertainment, new technologies allow a few "superstar" entertainers to capture global audiences, displacing many only slightly less skilled performers who previously served local audiences by being the best entertainment within traveling range. In 2017, Beyoncé, LeBron James, and J. K. Rowling each made nearly $100 million. This is perhaps one hundred times more than their midcentury counterparts. It is roughly one thousand times more than backup singers, players in the NBA's development league, and television scriptwriters—all skilled people, near but not at the tops of their professions—make today.

Finally, of course, technology has transformed manufacturing. Conventional wisdom emphasizes that technology has destroyed the traditional mid-skilled manufacturing jobs that helped to build the midcentury middle class, not just in St. Clair Shores but around the country. General Motors, the country's largest employer at midcentury, paid its unionized workers $60,000 per year, plus substantial benefits. Today, the U.S. auto industry deploys over twelve hundred robots per ten thousand employees, and the trend toward robot production is accelerating. (Robots play more prominent roles yet in manufacturing in Europe and Asia.) Overall, the United States has lost nearly eight million manufacturing jobs since the late 1970s. And to employ the same percentage of the American workforce in manufacturing today as worked in the sector in the mid-1960s, the economy would require perhaps twenty-five million more manufacturing jobs than it currently provides.

At the same time, although less familiarly, the new technologies have created a new group of glossy jobs staffed by super-skilled industrial workers who design, program, and manage automated production processes. Even as overall domestic manufacturing employment fell by roughly a third between 1992 and 2012, the number of manufacturing jobs for workers with college degrees increased by 2.4 percent, and the number of manufacturing jobs for workers with graduate degrees increased by 44 percent.

These super-skilled workers are more productive—much more productive—than the mid-skilled workers they replace, and their productivity has allowed manufacturing's share of real gross domestic product to hold steady even as its share of employment declined. They are also better paid: between 2007 and 2012, the average income of manufacturing workers increased by over 15 percent. In extreme cases, the shift from mid-skilled to glossy jobs can rival the effect in finance. Kodak at its peak employed 140,000 mid-skilled light manufacturing workers making cameras and film; and its founder, George Eastman, famously embraced the midcentury middle-class model of work, providing lifetime employment and extensive opportunities for workplace training and promotion. Today, the firm has been effectively displaced by digital alternatives such as Instagram, which employed a grand total of thirteen super-skilled workers when it was sold to Facebook for $1 billion. These thirteen became fabulously wealthy, of course.

All these examples (and many others not recounted here) tell and retell the same basic story, as many variations on a single theme. The democratic regime that governed the midcentury American workplace has yielded to meritocratic inequality today. A raft of technological innovations has eliminated the mass of mid-skilled, middle-class jobs that once dominated production and replaced these jobs with varying combinations of gloomy and glossy ones.

The economic sector most closely associated with middle-class work at midcentury—manufacturing—has suffered a steep decline in absolute and proportional employment, and the sectors most closely associated with both subordinate and superordinate work today—retail on the one hand and finance on the other—have experienced massive expansions. In addition, work has polarized within each sector: mid-skilled loan officers yield to subordinate clerks and superordinate analysts; middle managers yield to subordinate contract workers and superordinate executives; mid-skilled independent retailers yield to massive chains that employ subordinate checkout cashiers and superordinate e-commerce software developers; and mid-skilled tool- and diemakers yield to robots and superordinate engineers.

Aggregate data confirm and quantify the overall hollowing out of the middle of the labor market.* In the three and a half decades beginning in the early 1980s, the share of all jobs principally devoted to mid-skilled tasks has fallen at a steep and accelerating rate: by roughly 5 percent over the 1980s, roughly 7 percent over the 1990s, and nearly 15 percent since 2000. Over the same period, the share of jobs principally devoted to super-skilled tasks has risen steeply, by nearly 10 percent per decade, and the share principally devoted to unskilled tasks has also grown, mostly since 2000.

Altogether, fully a quarter of the economy's mid-skilled jobs have disappeared since 1980, and the share of jobs allocated specifically and exclusively to high-skilled workers has increased by more than a third, while the share of the overall workforce composed of technical and professional workers has more than doubled since 1950 and is today nearly 20 percent. Moreover, state-by-state comparisons suggest that the ascent of the rich and the stagnation of the middle class go together—that rising top incomes (as

---

* A graphical representation of these trends appears in Figure 8 on page 304.

measured by the richest 1 percent's share of total income) produce falling middle-class incomes. In addition, the trends are not peculiar to the United States. Rather, meritocracy undermines democratic equality at work throughout the world's rich societies.

These trends only grow stronger as the years advance. Low- and high-wage employment, once again, both increased during the first decade of the new millennium even as mid-wage employment declined. A similar pattern arose during the Great Recession and the subsequent recovery: with middle-class jobs accounting for three times as large a share of recession losses as recovery gains, while subordinate and superordinate jobs each accounted for greater shares of gains than of losses. In addition, the Bureau of Labor Statistics predicts that over the coming decade, the fastest-shrinking job categories will all be mid-skilled, and the ten fastest-growing will all be either low- or super-skilled. The McKinsey Global Institute—the consulting firm's research arm—forecasts an even more dramatic transformation, predicting that nearly one-third of the U.S. workforce, overwhelmingly in mid-skilled jobs, will be displaced by automation by 2030.

These developments, taken all together, constitute not a ripple but a tidal wave—even a sea change. The labor market has, bluntly put, abandoned the midcentury workforce's democratic center, and this has fundamentally transformed the nature of work.

Whereas work once underwrote midcentury America's apt self-image as an economy and society dominated by the broad middle class, work today underwrites the equally apt sense of a rising division between the rich and the rest. At midcentury, work united Americans around a shared, democratic experience, and the unionized middle-class autoworkers at General Motors embodied the labor market. Today, work divides Americans, in a labor market epitomized by Walmart greeters and Goldman Sachs bankers.

## TRAINING PAYS OFF

The democratic workplace that dominated the midcentury economy suited the habits of the American middle class. The many mid-skilled jobs and the associated opportunities for training that once characterized the workplace connected workers across ranks and skill levels. When pinboys in St. Clair

Shores could walk into lifetime employment—at middle-class wages and with workplace training and opportunities to advance—elaborate, competitive, and elite educations had no compelling purpose.

By contrast, the meritocratic workplace that dominates the economy today suits the habits of the American elite. The hollow middle of today's labor market segregates workers by type, and in particular isolates super-skilled workers from all others. Rich families run the gauntlet of elite education (which has displaced continuous workplace training in favor of discreet degrees, provided in universities) to give their children the exceptional training and skills required to get and to do superordinate jobs, so that they might land on the right side of the meritocratic divide.

Elite training succeeds. The investments that rich families make in their children's human capital pay off. Children from the richest fifth of households are roughly seven times more likely than children from the poorest fifth to end up in the top quintile of the income distribution as adults, roughly nine times more likely to end up in the top quintile of the wealth distribution, and roughly twelve times more likely to end up in the top quintile of the education distribution.

Education has become the labor market's preferred sorting mechanism, and the economic returns to schooling, especially at the best schools, have become astronomical. Education, that is, nearly perfectly maps the fault line that separates subordinate from superordinate workers in the newly polarized labor market, sorting workers into income classes that barely overlap. Intensive educations and glossy jobs run quite generally together; meritocratic inequality makes elite students and superordinate workers one and the same.

The completeness of the segmentation amazes.* The median college graduate will make more money over his lifetime than 93 percent of workers without a high school degree and than 86 percent of workers with a high school degree only; and the median professional school graduate will make more money than nearly 99 percent of high school dropouts, 98 percent of workers with a high school degree only, and 83 percent of workers with a BA only. This means that only about one worker in fifty from the bottom half of the educational distribution makes more than the median worker from the top tenth.

---

* A graphical representation of these trends appears in Figure 9 on page 305.

The absolute numbers at stake are massive. The median male worker with no more than a high school degree makes about $1.5 million over a lifetime, the median male college graduate makes about $2.6 million over a lifetime, and the median male professional degree holder makes more than $4 million over a lifetime. For women, the relevant numbers are $1.1 million, $1.9 million, and just over $3 million. The absolute numbers are also relatively large—compared both to America's own past and to other rich countries in the present. The college income premium is perhaps twice as large today as it was in 1980, and the present discounted value of a BA, net of tuition fees, is nearly three times greater today than it was in 1965. (The purely economic rate of return on university education—one prominent estimate yields a 13 to 14 percent return to a year of college—about doubles the long-run returns provided by the stock market.) The college premium is one and a half times bigger in the United States than in Britain and France and three times bigger than in Sweden.

As with grades and test scores, the top/middle lifetime income gap far exceeds the middle/bottom gap. A closer look at still more refined educational elites amplifies this pattern. BAs from even modestly higher-ranked schools boost incomes by 10 to 40 percent more than BAs from lower-ranked schools and nearly double the rate of return on the tuition. Super-elite BAs generate still greater income boosts, more than doubling the gains produced by an average BA, and the top incomes from super-elite schools more than triple the incomes of the top earners with average BAs. (The highest-paid 10 percent of Harvard graduates average salaries of $250,000 just six years after graduation.) A recent broader survey reports—incredibly—that nearly 50 percent of America's corporate leaders, 60 percent of its financial leaders, and 50 percent of its highest government officials attended only twelve universities.

Graduate and especially professional degrees yield a still greater income premium. In 1963, the postgraduate income premium, compared to a BA, was effectively zero. Today, by contrast, the postgraduate premium is nearly 30 percent, even for a generic postgraduate degree. The premium for an elite graduate or professional degree is much greater still. Professional school graduates at just the 75th percentile by income enjoy lifetime earnings of about $6.5 million, or nearly five times the median high-school-only graduate. And the very most elite professional schools produce yet greater incomes.

The enormous lawyers' incomes reported earlier—millions of dollars for top partners and hundreds of thousands of dollars for top associates—are concentrated in elite firms, which are dominated by graduates of elite schools. Median first-year pay for graduates of top-ten law schools is approaching $200,000; a recent study of Harvard Law School graduates roughly ten years out (which is to say, in their late thirties) reported a median annual income for men of nearly $400,000; and 96 percent of the partners at the most profitable law firm (making over $5 million per year) graduated from a top-ten school. Overall, graduates of top-ten law schools make on average a quarter more than graduates of schools ranked eleven to twenty and a half more than schools ranked twenty-one to one hundred. These outcomes produce massive stratification even within the legal profession. They also drive up the internal rate of return on attending law school to between 15 and 30 percent, depending on how much tuition assistance a law student receives.

In business schools, graduates of top-five programs make an average salary four years out of $215,000, while the highest-paid recent graduates capture incomes in excess of $1 million, and the top programs produce double to triple the gains of the fiftieth-ranked program. The jobs that top graduates get again explain their incomes. At Harvard Business School—where 1.3 percent of the class of 1941 took finance-sector jobs—fully 28 percent of the class of 2016 went to work on Wall Street and 25 percent joined consulting firms. As with law, top MBAs pay off almost at once: the five-year income gain associated with graduating from the top five business schools—increased salary minus tuition, fees, and forgone wages during the student years—now exceeds $75,000.

These numbers also emphasize just how narrowly meritocratic inequality frames the superordinate working class—how few truly glossy jobs there are. The generic college degree—which puts someone into the most educated third of U.S. adults—will keep a worker from falling into the bottom of a polarized labor market, but it will no longer carry her anywhere near the top (nor could it, when income growth is concentrated in the top 5, 1, and one-tenth of 1 percent). As the CEO of CareerBuilder.com says, "The B.A. gets you in the door—there's not much unemployment for people with a college degree—but it doesn't allow you the wage growth you'd expect." The nonelite BA, one might say, is being overtaken by technological advances, much as lower qualifications were earlier overtaken by prior advances, including those that once gave the BA its value.

The thought that a generic BA constitutes a general ticket of admission into the elite is less a symbol of labor market polarization than a holdover from a prepolarized, more democratic view of work—really, a midcentury idea.

## IDLED BUT EXCLUDED FROM LEISURE

In 1883, Paul Lafargue (who was Karl Marx's son-in-law) wrote a tract promoting *The Right to Be Lazy*. In the first decades of the twentieth century, on the heels of early victories in the fight for a forty-hour workweek, some labor unions began to push to reduce work further. Calls for a thirty-hour week became increasingly prominent, and some of the more radical unions sought still shorter hours (the Industrial Workers of the World even went so far as to print T-shirts calling for a "four-day week, four-hour day"). Disinterested observers took these calls to be expressing a serious proposition. No less than John Maynard Keynes, writing around 1930, predicted that technological innovation would effectively eliminate long (or even moderate) human hours and labor effort for the masses, imagining that a three-hour workday might be possible within a century.

Keynes and others hoped that these developments would usher in something approaching a utopia—a new world in which everyone might enjoy a form of life that, in their world, only elites could afford. These hopes were natural in their time. Work remained drudgery, and leisure still constituted honor. The idea that through industrialization, machine power would relieve the working classes of the yoke of their labor naturally captivated hopeful dreamers.

Much of what was predicted has in fact come to pass, although not in the way that was expected, and with results more nearly ruinous than utopian.

Technological innovation has indeed relieved the working and middle classes of much of the old burden of labor. Childhood and retirement take up larger shares of life than they used to, and participation in the labor force has fallen among adults of prime working age. Jobs themselves also require fewer hours than they used to, at least outside of the elite. The sixty-plus-hour weeks that dominated working-class life in 1900 are therefore almost

unheard of today, and even forty-hour weeks are rarer for middle-class workers than they were at midcentury. Moreover, unskilled and even mid-skilled
labor has become almost incomparably less physically strenuous and less dangerous than it once was. At the same time, middle- and working-class Americans are wealthier than ever before. Overall, the bottom two-thirds of the
economic distribution today expends massively less labor effort than its predecessors did, under less arduous work conditions, even as it enjoys material
comforts that they could hardly have imagined. These developments do not
perhaps go quite as far as Keynes and others imagined, but they make consid-
erable strides in the utopian direction.

If utopia remains far out of reach, then, this is because Keynes and others
got their predictions about values—about how the future would measure
honor—almost totally wrong.

The utopians all believed (as Keynes made explicit) that shorter workdays
would yield not just prosperity but also greater and widely shared leisure—
with leisure implicitly understood in the thick sense, associated with the aristocracy, of exploit that confers honor and status. They believed, in other
words, that technology would allow the masses to acquire a share in the form
of life that in their day constituted the elite. Innovation, according to this
view, would relieve the masses of not just the material burdens that working
involved, but also of the attendant social disabilities and status degradations.
The world ushered in by the technological revolution would be not just be-
neficent but inclusive. Even if it fell short of full economic equality, the new
order would undo gross distinctions of caste or class and sustain the dignity
and social participation of all its members. The spread of leisure—again understood not merely as the absence of drudgery but rather as the presence of
dignified recreation—would be both the warrant and the measure of the
coming equality. This is what made the visions utopian.

The utopian vision of universal leisure fell at the first hurdle. Technological innovation has not just changed the brute facts about how people spend
their hours; it has also, and by the same stroke, remade social meanings. As
new technologies revolutionize work to concentrate production in the elite,
they simultaneously fuse labor and leisure, so that industry and exploit become one and the same.

Even as the mass of workers have been released from drudgery, they have also (and by the same mechanism) been excluded from industry. The polarized labor market leaves the middle class with not enough—not nearly enough—to do. Once again, the enforced idleness—including not just unemployment but also involuntary underemployment and withdrawal from the labor market—that meritocratic inequality now imposes on mid-skilled workers roughly equals, in size and scope, the enforced idleness that gender discrimination imposed on women at midcentury.

Because industry now constitutes honor, this idleness no longer sustains status-conferring leisure but rather imposes its opposite—listless indolence and its attendant degradations. And even when middle-class workers do find work, their increasingly gloomy jobs—subject to intrusive, nerve-racking, and degrading surveillance and control—cannot give them the dignity and social standing that superordinate workers get. Amazon warehouse workers have their movements tracked and regulated to the footstep, and the company has patented a wristband that provides haptic feedback to steer workers' hands as they fill boxes and can identify when workers use the bathroom or just scratch themselves or fidget. Uber drivers must accept ride requests, to unknown destinations, within twenty seconds of receiving them.

Idleness under meritocracy produces almost precisely the social effect that toil produced under aristocracy (and the opposite of the effect that leisure once produced): just as toil was the antithesis of dignity in an aristocratic world that worshiped leisure, so idleness has become the antithesis of dignity today in a meritocratic world that worships industry. Gloomy jobs beget gloomy lives, and the bitter despair and resentment that the meritocracy trap imposes on the middle class draw from roots embedded deep in meritocratic inequality's economic and social logics.

This is why declining middle-class labor produces the polar opposite of the flourishing that Keynes and others so eagerly hoped for—why Americans today rightly understand middle-class idleness as a grave social malaise rather than a happy expansion of privilege, as more nearly heralding a coming hell than heaven. Even technological fantasies tend now toward not utopia but rather its opposite.

Meritocratic inequality prosecutes a pervasive, two-pronged attack on the middle class, as new economic facts deprive the middle class of industry and new norms deprive it of honor. Meritocracy's essential logic concentrates advantage and then frames disadvantage in terms of individual defects of skill and effort, as a failure to measure up. This explains the otherwise mysterious anger and contempt that increasingly overwhelm society: the populism that engulfs politics, even during an economic expansion, and the self-inflicted deaths (from addiction, overdose, and suicide) that increase overall mortality, even without plague or war. Both upheavals are concentrated in people with middle-class incomes but without college degrees—precisely the group that meritocratic inequality condemns as redundant.

Gloomy jobs cast a pall over those who must endure them. And meritocracy makes skill into a fetish—an object of desire, invested with almost magical powers, that frustrates those who cannot attain it.

## OVERWHELMED BY INDUSTRY

The work arrangement that once built the American middle class—lifetime employment in respectable mid-skilled work, rising up a smooth hierarchy of small but steady promotions—is simply no longer on the table. Loan officers and stockbrokers, middle managers, independent merchants, and skilled tradesmen are all disappearing. The hollow middle creates a "nonlinear relationship between earnings and hours," and more generally between eliteness and industry, so that "a flexible schedule often comes at a high price." The only real alternative to the exploitative intensity of superordinate work is subordinate work, and elites who rebel against glossy jobs consign themselves to gloomy ones. A "winner take all" society therefore arises, in which the distribution of income and status comes to resemble not a slope but a cliff.

At midcentury, bottom-heavy income growth pushed each rung of the income ladder nearer to the rung above it. By 1970 the consequences of rising from the 50th to the 75th percentile of the income distribution, or from the 75th to the 99th, and especially from the 99th to the 99.9th, had become so small that Americans from the middle class through the elite were all secure, with little to lose from falling down a rung and less to gain from clawing up one.

Since then, meritocratic inequality's top-heavy income growth has pulled the rungs of the income ladder ever farther apart, with the biggest gaps coming at the very top rungs. This makes the competition to climb the ladder most intense at the very top, where rising from the 90th to the 99th percentile, or from the 99th to the 99.9th (or for that matter the 99.9th to the 99.99th) makes the difference between economic stagnation and skyrocketing wealth, between the struggling middle class and the modern-day aristocracy. A meritocrat cannot truly succeed simply by beating ninety-nine out of every hundred competitors; she must beat ninety-nine out of the hundred who have already beaten ninety-nine out of a hundred. The most successful meritocrats therefore become the most insecure. The pressure inside meritocracy's shrinking cage rises inexorably.

In a labor market with this distribution of jobs, work/life balance is not on the menu. To recover leisure a person must altogether abandon superordinate work, and the income and status constituted by such work, and exit the elite. Moreover, the immense cost of elite education means that this choice will cascade down through the generations. A superordinate worker who rejects self-exploitation brings his whole world crashing down—on his children. The abrupt cutoff at the cliff's edge therefore puts intense pressure on those whose first choice would be to live halfway up a hill but who would rather scratch and claw to hang on to a cliff than be pushed off.

The mechanics of meritocratic production put additional upward pressure on elite industry, driving superordinate workers to yield ever more intense effort and ever-longer hours—more than anyone actually wants—in what economists call a *rat-race equilibrium*. Competitive rowers illustrate the effect in action. Victorious single scull rowers typically celebrate extravagantly when they cross the finish line; rowers in victorious eight-person boats, by contrast, slump immediately after the finish in displays of conspicuous exhaustion. The single scull rowers show, in the spirit of Veblen, that they did not exhaust their full capacities to achieve victory but rather won at their leisure, as one might say. But the eight-oared shell—an averaging device—disguises each rower's individual contribution to the boat's speed. Conspicuous exhaustion signals productivity where productivity cannot be measured directly.

Superordinate workers, doing sophisticated, fluid tasks, face the same problem. When individual effort influences group production but employers cannot measure individual productivity directly, they use long hours as a proxy and may even eliminate short-hours jobs entirely to screen out less effortful or productive workers. The rat-race effect is so powerful that when one elite firm, concerned that its employees were working too hard, granted unlimited vacation time, this triggered a reduction in vacation actually taken.

Together, these mechanisms drive up elite work hours. Cross-country comparisons show that work hours, especially for elites, are higher in countries with greater economic inequality. The cross-country effect is substantial: for example, according to one estimate, the difference between inequality in the United States and Sweden accounts for nearly 60 percent of the longer work hours in the United States. A similar effect exists within the United States but across industries: increases in long work hours correlate to increases in within-industry income inequality. Moreover, rat-race effects have been demonstrated empirically, for example, in connection with the hours that elite law firms require associates to bill in order to make partner. One prominent study estimated that nearly half of the associates it considered worked too many hours as a result of these perverse incentives.

The rich as a class do not benefit from any of this, as each person's increase imposes status losses on all others even as it confers status on himself. Competitive industry establishes a prisoner's dilemma, in which the elite earns and consumes collectively too much and must work collectively too hard in order to finance the excess. The stories of obviously self-destructive elite overwork recounted earlier may be multiplied so readily—effectively without end—that they have become a familiar trope among meritocrats. Managing directors, CEOs, and professional firm partners tell of owning extravagant apartments filled with just a mattress and sleeping bag, because they lack time to take delivery of furniture. The empty apartments capture the imagination because they symbolize lives devoid of everything but work.

Indeed, elite workers today are almost expected not to have personal lives. David Solomon, co-head of investment banking at Goldman Sachs, observes that while bankers worked long hours even in the 1980s, it was acceptable to leave the office in the evening and pick up voicemail in the morning. Now "if someone sends you a message and you don't respond in an hour they start to wonder if you've been hit by a car." Virtually no part of the meritocratic elite's personal life is proof against the encroachments of work. A prominent report of the American Bar Association observes that "stories of lawyers closing deals or drafting documents in hospital delivery rooms are disturbingly common," as are stories of missing children's performances and siblings' weddings on account of deadlines, and of shifting family funerals to make meetings.

These and other similar burdens cumulate. An ethnography of Wall Street reports a representative story of a "happy guy in college" who joined Morgan Stanley, gained thirty pounds, and became "a snappy . . . really uncomfortable guy to be around . . . [who] never smiled." And in one study of elite bankers, "eager and energetic" newly hired college graduates became, by their fourth year on the job, "a mess," suffering from "allergies and substance addictions" and even "long-term health conditions such as Crohn's disease, psoriasis, rheumatoid arthritis, and thyroid disorders."

Stress-related workers' compensation claims—especially brought by elite workers—have exploded, tripling in just the first half of the 1980s. The Palo Alto Medical Foundation, which sends a mobile doctor's office around the campuses of many of Silicon Valley's largest employers, has seen an epidemic of stress- and anxiety-related conditions among elite workers and commonly diagnoses vitamin D deficiency—in a climate that provides 260 annual days of sunshine.

Even efforts to combat elite overwork only emphasize the extent of the problem. The financial services firm UBS has resorted to asking junior bankers to take two hours off each week to attend to "personal matters." Goldman Sachs now instructs summer interns not to work through the night and has required analysts to take Saturdays off. And Morgan Stanley has rebranded vacations as four-week paid "sabbaticals" in the hope that vice presidents will take them and has committed to monitoring the scheme so that employees are not perceived as "weak" for taking time off.

These stories describe workers who do little besides working and addressing the essential needs that must be met in order to remain able to work. No amount of income and wealth can compensate for the burdens such hours impose on human flourishing, all things considered. Whereas additional income and consumption yield incrementally less and less well-being, additional hours spent working impose incrementally greater and greater burdens to well-being, as they force workers increasingly to cut essential activities out of their lives.

Superordinate workers increasingly understand this. The reports that those who now work over sixty hours per week wish, on average, that they worked twenty-five hours less document the vanguard of a broad and deep experience of elite overwork. Eighty percent of men and nearly 90 percent of women who work over fifty hours per week report that they would prefer to work fewer hours. Similarly, men with some graduate education or more report that they work 11.6 hours more per week than they would ideally like, and male managerial, professional, and technical workers again report nearly twelve hours of weekly overwork. For elite women, the overwork is still more extreme: women with some graduate education work nearly fifteen hours per week more than they'd like, and managerial, professional, and technical women report thirteen weekly hours of overwork. (Non-elite workers, remarkably, report significantly less overwork: both men and women with less than a high school education report only about five hours of overwork per week.)

In less formal settings, and less polite moments, elites treat the idea that high incomes might compensate them for their hours as frankly absurd. One young professional recently compared his income-and-work package to being paid $3 million to fight Mike Tyson. Others in the overworked elite call their work effort "sick and insane," say that theirs is "not a life," or "no way to have a child." The most graphic complaints are more gripping still. Analysts at banks such as JPMorgan and DLJ compare the demands of their jobs to the Bataan Death March, to slavery, and to the Holocaust. That the comparisons are offensive does not gainsay the experiences that generate them. Superordinate workers today routinely yield the kind of hours that labor reformers condemned as cruel and inhumane when they were worked in the past by the poor.

Finally, meritocrats do not just work too long and too hard; they also work in the wrong style—with the wrong motives and at the wrong tasks.

Work pursued authentically, as a vocation that reflects the worker's true interests and ambitions, can be a site of self-expression and self-actualization. After a point, long hours will make a mess of life no matter how work is constructed: constant hundred-hour workweeks are incompatible with being a spouse, parent, friend, or any kind of enthusiast, regardless of how work is imagined. But the idea of a vocation retains its power to humanize work nevertheless, enabling work to express rather than to alienate the worker's personality. A vocation integrates work with the other parts of a person's life, into a unified whole.

Meritocratic inequality increasingly precludes superordinate workers from pursuing work as a vocation. In this way, meritocracy makes skill into a fetish for elites also—an object of powerful desire that provides only shallow satisfaction even when it is obtained. Elites, trapped in the paradox of human capital, have too much invested in their skills—they hold too great a share of their total wealth as human capital—to be able to afford authenticity at work. When work dominates income, and industry dominates status, a worker who indulges ambitions and tastes other than the market's—who ignores wages and works for other ends—again expels himself (and his children) from the elite. Meritocratic success demands that elites yield not just immense but also alienated labor.

This effect has become so powerful that elites now dress their alienation up in the garb of authentic ambition, making status itself into their goal. This allows elite employers to exploit what one recent investment banking recruit calls elite workers' "desire to find the 'Harvard' of everything," and another calls a "Princeton-like job," by encouraging a culture in which those who forsake high-paying jobs in favor of leisure or freedom or even meaningful work are perceived as settling, as less ambitious, as "less smart." At the same time, jobs that provide meaningful work but little pay—teachers, public servants, even the military and the clergy—have all suffered dramatic declines in social status over the course of meritocracy's career.

But alienated labor remains so no matter how prayerfully embraced. The language of superordinate life in the end admits this: the very idea of work/life balance, so prominent among meritocrats today, presumes that work involves not vocational but alienated labor.

The meritocracy trap ensnares the elite in a twist of fate. The old associations between leisure and status, industry and subordination—the norms behind Veblen's leisure class—established a kind of collective bargain among the elite, a code of conduct that protected against overwork, exploitation, and alienation. By privileging leisure over the consumption of material goods, these norms protected the elite's time and attention. And by casting industrious work devoted to financing material consumption as degraded, they encouraged the elite to devote itself to authentic interests, sustaining the idea of a vocation.

The ideology of leisure constituted a kind of high-caste guild, which protected the elite not just against outsiders but also against itself—by helping the leisure class to avoid or at least dampen a mutually destructive one-way ratchet of ever-greater and endlessly more exploitative industry.

In order for meritocratic inequality to arise, the ideology of leisure had to be broken. The glossy jobs of the new polarized labor market simply cannot fulfill their economic function unless those who do them are trained to immense skill and are psychologically willing and socially encouraged to work very, very hard. The remaking of elite culture to replace leisure with industry as the badge of honor is the master innovation, which enables and sustains all the others.

The characteristic afflictions of the superordinate worker—exhaustion and alienation—follow this innovation as night follows day. Just at the historical moment when virtuous industry might sustain a just reward, work (especially elite work) has become alienated. Just when the prospect of a vocation would be more attractive and valuable to the elite than ever before, a transformation in the nature of work has made the concept itself almost quaint. The inner logics of meritocratic competition and reward—and the social economy of meritocratic status—tend inexorably toward alienated self-exploitation.

Meritocrats therefore suffer as well as gain from rising economic inequality and never recover the full measure of aristocratic advantage, and superordinate workers are not masters of the universe so much as high-class conscripts. Condemned to intensive and alienated labor by their own ascendancy. Collateral victims of their own success.

# Part Three

# A New Aristocracy

# SEVEN

# A COMPREHENSIVE
# DIVIDE

William Jefferson Clinton and George Walker Bush were born within fifty days of each other in the summer of 1946 and would eventually become the forty-second and forty-third presidents of the United States.

Although both men reached the presidency, they came from different segments of midcentury society. Bill Clinton's family was middle class. His father was a traveling salesman who died in an auto accident just before Clinton was born. His mother returned home to study nursing (before remarrying, to a car dealer), and the young Clinton was raised by his grandparents, who ran a small grocery store.

George Bush's family, by contrast, was unquestionably rich, even patrician. He was born while his father (of course himself a future president) was a student at Yale University. And Bush's grandfather, Prescott Bush (who would become a U.S. senator), was at the time a member of the Yale Corporation and a partner at the prestigious and profitable bank Brown Brothers Harriman & Co.

These vast nominal distinctions between the two families made astonishingly little difference to the lived experiences of the two boys' childhoods.

On the one hand, although the Clintons were anything but rich, this did not substantially determine the shape of the young Bill Clinton's life. His childhood home, at 117 South Hervey Street in Hope, Arkansas (which his grandparents had rented beginning in 1938 and then bought in the year Bill was born), belonged to a stable middle-class community near the vibrant center of a small town. The Clintons' modest frame house stood across the street from the larger brick house of Vince Foster, whose father was a prosperous real estate developer, and despite the economic distinction between their families, the two boys naturally became lifelong friends. As a child, Clinton made use of the opportunities that his hometown provided: he received an excellent formal education at a public high school that prepared him well for college; and he joined vibrant civic associations, including the American Legion's Boys Nation, where he served as a student senator and traveled to Washington, meeting President Kennedy and triggering a lifelong interest in government service. Eventually, Clinton attended an elite private college with the aid of scholarships, and further scholarships helped him attend Oxford University and Yale Law School, where he met Hillary Rodham, who came from a richer family, and whom he eventually married.

On the other hand, although the Bushes were unquestionably rich, this again had only a limited impact on the young George Bush's day-to-day experience. The family's fortune was small by today's standards, and they lived accordingly. Bush's childhood home, at 1412 West Ohio Avenue in Midland, Texas, was a modest fourteen hundred square feet and stood, like Clinton's, in a stable middle-class neighborhood. Bush's childhood church was economically integrated. He met his decidedly middle-class wife, Laura, a librarian, at a backyard barbecue. Laura Bush would wear an off-the-rack dress at her wedding (as did Hillary Clinton), and George and Laura would honeymoon relatively humbly, in Cozumel, Mexico.

Clinton and Bush were both born fully members of an American society that was more economically integrated than it had ever been before and that would, due to the economic boom and civil rights revolutions of the postwar years, become more broadly integrated also. Rising wages and powerful unions gave blue-collar workers a central place in midcentury American life. Moreover, the GI Bill drew a generation to college who would not otherwise have attended, opening up a wide path from blue-collar origins to a white-collar future.

The economic elite, for its part, enjoyed only moderate incomes. The income ratios not just of CEOs to production workers but also of doctors to nurses, lawyers to secretaries, and bank presidents to bank tellers were all between one-half and one-twentieth of their present levels. Moreover, these comparatively modest incomes faced comparatively immodest taxes—at top marginal rates above 90 percent throughout the 1950s, compared to perhaps 40 percent today. Finally, the elite was not just modest but also geographically dispersed, as wages across regions converged between 1950 and 1970.

These economic facts produced social habits and norms that established points of connection between the elite and middle class and sustained an economically integrated midcentury American culture.

The midcentury elite enjoyed few avenues along which to distinguish itself through high living. The luxurious extravagances that today's economic elite habitually indulge simply did not exist, at least not at any scale. The most expensive restaurant meals in a major American city in the early 1960s probably cost only about twice what an average restaurant meal cost then, the most expensive wines that might readily be bought cost only the equivalent of $50 in today's money, and the most expensive cars cost less than twice the price of an ordinary car. Houses also followed suit. The average house in one of the "toniest" neighborhoods in the country cost just twice the average price of all new houses built in a typical midcentury year. Even midcentury design, by embracing modernism, simplicity, and mass production, elevated a middle-class aesthetic to the pinnacle of good taste, including among elites.

The elite similarly did not, because it could not, avoid the middle class by retreating into physical, social, or cultural spaces that might set the rich comprehensively apart from the rest. The America of the 1950s was filled with institutions that bridged the anyway small divide between the middle class and the rich. The Boys Nation that brought the middle-class Clinton to meet President Kennedy was not unusual. Any number of massive national civic membership organizations (the American Legion, the Freemasons, the Farm Bureau, the United Methodist Women, and so on) all drew members from across class lines, including into leadership positions. Overall, the elite and middle class largely shared a single, integrated society. At midcentury, all of America resembled St. Clair Shores.

Moreover, Americans at midcentury self-consciously recognized that their economic order had merged the rich into the rest, and they embraced the ideals behind the merger and celebrated their classless society, including in popular culture. *Fortune* magazine, describing the daily lives of America's "top executives" in 1955, trumpeted that a typical member of this elite "lives on an economic scale not too different from that of the man on the next-lower income rung." The magazine, moreover, could back up its claim with details ready from experience. For example, Jack Warner, the "operating boss" of a paper firm that in 1954 produced five billion paper sacks and served one-fifth of the entire U.S. market, "live[d] in an unpretentious brick house on a 120-foot plot in Tuscaloosa, near the University of Alabama campus." And when Bill Stephenson became president of the largest banking chain in the Northwest, he "bought a new Ford, which he still drives; Mrs. Stephenson drives a three-year-old Buick. The Stephensons were obliged to do a little more entertaining, but they stayed right on in their seven-room house, and continued to get along quite satisfactorily with a part-time cleaning woman."

*Fortune* concluded that these cases constituted a trend. "The executive's home today is likely to be unpretentious and relatively small—perhaps seven rooms and two and a half baths"; similarly, "as executives' homes have dwindled in size, so have their parties," and "the large yacht has also foundered." The material modesty through which the elite merged into the middle class had become so well established at midcentury as to set a norm, which subjected violators to criticism bordering on mockery. *Fortune* expressly contrasted the socially integrated midcentury elite with its higher-living and socially detached pre-Depression predecessor. Indeed, the magazine took its hostility to conspicuous luxury personally: "The executive who feels, as apparently Robert R. Young does, that to be completely happy he needs a forty room 'cottage' in Newport and a thirty-one room Oceanside villa in Palm Beach is a rare bird these days," the magazine wrote, before adding that "the fact that Young paid only $38,000 for his Newport place, Fairholme, which cost Philadelphia banker John R. Drexel nearly a quarter of a million dollars to build in 1905, demonstrates the decline in the market for such outsize mansions." Stephenson himself made the point more diplomatically, but with no less force: "'Top executives . . . are not expected to get off the beam,' he says, meaning they are expected not to emerge obtrusively from the background."

Economic fundamentals produced cultural practices that reached deeply and broadly into people's lives, to influence not just how they lived but also how they thought about how they lived, building an imaginative field. As the sociologist William Julius Wilson has observed, there was at midcentury simply "no evidence of class effects on [American social structure] that could rival the effects of race." Throughout the Great Compression, the rich merged more or less seamlessly into the middle class. Insofar as income did insert a seam into American society, it lay between the middle class and the poor.

Outside of poverty, economic inequality at midcentury presented a social blur. Fitzgerald's remark that the very rich are different from ordinary people might have appealed to romantics or nostalgists, but by midcentury, Hemingway's dismissive rejoinder stated the unvarnished truth. As Clinton and Bush illustrate, and their broader social context demonstrates, the only real difference between the rich and the rest at midcentury was that the rich had (modestly) more money.

## INSERTING A SEAM

Matters look very different today.

Economic inequality now threatens to divide America against itself. Inequality threatens, in other words, to break the mechanisms through which American capitalism once sustained social solidarity and instead to transform America into a caste society.

Economic inequality is not the only axis of subordination in America. Racial bigotry—America's original sin—endures, and race remains one of American society's fault lines, which class cannot displace. But class, deployed alongside rather than to replace race, now provides an organizing principle for social and economic stratification that has comparable power (as Wilson himself has acknowledged). The earlier observation that class now has a greater effect on academic achievement than race—an effect so great that it matches the race effect under Jim Crow—highlights just one case in point among many. The comparison should not obscure race, but it does shine a light on class.

The bright line that meritocratic inequality now inserts between the elite and the middle class (displacing the midcentury blur) is no mere metaphor but instead captures concrete and measurable facts. The middle class is literally shrinking: the share of all households that might sensibly be called "middle class" has fallen by nearly a fifth from its peak, and the share of total income captured by middle-class households has fallen by roughly a third. These trends explain why an absolute majority of Americans are no longer middle class and why the surviving American middle class no longer stands out for its wealth. The decline of the middle class reverberates across all of American society: the center of the American economic distribution—whose mass at midcentury pulled the distribution and the society together—is no longer holding.

Middle-class culture is losing its imaginative command over American society writ large. St. Clair Shores no longer represents the American ideal—Palo Alto has taken its place. Inevitably, therefore, the forms of solidarity that waxed at midcentury are now waning. Today, meritocratic inequality determines virtually all aspects of the lives of the citizens who live under it. The rich and the rest now work, live, marry and reproduce, and shop, eat, play, and pray differently and in largely separate social worlds. Inequality produces an internally cohesive and externally insulated elite class, whose lived experience is constructed by its meritocratic eliteness.

Today, the rich and the rest each lead lives that the other could hardly recognize and cannot understand. Economic inequality comprehensively organizes both castes through patterns, practices, and worldviews that rarely intersect, interact only thinly and instrumentally, and grow increasingly distant, uncomprehending, and unsympathetic.

## WORK

A chasm between compulsive overwork and enforced idleness increasingly separates the rich from the rest. Each group, moreover, adjusts its attitudes to render its circumstances tolerable, so that values diverge alongside facts. The rich valorize long hours as heroic (even masculine) and despise idleness. The rest, by contrast, disparage excessive devotion to work as a kind of narcissism. In this way, the economic divisions imposed by meritocratic inequality lead directly to moral conflict.

Differences between elite and middle-class workplaces exacerbate this conflict. The rich and the rest might both work for a living, in the formal sense associated with the distinction between labor and capital. But they toil in different fields, on separate continents, even.

Midcentury employers hired without much screening. The story of the pinboys in St. Clair Shores was typical. In the 1960s, the Ford Motor Company—a high-wage employer at the time—openly declined to screen job applicants at all, at least for blue-collar jobs: in the words of one of Ford's managers, "If we had a vacancy, we would look outside in the plant waiting room to see if there were any warm bodies standing there. If someone was there and they looked physically OK and weren't an obvious alcoholic, they were hired." Even applicants for white-collar jobs received startlingly little scrutiny. For most midcentury workers, getting a job did not involve any application at all, in the competitive sense of the term.

Midcentury firms, moreover, pooled workers of all skill levels. The dispersed managerial technology embraced at midcentury, in which workers from across the skill distribution worked side by side in jobs that blended seamlessly into one another, secured this result. Workplace training provided the relatively modest skills that workers needed to move up a firm's hierarchy. Nor were workers sorted by skill across firms or even industries: recall that even finance workers were not appreciably more skilled, on average, than others. Indeed, the midcentury economy pooled the skilled and unskilled so pervasively at work that they were also pooled at home. In 1970, people with college degrees were "remarkably evenly distributed" across the country: between urban and rural locations, across geographic regions, and even within cities.

Today, by contrast, the workplace is methodically arranged around gradations of skill. Firms screen job candidates intensively at hiring, and they then sort elite and non-elite workers into separate physical spaces.

Only the very lowest-wage employers, seeking unskilled workers, hire casually. Middle-class employers screen using formal cognitive tests and lengthy interviews. And elite employers screen with urgent intensity, recruiting from only a select pool and spending millions of dollars to probe applicants over several rounds of interviews, lasting entire days.

The screening works, especially at the very top of the meritocratic hierarchy. The matching of workers to jobs by skill and training levels has become steadily more precise over time. And the most elite employers (such as the most profitable law firms) hire overwhelmingly, and sometimes almost exclusively, from the most elite colleges and universities.

Screening at hiring enables firms to segregate skilled from unskilled employees inside the workplace. Firms, moreover, have a strong incentive to segregate, as this enables them to embrace production techniques that specifically require skilled workers. The combination of means and motive has produced skill segregation with a vengeance.

The gutting of middle management—and the elimination of the career ladders that once connected workers throughout a firm's internal hierarchy—starkly segregates skilled managers from less skilled production workers within individual firms. Moreover, and more radically, American enterprise increasingly segregates skilled from unskilled workers into entirely separate firms. College-educated workers are increasingly unlikely to work for firms that also employ workers without college degrees.

Indeed, not just firms but entire industries have come to specialize in either low-skilled or high-skilled workers. Retail and finance both pooled workers and emphasized middle skills at midcentury, but today retail exemplifies low-skilled work and finance exemplifies super-skilled work. The idea that a person might begin her career as a Walmart associate and end as a managing director at Goldman Sachs has become laughable. Even the leap from production to management within a single firm—on the model of Ed Rensi's career at McDonald's—has become implausible.

Today, unskilled and skilled workers belong to separate tribes. Even the military no longer brings people from different class backgrounds together. The armed forces long drew citizens from all across society, and the mobilization in World War II and the subsequent GI Bill made military service a principal engine for social mobility. But today the military attracts virtually no one from the educated elite.

The transformation reveals itself most poignantly in memorials to the war dead. Nearly every major American university contains a wall inscribed with a long list of names of graduates who served and died in America's wars, from the Civil War through the two world wars and the Korean War. The lists become much shorter thereafter, however. Elite ideological opposition to the Vietnam War, coupled with the college draft deferment, kept the rich largely out of that war, and the rich almost entirely sat out the more recent wars in Iraq and Afghanistan, even though they largely supported the war efforts. The trend is so powerful that during the 1990–91 Gulf War, more Yale students were murdered in New Haven than were killed in Iraq.

When mid-skilled and super-skilled—middle-class and elite—workers are hired from distinct pools, chosen by different means, and segregated into separate firms and industries, the two classes inevitably come to embrace distinct and even competing cultures of work. Elite reverence and middle-class skepticism toward extreme ambition merely summarize or conclude pervasive differences in the life experience of work for the two groups.

Elite jobs subject superordinate workers to alienating and exploitative demands. But (partly on account of their expansive intensity) these demands are framed in a language of fellowship rather than opposition, of collaboration rather than command. Elite workplaces increasingly embrace informality over decorum: first names have replaced titles, and clothing tends toward informality or at least personal self-expression (uniforms—even of the gray flannel suit variety—are unheard of). Elite employers, moreover, increasingly blur the line between work and life, creating a "private-sector social world" centered on the workplace. Most significantly, elite employers prize responsibility taking and encourage initiative all across the elite workforce—from the most junior employee to the most senior—and employees think of themselves working with rather than for their nominal bosses. Reciprocity rather than contempt structures elite work today.

All these practices follow directly from meritocracy's economic and ideological structure. Where skill creates value and industry constitutes honor, work naturally acquires the gloss that attends exploit. The gloss on elite jobs is shallow, but it is real, and elite workplaces are carefully curated to preserve their sheen.

Non-elite workplaces adopt almost precisely the opposite approach along each of these dimensions. Not just the pay but also the culture of non-elite work increasingly reflects mid-skilled workers' subordinate status. Uniforms are common and serve to thwart self-expression and place workers in a hierarchy rather than to promote safe or efficient production (as craftsmen's technical work clothes once did). A former factory worker describes the jobs now open to him as requiring "throwing on a goofy hat." Workplaces rigidly enforce the distinction between work and life as employers tightfistedly limit break and personal time during the workday, and employers exercise increasing and in some cases—think of Amazon's warehouse practices—near-total command and control over employees' labor.

The stripping of managerial functions from production workers further enforces their separation from the superordinate workers who now exclusively wield managerial prerogatives. Indeed, employers increasingly micromanage mid-skilled workers so completely that they in effect buy the workers' outputs rather than their skill and effort. Accordingly, even as elite workplaces prize independence and initiative, non-elite workplaces reduce workers almost literally to tools deployed by management.

In all these ways, the culture of non-elite work denies the merit of the workers who do it and reinforces the gloom that low pay also expresses.

These distinctions collectively constitute a difference in kind between superordinate and subordinate workers. The difference becomes most pronounced at the extremes, which, although unusual, also display most clearly what is at stake in the run of common cases.

On the one hand, at the elite's very finest point in the extreme jobs described earlier, work completely subsumes life. The extreme worker looks single-mindedly to her productivity and the honor that she derives from it, and she throws all of her self into her work. The gloss of the extreme job is immensely bright but commensurately superficial, and the extreme worker's flourishing is limited to the shallow and instrumental virtues that meritocracy describes.

On the other hand, meritocracy flat-out banishes a large and growing class of subordinated persons from the status that work brings. Most conspicuously, the nearly 20 million people who have been imprisoned or carry a felony conviction—up from just 2.5 million in 1960—are excluded from all but the most marginal forms of employment and condemned to live under the gloomy shadow of the association between work and honor. This group is constructed through any number of racial biases, including in policing, criminal procedure, and the substantive criminal law, and it includes nonwhites and especially African Americans in such disproportion that mass incarceration and its consequences have been called the New Jim Crow.

The meritocratic idea that industry confers honor sheds a revealing new light on the workings of this caste order beyond the prison. Where prior convictions preclude subsequent employment, meritocratic inequality performs an astonishing inversion of the American race order. When leisure constituted status, racial subordination was imposed, under slavery, through legally compelled labor. Now that industry constitutes status, racial subordination is imposed through legally enforced idleness.

## FAMILY

Aristocrats once thought of themselves as above conventional morality and mocked the bourgeois propriety of middle-class sexual habits. Moreover, when the aristocratic elite did marry, parents gave little beyond wealth and pedigree to their children, who were typically raised by retainers or staff, and held at arm's length. Finally, even after the aristocracy began to fade, an ornamental wife, as Veblen observed, remained one of the last effective status symbols of the old leisure class—by demonstrating that a husband possessed sufficient wealth to sustain the household without her labor.

Today, the reverse is more nearly true. Meritocratic elites, both men and women, lead conservative personal lives and maintain distinctively stable marriages. They devote intense personal attention to raising children within these marriages. And a highly educated, successful wife elevates the social status of a male superordinate worker, while an un- or even undereducated wife produces status anxiety.

Meritocratic inequality explains these changes. Meritocracy remakes elite families as sites for the production of human capital, in the next generation of elite workers. These forces have transformed elite families, which today differ fundamentally from middle-class families in their composition, legal structure, and domestic habits.

Meritocrats' distinctive tendencies to marry each other, to stay married, and to raise children within their marriages all serve the imperatives of dynastic succession. Educated parents, and especially educated mothers, are better able to train their children. Divorce is costly, both directly and because it distracts from superordinate work and complicates the task of raising high-achieving children, and it is therefore rarer among the rich than the rest. And children born out of wedlock compound these complications and are therefore almost unheard of.

The elite's domestic ideals, moreover, have adjusted to give emotional and even moral expressions to these meritocratic imperatives. Elite children carry the burden of dynastic succession, as their accomplishments become the vehicles for the parents' meritocratic ambitions. Meritocratic competition even makes sibling rivalries discernibly more intense in elite than in middle-class households.

Among parents, meritocracy dominates attitudes toward marriage itself. While professional and working-class couples were roughly equally likely to report being "very happy" in their marriages in 1970, today the share of "very happy" working-class marriages has fallen by a third even as the share of "very happy" professional marriages, after recovering from a dip in the 1980s, remains where it was. Similarly, the share of women with college degrees who agreed that "divorce is usually the best solution when a couple can't seem to work out their marriage problems" fell by a quarter between 2002 and 2012. Meritocratic elites even tie sex distinctively to marriage: rich women do not just bear but also conceive children within marriages, and the abortion rate among rich women fell by nearly 30 percent over the past two decades, even as it grew by nearly 20 percent among poor women.

Marriage, that is, retains a distinctive ideological power for meritocrats. Elites may reject traditional morality and affirm sexual freedom as matters of abstract political principle. But they live distinctively chastely, as nonpracticing libertines.

Moreover, elite families engage their communities in increasingly distinctive ways. Extracurricular activities, for example, were conceived, in the late nineteenth century, "precisely . . . to teach soft life skills to working-class Americans." But although they served this function through the mid-twentieth century, they are again increasingly dominated by elites. Between the 1954 and 1986 birth cohorts, the gaps between the shares of twelfth graders from the highest and lowest socioeconomic status quartiles to participate in nonsports extracurricular activities, to participate in sports, and to captain sports teams grew by 240, 40, and 130 percent respectively.

Similarly, the differences between the number of days rich and poor children spend attending religious services and volunteering in community affairs both roughly tripled. And the differences in the shares of each group to report that "most people can be trusted" also tripled, while a generalized measure of social connectedness (constructed from answers to survey questions about loneliness, friendship, and interpersonal support) grew immensely for the top quartile and effectively not at all for the bottom.

Elite families—both parents and children—are increasingly more academically, vocationally, and emotionally invested and engaged in the meritocratic social order than non-elite families.

Even the gender dynamics of elite families are distinctive, although in surprisingly complex and even counterintuitive ways. Elites are socially more liberal than other Americans and therefore more likely to reject traditional gender norms that insist a woman's place is in the home, as wife and mother, and even to scorn the sexism of middle America. But the economic structure of elite households is distinctly at odds with their ideals (much as elite sexual practices disregard the elite's abstract sexual morality).

On the one hand, the most elite, highest-paying jobs in the economy belong among the most male-dominated. Only about 14 percent of the top executives (and just about 8 percent of the highest earners) in Fortune 500 companies are women, and more than a quarter of these companies have no women in top management; Wall Street remains overwhelmingly male-dominated; women make up only 18 percent of equity partners at American law firms; and the gender pay gap among doctors has widened in recent years.

The intense personal involvement that elite education now demands, when overlaid on gender norms that distinctively bind mothers to parenting, rationalizes these patterns. The hours that superordinate work requires are incompatible with bearing (let alone raising) children. Elite women therefore no longer stay home to signal their leisure, as Veblen imagined, but rather to labor intensively at training their children. Employers such as Facebook and Apple will pay tens of thousands of dollars to defray the cost of egg freezing in an effort to encourage superordinate women to delay childbirth and remain in the workforce. But the meritocratic imperatives of dynastic succession overpower these efforts.

On the other hand, middle-class men traditionally dominated the jobs—quintessentially in manufacturing—that have been lost or seen wage stagnation in recent decades, even as many of the service jobs that have displaced them are conventionally done by middle-class women. (In fact, progress in diminishing the gender pay gap overall principally comes courtesy of declining wages for men without a college degree.)

Moreover, poorer men are less successful than poorer women at acquiring the schooling needed to secure better jobs in a meritocratic labor market: men make up only 42 percent of college students from households with annual incomes below $30,000. Veblen's logic still applies to the middle class, although with a darkly ironic twist: in middle-class families, working women represent the no-longer adequacy of the male wage.

Together, these patterns entail that the wage gap between men and women has been growing among the elite even as it has been falling among the middle class and the poor. Indeed, among dual-earner households with incomes in the top quintile, just 29 percent of wives earn more than their husbands, whereas among dual-earner households in the bottom quintile, fully 69 percent of wives out-earn their husbands. This pattern actually helps account for declining marriage rates outside of the elite, as marriages are less likely to form when women out-earn men, an effect that accounts for 23 percent of the overall drop in marriage, and whose consequences are highly concentrated in the bottom of the economic distribution. In all these ways, meritocratic inequality penetrates even gender relations and the balance of economic power within the family.

The divisions are so deep and pervasive that they reach not just domestic habits but also the ideals of domesticity under whose flags habits are performed. Indeed, meritocratic inequality induces the rich and the rest to imagine the present challenges and future hopes for marriage and domestic life in terms that make no contact.

For the elite, the central marital question of the age concerns same-sex marriage. The rapid acceptance of same-sex marriage constitutes a triumph that foretells a bright future (although tempered, perhaps, by surprise at non-elite Americans' willingness to accept marriage equality even while retaining traditionalist views on other matters of sexual morality, including most notably abortion).

Non-elite Americans, by contrast, focus on—they cannot escape—the collapse of opposite-sex marriage. For them, the institutional foundations of family life are crumbling. And the question of whether or not a collapsing institution should be expanded to accommodate same-sex couples feels distant and almost academic.

## CULTURE

Sigmund Freud, on being asked how a person might flourish, once answered "love and work . . . work and love, that's all there is . . . love and work are the cornerstones of our humanness." When meritocracy organizes work and family, it reaches back into the wellsprings of life and channels the rich and the rest into divergent streams. But notwithstanding Freud's observation, people devote themselves to more than just love and work. They also worship, pursue politics, socialize, eat, shop, and amuse themselves. Collectively, these and other behaviors combine with work and family to construct a culture. And just as with family and with work, meritocratic inequality increasingly causes the rich and the rest to embrace vastly different cultures.

Religions in the United States today are remarkably segregated by education and income. Anglicans/Episcopalians, Jews, and Hindus are roughly twice as likely as the national average to hold a college degree and to have household incomes greater than $100,000 and roughly a quarter as likely to drop out of high school and half as likely to have household incomes less than $30,000. (Presbyterians are only slightly less educated and rich.) By contrast, Jehovah's Witnesses, National Baptists, and congregants of the Church of God in Christ are less than half as likely as the national average to hold a college degree or have household incomes greater than $100,000 and are roughly one and a half times as likely to have dropped out of high school or have household incomes less than $30,000. (Interestingly, Catholics closely resemble the national average in both income and education, perhaps because the Catholic Church's long history, broad reach, and institutional footprint have produced many subdenominations within its ranks, permitting internal segregation.)

Politics is also becoming increasingly segregated by caste, and the stark hostilities highlighted by Trump's populism reflect much broader preexisting divisions.

A student at Phillips Exeter Academy, one of the elite prep schools described earlier, recently answered a survey on elite values by commenting, "Morally, I'm a Democrat, but my wallet says I am a Republican." The student knows his caste. Most broadly stated, elite Americans, regardless of political party, are more socially progressive and more economically conservative than their middle- and working-class counterparts.

Widespread evidence underwrites the common wisdom that the rich are socially progressive. A meta-study of hundreds of broad surveys of Americans' values concludes that Americans in the top fifth (roughly) of the income distribution display more liberal attitudes than their less well-off compatriots concerning homosexuality, abortion, and the separation of church and state (to name a few examples).

The opinions of narrower economic elites are harder to document (as the truly rich are more difficult to identify and, once found, both busier and more concerned with privacy and less inclined to answer opinion surveys). But as scholarly interest in the narrow elite increases in tandem with rising inequality, a clearer picture of the cultural attitudes of the truly rich is beginning to emerge. This picture uniformly confirms that the narrow elite shares and even extends the broad elite's progressive social views. One recent study finds that Americans who have attended graduate or professional school are six times as likely as those with a high school degree or less to hold "consistently liberal" views. The Phillips Exeter survey revealed that nine out of ten students identified as liberal on social issues. Finally, a pilot study focusing on truly rich Chicago households (mean annual income $1 million, mean wealth $14 million) again reveals distinctively progressive attitudes on a broad range of issues relating to religion, culture, and moral values.

The elite's economic conservatism is less familiar: it is hidden from popular view by a misconceived synecdoche that takes a few rich economic progressives—with high media profiles but eccentric views—to stand in for a broader economic elite that in general thinks quite differently. But the broader elite's economic conservatism is no less distinctive or real.

The broad survey of opinion among Americans from the top fifth of the income distribution that revealed distinctive social liberalism also revealed distinctive—indeed more distinctive—economic conservatism: the richest fifth of Americans are much more hostile than the bottom four-fifths to progressive taxation, economic regulation, and social welfare spending. Americans from the top tenth of the income distribution display similarly conservative economic views: when compared to median Americans, the rich are substantially more hostile to high top marginal tax rates, substantially more inclined to reduce capital gains and inheritance taxes, substantially less inclined to raise the minimum wage or increase unemployment benefits, and substantially more skeptical of government regulation of corporations and industry. The Phillips Exeter survey also revealed that three to five times as many students were conservative on economic issues as on social ones.

Truly rich Americans are, if anything, more economically conservative still. The participants in the Chicago survey (of the top 1 percent) were less than one-third as likely as Americans overall to favor policies, across a wide range of specific measures, that are designed to secure jobs and increase pay for working-class Americans. They were only about half as likely to support various forms of government provision designed to secure health care and high-quality education (public schooling, college, and worker retraining) for all Americans. They were only about a third as likely to favor direct government redistribution to reduce income inequality. They harshly opposed increasing regulation of large corporations even as the broader population hugely favored it. And they were roughly four times as likely to think deficits the most pressing issue facing the nation and only roughly one-fourth as likely to think jobs the most pressing. Moreover, the very richest of the rich— the top one-tenth of 1 percent—tended to be the most conservative, favoring less economic regulation than the merely rich in the sample and tending distinctively to favor cutting domestic social welfare programs, including in particular Social Security.

Finally, although opinion surveys of the super-rich remain rare, adjacent studies confirm the result that the extremely rich are extremely economically conservative: a recent experimental study reveals that students at Yale Law School (median parental income, roughly $150,000 annually; modal income from first permanent lawyering job, roughly $180,000 at the time of the study) are much, much more efficiency-minded and much, much less equality-minded than typical Americans. The students claimed to prefer Democrats over Republicans by a factor of ten to one, but Yale Law Democrats acted—in their reluctance to sacrifice efficiency to redistribution—like national Republicans. Yale Law School is not unusual in this respect. A broader survey found that attending a college with a wealthy student body more powerfully predicts a student's economic conservatism than the student's race, gender, religion, academic achievement, or professed motivations to make money or to gain knowledge. Indeed, the study concludes that wealthy colleges *cause* their students to become more economically conservative and that this effect is strongest among the richest students, even as a long train of evidence shows that elite colleges encourage students to develop progressive views on social questions.

These divisions cumulate to compose a distinctive elite worldview, which separates the natural instincts and imaginative understandings of rich Americans from those of the rest. This worldview combines traditionally progressive ideals concerning privacy, diversity, and pluralism with traditionally conservative ideals concerning work, productivity, and individual responsibility. The rich are more likely than the rest to favor same-sex marriage, women's rights, and affirmative action and to oppose school prayer and law-and-order policing, and they are more likely than the rest to favor low taxes and free trade, and to oppose social spending and labor unions. The worldview reflects what one commentator calls a "greater attraction of the free market to the affluent"—including both the free market's indifference to religion and moralism and its hostility to government regulation and redistribution.

Elite Americans, that is, are more inclined to embrace—and middle- and working-class Americans more inclined to oppose—what intellectual historians call classical liberalism (including in its narrower, more contemporary neoliberal variety). This ideology—which is just a roundabout way of saying that meritocratic hierarchies are okay while others are not—attracts elites from all walks of life. It led Steve Jobs famously to declare that "Silicon Valley is a meritocracy"; it leads Goldman Sachs to trumpet rather than hide its aggressive pursuit of wealth; and it leads Yale University to embrace its students of color but oppose unions among its staff and graduate students. Finally, the ideology unites elites across the partisan divide. Small wonder, therefore, that Donald Trump, who combines nativist populism and social conservatism with a hostility to trade and the free market, is so reviled among the meritocratic elite.

Moreover, the rich and the rest increasingly part ways not just at worship and in politics but in their everyday pastimes also. To begin with, Americans whose annual household incomes exceed $100,000 spend 40 percent less time in passive leisure than do Americans whose incomes fall below $20,000. (Even among the unemployed, less educated men now spend roughly eleven more hours per week watching television and sleeping than more educated men.) By contrast, the rich spend longer exercising, with the top quintile devoting twice as many weekly minutes to exercise as the middle and five times as many as the bottom; and fitness has become a status symbol.

Even after adjusting for longer work hours, the rich spend more time alone and less time socializing than the rest. When they do socialize, high incomes allow them to choose their companions, gravitating toward friends (5.2 more evenings spent with friends per year for those in the top income quartile than the bottom) even as the rest favor family and neighbors (4.6 more evenings spent per year with family and 8.3 more evenings per year with neighbors in the bottom income quartile than in the top).

Indeed, the rich and the rest have very differently constructed social networks: rich networks are broad (national and even international) but shallow and cater to "a mobile, even migratory" or "cosmopolitan" self, while working- and middle-class networks are narrow but deep and cater to a "rooted self." Even activities as basic as cooking and conversation now divide the rich and the rest. Elites cook novel foods to impress people whom they would like "to know better," often for purposes of professional networking; the middle class, by contrast, cooks familiar food to share with family and long-standing friends. And the rich tend toward formal and polite conversational habits, while the rest are proudly straightforward and direct.

The rich and the rest also pursue strikingly different hobbies. The earlier report of behavior online reveals just how far apart their preoccupations have grown, as the rich distinctively search for tech, fitness, and travel while the poor distinctively search for chronic ailments, guns, and religion. Virtual pursuits find parallel expressions in the real world. Student organizations at the elite University of California at Berkeley and the middle-class Louisiana State University introduce the extent of the difference. Student organizations at Berkeley that have no counterparts at LSU include Amnesty International, the Anti-Trafficking Coalition, Building Sustainability, the Environmental

Sciences Student Association, and the Global Student Embassy; student organizations at LSU that have no counterparts at Berkeley include the Oilfield Christian Fellowship, the Agribusiness Club, and the Wargaming and Role-playing Society.

## CONSUMPTION

The differences between the rich and the rest reach even the banal everyday of consumption—the clothes, appliances, cars, electronics, and so on that people own, the services that they use, the foods that they eat, and the businesses from which they buy all these things. Banal, but important. Household consumption in the United States amounts to nearly 70 percent of GDP, and consumer goods therefore fix the tone for society writ large.

At midcentury, that tone was egalitarian: the middle class could afford its blossoming lifestyle, and good taste (and even virtue) required the rich to emulate the middle class. Today, by contrast, consumption segregates the rich from the rest, and both tastes and morals increasingly affirm luxury. The separation is so complete that the brands a person buys now reveal more about her income than about her race.

For most of human history, elites owned and consumed different things from the masses, not just in degree but in kind. In feudal orders, land ownership was restricted to a narrow caste, and ownership constituted elite status. Indeed, absolute land ownership was a distinctive prerogative of the monarch-sovereign who sat at the pinnacle of the elite. Moreover, sumptuary laws regulated myriad other forms of consumption, for example by forbidding all but the elite from wearing lavish fabrics or colors and eating opulent foods.

The bourgeois revolutions inaugurated a long erosion of this consumer caste order (indeed, some sumptuary laws sought to hold back the tide, taking express aim at public displays of commercial rather than aristocratic wealth). Early-twentieth-century capitalism accelerated the process, so that by midcentury, the caste distinction between the consumption habits of the top and the middle had effectively dissolved.

With respect to land and houses, federal government programs supporting home buyers had raised homeownership rates from 44 percent in 1940 to 63 percent by 1970. (There has been no further substantial increase since then.) And cars, refrigerators, ranges, clothes washers and dryers, and air conditioners were by the 1980s all widely dispersed throughout the middle class. Midcentury Americans bought the same modest cars and watches, and ate out in the same modest restaurants. They even bought the same brands from the same stores. In the 1970s, three out of every four adults entered a Sears store at least once a year, and half of American households had a proprietary Sears credit card.

Tastes and even morals grew to endorse these economic facts. The midcentury homes that built St. Clair Shores and countless similar suburbs, and the modernist furnishings that filled them, self-consciously relied on materials, designs, and techniques that suited the modest affluence of a broad middle class rather than the luxurious rich or the thrifty poor. Even the cars that made suburban life feasible were deliberately designed and built to suit middle-class budgets. Henry Ford's famous practice of paying his workers enough so that they might become his customers equally importantly required him to build mass-market rather than exclusive cars, whose quality and price made his workers want and be able to afford them. By midcentury, the aesthetic models behind these practices had colonized culture and become moralized. Their force was so powerful that it applied even inside the elite, as when *Fortune* ridiculed the few midcentury business leaders who— whether in Newport "cottages" or Palm Beach villas—continued to try to live in the style of the Gilded Age.

Today, meritocratic inequality reverses this trend. Consumption inequality—understood in terms of raw dollar sums—strikingly tracks income inequality, including at the very top of the distribution. Moreover, consumption divides the rich and the rest beyond the numbers. Middle-class and elite consumers buy increasingly different things from different stores. They even pay for them in different ways.

On the one hand, *thrift goods,* which appeal to people who struggle in economic inequality's shadow, increasingly dominate middle-class consumption. Thrift retail sells conventional consumer goods to households that are forced to economize. And thrift finance enables a middle class whose stagnant wages no longer match its needs to fund consumption through borrowing.

Thrift retail—low-cost supermarkets, dollar stores, and big-box stores— has grown astronomically in the past decades. Walmart alone has grown from a single store in 1962 to generate nearly $300 billion in U.S. revenue in 2016. And Dollar General and Family Dollar have averaged nearly 9 and 7 percent annual revenue growth in recent years. Shoppers at all three stores earn substantially less—in the case of Family Dollar nearly 40 percent less—than shoppers even at other less downmarket big-box stores like Target, and the earnings gap to shoppers at upmarket stores is much greater still. (When big-box chain stores displace mid-skilled for unskilled retail workers, they contribute directly to the demand for the goods that they sell. Just as Henry Ford's decision to pay his workers enough for them to desire and to afford his cars epitomized the Great Compression's egalitarian economy, so Walmart's practice of paying its workers so little that they cannot afford to shop other than at thrift retailers epitomizes today's unequal economy.)

Thrift finance has also grown rapidly, to become an inescapable part of middle-class life. Payday loans give this pattern an open and notorious illustration. Payday lending serves people who obviously cannot afford their own lives, even week to week. The obviousness of the shortfall gives the business a bad odor, but that has not stopped its increase. The payday lending industry has grown from fewer than five hundred stores in the early 1990s, to twelve thousand in 2002, to twenty-two thousand by 2016. There are more payday lending stores in the United States today than there are McDonald's and Starbucks franchises combined, and in 2012, Americans spent $7.4 billion on payday loans.

Moreover, this open expression of thrift finance is only the small tip of a massive iceberg. Middle-class households accumulated substantial savings at midcentury, and as recently as the late 1970s, the bottom 90 percent of the income distribution enjoyed a savings rate of between 5 and 10 percent. But since then, saving vanished, and borrowing largely replaced income as the source of funding for rising consumption. Household debt therefore accumulated rapidly for this group, coming to exceed income in the late 1990s, with debt accumulation highest between the 50th and 75th percentiles. The borrowing does not go to frivolous or extravagant purchases, but instead overwhelmingly serves socially legitimate (or even necessary) expenses, that nevertheless exceed the incomes mid-skilled labor can command. Indeed, seven out of every ten low- and middle-income households reported using credit cards as a "safety net," to pay unavoidable costs such as medical expenses and car and house repairs. Middle-class households quite generally subsist on what are functionally payday loans, required to paper over the widening gap between middle-class needs and stocks.

Especially against the backdrop of increasingly insecure earnings, debt used to finance consumption casts an inescapable shadow of catastrophe. As Charles Dickens's Mr. Micawber complained, "Annual income twenty pounds, annual expenditure nineteen pounds nineteen and six, result, happiness. Annual income twenty pounds, annual expenditure twenty pounds nought and six, result misery." Micawber faced debtor's prison, as had Dickens's own father. More recently, middle-class Americans face an unprecedented wave of foreclosures and bankruptcies.

The scale of enforced debt collection is remarkable: in a typical recent year, New York City alone saw 320,000 consumer debt cases filed in its civil courts, a number roughly equal to all the cases filed in all federal courts that year. Even with the threat of prison removed, debt remains an affliction for the middle class. And like imprisonment, foreclosures and bankruptcies cast their shadows across whole lives, and down the generations, breaking marriages and disrupting childhoods. Indeed, the effect is so powerful that the middle class has been renamed, by some, the *precariat*.

On the other hand, *luxury goods*—goods that appeal to those at the top, in the glare of economic inequality's light—increasingly dominate the spending and mold the self-image of the rich. The norms and habits that framed *Fortune*'s midcentury sensibilities have been ground away under the pressure of meritocratic inequality's inner logic, and the meritocratic elite now prizes the extravagances that the magazine then derided. Tastes and even morals, falling in line with new economic fundamentals, now disparage things that are ordinary, unexceptional, or merely adequate and valorize distinctive, extravagant opulence.

Meritocracy makes this turn inevitable. Where industry constitutes honor, meritocratic elites lack the time to cultivate the leisured habits that Veblen described, and (alongside conspicuously intense labor) luxury goods rather than exploit become the main avenue for establishing social and economic caste. The rich now consume conspicuously in order to shine rising inequality's light on their fortunes. Fine and expensive things become honor's physical manifestations: an embodiment of industry and of the elite's alienated personality; meritocratic virtue made flesh.

This is most obvious in brands that openly declare their luxurious exclusivity. Cars that cost ten times the price of an ordinary vehicle are readily available and in fact commonly seen in every major city today. Bentley Motors sold more cars priced over $150,000 in 2014 than the entire automotive industry did in 2000; the Geneva Auto Show has in recent years included unprecedented numbers of million-plus-dollar cars (including one, made by Lamborghini, that costs $4 million); and a recent study by Brand Finance found that Ferrari has become the world's "most powerful" brand. Similarly, there now exist stores that specialize in watches that cost tens of thousands of dollars. Luxury ovens and refrigerators—made by firms such as Viking, Sub-Zero, Bertazzoni, and La Cornue—cost ten and even one hundred times the price of ordinary appliances. And the best restaurants in New York, Washington, or San Francisco now cost easily fifty times the price of an ordinary dinner out—the French Laundry, opened in the 1990s to fulfill its chef's "longtime culinary dream: to establish a destination for fine French cuisine in the Napa Valley," costs a minimum of $310 per person, without including the $5,000 bottles of wine readily available from its cellars.

Overall, retail sales of conventional luxury goods have grown roughly four times faster than the broader economy, by an average of more than 10 percent annually since 1990; and Goldman Sachs predicts that sales will continue to outstrip economic growth going forward, doubling in the next decade. The prices of individual items bring the aggregate sales data concretely into particular lives. Whereas midcentury prices placed even luxuries within reach of the middle class, on special occasions or perhaps where a person cared especially about a particular luxury (as a car lover, for example), the new ratios place luxury goods forever out of reach of the middle class. At midcentury, Billy Joel's Sergeant O'Leary could aim to trade in his Chevy for a Cadillac. But a middle-class person today cannot credibly dream of owning a Bentley, or wearing a Blancpain watch, or cooking on a La Cornue range, or eating at the French Laundry.

Moreover, luxury has dramatically expanded its field of action. Vast swaths of the goods that were once aimed at mass, middle-class consumption have been transformed into luxury goods. The average ticket price to a concert in Beyoncé's most recent tour, for example, exceeded $350, and tickets to home games of the Los Angeles Lakers, Dallas Cowboys, and New York Yankees can easily cost over $200. At the same time, entirely new types of luxury goods are now being made and sold: cruise ships create elite floors with private concierges and swimming pools and no access to the mass of passengers (not even by using points from loyalty programs); resorts create limited-access passes and low-traffic attractions that cost ten times more than an ordinary entrance ticket; airlines increase the luxury of first class and ferry the highest-paying passengers between terminals in Porsches, as airports build separate line-free terminals for these travelers; and entirely new businesses claim and then scalp even nominally free goods—public parking spots (Monkey Parking) or restaurant reservations (Reservation Hop)—to those rich enough to pay. (These new businesses trigger especially robust resentment, as, perhaps unsurprisingly, does first-class air travel: the presence of a first-class cabin increases the incidence of air rage among passengers traveling steerage by the same amount as a nine-hour-twenty-nine-minute flight delay, and where steerage passengers must walk through first class to reach their seats, by the equivalent of a fifteen-hour delay.)

Other goods and especially services that people do not ordinarily associate with luxury—because they involve no sybaritic indulgence—are also now distinctively consumed by the rich.

Elite private schools and colleges are just one example, among very many. Concierge doctors, who charge patients fees and annual retainers paid out of pocket and free from price caps negotiated by insurance, provide luxury medical care. The higher fees allow them to see perhaps a quarter as many patients as ordinary doctors, provide leisurely consultations (as opposed to the 15.7 minutes of attention that comprises a doctor's median patient visit length), and offer same-day appointments, including on weekends. Concierge hospital wings provide accommodations that resemble luxury hotels—Frette bed linens, elaborate restaurant menus with dishes such as prosciutto di Parma or veal scallopini, and personal butlers—for cash customers who can pay several thousand dollars a night on top of medical bills. (Even luxury dentists now exist: a Frenchman named Bernard Touati, for example, fixes the teeth of oligarchs and pop stars, including Madonna, in a Paris office nestled among the city's Chanel, Dior, and Prada boutiques; and he charges nearly $2,000 for a single filling, although Diane von Furstenberg gave him an IOU for two dresses at her boutique instead.) Lawyers, accountants, and investment advisers, again paid for without insurance and on the concierge model, similarly provide luxury legal and financial services (including income defense) to rich clients. Elite households even buy distinctive groceries. High-socioeconomic-status Americans eat more healthy foods (fruits, vegetables, fish, nuts, whole grains, and legumes) than middle-class Americans, who eat more healthy foods than low-socioeconomic-status Americans. Both gaps are growing, and, as usual, the gap between the top and the middle exceeds the gap between the middle and the bottom.

All these goods and services are consumed almost exclusively by the rich and indeed as a self-conscious performance of eliteness through consumption. If elites view consuming them as responsible (fruits and vegetables), necessary (medical care), or even virtuous (education), then this just shows how fully meritocratic ideals have colonized the idea of luxury.

Finally, these joint trends reinforce each other and cumulate their effects, so that the rich and the rest increasingly buy not just different goods but different brands, at separate stores, paid for by different means.

Like the middle of the labor market, so the middle of the consumer market is literally being hollowed out as commerce shifts to the extremes of thrift and luxury. Middle-class restaurants such as Olive Garden and Red Lobster struggle even as fast-food chains like Taco Bell and upscale restaurants like the French Laundry both thrive. Middle-class hotel brands (Best Western) grow at half the pace of luxury brands (Four Seasons and St. Regis). And middle-class supermarkets and department stores (Sears and J. C. Penney) collapse even as bargain stores (Price Chopper, Dollar Tree, Family Dollar) and luxury stores (Whole Foods, and Nordstrom, Barneys, and Neiman Marcus) both expand, often into the very locations that the middle-class brands have abandoned. (Barneys, for example, famously moved into Loehmann's iconic Chelsea storefront.)

Even at the till, elites pay differently, using income or savings (one-percenters still save perhaps a third of their incomes) rather than borrowed funds. And when they do borrow, the rich use debt (for example, thirty-year fixed-rate prime mortgages) to leverage rather than to replace their incomes, and to multiply the economic returns from their investments.

When they cumulate in this way, differences produce not just distinction but segregation. Elite schools and universities separate rich from middle-class students. Concierge doctors eliminate common waiting rooms or even the shared experience of waiting in any room. Even for seemingly ordinary purchases, segmented sellers increasingly have neither customers nor even products in common.

The food department at Big Lots does not have a cheese cave or craft butcher and does not sell artisanal ice cream, while Whole Foods does not sell Coca-Cola, Oscar Mayer hot dogs, or Heinz ketchup. Meanwhile, Family Dollar and Neiman Marcus do not stock a single common designer. And Taco Bell and the French Laundry do not use a single ingredient in common, not even salt. Even the attitudes of the two restaurants toward their ingredients are oceans apart. Taco Bell's website says that its ingredients "do have weird names" but are all "safe and approved by the FDA." A request for ingredients sent to the French Laundry produced a fifty-page book, with full-color photographs and hand-signed by the chef, telling the personal story of every supplier. Butter, according to the book, comes from a farm in Vermont that declares, "To make butter, one must be willing to sacrifice a measure of free will and live according to the needs of animals."

Meritocratic inequality has transformed consumption so that elite and middle-class consumers have increasingly few spaces or even experiences in common. All of life is remade on the model of class-segregated airplane cabins.

## PLACE

The roughly equivalent middle-class prosperity of St. Clair Shores and Palo Alto exemplified the economic geography of midcentury America. Other towns were similar. In Sigmona Park, just outside Washington, D.C., for example, a neighborhood newsletter kept continuously since midcentury reveals that in the early 1970s, a land surveyor, a Marine major, an interior designer, a hairdresser, a policeman, a maintenance worker, and a secretary all lived side by side, on Overbrook Street.

The majority of Americans lived in comparable middle-class communities, distinguished by culture rather than income and caste, and neighborhoods owed their sense of place to climate, history, or even the characters who lived there, rather than to economic data.

Incomes across regions converged steadily between the end of the Second World War and the end of the 1970s (and this convergence accounted for perhaps 30 percent of the overall reduction in wage inequality that the country experienced over those years). Whereas the richest region had enjoyed nearly twice the per capita income of the poorest in 1945, the gap fell by roughly two-thirds between 1945 and 1979. Even wealth spread itself evenly over the American map: in the mid-1960s, the country's twenty-five richest metro areas included Rockford, Illinois; Milwaukee; Ann Arbor, Michigan; and Cleveland.

These developments expressed the economic logic of midcentury production in geographic terms. The rentier elite had economic reasons to live near the physical assets that sustained its rents. Both agricultural land and industrial machines and factories were (often of necessity) geographically dispersed. This encouraged capital's elite owners to spread themselves throughout the country, across its physical space. And as midcentury elites diluted themselves—college graduates, for example, were spread relatively evenly across cities—the middle class came to dominate almost everywhere. Economic geography made the midcentury elite's social merger into the middle class inevitable, as the elite's dilution and thin ranks required social mixing across class lines. As Bill Clinton's and George Bush's childhoods replicated themselves in neighborhoods across the country, a "single American standard of living" emerged.

Today, meritocratic inequality reverses these forces. Superordinate workers bring their human capital with them wherever they go; and they can find jobs that pay elite wages only by working together in close physical proximity, so that their labor-intensive production can benefit from economies of agglomeration and in particular knowledge spillovers. Furthermore, the new elite requires a collective training infrastructure, comprising both schools and out-of-school enrichment activities, in order effectively to transmit its human capital to its children. Finally, the luxury goods that today's elite favor can be economically supplied only where there are large concentrations of rich consumers, as in prosperous cities. These forces drive the new elite toward geographic concentration, and America is resegregating by income.

To begin with, the elite is moving out of the countryside and into cities. (Middle-class people, by contrast, increasingly stay put, so that moving itself now marks eliteness.) In 1970, rural and urban Americans possessed roughly similar levels of education; by the new millennium, young adults in rural areas were less than half as likely to possess college degrees as young adults living in the average city, and the difference has increased still further in the years since. This represents a brain drain from the countryside commensurate to the outmigration that signally slows economic development in many poor countries.

Moreover, elite migration is producing distinctive education and income profiles even among towns, as college graduates and high earners congregate in certain cities and not others. There were by the turn of the millennium sixty-two metro areas in which fewer than 17 percent of adults possessed college degrees and thirty-two metro areas in which more than 34 percent were college graduates. Some cities, with familiar names, still more powerfully repel or attract educated workers. Fewer than 10 percent of Detroit's residents have college degrees; by contrast, Austin, Boston, San Francisco, San Jose, and Washington, D.C., all average nearly 50 percent. New York City similarly experienced a 73 percent growth in the raw number of college-educated workers between 1980 and 2010, even as the number of workers without college degrees fell by 15 percent. And nearly half of couples in which both partners are highly educated live in a handful of large cities.

Incomes, under meritocracy, follow education. Indeed, differences in patent production alone (an excellent proxy for population education) account for nearly a third of the variation in wages across regions. It is therefore no surprise that between 1980 and 2012, the ratios of mean city incomes to the national mean grew by roughly 50 percent for New York, 40 percent for Washington, and nearly 30 percent for San Francisco. More broadly, since 1990, the ten best-educated metro areas have experienced more than twice the increase in per capita incomes of the ten worst-educated metro areas. And workers in the most educated cities now receive on average twice the salaries of workers in the least educated cities.

House prices and rents follow suit. The thought that a house in an elite part of Boston, New York, San Francisco, or Washington, or for that matter in Palo Alto, would cost just twice the price of the median new house in the country—or in St. Clair Shores—has become laughable. Even renting in these places is now out of reach of the middle class: rents in Los Angeles, San Francisco, Miami, and New York now cost 49, 47, 44.5, and 41 percent of the highly inflated incomes in those cities (up from 34.1, 24.7, 26.5, 23.7 percent as recently as 2000). For every 1 percent rise in the ratio of college graduates to nongraduates in a city, rents increase by 0.6 percent. The middle class simply cannot afford elite cities today.

Indeed, geographic isolation by class proceeds in a finer grain still, as the rich and the rest are increasingly separated even within cities. In 1970, nearly two-thirds of Americans lived in middle-class neighborhoods; today, only two-fifths do; and over the same period, the shares of Americans living in rich and poor neighborhoods both doubled. More generally, both the rich and the poor have become substantially more concentrated by census tract over the past forty years: demographic measures of residential segregation by income and education have increased by at least 25 and 100 percent respectively since 1970. Even mixed neighborhoods have become less mixed: between 1970 and 1990, the shares of neighbors of the average poor family that were also poor and of the average rich family that were also rich doubled and increased by one-fifth, respectively.

Socioeconomic segregation is especially extreme at the very top of the distribution. In New York's Upper East Side, the share of adults with college degrees more than tripled between 1960 and 2006, reaching 74 percent. Similarly, among the 9.1 million Americans aged twenty-five and over who live in the top 5 percent of zip codes by income and education, 63 percent have BAs, and the median annual household income is $141,000. The next neighborhoods over extend the isolation of the elite. Nearly 80 percent of the residents of zip codes in the top 5 percent by income and education live in clusters of such zip codes, and the average neighborhood that borders such an elite zip code is itself in the 86th percentile by income and education. Moreover, the association between the elite and certain neighborhoods holds in both directions: recall that half of Harvard, Princeton, and Yale college alumni live in the richest and most educated 5 percent of zip codes. Elite professional school graduates live in more prosperous places still. Three-fifths of Harvard Business School alumni live in top 5 percent zip codes.

Physical segregation catalyzes other varieties of segregation. Education and income jointly feed back into amenities and quality of life more generally—to give the cultural divergence just described a geographic cast. The richest, best-educated cities boast dramatically longer life expectancies, lower crime rates, less pollution, and more political clout. Perhaps most important, meritocratic parents use economic segregation to insulate themselves and their children from the disorder and disruption that have become facts of life among the less stable families that make up the rest of society. The 90 percent of children in elite zip codes who grow up in enduring marriages, with both biological parents present, have virtually no friends and neighbors who do not. The gates and guards that control crime in rich neighborhoods might receive the lion's share of attention from those who lament inequality. But the most consequential mechanisms of elite self-segregation deploy not security guards but rather rents and house prices.

It is difficult to aggregate all these effects into a single composite, but according to one estimate, neighborhood quality and other amenities associated with rich, well-educated cities push inequality of well-being a further 30 percent higher than inequality of dollar income. Economic inequality produces entirely distinct ecosystems for the rich and the rest. Small wonder then that not just the facts of geographic mobility but also the reasons behind it have changed: whereas Americans used to move to cities seeking better weather, they now move expressly to be around others like themselves.

Finally, these effects reach across not just facets of life but also generations. Poor neighborhoods obstruct and rich neighborhoods facilitate the training that children require to join the elite as adults. The effects, once again, are substantial and apply across the income distribution. At the bottom, upward mobility is highest in cities that still disperse poor families among middle-class and rich ones, in mixed-income neighborhoods of just the sort that are generally disappearing. And higher up the distribution, rich neighborhoods support the extraordinary top/middle per-pupil expenditure gaps documented earlier, which underwrite the enormous skew to wealth among students at elite colleges and universities.

Each city and each neighborhood reprises these trends in a distinctive way, refracting patterns that arise generally through its own sense of place. But unlike at midcentury, data concerning income and caste now capture and determine a great deal about a place. Even towns that have remained middle class, like St. Clair Shores, have become distinctively rather than generically so—literally remarkable for having few really rich and few really poor residents. And most towns have moved either up or down the caste order, to become identified as rich or poor. Economic trends, not quirks of personality, now determine what places are like.

Overbrook Street, as it happens, has followed the same path as Palo Alto. Today, median annual household income in the Sigmona Park zip code exceeds $100,000, and 60 percent of adults in the neighborhood are college educated. Overbrook Street houses lawyers, doctors, and elite government workers.

## FITZGERALD AND HEMINGWAY REDUX

Midcentury American culture did not allow the economic distinctions between their families to make a great difference to the lived experience of Bill Clinton's and George Bush's childhoods—rather, they shared a middle-class society, with each other and with most of the rest of their generation.

By contrast, the lives of Bill's daughter, Chelsea, and George's daughters, Barbara and Jenna, have been determined by their families' now-shared eliteness, making them unrecognizable to middle-class children today, and equally so to the elite of their parents' generation.

Chelsea Clinton attended an elite private high school (the last child before her to be raised in the White House, Jimmy Carter's daughter Amy, attended public school) and then Stanford, Columbia, and Oxford Universities. After finishing her studies, she worked for the management consultancy McKinsey & Company and the private equity and distressed securities investment firm Avenue Capital Group. Chelsea's husband—the son of two members of the House of Representatives who had been friendly with her parents in Washington—also graduated from Stanford and Oxford and then worked for Goldman Sachs before starting his own hedge fund. The couple met at a Renaissance weekend on Hilton Head Island; they married at Astor Court, a fifty-acre Beaux-Arts estate built on a bluff overlooking the Hudson River during the last gilded age (Chelsea wore a Vera Wang gown); and they spent over $10 million on an apartment (unsurprisingly, in Manhattan).

Barbara Bush graduated from Yale University and has worked for design museums and international development organizations. Jenna Bush has also worked for international charities, publishing a book about her work, as well as serving as a news correspondent for NBC. Jenna's husband—whose father has been, variously, assistant secretary of education, lieutenant governor of Virginia, and chairman of the Virginia Republican Party—works for Kohlberg Kravis Roberts, a leading private equity firm specializing in leveraged buyouts. The couple were married at a stone altar and cross specially commissioned for the occasion.

None of the Clinton or Bush children has ever lived in a middle-class setting. And just as Bill Clinton and George Bush exemplified midcentury America, so the younger Clinton and Bushes reflect their generation and the new age: they are typical of the elite today, at most an extreme case of a broader trend, and not in any way exceptional.

Meritocratic inequality's effects on the lives of the rich and the rest are no longer limited to income and wealth, understood as abstract dollar sums. Instead, meritocracy constitutes a caste system, which partitions the rich and the rest into separate and alien life-worlds. Unsurprisingly, when the rich and the rest work, marry, parent, worship, and assemble differently, a vast gulf opens up between them—separating them not just in their outer habits but also in their inner lives, giving them different hopes and fears. Less educated Americans display lower trust, lower participation in civic life, and greater pessimism about the future than their more educated counterparts, and these differences are greater in the United States than in most (and along some dimensions virtually all) other advanced economies.

The few class migrants who cross the meritocratic divide today reveal its enormous size, and the strains of foreignness touch both the grand arcs and the petty details of their lives. Even inside elite colleges, students from poorer backgrounds marry at lower rates than students from richer ones, for example. And work-study jobs, which typically require scholarship students to perform conventionally working-class tasks, are experienced as petty indignities. (The affront is intensified by the fact that elite student bodies skew so dramatically toward wealth that many financial aid recipients come from households sufficiently wealthy that the work-study jobs fall outside not just their aspirations but their past experience of class.) A student receiving financial aid from Yale College recently complained that "Yale has the ability to make people do unpleasant things and be thankful for it—office jobs, library jobs all of which I have held unwillingly but inevitably because I am not rich enough to own even my own time." The self-absorbed, even churlish tone of the complaint only emphasizes the student's impossible class position: as an outsider who cannot (yet) afford the life she is expected, by both her teachers and her peers, to lead.

Affinity groups—Yale Law School's is called "First Generation Professionals"—try to absorb the strains of this dilemma. But meritocracy possesses such ideological power that these groups cannot decide whether they aim to bring down the class structure or to ease their members' paths into the elite. The universities face the mirror image of this problem: they wish to affirm the backgrounds of their working- and middle-class students; but unlike for other minorities, they cannot credibly aim to dismantle the meritocratic hierarchy whose constitution is their core mission.

The meritocratic closure of the elite has become so pervasive that class migrants must now define themselves in terms of their relationship to it (as neither Bill Clinton nor George Bush ever needed to). As one college graduate remarked after returning home to his noncollege community, "I feel like I have changed sides in some very important game."

The metaphor of changing sides captures the essence of the lived experience of comprehensive inequality. Because meritocracy permits no overlap between the lives of the rich and the rest, there can be no middle ground for the classes to share, or even on which they might meet.

A final and more literal measure of comprehensive inequality looks to the health and longevity of the rich and the rest as they live on either side of it. These data cannot sustain a precise metric, of course, but they do yield "a good general indicator of accumulated advantage." Medical data draw meritocratic privilege's bottom line.

The rich and educated report massively lower rates of health-related limits on physical activity, difficulty seeing, heart disease, psychological distress, obesity, and generalized unwellness than both the poor and the middle class (and the rich/middle-class gaps are comparable to the middle-class/poor gaps). Elite Americans also smoke at massively lower rates than others—the percentage of smokers among Americans who have attended some college is roughly half that among Americans with a high school education only and among high school dropouts (and the last two percentages are virtually identical). Moreover, when they do get sick, elite Americans increasingly receive different and even separate health care, not just from the poor but also from the middle class. Even teeth now signal income and status, much as height did in the ancien régime. Rich Americans spend more than $1 billion each year on cosmetic dentistry, even as not just poor but also middle-class Americans increasingly rely on charity dental clinics (and even hospital emergency rooms), so that one out of five Americans over sixty-five has no real teeth left. Good teeth have thus become what one middle-class patient at a charity clinic recently called a "telltale, visible sign of wealth."

These and other differences in health produce enormous and increasing differences in life expectancy. Between 1999 and 2003, midlife mortality among middle-aged white non-Hispanic Americans with a high school education or less rose, even as mortality among people with some college but no degree held steady and mortality among those with a BA or more continued to fall. Indeed, mortality among less educated Americans rose so steeply that it outweighed falling mortality among the educated, so that mortality overall rose by about half a percent a year, reversing two decades of 2 percent annual mortality declines.

More broadly, between 1980 and 2010, the life expectancy (at age fifty) of the bottom two quintiles of the income distribution remained flat or fell slightly for men and declined significantly for women (including by nearly four years for women in the bottom quintile), the life expectancy of the middle two quintiles rose for men and remained flat or even fell slightly for women, and the life expectancy of the top quintile rose steeply for both men and women. The gap between life expectancy in the top and in the bottom two quintiles grew by about seven years for men (from five years to twelve years) and by about nine years for women (from four years to thirteen years).

Moreover, even within the elite, the very rich live longer than their merely rich counterparts, and even this very-rich/merely-rich gap has been growing. For both men and women, the differences in life expectancy at twenty-five between people with BAs or more education and people with some college but no BA exceed the gaps between people with some college and those with a high school degree only. Indeed, for both men and women, mortality rates are markedly lower among the top 1 percent by wealth than among the top 5 percent and lower among the top 5 percent than among the top 10 percent. These gaps have been growing, with the top-1/top-10-percent gap roughly doubling between the early 1980s and the mid-2000s.

Finally, and inevitably given where the rich and the rest live, these trends take on a geographic cast: the gap in life expectancy (at birth) between a rich state such as Connecticut and a poor state such as Mississippi is now nearly six years; and even as life spans increase steadily in rich places, those in poor places decline. The life span of women in eastern Kentucky, for example, fell by over a year between 2007 and 2011.

To grasp the size of this aggregated meritocratic advantage, consider that the gap between life expectancy in the United States and Nicaragua is about four years, and that curing all cancers would also increase life expectancy by only the same amount.

Although Hemingway may have won the argument with Fitzgerald at midcentury, meritocratic inequality increasingly vindicates Fitzgerald's view. A lifestyle runs through the body of the person who lives it, as the flesh surrounds us with its own decisions. Today, the very bodies of the rich are different from the rest.

The difference is so large that the rich and the rest might as well live in separate countries.

# EIGHT

# SNOWBALL
# INEQUALITY

Beginning in the 1970s, the American middle class, caught short by stagnating wages, ran out of income and began borrowing to fund its lifestyle.

Even as the median wage stagnated, social and economic imperatives insisted that middle-class consumption must keep rising. Deep-rooted ideals of national progress created a felt need for each new generation of Americans to be better off than the one before. And rising middle-class consumption remained necessary to sustain the aggregate demand on which employment and growth in a consumer economy depend. At the same time, the Reagan Revolution flatly rejected outright redistribution from the rich to the middle class, and taxes in fact became less progressive.

The collision between the overwhelming imperative to boost middle-class consumption above the levels that might be sustained by stagnant wages and the implacable objection to outright redistribution left few alternatives open. A person who does not increase her income can increase consumption only using funds that she steals, begs, or borrows. And where widespread theft is out of the question, and private charity has reached its outer limits, the meeting of the unbending constraint that taxes must become less rather than more progressive and the insistent demand that median consumption must increase even as median incomes stagnate effectively required expanding private borrowing. At the same time, rising top incomes produced excess savings in the new economic elite, which generated a ready supply of lending, even from rich people who were ideologically opposed to outright redistribution. Where stagnant incomes confront an imperative to sustain rising consumption without redistribution, debt follows inexorably—by an almost actuarial logic. In this way, rising economic inequality dramatically increased the demand for financial engineering, and the new demand (alongside other causes) made finance grow rapidly.

Government actively supported both sides of this equation, in gross and in fine. Loose monetary policy, a tolerance for asset bubbles, and promises to protect investors when the bubbles burst all generally promoted debt-financed middle-class consumption. Other policies pursued the same goal in specific contexts. The Clinton administration, for example, changed federal mortgage policy in order to promote "financing strategies fueled by the creativity and resources of the private and public sectors" that could "address . . . financial barriers to homeownership." The government was particularly motivated to encourage borrowing by people who "lack . . . cash available to accumulate the required down payment" and "do not have sufficient available income to make the monthly payments" on traditional loans.

These policies worked—often immediately. When low interest rates inflated house prices, for example, households borrowed between 25 and 30 cents out of every dollar of housing price appreciation. Taken all together, the policies transformed the bases of middle-class consumption. The midcentury middle class had financed its rising standard of living with income. But beginning in the 1970s, middle-class consumption began to be financed by debt.

The pattern is unmistakable. Mean income among the bottom 90 percent rose steadily (more or less in tandem with consumption) between roughly 1940 and roughly 1975, at which point income stopped rising almost completely, even as consumption continued its smooth growth. Mean debt, by contrast, rose more slowly than income from 1940 to 1975 and then, just a few years after incomes stopped growing, began a steep rise (again, more or less in tandem with still-rising consumption). Middle-class borrowing, in other words, bent upward just as middle-class incomes flattened out, and borrowing grew on a scale big enough to fill the income gap that middle-class households lost to stagnant wages.* The scale of the borrowing, moreover, approached the shift in wages from the middle to the top.

As the Nobel Prize–winning economist Joseph Stiglitz has observed, "The negative impact of stagnant real incomes and rising income inequality… was largely offset by financial innovation . . . and lax monetary policy that increased the ability of households to finance consumption by borrowing. . . . The support for the bubble thus depended on expansionary monetary policy together with financial sector innovation leading to ever-increasing asset prices that allowed households virtually unlimited access to credit." If the standard of living in midcentury America was funded by income, and the standard of living of the European middle class is increasingly supported by government redistribution, the American middle class increasingly relies on borrowed funds. The earlier observation that household credit has become functionally equivalent to payday lending stated a literal truth.

Finance rode to its current prominence atop this wave of inequality-induced borrowing, scaled to match the U.S. macroeconomy, which pushed new money through the sector not as a trickle, nor even as a stream, but as a geyser. The share of GDP attributable to financial services has roughly doubled since 1970. Finance now contributes nearly a tenth of the country's total economic output, which is beginning to converge on the share of GDP attributable to manufacturing.

These developments shifted the center of gravity of the American economy away from Main Street and toward Wall Street: economic activities such as agriculture, wholesale and retail trade, and manufacturing that produce directly useful goods and services became relatively less important; while financial activities such as banking, securities trading, investment management, and insurance that create and transfer claims to money became relatively more important. Even traditionally powerhouse industrial firms have come to be dominated by their financial offshoots. The most profitable unit of General Motors in the years leading to the financial crisis was its financing subsidiary, GMAC. At General Motors, Wall Street's debt-financed middle-class consumption swamped Main Street's industrial production.

Overall, about a quarter of finance's exceptional growth came immediately

---

* A graphical representation of these trends appears in Figure 10 on page 306.

and directly from the inequality-driven rise in household credit, and in particular the explosion of residential mortgages—though consumer credit, including credit card debt, also contributed substantially to this facet of finance. A further half of finance's growth came from economic inequality's other side, through the increased output of the securities industry. The securities boom was overwhelmingly propelled by the growth of asset management services—with especially rapid growth in private equity firms, venture capital firms, and hedge funds—which by nature serve the wealthy whose assets they manage. Indeed, the most rapid growth within asset management came from fixed-income assets, typically produced by securitizing loans—securitized home mortgages alone accounted for roughly half of *all* asset-backed securities issued between 2000 and 2008—which show the flip side of rising household borrowing. (By contrast, the functions that traditionally generated the securities industry's profits in the more equal midcentury—trading fees and commissions, trading gains, and securities underwriting fees—actually all generated declining shares of GDP over this period.)

It is only a slight exaggeration to say, with one prominent commentator, that by the time of the 2007–8 crisis, the "entire edifice" of the U.S. financial market "rested on the housing market." The housing market, for its part, rested on debt. And debt, once again, rested on economic inequality.

At almost the same historical moment as the demands on finance exploded, a new, super-skilled labor force came to Wall Street. The new supply of superordinate workers transformed how finance did business, attracting innovations that favored its own elite skills.

When the first wave of super-skilled finance workers reached Wall Street in the late 1970s, old-timers (still cast in the mid-skilled, midcentury mold) called them "rocket scientists." The reason is that they were. Military imperatives associated with World War II and the Cold War—the invention of radar, the Manhattan Project to build the atom bomb, and the arms and space races—had persuaded midcentury America that highly trained, meritocratic physicists and engineers were essential to the nation's prosperity and security. The Defense Department and the Department of Energy began liberally funding pure research, and academic faculties grew rapidly in both size and quality through the 1950s and 1960s.

But then the United States won the space race, a détente with the Soviet

Union slowed the arms race, and the unpopular conflict in Vietnam roused the public to oppose "science in the service of war." The tide turned against the military uses that had driven scientific research, government cut back its funding, and research dried up. A generation of newly minted PhDs in physics and engineering found themselves without academic jobs. The new supply of super-skilled workers went looking for demand.

At first, energy and communications companies, including most notably Exxon and Bell Labs, absorbed the new super-skilled workforce. But by 1980, Wall Street recognized that physicists and engineers could profitably develop and deploy new financial technologies and came calling—often literally. A physicist who entered finance early and eventually became a managing director at Goldman Sachs remembers that headhunters offered his cohort jobs "that paid \$150,000 . . . a huge amount in those days for an ex-physicist making less than \$50K."

When the rocket scientists arrived on Wall Street, they fundamentally transformed how the sector did business. The new, super-skilled workforce made complex financial techniques—long known in theory but too difficult for mid-skilled workers to implement—suddenly practicable. The match between the workforce that finance needed to reconstruct itself and the labor that physicists and engineers could provide was uncannily precise: the math deployed in finance and in physics closely resemble each other, and the pragmatic work ethic of physicists and engineers rendered them especially willing to step into subdisciplines not quite theirs and to construct makeshift solutions to practical problems and then move on. Finance had found a new type of human capital—"skilled mathematicians, modelers, and computer programmers who prided themselves on their ability to adapt to new fields and put their knowledge into practice"—that almost perfectly suited its growing needs.

This triggered innovations that had long lain dormant. The fundamental theoretical advances that ground modern, sophisticated finance (the capital asset pricing model and the Black-Scholes model that underwrite portfolio allocation and the pricing of options and other derivatives) were made in the 1950s, 1960s, and early 1970s, often a quarter century before finance transformed itself into a super-skilled sector by implementing them. (Indeed, the foundational ideas behind these models, which concern measuring, segregating, and then recombining risks, have been around since Pascal and other French mathematicians invented modern probability theory—an interest aroused by inquiries put to them when aristocratic gamblers sought to measure and manipulate the odds in their wagers.) Now, after a quarter century (or three centuries) of lying fallow as merely theoretical possibilities, these advances encountered a financial workforce capable of deploying them and a broader society that needed the services they made possible.

Practical innovation followed almost at once, with forty fundamentally new financial products and practices introduced between just 1970 and 1982. The innovators became rich. In the early 1980s, for example, super-skilled workers at Drexel Burnham Lambert pioneered the high-yield bond market: "There wasn't another firm in the world that knew how to price a junk bond," a Drexel insider remembers, which made the junk bond business immensely profitable. The profits of course drew competition from other newly minted super-skilled workers, and this competition generated new innovation, including in the mortgage-backed securities that proved so profitable in the early 2000s and in the high-frequency trading platforms that are so profitable today.

The innovations, moreover, drove mid-skilled, middle-class workers out of finance even as they attracted super-skilled replacements. Securitization, once again, encouraged banks to dispense with traditional loan officers, by aggregating and hedging away loan-specific risks, and therefore making the accurate initial lending decisions that traditional loan officers were charged with less valuable. (Indeed, literally all the increase in home mortgage loans over the past three decades was produced without mid-skilled loan officers, using financial technologies, and securitized and sold to shadow banks and other investors. The aggregate household credit issued on the midcentury model and held by banks constituted the same share of GDP in 2007 as it had in 1980, in spite of the massive rise in household borrowing.)

The match between elite education and finance was made. The sleepy, mid-skilled, middle-class model of the sector gave way to rapid growth, constant innovation, and a super-elite (immensely skilled and extravagantly paid) workforce. The transformation was so pervasive that it has changed finance's culture and language: old craft-based and autodidact practitioners, like chartists and stock tipsters, have been supplanted by new super-skilled, formally trained, university-certified "quants." Wall Street began to dominate hiring in the Ivy League, and entire groups at major banks came to be dominated by physicists, applied mathematicians, and engineers, many with PhDs. Finance has never been the same.

Finance abandoned its midcentury model of growing by hiring more mid-skilled workers, and even as its share of GDP rose rapidly, its share of employment actually began to fall. As finance used relatively fewer but more skilled workers to produce relatively more output, finance-sector incomes began to rise, and the elite workers who dominated the sector got rich. Today, "talent is the most precious commodity on Wall Street; it's what [banks] sell, so it's also what they have to pay for." Wages now capture nearly half a typical Wall Street firm's net revenue. The average finance worker now makes 70 percent more than average workers in other sectors (the college wage premium in finance nearly doubles that for other workers). And finance workers dominate the ranks of the really rich. Today, elite finance workers' enormous incomes exacerbate economic inequality, increasing the needs that finance serves.

This stylized story glosses over many complexities, but it captures an important core truth that applies far beyond finance, across the entire economy. The skill-biased technologies that account for superordinate workers' enormous incomes did not arise out of the blue—from beyond the meritocratic system. Instead, the appearance of super-skilled finance workers *induced* the innovations that then favored their elite skills. A rising supply of meritocrats stimulates its own demand.

Meritocratic inequality grows—and meritocracy builds and then reinforces its trap—through a series of feedback loops. The most important connects meritocratic inequality's two basic building blocks: the exceptional training that rich children receive in school and the extravagant incomes that elite skills sustain at work.

The returns to skill rationalize the elite's mania for training. Both parents and children accept oppressively intense education in order to secure glossy jobs, avoid gloomy ones, and transmit caste down through the generations. In this way, work remakes the home in its image.

The elite's exceptional training, for its part, rationalizes the labor market's fetish for skill. Most obviously, meritocracy promotes innovation. Innovators require training, often lots of it, and the scope and scale of research and development therefore increase where meritocratic education builds an innovator class—the physicists who came to Wall Street—and creates a "research and development sector." Less obviously, but no less important, meritocracy guides innovation, determining not just how many but which and what kinds of new technologies get invented. Meritocracy biases technological innovation toward skill because elaborately trained and intensely motivated superordinate workers can use skill-biased innovations in especially productive and profitable ways, in stark contrast to the aristocratic elite. (Imagine asking Bertie Wooster to trade collateralized debt obligations.) Meritocratic education both creates innovators and gives them a target to aim at. In this way, the home also remakes work in its image.

The feedback loop between elite training and elite work does not of course account for all economic inequality, or even just for all meritocratic inequality. Nevertheless, it constitutes the master mechanism that dominates social and economic life today. Meritocratic inequality exhibits neither self-correction nor even self-restraint; to the contrary, once it gains a foothold, new inequalities grow inexorably upon prior ones. The workplace fetish for skill induces elite parents to give their children exceptional educations, and superordinate workers bend the arc of innovation to increase the fetish for skill.

The cycle continues, and meritocratic inequality snowballs down through the generations, gathering size, mass, and momentum as it rolls down history's hill.

## REINVENTING MANAGEMENT

The Safeway supermarket chain was founded by the son of a Baptist minister, who promoted cash-and-carry grocery stores because he believed that credit-based grocers raised prices and produced household debt and dependency. The chain's founder, M. B. Skaggs, would later remark, "In 1919 I had never seen a cash-and-carry grocery store, but the plan made sense. My progress would be measured by the degree to which I could give better service, cut out waste, sell for cash, meet my customers' needs, and give them the benefit of my savings." For decades—through expansions, contractions, and restructurings—Safeway did business under mottos such as "Drive the Safeway; Buy the Safeway" and "Safeway Offers Security."

Throughout this period, the firm functioned on the midcentury model, embracing what *Fortune* magazine, in a 1940 article for which Ansel Adams provided pictures, called "a simple formula for success: it behaves as if it were operated for the benefit of its producers, employees, and consumers." The formula, moreover, was no empty slogan. The firm's 1939, 1940, and 1941 annual reports, for example, all proudly announced that although each year saw a decline in the number of Safeway stores in operation, this had not required the company to fire any of its employees. In 1968, Safeway worked to save a competitor food co-op that served the Bayview–Hunters Point neighborhood of San Francisco. In 1972, it was ranked first among food retailers for "social responsiveness and accountability to the public interest." And in the early 1970s, it seconded a director and senior vice president to the National Alliance of Businessmen, giving them paid leave to work on a crash program that aimed to create half a million good jobs for underprivileged minority workers.

Safeway's top managers, in this period, retained close connections to the rest of the firm. The 1965 annual report, in celebrating the company's fortieth anniversary, proudly declared that Safeway's president had worked for the firm for all forty years, beginning as a part-time food clerk when Safeway was incorporated in 1926 and working his way up to lead the firm. Safeway's policies enabled and even encouraged this trajectory: "We live and preach people development" the company announced; "we systematically forecast needs for trained and experienced managers; we identify them and provide the training and experience to qualify them for today's complex and demanding conditions; and we create opportunities for them to move up." Opportunities indeed followed: in 1939, all of Safeway's division managers save two started with the firm behind the checkout counter. One of these two started out as a bookkeeper and the other as a bakery helper.

Safeway's payroll was distributed broadly across its workers: a division manager might, with bonuses, take home half the pay of the CEO. And Safeway's CEOs were paid well but not exorbitantly: in each year between 1956 and 1964, Safeway paid its CEO, Robert Magowan, $135,000, which amounts to roughly $1.2 million in 2018 dollars—still a lot, but profoundly less than CEOs make today. *Fortune,* summing up the firm's culture, declared that "Safeway has rationalized its technique with so sound a concept of business that when it behaves in character it performs an act of public relations."

Finally, Safeway's approach suited its social circumstances. The nineteenth-century workforce—with low literacy rates, few high school graduates, and virtually no college graduates—had lacked the skills either to take or to give managerial direction, and nineteenth-century firms (like the Durant-Dort Carriage Company) therefore naturally did largely without managers. But by the twentieth century, universal high school education, the postwar college boom, and elaborate workplace training had produced a large class of workers capable of performing basic management tasks. At the same time, the valorization of leisure among midcentury elites and the uncompetitive mediocrity of midcentury universities produced top executives who were neither willing nor able to shoulder exceptional managerial burdens. The dispersed managerial technology and elaborate corporate hierarchies that Safeway (and other midcentury firms, including GM) adopted again matched the skill profile of their workforce.

Against this backdrop, and beginning in the late 1970s and accelerating through the 1980s, a series of interlocking innovations—in finance, in law, and in management itself—remade the American corporation and launched a new style of management: meritocratic rather than democratic, and with income intensely concentrated at the very top.

First, companies changed how they fund their businesses. Midcentury firms reinvested the lion's share of their profits in their own activities, rather than returning them to shareholders or creditors. This practice allowed the firms to fund nearly all their business investments from internal resources rather than requiring new money raised on the capital markets. But as the broader economy financialized, firms began to raise operating capital by borrowing. All in all, publicly traded firms today retain only a small share of their earnings and fund less than a quarter of major new expenditures from past profits.

This change requires firms now to devote profits to repaying creditors, on a fixed schedule. Indeed, part of the point of debt financing (especially combined with stock buybacks) is to bind managers to produce the revenues needed to pay creditors and to prefer owners over other stakeholders. Top managers lost the discretion that a large stock and steady flow of retained earnings supports and faced new pressures to promote their firms' bottom lines, including in particular by squeezing payrolls for everyone below them.

Where the midcentury firm's insulation from the capital markets had been so effective that "separation of ownership and control" became the organizing ideal of midcentury management, the contemporary firm's capital structure makes management intensely accountable to activist investors.

Second, new legal technologies created the market for corporate control that takeover artists might deploy—routinely rather than just in exceptional cases—to discipline management that failed to maximize shareholder value. The discipline came through many mechanisms, including perhaps most importantly the leveraged buyout—an arrangement whereby an acquirer seeking to take over a firm uses the target firm's own assets to secure a loan to buy the target's shares. Beginning in the 1980s, leveraged buyouts acutely increased the pressure that potential takeovers placed on incumbent managers.

Law firms such as Wachtell, Lipton, Rosen & Katz and Skadden, Arps, Slate, Meagher & Flom developed the legal frameworks to implement activist investing on a massive scale. And investment banks such as Drexel Burnham Lambert and private equity firms such as Kohlberg Kravis Roberts & Company embraced and expanded the tactics of earlier corporate raiders, bringing corporate takeovers from the eccentric fringes of finance to Wall Street's charismatic center. The dollar volume of mergers and acquisitions in the United States—a good if rough overall measure of the shareholder activism— grew by over 200 percent between 1982 and 1987 (similar years in the business cycle) and then by nearly 500 percent again between 1988 and 1999. By 1990, one-third of the firms in the Fortune 500 had been targeted by a hostile takeover bid, and two-thirds had feared such a bid sufficiently to implement anti-takeover defenses.

Third, these financial and legal innovations spurred managerial innovations, through which firms displaced the democratic management technologies deployed at midcentury with the meritocratic technologies that dominate management today. The change in who draws the corporation's bottom line induced an immense, concrete, and practical change in the corporate workplace.

The market for corporate control cannot directly incentivize workers outside of a firm's top management. Investors are too far removed from the firm's internal operations to monitor or control these workers directly; indeed, this distance is what makes them investors rather than being managers themselves. At the same time, the market for corporate control creates exceptionally high-powered incentives for top managers: investors can monitor top managers' performance and apply both carrots (stock- and option-based pay packages) and sticks (the threat of being ousted) to induce a firm's leadership to maximize shareholder value. This logic casts managerial discretion among non-elite workers as a cost to shareholders, and at the same time casts managerial capacity among a firm's elite, if properly incentivized, as a benefit. The market for corporate control therefore induced precisely the innovations in managerial technology that displaced the midcentury regime's widely dispersed management function in favor of the present-day practice of concentrating management at the very top of flattened corporate hierarchies.

These interlocking innovations together transformed the American corporation, displacing democratic practices in favor of meritocratic hierarchy. Finance has remade management in its image, bringing the fetish for skill into nonfinancial firms. One might even say, speaking loosely, that management has itself become financialized.

Like the innovations that transformed finance, the cascading innovations behind the managerial revolution did not arise spontaneously. Instead, they were all—every one—generated from within meritocracy, by and for the newly available supply of super-skilled, Stakhanovite workers coming out of America's newly meritocratic schools and universities.

The financial instruments through which corporate raiders accomplish their takeovers, like the other financial innovations just described, required super-skilled finance workers in order to construct, price, and trade them. (It is no coincidence that the takeover boom coincided with the rise of traders at places such as Drexel Burnham Lambert.)

Moreover, the new legal technologies that created the market for corporate control required super-skilled lawyers to develop and deploy them. The law firms that most consequentially created and developed these innovations—Wachtell and Skadden—were both intensely meritocratic. At midcentury, they set themselves self-consciously apart from the aristocratic lawyering elite, by rejecting the forms of discrimination based on breeding and religion that incumbent firms then still deployed. Today, Wachtell has become the embodiment of now-meritocratic elite lawyering, famously employing only the very top graduates from the very best schools. The firms' closest competitors, moreover, all cultivate similarly meritocratic reputations and actively contend for the same legal talent.

Most important, a corporate raider cannot improve a target firm's economic performance or increase its stock price unless he can replace incumbent managers with expert and industrious substitutes. The entire conceit of shareholder activism depends on deploying the increased elite managerial capacity that gives corporate takeovers their economic foundation. It requires a ready supply of Stakhanovite, super-skilled top managers who are willing and able effectively to exercise the vast powers of command that running a firm directly (without relying on middle managers) requires.

It is therefore again no happenstance that the 1980s takeover boom coincided with rapid expansions and repositionings in the institutions that produce managerial capacity. Chief financial officers rose to prominence at just this time and brought the perspective of the financial markets inside their firms. And both the business schools that grant MBAs and the management consulting firms—most notably McKinsey, Bain & Company, and the Boston Consulting Group (BCG)—through which MBAs provide essential technical support to top managers in flattened corporate hierarchies experienced transformative growth.

Management consulting, in particular, changed almost unrecognizably. The consulting industry remained "fledgling at best" through the Second World War and fully embraced the leisured norms of the aristocratic elite. Even McKinsey remained an aristocratic outfit, not hiring its first Harvard MBA until 1953 and continuing to require its consultants to wear fedoras until President Kennedy stopped wearing his.

But then, as the midcentury economy faded, consulting commenced a campaign to secure its eliteness by performing it. In 1965 and 1966, McKinsey took out "help wanted" ads in the *New York Times* and *Time* magazine with the express purpose of generating thousands of applicants who might be turned down; and throughout the 1970s it applied ruthlessly productivity-driven analytic methods to its own business. In the same decade, the Boston Consulting Group's Bruce Henderson, a "famed elitist," advertised in the Harvard Business School student newspaper that BCG sought to hire "not just the run-of-that-mill but, instead, scholars—Rhodes Scholars, Marshall Scholars, Baker Scholars (the top 5 percent of the class)." Today, 25 percent of top business school graduates join elite consulting firms, and the leading topic of career-building panels at the schools is "Investment Banking vs. Consulting."

The talent that flooded management consulting took relentless aim at middle managers, openly seeking to "foment a stratification within companies and society," induced not through respectful application of "silver-haired industry experience but rather from the brilliance of its ideas and the obvious candlepower of the people explaining them, even if those people were twenty-eight years old." The consultants attacked middle management with a dizzying array of often branded and even proprietary analytic methods.

MIT's Sloan School of Management, working with the consulting arm of the Computer Sciences Corporation, developed a process called corporate "reengineering," which aspired to "break an organization down into its components parts and then put some of them together again to create a new machine." The remaining parts, left out of the new machine, typically consisted of middle managers. And many firms, including GTE, Apple, and Pacific Bell, expressly cited reengineering as responsible for their downsizings. McKinsey, for its part, championed "Overhead Value Analysis," which the firm expressly cast as a response to the midcentury corporation's excessive embrace of middle management. McKinsey admitted that its "process, though swift, is not painless. Since overhead expenses are typically 70% to 85% people-related and most savings come from work-force reductions [to nonproduction employees], cutting overhead does demand some wrenching decisions."

The management consultant's mantra remained staunchly meritocratic throughout, and this legitimated the job cuts. The consultants insisted, in the words of one historian, that "we are *not* all in this together; some pigs are smarter than other pigs and deserve more money." In this way, meritocratic management "contributed to the fiercer feel of today's capitalism." Super-skilled bankers, lawyers, and consultants stimulated the managerial innovations that themselves favored skill.

Finally, all these managerial innovations again have their roots in the skill profile of American executives. Meritocratic education has created a cadre of super-skilled workers who are able to run even large and complex firms without relying on elaborate hierarchies of middle managers and are willing to work with an intensity that prior elites would have found degrading. These workers have spawned the innovations in finance, law, and management that strip the managerial powers and incomes from ordinary workers and concentrate them in top executives.

Safeway, as it happens, exemplifies these recent developments in management also. The firm's character changed dramatically in 1986 when, despite a sharply rising stock price, rising dividends, and record earnings, it succumbed to a leveraged buyout. Safeway's new corporate statement of purpose, advertised in the lobby of its headquarters, displaced the old mottos in favor of a promise that Safeway would pursue "Targeted Returns on Current Investment."

Divisions of the firm were shuttered, closing stores (often in struggling communities) and costing jobs. When the entire Dallas division was closed, nearly nine thousand employees (with an average tenure of seventeen years) were fired. The firm's middle management was sharply depleted—Safeway fired many admittedly "very good" employees from its corporate headquarters and eventually paid out millions of dollars to settle wrongful termination suits.

Elite management came increasingly from outside the firm. Safeway's present CEO is trained as a certified public accountant and got the job on account of running a competitor that acquired Safeway through a merger, and his predecessor came to the firm after twenty years in the transportation and energy industries. Meanwhile, the firm's top managers became immensely rich. Safeway's CEO's annual compensation was increased by about 40 percent in the year after the buyout, and his bonus nearly tripled, from 40 to 110 percent of base pay. The pay rise proved permanent and in fact only increased over time. In 2014, Safeway's CEO received $8,982,429 in total compensation, nearly ten times what his predecessor in the 1960s was paid.

# WHY INNOVATION TODAY
# FAVORS SKILL

New technologies did not always favor skilled workers. When elite incomes still depended on capital, innovation was biased against skilled labor. The technologies that inaugurated the Industrial Revolution replaced artisanal production with factory methods that separated previously complex tasks into simple components, which might be routinized and performed by less elite workers. Skilled artisans understood this and resisted. At the end of the eighteenth century in Leeds, England, well-paid artisanal weavers saw that the increasing use of automated looms would displace them in favor of fewer, less skilled, low-wage workers. The weavers organized (coming to be known as Luddites) and petitioned against the "scribbling machines" in local newspapers. When their arguments failed to protect their jobs, they conducted a campaign of sabotage and even riots against the machine looms.

A technological bias against skill endured deep into industrialization, as "many of the major technological advances of the nineteenth century . . . substituted physical capital, raw materials, and unskilled labor, as a group, for highly skilled artisans." In gunmaking, for example, cheap lumber from American forests, combined with lathes, allowed gun manufacturers to replace the skilled workers who had previously hand-fitted gun stocks with unskilled mass production using prefabricated parts.

Nor were guns exceptional: "The butcher, baker, glassblower, shoemaker, and smith were also skilled artisans whose occupations were profoundly altered by the factory system, machinery, and mechanization." Indeed, innovation's bias against skilled artisans continued into the early twentieth century. In the 1910s, for example, the development of assembly lines allowed the Ford Motor Company to build cars without the artisan-mechanics who had previously dominated production.

By the middle of the twentieth century, when unionized factory labor began to hold its own against capital and to sustain middle-class affluence, equality's champions had come to welcome innovation. Midcentury thinkers commonly supposed that technological innovation would favor middle-class workers and divert income from capital to labor. Moreover, as Joseph Spengler wrote in a 1953 note for the *American Journal of Sociology*, they believed that "a decrease in the fraction of national income going to property, coupled with an increase in the wage-salary fraction, tends to be accompanied by a decrease in income inequality." When economic battle lines were drawn based on the dispute between capital and mid-skilled labor, equality's champions embraced innovation as their friend.

The recent histories of finance and management suggest why innovation has changed course and now opposes economic equality. In each case, a rising supply of superordinate labor, produced by newly meritocratic elite education, bent the arc of innovation toward the skills that those workers possess. When economic battle lines were redrawn around a new conflict between mid- and super-skilled workers, innovation changed course to favor skill and promote inequality.

The shift follows an intelligible inner logic. Innovators are not dispassionate but rather work in a social milieu and have human and economic interests. Their context drives which thoughts and ideas, from the immense set of imaginative possibility, they actually discover and then take off the drawing board to develop and implement. This applies especially to innovations that are deployed in production, which are by nature pursued not for knowledge's own sake (if such a thing were even possible), but rather in response to practical considerations and opportunities for profit.

Interested innovators adjust the technologies that they invent to suit economic background conditions, including in particular the resource base that their society possesses—the broad set of assets that new technologies might exploit. This has been so from the very earliest days of innovation, indeed since the invention of agriculture. In the first agrarian economies, for example, a society in an arid country might develop drip irrigation, while a society with numerous rivers might develop paddy field farming. Later the abundance of slave labor in the ancient world is often said to help explain why even very advanced societies never industrialized. (Hero of Alexandria even devised a mechanism by which steam might spin a ball, but no one deployed this technology in productive engines.) And more recently, societies in which labor was scarce relative to land (such as the United States) developed very different agricultural techniques from societies in which land was scarce relative to labor (such as Japan).

One important resource that every society possesses is the skill and industry—the human capital—of its workers. Indeed, after millennia in which both wealth and economic production were dominated by land, and perhaps a century in which they were dominated by industrial machines, human capital has become the greatest source of economic wealth in the rich nations of the world. And just as the path of innovation once adjusted to suit society's natural or physical resources, so it now adjusts to suit society's human resources, and in particular the skill profile of the society's workforce.

The Industrial Revolution's bias against skill—early industrial technology's tendency to replace artisanal with factory production—shows this effect in action. Over the first half of the nineteenth century, England witnessed an immense and utterly unprecedented migration of unskilled workers from the countryside (and from famine-stricken Ireland) into its cities. Between 1811 and 1911, Greater London grew from around 1 million to over 7 million inhabitants, Greater Manchester grew from around 400,000 to 2.5 million, Greater Birmingham from around 250,000 to 1.75 million, and Greater Liverpool from around 150,000 to 1.4 million.

The central innovations of industrial production all targeted and exploited (and at the same time stimulated) this new labor source. The new style of production used standardized outputs, composed of interchangeable parts, to fragment previously integrated manufacture into discrete steps. This allowed unskilled workers, doing simple repetitive tasks coordinated by industrial engineers, to make goods whose production previously required the integrated efforts of a skilled artisan. Along the way, the innovations displaced older artisanal methods and the highly skilled workers who once deployed them.

Early industrial technology's bias against skill therefore responded directly to the shape of the human resources that it engaged—to the balance of skilled and unskilled labor available in industrializing England—just as early agricultural technologies responded to the balance of natural water resources that they might engage.

Present-day innovation's overwhelming bias in favor of skilled workers reflects the same mechanism. Only now the incentives to innovate push in the opposite direction. The boom in college education beginning in the 1960s produced a steep increase in the supply of skills, and the subsequent (and still ongoing) rise of an extraordinary concentration of training provided by the very top schools and universities produced a still steeper rise in super-elite skills and superordinate workers, capable of performing tasks of unprecedented complexity. At the same time, the transformation of social norms to celebrate hard work and deplore leisure primed newly super-skilled workers to deploy their training with intense industry. Moreover, the number and tenacity of the new elite workers allow technologies that mix with super-skilled labor to build on one another.

These trends provided economically fertile ground for new technologies that might productively be mixed with intensely effortful, super-skilled labor. Interested innovators responded to the new terrain—to the new labor supply that would make skill-biased innovations profitable. Their inventions focused on, and even fetishized, the newly available elite skills. At the same time, they neglected the more ordinary skills on which production had previously relied. Capital, naturally attracted to superordinate labor that it might exploit, funded the innovations. (The concentration of venture capital firms in Silicon Valley is just the most obvious instance of this phenomenon.)

Innovation acquired its now-famous bias in favor of skill not out of the blue, nor even on account of technology's necessary logic, but rather by tracking, even chasing, the new supply of skill that meritocratic education unleashed. The skilled-biased innovations—in finance and management, and also in retail, manufacturing, and across the economy—refocused production around super-skilled labor. This suppressed middle-class wages and increased elite ones. And meritocracy's trademark high-end inequality ensued.

Writing at the close of the Industrial Revolution, Sterling Bunnell remarked caustically that "highly skilled men need little outside of their tool chests" to be productive, while "cheap men need expensive jigs." Innovation's recent career turns this remark on its head. Today, not just in finance and management but across the broader economy, expensive workers induce innovators to invent jigs that make other workers cheap.

The growth in the supply of skill accelerated beginning in roughly 1970, as the post–World War II baby boom and the midcentury investment in college education intersected to produce an unprecedentedly large cohort of college graduates. The college wage premium unsurprisingly dropped precipitately in the subsequent decade, as the new supply of college skills outstripped the existing demand for them. But then, entering the 1980s, the wage premium took a surprising turn, increasing rapidly and almost without interruption through the present day. Moreover, the premium continued to rise steeply in subsequent decades, even as the relative supply of college skills also increased (with only a modest reduction in the pace of growth). This suggests a sudden, rapid increase in the demand for college skills, beginning roughly a decade after the sudden rise in the supply of college-educated workers. (An independent estimate finds that the demand for college skills grew more than one and a half times faster in the 1980s than over the previous four decades.)

The best explanation for this pattern—for the lagged timing of the rising demand for college skills—is that the rising supply of college-educated workers induced the innovations that would make their skills valuable and raise the wage premium that they enjoy.

These patterns and relationships replay themselves at the very top of the distribution also, in the premium captured by super-skilled workers with elite BAs or professional degrees. Meritocratic reforms at top universities, together with the elite's newfound embrace of industry instead of leisure, caused the supply of super-skilled labor to explode beginning in the early 1970s. Once again, the new supply initially suppressed the returns to super-skill, and the top 1 percent's income share reached its bottom not in the middle but rather at the very end of the midcentury era, falling from around 12 percent in the late 1960s to 10.4 percent in 1976. But then top incomes grew rapidly, beginning in the late 1970s and accelerating dramatically in the early and mid-1980s (so that by 1988, the top 1 percent's income share had increased by half to reach nearly 15 percent) and continuing to rise into the new millennium. The broader super-elite economy extends the microhistories of finance and management rehearsed earlier. The best explanation for this pattern, once again, is that the innovations that biased work and wages in favor of super-skills were induced by the new supply of super-skilled workers that the meritocratic revolution in elite education created.

Finally, international comparisons corroborate the historical lesson that connects skill-biased innovation to the rise of a super-skilled workforce. The division of labor into gloomy and glossy jobs is starker in the United States than in other rich countries, and elite education is more intensive and exceptional. Meritocratic inequalities at work and at school feed on each other.

Germany is, after the United States, the second-richest large country in the world, with a population of roughly eighty million and a GDP per capita of about $50,000. Indeed, the United States and Germany are (by one measure) the only two countries in the world with populations greater than fifty million and per capita GDPs greater than $50,000. But in spite of their being the only members of this exclusive club, the recent histories of education and work in Germany and in the United States have taken nearly opposite paths. The interconnected differences open a window into the relationship between training and labor, and in particular between elite education and the economic returns to super-skill.

On the one hand, U.S. and German education targets different populations by different means. The United States has concentrated its educational investments in an increasingly narrow elite. And it has delivered education increasingly in university settings, effectively eliminating workplace training. Germany, by contrast, has spread education increasingly broadly, over a larger and larger segment of its population. Moreover, all members of the broad German elite receive effectively equivalent educations: Germany has virtually no private schools or universities, and while there are elite faculties in the German public university system, there are virtually no exceptionally competitive or distinctively elite student bodies. Germany also provides intensive vocational training to those outside of the university-educated elite. Finally, the German state promotes egalitarian education from earliest childhood and backs its commitments by law. In Berlin, for example, the city government has gone so far as to enact an ordinance making free daycare available to all city residents and making elite daycare effectively illegal, by forbidding daycares from subjecting parents (no matter how rich) to surcharges greater than 90 euros a month.

On the other hand, American and German employers have in recent decades focused new investments and innovations on very different segments of the labor market. American firms allocate new investments in plants and machinery disproportionately to complement high-skilled workers. German firms, by contrast, channel new capital toward sectors in which unskilled or mid-skilled labor dominates production.

When a firm buys new equipment, this makes the workers who use that equipment more productive and therefore increases their wages. In this way, decisions about whether to invest in equipment used by mid-skilled or by super-skilled workers directly influence the pay of both types, and therefore also the wage premium that accompanies training and skill. Between just 1975 and 1991, for example, new investments—capital deepening—in manufacturing and retail in the United States increased the skill premium by about 8 percent. By contrast, capital deepening in these sectors decreased wage differentials in Germany. Overall, capital deepening in the United States is associated with increased wage dispersion and rising returns to skill, while in Germany it is associated with wage compression and falling returns to skill. Indeed, the effect was felt even in banking. American banks chase elite talent and have become some of the most economically unequal workplaces in the world. But in Germany, new investments in banking chased mid-skilled workers and decreased wage inequality in that sector by fully a third.

Adding other countries into the mix reinforces the connection between inequality at school and at work and reemphasizes that the U.S. elite's exceptional schooling and exceptional wages feed off of each other. Across developed economies, the college wage premium and the gap between elite and middle-class educational investments tend to rise and fall in tandem.* Where education concentrates training, firms focus investments on super-skilled workers and inflate the skill premium, and where education disperses training, firms focus investments on mid-skilled workers and reduce the skill premium. Meritocracy at school and meritocracy at work go together.

A meritocratic working elite, by its very existence, stimulates the demand for its own skills. The skill fetish that dominates the labor market today is a contingent and designed response to meritocratic developments in elite education. The elite then spends its enormous incomes on exceptional educations for its children, whose own skills induce further skill-biased innovations. And the cycle continues. One prominent commentator has gone so far as to speculate—more suggestively than literally—that "the Vietnam War draft laws and the high college enrollment rates of the baby boom cohorts . . . induced the development of computers." Simply put, glossy jobs were created in response to the emergence of super-educated workers who might do them.

Meritocratic inequality grows by feeding on itself.

## THE HUMAN RESOURCE CURSE

If society is a ladder, then opportunity to reach the top can be unequal in two ways.

First, a person's odds of reaching higher rungs can depend on the rung at which she starts. When meritocratic education concentrates training in children of rich parents and skews elite student bodies toward wealth, it damages

---

* A graphical representation of this pattern appears in Figure 11 on page 307.

equality of opportunity in just this way. Rich children exclude middle-class children from elite schools, and superordinate workers render mid-skilled workers redundant. Elite opportunities are middle-class obstacles, and the elite blocks the middle class on account of realizing rather than betraying meritocratic ideals.

Second, the value of any given climb depends on how far apart the rungs of the social and economic ladder lie—on how large the absolute differences of income and status across social classes actually are. It is one thing for a person to be confined to his birth rank in a narrowly compressed economic distribution, in which the classes lead materially and socially similar lives. It is quite another to be confined in a widely dispersed society, in which even adjacent ranks experience material and social conditions that render their lives mutually unrecognizable. When meritocracy polarizes work, replacing middle-class jobs with gloomy and glossy ones, it increases the separation between the rungs of the ladder. Not just individuals but entire castes come apart. This second development makes inequalities of opportunity in the first sense much worse.

The feedback loops that drive meritocratic inequality forward connect these two failures. The mechanisms through which meritocracy stretches the social and economic ladder, to increase the gaps between the rungs, also cause a person's chances of climbing to depend on where she starts. (The division between gloomy and glossy jobs causes elites to give their children the extraordinary investments needed to get the glossy jobs.) And the mechanisms through which meritocracy makes a person's chances of climbing the ladder depend on where she starts also drives the rungs of the ladder farther apart. (The rise of an elaborately educated elite induces innovations that bias work and income to favor the skills that this elite possesses.)

Together, these two effects have a devastating impact on absolute social mobility—the odds that a person will enjoy a greater income than her parents did. As with so many of meritocracy's burdens, the greatest decline is again concentrated in the broad middle class.

Virtually the entire generation born in 1940, which came of age during the postwar middle-class boom, grew richer than its parents. In this respect also, all of America resembled St. Clair Shores. A baby boomer had to be born into the richest tenth of households before her odds of becoming richer than her parents fell below nine in ten, and she had to be born into the richest 1 percent before her odds fell below half.

The generation born in 1980 faced a much bleaker future. Only the poor had a better than even chance of growing richer than their parents. Moreover, and crucially, the intergenerational decline in absolute mobility is by far biggest for children whose parents' incomes lie between roughly the 20th and roughly the 95th percentiles of the income distribution—that is, for the (very) broad middle class. This is the group whose opportunities were most expanded by open and democratic education at midcentury and whose outcomes most benefited from shared economic growth.* The broad middle class is also, of course, the group whose complaints of exclusion ring loudest and most discordantly today.

This lens focuses attention on the caste order that meritocratic inequality produces. Elite privilege and middle-class exclusion are not just individual but also, and essentially, collective affairs. The comprehensive divide described earlier in static terms also has a dynamic expression. When meritocracy guides innovation to favor meritocrats, the elite closes ranks. Exclusive education and the fetish for skill favor individual meritocrats, and the feedback loop between meritocracy's two movements favors the meritocratic elite as a class.

Deep social and economic forces drive this process forward. Inequality's critics commonly accuse elites, having got rich, of pulling the ladder of opportunity up behind them. But this is not quite accurate. At least, it does not capture the core objection to meritocratic inequality.

The critics are of course right that elite meritocrats are no more honorable than anyone else and therefore engage in all the familiar forms of self-dealing. But the principal mechanisms behind snowballing meritocratic inequality involve individually innocent choices—to educate children, to work industriously, and to innovate—that accumulate and feed on themselves, in ways that cause collective harm. Highlighting individual actions ignores the deeper structures within which people act. Emphasizing personal morality neglects politics.

A deeper, structural view now reveals that meritocratic inequality reenacts a familiar economic paradox, only in a novel setting.

Economists have long wondered why countries that are rich in natural

---

* A graphical representation of these trends appears in Figure 12 on page 308.

resources—such as oil, gold, or diamonds—are often less rich overall than countries with fewer resources. Part of the reason is that natural resources distort the economies of countries that are blessed with them. Such countries focus production on extractive industries, which get the resources through drilling, mining, and so on. These industries tend to concentrate wealth and power in a narrow caste of land and mineral owners, and they often also require a large class of oppressed labor to do the arduous and dangerous work of getting the wealth out of the earth.

Resource-rich countries therefore fail to invest in mass education and even suppress commerce and the professions, and they never develop a productive and dynamic middle class. They tend to develop undemocratic and even corrupt social and political institutions, designed to protect the private interests of their powerful elites at the expense of the public good. As a result, resource-rich countries grow less quickly than resource-poor ones—not always, but often enough that economists speak of a resource curse.

The feedback loops that drive meritocratic inequality forward present an unprecedented version of the resource curse. In the United States today, the cursed resource is not oil, gold, or diamonds, or any other kind of physical wealth, but rather human capital. The exceptional skills of superordinate workers distort economies that rely on them. Concentrated human capital induces innovations that refocus production on industries and jobs—finance, elite management—that use superordinate labor. And these industries concentrate wealth and power in an increasingly narrow caste of meritocratic workers, doing glossy jobs, who dominate a large class of subordinate workers doing gloomy jobs. They are in effect extractive industries, with the twist that they extract income not from natural wealth but rather from the human capital of the superordinate workers.

Meritocratic countries therefore also concentrate both education and commerce in a narrow elite, which closes ranks as ownership castes always do. The feedback loops between exclusive education and skill-biased innovation entrench and expand the elite's privilege and shrink and marginalize the middle class. The pathologies that familiarly plague natural-resource-rich societies—social and economic stratification, undemocratic politics, corruption, and low growth—all inexorably follow.

Meritocratic inequality casts a human resource curse.

# NINE

# THE MYTH OF MERIT

The word *meritocracy* is barely older than the practices that it describes. It was coined by the British sociologist Michael Young in his 1958 satire *The Rise of the Meritocracy*.

Young opposed meritocracy in scathing terms. *The Rise of the Meritocracy* is a cry of warning rather than a song of praise. A current of foreboding and even violence runs through the narrative. And Young himself regarded the book as a dystopian fantasy, along the lines of George Orwell's *1984* or, more immediately, Aldous Huxley's *Brave New World*.

Young imagined that meritocracy would use increasingly accurate and increasingly early tests for native intelligence ruthlessly to sort people into schools, universities, and eventually jobs. The sorting would produce a massive, stable, and complete social stratification by ability.

In this way, Young proposed, the most perfect formal equality of treatment—in which people of like native talent received like education, income, and status—would produce enormous substantive inequalities in the distribution of social and economic advantage. Ultimately, he warned, the inequalities would become too great for even meritocracy's ideological power to bear, producing revolutionary and often senseless violence.

Young was right to worry, it has turned out, although he worried about the wrong things. Believing in nature rather than nurture, he thought that even meritocrats would be born rather than made. This caused his fantasy to mistake the social technology that meritocratic inequality would employ. In fact, modern meritocracy operates not through more and more accurate testing for natural talent, deployed earlier and earlier, but rather through more and more intensive cultivation of nurtured talent, extending longer and longer.

Moreover, Young underestimated how pervasively meritocracy would transform society. He imagined that meritocracy might change the facts about how society allocates economic and social advantage without also changing the values—the moral and political ideals—by which the allocation of advantage is judged. And he did not see that meritocracy would bend the arc of innovation to favor the skills that it produced, so that meritocratic education and meritocratic work would come to rationalize and even require each other. Young underestimated both the powerful charisma that meritocracy would exert and the long shadow that meritocratic inequality would cast over economic, social, and ethical life.

Young's satire missed its mark by a mile. The term he introduced became widely embraced rather than reviled. And Young himself lamented this turn of events for all his life, even into the new millennium.

## NEW NORMS TO SUIT NEW FACTS

Epochal transformations cannot be criticized by deploying the norms of the old regime. Meritocracy has remade society so profoundly—launching interpenetrating upheavals at home and at work, in practical life and in the imagination—that the ideals concerning equality that Young inherited could not take the measure of the world that he imagined.

Present-day ideals concerning justice, entitlement, and even merit are all meritocracy's offspring and carry its genes inside them. Meritocracy has built a world that makes itself—in all its facets, including meritocratic inequality—seem practically and even morally necessary. This is the tyranny of no alternatives that makes the meritocracy trap so difficult to escape.

Coming to terms with the new facts that meritocracy has created—including the peculiar patterns of meritocratic inequality—demands new norms, designed and structured with the meritocratic world in mind. It takes a new imaginative frame—one that acknowledges meritocracy's charisma—to clarify and to vindicate the complaints of meritocracy's discontents, and eventually to escape the meritocracy trap.

Young's efforts help to build the new frame, even if his express arguments against meritocracy cannot convincingly fill it. He was forced to invent the word meritocracy because the natural and familiar word for rule by the "most virtuous"—aristocracy—was already taken and had (as a result of centuries of political activism and ideological work) acquired a pejorative sense. Young therefore replaced the Greek root for "most virtuous" with the Latin root for "earn," and coined his term.

Both Young's concept and its construction followed historical precedents. George Bernard Shaw (whom Young much admired) had written about what he variously called "aristocratic democracy" or "democratic aristocracy," by which he meant that good government required hierarchy, but one based on capacity, not breeding. Slightly earlier, the Frenchman Émile Boutmy created the Grande École Sciences Po (attended by six of the past seven French presidents) specifically to shore up the elite against the crumbling of aristocratic prerogatives—so that, he said, the "upper classes [could] preserve their political hegemony . . . by invoking the rights of the most capable." And Thomas Jefferson (who would have been farther than Shaw from Young's Fabian English mind and less coldly cynical than Boutmy) had even earlier embraced a "natural aristocracy" whose grounds were not "wealth and birth" but rather "virtue and talent." Young's wordplay was less revolutionary and more an effort to name an existing mood—which sought to replace an aristocratic hierarchy that modern democratic capitalism had rendered debased and even ridiculous with another hierarchy that it might embrace.

Although the common imagination casts meritocracy and aristocracy as opposites, these origins of the word meritocracy reveal (as Young himself believed) that the two social orders are in fact close cousins. This background insight provides more powerful ammunition against meritocracy than Young's express reasoning. The analogy to aristocracy weaves all the threads of the argument against meritocratic inequality together into a powerful unified critique of the meritocratic worldview.

Meritocracy, like aristocracy, comprehensively isolates an elite caste from the rest of society and enables this caste to pass its advantage down through the generations. Meritocratic education privileges rich students, glossy jobs privilege educated workers, and the feedback loops between training and work ensure that the two forms of privilege support each other and grow together. This dynastic quality—which operates both at the level of the individual family and at the level of the elite caste—is the key to understanding where meritocracy has gone wrong.

Aristocratic dynasties, based on hereditary landedness, were viable when land was the most valuable economic asset and (in consequence) wealth naturally endured across generations. But as Roscoe Pound (the Nebraska-born dean of Harvard Law School) remarked in 1922, "Wealth, in a commercial age, is made up largely of promises," including especially the promises contained in labor contracts. And the human capital that underwrites the value of labor must be arduously rebuilt in each new generation.

The legal regimes that had sustained aristocratic dynasties in the ancien régime—including primogeniture (which kept estates concentrated in single owners) and the fee tail (which kept estates within families)—were inadequate to these new conditions. Additional factors—inheritance taxes and wars (which confiscate and destroy physical wealth)—piled atop the structural shift and helped to speed aristocracy's demise. Land lost its value, aristocratic families lacked the skill and flexibility to adjust to new conditions, and bourgeois states eroded whatever vestiges of aristocratic legacies remained.

Now, meritocracy renovates the dynastic impulse for this new world. Meritocratic education passes human capital down through the generations, and elite training additionally grooms each new generation to resist indolence and decadence and instead to husband its caste. Elite schools and firms police caste to establish, in effect, a meritocratic version of *Debrett's Peerage and Baronetage*. This time also, law backstops dynastic succession. Legal rules insulate children from their parents' debts, to prevent the current generation from mortgaging the human capital of the next, in a meritocratic version of the fee tail that once kept aristocratic lands in the family. And inheritance and gift taxes pass over the massive wealth transfers that parents make in favor of minor children, by investing in their schooling to build their human capital. The meritocratic inheritance is the contemporary equivalent of aristocratic breeding.

The meritocratic reconstruction of dynastic privilege may be less secure than the aristocratic one was (although history, because its gaze selects for longevity, gives aristocracy an appearance of stability that it did not possess in lived experience). It is certainly costlier to elites. Each new generation of meritocrats must recapture its privilege anew, through genuine hard work. And the meritocrats' incomes depend on exploiting not others but rather themselves.

But although this explains why elites might join the ranks of meritocracy's discontents, it does not render meritocratic inequality any less hierarchical or meritocrats any less inclined toward dynasty. The shift from aristocratic to meritocratic dynasties does not reflect a rejection of social hierarchy so much as an adaptation or friendly amendment, made in order to preserve hierarchy in the face of economic and social changes that rendered the aristocratic version unsustainable.

## DEBUNKING MERIT

If one had asked an aristocrat of the ancien régime why he was entitled to a disproportionate share of wealth, status, and power, he would have answered (following Aristotle) that he possessed the greatest virtue. He would, moreover, have offered this answer in good faith—and possibly even credibly, given the broader circumstances of his age.

The aristocrat had the right relationship to wealth and especially to land. An agrarian economy, in which immobile capital sustained no real growth, debased commerce (which was nearly zero-sum). At the same time, this economic regime required that land be administered for the long term rather than exploited for present gain. The dynastic place of the land (including through the legal structures associated with entailment) ensured that each generation of aristocrats would take the long view, husbanding its land in "the interests of posterity, as embodied in their own family."

The aristocrat also, as this formulation suggests, aptly balanced loyalty to family and loyalty to the broader nation (at least in theory). A society that was scaling up—from local, almost clan-based social organization to the nation-state and even the multinational empire—needed a bridging institution that might expand formerly local varieties of social solidarity to operate across larger and larger social and physical distances. The aristocratic conflation of family and nation provided exactly the required bridge. (The bridge casts its shadow even into the present, for example in the use of the word *domestic* to refer to both household and national affairs).

Finally, aristocratic manners reliably navigated the transition from personal to impersonal governance. As society scaled up, administration necessarily grew detached from the personal charisma of individual leaders, slowly acquiring the impersonal authority of bureaucratic rationality. Courtly manners provided an intermediate administrative style to broker the transition—detached from individuals but without requiring the elaborate institutions of training and professional certification that would eventually confer bureaucratic authority but did not yet exist.

Aristocracy's self-conception as rule by the virtuous seems incredible today, of course. Partly, a rising commitment to equality of opportunity condemned the unfairness of the birthright lottery that inevitably ensues when heredity determines caste. Much more important, the bourgeois revolutions and the rise of a commercial economy reframed the aristocratic virtues as at best absurd and at worst debased. Stubborn conservatism about land impedes growth in an economy based on exchange, innovation, and skilled labor. Obsession with pedigree becomes self-serving in a society that frames membership in terms of a nation or even an ideal. And courtliness and etiquette appear amateurish and even incompetent where intense training and immense skill underwrite effortful and expert administration.

Aristocrats came to be mocked and disparaged, for precisely the character traits that once underwrote their authority. By the start of the seventeenth century, Cervantes could cast chivalry as ridiculous, and toward the century's end, La Rochefoucauld would skewer aristocratic vanity and greed. The aristocracy fared much worse in the revolutions of the eighteenth and nineteenth centuries, of course. And in the twentieth, an increasingly confident disdain for aristocracy came to pervade social and economic life, and the aristocratic virtues themselves were reframed as phony and corrupt. Corporate raiders sneeringly targeted firms run by the "third-generation Yale man." Ivy League admissions officers became no longer content to admit the "happy bottom quarter" of old-money students from aristocratic prep schools. Brewster's observation that even the privileged had come to prefer advancing on merit rather than breeding gave the Ivy League's seal of approval to an already completed revolution.

Meritocrats displaced aristocrats; and meritocracy's charisma explains why the aristocratic conception of virtue seems incredible today. Intense training and bureaucratic rationality have usurped breeding and mannerliness, democratic accountability has usurped patrician solicitude, and, above all, human capital has usurped land. The meritocratic virtues have become so dominant that they appear, especially to the elite, to articulate a natural and even necessary conception of human excellence—as fixed as the conception that once dominated aristocratic life.

But virtues almost always depend on context for validation. In some instances, a moment's reflection makes this clear. The athletic skill of a baseball pitcher is like this: obviously an artifact of the game that frames it, unsuited to other games, and worthless if the frame changes too dramatically or disappears altogether. The aristocratic virtues depended on context less obviously but not in the end any less completely, and they similarly became worthless (or worse) when the social and economic frame changed.

As the wheel makes another turn, the meritocratic virtues face a similar fate. Indeed, today's meritocratic elite strikingly resemble the baseball pitcher. Certainly, the training and capacities that make superordinate workers immensely productive in the present world would not have much value in a society of hunter-gatherers, or, for that matter, in a society devoted to subsistence agriculture, or to craft production on the early modern model, or even to industrial production on the model that dominated rich nations between the invention of Watt's steam engine and the middle of the twentieth century.

Moreover, one need not look so far afield to see that the value of the meritocratic virtues depends on context not just generally but in fact on a very particular context. Both the educations that now create elite skills and the forms of production that make these skills so valuable on the contemporary labor market can exist only at the end of a long cycle of feedback loops in which elite training and the skill fetish reciprocally encourage each other. Elite skills can exist and can command elite incomes only by sitting atop massive antecedent economic inequality. The meritocratic virtues, that is, are artifacts of economic inequality in just the fashion in which the pitching virtues are artifacts of baseball.

This insight fundamentally reframes meritocratic inequality, by changing the literal meaning of merit itself. Most immediately, it demolishes the leading argument of equality's enemies: that meritocratic inequality, although unfortunate and perhaps even lamentable, must be tolerated on account of elite workers' entitlements to be paid a wage commensurate to what they produce. It turns out that—even accepting that top incomes reflect merit rather than rent seeking or fraud—superordinate labor can be so productive only where massive inequality has distorted education to concentrate training and work to fetishize elite skills. But even immense productivity cannot justify an inequality that it in fact derives from and depends on. The proposed justification travels a circle, and so justifies nothing.

Even if superordinate workers deserve their hard-won skills, they cannot possibly deserve the unequal contrivance that makes these skills so peculiarly economically valuable. And with this recognition, the most politically potent argument in favor of meritocratic inequality—the argument captured in Mankiw's principle of just deserts—simply melts away.

Moreover, and more profoundly, the recognition that the immense productivity that allows superordinate workers to command enormous incomes is itself an artifact of economic inequality casts doubt on the very idea of skill, or merit. The doubt may be articulated in two ways: by an abstract argument and through a parable.

The commonplace conception of a particular worker's product—her contribution to output—looks to the difference between total output with and without her labor, where everyone else works in exactly the same way regardless of her participation. This quantity represents the conventional measure of her merit. Markets fix wages according to this model of productivity, which allows superordinate workers to capture enormous incomes. The model explains why the inequality that these incomes produce is commonly considered meritocratic.

But a better—both fairer and more accurate—accounting of a worker's product asks a different question. This accounting looks to the difference between total output with and without her labor, but now allowing everyone else to reorganize production optimally in her absence. This alternative approach yields a smaller measure of the worker's product (because of the offset for the gains achieved by others reorganized in her absence). The difference between the two measures becomes especially great when the worker's presence changes patterns of production generally, including how everyone else works. And the alternative measure becomes especially compelling when the worker prevents others from reorganizing production optimally without her.

In such a case, the worker may be massively productive according to the commonplace measure but not productive at all—indeed, she may even have a negative product—according to the alternative measure. This will happen whenever the direct gains that she produces, with everyone else's work fixed alongside her, are exceeded by the indirect losses that she produces, by preventing others from working more productively (as they could do without her).

Today, the meritocratic elite, not individually but as a class, is in precisely this position. Superordinate labor is essential to production given the current state of technology, which causes the labor market to fetishize elite skills. This entails that total output is much greater when elites work than when the remaining less skilled workers attempt to deploy current technologies without the elite. Deskilled loan officers, for example, could not possibly manage modern home mortgage finance without super-skilled workers to construct and trade mortgage-backed securities. And the super-skilled workers who administer securitization expect pay commensurate to the gains from securitization, which they regard as specifically their product. Similarly, line workers in downsized firms stripped of their own managerial capacities now depend on top managers to coordinate production. And the elite executives who have monopolized the management function congratulate themselves on their vast and productive powers of command and again expect to be paid commensurately. Superordinate workers of all stripes therefore insist that the inequality that their wages produce is meritocratic.

But the technologies that now fetishize increasingly extreme skill are not natural and inevitable. Rather, they are induced by the increasing concentration of training in a narrower and narrower elite—as the feedback loops between elite education and skill-biased innovation reveal. And in this case, superordinate workers as a class prevent everyone else from working in the ways—using the alternative technologies—that would be optimal without them. Securitization in home mortgage finance undermined and eventually eliminated the mid-skilled loan officer. Elite super-managers undermined and eventually eliminated middle management.

The gains that elite workers produce in a meritocratic world—where inequality-induced innovation has biased production toward their peculiar skills—should therefore be discounted by the reduced productivity that these innovations impose on non-elite workers. The precise balance between gain and loss of course remains speculative. But the best evidence suggests that the elite's true product may be near zero. For all its innovations, modern finance seems not to have reduced the total transaction costs of financial intermediation or to have reduced the share of fundamental economic risk borne by the median household, for example. And modern management seems not to have improved the overall performance of American firms (although it may have increased returns specifically to investors). More generally, rising meritocratic inequality has not been accompanied by accelerating economic growth or increasing productivity.

A parable presents the same argument less carefully but perhaps more vividly. Imagine that a society is composed of farmers, who are nurturing and cooperative, and warriors, who are cunning and strong. For decades, the society lives in prosperous harmony with its neighbors, as farmers raise crops and warriors keep the peace, and both do well. Then, one day, some warriors commence a border skirmish and, through a stream of provocations, steadily escalate hostilities until eventually harmony has been replaced by pervasive and constant warfare.

Once the society has adopted a war footing, the farmers become increasingly unproductive and the warriors increasingly essential to preserving safety and welfare. The warriors now claim disproportionate status, wealth, and power, on the ground that they deserve private advantages commensurate to their disproportionate contributions to the public good. To which the farmers might answer that the warriors would not be so productive if they had not started the wars. The warriors' true product must be offset by the general costs of the war, and especially by its suppression of farming.

The snowball mechanism behind meritocratic inequality casts middle-class workers in the role of farmers and superordinate workers in the role of warriors. Only after the rich have concentrated training in their children do the technologies of production adjust to fetishize elite skills. And superordinate workers who wish to justify their immense incomes on account of their productive merit will, like the warriors from the parable, falter over the observation that the elite would not be so exceptionally productive if it had not, through the intensive education it gives to its children, started the training war and set its consequences in motion. Like the warriors, the elite's true product must be offset by the costs of meritocratic inequality, and especially by meritocracy's suppression (through inducing innovation that fetishizes skill) of mid-skilled, middle-class production.

This raises a final and fatal analogy between contemporary meritocracy and the aristocracy of the ancien régime. It is easy to forget that aristocracy was, within the social and moral frames of its time, true to its name—it connected caste to a conception of virtue or excellence, and aristocratic elites disproportionately and indeed almost exclusively possessed virtue, so conceived. The ancien régime was discredited in the end not so much because aristocratic notions of heredity created a birthright lottery that violated equality of opportunity, but rather because the bourgeois revolutions unmasked the aristocratic conception of excellence and virtue as at best ridiculous and in fact a sham.

It is equally easy to accept the conception of merit at the heart of contemporary meritocracy as capturing genuine social contribution and real achievement. But the earlier accounts of training concentration and skill fetishism and of the ways in which the feedback loops between them constitute meritocratic inequality as snowball inequality unmask this conceit. The meritocratic achievement commonly celebrated today, no less than the aristocratic virtue acclaimed in the ancien régime, is a sham.

The problem with economic inequality is not, as progressives commonly propose, that elites use force or fraud or some other form of bad faith to inflate their incomes in excess of their merit. Nor is the problem, as progressives also say, that elites have not earned the training (from parents, schools, and colleges) behind the skills and dispositions that superordinate labor requires. Indeed, no version of the thought that economic life strays from true meritocracy captures the basic wrong in rising economic inequality.

Meritocratic inequality is wrong on account of meritocracy itself—even and indeed especially when fully realized—and the concept of merit is the taproot of the wrong. What is conventionally called merit is actually an ideological conceit, constructed to launder a fundamentally unjust allocation of advantage. Meritocracy is merely the most recent instance of the iron law of oligarchy. It is aristocracy's commercial and republican analog, renovated for a world in which prestige, wealth, and power derive not from land but from skill—the human capital of free workers.

## A COLOSSAL WRECK

These reflections transform the debate over economic inequality. They sidestep the difficult questions about individual desert, and they avoid the moralizing focus on private vices that befuddles meritocratic inequality's conventional progressive critics. Instead of attacking meritocrats, they attack the idea of merit itself. The new beginning sets the argument on a fresh path, which reaches a new and different conclusion.

Meritocracy—including the immense skill, effort, and industry of superordinate workers—increasingly clearly serves no one's interests. It renders the working and middle classes who once occupied the charismatic center of economic life surplus to economic requirements. It imposes idleness on the mass of citizens, whom it condemns to join a massive and growing lumpenproletariat. At the same time, meritocracy casts superordinate workers as rentiers of their own human capital, which they mix with their alienated labor, and it subjects rich children to the rigors and afflictions of ruthlessly instrumental elite education. Meritocratic inequality divides society into the useless and the used up.

Together, these patterns establish an effective but immensely costly mechanism for the dynastic transmission of caste: effective because they deny ordinary citizens a meaningful opportunity to join the elite, and costly because they draft the elite into a constant, exhausting, and insecure effort to preserve its caste. Along the way, meritocratic inequality undermines social solidarity and corrupts democratic self-government. Increasingly, meritocracy fails even to deliver economic growth. All these costs arise, moreover, not on account of private vices or even collective failures perfectly to realize the meritocratic ideal, but rather directly and specifically on account of meritocracy's structural commitments.

The meritocrat insists that all these immense costs—whose reality, and indeed whose origins in meritocracy she does not deny—must be borne on account of merit's moral footing: superordinate workers deserve incomes that reflect their immense skill and production; justice requires pay to track output and merit; and it is wrong to favor the less productive, less hardworking middle class over the more productive, harder-working rich. Meritocratic inequality must be accepted and should even be celebrated, notwithstanding all the distress that it imposes.

But the sheer size of meritocracy's burdens places such principled justifications of inequality—and the conception of merit at the heart of these justifications—under enormous pressure. And the conception of merit, once it is revealed as a sham, cannot withstand the pressure.

Meritocratic inequality's entire edifice—built, Ozymandias-like, on sand—comes tumbling down.

# CONCLUSION

## *What Should We Do?*

When meritocracy transformed economic inequality, it also transformed politics.

Equality's champions were slow to recognize the transformation, and they have still not fully understood it. This creates a political
opening, now filled by opportunists who instinctually sensed the change and
moved to exploit meritocracy's discontents.

Demagogues inflame middle-class resentments by railing against a corrupt establishment and attacking vulnerable outsiders. They promise,
through these attacks, to restore a mythical golden age. President Trump says
that abandoning the rule of law and deporting millions of undocumented
workers and families will Make America Great Again. Nigel Farage argues
that closing the border to the European Union will restore Britain's independence and self-respect. And German populists, seeking to recover "a thousand years of successful German history," accuse Angela Merkel of betraying
her country by admitting refugees.

Meanwhile, charlatans line up to sell a wearied elite cheap cures for deep
ills. Investment banks and other elite employers promise to restore work/life
balance by building on-site gyms and nap rooms, or paying for breast milk to
be shipped home from business trips, or even reimbursing the costs of

freezing eggs to extend fertility later into life. Colleges announce that they will fix the admissions frenzy by considering applicants' ethical and cooperative accomplishments, such as caring and communal engagement. And life coaches teach living in the present or promote New Year's resolutions to cut down on long hours rather than alcohol.

These promises are not really believed, even by those who for the moment embrace them. The rich and the rest both suspect, at the backs of their minds, that their self-professed advocates offer no real salvation and may even be playing them for fools.

A Trump-supporting businessman from St. Clair Shores discounted the president's promises and disdained his hard sell. And nearly half of Trump voters, surveyed after he won, expected that life in their communities would stay the same or get worse. Similarly, when the consulting firm Bain & Company recently asked more than a thousand elite workers what it takes to earn a promotion, a substantial majority, scorning work/life balance, answered "an unwavering commitment to long hours and constant work."

False prophets gain a foothold nevertheless because deeply discontented people care—often most and always first—about being heard and not just being helped. They will cling to the only ship that acknowledges the storm.

Populists may not restore the middle class's past glories, but they recognize that a form of life has been lost. They dignify the loss as a moral cost and place it at the center of their politics. And work/life programs may never achieve balance, but they recognize that superordinate workers yield alienated labor. They acknowledge that no amount of income can compensate a person for using herself up, for draining a resource that will in the end run dry.

Progressives cannot answer because they remain under meritocracy's thumb. They are captives who embrace their captor, through a sort of ideological Stockholm syndrome. As a result, progressives exacerbate problems that they do not even see.

When they focus on identity politics and poverty relief, progressives dismiss middle-class discontent as special pleading. For progressives, middle-class longing for the affluence and security that St. Clair Shores provided at midcentury—for unchallenged abundance—is just nostalgia for a form of life that is no longer viable, or even for lost (white, male) privilege. In effect, this tells the middle class that it cannot measure up.

And by focusing on purifying elite institutions of nonmeritocratic biases—on diversity and inclusion—progressives dismiss elite discontent as luxury's disappointment. For progressives, hypercompetitive admissions tournaments or Stakhanovite work hours become really wrong only when they discriminate against minorities or working mothers, or mask the operation of insider networks and cultural capital, rather than because they are simply, directly, and generally inhumane. In effect, this tells the elite to keep its nose to the grindstone in order to validate its privilege.

Both responses double down on meritocracy's most insulting and alienating elements. And progressives thereby drive the middle class into the arms of demagogues and the elite to resort to ineffectual gimmicks. When benevolent forces cannot see the despair that stares them in the face, politics turns dark.

Conventional views about how to cure economic inequality only compound the political problem.

Orthodox policy insists that economic redistribution is fundamentally a competitive affair: where a benefit can be achieved for the rest only by extracting a corresponding cost from the rich, and where the cost invariably exceeds the benefit. As Arthur Okun (who had served as chairman of Lyndon Johnson's Council of Economic Advisers) wrote in reflecting on the War on Poverty, the mechanisms of redistribution all carry money "from the rich to the poor in a leaky bucket." Some of the redistributed money "will simply disappear in transit, so the poor will not receive all the money that is taken from the rich."

This way of thinking insists that helping the middle class today requires hurting the elite—and that the hurt will necessarily exceed the help. Moreover, because the rich are few, the hurt must be concentrated. Poverty might be eliminated, even using leaky buckets, by imposing widely shared and individually small burdens on a large affluent class. The War on Poverty targeted no one and required no substantial sacrifices in St. Clair Shores. But high-end inequality cannot, by its nature, be reduced except through individually large assessments against the rich. A new War on Inequality, the common frame insists, cannot rebuild the middle class except by attacking the elite. Curing meritocratic inequality seems to require ravaging Palo Alto.

Orthodox opinion can neither muster the political will nor craft a policy to cure meritocratic inequality. Progressives inflame middle-class resentment and trigger elite resistance, while demagogues and charlatans monopolize and exploit meritocracy's discontents. Meritocratic inequality therefore induces not only deep discontent but also widespread pessimism, verging on despair.

When a recent book asked ten prominent economists (including four Nobel Prize winners) to predict what life will be like in a century, none expected economic inequality to recede; and several doubted society's capacity for "large-scale redistribution of income," because "those who are doing well will organize to protect what they have, including in ways that benefit them at the expense of the majority." A political scientist, after reviewing inequality across all of human experience, found only a single instance in which a society unwound concentrations of income and wealth as great as the United States suffers today without either losing a war or succumbing to a revolution. And a similar survey led a prominent historian to speculate that "only [an] all-out thermonuclear war might fundamentally reset the existing distribution of resources."

Nevertheless, in spite of all this, there are grounds for hope. The "single instance" of an orderly recovery from concentrated high-end inequality, it turns out, is the United States in the 1920s–1930s, which answered the Great Depression by adopting the New Deal framework that would eventually build the midcentury middle class. And human experience is anyway too limited to sustain iron laws (recorded history extends over only about fifty human life spans). Big things are still happening for the first time. And where the present is exceptional, what's past need not be prologue.

Most important, the orthodox frame is mistaken—about both politics and policy. Progressives can speak powerfully and directly to meritocracy's discontents. The meritocracy trap paints a much more compelling picture of middle-class frustrations and elite alienation than demagogues and life coaches can ever do.

This picture reveals that meritocracy has transformed not just inequality but also redistribution, so that it is no longer a competitive affair. Replenishing the middle class does not require draining the elite, and certainly not using leaky buckets. Instead, meritocracy's discontents give the rich and the rest a shared interest in dismantling inequality. Middle-class aspirations to recover lost income and status and elite aspirations to restore authentic freedom no longer compete but harmonize. The middle class and the elite are differently tormented, but by a single oppressor.

The rich and the rest cannot escape separately, but only together. To do this, they must dismantle meritocratic hierarchy and build democratic equality—a social and economic order that serves everyone and in which the status of each is valuable precisely *because* it is shared by all.

## TWO PATHS TO REFORM

Progressives have fought for an ideal like this before. In the ancien régime, kings and princes looked down on their subjects; and under slavery, and then Jim Crow, and in many ways still today, whites look down on people of color. Progressives know that democratic citizens look each other in the eye as equals. They also know, as abolitionists and civil rights campaigners emphasized, that this equality elevates everyone's humanity. Now progressives must apply this wisdom to economic life, to dismantle the meritocracy trap that consigns the rich and the rest to separate discontents and build an economy in which they can flourish together.

Unwinding meritocratic inequality is "the work of a civilization." It requires a comprehensive adjustment—to government, private associations, cultural habits, and individual consciousness—on a scale equivalent to the changes that built up meritocratic inequality to begin with. The meritocracy trap was constructed over generations and will take generations to dismantle. Nevertheless, studying the meritocracy trap shows reformers the way. Progressive reformers must take aim at each of the two mechanisms that produced meritocratic inequality. This basic insight lights two paths to reform.

First, education—now concentrated in the extravagantly trained children of rich parents—must become open and inclusive. Admissions must become less competitive, and training less all-consuming, even at the best schools and universities.

Second, work—now divided into gloomy and glossy jobs—must return mid-skilled labor to the center of economic production. Industry that is now concentrated in a superordinate working class must be dispersed widely across a broad middle class.

Of course, these precepts do not yield instructions for curing meritocratic inequality entirely. Like every generational project, the campaign to build democratic equality cannot be planned out in advance. Instead, it will require committed but also flexible and opportunistic action, on many fronts at once, in a movement that develops and adapts as it grows. It is a fool's errand to try to spell out a complete reform all in one place—in a policy wonk's checklist or even a politician's program—in advance of the first practical efforts to adopt any element of it. The two precepts are important not because they specify a reform agenda right through to its end, but because they tell campaigners where to begin, and because—by tackling meritocratic inequality at its roots—they show that meaningful progress is possible.

Education reformers should begin by leveraging the obvious unfairness of the status quo to their political and practical advantage, to attack meritocratic inequality head-on.

The meritocratic inheritance is at present entirely exempted from the estate taxes that normally apply to traditional bequests: the massive investments that rich parents make in their children's educations are simply not included in their estates. Moreover, private schools and colleges are taxed as if they were charities, devoted to the public interest: alumni donations are tax-deductible, and schools and colleges pay no taxes on income from their endowments.

These practices make meritocratic education in effect a tax shelter that only elites can exploit. Where parents' incomes and educations determine children's academic achievement, even purely meritocratic admissions fill elite schools and colleges with students whose parents also have elite degrees (even if not from the precise schools that their children attend).

Although elite schools and colleges are taxed as public charities, meritocratic inequality makes them functionally into exclusive clubs. The tax benefits that they enjoy are meritocratic analogs to the allowances that aristocracies once gave to princesses and princes. Middle-class families pay for elite educations that their own children will never receive.

The tax shelter, moreover, is massive. The meritocratic inheritance, for its

CONCLUSION 277

part, transfers roughly $10 million untaxed to each rich child. And in a recent year, Princeton University's tax exemption amounted to a subsidy of $105,000 per student, compared to public education spending of $12,300 per student at the State University of New Jersey at Rutgers and $2,400 per student at Essex County College in Newark. (Numbers like these lead cynics to call Harvard, Yale, and Princeton "hedge funds with universities attached.")

Finally, the shelter keeps growing. The ten largest university endowments now total over $180 billion, and they have in recent decades been growing at roughly 7 percent per year, which more than doubles the growth rate for the net wealth of U.S. households generally. Universities plan for the long haul: Yale, which built two residential colleges last year, expressly designed the new buildings to last forever. But if these rates of growth continue in the future, then inside of meritocracy's second century, the ten richest universities—even as they overwhelmingly educate the children of rich, well-educated parents—will own the entire country.

Something, literally, has to give.

These facts provide government with enormous leverage over elite schools and universities, including even—indeed especially—over the richest private colleges. (Princeton has in recent years derived as much as four-fifths of its total revenues from tax-free endowment income and tax-deductible alumni donations, and the top twenty universities on average derive a third of their revenues from these sources.) Reforms should use this leverage to break up the club, insisting that schools and universities should be taxed as charities only if they actually function as charities—that is, openly and inclusively to educate the broad public.

There are many ways to go about this. But the best is the most direct.

First, private schools and universities should lose their tax-exempt status unless they draw at least half of their students from families in the bottom two-thirds of the income distribution. And second, schools should be encouraged (including through public subsidies) to meet this requirement by expanding enrollments.

Together, these reforms would exchange meritocracy's exclusive, narrow, and profligately educated elite for an inclusive, broad, and yet still well-educated replacement. The reforms would spread the wealth that the meritocratic inheritance now concentrates, distributing "elite" education across a wider population and at the same time improving education generally by reducing the strain on resources outside the elite. In this way, they would dramatically shrink the educational gap between the rich and the rest.

The reforms' two prongs fit naturally together, as the second provides a road map to realizing the first. Elite education has become so extravagant that schools can afford to grow; and the schools that would need to grow the most (because their current students skew most toward wealth) are also the richest. The Ivy League could meet the condition for retaining not-for-profit status by doubling enrollments (drawing new students mostly from outside the elite) and still spend about as much per student as it did in 2000. Colleges generally could increase their enrollments by half and still spend roughly as much per student as they did in 1970. And private schools could double their enrollments and still have better student/teacher ratios than their public counterparts. Public funds paid to subsidize additional students would lend further support to already manageable growth. Certainly, the changes required today to make elite education inclusive are no greater than the revolution that elite schools and universities undertook by embracing meritocracy in the 1960s, and that then triggered meritocratic inequality's rise. Institutions once transformed may be transformed again.

Populists are already taking aim at private schooling, especially at elite universities (which they attack as hotbeds of liberalism and "political correctness"); and their efforts are beginning to succeed. After years in which similar proposals died in committee, a modest excise tax on the incomes of the very richest private universities became law as part of the most recent tax reform. Populists who say that colleges and universities are bad for America may have narrowly political motives, but a clear-eyed understanding of meritocratic inequality shows that they are not wrong.

Elites, for their part, should also support education reform. For all the financial subsidies that it bestows, the current regime leaves elites battered, bruised, and vulnerable. Extreme meritocratic competition imposes human costs on rich students, associated with the grinding and dehumanizing admissions tournament, that are increasingly unbearable. And the rigor of the tournament increasingly means that no child, no matter how elite her parents, is safe from elimination.

Reforms that made education inclusive by expanding elite student bodies would not require displacing anyone from the incumbent elite and would even (both inevitably and by design) modestly increase the number of rich students who get into competitive schools. (In this respect, the reforms model themselves on the reforms that brought women into elite universities by growing class sizes, so that adding women did not require excluding men.) Even a small increase in the number of places available to rich students can dramatically relax competition among rich applicants. And the increase to authentic freedom that the new breathing room affords is massively more valuable to elites than any associated decrease in the income or status conferred by degrees. Palo Alto would be transformed by inclusive education, but the change would on balance be benign—a relief and a blessing to the people who live there. The lesson of midcentury St. Clair Shores applies double in Palo Alto today: steady and true good is better than fleeting and false great.

Finally, although elite schools strenuously defend their tax exemptions against even the most modest incursions, this is a mistake. Inclusive education would reopen the pipelines through which schools and universities provided social mobility and rekindle the luster that even the most exclusive schools once held in the general imagination. The reforms would therefore actually advance the core mission of schools and colleges. And where something has to give—ten universities will never own all of America—these reforms would surely be more congenial to educators than their most likely populist alternatives.

A parallel policy agenda that may be pursued at the same time aims to reform work—to rebalance production away from superordinate and toward middle-class labor. The most direct way to promote middle-class labor is to promote ways of making goods and services that favor mid-skilled workers. Economic policy at present entirely ignores this possibility; it should be placed front and center going forward.

Government pervasively seeks to influence what goods and services are produced in order to ensure that basic needs are met or that products are safe. Health care policy, for example, promotes access to medicines, legal regulations promote access to justice, rules about corporate governance protect investors, and financial regulations protect consumers against exploitation and the financial system against crises.

But all of these regulations also influence what jobs exist in the regulated industries and how workers in these industries are paid. This generally over-looked effect is enormously consequential. Health care, for example, accounts for roughly one-sixth of GDP and finance for nearly one-tenth; and management, finance, medicine, and law together employ perhaps half of the richest 1 percent of workers. Reforms that promote mid-skilled production in these areas would therefore go a substantial way to securing equality overall.

Models for promoting mid-skilled production already exist. In medicine, San Francisco's proposed universal health care plan emphasizes nurse-practitioners rather than doctors, and clinics in Oregon and Wisconsin are even experimenting with deploying dentists to screen for health problems ordinarily diagnosed by doctors. In law, Washington State is experimenting with using mid-skilled special-purpose legal technicians rather than super-skilled JD lawyers to deliver routine legal services. In finance, regulations that limit exotic financial engineering and favor Main Street over Wall Street banks also shift finance jobs toward mid-skilled workers. And in management, governance regimes that rein in the market for corporate control, or that promote long-term employment over subcontracting, disperse the management function and its returns across a broad class of middle managers.

Conventional debates about all of these reforms focus on what effects they will have on the quantity, quality, and price of goods and services. Those are reasonable concerns. But the reforms also influence whether production is divided into gloomy and glossy jobs or unified around mid-skilled ones. Health care can be delivered by a few specialist doctors who deploy high-tech machines and deskilled technicians, or by a mass of mid-skilled GPs and nurse-practitioners. Which approach is best for patients of course matters. But even where health is at stake, whether one-sixth of the economy succumbs to meritocratic inequality or promotes democratic equality through mid-skilled work matters also. Indeed, it matters just as much.

Policymakers should therefore always attend to how their choices will impact the balance between elite and middle-class jobs. A mandatory review of this impact—an analog to the existing requirement that all new federal regulations must be subjected to a cost/benefit analysis—would help to promote and to coordinate these piecemeal reforms. It might even promote equality to simplify the regulatory process itself, as increasing evidence suggests that elaborate administrative procedures increase the influence that the rich have over the regulatory outcomes that the procedures produce.

A second reform should use taxes to encourage employers to create mid-skilled jobs. The existing tax structure—incredibly—actively promotes meritocratic inequality, by encouraging employers to displace mid-skilled in favor of super-skilled workers. A simple reform to the payroll tax would reverse these incentives, to favor mid-skilled, middle-class workers. The reformed payroll tax would also raise new revenues, and some of these might be deployed to generate further incentives for creating new middle-class jobs.

The federal payroll tax—in particular, the 12.4 percent tax on a person's first $132,900 of wages that funds Social Security—is starkly regressive, on account of the cap on the amount of a person's income to which it applies. Over much of the past half century, the regressiveness of the payroll tax has exceeded the progressiveness of the income tax, and this pattern entails that federal wage taxes burden lower-middle-class workers at effectively the same marginal rates as millionaires and burden upper-middle-class workers at significantly higher rates. The effect has been durable and large. Over the decades that produced meritocratic inequality, a married couple in which each partner earned the equivalent of about $100,000 (in 2018 dollars) could easily have faced the very highest aggregate marginal federal tax rate, with both capital income and income from superordinate labor often facing marginal tax rates that were only half as high. Overall, the existing tax structure makes middle-class labor the single most highly taxed factor of production in the entire economy.

A simple example illustrates the special burden that the payroll tax imposes specifically on middle-class labor. If a bank deploys midcentury financial technologies to issue home mortgages using twenty mid-skilled loan officers who each earn $100,000 per year, this costs the bank and the workers, taken together, $306,000 in payroll taxes. By contrast, if the bank were to switch to the current mode of production and displace the mid-skilled loan officers with a single Wall Street trader who earns $2 million, this would cost the bank and the trader only about $90,000. Where two technologies of production are economically equivalent, but one requires twenty mid-skilled workers while the other requires one super-skilled worker, the mid-skilled approach currently faces an average payroll tax rate over 10 percentage points higher than the meritocratic approach, which produces an aggregate payroll tax burden over three times as great.

The payroll tax, in other words, substantially suppresses mid-skilled employment and wages and fosters super-skilled employment and wages. (Indeed, if the super-skilled worker can get capital gains treatment for her income, by styling it as founder's shares or carried interest, the income tax adds a further bias, on the order of 20 percentage points.) Once again, middle-class workers subsidize superordinate jobs that they will never get.

Eliminating the income cap on the Social Security payroll tax would promote middle-class work. The new taxes would eliminate the present regime's substantial subsidy for production that deploys super-skilled rather than mid-skilled labor. They would therefore immediately reduce the appeal of organizing production around super-skilled workers and increase the appeal of organizing production around mid-skilled workers.

Eliminating the cap would also generate revenue. It is unclear just how much revenue would be raised, as the reform would influence both the labor market in particular and the economy in general. No fully dynamic model that takes all of these influences into account exists, but the Congressional Budget Office has built several semi-dynamic models. These predict that eliminating the cap would at once raise between $150 billion and $200 billion in new revenue and would in the long run increase payroll tax revenues by 1.1 percent of GDP.

These are large sums. They amount, for example, to roughly sixty times the total budget of the Department of Labor's Employment and Training Administration in recent years (and roughly ninety times its 2018 budget), and they amount to about one-third of the total budgets of all (public and private) U.S. colleges and universities.

Government might spend these additional revenues further to promote middle-class jobs. The optimal pattern of expenditures would require close study and experimentation. But imagine, by way of illustration, devoting half of the money to creating mid-skill jobs, by paying wage subsidies to employers who hire mid-skilled, middle-class workers, and allocating the other half to funding the expansion of private school and university student bodies required to make education open and inclusive. Combining the wage subsidies with a higher minimum wage can help to prevent employers from capturing the subsidies.

Wage subsidies are already gathering political support. Prominent political figures and businesspeople, including ones conventionally considered politically conservative, are warming to subsidies for middle-class wages. On the left, Senator Mark Warner has sponsored legislation to support middle-class jobs and wages, and the Center for American Progress's recently released Marshall Plan for America includes a proposal to create 4.4 million public-sector jobs, at a cost of roughly $150 billion per year. On the right, the leadership guru Peter Georgescu and Home Depot billionaire Ken Langone are actively campaigning for businesses to invest in workers and in the forms of production that make a middle-class workforce profitable. Georgescu even expressly backs federal wage subsidies.

Finally, the two pillars of this reform agenda arise directly out of the diagnosis of meritocratic inequality and fit closely together. They go to the heart of meritocratic inequality and, moreover, powerfully reinforce each other, to have a joint impact much greater than the sum of their parts. Together, they aim to commandeer the mechanisms that now drive meritocratic inequality forward and to shift these mechanisms into reverse.

Open and inclusive education would create a broader and less extravagant elite. The greater openness would at once increase social mobility into the elite and restore the avenues of opportunity that traditionally bound middle-class and elite Americans together. And the increased supply of educated workers would immediately reduce labor incomes and work hours in elite jobs, running all the way up the income scale.

At the same time, the payroll tax reform and wage subsidy would reverse the current tax preference for superordinate over middle-class labor and establish a clear preference for middle-class labor in its stead. A new demand would greet the surging supply of educated workers, especially in the broad middle of the skill distribution (where the current tax regime imposes the greatest tax burden).

The indirect effects of the two reforms would be greater still. Both reforms would give interested innovators an incentive to bend the arc of innovation away from technologies that favor superordinate workers and toward those that favor middle-class workers. Innovation would therefore further reduce the returns to extravagant skills and increase the returns to solid skills. This would reduce the appeal of elaborate training, making education still more open and inclusive. And a virtuous cycle of self-reinforcing equality would replace the snowballing inequality that meritocracy has produced.

Reforms to education and work, operating together and over time, can reestablish the middle class in its central role in economic and social life. The peculiar version of steady good that St. Clair Shores enjoyed at midcentury is of course lost to history. But the diagnosis of meritocratic inequality identifies a set of policies that put a twenty-first-century version of steady good— for all—back within reach.

## A NEW POLITICS OF DEMOCRATIC EQUALITY

In 1968—the last time the world experienced widespread unrest and rebellion against the status quo—radical students at the London School of Economics printed a poster that showed a cigar-smoking capitalist and a student fighting for control of a car with dollar and pound symbols inscribed on its headlights and "Strike Laws, Rent Increases, Student Repression" written on its license plate. The slogan on the poster read "Same Bosses, Same Fight."

The poster's slogan was a lie, or at best a fairy tale, only half believed even by its authors. The aristocratic regime that still prevailed in 1968 meant that rich students and poor workers did not have the same bosses and were decidedly not in the same fight. Rich students could still hope to join the leisure class, enjoying comfortable incomes as rentiers or at least organization men, while poor workers still suffered widespread deprivation at the hands of capital.

The middle class, having learned to hold its own against capital and prospering in the postwar boom, did not share the elite students' angst and was alternately bemused and put off. It might have been forgiven for suspecting that a part of the rich students' rebellion expressed an instinctual recognition, rising but as yet unconscious and inarticulate, that the meritocratic revolution then gathering steam would expose them to unwanted pressures— that meritocracy might not end well for the elite.

The poster's greatest irony is that its slogan, false when issued, would through these still unseen forces eventually be made true. Along the way, meritocracy would change the politics of economic inequality in fundamental ways. The transformation opens up new possibilities for an updated—and now apt—version of the grand alliance that the poster championed.

Today, meritocratic inequality benefits no one: neither the many whom meritocracy idles and thereby excludes from income and status, nor even the few whom meritocracy ensnares in a destructive tournament to exploit their human capital by yielding oppressively intense, pervasively alienated labor.

An opening therefore exists for a new politics to hear and to answer the real needs that demagogues, charlatans, and other false prophets now exploit. By unmasking merit as a sham, the diagnosis of meritocratic inequality pierces the ideologies that lead the elite to cling to its privilege and the middle class to direct its resentments at innocent outsiders. It is one thing for a person to suppress his humanity in order to protect real advantages; it is another to do so in the service of an illusion.

A clear-eyed view of meritocracy also shows that all meritocracy's discontents, although they appear unrelated, in fact share a common source—an excessive concentration of human capital and industry in an ever-narrowing elite that condemns the rich to Stakhanovite overwork and the rest to imposed idleness. A more equal social and economic order would therefore make everyone—both the rich and the rest—better off.

Moreover, democratic equality is the only cure for meritocracy's discontents. Meritocrats who hope to have their cake and to eat it too—who hope to reclaim their lost leisure and authentic freedom without sacrificing their income and status—are simply deceived. They ignore the grinding logic of meritocratic production—at their dire peril. Where human capital underwrites income and industry constitutes honor, there is simply no way for a person to dominate or overshadow others, as superordinate workers now do, and still remain true to herself. It is impossible to get rich off of human capital except by exploiting yourself and impoverishing your inner life. Just as citizens must each look the other in the eye in order to achieve their own civic self-respect, so workers must share income and industry in order to be free to become themselves. Meritocracy allows no route to domination besides through the destruction of the authentic self.

A more equal society benefits everyone. The elite can reclaim its freedom and leisure in exchange for a reduction of income and status that it can easily afford. Palo Alto, although it will be a little poorer, will get relief from burdens too intense to bear, and its still very rich residents will regain their liberty. At the same time, the middle class can get relief from enforced idleness, and renew its income and status, in exchange for letting go of resentments that anyway provide no satisfaction. St. Clair Shores will recover its wealth, restore its dignity, and regain its central place in the narrative of American life.

The right metaphor for redistribution today is not Okun's leaky bucket—a joint loss—but rather mutual gain. Where mature meritocracy produces universal discontent, democratic equality becomes a win-win deal—and a deal that requires cooperation between the rich and the rest, who can each escape the meritocracy trap only by working together.

Both groups benefit if they take the trade; and this makes the political pitch newly friendly to progressives.

Any victory will be long-fought and hard-won. It must be fought and won out of doors—by agitating and organizing—and not in the pages of a book. But a book can help to educate citizens to see what their true interests are and therefore what political movements they have reason to join. Meritocracy's bright shine blinds people to the ideological traps in which it ensnares them—creating false pride in the rich and false resentment in the rest, to obscure the harms that meritocratic inequality imposes on both groups. Reflection reveals the harms and, in this way, recommends equality to a broad spectrum of citizens, across the meritocratic divide. It also shows that the rich and the rest cannot escape the meritocracy trap except jointly—that although shallow advantage places them at odds, they can achieve their true interests only together.

To update an old slogan: the workers of the world—now both middle-class and superordinate—should unite. They have nothing to lose but their chains, and a whole world to win.

## ACKNOWLEDGMENTS

*The Meritocracy Trap* has been two decades in the writing, and I have accumulated innumerable debts of gratitude. It is impossible to list every one and difficult to repay any one. But that is no reason not to try.

I became interested in economic inequality—including in the peculiar problems that arise when inequality is built on human capital—while studying philosophy in graduate school under Bernard Williams, Derek Parfit, Ronald Dworkin, and G. A. Cohen. All had powerful and distinctive views about distributive justice. Probably more important, they all taught how difficult it is to think clearly about deep matters and how to get ideas to speak directly to lived experience. A little later, after I'd published some initial arguments about inequality, an exchange with Elizabeth Anderson persuaded me that these efforts had failed effectively to engage real life. The search for a better approach set me on the path that has led to this book.

That path itself has been anything but direct, and I have benefited from countless conversations with colleagues and friends, both at Yale and elsewhere, many of whom commented on early drafts. These include Muneer Ahmad, Anne Alstott, Ian Ayres, Monica Bell, Yochai Benkler, Phillip Bobbitt, Dani Botsman, Khiara Bridges, Steve Brill, Rick Brooks, John Buretta, Guido Calabresi, Jessica Cattelino, Bob Ellickson, Dan Esty, Crystal Feimster, Owen Fiss, James Forman, Robert Frank, Bryan Garsten, David Grewal, Oona Hathaway, Geneviève Helleringer, Robert Hockett, Michael Kades, Paul Kahn, Amy Kapczynski, Al Klevorick, Issa Kohler-Hausmann, Roy Kreitner, Doug Kysar, John Langbein, Marc Lipsitch, Zach Liscow, Yair Listokin, Ian

Malcolm, Benjamin Markovits, Inga Markovits, Julia Markovits, Rebecca Markovits, Richard Markovits, Stefanie Markovits, Noah Messing, Sam Moyn, David Owens, Przemek Palka, Ben Polak, Robert Post, Asher Price, Claire Priest, Jed Purdy, Aziz Rana, Rob Reich, Judith Resnik, Susan Rose-Ackerman, Scott Shapiro, Dan Sharfstein, Peter Schuck, Vicki Schultz, Reva Siegel, Tim Snyder, Kevin Stack, Tom Tyler, Rory Van Loo, Sharon Volckhausen, Philippe Wells, Leif Wenar, Patrick Wolff, Noah Zatz, and Taisu Zhang. Amy Chua and Jed Rubenfeld gave especially extensive and intensive help, and the book would (quite literally) not exist but for them.

In addition, I've presented the ideas in the book in many more formal settings, where questions improved both my presentation of the argument and often the argument itself. Venues that helped in this way include the American Constitution Society's Progressive Legal Scholarship Seminar; the Branford Money, Power, and Politics Series; the Bank of Japan; Ewha Women's University; the National University of Singapore Faculty of Law; the Interdisciplinary Center at Herzliya; the University of Tel Aviv Buchmann Faculty of Law; the Heidelberg Center for American Studies; the Universidad Pompeu Fabra; the Università di Bologna; the Centre for the Study of European Contract Law at the University of Amsterdam; the Humboldt-Universität zu Berlin; the Salon Polarkreis; the Berlin Inter-University Interdisciplinary Colloquium on Markets; the Recht im Kontext Seminar; the Yale Club of Chile; the Universidad de Chile Faculty of Law; the Money Talks Symposium at Yale; the Harvard Program in the Study of Capitalism; the James E. Rogers College of Law at the University of Arizona; the University of Arizona Center for Law and Philosophy; the Yale College Income Tax Assistance Project; the International University College of Turin; the Yale University Institution for Social and Policy Studies and Washington Center for Equitable Growth Conference on Inequality, Politics, and Prosperity; the Yale Law School Faculty Workshop; the Yale Law School commencement; the University of Toronto School of Law; the University of Texas School of Law; the American Constitution Society Conference on Law and Inequality; the Yale Law School alumni weekend; the Georgetown University Law Center; the Cegla Center; UCLA School of Law; Columbia Law School; the University of Texas Inequality and Human Rights Conference; Dartmouth College; Cornell Law School; the Yale College reunion; the

Seminario en Latinoamérica de Teoría Constitucional y Política; the Comenius Programme; the Fondazione Cariplo; the New York Institute for the Humanities; the NYU School of Law; Vanderbilt University Law School; the Conseil d'État; the Universidad de Buenos Aires Faculty of Law; the Federalist Society; the University of North Carolina School of Law; the Law and Political Economy Project; ETH Zurich and IAST Toulouse; the Humboldt-Universität Institut für Sozialwissenschaften; the Baldy Center at the University at Buffalo; the Northwestern University Pritzker School of Law; Brooklyn Law School; the Yale Law School First Generation Professionals; and the Italian Society of Law and Economics.

The participants in several seminars devoted to the penultimate draft of the book gave invaluable comments and suggestions as I was finishing the main task of writing. These include Giacomo Corneo, Felix Koch, Bertram Lomfeld, Christoph Möllers, Frauke Peter, Friedbert Rueb, and Jürgen Schupp at the Freie Universität Berlin; Oriana Bandiera, Lucy Barnes, Thorsten Bell, Richard Blundell (who suggested the book's title), Jeff King, Julian LeGrand, George Letsas, Philippa Malmgren, Claire Maxell, Avia Pasternak, Prince Saprai, and Paul Segal at University College London; Bruce Ackerman, David Brooks, Michael Graetz, Anthony Kronman, Rick Levin, Meira Levinson, Alec MacGillis, Jennifer Nedelsky, Alan Schwartz, John Witt, Portia Wu, and Gideon Yaffee at Yale Law School; and Emily Bazelon, Nicholas Dawidoff, Jacob Hacker, and Annie Murphy Paul at the New Haven reading group on inequality.

The Yale Law Library and its unmatched staff—including in particular Julian Aiken and Michelle Hudson—provided astonishing research support. And an absolutely exceptional group of research assistants assembled, evaluated, and organized mountains of data and other facts. These include: Yusef Al-Jarani, Matthew Ampleman, Molly Anderson, Kossi Anyinefa, Jessica Baker, Aaron Bartels-Swindells, Sarah Jane Bever-Chritton, Taly Bialostocki, Samuel M. Brill, John C. Calhoun, Michael Coenen, Ignacio Cofone, Jane Cooper, Lindsey Counts, Marcu DeWitt, Alexandra Eynon, Rhea Fernandes, Eric Fish, Edward Fox, Miguel Francisco de Figueiredo, Rueven Garrett, William Gaybrick, Adrian Gonzalez, Nathan Goralnik, Rohit Goyal, Casey Graetz, April Hu, Leora Kelman, Jeremy Kessler, David Kim, Daniel Knudsen, Dylan Kolhoff, Craig Konnoth, Chelsea Lane-Miller, Arthur Lau, Jeff Lingwall, Daniel Listwa, Catherine Logue, Lucas Mac-Clure, Marianna

Mao, Virginia McCalmont, Catherine McCarthy, Alex Mechanick, Marian Messing, Stratos Pahis, Jeremy Pilaar, Valida Prentice, Devin Race, Ravi Ramanathan, Conor Dwyer Reynolds, Eva Rigamonti, Rachel Rolnick, Claire Saint-Amour, Jackson Salovaara, Jonathan Sarnoff, George Shen, Erik Stegemiller, Emily Stolzenberg, Lilian Timmermann, Hong Tran, Jessica Vosburgh, Ting Wang, Megan Wright, Jeffery Zhang, Katherine Zhang, Carleen Zubrzycki. Two among this outstanding group especially stand out for their long and intense engagement with the book: Jeff Zhang at the beginning and middle of the work, and Catherine McCarthy at the end.

Yale Law School, and Deans Anthony Kronman, Harold Koh, Robert Post, and Heather Gerken, made intensive writing, extending over many years, possible; the Wissenschaftskolleg zu Berlin gave support for one year; and the British Library provided an open and congenial place to write and think over many, many shorter periods. Patty Milardo skillfully organized and nurtured my professional life throughout.

Tina Bennett, Tracy Fisher, Elizabeth Sheinkman, Fiona Baird, and Svetlana Katz have represented the book with grace and flair. Tina in particular took a speech and made it into a credible book proposal and then helped to take a rambling manuscript and make it into a book. I could not imagine a better agent.

Ann Godoff and Will Heyward at Penguin New York and Stuart Proffitt and Ben Sinyor at Penguin London edited the book with incredible care, skill, intelligence, and judgment. They spent many hours discussing the manuscript with me and many more reading and thinking about the argument. Their attentions remade my earlier efforts into something wholly new and dramatically better. Yuki Hirose vetted the manuscript with sympathetic care. And Casey Denis, Gail Brussel, Bruce Giffords, and the entire Penguin production crew made a physical book that is beautiful and, in its layout and visual language, enhances the book's ideas.

Finally, my wife, Sarah Bilston, read and helped to rewrite endless drafts, combining honest and even severe criticism with boundless kindness. Her voice is on every page. And at several crucial junctures, my three children (reversing the natural and proper order of things) set aside their own needs in order to help me to write.

Thank you all.

*Figures and Tables*

FIGURE 1

*Average Hours Worked per Week by Income Rank*
*(Ten-Year Moving Averages)*

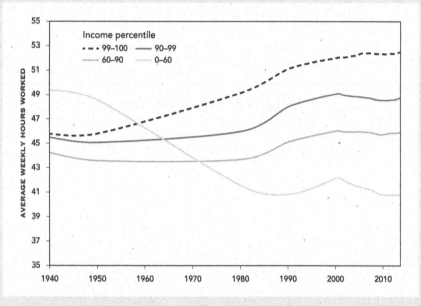

FIGURE 1 traces the association between income and industry over the past three-quarters of a century. Workers in the bottom 60 percent of the income distribution work nearly ten fewer hours per week today than they did in 1940, a decline of about 20 percent. Workers in the next 30 percent of the distribution (who lie between the 60th and the 90th percentiles) have worked effectively constant hours over this period. Work hours in the top tenth of the distribution, by contrast, have increased, with growing increases as incomes rise into the narrow elite. The top 1 percent in particular increased its work hours by nearly seven per week, which is more than any lower-income cohort. Uniquely, one-percenters also continued to increase their work hours even in the 2000s. The cumulative effects of this trend are enormous. At midcentury, one-percenters worked between three and four hours per week less than workers in the bottom 60 percent. To-day, they work roughly twelve hours per week more. The two components of this realignment (with the 1 percent working twelve hours more per week rather than three to four hours less per week) cumulate to roughly sixteen work hours, or two regulation workdays, per week. Finally, these numbers—because they report on only full-time, non-self-employed, prime-aged men—almost certainly understate the actual trends. Most important, they do not take into account trends in unemployment and especially labor force participation, which again shift work effort away from the middle class and toward the elite.

## FIGURE 2

### *Income Poverty, Consumption Poverty, and the Income Share of the Top 1 Percent (Five-Year Moving Averages)*

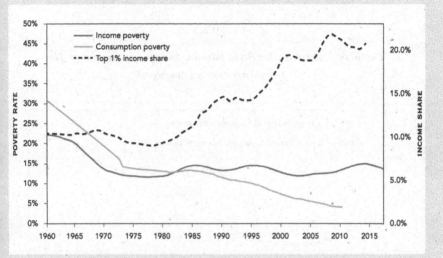

FIGURE 2 shows trends in income poverty and consumption poverty (on the left axis) and the income share of the top 1 percent (on the right axis) from 1960, at the center of the Great Compression, through the new millennium. The two solid gray lines that concern poverty both slope down. Although precise trends depend on how one counts, poverty has fallen to between about one-half and one-sixth of its 1960 levels. Income poverty rates have decreased from about 22.5 percent to about 12 percent. Consumption poverty rates have decreased from about 31 percent to less than 5 percent. By contrast, the dashed black line that concerns wealth slopes steeply up: the best-off 1 percent have roughly doubled their share of economic advantage since 1960—reflecting an absolute increase in the top 1 percent's income share from about 10 percent to about 20 percent.

## FIGURE 3

*Ratios of Representative High, Middle, and Low Incomes over Time
(Five-Year Moving Averages)*

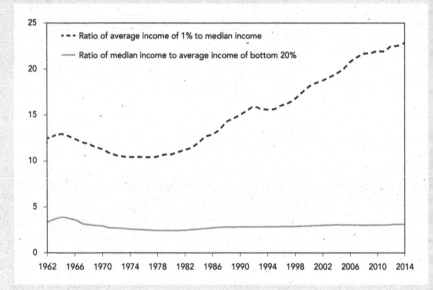

FIGURE 3 displays trends in the ratios of post-tax incomes at key points in the overall income distribution. The dark dashed line that slopes upward reports that the ratio of the average income of the top 1 percent to the income of the middle class (defined as the 50th percentile) has risen. The rich, that is, are getting richer relative to the middle class—they are leaving the middle class behind—and the average one-percenter today captures more than twenty times the median income, or nearly twice the multiple of his counterpart in the 1960s and 1970s. The light solid line reports the ratio of the median income to the average income of the poorest 20 percent. The line's slight downward slope overall reveals that the median earner captures a little less income relative to the poor today than at midcentury—that the poor and the middle class are converging.

**FIGURE 4**

*U.S. Top-End, Bottom-End, and Full Gini Coefficients over Time*
*(Five-Year Moving Averages)*

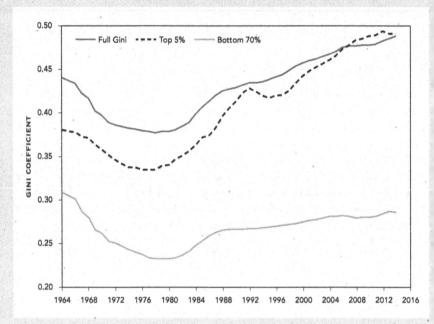

FIGURE 4 shows the Gini coefficients of the United States, calculated in three ways. The upward-sloping dark gray line displays the Gini for the entire U.S. economy. Its steep rise reflects the commonplace sense that inequality has shown a stark increase, from levels that resembled Norway in 1964 to levels that resemble India today. The light gray line is less familiar. It displays the Gini index for the bottom 70 percent of the U.S. income distribution, constructed not by redistributing any income but simply by discarding all income from the top 30 percent of households. The figure reveals that this bottom-end Gini has *fallen* (by about 10 percent) since midcentury, so that there has been a modest decrease in inequality across the bottom seven-tenths of the U.S. income distribution. Finally, the dashed black line with the steepest upward slope represents the Gini for the top 5 percent of the income distribution, now constructed by discarding all the income from the bottom 95 percent. This line shows that inequality *within the rich* has skyrocketed. Moreover, the difference between inequality within the large bottom and within the narrow top—the gap between black dashed and light gray lines—remained roughly steady between 1964 and 1984 but increased sharply beginning in 1984. Economic inequality's center of gravity is moving up the income distribution. Indeed, the black dashed and the dark gray lines have recently crossed: inequality within the rich now exceeds inequality in the overall economy, a result that would have been unimaginable at midcentury, when the central economic divide separated the poor from the middle class.

## FIGURE 5

### *Ratios of Education Expenditures by Income and Education*
### *(Five-Year Moving Averages)*

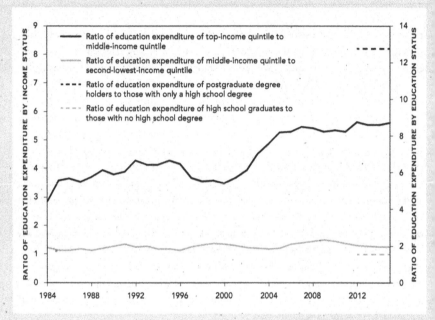

FIGURE 5 displays trends in the ratios of consumption expenditures specifically on education between rich and middle-class households on the one hand and between middle-class and poor households on the other. The figure reveals a massive increase in the investments that rich households make in children's education, relative to the investments made by the middle class. At the same time, investments made by middle-income households have not increased relative to investments made by poor households. A second, much briefer series—which reports ratios of education expenditures between super-educated and ordinarily educated households and between ordinarily educated and uneducated households—confirms the lesson of the first. The education series also selects out a narrower elite than the income series and, strikingly, reveals still more disproportionate educational investment, compared to the middle class.

Note the close correspondence between the expenditure ratios and the income ratios reported in Figure 3. In each case, a relatively stable midcentury order, in which the principal inequalities concerned differences between the middle class and the poor, gives way (beginning sometime in the 1980s) to a new order, in which the top separates itself from the middle, even as the middle and the bottom slowly converge.

## FIGURE 6

### 90/50 and 50/10 Income Achievement Gaps for Reading and Math

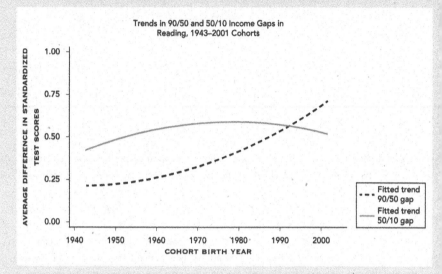

Trends in 90/50 and 50/10 Income Gaps in
Reading, 1943–2001 Cohorts

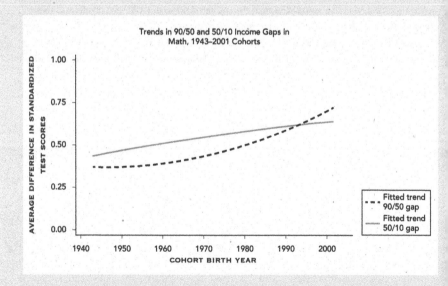

Trends in 90/50 and 50/10 Income Gaps in
Math, 1943–2001 Cohorts

FIGURE 6 (Top and Bottom), constructed by the sociologist Sean Reardon, reports the school achievement gaps for reading (top) and math (bottom) between the 90th and 50th percentiles of the income distribution on the one hand, and between the 50th and 10th percentiles on the other. This exercise reveals that the 90/50 gaps have been rising since midcentury and have been rising increasingly steeply since the early 1970s. The 50/10 gaps, by contrast, have been rising much more slowly and (for reading) have even begun to decline. The combined effect of the two trends entails that while at midcentury the 50/10 gaps roughly doubled the 90/50 gaps in reading and were about a third greater in math, by the mid-1990s the 90/50 gaps had caught up. Moreover, the 90/50 gaps have continued growing since, even as the 50/10 gaps have leveled off and even begun to fall. Today the school achievement gaps between rich and middle-class children are between a quarter and a third greater than the gaps between the middle class and the poor.

Note again the close correspondence between the achievement gaps and the income ratios reported in Figure 3. In each case, a relatively stable midcentury order, in which the principal inequalities concern differences between the middle class and the poor, gives way (beginning sometime in the 1980s) to a new order, in which the top separates itself from the middle, even as the middle and the bottom slowly converge.

FIGURE 7

### GDP Share, Employment Share, and Relative Income
### and Education for Finance, 1947–2005 (Five-Year Moving Averages)

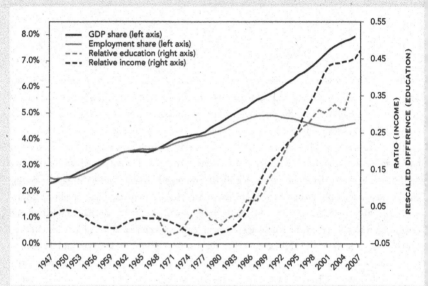

FIGURE 7 shows two pairs of trends—output and employment on the left axis and relative income and education on the right—in the finance sector over the past seventy years. From the end of the Second World War through the end of the 1970s, finance was a mid-skilled industry that grew by hiring more workers. Finance's shares of GDP and total employment grew together during this period. Moreover, and in line with their average productivity, finance-sector workers in this period were not appreciably better educated or paid than their private-sector counterparts. Then, from the 1980s onward, finance's share of GDP accelerated its growth, even as finance's employment share flattened and indeed began gently to decline. Furthermore, finance workers' rising relative productivity (as relatively fewer workers accounted for relatively more GDP) was unsurprisingly accompanied by their increasing relative education and relative income. Note, although the series is not included in the figure, that finance's share of total compensation paid rose steadily alongside its GDP share throughout both periods. Finance workers, in other words, did not take a bigger cut of their product. Instead, they became increasingly highly paid because they divided a stable slice of a growing pie among relatively fewer increasingly elite workers.

## FIGURE 8

### Percent Changes in Employment Shares for Routine and Fluid Skills

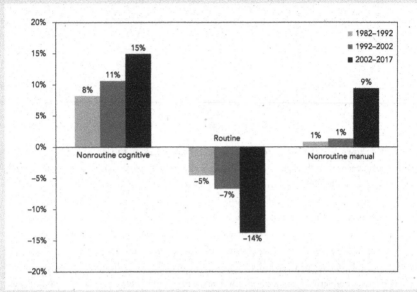

FIGURE 8, constructed by the economists Nir Jaimovich and Henry Siu, shows that each of the past three decades has seen a flight from mid-skilled routine-intensive work combined with a modest increase in manual, largely low-skilled fluid work and a massive increase in cognitive, high-skilled fluid work. Altogether, almost a quarter of the economy's mid-skilled jobs have disappeared since 1980, and the share of jobs allocated specifically and exclusively to high-skilled workers has increased by nearly a third.

## FIGURE 9

### *Earnings Segmentation by Education Level (Smoothed)*

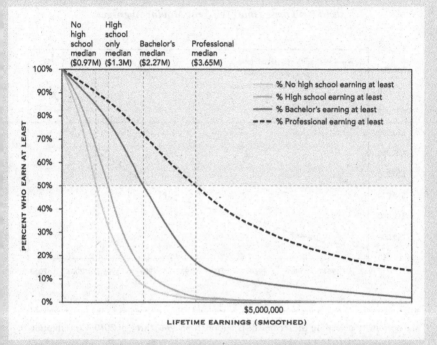

FIGURE 9 shows the segmentation of income according to education. The completeness of the segmentation amazes. Only 7.3 percent of workers without a high school degree and only 14.3 percent of workers with a high school degree only earn as much as the median college graduate. Just 1.3 percent of high school dropouts, just 2.4 percent of high-school-only workers, and just 17.2 percent of workers with a BA only earn as much as the median professional school graduate. These numbers reveal that uneducated and educated workers live in almost entirely separate worlds, which effectively never overlap. The least educated face a constant, demoralizing struggle to find work at all, while (contrary to popular stories of college graduates living in their parents' basements) the most educated enjoy full employment. And when they do find jobs, only about one worker in fifty from the bottom half of the educational distribution earns as much as the median worker from the top twentieth.

FIGURE 10

*Incomes of the Bottom 90 Percent and Per Capita Consumption
and Debt over Time (Ten-Year Moving Averages)*

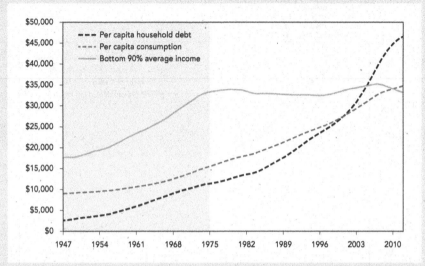

FIGURE 10 shows per capita consumption, household debt, and mean income for households in the bottom 90 percent of the income distribution, from 1947 through 2010. Consumption increased remarkably steadily over the seven decades depicted. The trends for income and borrowing, by contrast, each display a marked kink, and the kinks form a sort of mirror image. Mean income among the bottom 90 percent rose steadily (more or less in tandem with consumption) between 1947 and roughly 1975, at which point income stopped rising almost completely, even as consumption continued its smooth growth. Mean debt, by contrast, rose more slowly than rising incomes between 1947 and roughly 1975 and then, just a few years after incomes stopped growing, began a steep rise (more or less in tandem with still-rising consumption). The pattern is unmistakable: rising middle-class standards of living were once financed by growing middle-class incomes; then, beginning about 1975 and running through the present day, income stagnated and borrowing rose sharply. In the face of rising market inequality, the United States financed the lifestyle of its middle class not through redistribution, but rather through debt. Borrowing propped up consumption as income fell short. Credit issued to middle-class households is increasingly a thrift good, provided in the shadow of economic inequality and on the same basic model as payday lending.

## FIGURE 11

### The Returns to Skill and Unequal Investments in Education

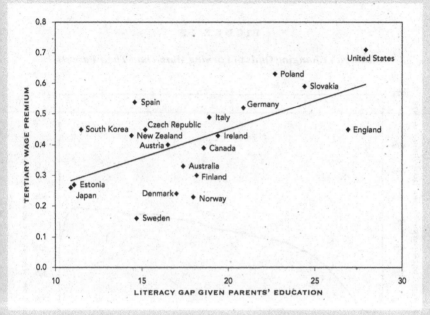

FIGURE 11 reports the relationship between the returns to skill and the inequality of educational investments across the OECD. The vertical axis displays the college wage premium, a straightforward measure of the economic returns to worker skill as measured by the ratio of the median hourly wages of workers with and without college degrees. The horizontal axis displays the effect of parents' status on children's skill (measured by an international test of facility in "understanding, using, reflecting on and engaging with written texts, in order to achieve one's goals, develop one's knowledge and potential, and participate in society"). Because parents' education correlates highly with investment in children's education, this is an excellent proxy for the degree of training concentration that a society produces. The striking correlation between the tertiary wage premium and the effect of parents' education on children's skill reveals that skill fetishism and training concentration vary across countries, not separately but together.

## FIGURE 12

### Children's Changing Odds of Earning More Than Their Parents

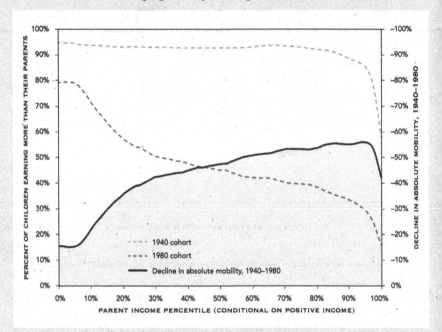

FIGURE 12 displays the percentage of children who earn more than their parents at midcentury and today, according to parents' income ranks. The dashed light gray line tracks this measure of social mobility at midcentury, for children born in 1940. Strikingly, virtually all of these children—right across the income distribution—came to earn more than their parents, with the only exception being children of the very top earners, for whom this test inevitably established a high bar. The dashed dark gray line tracks the same measure for children born in 1980. It is lower everywhere, simply on account of slower economic growth in recent decades. But it also has a very different shape. For children born in 1980, the odds of earning more than their parents fall swiftly as parental income ranks rise to escape poverty and then more or less plateau, until they fall swiftly again for children of the very richest parents (again on account of the high earnings bar that these parents set). Finally, the solid black line casts meritocratic inequality's effect on absolute mobility into sharp relief. The line reports the decline in absolute mobility across the two cohorts, again for every parental income rank. The decline is by far biggest for children whose parents' incomes fell between roughly the 20th and roughly the 95th percentiles of the income distribution—that is, for the (very) broad middle class whom wage stagnation has hit hardest.

## TABLE 1

### *Elites and Median Investments in Children's Education by Age*

| Phase of life | Elite investment | Median investment | Investment gap |
|---|---|---|---|
| preschool | 2 years of preschool at $15,000 per year | 1 year of preschool at $5,000 per year | $15,000 at age 3 $10,000 at age 4 |
| school years | 7 years of elementary school (K–6) at $25,000 per year | 7 years of elementary school (K–6) at $10,000 per year | $15,000 per year from ages 5–11 |
| | 6 years of middle and high school at $60,000 per year | 6 years of middle and high school at $10,000 per year | $50,000 per year from ages 12–17 |
| | 13 years of enrichment expenditures at $9,000 per year | 13 years of enrichment expenditures at $1,500 per year | $7,500 per year from ages 5–17 |
| college | 4 years at $90,000 per year | $0 The median American does not attend college. | $90,000 per year from ages 18–21 |
| graduate and professional school | 2 to 7 years at $90,000 per year | $0 The median American does not attend graduate or professional school. | $90,000 per year between ages 22 and 28 |

TABLE 1 rehearses, in rough numbers and counting conservatively, the difference between typical one-percenter and typical middle-class investments in human capital in each year of a child's life. The sums in the table surely understate the true difference between elite and ordinary educations. They capture only in-cash rather than in-kind contributions and measure only quantity and not quality. They do not allocate dollar values to the lower neonatal stress or safer neighborhoods or additional parental time and education that rich parents provide their children, for example, or to the peer effects of being surrounded by other elaborately trained children, or to the distinctive skill and effectiveness that rich and well-educated parents can bring to educating their children. But as long as the amounts are understood to represent rough quantities rather than a precise accounting, they vividly summarize the exceptional investments that the modern elite devotes to reproducing itself.

## TABLE 2

### Calculating the Meritocratic Inheritance

| Age of child at expenditure | Years from parents' death | Compound factor | | Expenditure gap ($) | Amount yielded at death ($) | |
|---|---|---|---|---|---|---|
| | | 8% | 6% | | 8% | 6% |
| 3 | 47 | 37.2 | 15.5 | 15,000 | 558,000 | 232,500 |
| 4 | 46 | 34.5 | 14.6 | 10,000 | 345,000 | 146,000 |
| 5 | 45 | 31.9 | 13.8 | 22,500 | 717,750 | 310,500 |
| 6 | 44 | 29.6 | 13.0 | 22,500 | 666,000 | 292,500 |
| 7 | 43 | 27.4 | 12.3 | 22,500 | 616,500 | 276,750 |
| 8 | 42 | 25.3 | 11.6 | 22,500 | 569,250 | 261,000 |
| 9 | 41 | 23.5 | 10.9 | 22,500 | 528,750 | 245,250 |
| 10 | 40 | 21.7 | 10.3 | 22,500 | 488,250 | 231,750 |
| 11 | 39 | 20.1 | 9.7 | 22,500 | 452,250 | 218,250 |
| 12 | 38 | 18.6 | 9.2 | 57,500 | 1,069,500 | 529,000 |
| 13 | 37 | 17.2 | 8.6 | 57,500 | 989,000 | 494,500 |
| 14 | 36 | 16.0 | 8.1 | 57,500 | 920,000 | 465,750 |
| 15 | 35 | 14.8 | 7.7 | 57,500 | 851,000 | 442,750 |
| 16 | 34 | 13.7 | 7.3 | 57,500 | 787,750 | 419,750 |
| 17 | 33 | 12.7 | 6.8 | 57,500 | 730,250 | 391,000 |
| 18 | 32 | 11.7 | 6.5 | 90,000 | 1,053,000 | 585,000 |
| 19 | 31 | 10.9 | 6.1 | 90,000 | 981,000 | 549,000 |
| 20 | 30 | 10.1 | 5.7 | 90,000 | 909,000 | 513,000 |
| 21 | 29 | 9.3 | 5.4 | 90,000 | 837,000 | 486,000 |
| 22 | 28 | 8.6 | 5.1 | 90,000 | 774,000 | 459,000 |
| 23 | 27 | 8.0 | 4.8 | 90,000 | 720,000 | 432,000 |
| 24 | 26 | 7.4 | 4.5 | 90,000 | 666,000 | 405,000 |
| 25 | 25 | 6.8 | 4.3 | 90,000 | 612,000 | 387,000 |
| Total equivalent inheritance | | | | | 16,841,250 | 8,773,250 |

TABLE 2 uses the numbers compiled in Table 1 to calculate the meritocratic inheritance, by computing what the distinctive expenditures devoted to elite education would sum up to if saved, invested, and then bequeathed to elite children on the death of their parents.

This requires making assumptions about how many years elite students spend in graduate and professional school and, more important, about when rich parents have children, when they die, and what rate of return they would get on investments. Where Table 1 reports a range of two to seven years in graduate and professional school, Table 2 uses a rough median of four years. In addition, the base case in Table 2 assumes that elites have children at thirty and die at eighty and would get an 8 percent annual rate of return. A robustness check assumes a lower 6 percent average rate of return.

These are conservative assumptions. The average age at first birth for a mother with a BA is roughly thirty; and the average life expectancy for Americans in the top 1 percent of the income distribution is roughly eighty-seven years for men and eighty-nine years for women. With dividends reinvested, the average annual nominal return for the S&P 500 from 1980 through 2018 was approximately 11.5 percent, and the average real rate of return was approximately 8 percent. Similarly, the average annual real rate of return for the entire U.S. stock market from 1926 to 2015, calculated using the CRSP 1–10 Index and the CPI-U Index, was 8.6 percent.

NOTES

## Introduction

ix **achievement rather than breeding:** This formulation closely tracks the definition given in the Oxford Dictionary of Sociology. See John Scott and Gordon Marshall, eds., *A Dictionary of Sociology*, 3rd ed., rev. (Oxford: Oxford Paperback Reference, 2009), 464 ("meritocracy"). Hereafter cited as Scott and Marshall, *A Dictionary of Sociology*.

ix **blocks the middle class from opportunity:** *Middle class* in these pages refers to the segment of the population that is neither poor nor inside the meritocratic elite and therefore includes many people who might, in other contexts, be called working class. This is not a definition so much as an implication of the book's overall argument. That is, the class that a person occupies depends on where he or she stands with respect to meritocratic inequality.

xi **a string of degrees along the way:** A BA in mathematics at Yale in 1991; an MSc in econometrics and mathematical economics at the London School of Economics in 1992; a BPhil and then a DPhil in philosophy at Oxford in 1994 and 1999; and a JD at Yale Law School in 2000. I spent two years at Harvard as a visiting graduate fellow but did not enroll toward a formal degree.

xi **"a haven for the world's most ambitious scholars":** "Mission, Vision, and History," Harvard College, accessed July 29, 2018, https://college.harvard.edu/about/mission-and-vision. Hereafter cited as "Mission, Vision, and History," Harvard College.

xi **"educate the citizens":** "Mission, Vision, and History," Harvard College.

xi **"probably the most elite work-society":** Karen Ho, *Liquidated: An Ethnography of Wall Street* (Durham, NC: Duke University Press, 2009), 39. Hereafter cited as Ho, *Liquidated*.

xi **the firm's website advertises:** "People and Culture," Goldman Sachs, accessed July 29, 2018, www.goldmansachs.com/who-we-are/people-and-culture/index.html; "Goldman Sachs Is Committed to Progress," Goldman Sachs, accessed July 29, 2018, www.goldmansachs.com/who-we-are/progress/.

xi **True to its Latin etymology:** See *Oxford English Dictionary*, s.v., "meritocracy, n.," Oxford University Press, March 2018, accessed July 29, 2018, www.oed.com/view/Entry/116806; and *Oxford English Dictionary*, s.v., "merit, n.," Oxford University Press, March 2018, accessed July 29, 2018, www.oed.com/view/Entry/11679. "Meritocracy" is an English formation from "merit," which we get from the Latin *meritum*, literally "that which is deserved."

xii **Bill Clinton:** "Yale's 309th Commencement," *YaleNews*, May 19, 2010, accessed July 29, 2018, https://news.yale.edu/2010/05/19/yales-309th-commencement.

xii **Joe Biden:** "Vice President Joe Biden to Be Yale's Class Day Speaker," *YaleNews*, May 4, 2008, accessed July 29, 2018, https://news.yale.edu/2015/04/08/vice-president-joe-biden-be-yale-s-class-day-speaker-0.

xii **Ruth Bader Ginsburg and Sonia Sotomayor:** Justices Ginsburg and Sotomayor gave unannounced speeches at the law school after receiving honorary degrees from the university.

xii **oldest continuously operating university in Europe:** Renaut Alain, "The Role of Universities in Developing a Democratic European Culture," in *The Heritage of European Universities*, ed. Nuria Sanz and Sjur Bergan (Strasbourg: Council of Europe Publishing, 2002), 119.

xii **old bottles to carry new wine:** *The New Revised Standard Version Bible* (Oxford: Oxford University Press, 1989). Hereafter cited as *The New Revised Standard Bible*. The Gospels say that when new wine is put into old bottles the bottles burst and perish and the wine spills out and is lost. See Matthew 9:14–17, Mark 2:21–22, and Luke 5:33–39. Meritocracy similarly bursts the social forms that it fills and spills out, destroying the inherited social order and undermining itself.

xiv **equality of opportunity:** In spite of this historical circumstance, and although even sophisticated political observers commonly conflate meritocracy and equality of opportunity, the abstract possibility that the two ideals may come apart has for some time been known to moral philosophers. Bernard Williams, "The Idea of Equality," in *Philosophy, Politics and Society* (Oxford: Basil Blackwell, 1969), 126 (discussing the example of the "warrior society"); Pierre Rosanvallon, *The Society of Equals*, trans. Arthur Goldhammer (Cambridge, MA: Harvard University Press, 2013), 254.

xiv **slow, devastating decline:** The phrase recalls Philip Larkin's "unbeatable slow machine that brings what you'll get." See Philip Larkin, "The Life with a Hole in It," in *The Complete Poems* (New York: Farrar, Straus & Giroux, 2012), 114. Hereafter cited as Larkin, *The Complete Poems*.

xv **adults would hold the office:** See U.S. Constitution, Article II, Section 1. For the framers' views about age and experience, see, e.g., Max Farrand, *The Records of the Federal Convention of 1787*, vol. 1, ed. Max Farrand (New Haven, CT: Yale University Press, 1911), 396. (George Mason argued that a requirement of twenty-five years of age was needed for the House because of his experience. "If interrogated [he would] be obliged to declare that his political opinions at the age of 21 were too crude and erroneous to merit an influence on public measures.") James Madison, *Federalist* No. 62. (The paper discusses why senators needed to be older than members of the House. Madison noted that senators need "greater extent of information and stability of character . . . that the senator should have reached a period of life most likely to supply these advantages." Madison, incidentally, also discusses a fear of powerful families trying to put their children into offices in a dynastic manner.) James Monroe, "Observations upon the

Proposed Plan of Federal Government. With an Attempt to Answer Some of the Principal Objections That Have Been Made to It," *Virginia Gazette*, April 2, 1788. (Monroe echoed the idea that the age requirement would help to prevent dynasties: "The Constitution has provided, that no person shall be eligible to the office, who is not thirty five years old; and in the course of nature very few fathers leave a son who has arrived to that age.")

xvi **"collective frenzy":** See Susan Sturm and Kinga Makovi, "Full Participation in the *Yale Law Journal*," report released in partnership with the *Yale Law Journal* (2015), 5, accessed July 29, 2018, www.yalelawjournal.org/files/FullParticipationintheYale LawJournal_e929dpx1.pdf. Hereafter cited as Sturm and Makovi, "Full Participation."

xvi **"collective anxiety":** See Sturm and Makovi, "Full Participation," 9.

xvi **in interlocking battalions:** William Shakespeare, *Hamlet, Prince of Denmark*, ed. Philip Edwards (Cambridge: Cambridge University Press, 1985), act 4, scene 5, lines 77–78 (p. 196).

xvii **"this American carnage":** Donald Trump, "The Inaugural Address," WhiteHouse.gov, January 20, 2017, accessed July 29, 2018, www.whitehouse.gov/briefings-statements/the-inaugural -address/. Hereafter cited as Trump, "The Inaugural Address." Other telling phrases from that text include: "[We've] subsidized the armies of other countries while allowing for the very sad depletion of our military"; "We've defended other nations' borders while refusing to defend our own"; "We've made other countries rich while the wealth, strength, and confidence of our country has disappeared over the horizon"; and "The wealth of our middle class has been ripped from their homes and then redistributed across the entire world."

xvii **"the forgotten men and women":** Trump, "The Inaugural Address."

xvii **feelings about the country:** When asked, "Regardless of how you plan to vote, do you think Trump's speech reflected the way you, personally, feel about things in the United States today or not?," 60 percent of whites without a BA said the speech "Reflected your feelings" while 34 percent said it "Did not reflect your feelings." Among whites with a BA, these shares were 39 and 53 percent respectively. See Greg Sargent, "This Is the Single Most Depressing Finding in Today's Polls Showing Trump Ahead," *Washington Post*, July 25, 2016, accessed July 29, 2018, www.washingtonpost.com/blogs/plum-line/wp/2016/07/25 /this-is-the-single-most-depressing-finding-in-todays-polls -showing-trump-ahead/.

xvii **universities are bad for America:** See "Sharp Partisan Divisions in Views of National Institutions," Pew Research Center, July 10, 2017, accessed July 29, 2018, www.people-press.org/2017/07/10 /sharp-partisan-divisions-in-views-of-national-institutions/.

xix **one for the rich and the other for the rest:** The idea that economic inequality has produced "two Americas" was a leading theme for the progressive politician John Edwards, pursued across two campaigns to become the Democratic Party's candidate for president and in a prominent speech accepting that party's 2004 nomination for vice president. See John Edwards, "Vice Presidential Nomination Speech," Democratic National Convention, Wells Fargo Center, Philadelphia, Pennsylvania, July 28, 2004, and John Edwards, "Two Americas" (speech), Reno Town Hall, June 23, 2007.

xx **is coming apart:** *Coming Apart* is the title of a recent book by the conservative political scientist Charles Murray. See Charles Murray, *Coming Apart: The State of White America, 1960–2010* (New York: Random House, 2013). Hereafter cited as Murray, *Coming Apart*.

xxii **not seen since the Black Death:** See Simon Szreter and Anne Hardy, "Urban Fertility and Mortality Patterns," in *The Cambridge Urban History of Britain, 1840–1950*, ed. Martin Daunton (Cambridge: Cambridge University Press, 2000), 671: "The 1830s and 1840s may well have been the worst decades ever for life expectancy since the Black Death in the history of those parishes which were now experiencing industrialization."

## Chapter One: The Meritocratic Revolution

3 **sixty-four hours a week:** Hans-Joachim Voth, "The Longest Years: New Estimates of Labor Input in England, 1760–1830," *Journal of Economic History* 61, no. 4 (2001): 1074. Hereafter cited as Voth, "The Longest Years."

3 **exceeded fifty hours:** U.S. Census Bureau, *Historical Statistics of the United States, 1789–1945* (Washington, DC, 1949), 67, accessed May 24, 2018, www2.census.gov/prod2/statcomp/doc uments/HistoricalStatisticsoftheUnitedStates1789-1945.pdf.

3 **the elite despised industry:** Thorstein Veblen, *The Theory of the Leisure Class: An Economic Study of Institutions* (New York: Macmillan, 1899), 19. Hereafter cited as Veblen, *Theory of the Leisure Class*.

4 **how hard they worked:** This formulation borrows from Voth, "The Longest Years," 1066, 1075.

4 **two generations ago:** See Chapter 6.

4 **high school degree or less:** See Steven F. Hipple, "Labor Force Participation: What Has Happened Since the Peak?," *Monthly Labor Review*, September 2016, accessed November 17, 2018, table 3 (pp. 10–11), www.bls.gov/opub/mlr/2016/article/pdf /labor-force-participation-what-has-happened-since-the-peak .pdf.

4 **enjoy less leisure:** See Chapter 4.

4 **than they did at midcentury:** See Chapter 4.

5 **Top jobs commonly pay:** In 2010, for instance, Steven Kaplan and Joshua Rauh reported that a Wall Street managing director typically made at least $500,000 per year and a partner at one of the nation's top ten law firms made, on average, $1 million per year. See Steven N. Kaplan and Joshua Rauh, "Wall Street and Main Street: What Contributes to the Rise in the Highest Incomes?," *Review of Financial Studies* 23, no. 3 (2010): 1004–50, accessed November 17, 2018, www.jstor.org/stable/40604776. Hereafter cited as Kaplan and Rauh, "Wall Street and Main Street." Robert S. Khuzami was paid upward of $5 million a year when he worked as partner for corporate law firm Kirkland & Ellis from 2013 to 2018. See Ben Protess and Peter Lattman, "A Legal Bane of Wall Street Switches Sides," *New York Times*, July 23, 2013, accessed June 2, 2018, https://dealbook.nytimes .com/2013/07/22/a-legal-bane-of-wall-street-switches-sides/. Total annual compensation among the two hundred highest-paid chief executives in the country ranges from roughly $10 million to roughly $100 million. See "The Highest-Paid C.E.O.s in 2017," *New York Times*, May 25, 2018, accessed June 2, 2018, www.nytimes.com/interactive/2018/05/25/business/ceo-pay -2017.html. For the years 2015–17, Amazon CEO Jeff Bezos received an annual compensation of over $1.6 billion. See Amazon.com, Inc., Proxy Statement, Annual Meeting of Shareholders, May 30, 2018, accessed June 2, 2018, www.sec.gov/Archives/ed gar/data/1018724/000119312518121077/d514607ddef14a.htm.

5 **dominant path to wealth:** See Chapter 4.

5 **Instead, it embraces:** This formulation again tracks the definition given in Scott and Marshall, *A Dictionary of Sociology*.

5 **superordinate working class:** The term comes from Jonathan Gershuny, "Busyness as the Badge of Honor for the New Superordinate Working Class," *Social Research* 72, no. 2 (2005): 287–314, accessed June 2, 2018, www.jstor.org/stable/40971766. Hereafter cited as Gershuny, "Busyness as the Badge of Honor."

6 **"You'll get in if you apply":** See Yale Law School Digital Repository Special Collections series, "Lives of Lawyers," https://digi talcommons.law.yale.edu/ylsiol/.

6 **the top-ranked school:** "The Best Law Schools in America, Ranked," *U.S. News & World Report*, 2018, accessed June 5, 2018, www.usnews.com/best-graduate-schools/top-law -schools/law-rankings?int=9c0f08.

7 **Law School Admission Test:** The Yale Law School class of 2020 had a median GPA of 3.91 and a median LSAT score of 173. Of students who took the LSAT between June 2016 and February 2017, 99.2 percent scored below 173. See Lisa Anthony, "Score Distribution—Law School Admission Test," Law School Admissions Council, June 20, 2017, accessed June 5, 2018, www .lsac.org/docs/default-source/data-(lsac-resources)-docs/lsat -score-distribution.pdf, and "Entering Class Profile," Yale Law School, 2018, accessed June 5, 2018, https://law.yale.edu/admis sions/profiles-statistics/entering-class-profile.

7 **Roughly 80 percent:** To be precise, 85 percent of new offers and 83 percent of total offers of admission were accepted last year. See "Entering Class Profile," Yale Law School, 2018, accessed June 5, 2018, https://law.yale.edu/admissions/profiles-statistics /entering-class-profile.

7 **15 percent of applicants:** The ABA Standard 509 required disclosures for the top five law schools give the following acceptance

rates, total admittees, and class sizes for the cohort of students accepted in 2017: Yale—8.4%, 240, 205; Stanford—9.9%, 392, 180; Harvard—15.8%, 900, 560; Chicago—21.5%, 958, 188; Columbia—20.4%, 1,188, 389. The average acceptance rate among these five schools was 15.2 percent that year. See "ABA Required Disclosures: Standard 509 Disclosure," American Bar Association Section of Legal Education and Admissions to the Bar, 2018, accessed June 6, 2018, www.abarequireddisclosures .org/Disclosure509.aspx.

7 **The median students at all five:** Median GPAs among students enrolling in the top five law schools ranged from 3.7 to 3.91 in 2017. Median LSAT scores were between 170 and 173, or between the 97.5th and the 99.2nd percentile scores. See Lisa Anthony, "Score Distribution—Law School Admission Test," Law School Admissions Council, June 20, 2017, accessed June 5, 2018, www .lsac.org/docs/default-source/data-(lsac-resources)-docs/lsat -score-distribution.pdf, and "ABA Required Disclosures: Standard 509 Disclosure," American Bar Association Section of Legal Education and Admissions to the Bar, 2018, accessed June 6, 2018, http://www.abarequireddisclosures.org/Disclosure509.aspx.

7 **no more than five:** This claim reflects the author's informed estimate.

7 **is three times as intense today:** See Chapter 5. Admissions competition for places at the broader elite of colleges has also intensified, although from a lower base. The University of Chicago, for example, is more than five times harder to get into than it was just twenty years ago.

7 **(more than six times the national public school average):** See Chapter 5.

7 **$90,000 per student per year:** See Chapter 5.

8 **"no law school better prepares":** John F. Manning, "Dean's Welcome," Harvard Law School, 2018, accessed June 6, 2018, https://hls.harvard.edu/about/deans-welcome/.

8 **"quite simply, the finest":** Robert Post, "Yale Law School Graduation Speech," May 18, 2015, accessed June 6, 2018, https://law.yale.edu/system/files/area/department/studen taffairs/document/postspeech.pdf.

9 **Automated industrial robots:** See Chapter 6.

9 **Innovations in distribution:** See Chapter 6.

9 **Derivatives and other new financial technologies:** See Chapter 6.

9 **And new management techniques:** See Chapter 6.

10 **"there are . . . approximately":** American Bar Association Committee on Economics of Law Practice, *The Lawyer's Handbook* (St. Paul, MN: West Publishing Company, 1962), 287.

10 **"if properly managed":** Deborah L. Rhode, *Balanced Lives: Changing the Culture of Legal Practice* (American Bar Association Commission on Women in the Profession, 2001), 14, http://womenlaw.stanford.edu/pdf/balanced.lives.pdf. Hereafter cited as Rhode, *Balanced Lives*, citing Edward Fennell, "The Lure of the Yankee Dollar," *Times* (London), July 18, 2000 (quoting Andrew Wilkinson, the managing partner of Cadwalader, Wickersham & Taft's London office).

10 **any light work:** See "bankers' hours, n.," OED Online, accessed June 7, 2018, www.oed.com/view/Entry/15246?rskey=aod4XK &result=2&isAdvanced=false#eid. Early uses even deployed the phrase to contrast the elite's leisure with the intense labor of working men. As one newspaper observed, "The millionaire doesn't put in his eight hours steady every day, like the poor man, but for the sake of argument, we'll take a banker's hours—ten to three, one hour off for lunch—four hours work." John T. McCutcheon, "The Pipe Dreamer's Club—Session No. 3: Where the Millionaire Has the Better of the Poor Man," *Indianapolis News*, July 12, 1902, 15. As recently as 1963, the *Washington Post* thought it newsworthy to observe, admiringly, "It is wellknown that Secretary of Defense Robert McNamara doesn't keep bankers' hours at the Pentagon." Winzola McLendon, "This Early Bird Beats Boss's Record at Pentagon," *Washington Post*, June 30, 1963, F11. These examples come from the expert researches of Fred Shapiro of the Yale Law Library.

10 **"organization men":** William H. Whyte Jr., *The Organization Man* (New York: Simon & Schuster, 1956), 3.

10 **"17 hours a day":** Ho, *Liquidated*, 89.

10 **"until midnight or one a.m.":** Ho, *Liquidated*, 97.

10 **the *extreme* job:** Sylvia Ann Hewlett and Carolyn Buck Luce, "Extreme Jobs: The Dangerous Allure of the 70-Hour

Workweek," *Harvard Business Review*, December 2006, 49–59. Hereafter cited as Hewlett and Luce, "Extreme Jobs."

10 **"physical presence" . . . "more than one job":** Hewlett and Luce, "Extreme Jobs," 51.

10 **More than half of the richest:** In 2010, 62 percent of households in the top 1 percent of the income distribution included someone who worked more than fifty hours a week (up from 46 percent as recently as 1983). Only 4 percent of households in the bottom quintile did. See Board of Governors of the Federal Reserve System, Survey of Consumer Finances, www.federalre serve.gov/econres/scfindex.htm. These data are based on intensive, structured, and probing interviews, and they are therefore unusually reliable. In addition, the survey oversamples the richest households. For both reasons, the survey presents an unusually authoritative measure of elite work.

10 **Overall, prime-aged men:** See Chapter 4.

11 **the badge of honor:** See Chapter 4 and Gershuny, "Busyness as the Badge of Honor."

11 **First-year associates:** Martha Neil, "First-Year Associate Pay Will Be $180K at Multiple BigLaw Firms Following Cravath's Lead," *ABA Journal*, June 8, 2016, accessed June 8, 2018, www .abajournal.com/news/article/cravath_raises_first_year_associ ate_pay_to_180k_effective_july_1.

11 **A law firm now exists:** Gina Passarella Cipriani, "The 2018 Am Law 100 Ranked by Profits Per Equity Partner," *American Lawyer*, April 24, 2018, accessed June 8, 2018, www.law.com /americanlawyer/2018/04/24/the-2018-am-law-100-ranked -by-profits-per-equity-partner/.

11 **the "top ten" . . . "top five":** These are the fourteen and six schools that, on account of ties and yearly fluctuations, are conventionally understood to constitute the "top five" and "top ten" schools in the *U.S. News & World Report* rankings. They are: Yale, Harvard, Stanford, Chicago, Columbia, and NYU (the "top five"), and Pennsylvania, Michigan, Virginia, Duke, Northwestern, Berkeley, Cornell, and Georgetown (to round out the "top ten").

Law firm profits are conventionally calculated in three ways: total profits, profits per lawyer, and profits per partner. The third—profits per partner—is the most commonly used and also, because partners are the highest-paid workers in the firms, the most relevant for present purposes. In 2015, the five most profitable firms were: Wachtell, Lipton, Rosen & Katz; Quinn Emanuel Urquhart & Sullivan; Paul Weiss; Sullivan & Cromwell; and Kirkland & Ellis. See Gina Passarella Cipriani, "The 2018 Am Law 100 Ranked by Profits Per Equity Partner," *American Lawyer*, April 24, 2018, accessed June 8, 2018, www .law.com/americanlawyer/2018/04/24/the-2018-am-law-100 --ranked-by-profits-per-equity-partner/.

As of 2018, 80 percent of Wachtell partners graduated from a top-five-ranked law school, while 96 percent graduated from a top-ten law school. As of 2018, 36 percent of Quinn Emanuel partners graduated from a top-five-ranked law school, while 53 percent graduated from a top-ten law school. As of 2018, 63 percent of Paul Weiss partners graduated from a top-five-ranked law school, while 79 percent graduated from a top-ten law school. As of 2018, 57 percent of Sullivan & Cromwell partners graduated from a top-five-ranked law school, while 72 percent graduated from a top-ten law school. As of 2018, 30 percent of Kirkland & Ellis partners graduated from a top-five-ranked law school, while 57 percent graduated from a top-ten law school. See "Best Law Schools," *U.S. News & World Report*, accessed July 25, 2018, www.usnews.com/best-graduate-schools /top-law-schools/law-rankings?int=9c0f08; "Attorney Search," Wachtell, Lipton, Rosen & Katz, accessed July 25, 2018, www.wlrk.com/Attorneys/List.aspx?LastName=; "Attorneys," Quinn Emanuel Trial Lawyers, accessed July 25, 2018, www .quinnemanuel.com/attorneys; "Professionals," Paul Weiss, accessed July 25, 2018, www.paulweiss.com/professionals; "Lawyers," Sullivan & Cromwell LLP, accessed July 25, 2018, www .sullcrom.com/lawyers; "Lawyers," Kirkland & Ellis LLP, accessed July 25, 2018, www.kirkland.com/sitecontent.cfm?con tentID=184.

The most profitable law firms, moreover, do not change much year by year. The five firms just listed ranked within the top eight in every year between 2012 and 2016. Other firms that make regular appearances in the top five—for example, Cravath,

Swaine & Moore and Cahill, Gordon & Reindel—have similarly composed partnerships.

11   **As in law, the top employers:** Ho, *Liquidated*, 11–12.

11   **Often, they do not:** See Chapter 6.

11   **The economic returns to schooling:** See Chapter 6.

12   **the returns to investments in stocks or bonds:** See Chapter 6.

12   **do their own chores:** See Hewlett and Luce, "Extreme Jobs."

12   **the lion's share become gloomy:** See Chapter 6.

12   **gives glossy jobs a false sheen:** It is increasingly common, especially among progressives, to insist that rising inequality has little to do with training or technology and much to do, instead, with the dominance of right-wing (really, neoliberal) politics, which attacks unions and deregulates the economy, in order to shift income from working- and middle-class workers to elites. See, e.g., Jared Bernstein, "It's Not a Skills Gap That's Holding Wages Down: It's the Weak Economy, Among Other Things," *American Prospect*, October 7, 2014, accessed June 13, 2018, http://prospect.org/article/it's-not-skills-gap-that's-holding -wages-down-its-weak-economy-among-other-things.

This is the within-labor analog to the earlier argument that rising inequality stems from a shift of income away from labor and toward capital. As before, the argument is not so much wrong as too imprecise concerning skill, too narrow concerning technology, and too shallow concerning causes. It is too imprecise concerning skill because it focuses exclusively on the returns to a generic college degree. Even if these have ceased to rise in recent years, the returns to elite college and elite graduate or professional school educations continue to grow, and these returns increasingly drive income inequality. The view is too narrow concerning technology because it fails to recognize that many of the policies that it complains of (and even associated social norms) are best understood as themselves being technological innovations, produced by a new supply of super-skilled workers. And it is too shallow because it does not seek the root causes of the disproportionate influence that the present-day elite wield over policy, which is itself a consequence of new patterns in training, work, and pay.

All in all, then, this expression of the progressive view recapitulates the errors of the earlier suggestion that economic inequality stems from a shift of income away from labor and toward capital. It inclines to moralize inequality as a product of individual choices, private vices, rather than seeking the deeper economic and social structures that govern behavior across the economic divide.

13   **owe perhaps two-thirds:** Tax data from 2015 suggest that an average member of the top 1 percent owed 56.4 percent of his total fiscal income to labor. See Facundo Alvaredo et al., World Inequality Database, distributed by WID.world, accessed July 3, 2018, https://wid.world/data/ (see "Average Fiscal Labour Income," wid.world code afilin992t, and "Average Fiscal Income," wid.world code afilinc992t, by tax unit for adults). This number is an underestimate of the labor component of total income, however, because much of what tax forms designate "capital income" is (as Chapter 4 will explain) actually attributable to labor.

13   **The top 1 percent of households now capture:** According to one estimate, in 2015, the top 1 percent of the income distribution captured 22.03 percent of all income earned in the United States and the top one-tenth of 1 percent captured 10.9 percent. See Thomas Piketty and Emmanuel Saez, "Income Inequality in the United States, 1913–1998," Updated Series (2015), accessed July 3, 2018, Table A3, https://eml.berkeley.edu//~saez/index .html. Hereafter cited as Piketty and Saez, "Income Inequality in the United States." Another estimate allocates a slightly more modest 20.2 percent of all income to the top 1 percent. See World Inequality Database, United States / Pre-tax national income / P99-P100 / Share, accessed October 29, 2018, https://wid .world/country/usa/.

13   **Compared to the period:** In the years between 1950 and 1970, the top 1 percent of the income distribution captured, on average, 10.6 percent of all income earned in the United States, less than half of the current share. The top one-tenth of 1 percent earned, on average, 3.5 percent, less than a third of the current share. See Piketty and Saez, "Income Inequality in the United States," Table A3, https://eml.berkeley.edu//~saez/index.html.

13   **between two-thirds and three-quarters:** See Chapter 4.

13   **toward superordinate labor:** See Chapter 4.

13   **Canada, Japan, and Norway:** See Table 5 of Carola Grün and Stephan Klasen, "Growth, Inequality, and Well-Being: Intertemporal and Global Comparisons," Discussion Paper no. 95, Ibero-America Institute for Economic Research, Ibero-Amerika Inst. Für Wirtschaftsforschung, Göttingen (2003), 21–23 (listing Gini coefficients for over 150 countries from 1960 to 1998).

13   **India, Morocco, Indonesia, Iran, Ukraine, and Vietnam:** Recent Gini index figures for these countries are: the United States, 41.5 (2016); India, 35.1 (2011); Morocco, 39.2 (2006); Indonesia, 39.5 (2013); Iran, 38.8 (2014); Ukraine, 25.0 (2016); Vietnam, 34.8 (2014). See World Bank, Development Research Group, "GINI index (World Bank estimate)," World Bank Group, 2018, accessed June 13, 2018, http://databank.world bank.org/data/reports.aspx?source=2&series=SI.POV.GINI& country=, and http://data.woddbank.org/indicator/SI.POV .GINI.

13   **Bangkok, Thailand:** The U.S. Census Bureau's American Community Survey estimates that Fairfield County had a Gini coefficient of 53.52 in 2011. Bangkok's Gini coefficient that year, as reported by the UN, was 40.0. See U.S. Census Bureau, "2007–2011 American Community Survey," accessed June 13, 2018, https://factfinder.census.gov/faces/nav/jsf/pages/index.xhtml, and United Nations Human Settlements Programme, Urbanization and Development: Emerging Futures, World Cities Report 2016 (2016), accessed June 13, 2018, 206–7, Table C.1, http:// wcr.unhabitat.org/wp-content/uploads/2017/02/WCR-2016 -Full-Report.pdf.

15   **render it increasingly indispensable:** See Stephen M. Hedrick, "The Acquired Immune System: A Vantage from Beneath," *Immunity* 21, no. 5 (2004): 607–15, accessed June 13, 2018, www .sciencedirect.com/science/article/pii/S1074761304003073 ?via%3Dihub. "By selecting for evermore-devious parasites [superordinate workers], the immune system [snowball inequality] is the cause of its own necessity." John Fabian Witt proposed this analogy.

15   **seem necessary, natural, and inevitable:** See Chapter 8.

15   **tyranny of no alternatives:** See Roberto Mangabeira Unger, *The Left Alternative* (London: Verso, 2009), 1.

15   **both the left and the right:** On the left, this view appears in some of the outwardly directed, public-facing arguments presented by the Occupy Wall Street movement. (Internally, Occupy embraced a radically egalitarian, participatory form of collective life, which came much nearer to rejecting meritocracy than the movement's outward expression acknowledged.) On the right, the view appears in certain strands of Trumpism. (Other strands take a much more elitist, and even oligarchic line.)

15   **intelligence or academic ability:** See, e.g., Lani Guinier, *The Tyranny of the Meritocracy* (Boston: Beacon, 2015), 21, and Richard D. Kahlenberg, "Affirmative Action for the Rich," *New York Times*, May 10, 2013, accessed June 14, 2018, www.nytimes .com/roomfordebate/2011/11/13/why-do-top-schools-still -take-legacy-applicants/affirmative-action-for-the-rich .

15   **skill or talent:** See, e.g., Lauren Rivera, *Pedigree: How Elite Students Get Elite Jobs* (Princeton, NJ: Princeton University Press, 2015), 15–25. Hereafter cited as Rivera, *Pedigree*. See also Bourree Lam, "Recruitment, Resumes, Interviews: How the Hiring Process Favors Elites," *Atlantic*, May 27, 2015, accessed June 14, 2018, www.theatlantic.com/business/archive/2015/05/recruit ment-resumes-interviews-how-the-hiring-process-favors-elites /394166/.

15   **outright fraud:** See, e.g., Russell Sobel, "Crony Capitalism Pays Well for Rent-Seeking CEOs," *Investor's Business Daily*, July 9, 2014, accessed June 14, 2018, www.investors.com/politics/com mentary/political-activity-and-connections-dont-make-business -profitable/.

15   **a rising oligarchy:** See Thomas Piketty, *Capital in the Twenty-First Century*, trans. Arthur Goldhammer (Cambridge, MA: Belknap Press of Harvard University Press, 2014). Hereafter cited as Piketty, *Capital*.

17   **denounce real targets:** In addition to Piketty's work, canonical accounts along these lines include Joseph E. Stiglitz, *The Price of Inequality* (New York: W. W. Norton, 2012), and Anthony B. Atkinson, *Inequality: What Can Be Done?* (Cambridge, MA: Harvard University Press, 2015).

17   **good-faith judgments of merit:** See Chapter 5.

17  **even without nepotism:** See Chapter 5.

17  **legacy preference declines:** See Thomas J. Espenshade, Chang Y. Chung, and Joan L. Walling, "Admission Preferences for Minority Students, Athletes, and Legacies at Elite Universities," *Social Science Quarterly* 85, no. 5 (December 2004): 1422–46, 1443, Figure 1. See also Douglas S. Massey and Margarita Mooney, "The Effects of America's Three Affirmative Action Programs on Academic Performance," *Social Problems* 54, no. 1 (2007): 99–117, 100 ("The only comprehensive study of all [preferential admissions] that has sought to control for variation in qualifications is that of Espenshade and associates (2004).")

17  **the entire bottom half:** See Chapter 5.

17  **was betting against them:** Goldman Sachs's ABACUS Flipbook is available on the webpage of the director of financial mathematics at NYU's Courant Institute of Mathematical Sciences. See ACA Management, LLC, ABACUS 2007-AC1, February 26, 2007, accessed June 19, 2018, www.math.nyu.edu/faculty/avellane/ABACUS.pdf. For more on the ABACUS deal, see Louise Story and Gretchen Morgenson, "S.E.C. Accuses Goldman of Fraud in Housing Deal," *New York Times*, April 16, 2010, accessed June 19, 2018, www.nytimes.com/2010/04/17/business/17goldman.html; Dan Wilchins, Karen Brettell, and Richard Change, "Factbox: How Goldman's ABACUS Deal Worked," Reuters, April 16, 2010, accessed January 27, 2019, www.reuters.com/article/us-goldmansachs-abacus-factbox/factbox-how-goldmans-abacus-deal-worked-idUSTRE63F5CZ20100416; Securities and Exchange Commission, "Goldman Sachs to Pay Record $550 Million to Settle SEC Charges Related to Subprime Mortgage CDO," July 15, 2010, accessed January 27, 2019, www.sec.gov/news/press/2010/2010-123.htm; and Michael A. Santoro and Ronald J. Strauss, *Wall Street Values: Business Ethics and the Global Financial Crisis* (Cambridge: Cambridge University Press, 2012), 116–17, 134–36.

17  **Goldman's total earnings:** For 2015, Goldman Sachs reported net earnings of $6.08 billion, net revenues of $33.82 billion, and average global core liquid assets of $199 billion. For 2016, the company reported net earnings of $7.40 billion, net revenues of $30.61 billion, and average global core liquid assets of $226 billion. For 2017, net earnings were $4.29 billion, net revenues were $32.07 billion, and global core liquid assets averaged $211 billion. The Goldman Sachs Group, Inc., Annual Earnings Press Releases, January 20, 2016; January 18, 2017; January 17, 2018, accessed June 19, 2018, www.goldmansachs.com/media-relations/press-releases-and-comments/archive/index.html.

17  **amount to trillions:** See Chapter 4.

18  **performance-related pay:** See Chapter 4.

18  **exploding wages for superordinate workers:** See Chapter 4.

18  **three hundred times as much today:** In 1965, a typical American large-firm CEO earned about twenty times the income of the average production worker; in 2014, the CEO of a comparable company took home about three hundred times as much as the average production worker. Lawrence Mishel and Alyssa Davis, *Top CEOs Make 300 Times More Than Typical Workers: Pay Growth Surpasses Stock Gains and Wage Growth of Top 0.1 Percent* (Washington, DC: Economic Policy Institute, 2015), accessed June 21, 2018, www.epi.org/publication/top-ceos-make-300-times-more-than-workers-pay-growth-surpasses-market-gains-and-the-rest-of-the-0-1-percent/.

18  **A cardiologist earned:** Private-duty nurses charged between $14 and $27.50 per day in 1965. Office nurses reported average monthly salaries between $350 and $397 in 1964. The average annual salary for a public health nurse employed by a local government was $5,313 in 1964.

Data on doctors' incomes by specialty are not available for the mid-1960s, but medical school graduates employed by the federal government in 1965 received annual starting salaries between $10,420 and $12,075—four times the salary of a government-employed nurse—and the net income of doctors in private practice overall averaged about $19,000 in 1963. See U.S. Department of Labor, Bureau of Labor Statistics, *Occupational Outlook Handbook 1966–67*, 117–25, accessed June 21, 2018, https://fraser.stlouisfed.org/files/docs/publications/bls/bls_1450_1965_1.pdf.

18  **more than seven times as much in 2017:** In 2017, the median annual salary for a registered nurse was $70,000. See U.S.

Department of Labor, Bureau of Labor Statistics, "Registered Nurses," *Occupational Outlook Handbook*, last updated April 13, 2018, accessed June 21, 2018, www.bls.gov/ooh/healthcare/registered-nurses.htm. The average salary for a male cardiologist exceeds $500,000. See Reshma Jagsi et al., "Work Activities and Compensation of Male and Female Cardiologists," *Journal of the American College of Cardiology* 67, no. 5 (2016): 535.

18  **less than five times:** According to the *Occupational Outlook Handbook* published by the Bureau of Labor Statistics (BLS), the average secretary (across all types of firms) made $99.50 per week, or roughly $5,000 per year, in 1963–64. See U.S. Department of Labor, Bureau of Labor Statistics, *Occupational Outlook Handbook 1966–67*, 283, accessed June 21, 2018, https://fraser.stlouisfed.org/files/docs/publications/bls/bls_1450_1965_2.pdf. According to the BLS's 1965 National Survey of Professional, Administrative, Technical, and Clerical Pay, attorneys in the highest earning bracket had average annual salaries of $24,804. See U.S. Department of Labor, Bureau of Labor Statistics, *National Survey of Professional, Administrative, Technical, and Clerical Pay 1965*, 16, accessed June 21, 2018, https://fraser.stlouisfed.org/content/?item_id=498147&filepath=/files/docs/publications/bls/bls_1469_1965.pdf.

18  **forty times as much today:** According to the BLS's *Occupational Outlook Handbook* for 2018, the median annual salary for a secretary or administrative assistant was $37,870. See U.S. Department of Labor, Bureau of Labor Statistics, "Secretaries and Administrative Assistants," *Occupational Outlook Handbook*, last updated April 13, 2018, accessed June 21, 2018, www.bls.gov/ooh/office-and-administrative-support/secretaries-and-administrative-assistants.htm. The average profits per partner among firms in the *American Lawyer*'s top one hundred firms (ranked by gross revenues) was $1.55 million. See "The AmLaw 100: A Special Section," *American Lawyer* (May 2015), 92–93, www.siia.net/archive/neals/2016/filez/442072/688_1732_442072_c9f58ffc-510d-40fb-9133-5863e7854558_82357_3_1.pdf.

18  **David Rockefeller received:** Rockefeller's salary was typical for the time. Rudolph Peterson made roughly a base salary of $137,500 plus $37,500 in deferred compensation as CEO of Bank of America in 1963; Thomas Gates made roughly $267,250 as chairman of the Morgan Guaranty Trust Company in 1968; and Walter Wriston was paid $128,139 as chairman and CEO of Citibank in 1967. See Nomi Prins, *All the Presidents' Bankers: The Hidden Alliances That Drive American Power* (New York: Nation Books, 2014), 271–72. Bank tellers' earnings ranged from $45 to $150 per week in 1964, depending on the metropolitan areas in which they worked. See U.S. Department of Labor, Bureau of Labor Statistics, *Occupational Outlook Handbook 1966–67*, 618, accessed June 21, 2018, https://fraser.stlouisfed.org/files/docs/publications/bls/bls_1450_1965_4.pdf.

18  **Last year Jamie Dimon:** Dimon was paid $29.5 million in total compensation for his work in 2017. See Anders Melin, Hugh Son, and Jenn Zhao, "JPMorgan Boosts Dimon's Pay 5.4% to $29.5 Million for 2017," Bloomberg, January 18, 2018, accessed June 21, 2018, www.bloomberg.com/news/articles/2018-01-18/jpmorgan-boosts-dimon-s-pay-5-4-to-29-5-million-for-last-year. For that same year, the median annual pay for a bank teller was $28,110. See U.S. Department of Labor, Bureau of Labor Statistics, "Tellers," *Occupational Outlook Handbook*, last updated April 13, 2018, accessed June 21, 2018, www.bls.gov/ooh/office-and-administrative-support/tellers.htm.

18  **All told, nearly a million:** See Chapter 4.

18  **over middle-class workers:** See Chapter 4.

## Chapter Two: The Harms of Meritocracy

20  **Median incomes nearly doubled:** See Chapter 4.

20  **richer than their parents:** A child born in 1940 to median-income parents had a 93 percent chance of earning more than her parents. A child born to median-income parents in 1980 had a 45 percent chance of earning more than her parents. See Raj Chetty et al., "The Fading American Dream: Trends in Absolute Mobility Since 1940," *Science* 356, no. 6336 (April 2017): 398–406.

20  **$40,000 a year today:** Anonymous resident in conversation with the author, St. Clair Shores, Michigan, May 2018.

21  **Shore Club Highrise Apartments:** "Groundbreaking Today: 750 Apartments in Shores Project," *Detroit Free Press,* July 31, 1962, A3, and Proctor Homer Warren, Inc., "With Every Great Apartment and Sky House, We'll Throw in a Great Lake Free," advertisement, *Detroit Free Press,* November 19, 1970. The building is visible from Detroit and is so prominent that city residents call it 9 Mile Tower.

21  *The Affluent Society:* See John Kenneth Galbraith, *The Affluent Society* (Boston: Houghton Mifflin, 1958). Hereafter cited as Galbraith, *The Affluent Society.*

21  **matches the national median:** Median annual family income in St. Clair Shores is $69,878, according to 2012–2016 U.S. Census Bureau estimates. The national median is $67,871. Median annual *household* income in St. Clair Shores is an estimated $54,590; the national median is $55,322. See U.S. Census Bureau, 2012–2016 American Community Survey 5-Year Estimates, *Selected Economic Characteristics,* United States and St. Clair Shores city, Michigan, accessed June 21, 2018, www.census.gov/programs-surveys/acs/.

21  **triples the poverty threshold:** Average household size in St. Clair Shores is between two and three residents. The 2016 poverty threshold for an average three-person family was $19,105, less than one-third of St. Clair Shores' median family income. See U.S. Census Bureau, 2012–2016 American Community Survey 5-Year Estimates, *Selected Social Characteristics in the United States,* St. Clair Shores city, Michigan, accessed June 21, 2018, www.census.gov/programs-surveys/acs/, and U.S. Census Bureau, *Poverty Thresholds for 2016 by Size of Family and Number of Children,* accessed June 21, 2018, www.census.gov/data/tables/time-series/demo/income-poverty/historical-poverty-thresholds.html.

21  **falls below the nationwide rate:** The national poverty rate is 15.1 percent for all people and 11.0 percent for families. The rate in St. Clair Shores is 9.1 percent for all people and 6.4 percent for families. See U.S. Census Bureau, 2012–2016 American Community Survey 5-Year Estimates, *Selected Economic Characteristics,* United States and St. Clair Shores city, Michigan, accessed June 21, 2018, www.census.gov/programs-surveys/acs/.

21  **eleven hundred square feet:** Over half of the 144 single-family homes for sale on Zillow in St. Clair Shores in mid-June 2018 were between 1,000 and 1,500 square feet and over two-thirds are three-bedroom homes. Zillow, accessed June 21, 2018, www.zillow.com/homes/for_sale/Saint-Clair-Shores-MI/. The nationwide median new single-family house sold in 2017 was 2,457 square feet. See U.S. Census Bureau, *Highlights of Annual 2017 Characteristics of New Housing,* accessed June 23, 2018, www.census.gov/construction/chars/highlights.html.

21  **issuing citations:** Anonymous residents in conversation with the author, St. Clair Shores, Michigan, May 2018. One resident reported getting a ticket from the town for flaking paint; she said it would do the same for a sagging roof, an uneven sidewalk, or failure to remove snow. A couple reported that their elderly neighbor was cited for feeding the birds.

22  **boards, commissions, and committees:** There are currently thirty-two volunteer organizations listed in the St. Clair Shores Boards, Commissions & Committees Handbook, including an Activities Committee, an Ethics Committee, and a Dog Park Committee. *Boards, Commissions & Committees Handbook,* 2000, rev. 2012, accessed June 23, 2018, www.scsmi.net/DocumentCenter/View/11/Boards-and-Commissions-Committees?bidId=.

22  **largest Memorial Day parade in Michigan:** Anonymous resident in conversation with the author, St. Clair Shores, Michigan, May 3, 2018. See also Mitch Hotts, "Olympic Figure Skater Nancy Kerrigan to Appear at St. Clair Shores Memorial Day Parade," *Macomb Daily,* May 2, 2018, accessed June 23, 2018, www.macombdaily.com/general-news/20180502/olympic-figure-skater-nancy-kerrigan-to-appear-at-st-clair-shores-memorial-day-parade.

22  **down Harper Avenue:** See Mitch Hotts, "Harper Charity Cruise Ready to Roll Down the Avenue," *Macomb Daily,* August 29, 2016, accessed June 23, 2018, www.macombdaily.com/article/MD/20160829/NEWS/160829618.

22  **still dominate the town:** Anonymous residents in conversation with the author, St. Clair Shores, Michigan, May 3, 2018.

22  **the largest municipal bankruptcy:** See Monica Davey and Mary Williams Walsh, "Billions in Debt, Detroit Tumbles into Insolvency," *New York Times,* July 18, 2013, accessed June 23, 2018, www.nytimes.com/2013/07/19/us/detroit-files-for-bankruptcy.html.

22  **Fewer than a quarter:** According to 2016 estimates, 24.4 percent of St. Clair Shores residents twenty-five years old or older have finished a bachelor's degree compared to 30.0 percent nationally, and 8.3 percent have finished a graduate or professional degree compared to 11.5 percent nationally. U.S. Census Bureau, 2012–2016 American Community Survey 5-Year Estimates, *Educational Attainment,* United States and St. Clair Shores city, Michigan, accessed June 28, 2018, https://factfinder.census.gov/faces/tableservices/jsf/pages/productview.xhtml?pid=ACS_16_5YR_S1501&src=pt.

22  **outside the top 1 percent:** Anonymous resident in conversation with the author, St. Clair Shores, Michigan, May 3, 2018. According to the IRS's Statistics of Income Bulletin for Winter 2018, the minimum adjusted gross income for top 1 percent tax returns in tax year 2015 was $480,930. See Adrian Dungan, "Individual Income Tax Shares, 2015," *IRS Statistics of Income Bulletin,* Winter 2018, accessed June 28, 2018, www.irs.gov/pub/irs-soi/soi-a-ints-id1801.pdf.

22  **Gilbert's Lodge:** "Menu," Gilbert's Lodge, accessed June 28, 2018, www.gilbertslodge.com/menu/0/menus.aspx.

23  **"people going to Gilbert's":** Anonymous resident in conversation with the author, Gilbert's Lodge, St. Clair Shores, Michigan, May 2, 2018.

23  **When Gilbert's burned down:** Anonymous resident in conversation with the author, Gilbert's Lodge, St. Clair Shores, Michigan, May 2, 2018. See also Mitch Hotts, "Gilbert's Lodge Re-opens After Two Fires," *Macomb Daily,* July 9, 2014, accessed June 28, 2018, www.macombdaily.com/article/MD/20140709/NEWS/140709659.

23  **reupholstered a few years ago:** In 2002, the library had 24 full- and part-time employees. See City of St. Clair Shores, Michigan, *Comprehensive Annual Financial Report with Supplemental Information Prepared by the Department of Finance for the Fiscal Year Ended June 30, 2006* (St. Clair Shores, MI: 2006), 108. By 2018, the library's staff had fallen to 16.5 full- and part-time employees. See City of St. Clair Shores, Michigan, *Comprehensive Annual Financial Report for the Fiscal Year Ended June 30, 2018* (St. Clair Shores, MI: 2018), 6–20. On part-time positions and high staff turnover, see Kristyne E. Demske, "Shores Council Debates Additional Money, Staffing for Library," *St. Clair Shores Sentinel,* May 3, 2017, accessed March 17, 2019, https://www.candgnews.com/news/council-debates-additional-money-staffing-library-101124. For the dependence on private charity, see Kristyne E. Demske, "Friends Promoting Buy a Chair Campaign for Library," *St. Clair Shores Sentinel,* March 3, 2015, accessed March 17, 2019, https://www.candgnews.com/news/friends-promoting-buy-chair-campaign-library-81642. The claim about the old tables and chairs relies on an anonymous staff member in conversation with the author, St. Clair Shores, Michigan, May 3, 2018.

23  **has lost nearly a third of its residents:** St. Clair Shores first appears on the U.S. Census in 1930 with a population of 6,745 and grew rapidly through the middle of the twentieth century to peak at 88,093 in 1970. Since then, the population has been slowly but consistently declining. The population recorded in the 2010 Census was 59,715. See U.S. Census Bureau, "Decennial Census of Population and Housing," accessed June 28, 2018, www.census.gov/programs-surveys/decennial-census/decade/decennial-publications.2010.html.

23  **tallest building in town:** See "History of City," City of St. Clair Shores Michigan, accessed June 28, 2018, www.scsmi.net/98/History-of-City.

23  **the only hotel in town:** The Shore Pointe Motor Lodge was incorporated in Michigan in 1967 as the Shorian Motor Inn and changed its name around 1980. See Michigan Department of Licensing and Regulatory Affairs, "Summary for Shorian Motor Inn, Incorporated," *LARA Corporations Online Filing System,* accessed June 28, 2018, https://cofs.lara.state.mi.us/CorpWeb/CorpSearch/CorpSummary.aspx?ID=80002201.

23  **nearly ten million middle-class jobs:** See Chapter 6.

23  **As the incomes of the top:** In 1975, median household income was $47,879 (in 2016 dollars). In 2016, median household income was $59,039 (in 2016 dollars). That is an increase of 23.3

percent. In 2000, median household income was $58,544 in 2016 dollars. Between 2000 and 2016, median incomes increased less than 1 percent. U.S. Census Bureau, "Historical Income Tables: Households," Current Population Survey, last modified August 28, 2018, accessed June 28, 2018, Table H-5, www.census.gov /data/tables/time-series/demo/income-poverty/historical -income-households.html.

    In 1975, the average income (including capital gains) of a household in the top 1 percent of the income distribution was $345,565 (in 2014 dollars). In 2014, that average was $1,283,775 (in 2014 dollars). That is an increase of 271.5 percent. See Facundo Alvaredo et al., World Inequality Database, distributed by WID.world, accessed July 3, 2018, https://wid.world/data/, Average Fiscal Income (wid.world code afiinc992t, by tax unit for all adults).

24   **narrow cadre of exceptional students:** See, e.g., Dominic J. Brewer, Eric R. Eide, and Ronald G. Ehrenberg, "Does It Pay to Attend an Elite Private College? Cross-Cohort Evidence on the Effects of College Type on Earnings," *Journal of Human Resources* 34, no. 1 (Winter 1999): 104–23, 114.

24   **radio and television advertisements:** "Macomb trains the workforce that keeps our communities healthy, safe, and secure," says one such television commercial over footage of students in scrubs and firefighters' suits. Macomb College, "Macomb: Comcast Advertisement," YouTube video, 0:30, January 17, 2012, accessed June 28, 2018, www.youtube.com/watch?v =v99EWhqhvP0. See also Pat Vitale and Joe Petroskey, "The Community College Corner," Macomb Community College radio advertisement.

24   **Some students:** Niche.com allows high school students to report where they are interested in going to college. The colleges with over a hundred reports of interest from St. Clair Shores public high schools are Saginaw Valley State University, Grand Valley State University, Eastern Michigan University, Western Michigan University, Central Michigan University, Oakland University, Michigan State University, Wayne State University, Macomb Community College, and the University of Michigan at Ann Arbor, as of July 2018. Only the last of these is elite. See "Lake Shore High School," Niche.com, accessed July 25, 2018, www.niche.com/k12/lake-shore-high-school-saint-clair -shores-mi/; "Lakeview High School," Niche.com, accessed July 25, 2018, www.niche.com/k12/lakeview-high-school-saint-clair -shores-mi/academics/; and "South Lake High School," Niche .com, accessed July 25, 2018, www.niche.com/k12/south-lake -high-school-saint-clair-shores-mi/.

24   **make the local paper:** Anonymous residents in conversation with the author, St. Clair Shores, Michigan, May 2–3, 2018.

24   **are barely better represented:** See Chapter 5.

25   **by nearly six to one:** See Chapter 5.

25   **the entire bottom half:** See Chapter 5.

25   **an advanced (post-BA) degree:** In 2015, 12 percent of American adults reported having finished an advanced degree. See Camille L. Ryan and Kurt Bauman, "Educational Attainment in the United States: 2015," U.S. Census Bureau, Current Population Reports no. P20-578 (March 2016), accessed June 30, 2018, 2, Table 1, www.census.gov/content/dam/Census/library /publications/2016/demo/p20-578.pdf.

25   **Top public schools:** In the 2013–14 fiscal year, Lakeview Public Schools, one of three school districts serving St. Clair Shores, spent a total of $10,309 per student. Michigan's wealthiest school districts spent twice as much (see, e.g., Bloomfield Hills Schools, $24,166 per student). The nation's wealthiest districts spent three times as much (e.g., Cold Spring Harbor Central School District, $32,540 per student). See National Center for Education Statistics, *Common Core of Data (CCD)*, distributed by the Institute of Educational Sciences, accessed June 30, 2018, https://nces.ed.gov/ccd/districtsearch/index.asp.

25   **might share a music teacher:** Anonymous resident in conversation with the author, St. Clair Shores, Michigan, May 2, 2018.

25   **Newton, Massachusetts:** Robert Reich, "Back to School, and to Widening Inequality," *Robert Reich*, August 25, 2014, accessed June 30, 2018, http://robertreich.org/post/95749 31970. Hereafter cited as Reich, "Back to School."

25   **Coronado, California:** Motoko Rich, "Nation's Wealthy Places Pour Private Money into Public Schools, Study Finds," *New York Times*, October 21, 2014, accessed November 17, 2018,

www.nytimes.com/2014/10/22/us/nations-wealthy-places -pour-private-money-into-public-schools-study-finds.html.

25   **A careful study of one large county:** Sharon Jank and Lindsay Owens, Stanford Center on Poverty and Inequality, "Inequality in the United States: Understanding Inequality with Data," slide 16 (referencing Demetra Kalogrides and Susanna Loeb for the Center for Education Policy Analysis, Stanford University 2012, Data from Miami-Dade County School District Administrative Staff Data, 2003–2011), accessed June 30, 2018, https:// nces.ed.gov/pubs2017/2017094.pdf, and https://inequality.stan ford.edu/sites/default/files/Inequality_SlideDeck.pdf. Hereafter cited as Jank and Owens, "Inequality in the United States."

26   **a teacher in St. Clair Shores observes:** Anonymous resident in conversation with the author, St. Clair Shores, Michigan, May 2, 2018.

26   **six times the national public school average:** See Chapter 5.

26   **more than twice as many teachers:** Student/teacher ratios at elite private schools are roughly 7:1, while the average student /teacher ratio at public schools nationwide is 16:1. See Thomas D. Snyder, Cristobal de Brey, and Sally A. Dillow, *Digest of Education Statistics: 2016* (February 2018): 149, Table 208.10, accessed July 3, 2018, https://nces.ed.gov/pubs2017/2017094.pdf, and U.S. Department of Education, National Center for Education Statistics, "Pupil/Teacher Ratio of Private Schools, by School Level and Selected School Characteristics: United States, 2013–14," *Private School Universe Survey (PSS)*, accessed July 3, 2018, https://nces.ed.gov/surveys/pss/tables/table_2013_12.asp.

26   **fully three-quarters of the teachers:** Among *Forbes*'s 20 Best Prep Schools, the average percentage of teachers with an advanced degree is 76.3 percent. See Raquel Laneri, "America's Best Prep Schools," *Forbes*, April 29, 2010, accessed July 3, 2018, www.forbes.com/pictures/fl45mj/americas-best-prep-sc/#7ce 0256e4ea0.

26   **Brown v. Board of Education:** For children born in the 1940s through the 1960s, the achievement gap between black and white children was much larger than that between the richest and the poorest students. For children born in the last two decades, the achievement gap between the richest and the poorest children entering kindergarten is "two to three times larger than the black-white gap at the same time." See Sean F. Reardon, "The Widening Academic Achievement Gap Between the Rich and the Poor: New Evidence and Possible Explanations," in *Whither Opportunity? Rising Inequality and the Uncertain Life Chances of Low-Income Children*, ed. Richard Murnane and Greg Duncan (New York: Russell Sage Foundation, 2011), 99. Hereafter cited as Reardon, "The Widening Academic Achievement Gap." Sean Reardon, "No Rich Child Left Behind," *New York Times*, April 27, 2013, accessed July 3, 2018, https://opinionator.blogs .nytimes.com/2013/04/27/no-rich-child-left-behind/. Hereafter cited as Reardon, "No Rich Child Left Behind."

26   **Economic inequality today:** See Chapter 5.

26   **The academic achievement gap:** See Chapter 5.

26   **Rich children now outscore:** See Chapter 5.

26   **Only about one in two hundred:** See Chapter 5.

27   **fewer than one out of every fifty:** See generally, Gary Solon, "Intergenerational Mobility in the Labor Market," in *Handbook of Labor Economics*, vol. 3, ed. Orly Aschenfelter and David Card (Amsterdam: Elsevier, 1999).

27   **A poor or middle-class child:** See Isabel Sawhill and John E. Morton, "Economic Mobility: Is the American Dream Alive and Well?" Economic Mobility Project, 2007, www.economic mobility.org/reports_and_research/mobility_in_america; Miles Corak, "Do Poor Children Become Poor Adults? Lessons from a Cross Country Comparison of Generational Earnings Mobility," *Research on Economic Inequality* 13 (2006): 143–88; Anders Bjorklund and Markus Jäntti, "Intergenerational Income Mobility in Sweden Compared to the United States," *American Economic Review* 87, no. 5 (1997): 1009–18; Markus Jäntti et al., "American Exceptionalism in a New Light: A Comparison of Intergenerational Earnings Mobility in the Nordic Countries, the United Kingdom and the United States," IZA Discussion Paper 1938, Institute for the Study of Labor (IZA) (2006); Miles Corak, "Income Inequality, Equality of Opportunity, and Intergenerational Mobility," *Journal of Economic Perspectives* 27, no. 3 (2013): 79–102; Simon Boserup, Wojciech Kopczuk, and Claus Kreiner, "Intergenerational Wealth Mobility: Evidence from

Danish Wealth Records of Three Generations," University of Copenhagen mimeograph (2013), http://web.econ.ku.dk/eprn_epru/Seminar/WealthAcrossGen.pdf; and Emily Beller and Michael Hout, "Intergenerational Social Mobility: The United States in Comparative Perspective," *Future Child* 16, no. 2 (2006): 19–36.

27   **The odds that a middle-class child:** See Chapter 8.

28   **that he could *not* buy:** Canlis restaurant in Seattle, to name just one example, offers only one dinner option—a four-course menu for $125. A bottle of beer costs up to $136; and a bottle of wine costs up to $22,500 (although this admittedly buys a magnum). Canlis, "Menu," accessed August 1, 2018, https://canlis.com/menu; Canlis, "Wine List," accessed August 1, 2018, https://canlis.com/uploads/Canlis%20Wine%20List%206.19.18.pdf.

28   **When asked who is important:** Anonymous residents in conversation with the author, St. Clair Shores, Michigan, May 2–3, 2018.

28   **"People don't like the elite":** Anonymous resident in conversation with the author, St. Clair Shores, Michigan, May 3, 2018.

28   **"I've never hired anybody":** Anonymous resident in conversation with the author, St. Clair Shores, Michigan, May 3, 2018.

29   **"you can't feel successful":** Anonymous resident in conversation with the author, St. Clair Shores, Michigan, May 3, 2018.

29   **"You've either made it or not":** Anonymous resident in conversation with the author, St. Clair Shores, Michigan, May 3, 2018.

29   **"felt middle class" here:** Anonymous resident in conversation with the author, St. Clair Shores, Michigan, May 2, 2018.

29   **"Steady good":** Anonymous resident in conversation with the author, St. Clair Shores, Michigan, May 3, 2018.

29   **It feels better:** See generally Robert H. Frank, *Choosing the Right Pond: Human Behavior and the Quest for Status* (New York: Oxford University Press, 1987), and Richard Wilkinson and Kate Pickett, *The Inner Level: How More Equal Societies Reduce Stress, Restore Sanity, and Improve Everyone's Well-Being* (London: Penguin Press, 2019). I owe this formulation of the thought—better to be at the center of your own society than on the margins of someone else's—to Maisie Bilston.

29   **it will never be in St. Clair Shores:** See Dennis Quaid's speech in the 1979 film *Breaking Away:* "You know, I used to think I was a really great quarterback in high school. Still think so, too. Can't even bring myself to light a cigarette 'cause I keep thinkin' I gotta stay in shape. You know what really gets me, though? I mean, here I am, I gotta live in this stinkin' town, and I gotta read in the newspapers about some hot-shot kid, new star of the college team. Every year, it's gonna be a new one. Every year it's never gonna be me." Steve Tesich, *Breaking Away*, DVD, directed by Peter Yates, Los Angeles: 20th Century Fox, 1979.

30   **less safe and less controlled:** Anonymous resident in conversation with the author, St. Clair Shores, Michigan, May 3, 2018.

30   **mortality rates (especially among middle-aged men) rise:** In 1999, midlife mortality rates among white non-Hispanics stopped falling and began to rise, even as mortality rates among older people and other racial and ethnic groups continued to fall. Anne Case and Angus Deaton note that "deaths of despair"—deaths related to drug overdoses, suicides, and alcohol poisoning—account for much of this increase. Their data collect suicide, overdose, and alcohol-related deaths per 100,000 persons for white, non-Hispanic fifty- to fifty-four-year-old men and women, by their level of education. For men with a high school degree or less, this rate increased by 130 percent between 1998 and 2015; for men with a BA or more, it increased by 44 percent. For women with a high school degree or less, this rate increased 381 percent; for women with a BA or more, it increased by 70 percent. Case and Deaton argue that declining job prospects and economic insecurity are the most compelling explanations for this trend. See Anne Case and Angus Deaton, "Mortality and Morbidity in the 21st Century," *Brookings Papers on Economic Activity* (Spring 2017), accessed July 5, 2018, www.brookings.edu/bpea-articles/mortality-and-morbidity-in-the-21st-century/. Hereafter cited as Case and Deaton, "Mortality and Morbidity." David Autor, David Dorn, and Gordon Hanson demonstrate a similar correlation between manufacturing trade shocks and declining rates of marriage and fertility. See David Autor, David Dorn, and Gordon Hanson, "When Work Disappears: Manufacturing Decline and the Falling Marriage

Market Value of Young Men," NBER Working Paper No. 23173 (January 2018), www.nber.org/papers/w23173.

30   **a college degree or more:** See Chapter 5.

30   **For two straight years now:** For increases in mortality among middle-aged white Americans, see Anne Case and Angus Deaton, "Rising Morbidity and Mortality in Midlife Among White non-Hispanic Americans in the 21st Century," *Proceedings of the National Academy of Sciences of the United States of America* 112, no. 49 (December 2015): 15078–83, accessed July 5, 2018, www.pnas.org/content/pnas/112/49/15078.full.pdf. Hereafter cited as Case and Deaton, "Rising Morbidity." For decreases in American life expectancy, see Kenneth D. Kochanek et al., "Mortality in the United States," NCHS Data Brief No. 293 (December 2017), 1–2, accessed July 5, 2018, www.cdc.gov/nchs/data/databriefs/db293.pdf.

31   **The last two-year decrease:** More recently, the AIDS epidemic produced a one-year decrease in life expectancy in 1993. See Elizabeth Arias, Melonie Heron, and Jiaquan Xu, "United States Life Tables, 2014," *National Vital Statistics Reports* 66, no. 4 (August 2017): 45–46, accessed July 5, 2018, www.cdc.gov/nchs/data/nvsr/nvsr66/sr66_04.pdf.

31   **The billboards along I-94 East:** I took the drive on May 2, 2018.

31   **seven times as many:** See Jameson Cook, "Deaths from Heroin and Opioid Overdoses Rise in Macomb County, State," *Macomb Daily*, April 24, 2017, www.macombdaily.com/article/MD/20170424/NEWS/170429741.

31   **rising mortality overall:** See Case and Deaton, "Rising Morbidity." If midlife white mortality rates had continued to decline at their 1979–98 rate, Case and Deaton report, half a million deaths would have been avoided during 1999–2013—roughly comparable to the death toll of the U.S. AIDS epidemic through 2015.

31   **"deaths of despair":** The phrase was coined by Case and Deaton and popularized by media coverage of their 2017 study. See Drake Baer, "Economic Forces Making US Men Less Appealing Partners, Researchers Say," CNN, September 28, 2017, accessed July 6, 2018, www.cnn.com/2017/09/28/health/american-men-less-marriageable-partner/index.html; Joel Achenbach and Dan Keating, "New Research Identifies a 'Sea of Despair' Among White, Working-Class Americans," *Washington Post*, March 23, 2017, accessed July 6, 2018, www.washingtonpost.com/national/health-science/new-research-identifies-a-sea-of-despair-among-white-working-class-americans/2017/03/22/c777ab6e-0da6-11e7-9b0d-d27c98455440_story.html?hpid=hp_hp-top-table-main_whitedeaths-1am-1%3Ahomepage%2Fstory&utm_term=.04bad358697c.

32   **make such extreme demands:** One study surveyed 4,317 students from ten high-performing public and private schools in upper-middle-class communities and found that students spent an average of 3.11 hours on homework per night. Students at one of the ten schools reported spending 3.59 hours on homework per night. See Mollie Galloway, Jerusha Conner, and Denise Pope, "Nonacademic Effects of Homework in Privileged, High-Performing Schools," *Journal of Experimental Education* 81, no. 4 (2013): 498, accessed July 10, 2018, www.tandfonline.com/doi/pdf/10.1080/00220973.2012.745469#.Ux3fF_ldXTo. See also Pope's anecdotal evidence in Denise Pope, *"Doing School": How We Are Creating a Generation of Stressed Out, Materialistic, and Miseducated Students* (New Haven, CT: Yale University Press, 2001), 83. One student with whom Pope spoke at an elite California school spent "at least five hours" per day on homework.

32   **schoolwork-induced sleep deprivation:** See, e.g., Anne G. Wheaton, Daniel P. Chapman, and Janet B. Croft, "School Start Times, Sleep, Behavioral, Health, and Academic Outcomes: A Review of the Literature," *Journal of School Health* 86, no. 5 (May 2016): 363–81, accessed July 10, 2018, https://stacks.cdc.gov/view/cdc/38887/cdc_38887_DS1.pdf. Wheaton et al. name schoolwork as one of a few significant factors in adolescent sleep deprivation, citing Mary A. Carskadon, "Factors Influencing Sleep Patterns of Adolescents," in *Adolescent Sleep Patterns: Biological, Social, and Psychological Influences*, ed. M. A. Carskadon (Cambridge: Cambridge University Press, 2002), 8–9.

32   **twenty-four hours a day:** Anonymous lawyer in conversation with the author. Email record on file with author.

32   **advance through the hierarchy:** Ho, *Liquidated*, 87.

32 **"the hardest working":** Arlie Russell Hochschild, *The Time Bind: When Work Becomes Home and Home Becomes Work* (New York: Metropolitan Books, 1997), 56. Hereafter cited as Hochschild, *The Time Bind*. The executive added, "It's going to be a long time before somebody becomes the CEO of a company saying, 'I'm going to be a wonderfully balanced person'—because there are just too many others who aren't. The environment here is very competitive" (56–57).

32 **twenty-five fewer weekly hours:** Jerry Jacobs and Kathleen Gerson, *The Time Divide: Work, Family, and Gender Inequality* (Cambridge, MA: Harvard University Press, 2004), 65–66. Hereafter cited as Jacobs and Gerson, *The Time Divide*. Nearly two-thirds of all workers would reduce their workweek by an average of ten hours. Steven Ginsberg, "Raising Corporate Profits by Reaching Out to Families," *Washington Post*, April 19, 1998, H7; Sue Shellenbarger, "Study of U.S. Workers Finds Sharp Rise Since 1992 in Desire to Reduce Hours," *Wall Street Journal*, April 15, 1998, A10. For discussion of the generational shift in priorities within law and accounting firms as young men as well as women express greater desire for time with their families, see Douglas McCracken, "Winning the Talent War for Women: Sometimes It Takes a Revolution," *Harvard Business Review*, November–December 2000, 159, 161; Bruce Balestier, "'Mommy Track' No Career Derailment," *New York Law Journal*, June 9, 2000, 24; Terry Carter, "Your Time or Your Money," *ABA Journal*, February 2001, 26. One survey by Harris Interactive and the Radcliffe Public Policy Center found that almost three-quarters of men in their middle thirties, compared to only a quarter of men over sixty-five, would be willing to take lower salaries in exchange for more time available for their family. Kirstin Downey Grimsley, "Family a Priority for Young Workers: Survey Finds Changes in Men's Thinking," *Washington Post*, May 3, 2000, E1. See generally Bruce Tulgan, *The Manager's Pocket Guide to Generation X* (Pelham, MA: HRD Press, 1997).

32 **They say this because:** Nearly three-quarters found that work interfered with their capacity to maintain their home, 58 percent experienced work as an obstacle to strong relationships with their children, 46 percent found that work obstructed good relations with their spouses (45 percent reported being too tired, on seeing their spouses at the end of a working day, to say anything to them at all), and 50 percent reported that their jobs made it impossible to have a satisfying sex life. Hewlett and Luce, "Extreme Jobs."

33 **"time famine":** American Bar Association, *The Report of "At the Breaking Point," a National Conference on the Emerging Crisis in the Quality of Lawyers' Health and Lives, Its Impact on Law Firms and Client Services* (American Bar Association, 1991), 3.

33 **one in ten applicants:** Preschool admissions consultants, whose hourly fees often climb well into the hundreds, say that some elite Manhattan preschools accept as few as 4 or 5 percent of applicants per year. See Elyse Moody, "Confessions of a Preschool Admissions Coach," LearnVest, June 18, 2013, accessed July 10, 2018, www.learnvest.com/2013/06/confessions-of-a-preschool-admissions-coach, and Emily Jane Fox, "How New York's 1% Get Kids into Preschool," CNN Money, June 19, 2014, accessed July 10, 2018, http://money.cnn.com/2014/06/10/luxury/preschool-new-york-city/. For comparison, the acceptance rates for the classes of 2021 at Harvard, Yale, and West Point are 5.2, 6.9, and 9.5 percent respectively. See "Admissions Statistics," Harvard University, accessed July 10, 2018, https://college.harvard.edu/admissions/admissions-statistics; "Class of 2021 Is One for the Record Books," *YaleNews*, May 16, 2017, accessed July 10, 2018, https://news.yale.edu/2017/05/16/class-2021-one-record-books; and "Class of 2021—By the Numbers," U.S. Military Academy, accessed July 10, 2018, www.usma.edu/parents/SiteAssets/RDayWelcomeBrief2017.pdf.

33 **now commonly apply:** See "An Hereditary Meritocracy," *The Economist*, January 24, 2015, accessed July 10, 2018, www.economist.com/briefing/2015/01/22/an-hereditary-meritocracy, describing the practice of Jennifer Brozost of the Peas educational consultancy. See also David Kirp, *The Sandbox Investment: The Preschool Movement and Kids-First Politics* (Cambridge, MA: Harvard University Press, 2009), hereafter cited as Kirp, *The Sandbox Investment*, and Liz Moyer, "The Most Expensive Preschools," *Forbes*, September 19, 2007, accessed July 10, 2018, www.forbes.com/2007/09/18/education-preschool-kindergarten-biz-cx_lm_0919preschool.html.

33 **Nearly thirty thousand students:** See Leslie Brody, "Who Got into Stuyvesant and New York's Other Elite Public High Schools," *Wall Street Journal*, March 7, 2018, www.wsj.com/articles/who-got-into-stuyvesant-and-new-yorks-other-elite-public-high-schools-1520465259.

33 **Elite universities that:** For instance, in 1991, Columbia University, the Massachusetts Institute of Technology, and the California Institute of Technology admitted 32 percent, 31 percent, and 30 percent of applicants respectively; in 2016 they admitted 6 percent, 8 percent, and 8 percent. Among "top ten" universities, the average acceptance rate in 1991 was 27 percent. In 2016 it was 8 percent. The "top ten" universities, for purposes of this claim, are: the California Institute of Technology, Columbia, Dartmouth, Duke, Harvard, MIT, Princeton, Stanford, the University of Chicago, the University of Pennsylvania, and Yale. The construction of the list is obviously imprecise, but these eleven universities commonly appear (with strikingly little fluctuation) among the top ten universities in the *U.S. News & World Report* rankings. For 1991 acceptance rates, *see Peterson's Guide to Four-Year Colleges*, 13th ed. (Princeton, NJ: Peterson's Guides, 1993). For 1995 acceptance rates, see *America's Best Colleges 1997* (Washington, DC: *U.S. News & World Report*, 1996–97). For 2016 acceptance rates, see "National University Rankings," *U.S. News & World Report*, accessed July 26, 2018, www.usnews.com/best-colleges/rankings/national-universities?_sort=acceptance-rate&_sort-direction=asc.

33 **can reach twenty to one:** See Debra Cassens Weiss, "These BigLaw Firms Had the Highest Spreads in Partner Compensation," *ABA Journal Daily News*, June 19, 2013, accessed July 13, 2018, www.abajournal.com/news/article/these_biglaw_firms_had_the_highest_spreads_in_partner_compensation/, and Aric Press, "Revealed: Compensation Spreads of the American Law 200," *American Lawyer*, June 17, 2013, accessed July 13, 2018, www.law.com/americanlawyer/almID/1202600641230/.

33 **and the firms expel:** See Joe Patrice, "Biglaw Partners on the Hot Seat: Firms Are Demoting Partners Hand over Fist," *Above the Law*, October 11, 2016, accessed July 13, 2018, https://abovethelaw.com/2016/10/biglaw-partners-on-the-hot-seat-firms-are-demoting-partners-hand-over-fist/, and Sara Randazzo, "Law Firms Demote Partners as Pressure Mounts over Profits," *Wall Street Journal*, October 10, 2016, accessed July 13, 2013, www.wsj.com/articles/law-firms-demote-partners-as-pressure-mounts-over-profits-1476137818/.

33 **an annual "bonus day":** See Kevin Roose and Susanne Craig, "It's Goldman Bonus Day," *New York Times*, January 19, 2012, accessed July 16, 2018, https://dealbook.nytimes.com/2012/01/19/its-goldman-sachs-bonus-day/, and Susanne Craig, "It's Bonus Week on Wall Street," *New York Times*, January 15, 2013, accessed July 16, 2018, https://dealbook.nytimes.com/2013/01/15/its-bonus-week-on-wall-street/.

33 **Large corporations distinguish:** See, e.g., "Ascending to the C-Suite," McKinsey & Company, April 2015, accessed July 16, 2018, www.mckinsey.com/featured-insights/leadership/ascending-to-the-c-suite.

34 **even CEOs get their compensation:** See Chapter 4.

34 **the battle to win intensifies:** See Robert Frank and Philip Cook, *The Winner-Take-All Society: Why the Few at the Top Get So Much More Than the Rest of Us* (New York: Penguin, 1995). Hereafter cited as Frank and Cook, *The Winner-Take-All Society*.

35 **the alternative to victory is elimination:** See, e.g., Marc Galanter and Thomas Palay, *Tournament of Lawyers: The Transformation of the Big Law Firm* (Chicago: University of Chicago Press, 1991).

36 **liberates its owners:** This liberating power of conventional wealth has in fact grown over time, as the social and economic structures within which physical and financial capital is owned increasingly separate ownership from control over the capital. An aristocratic landowner, in the ancien régime, may have been bound by a combination of legal and social institutions actively to administer his lands in a particular way, with designated tenant farmers selling to designated markets. The rise of a commercial economy effectively commodified physical capital—most notably land, but also the tools and materials deployed in traditional, guild-based trades. In this way, the commercial economy pulled wealth out of its fixed social context and freed

owners of physical or financial capital from the constraints that had bound aristocrats and artisans.

The midcentury American joint stock corporation, owned by dispersed shareholders and professionally run by (modestly) salaried managers, whose incomes were independent of profits, represented the high point of this separation. See generally Adolf Berle and Gardiner Means, *The Modern Corporation and Private Property* (Piscataway, NJ: Transaction Publishers, 1991), and Walther Rathenau, *In Days to Come*, trans. Eden and Cedar Paul (London: G. Allen & Unwin Ltd., 1921). Wealth constituted in this fashion frees its owner from every thick, personal connection to her assets and from every call that these assets might previously have asserted on her time and attention. The only rational—indeed, the only possible—course of conduct for an owner of such wealth is passively to let rents come to him as income, and then to devote his active energies to whatever projects or passions incite his authentic ambition. Commodified physical and financial wealth emancipates the rich.

36  **human capital:** The term *human capital* is itself deeply embedded in meritocracy's career. Long disfavored as crass, it rose to prominence in the 1960s, just as the meritocracy that is now fully leaved was first conceived, at least as a serious enterprise. Indeed, the term entered mainstream thought through the economist Gary Becker—meritocracy's most formidable ideologue, both for better and for worse—who used it as the title of a book published in 1964. See Gary Becker, *Human Capital: A Theoretical and Empirical Analysis with Special Reference to Education* (New York: Columbia University Press, 1964). The use of "leaved" and "conceived" borrows from Philip Larkin, "Long Lion Days," in Larkin, *The Complete Poems*, 323.

37  **"devours everything in its path":** See Anton Chekhov, *The Cherry Orchard*, in *Anton Chekhov, Plays*, trans. Elisaveta Fen (New York: Viking Penguin, 1959), 363.

38  **"Human Capital Management":** See Kevin Roose, *Young Money: Inside the Hidden World of Wall Street's Post-Crash Recruits* (New York: Grand Central Publishing, 2014), 35, and "Human Capital Management," Goldman Sachs, accessed July 16, 2018, www.goldmansachs.com/careers/divisions/human-capital -management/.

39  **Fewer than one in one hundred jobs:** Here see the calculations reported in Daniel Markovits, "How Much Redistribution Should There Be?," *Yale Law Journal* 112 (2003): 2311–13.

40  **enslaves them in production:** This metaphor runs surprisingly deep. It has been observed that one of the deepest pathologies of slavery was to make every human excellence—intelligence, strength, or beauty—an additional source of vulnerability for the slave, a new invitation and avenue for ruthless exploitation by a slaveowner. Meritocratic inequality based on superordinate labor adds self-ownership to this regime, which makes a massive moral difference: it enables the superordinate worker to capture the benefits that come from her own exploitation. But capturing the benefits does not erase the burdens, and self-ownership inserts exploitation inside the elite's own lives. Self-ownership is no mere metaphor but rather a literal social and economic fact, with immediate and concrete consequences. An owner of human capital is not just the person who owns but also the person who is owned.

40  **useful without fuss:** This formulation borrows from Arthur Koestler, *Darkness at Noon*, trans. Daphne Hardy (New York: Macmillan, 1941), 174. Hardy's translation reads, "Honour is to be useful without vanity." George Orwell's essays on Koestler use the word "fuss."

40  **"gold stars" and "shiny things":** See Sturm and Makovi, "Full Participation," 37.

40  **the right food:** See John Updike, *Rabbit, Run* (New York: Alfred A. Knopf, 1960), 48. "Oh Harry," the protagonist's old basketball coach complains, "you can't understand an old man's hunger, you eat and eat and it's never the right food. You can't understand that."

40  **up the class structure:** These formulations benefited from a discussion with Julieta Lemaitre.

41  **bright, unreal path:** The phrase borrows from Philip Larkin, "Nothing Significant Was Really Said," in Larkin, *The Complete Poems*, 178.

41  **No quantity of income:** An astute and timely reflection on why this is so appears in Robert Skidelsky and Edward Skidelsky, *How Much Is Enough? Money and the Good Life* (New York:

Other Press, 2013). Hereafter cited as Skidelsky and Skidelsky, *How Much Is Enough?*

41  **White-Collar Salt Mines:** This phrase follows Tony Schwartz and Christine Porath, "Why You Hate Work," *New York Times*, May 30, 2014, accessed July 17, 2018, www.nytimes.com/2014 /06/01/opinion/sunday/why-you-hate-work.html.

41  **she urinated on herself:** See Frank Bruni, "Naked Confessions of the College-Bound," *New York Times*, June 14, 2014, accessed July 17, 2018, www.nytimes.com/2014/06/15/opinion/sunday /frank-bruni-oversharing-in-admissions-essays.html.

41  **"Duck Syndrome":** See Julie Scelfo, "Suicide on Campus and the Pressure of Perfection," *New York Times*, July 27, 2015, accessed July 17, 2018, www.nytimes.com/2015/08/02/education /edlife/stress-social-media-and-suicide-on-campus.html? mcubz=0.

41  **"The 10 minutes that I give":** See Boris Groysberg and Robin Abrahams, "Manage Your Work, Manage Your Life," *Harvard Business Review*, March 2014, accessed July 17, 2018, https:// hbr.org/2014/03/manage-your-work-manage-your-life. See also Anne Weisberg, "The Workplace Culture That Flying Nannies Won't Fix," *New York Times*, August 24, 2015, accessed July 17, 2018, www.nytimes.com/2015/08/24/opinion/the-workplace -culture-that-flying-nannies-wont-fix.html?mcubz=0.

41  **where four-fifths of adults:** See U.S. Census Bureau, American Community Survey 5-Year Estimates 2012–2016, *Educational Attainment*, Palo Alto city, California, accessed July 17, 2018, https://factfinder.census.gov/faces/tableservices/jsf/pages/pro ductview.xhtml?src=CF. According to these estimates, 80.0 percent of Palo Alto's adult population hold BAs and 51.5 percent hold graduate or professional degrees.

41  **triples the national median:** Median family income in Palo Alto nearly triples the national median, and median home values are about ten times the national median.

Median family income in Palo Alto is about $176,000. See U.S. Census Bureau, American Community Survey 5-Year Estimates 2012–2016, *Selected Economic Characteristics*, Palo Alto city, California, accessed July 17, 2018, https://factfinder.cen sus.gov/faces/tableservices/jsf/pages/productview.xhtml?src =CF. The national median is about $68,000. See U.S. Census Bureau, American Community Survey 5-Year Estimates 2012– 2016, *Selected Economic Characteristics*, United States, accessed July 17, 2018, https://factfinder.census.gov/faces/tableservices /jsf/pages/productview.xhtml?src=CF.

According to the Census Bureau, median house prices in Palo Alto and St. Clair Shores, for the period between 2012 and 2016, were $1,702,100 and $102,400 respectively. See U.S. Census Bureau, American Community Survey 5-Year Estimates 2012–2016, *Selected Housing Characteristics*, Palo Alto city, California, and St. Clair Shores city, Michigan, accessed July 17, 2018, https://factfinder.census.gov/faces/nav/jsf/pages/index .xhtml. According to Zillow, average home values in Palo Alto in July 2018 were $2,572,300. See "Palo Alto CA Real Estate," Zillow, accessed July 18, 2018, www.zillow.com/homes/for_sale /Palo-Alto-CA/26374_rid/globalrelevanceex_sort/71.483 085,-113.07129,24.407137,-173.188477_rect/3_zm/. And according to Realtor, the median prices of homes for sale in Palo Alto on July 18, 2018, was $2,390,000—between seven and ten times the national median. See "Palo Alto, CA Real Estate & Homes for Sale," Realtor.com, accessed July 18, 2018, www.real tor.com/realestateandhomes-search/Palo-Alto_CA; "United States Home Prices & Values," Zillow, accessed July 18, 2018, www.zillow.com/home-values/; and U.S. Census Bureau, "Median Sales Price of Houses Sold for the United States," Federal Reserve Bank of St. Louis, updated April 24, 2018, accessed July 18, 2018, https://fred.stlouisfed.org/series/MSPUS.

Silicon Valley, moreover, enfolds Palo Alto in a mantle of wealth and education, stretching from San Francisco to San Jose. The technology and venture capital firms that dominate the local economy—companies like Apple and Google, and New Enterprise Associates and Sequoia Capital—pay immense wages to one of the best-educated and most elite workforces ever assembled, anywhere.

41  **St. Clair Shores:** According to estimates based on data from the 2013–14 school year, St Clair Shores' Lakeview Public Schools spend $10,309 per student per year. Palo Alto Unified school district spends $18,795 per student per year. See National Center for Education Statistics, *Common Core of Data (CCD)*,

distributed by the Institute of Educational Sciences, accessed June 30, 2018, https://nces.ed.gov/ccd/districtsearch/index.asp.

41 **nationwide on the SAT:** In 2017, the average student at Henry M. Gunn High School scored 663 (about the 90th percentile score nationally) on the Evidence-Based Reading and Writing section of the new SAT and 706 (about the 95th-percentile score nationally) on the Math section. The average student at Palo Alto High scored 664 in Evidence-Based Reading and Writing and 680 in Math (both about 90th-percentile scores according to national rubrics). See Palo Alto High School, *Palo Alto High School 2017–2018 School Profile*, accessed July 18, 2018, https://paly.net/sites/de fault/files/Paly1718_profile_and_grading_key.pdf; Henry M. Gunn High School, *Henry M. Gunn High School 2017–18 School Profile*, accessed July 18, 2018, https://gunn.pausd.org/sites /default/files/2017-2018%20Gunn%20School%20Profile .pdf; and College Board, *SAT: Understanding Scores 2017*, accessed July 18, 2018, https://collegereadiness.collegeboard.org/ pdf/under standing-sat-scores.pdf.

42 **to Stanford alone:** See Kai Oda and Edan Sneh, "College Acceptance Rates for PALY Students," *The Campanile*, January 25, 2017, https://thecampanile.org/2017/01/25/collegeinfo/. These numbers have been checked for accuracy by comparing them to various online reports posted in student forums and other places that collect college admissions news and gossip.

42 **four to five times the national average:** See Hanna Rosin, "The Silicon Valley Suicides: Why Are So Many Kids with Bright Prospects Killing Themselves in Palo Alto?," *Atlantic*, December 2015, accessed July 18, 2018, www.theatlantic.com/magazine /archive/2015/12/the-silicon-valley-suicides/413140/. Hereafter cited as Rosin, "The Silicon Valley Suicides."

42 **"like the cannon that goes off":** See Rosin, "The Silicon Valley Suicides."

42 **higher rates of drug:** See Suniya Luthar and Karen D'Avanzo, "Contextual Factors in Substance Use: A Study of Suburban and Inner-City Adolescents," *Development and Psychopathology* 11, no. 4 (December 1999): 845–67.

42 **double or triple the national average:** See Suniya Luthar, "The Culture of Affluence: Psychological Costs of Material Wealth," *Child Development* 74, no. 6 (November–December 2003): 1582.

42 **In a recent study:** See Vicki Abeles, "Is the Drive for Success Making Our Children Sick?," *New York Times*, January 2, 2016, accessed November 18, 2018, www.nytimes.com/2016/01/03 /opinion/sunday/is-the-drive-for-success-making-our-children -sick.html. This study was performed by Stuart Slavin, of the Saint Louis University School of Medicine.

42 **College students, similarly:** The absolute rate, moreover, is large: roughly 20 percent today versus roughly 10 percent in 2000. See American College Health Association, *National College Health Assessment Institutional Data Report—Spring 2000* (Baltimore: American College Health Association, 2000), accessed July 18, 2018, www.acha-ncha.org/docs/ACHA-NCHA _Reference_Group_Report_Spring2000.pdf, and American College Health Association, *National College Health Assessment Undergraduate Student Reference Group Data Report—Fall 2017* (Hanover, MD: American College Health Association, 2018), accessed July 18, 2018, www.acha-ncha.org/docs/NCHA-II _FALL_2017_REFERENCE_GROUP_DATA_REPORT _UNDERGRADS_ONLY.pdf.

Systematic data on college students' mental health are a surprisingly recent invention, so comparisons to periods before the millennium are difficult to draw. Nevertheless, individual colleges have reported steep increases in their students' mental health troubles beginning earlier, in the mid-1990s. In 2002, Columbia reported that use of mental health services had increased 40 percent since the 1994–95 academic year. In November 2001, MIT reported a 50 percent increase in the use of mental health services between 1995 and 2000. And in 2002, SUNY at Purchase reported a 48 percent increase over the past three years. See Leslie Berger, "The Therapy Generation," *New York Times*, January 13, 2002, accessed July 18, 2018, www .nytimes.com/2002/01/13/education/the-therapy-generation .html. Similarly, in 2002, the University of Cincinnati reported a 55 percent increase in the number of students seeking counseling over the previous six years and Xavier University reported a 40 percent increase in counseling visits compared to the previous year, with depression the most common problem. See Kristina Goetz, "Counseling Demand Overwhelms Colleges,"

*Cincinnati Enquirer*, March 18, 2002, accessed July 18, 2018, http://enquirer.com/editions/2002/03/18/loc_counseling _demand.html. See also Martha Anne Kitzrow, "The Mental Health Needs of Today's College Students: Challenges and Recommendations," *NASPA Journal* 41, no. 1 (Fall 2003): 167–81, accessed July 18, 2018, www.tandfonline.com/doi/abs /10.2202/1949-6605.1310?journalCode=uarp19.

42 **"demoralization, alienation":** See University of Pennsylvania, *Report of the Task Force on Student Psychological Health and Welfare* (Philadelphia: University of Pennsylvania, 2015), accessed July 18, 2018, https://almanac.upenn.edu/archive/volumes/v61 /n23/pdf/task-force-psychological-health.pdf. See also Julie Scelfo, "Suicide on Campus and the Pressure of Perfection," *New York Times*, July 27, 2015, accessed July 18, 2018, www.nytimes .com/2015/08/02/education/edlife/stress-social-media-and -suicide-on-campus.html.

42 **A broader report:** See Frank Bruni, "Rethinking College Admissions," *New York Times*, January 19, 2016, accessed July 18, 2018, www.nytimes.com/2016/01/20/opinion/rethinking-col lege-admissions.html?mcubz=0.

42 **A junior banker:** See Dawn Kopecki, "Young Bankers Fed Up with 90-Hour Weeks Move to Startups," Bloomberg, May 9, 2014, accessed July 18, 2018, www.bloomberg.com/news/arti cles/2014-05-09/young-bankers-fed-up-with-90-hour-weeks -move-to-startups.

43 **A former lawyer:** Elie Mystal, "In Re the Passing of a Skadden Associate," *Above the Law*, June 30, 2011, accessed July 18, 2018, https://abovethelaw.com/2011/06/in-re-the-passing-of-a -skadden-associate/?rf=1. Hereafter cited as Mystal, "In Re the Passing of a Skadden Associate."

43 **commitment to her job:** Mystal, "In Re the Passing of a Skadden Associate."

43 **Bankers have in some cases:** See Andrew Ross Sorkin, "Reflections on Stress and Long Hours on Wall Street," *New York Times*, June 17, 2015, accessed November 18, 2018, www.ny times.com/2015/06/02/business/dealbook/reflections-on -stress-and-long-hours-on-wall-street.html.

43 **NFL player Ronnie Lott's:** Tom Pedulla, "Giants' Jason Pierre-Paul Should Be Able to Overcome Loss of Finger, Former Players Say," *New York Times*, July 9, 2015, accessed July 18, 2018, www .nytimes.com/2015/07/10/sports/football/giants-jason-pierre -paul-should-be-able-to-overcome-loss-of-finger-former-play ers-say.html.

43 **"deliver results":** See Amazon, "Leadership Principles," accessed July 18, 2018, www.amazon.jobs/principles. Hereafter cited as Amazon, "Leadership Principles."

43 **"even when doing so" . . . "vocally self-critical":** See Amazon, "Leadership Principles."

43 **"nearly every person":** Jodi Kantor and David Streitfeld, "Inside Amazon: Wrestling Big Ideas in a Bruising Workplace," *New York Times*, August 15, 2015, accessed July 18, 2018, www.ny times.com/2015/08/16/technology/inside-amazon-wrestling -big-ideas-in-a-bruising-workplace.html. Hereafter cited as Kantor and Streitfeld, "Inside Amazon."

43 **"Congratulations, you're being promoted":** Kantor and Streitfeld, "Inside Amazon."

43 **even banal:** See, e.g., David Auerbach, "I've Worked Insanely Demanding Tech Jobs—and I Really Doubt Amazon Is Much Worse Than Google—or Even Microsoft," *Slate*, August 17, 2015, accessed July 18, 2018, www.slate.com/articles/technology /bitwise/2015/08/amazon_abuse_of_white_collar_workers_i _worked_at_microsoft_and_google_and.html; Anne Weisberg, "The Workplace Culture That Flying Nannies Won't Fix," *New York Times*, August 24, 2015, accessed July 18, 2018, www.ny times.com/2015/08/24/opinion/the-workplace-culture-that -flying-nannies-wont-fix.html?mcubz=0; "Depiction of Amazon Stirs a Debate About Work Culture," *New York Times*, August 18, 2015, accessed July 18, 2018, www.nytimes.com/2015 /08/19/technology/amazon-workplace-reactions-comments .html.

43 **not materially different:** The language of worker competition changes across firms and over time. The particular phrases just rehearsed belong peculiarly to Amazon. However, American corporations constantly measure their managers against one another, at every level in their hierarchies, and promote the best while eliminating the worst. GE "ranked and yanked" managers in the 1990s. Herman Aguinis and Charles A. Pierce,

"Enhancing the Relevance of Organizational Behavior by Embracing Performance Management Research," *Journal of Organizational Behavior* 29, no. 1 (January 2008): 142. Microsoft employed "stack ranking" in the 2000s. See Margaret Heffernan, "Lose the Competition," *RSA Journal* 160, no. 5558 (2014): 42. And Netflix employs the "keeper test." See Netflix, "Netflix Culture," accessed July 18, 2018, https://jobs.netflix .com/culture. And while particular implementations may fall into disrepute for being clumsy or creating perverse incentives (to avoid taking chances at work, or to undermine rather than support colleagues), the basic idea of sifting and winnowing elite workers according to measured performance necessarily endures.

43  **Burnout pervades the elite workplace:** In a recent study of senior corporate leaders, nearly every subject diagnosed symptoms of burnout in her or his own life, and one-third described their burnout as extreme. See Leslie Kwoh, "When the CEO Burns Out: Job Fatigue Catches Up to Some Executives Amid Mounting Expectations," *Wall Street Journal*, May 7, 2013, www.wsj .com/articles/SB10001424127887323687604578469124008524696. See also Tony Schwartz and Christine Porath, "Why You Hate Work," *New York Times*, May 30, 2014, accessed July 18, 2018, www.nytimes.com/2014/06/01/opinion/sunday/why-you -hate-work.html?mcubz=0&_r=0.

44  **"hit the wall"** . . . **"climb the wall":** Kantor and Streitfeld, "Inside Amazon."

44  **"it's hard to be":** Reed Abelson, "A Survey of Wall St. Finds Women Disheartened," *New York Times*, July 26, 2001, accessed July 18, 2018, www.nytimes.com/2001/07/26/business/a-survey -of-wall-st-finds-women-disheartened.html.

44  **"Some people flame out":** Hochschild, *The Time Bind*, 56.

44  **An unhappy, even disconsolate:** See, e.g., Brigid Schulte, *Overwhelmed: Work, Love, and Play When No One Has the Time* (New York: Farrar, Straus & Giroux, 2014).

44  **Roughly two-thirds:** Hewlett and Luce, "Extreme Jobs."

44  **"Vietnam moment":** See John Thornhill, "A Universal Basic Income Is an Old Idea with Modern Appeal," *Financial Times*, March 14, 2016, accessed July 18, 2018, www.ft.com /content/a9758f1a-e9c0-11e5-888e-2eadd5fbc4a4.

44  **Does anyone actually want it?:** Larry Kramer, "From the Dean," *Stanford Lawyer* 77 (Fall 2007), accessed July 18, 2018, https://law.stanford.edu/stanford-lawyer/articles/from-the -dean-15/.

## Chapter Three: The Coming Class War

46  **sumptuary codes:** See, e.g., Alan Hunt, *Governance of the Consuming Passions: A History of Sumptuary Law* (Basingstoke: Macmillan, 1996).

46  **mostly did not:** The poor provided an exception to this rule, even at midcentury—and indeed more so at midcentury than they do today. For more on the recent history of poverty in America, see Chapter 4.

46  **Jerry Garcia settled in Palo Alto:** See "The Grateful Dead: Making the Scene in Palo Alto," Palo Alto History, accessed July 18, 2018, www.paloaltohistory.org/the-grateful-dead.php.

46  **Bob Seger played the Crow's Nest:** See, for instance, "Crow's Nest East," The Concert Database, accessed July 18, 2018, http://theconcertdatabase.com/venues/crows-nest-east.

46  **were similar in both towns:** In 1960, the median family income in St. Clair Shores was only about one-seventh lower than in Palo Alto, and median house prices were only about one-third to one-half lower. For incomes, see U.S. Census Bureau, "General Social and Economic Characteristics: Michigan," in 1960 Census of Population, 182, Table 33, www2.census.gov/library /publications/decennial/1960/population-volume-1/377 22966v1p24ch4.pdf, and U.S. Census Bureau, "General Social and Economic Characteristics: California," in 1960 Census of Population, 224, Table 33, www2.census.gov/library/publica tions/decennial/1960/population-volume-1/vol-01-06-f.pdf. For house prices, the one-third figure comes from the Census Bureau. See U.S. Census Bureau, "Michigan," in 1960 Census of Housing, 6, Table 1, https://www2.census.gov/library/publica tions/decennial/1960/housing-volume-1/41962442v1p5ch2 .pdf, and U.S. Census Bureau, "California," in 1960 Census of Housing, 5, Table 1, https://www2.census.gov/library/publi cations/decennial/1960/housing-volume-1/41962442v1p2ch4

.pdf. The one-half figure comes from comparing the median prices of the sixty-two houses in Palo Alto listed for sale in the *San Francisco Chronicle* in 1960 and the median prices of the sixty houses in St. Clair Shores listed for sale in the *Detroit Free Press* in 1960.

46  **places to shop:** Brian Edwards, *University Architecture* (Milton Park: Taylor & Francis, 2014), 19.

46  **places to live in St. Clair Shores:** "Groundbreaking Today: 750 Apartments in Shores Project," *Detroit Free Press*, July 31, 1962, A3, and Proctor Homer Warren, Inc., "With Every Great Apartment and Sky House, We'll Throw in a Great Lake Free," advertisement, *Detroit Free Press*, November 19, 1970.

47  **converged between 1950 and 1970:** Bill Bishop, *The Big Sort: Why the Clustering of Like-Minded America Is Tearing Us Apart* (Boston: Houghton Mifflin Harcourt, 2008), 130. Hereafter cited as Bishop, *The Big Sort*. See also Christopher Berry and Edward Glaeser, "The Divergence of Human Capital Levels Across Cities," *Papers in Regional Science* 84, no. 3 (2005): 407–44, accessed July 26, 2018, www.nber.org/papers/w11617. Hereafter cited as Berry and Glaeser, "The Divergence of Human Capital."

47  **even within cities:** See also Berry and Glaeser, "The Divergence of Human Capital."

47  **Americans bought 90 percent:** In 1965, Americans bought 90.7 percent of their cars from these three companies. See Figure B: Percent of total U.S. auto industry market share, by automaker, 1961–2014, in Joel Cutcher-Gershenfeld, Dan Brooks, and Martin Mulloy, *The Decline and Resurgence of the U.S. Auto Industry* (Washington, DC: Economic Policy Institute, 2015), accessed July 18, 2018, www.epi.org/publication/the-decline -and-resurgence-of-the-u-s-auto-industry/. General Motors' Corvette sold for about $3,000 in 1956. See Richard Prince, *Corvette Buyers Guide, 1953–1967* (Minneapolis: Motorbooks International, 2002), 39. See also "How Much Cars Cost in the 60s," *The People History*, accessed October 7, 2018, www.the peoplehistory.com/60scars.html.

47  **half of their appliances:** See Sears, "Kenmore Chronology," accessed January 29, 2019, www.searsarchives.com/brands/detail /kenmore/1950s.htm; Chris Isidore, "Here's What's Killing Sears," CNN, February 12, 2018, accessed January 29, 2019, https://money.cnn.com/2018/02/12/news/companies/sears -downfall/index.html.

47  **a third of their watches:** See Amy Glasmeier, *Manufacturing Time: Global Competition in the Watch Industry, 1795–2000* (New York: Guilford Press, 2000), 189–192; "Corporations: Watches for an Impulse," *Time*, March 15, 1963, accessed November 19, 2018, http://content.time.com/time/magazine/article /0,9171,870225,00.html; Timex, "Every Third Watch Sold Is a Timex," advertisement, *Life*, December 7, 1959.

47  **"they have more money":** "Let me tell you about the very rich," Fitzgerald wrote in 1924. "They are different from you and me. They possess and enjoy early, and it does something to them, makes them soft where we are hard, and cynical where we are trustful, in a way that, unless you were born rich, it is very difficult to understand. They think, deep in their hearts, that they are better than we are because we had to discover the compensations and refuges of life for ourselves. Even when they enter deep into our world or sink below us, they still think they are better than we are. They are different." F. Scott Fitzgerald, "The Rich Boy," in *The Rich Boy* (London: Hesperus Press Limited, 2003), 3. Twelve years later, Hemingway published "The Snows of Kilimanjaro" in *Esquire*. "The rich were dull and they drank too much, or they played too much backgammon. They were dull and they were repetitious. He remembered poor Scott Fitzgerald and his romantic awe of them and how he had started a story once that began, 'The very rich are different from you and me.' And how someone had said to Scott, Yes, they have more money. But that was not humorous to Scott. He thought they were a special glamorous race and when he found out they weren't it wrecked him just as much as any other thing that wrecked him." Ernest Hemingway, "The Snows of Kilimanjaro," *Esquire*, August 1936, 200.

47  **incomes in the middle and bottom quintiles have converged:** See Chapter 4.

48  **The rich and the rest now marry:** See Murray, *Coming Apart*, 62. See also Christine Schwartz and Robert Mare, "Trends in

Educational Assortative Marriage from 1940 to 2003," *Demography* 42, no. 4 (November 2005): 629–30 (reporting that both partners had sixteen or more years of schooling in 3.95 percent of married couples in 1960 and in 18.02 percent of married couples in 2000).

48 **The rich and the rest parent:** See Chapter 5.

48 **fitness is now a status symbol:** See "Spin to Separate: Sweating on Purpose Is Becoming an Elite Phenomenon," *The Economist*, August 1, 2015, accessed July 19, 2018, www.economist.com/news/united-states/21660170-sweating-purpose-becoming-elite-phenomenon-spin-separate.

48 **The rich and the rest worship:** See Caryle Murphy, "The Most and Least Educated U.S. Religious Groups," Pew Research Center, November 4, 2016, accessed July 19, 2018, www.pewresearch.org/fact-tank/2016/11/04/the-most-and-least-educated-u-s-religious-groups/. Hereafter cited as Murphy, "The Most and Least Educated U.S. Religious Groups." David Masci, "How Income Varies Among U.S. Religious Groups," Pew Research Center, October 11, 2016, accessed July 19, 2018, http://www.pewresearch.org/fact-tank/2016/10/11/how-income-varies-among-u-s-religious-groups/. Hereafter cited as Masci, "How Income Varies Among U.S. Religious Groups."

48 **Google data on searches:** See David Leonhardt, "In One America, Guns and Diet. In the Other, Cameras and 'Zoolander,'" *New York Times*, August 18, 2014, accessed July 19, 2018, www.nytimes.com/2014/08/19/upshot/inequality-and-web-search-trends.html.

48 **roughly twenty times as high:** Median household incomes in Palo Alto and St. Clair Shores, for the period between 2012 and 2016, were $137,043 and $54,590 respectively. See U.S. Census Bureau, American Community Survey 5-Year Estimates 2012–2016, *Selected Economic Characteristics*, St. Clair Shores city, Michigan, and Palo Alto city, California, accessed July 19, 2018, https://factfinder.census.gov/faces/tableservices/jsf/pages/productview.xhtml?src=CF. According to the Census Bureau, median house prices in Palo Alto and St. Clair Shores, for the period between 2012 and 2016, were $1,702,100 and $102,400 respectively. U.S. Census Bureau, American Community Survey 5-Year Estimates 2012–2016, *Selected Housing Characteristics*, St. Clair Shores city, Michigan, and Palo Alto city, California, accessed July 19, 2018, https://factfinder.census.gov/faces/tableservices/jsf/pages/productview.xhtml?src=CF. According to Zillow, average home values in Palo Alto and St. Clair Shores in July 2018 were $2,709,700 and $132,000 respectively. See "Palo Alto Real Estate," Zillow, accessed July 19, 2018, www.zillow.com/homes/for_sale/Palo-Alto-CA/26374_rid/37.375477,-121.949273,37.053944,-122.191315_rect/11_zm/, and "St. Clair Shores Real Estate," Zillow, accessed July 19, 2018, www.zillow.com/homes/for_sale/St-Clair-Shores-MI/37.375477,-121.949273,37.053944,-122.191315_rect/11_zm/. And according to Realtor, the median prices of homes for sale in Palo Alto and St. Clair Shores in July 2018 were $2,400,000 and $150,000 respectively. See "Palo Alto, CA Real Estate & Homes for Sale," Realtor.com, accessed July 19, 2018, www.realtor.com/realestateandhomes-search/Palo-Alto_CA, and "St. Clair Shores, MI Real Estate & Homes for Sale," Realtor.com, accessed July 19, 2018, www.realtor.com/realestateandhomes-search/Saint-Clair-Shores_MI.

48 **residents of St. Clair Shores:** See U.S. Census Bureau, American Community Survey 5-Year Estimates 2012–2016, *Educational Attainment*, St. Clair Shores city, Michigan, and Palo Alto city, California, accessed July 19, 2018, https://factfinder.census.gov/faces/tableservices/jsf/pages/productview.xhtml?src=CF.

48 **half that of the average city:** Bishop, *The Big Sort*, 132.

48 **large metropolitan areas:** See Dora L. Costa and Matthew E. Kahn, "Power Couples: Changes in the Locational Choice of the College Educated, 1940–1990," *Quarterly Journal of Economics* 115, no. 4 (November 2000): 1287–1315, accessed July 19, 2018, http://econ2.econ.iastate.edu/classes/econ321/orazem/costa_dual-career.pdf. Hereafter cited as Costa and Kahn, "Power Couples." Similar trends arise internationally. Across the planet, roughly a quarter of all people with a two-year college education or more live in the world's hundred largest cities. And the share of residents of these cities to have this much education doubles the share of the population worldwide and grew by a

sixth (from 18 to 21 percent) in just the decade between 2005 and 2014. See Emily Badger, "A Quarter of the World's Most Educated People Live in the 100 Largest Cities," *Washington Post*, July 18, 2014, accessed July 19, 2018, www.washingtonpost.com/news/wonk/wp/2014/07/18/a-quarter-of-the-worlds-most-educated-people-live-in-the-100-largest-cities/?utm_term=.2e8e2e0ce30c, and Ugne Saltenyte, "One Quarter of the World's Educated Population Resides in Just 100 Cities," *Euromonitor International*, July 15, 2014, accessed July 19, 2018, https://blog.euromonitor.com/2014/07/one-quarter-of-the-worlds-educated-population-resides-in-just-100-cities.html.

49 **zip codes in the top 1 percent:** See Murray, *Coming Apart*, 78, 82, 87, and Appendix B. See also Charles Murray, "Charles Murray, Author of *Coming Apart*, Examines Demographic Shifts in This New Decade," Debate This Book, April 25, 2013, accessed July 19, 2018, http://debatethisbook.com/2013/04/25/charles-murray-author-of-coming-apart-examines-demographic-shifts-in-this-new-decade/.

49 **high school degrees only:** A longitudinal study based on data from the years between 1979 and 1996 found that 19.2 percent of young adults with just a high school education moved states, while 36.6 percent of college graduates and 45.0 percent of people with more than a college education moved to a different state. See Yolanda K. Kodrzycki, "Migration of Recent College Graduates: Evidence from the National Longitudinal Survey of Youth, *New England Economic Review*, January–February 2001, 15. See also Costa and Kahn, "Power Couples"; Bishop, *The Big Sort*.

49 **an axis of economic segregation:** See Costa and Kahn, "Power Couples"; Bishop, *The Big Sort*, 130–33.

50 **forbidden by law:** See, e.g., Janelle Jones, "The Racial Wealth Gap: How African-Americans Have Been Shortchanged out of the Materials to Build Wealth," Economic Policy Institute, February 13, 2017, accessed July 19, 2018, https://www.epi.org/blog/the-racial-wealth-gap-how-african-americans-have-been-shortchanged-out-of-the-materials-to-build-wealth/.

50 **racial differences at midcentury:** In 1960, 34.5 percent of African Americans owned their own homes, for example; 34.9 percent of low-income families do so today. See U.S. Census Bureau, Census of Housing, "Historical Census of Housing Tables: Ownership Rates," accessed October 31, 2018, www.census.gov/hhes/www/housing/census/historic/ownrate.html; Felipe Chacon, "The Home Ownership Gap Is on the Wane," Trulia, August 10, 2017, www.trulia.com/research/homeownership-gap/.

In 1970, the unemployment rate for African Americans was 9.2 percent; in 2017, the unemployment rate for low-income Americans was 13 percent. See Robert W. Fairlie and William A. Sundstrom, "The Racial Unemployment Gap in Long-Run Perspective," *American Economic Review* 87, no. 2 (May 1997), www.jstor.org/stable/2950936?seq=1#metadata_info_tab_contents; Janet L. Yellen, "Addressing Workforce Development Challenges in Low-Income Communities," Federal Reserve, March 28, 2017, www.federalreserve.gov/newsevents/speech/yellen20170328a.htm.

50 **a 5 percent chance:** See Becky Pettit and Bruce Western, "Mass Imprisonment and the Life Course: Race and Class Inequality in U.S. Incarceration," *American Sociological Review* 69, no. 2 (April 2004): 162.

50 **"two nations":** Benjamin Disraeli, *Sybil; or, The Two Nations* (London: Henry Colburn, 1845), 149.

51 **vulnerable and insecure:** See, e.g., Christopher Hayes, *Twilight of the Elites: America After Meritocracy* (New York: Broadway Books, 2012), hereafter cited as Hayes, *Twilight of the Elites*, and Jacob Hacker, *The Great Risk Shift* (Oxford: Oxford University Press, 2006), hereafter cited as Hacker, *The Great Risk Shift*.

51 **defend their position:** See, e.g., Joseph E. Stiglitz, *The Price of Inequality* (New York: W. W. Norton, 2012).

51 **the midcentury unity of ideals:** See Chapter 7.

51 **"the problem of our age":** Andrew Carnegie, "The Gospel of Wealth," in *The Gospel of Wealth and Other Timely Essays* (Cambridge, MA: Belknap Press of Harvard University Press, 1962 [originally published by the Century Company, New York, 1900]), 14.

51 **"If all the cleavages":** See Robert Dahl, *Democracy in the United States: Promise and Performance* (Skokie, IL: Rand McNally, 1972), 309.

52 **"the continuing responsiveness":** Robert Dahl, *Polyarchy: Participation and Opposition* (New Haven, CT: Yale University Press, 1971), 1.

The general formulation requires much filling in. On the one hand, simply counting votes—even when all votes get the same weight—cannot on its own sustain a democracy. Opinion polls might add up citizens' preferences, but without democratic institutions—political parties, campaigns, debates, and a political press—the polls merely balance private preference. They cannot sustain or guide a collective choice. On the other hand, the processes of collective engagement that democracy requires necessarily enable some citizens—who are advantaged, or even just skilled or trusted, and therefore unusually persuasive—to exert vastly greater influence over public affairs than others (even if all votes are counted equally and thus retain the same direct impact on elections). The very processes needed for politics to sustain collective choices thus undermine individual equality. Almost all of the deepest puzzles in democratic thought trace back eventually to this dilemma. For the distinction between influence and impact over democratic decision, see Ronald Dworkin, "What Is Equality? Part 3: The Place of Liberty," *Iowa Law Review* 73, no. 1 (October 1987): 1–50.

52 **the bottom 75 percent combined:** The richest 1 percent of Americans supplies over half of all campaign contributions (the richest quarter of a percent supplies about a third). Martin Gilens, *Affluence and Influence: Economic Inequality and Political Power in America* (Princeton, NJ: Princeton University Press, 2012), 242 (citing Lynda Powell and data from the Congressional Campaign Study, but there is no full reference). Hereafter cited as Gilens, *Affluence and Influence.* In 1990, the richest quarter supplied nearly three-fourths of campaign contributions. The poorest fifth accounted for only one-fiftieth of campaign contributions. See Sidney Verba, Kay Lehman Schlozman, and Michael Brady, *Voice and Equality: Civic Voluntarism in American Politics* (Cambridge, MA: Harvard University Press, 1995), 194. See also Henry E. Brady, Sidney Verba, and Kay Lehman Schlozman, "Beyond SES: A Resource Model of Political Participation," *American Political Science Review* 89, no. 2 (June 1995): 271–84, and Larry Bartels, *Unequal Democracy: The Political Economy of the New Gilded Age* (Princeton, NJ: Princeton University Press, 2008), hereafter cited as Bartels, *Unequal Democracy.*

52 **collectively contributed $176 million:** Twenty backed Democrats and 138 backed Republicans. See Nicholas Confessore, Sarah Cohen, and Karen Yourish, "The Families Funding the 2016 Presidential Election," *New York Times,* October 10, 2015, accessed July 19, 2018, www.nytimes.com/interactive/2015/10/11/us/politics/2016-presidential-election-super-pac-donors.html?_r=0.

52 **promoting free-market policies:** See generally Jane Mayer, *Dark Money: The Hidden History of the Billionaires Behind the Rise of the Radical Right* (New York: Doubleday, 2016). By broadcasting their intentions, the Koch brothers could use their money to exert influence long before the first dollar was spent. See Matea Gold, "Koch-Backed Network Aims to Spend Nearly $1 Billion on 2016 Elections," *Washington Post,* January 26, 2015, and later "Correction," accessed August 1, 2018, www.washingtonpost.com/politics/koch-backed-network-aims-to-spend-nearly-1-billion-on-2016-elections/2015/01/26/77a44654-a513-11e4-a06b-9df2002b86a0_story.html. Progressive billionaires also spend lavishly. Tom Steyer planned to spend over $100 million on the 2018 midterm elections. See Edward-Isaac Dovere, "Tom Steyer's $110 million Plan to Redefine the Democrats," *Politico,* July 31, 2018, accessed August 1, 2018, www.politico.com/story/2018/07/31/steyer-democrats-millions-midterms-751245.

52 **98 percent of the increase:** Whereas there were roughly seventy-five hundred registered lobbyists in Washington in 1981, there are roughly thirteen thousand today. See Matthew P. Drennan, *Income Inequality: Why It Matters and Why Most Economists Didn't Notice* (New Haven, CT: Yale University Press, 2016), 31. Hereafter cited as Drennan, *Income Inequality.* Drennan cites Lee Drutman, "The Business of America Is Lobbying: The Expansion of Corporate Political Activity and the

Future of American Pluralism" (PhD dissertation, University of California, Berkeley, 2010), 141, https://cloudfront.escholarship.org/dist/prd/content/qt1mh761v2/qt1mh761v2.pdf?t=mtgaay.

52 **exceed $3 billion:** See Lee Drutman, *The Business of America Is Lobbying: How Corporations Became Politicized and Politics Became More Corporate* (Oxford: Oxford University Press, 2015), 8. Hereafter cited as Drutman, *The Business of America Is Lobbying.*

52 **spend perhaps ten times as much:** See Jeffrey Milyo, David Primo, and Timothy Groseclose, "Corporate PAC Campaign Contributions in Perspective," *Business and Politics* 2, no. 1 (2000): 83.

52 **as recently as the late 1990s:** See Drutman, *The Business of America Is Lobbying,* 11–12.

53 **the tax deduction for charitable giving:** See Marianne Bertrand et al., "Tax-Exempt Lobbying: Corporate Philanthropy as a Tool for Political Influence," NBER Working Paper No. 24451 (March 2018), accessed July 20, 2018, www.nber.org/papers/w24451.

53 **the Walton Foundation:** See, e.g., Motoko Rich, "A Walmart Fortune, Spreading Charter Schools," *New York Times,* April 25, 2014, accessed July 20, 2018, www.nytimes.com/2014/04/26/us/a-walmart-fortune-spreading-charter-schools.html; Valerie Strauss, "The 'Walmartization' of Public Education," *Washington Post,* March 17, 2016, accessed July 20, 2018, www.washingtonpost.com/news/answer-sheet/wp/2016/03/17/the-walmartization-of-public-education/?utm_term=.01a53a2035db. For more on philanthropy as a form of political power, see, e.g., Iain Hay and Samantha Muller, "Questioning Generosity in the Golden Age of Philanthropy," *Progress in Human Geography* 38, no. 5 (2014): 635–53; Lenore Ealy, "The Intellectual Crisis in Philanthropy," *Society* 51, no. 1 (February 2014): 87–96; Kenneth Saltman, "From Carnegie to Gates: The Bill and Melinda Gates Foundation and the Venture Philanthropy Agenda for Public Education," in *The Gates Foundation and the Future of U.S. "Public" Schools,* ed. Philip Kovacs (New York: Taylor & Francis, 2011), 1–20; Robin Rogers, "Why Philanthro-Policymaking Matters," *Society* 48, no. 5 (September 2011): 376–81; Ben Williamson, "Mediators and Mobilizers of Curriculum Reform: Education Policy Experts of the Third Sector," paper presented at the University of Stirling School of Education, December 5, 2012; Georgia Levenson Keohane, *Social Entrepreneurship for the 21st Century: Innovation Across the Nonprofit, Private, and Public Sectors* (New York: McGraw Hill Education, 2013); and Amy Brown, "Philanthrocapitalism: Race, Political Spectacle, and the Marketplace of Beneficence in a New York City School," in *What's Race Got to Do with It? How Current School Reform Policy Maintains Racial and Economic Inequality* (New York: Peter Lang, 2015), 147–66.

53 **Elections begin:** See, e.g., Nicholas Confessore and Jonathan Martin, "G.O.P. Race Starts in Lavish Haunts of Rich Donors," *New York Times,* February 28, 2015, accessed July 20, 2018, www.nytimes.com/2015/03/01/us/politics/gop-race-starts-in-lavish-haunts-of-rich-donors.html.

53 **every day in office:** See Ezra Klein, "The Most Depressing Graphic for Members of Congress," *Washington Post,* January 14, 2013, accessed July 20, 2018, www.washingtonpost.com/news/wonk/wp/2013/01/14/the-most-depressing-graphic-for-members-of-congress/?utm_term=.072d62e69b40. Hereafter cited as Klein, "The Most Depressing Graphic."

53 **This roughly triples:** See Klein, "The Most Depressing Graphic."

53 **said to resemble telemarketers:** See, e.g., David Jolly, interview with Norah O'Donnell, "Dialing for Dollars," *60 Minutes,* CBS, April 24, 2016.

53 **"If you're a lobbyist":** See James Hohmann, "The Daily 202: Mick Mulvaney's Confession Highlights the Corrosive Influence of Money in Politics," *PowerPost* (blog), *Washington Post,* April 25, 2018, accessed July 20, 2018, www.washingtonpost.com/news/powerpost/paloma/daily-202/2018/04/25/daily-202-mick-mulvaney-s-confession-highlights-the-corrosive-influence-of-money-in-politics/5adfea2230fb043711926869/?utm_term=.0bf524639cc0.

53 **whose views they promote:** See Richard Hall and Alan Deardorff, "Lobbying as Legislative Subsidy," *American Political*

*Science Review* 100, no. 1 (February 2006): 69–84. For lobbying in general, see Beth Leech, "Lobbying and Interest Group Advocacy," in *The Oxford Handbook of the American Congress*, ed. Frances Lee and Eric Schickler (New York: Oxford University Press, 2011), and Beth Leech, "Lobbying and Influence," in *The Oxford Handbook of American Political Parties and Interest Groups*, ed. Jeffrey Berry and L. Sandy Maisel (New York: Oxford University Press, 2010). See also Anthony Nownes, *Total Lobbying: What Lobbyists Want (and How They Try to Get It)* (New York: Cambridge University Press, 2006).

53  **"in effect . . . subsidized":** Motoko Rich, "A Walmart Fortune, Spreading Charter Schools," *New York Times*, April 25, 2014, accessed July 20, 2018, www.nytimes.com/2014/04/26/us/a -walmart-fortune-spreading-charter-schools.html.  Similarly, the Gates Foundation's belief that smaller schools foster competition produced over three hundred small schools in New York City in a decade. See Jessica Shiller, "City Prep: A Culture of Care in an Era of Data-Driven Reform," in *Critical Small Schools: Beyond Privatization in New York City Urban Educational Reform*, ed. Maria Hantzopoulos and Alia Tyner-Mullings (Charlotte, NC: Information Age Publishing, 2012), 4.

Similar examples may be multiplied almost endlessly. In Illinois, a challenger with strong anti-union views recently unseated an incumbent governor after just ten people made donations equal to the incumbent's entire campaign budget and one family contributed more than the incumbent received from 244 labor unions combined. The new governor at once promoted an aggressively anti-union agenda. See Nicholas Confessore, "A Wealthy Governor and His Friends Are Remaking Illinois," *New York Times*, November 29, 2015, accessed July 20, 2018, www.nytimes.com/2015/11/30/us/politics/illinois-campaign -money-bruce-rauner.html.

54  **stabilize commodity prices:** See, e.g., Edward Wyatt and Eric Lichtblau, "A Finance Overhaul Fight Draws a Swarm of Lobbyists," *New York Times*, April 19, 2010, accessed July 26, 2018, www.nytimes.com/2010/04/20/business/20derivatives.html, and Binyamin Appelbaum and Eric Lichtblau, "Banks Lobbying Against Derivatives Trading Ban," *New York Times*, May 9, 2010, accessed July 26, 2018, www.nytimes.com/2010/05/10 /business/10lobby.html, The effort bore fruit, and proposed outright bans on certain forms of derivatives trading were weakened into partial restrictions. See Edward Wyatt, "For Securities Industry, Finance Law Could Bring New Light to Derivatives," *New York Times*, July 15, 2010, accessed August 1, 2018, www .nytimes.com/2010/07/16/business/16deriv.html?action =click&contentCollection=Business%20Day&module=Relat edCovera&region=Marginalia&pgtype=article.

54  **committing tax fraud:** See 26 U.S.C. §§ 1441(c)(11) and 871(j).
54  **only minimally responsive to the 70th:** Gilens, *Affluence and Influence*, 82. (The regression coefficient for the 70th percentile is small and not statistically significant.)
54  **ignores the shared preferences:** Gilens, *Affluence and Influence*, 84–85.
54  **the Rule of Law:** For more on the income defense industry and its relationship to the rule of law, see Jeffrey Winters, *Oligarchy* (New York: Cambridge University Press, 2011), 18–19. Hereafter cited as Winters, *Oligarchy*.
54  **The trusts and estates bar:** In 2003, there were roughly sixteen thousand lawyers in the United States who specialized in trusts and estates. See David Cay Johnston, *Perfectly Legal: The Covert Campaign to Rig Our Tax System to Benefit the Super Rich—and Cheat Everyone Else* (New York: Portfolio, 2003), 5.
54  **The total revenues:** See Ben Seal, "The 2018 Am Law 100 by the Numbers," *American Lawyer*, April 24, 2018, accessed July 20, 2018, www.law.com/americanlawyer/2018/04/24/the-2018 -am-law-100-by-the-numbers/.
54  **the revenues of the big four:** Ernst and Young reported combined global revenues of $31.4 billion for the financial year ending June 30, 2017. "EY Reports Strong Global Revenue Growth in 2017," *EY News*, September 5, 2017, accessed July 20, 2018, www.cy.com/gl/en/newsroom/news-releases/news-ey-reports -strong-global-revenue-growth-in-2017. PricewaterhouseCoopers reported revenues of $37.7 billion for the financial year ending June 30, 3017. *PwC's Global Annual Review 2017*, accessed July 20, 2018, www.pwc.com/gx/en/about/global-annual-review-2017

.html. Deloitte reported making $38.8 billion in the fiscal year ending May 31, 2017. "Deloitte Announces Record Revenue of US$38.8 Billion," press release, Deloitte, September 14, 2017, accessed July 20, 2018, www2.deloitte.com/global/en/pages /about-deloitte/articles/global-revenue-announcement.html. KPMG reported making $26.4 billion in the financial year ending September 30, 2017. KPMG International Cooperative, *2017 International Annual Review*, accessed July 20, 2018, https:// assets.kpmg.com/content/dam/kpmg/xx/pdf/2017/12/inter national-annual-review-2017.pdf.

54  **the revenues of the ten largest:** For more on the growth hedge fund and asset management industries and thus of income defense, see Robin Greenwood and David Sharfstein, "The Growth of Finance," *Journal of Economic Perspectives* 27, no. 2 (Spring 2013): 3–28, www.people.hbs.edu/dscharfstein /Growth_of_Finance_JEP.pdf. Hereafter cited as Greenwood and Sharfstein, "The Growth of Finance."
55  **According to this view:** See Winters, *Oligarchy*, 24.
55  **even a favorable pitch:** The phrase "swollen fortune" and the emphasis that property is not scale-blind recall Teddy Roosevelt's famous "New Nationalism" speech.
55  **ten or even twenty times the median wage:** In Great Britain, the United States, and Norway, for example, elite civil servants received 17.8, 7.8, and 5.3 times the average wage at the century's start and still received 8.9, 4.1, and 2.1 times the average wage at midcentury. See Henry Phelps Brown, *The Inequality of Pay* (New York: Oxford University Press, 1977), Table 3.4, 84. Michael Walzer also reports these numbers in *Spheres of Justice: A Defense of Pluralism and Equality* (New York: Basic Books, 1983), 158.
55  **In 1969, a congressperson:** A congressional staffer earned $10,000 in 1969; a congressperson earned $42,500; a full-time lobbyist might earn $15,000. See Norman Ornstein, "District of Corruption," *New Republic*, February 4, 2009, accessed July 21, 2018, https://newrepublic.com/article/61705/district-corrup tion, and "Registrations by Lobbyists," *CQ Almanac 1970*, 26th ed. (Washington, DC: Congressional Quarterly, 1971), 11-1214–1245, accessed July 21, 2018, http://library.cqpress.com /cqalmanac/cqal70-1290625. The $15,000 estimate is a rough average of the annual salaries of lobbyists registered between December 23, 1969, and January 3, 1971.
56  **a federal judge received:** In 1969, a district judge earned $30,000, while roughly the top 13 percent of lawyers earned $50,000 or more. See "Judicial Compensation," United States Courts, accessed July 21, 2018, http://www.uscourts.gov /judges-judgeships/judicial-compensation#fn7, and "In Search of the Average Lawyer," *ABA Journal* 56, no. 12 (December 1970): 1164.
56  **the secretary of the treasury:** In 1964, secretaries of executive departments made $35,000. See Arthur Sackley, "Salaries of Major Federal Officials, 1789–1965," *Monthly Labor Review* 87 (October 1964): 1145. A well-compensated financial analyst might make $40,000 a year. See William Norby, "Profile and Compensation of the Financial Analyst," *Financial Analysts Journal* 28, no. 2 (March–April 1972): 36. See also Chrystia Freeland, *Plutocrats: The Rise of the New Global Super-Rich and the Fall of Everyone Else* (New York: Penguin Press, 2012), 226. Hereafter cited as Freeland, *Plutocrats*. Freeland reports that as recently as 1980, top regulators earned one-tenth of the salaries of leaders of the businesses that they regulated. By 2005, they earned one-sixtieth.
56  **the military or the clergy:** See Zouheir Jamoussi, *Primogeniture and Entail in England: A Survey of Their History and Representation in Literature* (Newcastle upon Tyne: Cambridge Scholars Publishing, 2011), 61.
56  **now earn many times more:** Non-elite public-sector employees, incidentally, also receive lower wages than their private-sector counterparts. "On average, total compensation is 6.8 percent lower for state employees and 7.4 percent lower for local workers, compared with comparable private sector employees." See Keith Bender and John Heywood, *Out of Balance? Comparing Public and Private Sector Compensation over 20 Years* (Center for State & Local Government Excellence and National Institute on Retirement Security, April 2010), 3.
56  **perhaps $2 million:** For the salaries that a congressperson might make as a legislator and as a lobbyist, see Christopher Lee,

"Daschle Moving to K Street: Dole Played a Key Role in Recruiting Former Senator," *Washington Post*, March 14, 2005, A17, accessed July 22, 2018, www.washingtonpost.com/wp-dyn /articles/A32604-2005Mar13.html ("Other influential former members of Congress have drawn annual compensation packages of as much as $1 million and higher after making such moves," Lee reports. "[Former Republican senator Robert J.] Dole has been reported to earn $800,000 to $1 million annually, a range the Republican called 'more or less' accurate in an interview Friday."). Similarly, Congressman Billy Tauzin left office to be paid $2 million a year as a pharmaceutical lobbyist, and Congressman Eric Cantor, after losing a bid for reelection, now receives roughly $2 million a year to work as an investment banker. See Paul Blumenthal, "The Legacy of Billy Tauzin: The White House-PhRMA Deal," *Sunlight Foundation* (blog), February 12, 2010, accessed July 22, 2018, http://blog.sunlightfounda tion.com/2010/02/12/the-legacy-of-billy-tauzin-the-white -house-pharma-deal, and Taylor Wofford, "Eric Cantor Lands $3.4 Million Investment Banking Job," *Newsweek*, September 2, 2014, accessed July 22, 2018, www.newsweek.com/eric-cantor -lands-34-million-investment-banking-job-267924. The current salary for a member of the House of Representatives is $174,000. See Ida Brudnick, *Congressional Salaries and Allowances: In Brief* (Washington, DC: Congressional Research Service, April 11, 2018), 9.

A congressional staffer might quintuple his income, from $50,000 to $250,000. For average staffer salaries, see Daniel Schuman, "What's the Average Salary of House Staff?," *Open House Project*, December 2, 2009, accessed July 22, 2018, www .webcitation.org/5xkbywzmS. (Staffers in 2009 earned between $29,890.54 and $120,051.55, and roughly 80 percent earned between $29,890.54 and $61,389.93.) For salaries on becoming lobbyists, see Kevin Bogardus and Silla Brush, "Democratic Aides May Get Cold Shoulder from K Street After Midterms," *The Hill*, September 14, 2010, accessed July 22, 2018, http://the hill.com/business-a-lobbying/118495-democratic-party-aides -see-value-drop-on-k-street ("Lobbying salaries offered to Democratic staffers leaving Congress for K Street about a year ago [in 2009] ranged from $250,000 to $500,000.").

For a general synthesis of many of these reports, See Richard Hasen, "Lobbying, Rent-Seeking, and the Constitution," *Stanford Law Review* 64, no. 1 (February 2012): 2224–25. See also Robert Reich, *Supercapitalism: The Transformation of Business, Democracy, and Everyday Life* (New York: Alfred Knopf, 2007), 139. Hereafter cited as Reich, *Supercapitalism*. By 2006, well-connected staffers would get $500,000 per year as lobbyists; former chairs of congressional committees could get up to $2 million.

56  **is now $400,000:** In 2017, the chief justice of the Supreme Court made $263,300. That same year, the average partner compensation at Wachtell, Lipton, Rosen & Katz was $5.7 million. See "Judicial Salaries: Supreme Court Justices," Federal Judicial Center, accessed July 23, 2018, www.fjc.gov/history/judges/ju dicial-salaries-supreme-court-justices, and Gina Passarella Cipriana, "The 2018 Am Law 100 Ranked by Compensation—All Partners," *American Lawyer*, April 24, 2018, accessed July 23, 2018, www.law.com/americanlawyer/2018/04/24/the-2018-am -law-100-ranked-by-compensation-all-partners/. Jones Day, Kirkland & Ellis, Orrick, Paul Weiss, Skadden Arps, and Susman Godfrey now all offer Supreme Court clerks $400,000 signing bonuses. Staci Zaretsky, "$400K Is Now the Official Market Rate for Supreme Court Bonuses," *Above the Law*, November 15, 2018, accessed January 8, 2019, abovethelaw.com/2018/11 /400k-is-now-the-official-market-rate-for-supreme-court-clerk -bonuses/.

56  **a hundred times as much:** In 2018, the secretary of the treasury and other officials on the Executive Schedule Level I made $210,700. See U.S. Office of Personnel Management, "Salary Table No. 2018-EX: Rates of Basic Pay for the Executive Schedule," 2018 Executive & Senior Level Employee Pay Tables, accessed July 23, 2018, www.opm.gov/policy-data -oversight/pay-leave/salaries-wages/salary-tables/18Tables /exec/html/EX.aspx. In 2017, total CEO compensation at Goldman Sachs, JPMorgan Chase, and Morgan Stanley averaged $26.8 million. See JPMorgan Chase & Co., Schedule 14A: Preliminary Proxy Statement (filed April 4, 2018), accessed July 23,

2018, www.sec.gov/Archives/edgar/data/19617/0000019617 18000067/jpmc2018preliminaryproxy.htm; the Goldman Sachs Group, Form 8-K (filed February 15, 2018), accessed July 23, 2018, www.sec.gov/Archives/edgar/data/886982/000119 312518047491/d518947d8k.htm; and Morgan Stanley, Schedule 14A: Definitive Proxy Statement (filed April 6, 2018), accessed July 23, 2018, www.sec.gov/Archives/edgar/data/895 421/000119312518109962/d492849ddef14a.htm. See also Freeland, *Plutocrats*, 226, who reports that as recently as 1980, top regulators earned one-tenth of the salaries of leaders of the businesses that they regulated. By 2005, they earned one -sixtieth.

57  **daughter of Pakistani immigrants:** See, e.g., Seth Stern, "The Dealmaker: Top M&A Attorney Faiza Saeed is Cravath's Presiding Partner," *Harvard Law Bulletin*, May 18, 2017, accessed July 23, 2018, https://today.law.harvard.edu/the-dealmaker/.

57  **"barely disguised employment agencies":** Thomas Ferguson and Robert Johnson, "When Wolves Cry 'Wolf': Systematic Financial Crises and the Myth of the Danaid Jar," paper presented at INET Inaugural Conference, King's College, Cambridge, April 2010, accessed July 23, 2018, www.ineteconomics .org/uploads/papers/INET-C@K-Paper-Session-8-Ferguson -Rob-Johnson.pdf, 21.

57  **on leaving public office:** See Mark Leibovich, *This Town: Two Parties and a Funeral—Plus Plenty of Valet Parking!—in America's Gilded Capital* (New York: Blue Rider Press, 2013), 148–64. See also Christopher Lee, "Daschle Moving to K Street: Dole Played a Key Role in Recruiting Former Senator," *Washington Post*, March 14, 2005, A17, accessed July 23, 2018, www .washingtonpost.com/wp-dyn/articles/A32604-2005Mar13 .html.

57  **"has long been seen":** The entire story is reported in Juliet Lapidos, "Eric Cantor Cashes In, Goes to Wall Street," *New York Times*, September 2, 2014, accessed July 23, 2018, https://taking note.blogs.nytimes.com/2014/09/02/eric-cantor -cashes-in-goes-to-wall-street/. For the *New York Times* prediction, see Editorial Board, "Eric Cantor's Big Payoff," *New York Times*, August 3, 2014, accessed July 23, 2018, www.nytimes .com/2014/08/10/opinion/sunday/eric-cantors-big-payoff .html; for the *Wall Street Journal*'s reflections after the fact, see Dana Cimilluca and Patrick O'Connor, "Eric Cantor to Join Wall Street Investment Bank," *Wall Street Journal*, September 2, 2014, accessed July 23, 2018, www.wsj.com/articles/eric-cantor -to-join-wall-street-investment-bank-1409630638.

57  **sold out years in advance:** See Greg Jaffe and Jim Tankersley, "Capital Gains: Spending on Contracts and Lobbying Propels a Wave of New Wealth in D.C.," *Washington Post*, November 17, 2013, accessed July 23, 2018, www.washingtonpost.com/na tional/capital-gains-spending-on-contracts-and-lobbying-pro pels-a-wave-of-new-wealth-in-d-c/2013/11/17/6bd938aa-3c25 -11e3-a94f-b58017bfee6c_story.html?utm_term=.44ae 6632d430. Hereafter cited as Jaffey and Tankersley, "Capital Gains."

57  **Washington is now among:** See Jaffe and Tankersley, "Capital Gains." See also Richard Florida, "Venture Capital Remains Highly Concentrated in Just a Few Cities," *City Lab*, October 3, 2017, accessed July 23, 2018, www.citylab.com/life/2017/10 /venture-capital-concentration/539775/.

58  **any other major metro area:** See Jaffe and Tankersley, "Capital Gains."

58  **$200 per person, before wine:** See Jaffe and Tankersley, "Capital Gains." For Washington restaurants, see, e.g., Maura Judkis, "One of the Most Expensive Restaurants in Washington Is Going to Increase Its Prices," *Washington Post*, January 23, 2017, accessed July 23, 2018, www.washingtonpost.com/news/going -out-guide/wp/2017/01/23/one-of-the-most-expensive-restau rants-in-washington-is-about-to-increase-its-prices/?utm_term =.3884ea4ce2ca.

58  **"ways of expropriating wealth":** Ajay Kapur, Niall Macleod, and Narendra Singh, "Equity Strategy: Plutonomy: Buying Luxury, Explaining Global Imbalances," Citigroup, Industry Note, October 16, 2005, accessed July 23, 2018, https://delong.type pad.com/plutonomy-1.pdf. I borrow the term "income defense" from Winters, *Oligarchy*, 18–19.

58  **"only morons pay the estate tax":** See Julie Hirschfeld Davis and Kate Kelly, "Two Bankers Are Selling Trump's Tax Plan. Is

Congress Buying?," *New York Times*, August 28, 2017, accessed July 23, 2018, www.nytimes.com/2017/08/28/us/politics/trump-tax-plan-cohn-mnuchin.html.

58 **paid any estate tax at all:** See Brian O'Connor, "Heirs Inherit Uncertainty with New Estate Tax," *New York Times*, February 23, 2018, accessed July 23, 2018, www.nytimes.com/2018/02/23/business/estate-tax-uncertainty.html.

Elite lobbying and lawyering are now conspiring to create changes to the law of trusts that might in effect eliminate estate taxes entirely, even for the super-rich. A doctrine known as the rule against perpetuities has for generations prevented people from establishing perpetual trusts, which allow the dead to control assets indefinitely from beyond the grave, including for the benefit of their descendants. Recently, two rich brothers—one a New York lawyer and the other an Alaska banker—hatched a plan to repeal the rule in Alaska, by statute, to bring more trusts and estates business to the state. They succeeded, and other states are now following suit. See Ray Madoff, *Immortality and the Law: The Rising Power of the American Dead* (New Haven, CT: Yale University Press, 2010), 81.

58 **$18 trillion of assets offshore:** This sum represents 10, 20–30, and 50 percent of the total assets owned by the rich in North America, Europe, and Latin America respectively. See Winters, *Oligarchy*, 233. Wealth in tax havens is, for obvious reasons, difficult to find and measure. For some of the complexities, see Annette Alstadsaeter, Niels Johannesen, and Gabriel Zucman, "Who Owns Wealth in Tax Havens: Macro Evidence and Implications for Global Inequality," NBER Working Paper No. 23805 (September 2017), 8, www.nber.org/papers/w23805.pdf.

58 **fell by perhaps a third:** For the share of national income belonging to the top 1 percent of earners, see Michael Greenstone and Adam Looney, *Just How Progressive Is the US Tax Code?* (Washington, DC: The Hamilton Project, April 13, 2012), 3, accessed July 23, 2018, www.hamiltonproject.org/assets/legacy/files/downloads_and_links/0413_tax.pdf; for tax rates among the 1 percent, see Emmanuel Saez, "Reported Incomes and Marginal Tax Rates, 1960–2000: Evidence and Policy Implications," *Tax Policy and the Economy* 18 (2004): 117–73. Hereafter cited as Saez, "Reported Incomes and Marginal Tax Rates."

58 **lower rate than his secretary:** See Warren Buffett, "Stop Coddling the Super-Rich," *New York Times*, August 14, 2011, accessed July 23, 2018, www.nytimes.com/2011/08/15/opinion/stop-coddling-the-super-rich.html?_r=0, and Chris Isidore, "Buffett Says He's Still Paying Lower Tax Rate Than His Secretary," CNN Money, March 4, 2013, accessed July 23, 2018, https://money.cnn.com/2013/03/04/news/economy/buffett-secretary-taxes/index.html.

58 **become effectively flat:** When the payroll taxes that fund Social Security and Medicare and also state and local taxes are taken into account, the average overall tax rates in the United States today are almost totally flat. In a typical recent year, the bottom fifth of earners receive 3 percent of income and pay 2 percent of taxes; the middle fifth receive 11 percent and pay 10 percent; and the top 1 percent receive 21 percent and pay 22 percent. See D.R., "Taxes and the Rich: Looking at All the Taxes," *The Economist*, July 19, 2012, accessed December 29, 2018, www.economist.com/blogs/democracyinamerica/2012/07/taxes-and-rich-0.

58 **left for private-sector jobs:** See Jesse Eisinger, "Why the S.E.C. Didn't Hit Goldman Sachs Harder," New Yorker, April 21, 2016, accessed July 23, 2018, www.newyorker.com/business/curren/why-the-s-e-c-didnt-hit-goldman-sachsharder.

60 **"hate cannot drive out hate":** Martin Luther King Jr., *Strength to Love* (New York: Simon & Schuster, 1964), 47.

60 **"that he, who best deserves":** This is from Dryden's translation of the fourth book of Virgil's *Georgics*. Virgil, *The Georgics, with John Dryden's Translation* (Ashington: Mid Northumberland Arts Group, 1981), 147.

61 **"economically . . . negative assets":** See Kevin Williamson, "Chaos in the Family, Chaos in the State: The White Working Class's Dysfunction," *National Review*, March 17, 2016, accessed July 23, 2018, www.nationalreview.com/article/432876/donald-trump-white-working-class-dysfunction-real-opportunity-needed-not-trump. See also Edward Luce, "The New Class Warfare in America," *Financial Times*, March 20,

2016, accessed July 23, 2018, www.ft.com/content/63b061be-ecfc-11e5-bb79-2303682345c8.

61 **"the stagnant pool":** See Bret Stephens, "Only Mass Deportation Can Save America," *New York Times*, June 16, 2017, accessed July 23, 2018, www.nytimes.com/2017/06/16/opinion/only-mass-deportation-can-save-america.html.

61 **"takers" and "makers":** See Ezra Klein, "Romney's Theory of the 'Taker Class,' and Why It Matters," *Wonkblog, Washington Post*, September 17, 2012, accessed July 23, 2018, www.washingtonpost.com/news/wonk/wp/2012/09/17/romneys-theory-of-the-taker-class-and-why-it-matters/?utm_term=.ad5165f4407f. Ryan has since said that he regrets this phrase. See "Speaker Ryan on the State of American Politics," press release, Speaker.gov, March 23, 2016, accessed July 23, 2018, www.speaker.gov/press-release/full-text-speaker-ryan-state-american-politics.

61 **"are dependent upon government":** See Amy Davidson Sorkin, "Mitt's Forty-Seven-Per-Cent Problem," *New Yorker*, September 18, 2012, accessed July 23, 2018, www.newyorker.com/news/amy-davidson/mitts-forty-seven-per-cent-problem. Romney subsequently expressed regret at the remark. See Ashley Parker, "Romney, Buoyed by Debate, Shows Off His Softer Side," *New York Times*, October 6, 2012, accessed July 23, 2018, www.nytimes.com/2012/10/07/us/politics/mitt-romney-after-debate-success-shows-softer-side.html?pagewanted=all.

61 **"bitter" working-class conservatives:** See Jeff Zeleny, "Opponents Call Obama Remarks 'Out of Touch,'" *New York Times*, April 12, 2008, accessed July 23, 2018, www.nytimes.com/2008/04/12/us/politics/12campaign.html?action=click&contentCollection=Politics&module=RelatedCoverage&region=EndOfArticle&pgtype=article. Obama later said he had expressed himself badly. See Katharine Seelye and Jeff Zeleny, "On the Defensive, Obama Calls His Words Ill-Chosen," *New York Times*, April 13, 2008, accessed July 23, 2018, www.nytimes.com/2008/04/13/us/politics/13campaign.html.

61 **"basket of deplorables":** See Amy Chozick, "Hillary Clinton Calls Many Trump Backers 'Deplorables,' and G.O.P. Pounces," *New York Times*, September 10, 2016, accessed July 23, 2018, www.nytimes.com/2016/09/11/us/politics/hillary-clinton-basket-of-deplorables.html. Clinton also expressed regret for what she said. See Dan Merica and Sophie Tatum, "Clinton Expresses Regret for Saying 'Half' of Trump Supporters are 'Deplorables,'" CNN, September 12, 2016, accessed July 23, 2018, www.cnn.com/2016/09/09/politics/hillary-clinton-donald-trump-basket-of-deplorables/.

63 **by their own land:** The phrase recalls Arlie Russell Hochschild's *Strangers in Their Own Land: Anger and Mourning on the American Right* (New York: New Press, 2016). Hereafter cited as Hochschild, *Strangers in Their Own Land*. Hochschild narrativizes white nativism in terms of what she calls a "deep story" that white working- and middle-class people construct to explain their lives: they have waited patiently in line for prosperity, but others—blacks, women, immigrants—are joining the line, and elites, flying flags of civil rights, feminism, multiculturalism, and always meritocracy, use government handouts to help the others cut to the front. See Hochschild, *Strangers in Their Own Land*, 136–37. Earlier studies of white working-class discontent confirm this interpretation. In 1985, Stanley Greenberg surveyed white UAW workers and retirees in Macomb County, Michigan, and found that the almost all of his subjects attributed their lack of personal advancement to "discrimination against whites" and the "special status of blacks." See Stanley Greenberg, *Middle Class Dreams: The Politics and Power of the New American Majority* (New Haven, CT: Yale University Press, 1995), 40, 47. Another 1985 study of working-class white voters by the marketing and polling firm CRG similarly concluded that these voters believed that the Democratic Party was "not helping them" and was "helping blacks, Hispanics, and the poor" instead, and that "they feel betrayed." The CRG study was never published because Democratic leaders worried about its depiction of "controversial sources of dissent from liberal orthodoxy," but it is quoted in Thomas Edsall and Mary Edsall, "When the Official Subject Is Presidential Politics, Taxes, Welfare, Crime, Rights, or Values, the Real Subject Is Race," *Atlantic*, May 1991, accessed July 23, 2018, www.theatlantic.com/past/docs/politics/race/edsall. The deep story casts the

white working and middle class as "stay-at-home migrants," whose values remain constant even as the world around them shifts. See Hochschild, *Strangers in Their Own Land*, 49.

63  **"anesthesia" or "narcotic":** Friedrich Nietzsche, *On the Genealogy of Morality*, trans. Carol Diethe, ed. Keith Ansell-Pearson (New York: Cambridge University Press, 2014), III:15, 93. Nietzsche says that, for the proponent of slave morality, "the release of emotions is the greatest attempt at relief, or should I say, at *anaesthetizing* on the part of the sufferer, his involuntarily longed-for narcotic against pain of any kind."  /

63  **slave-owning settler society of the colonial era:** See Aziz Rana, *The Two Faces of American Freedom* (Cambridge, MA: Harvard University Press, 2014).

63  **"victims without a language of victimhood":** Hochschild, *Strangers in Their Own Land*, 131.

63  **"the whole idea":** Jamie Walsh, quoted in Gary Younge and Laurence Mathieu-Léger, "The View from Middletown: 'Trump Speaks to Us in a Way Other People Don't,'" *Guardian*, October 2, 2016, accessed October 23, 2018, www.theguardian.com/membership/2016/oct/27/middletown-trump-muncie-clinton. Hereafter cited as Younge and Mathieu-Léger, "The View from Middletown."

64  **"And you've got people":** Jamie Walsh, quoted in Younge and Mathieu-Léger, "The View from Middletown."

64  **as claims of injustice:** Other, more subtle meritocratic logics are also at play. When meritocracy associates learning with elites, it casts intellectualism outside of the elite as class betrayal. Religiosity becomes an acceptable outlet for intellectually inclined but loyal middle-class people. As one intellectual raised middle-class reflects on her childhood society, "Learnedness itself was suspect, and making a display of learning was simply not done; in school as elsewhere, the worst failure of character was to get 'a swelled head.' You could do intellectual work, though, if you called it something else. We called it religion." Suzanne Lebsock, "Snow Falling on Magnolias," in *Shapers of Southern History: Autobiographical Reflections*, ed. John Boles (Athens: University of Georgia Press, 2004), 291.

64  **"are more educated":** See Joan Williams, interview with Curt Nickisch, "Why the White Working Class Voted for Trump," *Harvard Business Review*, November 18, 2016, accessed July 23, 2018, https://hbr.org/ideacast/2016/11/why-the-white-working-class-voted-for-trump. Hereafter cited as "Why the White Working Class Voted for Trump," interview with Joan C. Williams. See also Michèle Lamont, *The Dignity of Working Men: Morality and the Boundaries of Race, Class, and Immigration* (Cambridge, MA: Harvard University Press, 2000).

65  **to own a company:** Joan Williams, *White Working Class: Overcoming Class Cluelessness in America* (Boston: Harvard Business Review Press, 2017), 26. Hereafter cited as Williams, *White Working Class*.

65  **the epidemic of addiction, overdose, and suicide:** See Case and Angus, "Rising Morbidity," Table 1.

66  **Columbia College and Harvard Law School:** David Mendell, *Obama: From Promise to Power* (New York: HarperCollins, 2007), 59–63, 83–92.

66  **his all-star first cabinet:** In 2009, nearly half of Obama's confirmed executive and judicial nominees had a degree from the Ivy League and nearly one-third of all degrees earned were from an Ivy League school. Secretary of Energy Steven Chu received the Nobel Prize in Physics in 1997; several members of the administration received Rhodes and Marshall scholarships. See "Obama Cabinet Nominations," United States Senate, accessed July 28, 2018, www.senate.gov/reference/Obama_cabinet.htm#1; "About the Governor," Governor Gary Locke, accessed July 28, 2018, www.digitalarchives.wa.gov/governorlocke/bios/bio.htm; "Attorney General: Eric H. Holder, Jr.," United States Department of Justice, accessed July 28, 2018, www.justice.gov/ag/bio/attorney-general-eric-h-holder-jr; "Secretary Tom Vilsack," Feeding America, accessed July 28, 2018, http://www.feedingamerica.org/about-us/leadership/Secretary-Tom-Vilsack.html; "Dr. Robert M. Gates," Department of Defense, accessed July 28, 2018, www.defense.gov/About/Biographies/Biography-View/Article/602797/; "Arne Duncan, U.S. Secretary of Education—Biography," U.S. Department of Education, accessed July 28, 2018, www2.ed.gov/news/staff/bios/duncan

.html; "Dr. Steven Chu," Energy.gov, accessed July 28, 2018, www.energy.gov/contributors/dr-steven-chu; "Bio," Sebelius Resources, accessed July 28, 2018, www.sebeliusresources.com/welcome-1/; "Janet Napolitano, Secretary of Homeland Security 2009–2013," Homeland Security, accessed July 28, 2018, www.dhs.gov/janet-napolitano; "Shaun Donovan," White House blog, accessed July 28, 2018, https://obamawhitehouse.archives.gov/blog/author/Shaun-Donovan; "Ken Salazar," WilmerHale, accessed July 28, 2018, www.wilmerhale.com/en/people/ken-salazar; "Biography," Supervisor Hilda L. Solis, accessed July 28, 2018, http://hildalsolis.org/biography/; "About Hillary," Office of Hillary Rodham Clinton, accessed July 28, 2018, www.hillaryclinton.com/about/; "Ray LaHood," DLA Piper, accessed July 28, 2018, www.dlapiper.com/en/us/people/l/lahood-ray/?tab=credentials; "Timothy F. Geithner," Warburg Pincus, accessed July 28, 2018, www.warburgpincus.com/people/timothy-f-geithner/; and "Class of 1951 Leadership Chair," West Point, accessed July 28, 2018, www.usma.edu/bsl/sitepages/the%20honorable%20eric%20k%20shinseki.aspx.

67  **"summer of silliness":** See Governor Bobby Jindal on Fox News, *America's Newsroom*, "Rove Predicts GOP Race Will Be 'Unsettled for a Long Time,'" August 31, 2015, accessed November 18, 2018, http://video.foxnews.com/v/4454547303001/?#sp=show-clips.

67  **"eat a bug":** Sam Wang, "Sound Bites and Bug Bites," Princeton Election Consortium, November 4, 2016, accessed July 23, 2018, http://election.princeton.edu/2016/11/04/sound-bites-and-bug-bites/.

67  **"a failed and corrupt political establishment":** See Team Trump, "Donald Trump's Argument for America," advertisement, November 4, 2016, accessed July 24, 2018, www.youtube.com/watch?v=vST61W4bGm8.

67  **neared an all-time high:** For poverty, see Chapter 4. For unemployment, see Bureau of Labor Statistics, Unemployment Rate, https://data.bls.gov/timeseries/LNS14000000. For consumption, see Chapter 8. For crime, see Matthew Friedman, Ames Grawert, and James Cullen, *Crime Trends: 1990–2016* (New York: Brennan Center for Justice, 2017), accessed July 24, 2018, www.brennancenter.org/sites/default/files/publications/Crime%20Trends%201990-2016.pdf.

67  **He portrayed a country:** Trump, "The Inaugural Address." "[We've] Subsidized the armies of other countries while allowing for the very sad depletion of our military; we've defended other nations' borders while refusing to defend our own; . . . We've made other countries rich while the wealth, strength, and confidence of our country has disappeared over the horizon"; "The wealth of our middle class has been ripped from their homes and then redistributed across the entire world"; and "Mothers and children trapped in poverty in our inner cities; rusted-out factories scattered like tombstones across the landscape of our nation; an education system, flush with cash, but which leaves our young and beautiful students deprived of knowledge; and the crime and gangs and drugs that have stolen too many lives and robbed our country of so much unrealized potential."

68  **voters who had supported Barack Obama:** See Nate Cohn, "The Obama-Trump Voters Are Real. Here's What They Think," *New York Times*, August 15, 2017, accessed July 24, 2018, www.nytimes.com/2017/08/15/upshot/the-obama-trump-voters-are-real-heres-what-they-think.html?_r=0, and "Democrats Will Struggle to Win Back Obama-Trump Voters," *The Economist*, November 2, 2017, accessed July 24, 2018, www.economist.com/united-states/2017/11/02/democrats-will-struggle-to-win-back-obama-trump-voters.

68  **"That was some weird shit":** Yashar Ali, "What George W. Bush Really Thought of Donald Trump's Inauguration," *New York Magazine*, March 29, 2017, accessed July 24, 2018, http://nymag.com/daily/intelligencer/2017/03/what-george-w-bush-really-thought-of-trumps-inauguration.html.

68  **"a blue-collar billionaire":** Sharon Galicia quoted by Arlie Russell Hochschild, "I Spent 5 Years with Some of Trump's Biggest Fans. Here's What They Won't Tell You," *Mother Jones*, September/October 2016, accessed July 24, 2018, www.motherjones.com/politics/2016/08/trump-white-blue-collar-supporters/, adapted from Hochschild, *Strangers in Their Own Land*.

68 **"I love the poorly educated"**: See Edward Luce, "The End of American Meritocracy," *Financial Times*, May 8, 2016, accessed July 24, 2018, www.ft.com/content/c17d402a-12cf-11e6-839f-2922947098f0?mhq5j=e1.

68 **"under[stood] the depth"**: See "Why the White Working Class Voted for Trump," interview with Joan C. Williams.

69 **"believe that the modern"**: See J. D. Vance, *Hillbilly Elegy* (New York: Harper, 2016), 191.

69 **thought the same of them**: See Chris Cillizza, "Donald Trump's Appeal Was Just Perfectly Summed Up by Chris Matthews," *Washington Post*, September 30, 2016, accessed July 24, 2018, www.washingtonpost.com/news/the-fix/wp/2016/09/30/chris-matthews-just-nailed-donald-trumps-appeal/?utm_term=.24ba2184ad30.

69 **agreed with both statements**: The survey was conducted by the *Huffington Post* in conjunction with YouGov. See Michael Tesler, "Trump Voters Think African Americans Are Much Less Deserving Than 'Average Americans,'" *Huffington Post*, December 19, 2016, accessed July 24, 2018, www.huffingtonpost.com/michael-tesler/trump-voters-think-africa_b_13732500.html. See also Victor Tan Chen, "The Spiritual Crisis of the Modern Economy," *Atlantic*, December 21, 2016, accessed July 24, 2018, www.theatlantic.com/business/archive/2016/12/spiritual-crisis-modern-economy/511067/. Hereafter cited as Tan Chen, "The Spiritual Crisis of the Modern Economy."

69 **"profound contempt"**: See Alec MacGillis, "Revenge of the Forgotten Class," ProPublica, November 10, 2016, accessed July 23, 2018, www.propublica.org/article/revenge-of-the-forgotten-class.

69 **by 39 percentage points**: See Thomas Edsall, "The Not-So-Silent White Majority," *New York Times*, November 17, 2016, accessed July 24, 2018, www.nytimes.com/2016/11/17/opinion/the-not-so-silent-white-majority.html.

69 **between $50,000 and $100,000**: Jon Huang et al., "Election 2016: Exit Polls," *New York Times*, November 8, 2016, accessed July 24, 2018, www.nytimes.com/interactive/2016/11/08/us/politics/election-exit-polls.html. For a largely congruent analysis of the sources of Trump's support using a massive data set of preelection Gallup surveys, see Jonathan Rothwell and Pablo Diego-Rosell, "Explaining Nationalist Political Views: The Case of Donald Trump," SSRN working paper (November 2, 2016), https://papers.ssrn.com/sol3/papers.cfm?abstract_id=2822059.

69 **over Romney's 2012 results**: See Nate Silver, "Education, Not Income, Predicted Who Would Vote for Trump," FiveThirtyEight, November 22, 2016, accessed July 24, 2018, http://fivethirtyeight.com/features/education-not-income-predicted-who-would-vote-for-trump/. For a similar analysis, see Neera Tanden et al., "Towards a Marshall Plan for America," Center for American Progress, May 16, 2017, accessed July 24, 2018, www.americanprogress.org/issues/economy/reports/2017/05/16/432499/toward-marshall-plan-america/.

69 **"Of course he wasn't"**: Anonymous resident in conversation with the author, St. Clair Shores, Michigan, May 2, 2018.

70 **roughly the same amount**: See Jed Kolko, "Trump Was Stronger Where the Economy Is Weaker," FiveThirtyEight, November 10, 2016, accessed July 24, 2018, https://fivethirtyeight.com/features/trump-was-stronger-where-the-economy-is-weaker/. Moreover, the shift from Obama to Trump was greatest where routine jobs were most prevalent. See Neera Tanden et al., "Towards a Marshall Plan for America," Center for American Progress, May 16, 2017, accessed July 24, 2018, www.americanprogress.org/issues/economy/reports/2017/05/16/432499/toward-marshall-plan-america/.

70 **outside of (and even in opposition to) work**: See Michèle Lamont, *The Dignity of Working Men: Morality and the Boundaries of Race, Class, and Immigration* (Cambridge, MA: Harvard University Press, 2000), 19–20; Williams, *White Working Class*, 16–17, 20, 31, 37.

70 **worst hit by the opioid epidemic**: See Timothy Snyder, *The Road to Unfreedom: Russia, Europe, America* (New York: Tim Duggan, 2018), 263–66.

70 **25 percentage point landslide**: See Board of County Canvassers, Canvass of Votes Cast at the General Election Held on Tuesday, the 8th Day of November, A.D. 1960, November 8, 1960, accessed July 24, 2018, http://clerk.macombgov.org/sites/default/files/content/government/clerk/pdfs/electionresults/1960-11-08-GENERAL-ELECTION.pdf. St. Clair Shores voted about 62 percent Kennedy-Johnson and 37 percent Nixon-Lodge.

70 **10 percentage point victory in 2016**: Michigan Department of State, Michigan Election Precinct Results, 2016 General Election, President of the United States, St. Clair Shores City, accessed July 24, 2018, http://miboecfr.nictusa.com/cgi-bin/cfr/precinct_srch_res.cgi. St. Clair Shores voted 53 percent Trump-Pence and 42 percent Clinton-Kaine.

70 **"Donald Trump's speeches"**: See Kevin Williamson, "Chaos in the Family, Chaos in the State: The White Working Class's Dysfunction," *National Review*, March 17, 2016, accessed July 23, 2018, www.nationalreview.com/article/432876/donald-trump-white-working-class-dysfunction-real-opportunity-needed-not-trump. See also Edward Luce, "The New Class Warfare in America," *Financial Times*, March 20, 2016, accessed July 24, 2018, www.ft.com/content/63b061be-ecfc-11e5-bb79-2303682345c8.

70 **any winning candidate since 1980**: See American National Election Studies, "Time Series Cumulative Data File" (2012), www.electionstudies.org/studypages/anes_timeseries_cdf/anes_timeseries_cdf.htm; American National Election Studies, "2016 Time Series Study" (2016), www.electionstudies.org/studypages/anes_timeseries_2016/anes_timeseries_2016.htm.

70 **nearly 70 percentage points**: See "Past Election Results," Santa Clara County Registrar of Voters, www.sccgov.org/sites/rov/Resources/Pages/PastEResults.aspx (see "Statement of Vote" for the November 8, 2016, Presidential General Election).

71 **This was Thomas Jefferson's dream**: See "The Virginia Constitution: First Draft by Jefferson," *The Papers of Thomas Jefferson*, volume 1, *1760–1776*, ed. Julian Boyd, Lyman Butterfield, and Mina Bryan (Princeton, NJ: Princeton University Press, 1950), 337. Jefferson's guarantees were, of course, limited to free white men. The contemporary version of Jefferson's ideal universalizes them.

71 **"we can have a democratic society"**: It is not clear that Brandeis ever said this. Scott Campbell, the librarian at Brandeis Law School in Louisville, reports that Brandeis's scholars and biographers have not found a source for the quote. See Ronald Smith, *Thomas Ewing, Jr., Frontier Lawyer and Civil War General* (Columbia: University of Missouri Press, 2008), 307 n.59.

## Chapter Four: The Working Rich

77 **"What, 'work'?"**: The precise lines are from Stephen Fry's and Hugh Laurie's television adaptation of Wodehouse's story "Jeeves Takes Charge," first published in the *Saturday Evening Post*, November 1916. See *Jeeves and Wooster*, "In Court After the Boat Race," ITV, April 22, 1990, written by Clive Exton, directed by Robert Young.

77 **"a chicken in every pot"**: The slogan is commonly attributed to Herbert Hoover's 1928 presidential campaign, but it appears that Hoover himself never used it. Rather, it was first used by King Henry IV of France in the sixteenth century and eventually made the title of a 1928 Republican campaign flyer. Democrats then mocked Republicans for delivering, instead, the deprivation of the Great Depression. As late as 1960, John F. Kennedy used this line of attack at a rally in Bristol, Tennessee, saying, "It is my understanding that the last candidate for the presidency to visit this community in a presidential year was Herbert Hoover in 1928. President Hoover initiated on the occasion of his visit the slogan, 'Two chickens for every pot,' and it is no accident that no presidential candidate has ever dared come back to this community since." See "chicken in every pot," William Safire, *Safire's Political Dictionary* (Oxford: Oxford University Press, 2008), 115.

77 **reasonable estimates suggest**: Modern poverty statistics were not kept in the Great Depression. But the most reliable estimate suggests a poverty rate as high as 66 percent in 1914 and 78 percent in 1932. See Robert Plotnick et al., "The Twentieth Century Record of Inequality and Poverty in the United States," Institute for Research on Poverty, Dischssion Paper no. 1166-98 (July 1998), University of Wisconsin–Madison, 58, accessed

August 7, 2018, www.irp.wisc.edu/publications/dps/pdfs/dp116698.pdf. See also Robert Plotnick et al., "The Twentieth-Century Record of Inequality and Poverty in the United States," in *The Cambridge Economic History of the United States*, vol. 3, ed. S. L. Engerman and R. E. Gallman (Cambridge: Cambridge University Press, 2000), 249–99, Figure 4.4; G. Fisher, "Estimates of the Poverty Population Under the Current Official Definition for Years Before 1959," mimeograph, Office of the Assistant Secretary for Planning and Evaluation, U.S. Department of Health and Human Services, 1986.

78  **By one estimate:** See Christine Ross, Sheldon Danziger, and Eugene Smolensky, "The Level and Trend of Poverty in the United States, 1939–1979," *Demography* 24, no. 4 (November 1987): 589.

78  **War on Poverty:** See, e.g., "Johnson State of Union Address Provides Budget $97.9 Billion, War on Poverty, Atomic Cutback," *New York Times*, January 9, 1964, accessed August 11, 2018, www.nytimes.com/1964/01/09/archives/johnson-state-of-union-address-provides-budget-of-979-billion-war.html.

79  **Thorstein Veblen:** John Patrick Diggins, *Thorstein Veblen: Theorist of the Leisure Class* (Princeton, NJ: Princeton University Press, 1999), 33, 135.

79  **"are by custom exempt":** Veblen, *Theory of the Leisure Class*, 1.

79  **"a steady application":** Veblen, *Theory of the Leisure Class*, 8.

80  **"music, or diversion, or conversation":** See Benjamin Franklin, *The Autobiography of Benjamin Franklin*, ed. Frank Woodworth Pine (New York: Henry Holt, 1916), 69.

80  **"indolence or quiescence":** Veblen, *Theory of the Leisure Class*, 43.

80  **"elaborating the material means of life":** Veblen, *Theory of the Leisure Class*, 10.

80  **"non-productive consumption of time":** Veblen, *Theory of the Leisure Class*, 43.

80  **"a degree of honor attaches":** Veblen, *Theory of the Leisure Class*, 1.

80  **exploit:** Veblen, *Theory of the Leisure Class*, 8.

80  **public merrymaking:** Veblen, *Theory of the Leisure Class*, 8–15.

80  **English spelling:** Veblen, *Theory of the Leisure Class*, 394–400.

81  **did not sully themselves with work:** Veblen, *Theory of the Leisure Class*, 171. Veblen writes, "The pleasing effect of neat and spotless garments is chiefly, if not altogether, due to their carrying the suggestion of leisure—exemption from personal contact with industrial processes of any kind. Much of the charm that invests the patent leather shoe, the stainless linen, the lustrous cylindrical hat, and the walking-stick, which so greatly enhance the native dignity of a gentleman, comes of their pointedly suggesting that the wearer cannot when so attired bear a hand in any employment that is directly and immediately of any human use. Elegant dress serves its purpose of elegance not only in that it is expensive, but also because it is the insignia of leisure. It not only shows that the wearer is able to consume a relatively large value, but it argues at the same time that he consumes without producing."

81  **"if you destroy":** "Destruction of the Leisure Class, Says Morgan, Would Cause Whole Civilization to Perish," Associated Press via *Reading (PA) Times*, February 5, 1936, accessed August 8, 2018, www.newspapers.com/image/47578199/.

81  **"began at ten":** Steve Fraser, *Every Man a Speculator: A History of Wall Street in American Life* (New York: HarperCollins, 2005), 542. Hereafter cited as Fraser, *Every Man a Speculator.*

81  **"the banks close at three":** Martin Mayer, *Wall Street: Men and Money*, rev. ed. (New York: Collier, 1962), 39–40. Hereafter cited as Mayer, *Wall Street*. An erratum in the book replaces "Dow" with "Down."

81  **around six-thirty":** Mayer, *Wall Street*, 39–40.

81  **"third-generation Yale man":** Fraser, *Every Man a Speculator*, 487.

81  **"treated as uncouth ruffians":** Fraser, *Every Man a Speculator*, 488.

81  **threatened with legislative sanction:** Fraser, *Every Man a Speculator*, 487–90.

81  **gentlemen of independent means:** Fraser, *Every Man a Speculator*, 488.

81  **"dressed in a suit":** See Michael Young, *The Rise of the Meritocracy* (New Brunswick, NJ: Transaction Publishers, 1994), 18. Hereafter cited as Young, *The Rise of the Meritocracy*.

82  **"nourished themselves":** Young, *The Rise of the Meritocracy*, 18.

82  **reflected long-standing conventional wisdom:** American Bar Association Committee on Economics of Law Practice, *The Lawyer's Handbook* (St. Paul, MN: West Publishing Company, 1962), 287. William Ross similarly cites a 1965 American Bar Association Survey that reported that law firm associates typically billed just fourteen hundred to sixteen hundred hours annually and partners just twelve hundred to fourteen hundred. See William G. Ross, *The Honest Hour: The Ethics of Time-Based Billing by Attorneys* (Durham, NC: Carolina Academic Press, 1996), 2–3, citing Clark Sloat and Richard Fitzgerald, *Administrative and Financial Management in a Law Firm* (Standing Committee on Economics of Law Practice of the American Bar Association, Economics of Law Practice Series, Pamphlet 10, 1965), 2. Hereafter cited as Sloat and Fitzgerald, *Administrative and Financial Management in a Law Firm*.

82  **only fourteen hundred hours in a year:** See Peter Giuliani, "Financial Planning and Control for Lawyers," *ABA Journal* 63 (January 1977): 60–70, accessed January 31, 2019, https://books.google.com/books?id=MMPODtsVJGIC&pg=PA3&lpg=PA3&dq=%22financial+planning+and+control+for+lawyers%22&source=bl&ots=TGFj64ggsb&sig=6r8Uyltb2dxjlihoOjw3UVlkphM&hl=en&sa=X&ved=2ahUKEwj7_9GM7d3cAhWKAXwKHUwuDbUQ6AEwAXoECAMQAQ#v=onepage&q=%22financial%20planning%20and%20control%20for%20lawyers%22&f=false.

82  **others report similar hours:** See, e.g., Sloat and Fitzgerald, *Administrative and Financial Management in a Law Firm*, 2–3 ("Experience with a number of firms indicates that a yearly schedule of 1400 to 1600 hours for each associate and from 1200 to 1400 hours for each partner represents a norm. Naturally, there will be individual variations."); Deborah Rhode, "Institutionalizing Ethics," *Case Western Reserve Law Review* 44, no. 2 (1994): 711, accessed August 8, 2018, https://scholarlycommons.law.case.edu/cgi/viewcontent.cgi?article=1977&context=caselrev ("Conventional wisdom just a few decades ago was that lawyers could not reasonably expect to charge for more than 1200 to 1500 hours per year."); Carl Bogus, "The Death of an Honorable Profession," *Indiana Law Journal* 71, no. 4 (Fall 1996): 924, accessed August 8, 2018, www.repository.law.indiana.edu/cgi/viewcontent.cgi?article=1802&context=ilj (reporting that median hours for partners and associates alike were 1,500). Indeed, as recently as 1984, the Altman Weil Survey of Law Firm Economics could report that average billable hours for partners in the firms that it surveyed were 1,531 per year. See Marci Krufka, *Mining the Surveys: Law Firm Partners Working Harder Than Ever* (Newtown Square, PA: Altman Weil, Inc., 2003), 1.

82  **Young investment bankers:** See Leslie Kwoh, "Hazard of the Trade: Bankers' Health," *Wall Street Journal*, February 15, 2012, accessed August 8, 2018, www.wsj.com/articles/SB10001424052970204627045772236238249444472.

82  **In a story familiar:** Ho, *Liquidated*, 88.

82  **A standard "disciplinary joke":** Ho, *Liquidated*, 88.

82  **"the stamina to work":** Brian Dumaine and Lynn Fleary, "A Hot New Star in the Merger Game," *Fortune*, February 17, 1986, accessed July 18, 2018, http://archive.fortune.com/magazines/fortune/fortune_archive/1986/02/17/67133/index.htm.

82  **"banker nine-to-five":** Kevin Roose, *Young Money: Inside the Hidden World of Wall Street's Post-Crash Recruits* (New York: Grand Central Publishing, 2014), 114.

82  **"purposeful Darwinism"** . . . **"unreasonably high":** Kantor and Streitfeld, "Inside Amazon."

82  **"can work long":** Kantor and Streitfeld, "Inside Amazon."

82  **"a continual performance improvement":** Kantor and Streitfeld, "Inside Amazon."

83  **cull less productive workers:** The firm, being "driven by data," will stop this only "if the data says it must." Kantor and Streitfeld, "Inside Amazon."

83  **Amazon also imposes:** Kantor and Streitfeld, "Inside Amazon."

83  **Apple, for example:** See Ben Lovejoy, "Former Apple Managers Talk of the 24/7 Work Culture: 'These People Are Nuts,'" 9to5Mac, October 1, 2014, accessed August 11, 2018, http://9to5mac.com/2014/10/01/former-apple-managers-talk-of-the-247-work-culture-these-people-are-nuts/. Recall also the law firm that tracks partners' contributions in a database, updated

every twenty minutes, that may be accessed by every partner, at any time and from anywhere, by computer or smartphone. Report of anonymous partner given to author by email, December 7, 2016.

83 **wrung out of American firms:** The connection between corporate restructuring and increased managerial workloads is well documented. In one detailed study from the telecommunications sector in the mid-1990s, for example, 93 percent of middle managers reported increased workloads following restructuring. See Rosemary Batt, "From Bureaucracy to Enterprise? The Changing Jobs and Careers of Managers in Telecommunications Service," in Paul Osterman, ed., *Broken Ladders: Managerial Careers in the New Economy* (Oxford: Oxford University Press, 1996), 73. See also Peter Cappelli, *The New Deal at Work: Managing the Market-Driven Workforce* (Boston: Harvard Business School Press, 1999), 129–30. Hereafter cited as Cappelli, *The New Deal at Work.*

83 **Managers' hours grew steadily:** Daniel Feldman, "Managers' Propensity to Work Long Hours: A Multilevel Analysis," *Human Resource Management Review* 12 (2002): 339.

83 **exceeded fifty-five per week:** Juliet Schor, *The Overworked American: The Unexpected Decline of Leisure* (New York: HarperCollins, 1991), 181, citing a Korn/Ferry International poll. Hereafter cited as Schor, *The Overworked American.*

83 **over sixty hours per week:** Schor, *The Overworked American,* 181, citing a Heidrick and Struggles poll, also cited in Ford S. Worthy, "You're Probably Working Too Hard," *Fortune,* April 27, 1987, 136.

83 **over the course of the 1980s:** Schor, *The Overworked American,* 181, citing Sally Solo, "Stop Whining and Get Back to Work," *Fortune,* March 12, 1990, 49.

The rate of increase perhaps slowed after this, as the initial work efficiencies it aimed at had mostly been achieved. See Peter Kuhn and Fernando Lozano, "The Expanding Workweek? Understanding Trends in Long Work Hours Among U.S. Men, 1979–2006," *Journal of Labor Economics* 26, no. 2 (2008): 311–43. Hereafter cited as Kuhn and Lozano, "The Expanding Workweek?" This article uses data from the Current Population Survey between 1979 and 2006 to show that managerial work hours increased most rapidly in the 1980s. But the trend has not reversed, or even stopped, and *Fortune* magazine reports that executives today "are working harder than ever." Patricia Sellers, "You're Working Too Hard!" *Fortune* (blog), August 20, 2009, accessed August 11, 2018, http://postcards.blogs.fortune.cnn.com/2009/08/20/youre-working-too-hard/.

A 1990s poll of 1,344 middle managers similarly reported that 33 percent of managers work forty to forty-nine hours per week, 57 percent work fifty-one to sixty hours per week, and 6 percent work more than sixty hours per week. See Anne Fisher, "Welcome to the Age of Overwork," *Fortune,* November 30, 1992, 64–71, and Jeanne Brett and Linda Stroh, "Working 61 Plus Hours a Week: Why Do Managers Do It?," *Journal of Applied Psychology* 88, no. 1 (2003).

Other reports of managers' work hours include Arlie Hochschild's conclusion that top executives work fifty to seventy hours per week. See Hochschild, *The Time Bind,* 57. See also a mid-1980s poll conducted by Korn/Ferry (Ford S. Worthy, "You're Probably Working Too Hard," *Fortune,* April 27, 1987, 136), which showed that senior executives worked an average of fifty-six hours per week.

83 **"the members of the Management Committee":** Hochschild, *The Time Bind,* 56. The executive added, "It's going to be a long time before somebody becomes the CEO of a company saying, 'I'm going to be a wonderfully balanced person'—because there are just too many others who aren't. The environment here is very competitive." Hochschild, *The Time Bind,* 56–57.

83 **"I don't think":** Hochschild, *The Time Bind,* 70.

The demands on small businesspeople have grown similarly. A detailed study of businesses operating in Dallas, for example, reveals that whereas only 6.8 percent of existing businesses failed in 1970, by the mid-1980s, over 20 percent of existing businesses failed each year. See Louis Richman, "How Jobs Die—and Are Born," *Fortune,* July 26, 1993.

83 **"62% of high-earning individuals":** Hewlett and Luce, "Extreme Jobs."

83 **"The majority of them":** Hewlett and Luce, "Extreme Jobs."

84 **averaged across four weeks:** See Julia Szymczack et al., "To Leave or to Lie? Are Concerns About a Shift-Work Mentality and Eroding Professionalism as a Result of Duty-Hour Rules Justified?," *Milbank Quarterly* 88, no. 3 (September 2010): 350–81.

84 **increased by nearly half:** Renée M. Landers, James B. Rebitzer, and Lowell J. Taylor, "Rat Race Redux: Adverse Selection in the Determination of Work Hours in Law Firms," *American Economic Review* 86, no. 3 (June 1996): 329–48, 330, citing American Bar Association, Young Lawyers Division, *The State of the Legal Profession* (American Bar Association, 1991), 22, Table 19. The ABA study reports that in 1984, 4 percent of lawyers worked more than 240 hours a month and 31 percent worked 200 to 239. By 1990, 13 percent worked more than 240 hours a month and 37 percent worked 200 to 239. Hereafter cited as Landers, Rebitzer, and Taylor, "Rat Race Redux."

84 **during busy periods:** Landers, Rebitzer, and Taylor, "Rat Race Redux," 337. Other surveys report equivalent results. For example, a University of Michigan School of Law survey of its graduates reports that 70 percent average over fifty hours work per week and over a quarter average over sixty hours. University of Michigan Law School, "Class of 1995 Five Year Report" (2002), accessed August 11, 2018, http://repository.law.umich.edu/cgi/viewcontent.cgi?article=1145&context=alumni_survey_reports. See also Patrick Schiltz, "On Being a Happy, Healthy, and Ethical Member of an Unhappy, Unhealthy, and Unethical Profession," *Vanderbilt Law Review* 52, no. 4 (May 1999): 870–951. Hereafter cited as Schiltz, "An Unhappy, Unhealthy, and Unethical Profession."

84 **"work weeks of more":** See Rhode, *Balanced Lives,* 14; Deborah L. Rhode, *In the Interests of Justice: Reforming the Legal Profession* (Oxford: Oxford University Press, 2000); Cameron Stracher, "Show Me the Misery," *Wall Street Journal,* March 6, 2000, A31; Carl Bogus, "The Death of an Honorable Profession," *Indiana Law Journal* 71, no. 4 (Fall 1996): 924, accessed August 8, 2018, www.repository.law.indiana.edu/cgi/viewcontent.cgi?article=1802&context=ilj; and Sheila Wellington, "Women in Law: Making the Case," *Women Lawyers Journal* 88, no. 2 (Winter 2003): 11–15.

84 **An anonymous lawyer recently described:** Anonymous mid-level/senior associate at a large law firm, "My Typical Day Shows Why Lawyers Are Miserable and Lonely," *Business Insider,* November 12, 2013, accessed August 12, 2018, originally posted by Anonymous at "Why are so many lawyers unhappy with their jobs?," Quora, accessed August 12, 2018, www.quora.com/Attorneys/Why-are-so-many-lawyers-unhappy-with-their-jobs.

84 **"When you wake up":** Blake Edwards, "Big Firm Burnout and the New Virtual Lawyers," Bloomberg Law, August 27, 2015, accessed August 12, 2018, https://bol.bna.com/big-firm-burnout-and-the-new-virtual-lawyers/ (reporting on Patrick Murdoch, former associate at Shearman & Sterling).

84 **"the only quantitative requirement":** See Casey Sullivan, "Law Firm Leaders Weigh In on Partner Dismissals," Reuters Legal, October 22, 2013, accessed November 18, 2018, https://content.next.westlaw.com/Document/I4d4fcbf03b0411e389b0e1bebc789156/View/FullText.html?contextData=(sc.Default)&transitionType=Default&firstPage=true&bhcp=1.

84 **did not know that they were happening:** See generally C. B. Fry, *Life Worth Living: Some Phases of an Englishman* (London: Eyre & Spottiswoode, 1939).

84 **famously resisted practicing:** Dave McKibben, "Fleming Has Classic Memories of Partnership with McEnroe," *Los Angeles Times,* October 1, 1992, accessed September 2, 2018, http://articles.latimes.com/1992-10-01/sports/sp-145_1_tennis-classic.

84 **nearly seven hours a day:** Dominic Bliss, "Service Charged," *GQ* (UK), March 29, 2012, accessed August 12, 2018, www.gq-magazine.co.uk/article/gq-sport-rafael-nadal-tennis-fitness-training-tips-workout.

85 **eighty- to one-hundred-hour weeks:** See, e.g., Lynette Pinchess, "How This Nottinghamshire Lad Went from Shippo's Pub Kitchens to Cooking for Hollywood Stars," *Nottingham Post,* October 13, 2017, accessed August 12, 2018, www.nottinghampost.com/whats-on/food-drink/how-nottinghamshire-lad-went-shippos-623239; *Guardian* readers, "What It's Like to Work in the Restaurant Industry—Our Readers' Stories," *Guardian,* March 25, 2017, accessed August 12, 2018, www

.theguardian.com/lifeandstyle/2017/mar/25/what-its -like-to-work-in-the-restaurant-industry-our-readers-stories.

85   **"all train like it's the . . . Olympics":** Brooke Shunatona, "10 Victoria's Secret Models Reveal How They Really Feel About Their Bodies," *Cosmopolitan*, December 15, 2014, accessed August 12, 2018, www.cosmopolitan.com/style-beauty/fashion /a34249/victorias-secret-models-body-image/ (attributing the quoted text to Elsa Hosk). See also Deni Kirkova, "'I Thought, Oh My God, They Don't Want Me Here!': Naomi Campbell on Her Nerves About Her Emotional Return to the Versace Cat- walk," *Daily Mail*, October 7, 2013, accessed August 12, 2018, www.dailymail.co.uk/femail/article-2443934/I-want-people -know-hard-models-work-Naomi-Campbell-reveals-drank-just -juice-days-Versace-catwalk.html; Radar Staff, "Kendall Jenner: 'In Reality, I Worked Pretty Hard' for Modeling Success, 'Not Trying to Use a Family Name' to Get Ahead," Radar Online, November 17, 2014, accessed November 18, 2018, http:// radaronline.com/exclusives/2014/11/kendall-jenner-model -career-hard-work-nightline-kim-kardashian/.

85   **effortfully cultivate their fame:** Kim Kardashian sleeps with her BlackBerry and iPhone, wakes at 6 a.m., and sets almost im- mediately to work. See Kim Kardashian, interview with Char- lotte Cowles, "Exclusive: 24 Hours with Kim Kardashian," *Harper's Bazaar*, April 14, 2005, accessed August 12, 2018, www.harpersbazaar.com/culture/features/a10567/kim -kardashian-0515/.

85   **the *time divide*:** See Jacobs and Gerson, *The Time Divide*.

85   **According to one measure:** Kuhn and Lozano, "The Expand- ing Work Week?," 311. The data come from the U.S. Census, and the share working over forty-eight hours rose from 15.4 per- cent to 23.3 percent.

85   **between 1980 and 2005:** Kuhn and Lozano, "The Expanding Work Week?," 312. The data come from the U.S. Census and the American Community Survey, and the share working over forty-eight hours rose from 16.6 percent to 24.3 percent.

85   **increased by roughly half:** See Jacobs and Gerson, *The Time Divide*, 50. For couples with children, the percentage rose from 8.2 to 12.2 percent. For childless couples, the percentage nearly doubled, rising from 9.5 to 17.5 percent. Jacobs and Gerson also report that between 1970 and 2000, the percentage of families working one hundred hours or more per week tripled, from 3.1 percent to 9.3 percent (p. 43), and that the percentage of hus- bands and wives working one hundred hours or more rose from 8.7 percent to 14.5 percent (p. 45).

85   **leisure:** Leisure, as it is used in the data reported here, includes directly recreational activities and also some activities—such as sleeping, eating, and personal care—that involve relatively little burden and contribute indirectly to well-being. Market work and leisure therefore do not exhaust the activities that people engage in or the hours that they devote to them. A third cate- gory, nonmarket work, refers to nonrecreational activities that are nevertheless not performed for pay. Domestic chores and (some) childcare are the most notable components of nonmarket work. Although the text will occasionally refer to trends in non- market work, the larger argument focuses its principal attention on labor sold in the market, for pay.

For more on conceptualizing leisure, see Mark Aguiar and Erik Hurst, "Measuring Trends in Leisure: The Allocation of Time over Five Decades," *Quarterly Journal of Economics* 122, no. 3 (August 2007): 969–1006. Hereafter cited as Aguiar and Hurst, "Measuring Trends in Leisure." Lonnie Golden, "A Brief History of Long Work Time and the Contemporary Sources of Overwork," *Journal of Business Ethics* 84 (Supp. 2) (January 2009): 217–27. Hereafter cited as Golden, "A Brief History of Long Work Time." Orazio P. Attanasio and Luigi Pistaferri, "Consumption Inequality," *Journal of Economic Perspectives* 30, no. 2 (April 2016): 3. Hereafter cited as Attanasio and Pistaferri, "Consumption Inequality."

85   **between 1965 and 2003:** Aguiar and Hurst, "Measuring Trends in Leisure," 971.

85   **Moreover, income inequality:** Might these results be mere ar- tifacts of changing work and pay patterns not across but rather within individual workers? More specifically, might they show only that the representative worker supplies roughly the same total labor over longer periods but concentrates this labor in shorter periods of more intense work punctuated by longer

periods of unemployment? The data clearly reject this alterna- tive explanation. The same workers who earned increasingly higher wages and worked increasingly longer hours over the years in question also became increasingly less likely to become unemployed. See Kuhn and Lozano, "The Expanding Work Week?," 321–22.

85   **less educated workers:** See Kuhn and Lozano, "The Expanding Work Week?," 312. See also *Fighting for Time: Shifting Bound- aries of Work and Social Life*, ed. Cynthia Fuchs Epstein and Arne L. Kalleberg (New York: Russell Sage Foundation, 2004).

Dividing the population by education levels rather than by hourly wages produces results analogous to those in the main text. Both the absolute association between hours and earnings and the increase in the association between 1980 and 2000 were higher for salaried, typically better-educated, than for hourly, typically worse-educated, workers. See Kuhn and Lozano, "The Expanding Work Week?," 331, Figure 5. Educa- tion correlates to lifetime and not just hourly earnings. The con- nection between education and hours thus reinforces the point, made earlier, that the new association between high incomes and long hours arises across workers, over their entire lifetimes, rather than within workers who alternate periods that combine high income and long hours with periods of low income and idleness.

85   **The match between:** See Kuhn and Lozano, "The Expanding Work Week?," 331, Figure 5.

86   **roughly one in seven:** See Kuhn and Lozano, "The Expanding Work Week?," 317, Table 1, and 318, Figure 3.

86   **the bottom wage earner:** See Kuhn and Lozano, "The Expand- ing Work Week?," 317, Table 1.

86   **loss of leisure:** Aguiar and Hurst, "Measuring Trends in Lei- sure," 992, Table V, 995, Table VII.

86   **still notable for women:** In 1993, for example, roughly 25 per- cent of women managers worked forty-nine or more hours per week, compared with about 9 percent of women laborers, and female college graduates have experienced a very modest increase in leisure since the 1960s (although this increase is much smaller than the increase experienced by uneducated women and much, much less than the time freed up by labor-saving domestic de- vices). See Philip L. Rones, Randy E. Ilg, and Jennifer M. Gard- ner, "Trends in Hours of Work Since the Mid-1970s," *Monthly Labor Review* (April 1997): 9. For the claim about women's lei- sure, see Aguiar and Hurst, "Measuring Trends in Leisure," 992, Table V.

86   **the bottom quintile:** See Stuart Butler, "Can the American Dream Be Saved?," *National Affairs* 14 (Winter 2013): 40–57, 42. The exact numbers are 74.1 percent for the top quintile and 4.5 percent for the bottom quintile. Butler takes his data from U.S. Census Bureau, Current Population Survey (CPS) Annual Social and Economic (ASEC) Supplement, at U.S. Census Bu- reau, "HINC-01. Selected Characteristics of Households by Total Money Income," accessed August 12, 2018, www.census .gov/data/tables/time-series/demo/income-poverty/cps-hinc /hinc-01.2016.html. Taking the top quintile of households in 2010 to be at $100,000 or more (24,421 out of 119,927 house- holds), 18,111 households, so 74.1 percent, had two or more earners. Taking the bottom quintile to be at $19,999 or less (23,892 out of 119,927 households), 1,085 households, so 4.5 percent, had two or more earners.

86   **worked outside the home:** See Chinhui Juhn and Simon Pot- ter, "Changes in Labor Force Participation in the United States," *Journal of Economic Perspectives* 20, no. 3 (Summer 2003): 27– 46, 33, Table 2, which used data from the March CPS survey.

86   **their husbands had lost:** Veblen, *Theory of the Leisure Class*, 81.

87   **how data on work hours are collected:** Intensive and highly reliable in-person interviews conducted by the Federal Reserve Bank, in connection with its Survey on Consumer Finance, con- firm the explosion of elite work effort. The interviews are struc- tured, serious, and probing, and the survey oversamples the richest households, and for both reasons, the survey presents an unusually authoritative measure of elite work. According to the survey, the average total hours worked in households in the top 1 percent of the income distribution grew by 9.5 hours per week between 1983 and 2010. Over the same period, the percentage of households in this elite group whose hardest-working member

put in more than fifty hours per week grew by 16 percentage points, rising from 46 percent to 62 percent (so that by 2010, the median 1 percent household contained a fifty-hour worker). Over the same period, the share of households with a fifty-plus -hour worker fell with every step down the income distribution, until only 4 percent of households in the bottom quintile of the income distribution had a member regularly working more than fifty hours per week. See Board of Governors of the Federal Reserve System, "Survey of Consumer Finances," www.federal reserve.gov/econres/scfindex.htm.

87 **about 1.5 million households:** In 2014, the minimum income for tax units in the top 1 percent of the income distribution was $477,514. That year, 148,646,000 tax returns were filed. See Facundo Alvaredo et al., World Inequality Database, distributed by WID.world, accessed August 23, 2018, https://wid .world/data/ (see "Pre-Tax National Income Threshold," wid .world code tptinc992j, and "Number of Tax Returns," wid .world code ntaxre999t).

87 **vice presidents or above:** An October 2018 search of the D&B Hoovers database of business professionals turned up 241,113 workers at S&P 1500 companies under the categories Board of Directors, Directors, Executive Vice Presidents, Senior Officers C-level, Senior Vice Presidents, and Vice Presidents. (D&B Hoovers is a database commonly used for sales leads and marketing containing over 125 million [125,533,312] employee contacts ranging from nonmanagerial to the board of directors representing over 140 million firms [141,266,092]. The company answered an inquiry from the author confirming that each employee contact appears in its database only once, so that the search does not double-count.) The search turned up a further 398,087 Managers or Supervisors. The search downloaded the S&P 1500 constituents for 2017 from Compustat. DUNS numbers were matched by suppling Mergent with CUSIPs to generate the corresponding DUNS. A list of the S&P 1500 DUNS was uploaded in the D&B Hoovers and searched using the criteria for "Contact Level" under the search category of "Contact Type." There were 1,511 companies in the "S&P 1500" data set, on account of changes in the registry's composition over the course of the year.

87 **professionals in the finance sector:** The Financial Industry Regulatory Authority records over 630,132 registered financial representatives in the United States in 2017. See Financial Industry Regulatory Authority, "Statistics," accessed August 15, 2018, www.finra.org/newsroom/statistics#currentmonth. And the Bureau of Labor Statistics reports that as of May 2018, more than 250,000 people worked in supervisory roles in the broad "Securities, Commodity Contracts, and Other Financial Investments and Related Activities" industry category. See Bureau of Labor Statistics, "Industries at a Glance: Securities, Commodity Contracts, and Other Financial Investments and Related Activities," accessed August 15, 2018, www.bls.gov/iag/tgs/iag523 .htm#about. Reached by subtracting employment numbers for production and nonsupervisory employees from full employment numbers. The average hourly earnings in this sector, according to the BLS, is $54, for annual earnings of about $100,000. The supervisory employees may reasonably be thought to earn well above average wages, and given that they represent only about one-third of the total employees, this makes it reasonable to suppose that they earn in the neighborhood of a 1 percent threshold.

87 **the top five management consultancies:** The top five consulting firms are McKinsey & Company, the Boston Consulting Group, Inc., Bain & Company, Deloitte Consulting LLP, and Oliver Wyman, according to Phil Stott, "Vault's Top 50 Consulting Firms for 2018," Vault, August 22, 2017, accessed August 15, 2018, www.vault.com/blog/consult-this-consulting-careers -news-and-views/2018-vault-consulting-rankings. McKinsey employed 23,000 people in 2017. "McKinsey & Company: Overview," Vault, accessed August 15, 2018, www.vault.com /company-profiles/management-strategy/mckinsey-company /company-overview.aspx. Boston Consulting employed 14,000. "The Boston Consulting Group: Overview," Vault, accessed August 15, 2018, www.vault.com/company-profiles/management -strategy/the-boston-consulting-group,-inc/company-overview .aspx. Bain employed 7,000. "Bain & Company: Overview," Vault, accessed August 15, 2018, www.vault.com/company

-profiles/management-strategy/bain-company/company -overview.aspx. Deloitte employed 40,513. "Deloitte Consulting LLP: Overview," Vault, accessed August 15, 2018, www .vault.com/company-profiles/management-strategy/deloitte -consulting-llp/company-overview.aspx. Oliver Wyman employed 4,500. "Oliver Wyman: Overview," Vault, accessed August 15, 2018, www.vault.com/company-profiles/management -strategy/oliver-wyman/company-overview.aspx. If two-thirds of these are professionals, this is a total of about 60,000.

87 **partners at law firms:** In 2018, all but twelve of the AmLaw 200 had profits per partner above $475,000, the rough cutoff for top-1-percent income. See Ben Seal, "The 2018 Am Law Second Hundred: A to Z," *American Lawyer*, May 22, 2018, accessed August 23, 2018, www.law.com/americanlawyer/2018/05/22 /the-2018-am-law-second-hundred-at-a-glance/, and Gina Passarella Cipriani, "The 2018 Am Law 100 Ranked by: Profits per Equity Partner," *American Lawyer*, April 24, 2018, accessed August 23, 2018, www.law.com/americanlawyer/2018/04/24 /the-2018-am-law-100-ranked-by-profits-per-equity-partner/. And according to the *American Lawyer* "2012 Global 100: Profits Per Partner" list, the 75 U.S. firms in the Global 100 averaged 209 partners each: "The 2012 Global 100: Profits Per Partner," *American Lawyer*, September 28, 2012, accessed August 23, 2018, www.americanlawyer.com/PubArticleTAL.jsp?id=1202 571229443&The_2012_Global_100_Profits_Per_Partner& slreturn=20130225100009.

   If the remaining 45 firms were the same size, this would yield 25,000 equity partners at firms whose per-partner profit exceeded $400,000 in 2012.

87. **specialist doctors:** According to data from Redi-Direct, the number of specialist doctors in the United States was 501,296 as of March 2018. "Professionally Active Physicians," Henry J. Kaiser Family Foundation, March 2018, accessed August 15, 2018, www.kff.org/other/state-indicator/total-active-physicians /?currentTimeframe=0&sortModel=%7B%22colId%22: %22Location%22,%22sort%22:%22asc%22%7D.

88 **of 1 percent households overall:** More intensive and precise studies similarly reduce the composition of still narrower elites to known and named jobs. Steven Kaplan and Joshua Rauh, for example (using methods that they repeatedly admit are seriously underinclusive), estimate that the five highest-paid executives at America's largest firms, finance workers at the level of managing director or above, partners at the hundred largest law firms, professional athletes, and top celebrities collectively together compose roughly 20 percent (give or take a few percentage points) of the top 0.1 percent, 0.01 percent, 0.001 percent, and 0.0001 percent of tax units. See Kaplan and Rauh, "Wall Street and Main Street," Table 14.

88 **capital's renewed dominance:** See, e.g., Josh Bivens and Lawrence Mishel, "Understanding the Historic Divergence Between Productivity and a Typical Worker's Pay: Why It Matters and Why It's Real," Economic Policy Institute Briefing Paper no. 406 (September 2, 2015), accessed August 23, 2018, www.epi .org/publication/understanding-the-historic-divergence -between-productivity-and-a-typical-workers-pay-why-it -matters-and-why-its-real/; Angelo Young, "CBO Reports Suggests [*sic*] Growth in US Income Inequality Will Continue Through 2035 (but, Hey, as Long as Capital Markets Are Doing Great, Right?)," *International Business Times*, June 5, 2013, accessed August 23, 2018, www.ibtimes.com/graphic-cbo-reports -suggests-growth-us-income-inequality-will-continue-through -2035-1292085.

88 **the decline of labor unions:** See, e.g., Louis Uchitelle, "How the Loss of Union Power Has Hurt American Manufacturing," *New York Times*, April 20, 2018, accessed August 15, 2018, www.nytimes.com/2018/04/20/business/unions-american -manufacturing.html.

88 **market power among large employers:** See, e.g., Alan B. Krueger and Eric A. Posner, "A Proposal for Protecting Low-Income Workers from Monopsony and Collusion," The Hamilton Project, Policy, Proposal no. 2018-05 (February 2018), accessed October 24, 2018, www.brookings.edu/wp-content /uploads/2018/02/es_2272018_protecting_low_income _workers_from_monopsony_collusion_krueger_posner _pp.pdf; Eric Posner and Glen Weyl, "The Real Villain Behind Our New Gilded Age," *New York Times*, May 1, 2018, accessed

August 15, 2018, www.nytimes.com/2018/05/01/opinion/mo
nopoly-power-new-gilded-age.html.

88  **outsourcing and globalization:** See Chrystia Freeland, "For
U.S. Workers, Global Capitalism Fails to Deliver," *New York
Times*, April 14, 2011, accessed August 18, 2018, www.nytimes
.com/2011/04/15/us/15iht-letter15.html.

88  **Labor's share of national income:** See, e.g., Robert J. Gordon
and Ian Dew-Becker, "Controversies About the Rise of American Inequality: A Survey," NBER Working Paper No. 13982
(April 21, 2008), http://economics.weinberg.northwestern
.edu/robert-gordon/files/RescPapers/ControversiesRiseAmer
icanInequality.pdf; Paul Gomme and Peter Rupert, "Measuring
Labor's Share of Income," Federal Reserve Bank of Cleveland
Policy Discussion Paper No. 7 (November 2004), accessed August 23, 2018, https://papers.ssrn.com/sol3/papers.cfm?ab
stract_id=1024847; Brian I. Baker, "The Laboring Labor Share
of Income: The 'Miracle' Ends," *Monthly Labor Review*, January
2016, accessed August 26, 2018, www.bls.gov/opub/mlr/2016
/beyond-bls/the-laboring-labor-share-of-income-the-miracle
-ends.htm; Loukas Karabarbounis and Brent Neiman, "The
Global Decline of the Labor Share," *Quarterly Journal of Economics* 129, no. 1 (February 2014): 61–103; International Labour Organization, Global Wage Report 2012/12: Wages and
Equitable Growth (Geneva: International Labour Organization, 2013), 41–53. Note that the global trend—which spans
countries with vastly different political systems and domestic
policy regimes—strongly implies that labor's decline stems from
economic fundamentals rather than shallow political or policy
choices.

89  **Eight of the ten richest Americans:** The ten richest Americans, according to *Forbes* magazine, are (in order): Bill Gates,
Jeff Bezos, Warren Buffett, Mark Zuckerberg, Larry Ellison,
Charles Koch, David Koch, Michael Bloomberg, Larry Page,
and Sergey Brin. See "Forbes 400," *Forbes*, accessed August 26,
2018, www.forbes.com/forbes-400/list/. Of these, all but the
Koch brothers are self-made, and the Koch brothers inherited a
relatively small business (from its entrepreneur-founder), which
they built into a much larger one, at a growth rate that resembles
self-made entrepreneurship. Broadening the inquiry to the fifty
richest Americans reveals that thirty-three owe their wealth
principally to founder's stock, partnership shares, carried interest, or executive compensation—that is, to their own labor—
and that a further eight owe their wealth to labor from just one
generation earlier. A similar point appears in Victor Fleischer,
"Alpha: Labor Is the New Capital" (unpublished manuscript on
file with author), table in appendix. Hereafter cited as Fleischer,
"Alpha." See also Dan Primack, "Are Entrepreneurs Exploiting a
Tax Loophole? (Part II)," *Fortune*, December 30, 2010, accessed
August 26, 2018, http://fortune.com/2010/12/29/are-entre
preneurs-exploiting-a-tax-loophole-part-ii/.

89  **nearly seven in ten are:** See Steven Kaplan and Joshua Rauh,
"Family, Education, and Sources of Wealth Among the Richest
Americans, 1982–2012," *American Economic Review* 103, no. 3
(May 2013): 158–62, 159. Hereafter cited as Kaplan and Rauh,
"Family, Education, and Sources of Wealth." Between 1982 and
2011, the share of Forbes 400 members who grew up with wealth
dropped from 60 percent to 32 percent. See also James Pethokoukis, "How Super-Rich Americans Get That Way Is Changing," *AEIdeas*, American Enterprise Institute, March 23, 2016,
www.aei.org/publication/how-super-rich-americans-get-that
-way-is-changing/.

89  **outnumber purely inherited ones:** See James Pethokoukis,
"More and More of America's Superrich May Be Getting That
Way Through Entrepreneurship," *AEIdeas*, American Enterprise Institute, December 22, 2014, accessed August 26, 2018,
www.aei.org/publication/americas-superrich-getting-way
-entrepreneurship/.

89  **between 1961 and 2007:** See Winters, *Oligarchy*, 247, Table
5.4. The percentages are: 1961, 22.3 percent; 1992, 47.4 percent;
2007, 34.4 percent. The *Forbes* list was inaugurated in 1982, but
we have data for 1961 on account of the fluke that, in that year,
398 taxpayers had income sufficient to get into the highest tax
bracket, and so were counted by the IRS. David Cay Johnston,
"Is Our Tax System Helping Us Create Wealth?," *Tax Notes*,
December 21, 2009, www.taxnotes.com/tax-notes/budgets
/our-tax-system-helping-us-create-wealth/2009/12/21/qjq2.

89  **between 1982 and 2011:** From 17 percent in 1982 to just 5 percent by 2011. See Kaplan and Rauh, "Family, Education, and
Sources of Wealth," 158–62, 160.

89  **24 percent from finance:** See Les Leopold, "Five Obscene Reasons the Rich Grow Richer," *Salon*, October 1, 2012, accessed
August 26, 2018, www.salon.com/2012/10/01/five_obscene
_reasons_the_rich_grow_richer/. In 2017, ninety-two of the
four hundred (approximately 23 percent) richest people worked
in finance or finance and investments, and fifteen (3.75 percent)
worked in manufacturing. See "Forbes 400," *Forbes*, accessed
August 26, 2018, www.forbes.com/forbes-400/list/.

90  **do not make the papers:** See Nathan Vardi, "The 25 Highest-
Earning Hedge Fund Managers & Traders," *Forbes*, March 14,
2017, accessed August 26, 2018, www.forbes.com/sites/nathan
vardi/2017/03/14/hedge-fund-managers/#3402d78d6e79.

90  **on average $2.4 million:** See Will Wainewright and Lindsay
Fortado, "Hedge Fund Manager Compensation Rises 8% to
$2.4 Million," Bloomberg, November 6, 2014, accessed August
26, 2018, www.bloomberg.com/news/articles/2014-11-06/hedge
-fund-manager-compensation-rises-8-to-2-4-million.

90  **reached over $420,000:** See "The Securities Industry in New
York City," Office of the New York State Comptroller, September 2018, accessed October 24, 2018, www.osc.state.ny.us/osdc
/rpt6-2019.pdf. Incredibly, bonuses were even higher just before
the 2007–8 financial crisis, when they reached over $190,000.
See "New York City Securities Industry Bonuses," Office of
the New York State Deputy Comptroller, January 28, 2009,
accessed August 20, 2018, www.osc.state.ny.us/osdc/wallst
_bonuses/2009/bonus2009.pdf, and "New York City Securities
Industry Bonus Pool," Office of the New York State Comptroller, March 26, 2018, accessed August 20, 2018, www.osc.state
.ny.us/press/releases/mar18/wall-st-bonuses-2018-sec-industry
-bonus-pool.pdf.

Small wonder that according to one calculation, the
financial sector's overall representation in the top tiers of wealth
has increased by a factor of ten since the 1970s. See Eric Posner
and E. Glen Weyl, "Against Casino Finance," *National Affairs*
14 (Winter 2013): 58–77, 62, accessed November 18, 2018,
www.nationalaffairs.com/publications/detail/against-casino
-finance. Hereafter cited as Posner and Weyl, "Against Casino
Finance." Posner and Weyl cite Kaplan and Rauh, "Wall Street
and Main Street," which examines the composition of the top
0.1 percent, 0.01 percent, 0.001 percent, and 0.0001 percent of
income distribution by employment sector.

90  **an owner of bank stocks:** See, e.g., "Going Overboard," *The
Economist*, July 16, 2009, accessed August 21, 2018, www.econ
omist.com/node/14034875/print?story_id=14034875.

90  **nearly $14 million:** "Executive Paywatch," AFL-CIO, accessed
August 21, 2018, https://aflcio.org/paywatch.

The highest-paid CEO in 2013 made $141.9 million and
the two-hundredth-highest-paid CEO made $12.4 million. See
Karl Russell, "The Pay at the Top," *New York Times*, June 7,
2014, accessed August 26, 2018, www.nytimes.com/interac
tive/2014/06/08/business/the-pay-at-the-top.html.

In 2014, the highest-paid CEO made $156.1 million and
the two-hundredth-highest-paid CEO made $12.6 million. See
"Highest-Paid Chiefs in 2014," *New York Times*, May 16, 2015,
accessed August 26, 2018, www.nytimes.com/interactive/2015
/05/14/business/executive-compensation.html.

In 2015, the highest-paid CEO made $94.6 million and
the two-hundredth-highest-paid CEO made $12.2 million. See
Karl Russell and Josh Williams, "Meet the Highest-Paid
C.E.O.s in 2015," *New York Times*, May 27, 2016, accessed August 26, 2018, www.aflcio.org/Corporate-Watch/Paywatch
-2014/100-Highest-Paid-CEOs.

In 2016, the highest-paid CEO made $98.0 million and
the two-hundredth-highest-paid made $13.0 million. Jon
Huang and Karl Russell, "The Highest-Paid C.E.O.s in 2016,"
*New York Times*, May 26, 2017, accessed August 21, 2018, www
.nytimes.com/interactive/2017/05/26/business/highest-paid
-ceos.html.

In 2017, the highest-paid CEO made $103.2 million and
the two-hundredth-highest-paid made $13.8 million. "The
Highest-Paid C.E.O.s in 2017," *New York Times*, May 25, 2018,
accessed August 21, 2018, www.nytimes.com/interactive/2018
/05/25/business/ceo-pay-2017.html.

90 **collective profits:** A 2005 analysis of compensation for top five highest-paid officers in the ExecuComp database (which includes "all the S&P 500, Mid-Cap 400, and Small-Cap 600 companies … also known as the S&P 1,500") found that, between 2001 and 2003, the "ratio of aggregate [top-five] executive compensation to aggregate [S&P 1500] earnings" was 9.8 percent. See Lucian Bebchuk and Yaniv Grinstein, "The Growth of Executive Pay," *Oxford Review of Economic Policy* 21, no. 2 (2005): 283–303, 284, 297, accessed August 26, 2018, www.law.harvard.edu/faculty/bebchuk/pdfs/Bebchuk-Grinstein.Growth-of-Pay.pdf.

90 **a war that talent is winning:** See Roger L. Martin and Mihnea C. Moldoveanu, "Capital Versus Talent: The Battle That's Reshaping Business," *Harvard Business Review*, July 2003, accessed August 26, 2018, https://hbr.org/2003/07/capital-versus-talent-the-battle-thats-reshaping-business (concluding that talent has "started taking more of the profits from capital").

91 **nine-tenths of their income from capital:** Thomas Piketty, Emmanuel Saez, and Gabriel Zucman, "Distributional National Accounts: Methods and Estimates for the United States," NBER Working Paper No. 22945 (2016), 26, 49, Figure 8, http://gabriel-zucman.eu/files/PSZ2016.pdf. Hereafter cited as Piketty, Saez, and Zucman, "Distributional National Accounts."

91 **reaching bottom in 2000:** Piketty, Saez, and Zucman, "Distributional National Accounts," 26, 49, Figure 8.

91 **(roughly 49 percent and 53 percent, respectively):** Thomas Piketty, Emmanuel Saez, and Gabriel Zucman, "Distributional National Accounts: Methods and Estimates for the United States," *Quarterly Journal of Economics* 133, no. 2 (May 2018): 553–609, Figure VIII.

91 **(when the data series runs out):** Piketty, Saez, and Zucman, "Distributional National Accounts," 26, 49, Figure 8. In calculating these shares the authors allocated 70 percent of the income received by owners of unincorporated businesses to labor and 30 percent to capital. Piketty, Saez, and Zucman, "Distributional National Accounts," 42n.

Other sources tell a compatible tale. For example, tax data from 2015 suggest that an average member of the top 1 percent owed 56.4 percent of his total fiscal income to labor. Facundo Alvaredo et al., World Inequality Database, distributed by WID.world, accessed July 3, 2018, https://wid.world/data/ (see "Average Fiscal Labour Income," wid.world code aflinc992t, and "Average Fiscal Income," wid.world code aflinc992t).

91 **on their tax returns:** Either directly, as restricted stock grants, or through the exercise of stock options.

91 **pensions and owner-occupied housing:** Employers fund pensions as payment for workers' labor, and the payment anticipates that the pensions will accumulate between when the contributions are made and when the funds are withdrawn. The entire accumulated pensions therefore represent, both economically and morally, wages deferred until retirement, which is to say labor income. And at least insofar as a worker pays for her house with her wages (often, over time, facilitated by a mortgage), any economic return that the house generates again stems naturally from labor.

92 **the founders who built the firms:** Luisa Kroll and Kerry A. Dolan, eds., "Forbes 400: The Definitive Ranking of the Wealthiest Americans," *Forbes*, October 3, 2018, www.forbes.com/forbes-400/#7de6813e7e2f. Hereafter cited as Kroll and Dolan, "Forbes 400." The founders who hold these shares include: Jeff Bezos (1), Bill Gates (2), Warren Buffett (3), Mark Zuckerberg (4), Larry Ellison (5), Larry Page (6), and Sergey Brin (9). Others among the top one hundred—for example, George Soros (60) and Carl Icahn (31)—owe their fortunes to carried interest.

92 **reported by one-percenters:** Victor Fleischer, "How a Carried Interest Tax Could Raise $180 Billion," *New York Times*, June 5, 2015, http://nytimes.com/2015/06/06/business/dealbook/how-a-carried-interest-tax-could-raise-180-billion.html. Fleischer reaches this result by inference from the legal structures typically employed by investment funds. In particular, investment funds are generally organized as partnerships, and the fund managers of investment funds are themselves also organized as partnerships. Income reported to the IRS as accruing to "partnership general partners"—that is, to general partners in one partnership that are themselves organized as a second partnership—therefore overwhelmingly goes to fund managers of investment funds. This is the "carried interest" that receives capital gains treatment, although it is, economically, just a return on the labor of the

investment fund managers. The precise share is difficult to determine, because the IRS breaks its data into overlapping categories, which raises a specter of double counting. Fleischer, "Alpha"; Internal Revenue Service, "SOI Tax Stats—Partnership Statistics by Sector or Industry," last modified June 20, 2018, www.irs.gov/statistics/soi-tax-stats-partnership-statistics-by-sector-or-industry; www.treasury.gov/resource-center/tax-policy/Documents/OTP-CG-Taxes-Paid-Pos-CG-1954-2009-6-2012.pdf; "SOI Tax Stats—Individual Statistical Tables by Size of Adjusted Gross Income," last modified November 5, 2018, www.irs.gov/statistics/soi-tax-stats-individual-statistical-tables-by-size-of-adjusted-gross-income; Victor Fleischer, email correspondence with author, October 30, 2018.

Moreover, simulations of the investment structures deployed by the Blackstone Group suggest that perhaps three-quarters of the capital gains income taxed to individual taxpayers (as opposed to firms, foundations, or investment funds) through these structures in fact constitutes a return to labor. Blackstone manages over $250 billion, including (by investing for public pension funds) portions of the retirement holdings of more than half of all retirees in the United States. Fleischer, "Alpha," 15–17.

92 **stock or stock options:** K. J. Martijn Cremers, Saura Masconale, and Simone N. Sepe, "CEO Pay Redux," *Texas Law Review* 96 (2017): 242, Figure 2. Hereafter cited as Cremers, Masconale, and Sepe, "CEO Pay Redux." Not all of this income is taxed as capital gains, of course.

92 **in the 1960s:** In recent years, returns to pensions and imputed rents from owner-occupied housing together have constituted about 12 percent of the top 1 percent's income and 6 percent of the top 0.1 percent's income, compared to about 6 and 3 percent of income, respectively, in the 1960s. For the 1 percent, these shares have held roughly steady since the late 1980s; for the 0.1 percent, the shares were greater in the 1990s and fell off in the first decade of the new millennium. These numbers are calculated from the distributional series included in Piketty, Saez, and Zucman, "Distributional National Accounts," Appendix II, http://gabriel-zucman.eu/files/PSZ2016DataAppendix.pdf. The calculations for the 1 percent are based on Table B2b (also labeled TA2b) and divide the sum of columns 20 and 22 by column 17. The calculations for the 0.1 percent are based on Table B2c (also labeled TA2c) and divide the sum of columns 12 and 14 by column 9.

92 **survey of elite jobs:** The phenomenon is so powerful that it applies even during the life phase once devoted to "retirement." The top quintile of earners over sixty-five today owes more than four-fifths (83.3 percent) of its income to wages, Social Security, or pensions—that is, to its own present or prior labor. Ke Bin Wu, *Sources of Income for Older Americans* (Washington, DC: AARP Public Policy Institute, 2013), 3, Figure 4, www.aarp.org/money/low-income-assistance/info-12-2013/sources-of-income-for-older-americans-2012-AARP-ppi-econ-sec.html.

92 **now literally works for a living:** A recent, detailed, and sophisticated argument for this conclusion, which emphasizes non-wage labor income associated with "pass-through" business profits, appears in Matthew Smith, Danny Yagan, Owen Zidar, and Eric Zwick, "Capitalists in the Twenty-First Century" (working paper, May 15, 2019), 51–52, Figures 7 and 8.

93 **total national income:** A rough-and-ready calculation underwrites this claim. Begin by measuring the overall income shift from labor to capital. Reasonable estimates of labor's overall share of total national income range from finding an increase since 1950, from roughly 65 to 70 percent of total income, to finding a larger but still modest decline, from 62 percent in 1950 to perhaps 56 percent today. Robert J. Gordon and Ian Dew-Becker, "Controversies About the Rise of American Inequality: A Survey," NBER Working Paper No. 13982 (May 2008), 5; Paul Gomme and Peter Rupert, *Measuring Labor's Share of Income*, Policy Discussion Paper (Cleveland: Federal Reserve Bank of Cleveland, November 2004), 8, 9, Figure 6; Brian I. Baker, *The Laboring Labor-Share of Income: The "Miracle" Ends* (Washington, DC: U.S. Bureau of Labor Statistics, January 2016), 1, www.bls.gov/opub/mlr/2016/beyond-bls/the-laboring-labor-share-of-income-the-miracle-ends.htm; Loukas Karabarbounis and Brent Neiman, "The Global Decline of the Labor Share," *Quarterly Journal of Economics* 129, no. 1 (February 2014): 61, https://doi.org/10.1093/qje/qjt032; International Labor Organization, *Global*

*Wage Report 2012/13: Wages and Equitable Growth* (Geneva: International Labour Organization, 2013), 43, Figure 31.

It is better to consider the span of responsible assessments rather than any single specific estimate because measuring these shares turns out to require judgment, and reasonable people can disagree. How should the rental value of owner-occupied housing, which is included in national income, be apportioned between treating the owner as capitalist who rents to herself and as worker who superintends her own dwelling, for example? How should the income received by proprietors of owner-operated businesses be treated? And what return to the capital stock of the government should be included as a counterbalance to the labor income of public employees? Note that the global trend—which spans countries with vastly different political systems and domestic policy regimes—strongly implies that labor's decline stems from economic fundamentals rather than shallow political or policy choices.

Next, ask what share of capital is owned by top earners. Serious estimates of the share of total wealth held by the wealthiest 1 percent of Americans range from 20 percent to 42 percent, and the top 1 percent of Americans sorted by income can own no greater share of capital than this. The 20 percent estimate, which tabulates individuals rather than households, comes from Wojciech Kopczuk and Emmanuel Saez, "Top Wealth Shares in the United States, 1916–2000: Evidence from Estate Tax Returns," *National Tax Journal* 57, no. 2 (June 2004): 453. The 42 percent estimate, which uses household data, comes from Emmanuel Saez and Gabriel Zucman, "Wealth Inequality in the United States Since 1913: Evidence from Capitalized Income Tax Data," *Quarterly Journal of Economics* 131, no. 2 (May 2016): 520. Hereafter cited as Saez and Zucman, "Wealth Inequality in the United States."

Finally, combine these facts. The overall shift in income from labor to capital amounts to at most 6 percent of total income, and the richest 1 percent of households measured by income own at most two-fifths of the capital. This entails that the labor-to-capital shift can have augmented the 1 percent's income share by about 2.5 percent (which is a little more than two-fifths times 6 percent) of total national income. (This approach assumes that the rich do not enjoy materially higher rates of return on their wealth than the rest of the population. The best evidence supports this assumption and reveals only modest differences in the overall performance of investments held by wealthy versus ordinary Americans. Saez and Zucman, "Wealth Inequality in the United States Since 1913," Appendix, Figures B29–B31, B33, Tables B30–B31, http://gabriel-zucman.eu/files /SaezZucman2016QJEAppendix.pdf.)

93  **roughly 20 percent today:** See World Top Incomes Database, United States / Pre-tax national income / P99-P100 / Share, October 29, 2018, https://wid.world/country/usa/.

93  **rising top income shares:** Some studies appear to show a more modest labor contribution to rising overall inequality. For example, see Congressional Budget Office, Trends in the Distribution of Household Income Between 1979 and 2007 (Washington, DC: U.S. Government Printing Office, October 2011), www.cbo.gov/publication/42729. Hereafter cited as Congressional Budget Office, "Trends in the Distribution of Household Income." But these studies reach their conclusions by failing to attribute any business income or capital gains to labor, and the studies even so conclude that labor is the dominant cause of rising top incomes.

93  **top lawyers, bankers, managers, and so on:** Saez, "Reported Incomes and Marginal Tax Rates," 155–56, Figure 6 [top 10 percent], 156, Figure 7 [top 1 percent], 158, Figure 8 [top 0.01 percent]. Another related study thus concludes that "the increase in top income shares in the last three decades is the direct consequence of the surge in top wages." Thomas Piketty and Emmanuel Saez, "Income Inequality in the United States, 1913–1998," *Quarterly Journal of Economics* 118, no. 1 (February 2003): 3.

93  **elite labor income:** Saez, "Reported Incomes and Marginal Tax Rates," 158, Figure 8 (calculation from the figure, following the practice noted earlier of treating 70 percent of profits from S-corporations, partnerships, and sole proprietorships as labor income).

94  **an open letter:** Mark Zuckerberg, "A Letter to Our Daughter," Facebook, December 1, 2015, www.facebook.com/notes/mark -zuckerberg/a-letter-to-our-daughter/10153375081581634/. When Zuckerberg wrote the letter, he was the sixth-richest

person in the world. Kerry A. Dolan and Luisa Kroll, "Forbes 2016 World's Billionaires: Meet the Richest People on the Planet," *Forbes*, March 1, 2016, www.forbes.com/sites/luisak roll/2016/03/01/forbes-2016-worlds-billionaires-meet-the -richest-people-on-the-planet/#5d8c660277dc.

94  **"advance human potential":** Zuckerberg, "A Letter to Our Daughter."

94  **constituted social status:** For a similar point, see John Langbein, "The Twentieth-Century Revolution in Family Wealth Transmission," *Michigan Law Review* 86 (February 1988): 722– 51. Hereafter cited as Langbein, "Twentieth-Century Revolution."

94  **govern dynastic succession:** "The right of the father to dispose of his property, when given to him and the heirs of his body, depended upon his first having a son, who was capable of the inheritance." Charles Neate, *The History and Uses of the Law of Entail and Settlement* 7 (London: W. Ridgway, 1865).

94  **Blenheim Palace:** The example is chosen because this dukedom, exceptionally, can pass through the female line, and the current holders of the title do trace their succession to this contingency. Noel Cox, "Property Law, Imperial and British Titles: The Duke of Marlborough and the Principality of Mindelheim," *Legal History Review* 77, no. 1–2 (2009): 193, https://doi .org/10.1163/004075809X403433.

94  **the entire aristocratic order:** It might even, eventually, have dissolved the family title. Moreover, even these consequences would have followed only if the regnant legal order governing titles and property permitted the divestiture at all, rather than entailing the estate to guarantee that it remained in the family. See Langbein, "Twentieth-Century Revolution," 725–26.

95  **upon their deaths:** "History of the Pledge," The Giving Pledge, accessed October 12, 2018, https://givingpledge.org. Signatories include Bill Gates, Warren Buffett, Mark Zuckerberg, Larry Ellison, and Michael Bloomberg, all in the top ten of 2018's Forbes 400. Kroll and Dolan, "Forbes 400."

96  **An advertisement for the *Wall Street Journal*:** "People who don't have time make time to read the *Wall Street Journal*," *Wall Street Journal*, accessed October 12, 2018, www.wsj.com/maketime.

96  **When law students were recently asked:** This is reported in an unpublished early draft of Heather Kappes et al., "'Who You Are' Heightens Entitlement More Than 'What you Did'" (manuscript on file with author).

96  **more important than studying:** Stephanie Addenbrooke and Emma Platoff, "2019 by the Numbers: First Impressions," *Yale Daily News*, August 28, 2018, accessed November 18, 2018, http://features.yaledailynews.com/blog/2015/08/28/2019-by -the-numbers-first-impressions/.

In 2016, the Yale College Council Health Task Force found that the average Yale student slept only 6.7 hours on a weekday and that more than 10 percent of students slept less than 5 hours on average on a weekday. Paddy Gavin, "UP CLOSE: Unhealthy Sleep Culture at Yale," *Yale Daily News*, September 9, 2016, accessed November 18, 2018, http://fea tures.yaledailynews.com/blog/2016/09/09/up-close -unhealthy-sleep-culture-at-yale/. Similarly, a 2014 Harvard University Health Services Assessment survey of two thousand Harvard undergraduate students found that 10 percent of students reported getting less than 6 hours of sleep a night on average and that a full two-thirds of students averaged just 6–7 hours of sleep a night. Quynh-Nhu Le and Zara Zhang, "The State of the Student Body," *Harvard Crimson*, November 11, 2014, accessed November 18, 2018, www.thecrimson.com/article /2014/11/11/state-of-the-student-body/.

96  **self-identify as workaholics:** Golden, "A Brief History of Long Work Time," 223 (citing Daniel S. Hamermesh and Joel Slemrod, "The Economics of Workaholism: We Should Not Have Worked on This Paper," NBER Working Paper No. 11566 [2005], www.nber.org/papers/w11566).

96  **"whatever it takes to get things done":** Ho, *Liquidated*, 103.

96  **"wear their commitments":** Hewlett and Luce, "Extreme Jobs."

97  **"shouldn't wear suspenders":** Ho, *Liquidated*, 73.

97  **Exploit has been reconstituted:** Gershuny, "Busyness as the Badge of Honor," 296. Gershuny attributes this point to Pierre Bourdieu, *Distinction: A Social Critique of the Judgment of Taste* (London: Routledge & Kegan Paul, 1984).

97　**Even celebrity—fame for its own sake:** Kim Kardashian, for example, has stated, "The biggest misconception about my family and me is that we're lazy. . . . I work hard; the show is a full-time job. Sometimes, I don't think people realise that—we work 7am until 7pm on the programme." Ella Alexander, "How Alaïa and Valentino Inspired the Kardashians' Lipsy Collection," *Vogue UK*, October 21, 2013, accessed November 18, 2018, www.vogue.co.uk/gallery/kardashians-lipsy-collection-launches-kim-kardashian-interview.

97　**a disciplinary tool:** Elaine K. Yakura, "Billables: The Valorization of Time in Consulting," *American Behavioral Scientist* 44, no. 7 (March 1, 2001): 1090, https://doi.org/10.1177/00027 64201044007003.

97　**"the right to expect":** Schiltz, "An Unhappy, Unhealthy, and Unethical Profession," 942.

97　**"a fair trade":** Schor, *The Overworked American*, 140.

97　**"pay us lots and lots":** Jeanne M. Brett and Linda K. Stroh, "Working 61 Plus Hours a Week: Why Do Managers Do It?," *Journal of Applied Psychology* 88, no. 1 (February 2003): 76, https://doi.org/10.1037/0021-9010.88.1.67.

97　**"consider their over-the-top efforts":** Hewlett and Luce, "Extreme Jobs."

97　**"just deserts" of their industry:** N. Gregory Mankiw, "Spreading the Wealth Around: Reflections Inspired by Joe the Plumber," *Eastern Economic Journal* 36, no. 3 (2010): 295, https://doi.org/10.3386/w15846; N. Gregory Mankiw, "Defending the One Percent," *Journal of Economic Perspectives* 27, no. 3 (Summer 2013): 32–33, https://doi.org/10.1257 /jep.27.3.21. See also N. Gregory Mankiw, "Yes, the Wealthy Can Be Deserving," *New York Times*, February 15, 2014, accessed November 18, 2018, www.nytimes.com/2014/02/16/business /yes-the-wealthy-can-be-deserving.html.

98　**"outside [non-elite] world":** Ho, *Liquidated*, 103. Ho adds that even the banks' own back-office workers were disrespected on account of their shorter work hours: "To say that Wall Street had little respect for back-office workers is an understatement. Although they were not openly disparaged, they were casually dubbed career nine-to-fivers; their work ethic was questioned, as was their smartness, drive, and innovation." Ho, *Liquidated*, 17.

98　**raising Social Security's retirement age:** Jordan Weissmann, "The Head of Goldman Sachs Wants to Raise Your Retirement Age," *Atlantic*, November 20, 2012, www.theatlantic.com/busi ness/archive/2012/11/the-head-of-goldman-sachs-wants -to-raise-your-retirement-age/265475/.

98　**"the badge of honor":** Gershuny, "Busyness as the Badge of Honor." See also Golden, "A Brief History of Long Work Time," 222 (citing Fredrik Carlsson, Olof Johansson-Stenman, and Peter Martinsson, "Do You Enjoy Having More Than Others? Survey Evidence of Positional Goods," *Economica* 84, no. 296 (November 2007), https://doi.org/10.1111/j.1468-0335.2006. 00571.x).

98　**The social order that Veblen discerned:** In a "remarkable historical reversal" that exchanges Veblen's social world for its polar opposite, "'being busy' [has] replaced leisure as a sign of social status." Jacobs and Gerson, *The Time Divide*, 120. See also Gershuny, "Busyness as the Badge of Honor," 306–7.

98　**"was, after all":** Gershuny, "Busyness as the Badge of Honor," 290–91 (emphasis removed).

99　**a "collaboration between":** Fraser, *Every Man a Speculator*, 476.

99　**The median real income:** In nominal dollars, individual income for men stood at $2,230 in 1947 and $5,553 in 1967. U.S. Census Bureau, "Historical Income Tables: People," Current Population Survey, last modified August 28, 2018, accessed October 11, 2018, Table P-2, www.census.gov/data/tables/time -series/demo/income-poverty/historical-income-people.html.

99　**the number of American households:** The homeownership rate stood at 43.6 percent in 1940 and 61.9 percent in 1960. U.S. Census Bureau, Census of Housing, "Historical Census of Housing Tables: Homeownership," last modified October 31, 2011, www.census.gov/hhes/www/housing/census/historic/owner .html.

99　**"voiceless minority":** See Galbraith, *The Affluent Society*, 79.

99　**Harrington was a graduate:** Maurice Isserman, *The Other American: The Life of Michael Harrington* (New York: Perseus, 2000), 154. Hereafter cited as Isserman, *The Other American*.

99　**"the only responsible radical in America":** Isserman, *The Other American*, 219.

99　**the circumstances of America's poor:** Isserman, *The Other American*, 175–220.

99　**"alarming . . . pockets of despair":** Herbert Mitgang, "Books of the Times," *New York Times*, March 21, 1962, accessed November 18, 2018, https://timesmachine.nytimes.com/timesma chine/1962/03/21/83217578.pdf.

99　**"the minimal levels of health":** Michael Harrington, *The Other America: Poverty in the United States* (New York: Simon & Schuster, 1997 [originally published in 1962 by Macmillan]), 179. Hereafter cited as Harrington, *The Other America*.

99　**"angry thesis":** A. H. Raskin, "The Unknown and Unseen," *New York Times*, April 8, 1962, accessed November 18, 2018, https://timesmachine.nytimes.com/timesmachine/1962/04 /08/113424067.pdf.

100　**Harrington claimed that:** Harrington, *The Other America*, 190.

100　**still lived in poverty:** Robert D. Plotnick et. al, "The Twentieth Century Record of Inequality and Poverty in the United States," Institute for Research on Poverty, Discussion Paper no. 1166- 98 (July 1998), University of Wisconsin–Madison, 57, www.irp .wisc.edu/publications/dps/pdfs/dp116698.pdf. While no official statistics exist for the poverty rate before the 1960s, one estimate in 1955 was 26.2 percent. In 1959, the earliest year in the Census Bureau's Official Poverty Measure time series, the official poverty rate remained 22.4 percent. For complete historical data on the Official Poverty Measure, see U.S. Census Bureau, "Historical Poverty Tables: People and Families—1959 to 2017," Current Population Survey, last modified August 28, 2018, Table 3, www.census.gov/data/tables/time-series/demo /income-poverty/historical-poverty-people.html.

100　**"I would beg the reader":** Harringon, *The Other America*, 191.

100　**"an American Dickens":** Harrington, *The Other America*, 17.

100　**"no telephone in the house":** Gabriel Kolko, *Wealth and Power in America: An Analysis of Social Class and Income Distribution* (New York: Frederick A. Praeger, 1962), 98.

101　**no broader impact:** Isserman, *The Other American*, 198–208.

101　**soon after publication:** Isserman, *The Other American*, 198– 208.

101　**"Our Invisible Poor":** Dwight Macdonald, "Our Invisible Poor," *New Yorker*, January 19, 1963, accessed November 18, 2018, www.newyorker.com/magazine/1963/01/19/our-invisible -poor.

101　**in the magazine's history:** Isserman, *The Other American*, 208.

101　**"more widely read":** Carl M. Brauer, "Kennedy, Johnson, and the War on Poverty," *Journal of American History* 69, no. 1 (June 1982): 103, https://doi.org/10.2307/1887754. Hereafter cited as Brauer, "Kennedy."

101　**to the president himself:** Peter Dreier, "How Rachel Carson and Michael Harrington Changed the World," *Contexts* 11, no. 2 (Spring 2012): 44, https://doi.org/10.1177/153650421244 6459. It is difficult to be certain of whether President Kennedy saw the book or the review; historians tell both versions.

101　**"that The Other America helped":** Arthur M. Schlesinger Jr., *A Thousand Days: John F. Kennedy in the White House* (Boston: Houghton Mifflin, 1965), 1010.

101　**"widely assumed in Washington":** Isserman, *The Other American*, 208.

101　**"outskirts of poverty":** Annual Message to the Congress on the State of the Union, 1 Pub. Papers 13 (January 14, 1963).

101　**"Poverty in the midst":** Letter to the President of the Senate and to the Speaker of the House Proposing the Establishment of a National Service Corps, 1 Pub. Papers 320 (April 10, 1963).

101　**how could a society:** This formulation loosely follows one of John Rawls's main lines of argument in John Rawls, *A Theory of Justice* (Cambridge, MA: Belknap Press of Harvard University Press, 1971).

101　**1964 legislative program:** Byron G. Lander, "Group Theory and Individuals: The Origin of Poverty as a Political Issue in 1964," *Western Political Quarterly* 24, no. 3 (September 1971): 524, https://doi.org/10.2307/446920. Hereafter cited as Lander, "Group Theory."

101　**the newly sworn-in President Johnson:** Lander, "Group Theory," 524.

101 **The program appealed:** Brauer, "Kennedy," 114. Johnson was eager to disabuse Kennedy's advisers of the view that he was a fiscal conservative.

101 **"carry on the fight":** Address Before a Joint Session of the Congress, 1 Pub. Papers 9 (November 27, 1963).

102 **The popular press:** Lander, "Group Theory," 524, citing James Reston, "Washington: On Exploring the Moon and Attacking the Slums," *New York Times*, December 20, 1963, accessed November 18, 2018, https://timesmachine.nytimes.com/timesmachine/1963/12/20/89995256.pdf; Editorial, "Assault on Poverty," *New York Times*, December 30, 1963, accessed November 18, 2018, https://timesmachine.nytimes.com/timesmachine/1963/12/30/81832524.pdf; Editorial, "Price of Poverty," *New York Times*, January 3, 1964, accessed November 18, 2018, https://timesmachine.nytimes.com/timesmachine/1964/01/03/118649586.pdf; and James Reston, "A Modified New Deal," *New York Times*, January 9, 1964, accessed November 18, 2018, https://timesmachine.nytimes.com/timesmachine/1964/01/09/106931619.pdf.

102 **"unconditional War on Poverty in America":** Annual Message to the Congress on the State of the Union, 1 Pub. Papers 114 (January 8, 1964). For another version of the story, see Brauer, "Kennedy."

102 **poverty has worsened in recent years:** There are many reasons for this. But one important reason is that transfer programs have both shrunk and, additionally, lost some of their initial focus on the poor. Whereas households in the bottom fifth of the income distribution received 54 percent of all federal transfer payments in 1979, their share had fallen to 36 percent by 2007. See Congressional Budget Office, "Trends in the Distribution of Household Income." Nevertheless, economic growth renders relatively reduced redistribution consistent with stable or falling absolute poverty.

102 **11.1 percent in 1973:** U.S. Census Bureau, "Historical Poverty Tables: People and Families—1959 to 2017," Current Population Survey, last modified August 28, 2018, Table 3, www.census.gov/data/tables/time-series/demo/income-poverty/historical-poverty-people.html.

102 **between 11 and 15 percent since then:** U.S. Census Bureau, "Historical Poverty Tables: People and Families—1959 to 2017," Current Population Survey, last modified August 28, 2018, Table 3, www.census.gov/data/tables/time-series/demo/income-poverty/historical-poverty-people.html. Poverty rose to slightly over 15 percent in the early 1980s and fell slightly toward the end of that decade. Poverty rates then rose above 15 percent again in the early 1990s before falling back down to a little over 11 percent in 2000, rising through the Bush years and the Great Recession, and then falling again, slightly, to 12.3 percent in 2017.

Additional statistics confirm this impression about income poverty, as a kind of reality check. According to a 2007 CBO study, after-tax annual income for the bottom quintile grew by 6 percent between 1979 and 2005. See David A. Zalewski and Charles J. Whalen, "Financialization and Income Inequality: A Post Keynesian Institutional Analysis," *Journal of Economic Issues* 44, no. 3 (2010): 757, https://doi.org/10.2753/JE10021-3624440309. Another study that adjusts the income of the poor to take into account government transfers, health insurance paid for by others, and the decline in household size found that the real income of the bottom quintile grew by 26.4 percent between 1979 and 2007. See Richard Burkhauser, Jeff Larrimore, and Kosali I. Simon, "A 'Second Opinion' on the Economic Health of the American Middle Class," *National Tax Journal* 65, no. 1 (March 2012): 23, https://dx.doi.org/10.17310/ntj.2012.1.01.

102 **Supplemental Poverty Measure:** Trudi Renwick, "What Is the Supplemental Poverty Measure and How Does It Differ from the Official Measure?," U.S. Census Bureau, Census Blogs, November 8, 2012, www.census.gov/newsroom/blogs/random-samplings/2012/11/what-is-the-supplemental-poverty-measure-and-how-does-it-differ-from-the-official-measure.html. As compared to the Official Poverty Measure, the Supplemental Poverty Measure increases both the poverty threshold and the resource measure of the poor. Very roughly, the new measure makes modest changes in the composition of household units, sets the poverty threshold at 1.2 times the 33rd-percentile expenditure on food, clothing, shelter, and utilities of households with exactly two children, makes geographic adjustments for cost of living, changes the formula for updating for inflation, and changes the resource measure to include in-kind benefits (such as nutritional assistance, subsidized housing, and home energy assistance) and exclude taxes, work expenses, and medical expenses.

102 **substantially more than the Official Measure:** The Supplemental Measure reports that poverty has fallen from 25.8 percent in 1967 to 14.3 percent in 2015—an 11.5 percent drop, versus effectively no secular decline in the Official Poverty Measure over these years (as the real decline in poverty according to the Official Measure came between 1959 and 1967). See Trudi Renwick and Liana Fox, *The Supplemental Poverty Measure: 2015*, U.S. Census Bureau, Current Population Reports no. P60-258 (September 2016), accessed October 24, 2018, www.census.gov/content/dam/Census/library/publications/2016/demo/p60-258.pdf. See also Christopher Wimer et al., "Trends in Poverty with an Anchored Supplemental Poverty Measure," Columbia Population Center Working Paper no. 13-01 (December 5, 2013), Columbia Population Research Center, New York, NY, Figure 2, https://doi.org/10.7916/D8RN3853.

102 **still more dramatic declines:** These approaches all focus on absolute rather than relative poverty and therefore privilege material deprivation over social exclusion. Measures that incorporate an element of relative poverty report more modest declines in poverty, but even these are falling. For example, a poverty rate calculated by the OECD, which sets the poverty threshold at one-half of median income, remained lower in 2013 (17.2 percent) than it was in 1947 during the Great Compression (18.9 percent). See OECD, "OECD Data: Poverty Rate," accessed October 10, 2016, https://data.oecd.org/inequality/poverty-rate.htm; Victor Fuchs, "Redefining Poverty and Redistributing Income," *The Public Interest* 8 (Summer 1967): 90.

102 **below 5 percent:** Christopher Jencks, "The War on Poverty: Was It Lost?," *New York Review of Books*, April 2, 2015, accessed November 18, 2018, www.nybooks.com/articles/2015/04/02/war-poverty-was-it-lost/. Social scientist Jencks takes the official poverty rate and discounts it by nearly 10 percentage points to account for expanded food and housing benefits, the earned income tax credit and child tax credit, and the use of an alternative inflation measure.

103 **4.5 percent by 2010:** Bruce D. Meyer and James X. Sullivan, "Winning the War: Poverty from the Great Society to the Great Recession," NBER Working Paper No. 18718 (January 2013), Table 1, www.nber.org/papers/w18718.pdf. Hereafter cited as Meyer and Sullivan, "Winning the War."

103 **remained about 6 percent:** U.S. Census Bureau, *2010 Annual Social and Economic Supplement*, Current Population Survey (2010), ftp://ftp.census.gov/programs-surveys/cps/techdocs/cpsmar10.pdf. In 2009, 19,028,000 Americans lived below 50 percent of the poverty line (i.e., in deep poverty). This represented 6.26 percent of the total population.

103 **below 1 percent:** Meyer and Sullivan, "Winning the War," Figure 6.

103 **The poor can afford:** Bernadette D. Proctor, Jessica L. Semega, and Melissa A. Kollar, *Income and Poverty in the United States: 2015*, U.S. Census Bureau, Current Population Reports no. P60-256 (September 2016), accessed December 30, 2018, 31, Table A-2, www.census.gov/content/dam/Census/library/publications/2016/demo/p60-256.pdf. Between 1967 and 2015, the mean real income of the bottom fifth of households grew by 25.4 percent.

103 **A typical poor family:** Liana Fox et al., "Trends in Deep Poverty from 1968 to 2011: The Influence of Family Structure, Employment Patterns, and the Safety Net," *Russell Sage Foundation Journal of the Social Sciences* 1, no. 1 (November 2015): 16, https://doi.org/10.7758/RSF.2015.1.1.02. Hereafter cited as Fox et al., "Trends in Deep Poverty," citing Nathan Hutto et al., "Improving the Measurement of Poverty," *Social Service Review* 85, no. 1 (March 2011): 47, https://doi.org/10.1086/659129. A typical poor family now spends one-sixth of its income on food, as opposed to one-third.

103    **In 1960, the poor:** In 1960, 21.7 percent of the population made less than $3,000. *Consumer Income*, U.S. Census Bureau, Current Population Reports no. P60-36 (June 9, 1961), accessed December 30, 2018, 2, Table 1, www2.census.gov/library/publications/1961/demographics/p60-36.pdf. U.S. Census Bureau, Statistical Abstract of the United States 1971, 321 (1971). The shares in the main text are derived by combining this fact with Census Bureau data on ownership of consumer durables by income. U.S. Census Bureau, Statistical Abstract of the United States 1971, 321 (1971).

103    **By 2009, over 80 percent:** Bruce D. Meyer and James X. Sullivan, "The Material Well-Being of the Poor and the Middle Class Since 1980," American Enterprise Institute for Public Policy Research Working Paper 2011-04, October 25, 2011, 44, Table 2, www.aei.org/wp-content/uploads/2011/10/Material-Well-Being-Poor-Middle-Class.pdf. Hereafter cited as Meyer and Sullivan, "Material Well-Being of the Poor." See also U.S. Census Bureau, American Housing Survey (2013); Attanasio and Pistaferri, "Consumption Inequality," 19. These outcomes reflect steady increases. At the end of the 1980s (roughly midway between 1960 and 2009), 54 percent of the poorest quintile of American households had air conditioners, 48 percent had clothes dryers, 22 percent had dishwashers, and more than 70 percent owned a car. See Meyer and Sullivan, "Material Well-Being of the Poor," Table 2.

103    **during the same period:** Attanasio and Pistaferri, "Consumption Inequality," 21. See Aguiar and Hurst, "Measuring Trends in Leisure," 993–94.

103    **its attendant harms:** Aguiar and Hurst, "Measuring Trends in Leisure," 969–1006. The increased divide in leisure time between rich and poor cannot be attributed solely to changing incomes or expenditures, and may be a result of a shift out of market work for lower-income groups.

103    **as much as 75 percent:** Alan Barreca et al., "Adapting to Climate Change: The Remarkable Decline in the US Temperature-Mortality Relationship over the Twentieth Century," *Journal of Political Economy* 124, no. 1 (January 5, 2016): 152, https://doi.org/10.1086/684582. "There were roughly 5,900 premature fatalities annually due to high temperatures [between 1960 and 2004]. . . . The diffusion of residential AC during the 1960–2004 period reduced premature fatalities by about 18,000 annually." 18,000/(18,000 + 5,900) = 0.753.

103    **The mortality rate:** "Mortality Rate, Under-5 (per 1,000 Live Births)," World Bank Open Data, World Bank, accessed October 12, 2018, https://data.worldbank.org/indicator/SH.DYN.MORT?locations=US. In addition, teenage birth rates have dropped by roughly 75 percent since 1957. Birth rates for persons aged fifteen to nineteen have fallen from 96 per thousand in 1957 to 24.2 per thousand in 2014. Centers for Disease Control and Prevention, National Vital Statistics Reports 49, no. 10 (September 25, 2001): 2, accessed November 18, 2018, www.cdc.gov/nchs/data/nvsr/nvsr49/nvsr49_10.pdf; "Trends in Teen Pregnancy and Childbearing," Department of Health and Human Services, accessed October 12, 2018, www.hhs.gov/ash/oah/adolescent-development/reproductive-health-and-teen-pregnancy/teen-pregnancy-and-childbearing/trends/index.html.

104    **increased by about 10 percent:** "Human Development Data," United Nations Development Programme, accessed October 12, 2018, www.hdr.undp.org/en/indicators/137506. The United Nations Development Programme's Human Development Index (HDI) measures "average achievement in three basic dimensions of human development: a long and healthy life, knowledge and a decent standard of living." The HDI for the United States was 0.826 in 1980, and increased to 0.915 in 2014.

104    **by richer Americans:** See Social Security Administration, Office of Retirement and Disability Policy, "Trends in Mortality Differentials and Life Expectancy for Male Social Security–Covered Workers, by Socioeconomic Status," *Social Security Bulletin* 67, no. 3 (2007): Table 4, www.ssa.gov/policy/docs/ssb/v67n3/v67n3p1.html. See also Lawrence Summers, "The Rich Have Advantages That Money Cannot Buy," *Financial Times*, June 8, 2014, accessed November 18, 2018, www.ft.com/content/36d0831a-eca2-11e3-8963-00144feabdc0. Hereafter cited as Summers, "The Rich Have Advantages."

104    **between half and a sixth:** For income poverty over time, see U.S. Census Bureau, "Historical Poverty Tables: People and Families—1959 to 2017," Current Population Survey, last modified August 28, 2018, Tables 2–3, www.census.gov/data/tables/time-series/demo/income-poverty/historical-poverty-people.html. For consumption poverty over time, see Meyer and Sullivan, "Winning the War," Table 1. See also Meyer and Sullivan, "Material Well-Being of the Poor," 19–20.

104    **no longer dominates the American scene:** An honest accounting must, however, recognize another historical trend that analyses of poverty all too often simply ignore. Incarceration rates have exploded even as poverty rates have fallen. Official poverty rates do not include prisoners, as the population base for these measures excludes those living in institutions or "group quarters." See Fox et al., "Trends in Deep Poverty," 30. (Quite absurdly, university students living in dormitories are excluded under the same principle. See Fox et al., "Trends in Deep Poverty," 17.)

        Nevertheless, even as the state provides prisoners with food, shelter, and medical care, prisoners earn effectively no income and (especially in the harsher state prison systems) consume at levels that would count as deep poverty were they the consumption of free citizens. This makes it natural to ask how properly to account for the poverty status of prisoners. Studies that have analyzed the link between poverty and incarceration have found that the intensity of American poverty may be understated by as much as a sixth of the official measure. See Ian Irvine and Kuan Xu, "Crime, Punishment and the Measurement of Poverty in the United States, 1979–1997," 22, Dalhousie University Economics Working Paper (July 29, 2003), Dalhousie University, Halifax, NS. This effect does not, however, undermine the broader downward trend in poverty, as the overall poverty rate has fallen by a much, much greater proportion—between a half and five-sixths, depending on the measure used.

104    **Once again, wealth has advanced:** "Income Inequality, USA, 1970–2014," World Inequality Database, accessed October 12, 2018, https://wid.world/country/usa/.

        It would be instructive to construct a series for the top 1 percent's consumption share, but existing data do not allow this. The Consumer Expenditure Survey tracks expenditure shares by quintiles of pretax income, and (beginning more recently) by deciles of pretax income. See, e.g., Bureau of Labor Statistics, Consumer Expenditure Survey (2015), Table 1101, www.bls.gov/cex/2015/combined/quintile.pdf, and Bureau of Labor Statistics, Consumer Expenditure Survey (2015), Table 1110, www.bls.gov/cex/2015/combined/decile.pdf. The survey also currently tracks consumption by income buckets that range from "less than $15,000" to "$200,000 or more" (which represents roughly the top 5 percent in 2015). See Bureau of Labor Statistics, Consumer Expenditure Survey (2015), Table 1203, www.bls.gov/cex/2015/combined/income.pdf. But decile tracking began only recently and the income buckets used by the survey have changed over time, so that no good time series for top/bottom ratios can be constructed using these categories. Moreover, the survey still does not track consumption in still narrower economic elites. Time trends in consumption by quintile are summarized over 1984–2010 by Kevin A. Hassett and Aparna Mathur, who find only a modest increase in the top/bottom-quintile consumption ratios over the period of their study. Kevin A. Hassett and Aparna Mathur, *A New Measure of Consumption Inequality*, American Enterprise Institute (June 2012), 5, www.aei.org/wp-content/uploads/2012/06/-a-new-measure-of-consumption-inequality_142931647663.pdf.

105    **twenty-three times as large:** In 2014, the average income within the bottom quintile was $13,132, the median income was roughly $43,955, and the average income among the top 1 percent was $1,012,549 (all in nominal 2014 dollars). See World Top Incomes Database / United States, Post-tax national income / Average income / Equal-split adults / P0-P20, P49-P51, P99-P100, https://wid.world/country/usa/.

        In 1964, the average income within the bottom quintile was $990, the median income was roughly $4,185, and the average income among the top 1 percent was $54,530 (all in nominal

1964 dollars). See World Top Incomes Database / United States, Post-tax national income / Average income / Equal-split adults / P0-P20, P49-P51, P99-P100, https://wid.world/country/usa/.

105 **were not middle class:** "The American Middle Class Is Losing Ground," Pew Research Center, December 9, 2015, accessed October 14, 2018, www.pewsocialtrends.org/2015/12/09/the -american-middle-class-is-losing-ground/. Hereafter cited as Pew Research Center, "The American Middle Class Is Losing Ground."

105 **no longer the richest in the world:** David Leonhardt and Kevin Quealy, "The American Middle Class Is No Longer the World's Richest," *New York Times,* April 22, 2014, accessed November 18, 2018, www.nytimes.com/2014/04/23/upshot/the -american-middle-class-is-no-longer-the-worlds-richest.html ?_r=0. Leonhardt and Quealy use data from the Luxembourg Income Study to show that around 2010, median incomes in Canada and Norway overtook those in the United States, and that median incomes in almost every other rich nation have been catching up rapidly over the past three decades.

105 **as high as 0.49 today:** These figures are calculated using date from the World Top Incomes Database. See World Top Incomes Database / United States / Post-tax national income / Gini (P0—P100) / Equal-split adults, October 29, 2018, https://wid .world/country/usa/. The calculation uses post-tax and -transfer incomes, in order to capture the true circumstances of the various segments of the economy that the Gini coefficients describe. In addition, the calculation uses one hundred data points for each year, corresponding to income levels at each percentile in the distribution. This increases accuracy and, more important for present purposes, makes it possible to calculate Gini coefficients for parts of the distribution, as the main text does. Many alternative U.S. Gini series, by contrast, calculate the Gini Index using only far fewer data points per year—often just five, corresponding to incomes for each quintile (with various methods of interpolation used within quintiles). This difference affects the absolute level of the calculated Ginis, and the series behind the claims made here departs from other prominent series, which depart from each other. At the same time, the trends revealed by all the series coincide, so that they rise and fall together.

105 **the bottom nine-tenths of the U.S. income distribution:** Congressional Budget Office, "Trends in the Distribution of Household Income," 16.

105 **as high as 0.5 today:** The data used to calculate these Ginis come from the World Top Incomes Database, Post-tax national income / equal-split adults / Average / Adults / constant 2015 local currency, https://wid.world/country/usa/.

106 **within the top twentieth:** Some studies go even further and question whether there has been any steady or even significant rise in economic inequality since 1993 across the bottom *99* percent of the distribution. For a review, see Robert J. Gordon, "Misperceptions About the Magnitude and Timing of Changes in American Income Inequality," NBER Working Paper No. 15351 (September 2009), 1, www.nber.org/papers/w15351.pdf.

107 **"You didn't build that":** Aaron Blake, "Obama's 'You Didn't Build That' Problem," *Washington Post,* July 18, 2012, accessed November 18, 2018, www.washingtonpost.com/blogs/the-fix /post/obamas-you-didnt-build-that-problem/2012/07/18 /gJQAJxyotW_blog.html; Lucy Madison, "Elizabeth Warren: 'There Is Nobody in This Country Who Got Rich on His Own,'" CBS News, September 22, 2011, accessed October 14, 2018, www.cbsnews.com/news/elizabeth-warren-there-is-nobody -in-this-country-who-got-rich-on-his-own/.

107 **a moral imperative:** This view is powerfully expressed by many thinkers and activists, including Matthew Desmond, *Evicted: Poverty and Profit in the American City* (New York: Crown, 2016); Donald S. Shepard, Elizabeth Setren, and Donna Cooper, "Hunger in America: Suffering We All Pay For," Center for American Progress, October 2011, www.americanprogress.org /wp-content/uploads/issues/2011/10/pdf/hunger_paper.pdf; H. Luke Shaefer and Kathryn Edin, "Extreme Poverty in the United States, 1996 to 2011," Policy Brief 28 (February 2012), National Poverty Center, http://npc.umich.edu/publications /policy_briefs/brief28/policybrief28.pdf; H. Luke Shaefer and Marci Ybarra, "The Welfare Reforms of the 1990s and the Stratification of Material Well-Being Among Low-Income Households with Children," National Poverty Center Working Paper

Series 12-12, National Poverty Center, Ann Arbor, MI, May 2012, http://npc.umich.edu/publications/u/2012-12-npc-work ing-paper.pdf; Yonatan Ben-Shalom, Robert Moffitt, and John Karl Scholz, "An Assessment of the Effectiveness of Anti-Poverty Programs in the United States," National Poverty Center Working Paper Series 11-19, National Poverty Center, Ann Arbor, MI, June 2011, http://npc.umich.edu/publications/u/2011 -19_NPC_Working_Paper.pdf.

Official statistics that document the suffering of the poor today include U.S. Department of Agriculture, Economic Research Service, *Food Security in the United States,* accessed October 3, 2016, www.ers.usda.gov/topics/food-nutri tion-assistance/food-security-in-the-us.aspx; *Key Statistics and Graphics,* accessed October 3, 2016, www.ers.usda.gov/topics /food-nutrition-assistance/food-security-in-the-us/key-statis tics-graphics.aspx; *Food Security in the United States,* accessed October 3, 2016, www.ers.usda.gov/data-products/food-secu rity-in-the-united-states.aspx; Current Population Survey Food Security Supplement, accessed October 3, 2016, www.ers.usda .gov/data-products/food-security-in-the-united-states.aspx #26502.

108 **outnumbered elites:** See Aristotle, *Aristotle's Politics,* Book IV; James Madison, *Federalist* No. 10, in *The Federalist Papers,* ed. Clinton Rossiter (New York: New American Library, 1961), 77–84.

108 **the top marginal tax rate:** See, e.g., Internal Revenue Code (I.R.C.) § 1 (1954); I.R.C. § 1 (1971); I.R.C. § 1 (1976); I.R.C. § 1 (1981); I.R.C. § 1 (1986); I.R.C. § 1 (1991) I.R.C. § 1 (1996); I.R.C. § 1 (2001); I.R.C. § 1 (2006); I.R.C. § 1 (2011); I.R.C. § 1 (2016). See also "Historical Highest Marginal Income Tax Rates," Tax Policy Center, accessed October 14, 2018, www.tax policycenter.org/statistics/historical-highest-marginal-income -tax-rates. The top marginal rate was raised to 91 percent in 1951 and to 92 percent in 1952 and 1953. It then fell back to 91 percent, where it remained until 1963. Internal Revenue Service, "Historical Table 23: U.S. Individual Income Tax: Personal Exemptions and Lowest and Highest Bracket Tax Rates, and Tax Base for Regular Tax, Tax Years 1913–2015" (2018), www.irs .gov/statistics/soi-tax-stats-historical-table-23.

108 **"significant advances in recent centuries":** Winters, *Oligarchy,* 4.

109 **political economy in mass democracies:** The mystery is so confounding that the American Political Science Association made studying it the central goal of its 2001 Task Force on Inequality and American Democracy, "Task Force on Inequality and American Democracy," American Political Science Association, accessed October 14, 2018, www.apsanet.org/PUBLICA TIONS/Reports/Task-Force-on-Inequality-and-American -Democracy.

109 **People who feel that they have worked:** Ran Kivetz and Yuhuang Zheng, "Determinants of Justification and Self-Control," *Journal of Experimental Psychology: General* 135, no. 4 (2006): 572–87, https://doi.org/10.1037/0096-3445.135 .4.572.

109 **support for economic redistribution declines:** Alberto Alesina and George-Marios Angeletos, "Corruption, Inequality, and Fairness," *Journal of Monetary Economics* 52, no. 7 (October 2005): 1227–44, https://doi.org/doi:10.1016/j.jmoneco.2005 .05.003.

109 **"When people can see":** N. Gregory Mankiw, "Yes, the Wealthy Can Be Deserving," *New York Times,* February 15, 2014, accessed November 18, 2019, www.nytimes.com/2014 /02/16/business/yes-the-wealthy-can-be-deserving.html. This effect applies even at the very top of the distribution, to block even progressive taxes aimed narrowly at the super-rich. A rare case in which the next 19 defeated the top 1 percent in a political dispute over taxes presents the exception that proves the rule. In the most recent reforms of the estate tax, the merely rich sought to increase the amount exempted from the tax, while the super-rich sought to reduce the rates at which the tax applied, or to eliminate it entirely. (This is natural: estates left by the merely rich will fall overwhelmingly within the higher exemption, making rates unimportant compared to the exemption, and estates left by the super-rich will massively exceed virtually any exemption, making the exemption unimportant compared to the rates. Indeed, in 2015, fewer than five thousand estates owed

any tax at all, and in 2013, the average size of an estate that paid the tax was $22.7 million. Brian J. O'Connor, "Once Again, the Estate Tax May Die," *New York Times*, February 18, 2017, accessed October 24, 2018, www.nytimes.com/2017/02/18/your -money/taxes/once-again-the-estate-tax-may-die.html.) Save for a fleeting repeal in 2010, the merely rich won the recent political battles: the exemption to the estate tax has increased even as the rates applied above the exemption have not fallen. For more on the politics of the estate tax, see Michael J. Graetz and Ian Shapiro, *Death by a Thousand Cuts: The Fight over Taxing Inherited Wealth* (Princeton, NJ: Princeton University Press, 2006).

109    **unjustly abuse industrious workers:** For related observations, see Skidelsky and Skidelsky, *How Much Is Enough?*, 191–92.

Lyndon Johnson once described the Great Society as "a place where every child can find knowledge to enrich his mind and to enlarge his talents . . . where the city of man serves . . . the desire for beauty and the hunger for community . . . where men are more concerned with the quality of their goals than the quantity of their goods." LBJ Presidential Library, "Social Justice Gallery," accessed October 15, 2018, www.lbjlibrary.org /exhibits/social-justice-gallery. Today, Paul Ryan divides society into "makers," whose work ethic serves the common good, and "takers," who exploit the programs that LBJ established. Nick Baumann and Brett Brownell, "VIDEO: Paul Ryan's Version of '47 Percent'—the 'Takers' vs. the 'Makers,'" *Mother Jones*, October 5, 2012, accessed October 15, 2018, www.motherjones.com /politics/2012/10/paul-ryans-47-percent-takers-vs-makers -video/. (Ryan would later express regret at the formulation. See, e.g., Paul Ryan, "Speaker Ryan on the State of American Politics," March 23, 2016, www.speaker.gov/press-release/full-text -speaker-ryan-state-american-politics. But the regret attaches more to style than to substance, and Ryan continued to dismantle the welfare state.)

Economic inequality's meritocratic turn explains both sides of this rhetorical contrast. Johnson could draw a sharp distinction between the "quality of . . . goals" and the "quantity of . . . goods" because the midcentury economy associated income with unearned means. Meritocratic inequality, by contrast, associates income with industry and therefore with virtue. This dissolves the contrast that Johnson relied on and erects the contrast Ryan evokes.

109    **accords to the industrious:** Conservatives especially disdain progressive intellectuals—including writers and professors—whose incomes do not match their educations and who moralize loudly but enviously against the wealth of a commercial class that they (clinging to the wreckage of aristocratic values) regard as inferior. See, e.g., David Brooks, "Bitter at the Top," *New York Times*, June 15, 2004, accessed November 18, 2018, www .nytimes.com/2004/06/15/opinion/bitter-at-the-top.html. Edward Conrad, a former venture capitalist and conservative writer, calls the type "art-history majors," which he uses as a "derisive term for pretty much anyone who was lucky enough to be born with the talent and opportunity to join the risk-taking, innovation-hunting mechanism but who chose instead a less competitive life." Adam Davidson, "The Purpose of Spectacular Wealth, According to a Spectacularly Wealthy Guy," *New York Times*, May 1, 2012, accessed November 18, 2018, www .nytimes.com/2012/05/06/magazine/romneys-former-bain -partner-makes-a-case-for-inequality.html. The derision suggests that the working rich, for their part, may mirror the intellectuals' income envy, only now taking aim at the freedom and leisure that intellectuals still enjoy, untaxed.

109    **"My neighbor has a cow":** See, e.g., U.S. Congress, House, Committee on International Relations, *Russian Foreign Policy: Proliferation to Rogue Regimes: Hearings Before the Committee on International Relations*, 106th Cong., 1st sess., 1999, 35 (statement of Representative James Woolsey).

109    **middle-class envy is exhausted:** Arthur C. Brooks, *The Road to Freedom: How to Win the Fight for Free Enterprise* (New York: Basic Books, 2012).

109    **grasping rather than magnanimous:** Moderate egalitarians especially succumb to just this fear. For example, former treasury secretary Larry Summers recently worried that "unless one regards envy as a virtue, the primary reason for concern about inequality is that lower- and middle-income workers have too

little—not that the rich have too much." Summers, "The Rich Have Advantages."

110    **launder the currency of middle-class desire:** The phrase "launder the currency of desire" borrows from Bernard Williams, *Ethics and the Limit of Philosophy* (London: Routledge, 2011), 56.

110    **"We are Wall Street":** Quoted in Freeland, *Plutocrats*, 53.

## Chapter Five: The Meritocratic Inheritance

111    **"Getting admitted to college":** Nicholas Lehman, *The Big Test: The Secret History of American Meritocracy* (New York: Farrar, Straus & Giroux, 1999), 141. Hereafter cited as Lehman, *The Big Test*.

111    **Yale, for example:** Geoffrey Kabaservice, "The Birth of a New Institution: How Two Yale Presidents and Their Admissions Directors Tore Up the 'Old Blueprint' to Create a Modern Yale," *Yale Alumni Magazine*, December 1999, accessed November 18, 2018, http://archives.yalealumnimagazine.com/issues/99_12 /admissions.html. Hereafter cited as Kabaservice, "The Birth of a New Institution."

111    **"that the admission":** Brooks Mather Kelley, *Yale: A History* (New Haven, CT: Yale University Press, 1999), 407; Kabaservice, "The Birth of a New Institution."

112    **coat-and-tie dress code:** Kabaservice, "The Birth of a New Institution."

112    **"a beetle-browed":** Kabaservice, "The Birth of a New Institution."

112    **"happy bottom quarter":** Kabaservice writes, "Indeed, while private school students made up more than 60 percent of the Class of 1957, they made up less than half of the membership of Phi Beta Kappa and one-sixth of the membership of Tau Beta Pi, the national engineering honor society. The largest feeder schools (Andover, Exeter, Lawrenceville, Hotchkiss, and St. Paul's), which Griswold considered the epitome of academic excellence and which collectively sent approximately 200 students (or 20 percent of the class), each accounted for only one of the 64 members of Phi Beta Kappa. Other traditional feeder schools such as Groton, Hill, Kent, St. Mark's, St. George's, and Taft contributed no members to Phi Beta Kappa at all." Kabaservice, "The Birth of a New Institution."

112    **academic honor rolls:** Elite Harvard undergraduates in the 1930s, for example, "lived in private apartments, attended by butlers and maids, in a district called the Gold Coast, went to debutante balls in Boston, did not customarily attend classes, and enrolled briefly in special tutoring schools at the end of each semester so they would be able to pass their exams." Similarly, gentlemen's Cs abounded well into the post–World War II years. Lehman, *The Big Test*, 20.

112    **more than three to one:** Kabaservice, "The Birth of a New Institution."

112    **the country's most prestigious university:** Jacques Steinberg, *The Gatekeepers: Inside the Admissions Process of a Premier College* (New York: Penguin Books, 2002), xii.

112    **first great successes:** Jerome Karabel, *The Chosen: The Hidden History of Admission and Exclusion at Harvard, Yale, and Princeton* (Boston: Mariner Books, 2014), 177.

112    **by the late 1940s:** Kabaservice, "The Birth of a New Institution."

112    **"the greatest change":** For Harvard's SAT revolution at midcentury, see Murray, *Coming Apart*, 54–55. Note that though Murray alternates between calling the dean William and Wilbur, his name is Wilbur. For the remark by Harvard's dean of admissions, see W. J. Bender, *Final Report of W. J. Bender, Chairman of the Admissions and Scholarship Committee and Dean of Admissions and Financial Aids, 1952–1960* (Cambridge, MA: Harvard University, 1960), 4.

112    **by 1955:** Kabaservice, "The Birth of a New Institution."

112    **Phillips Academy Andover:** Kabaservice, "The Birth of a New Institution."

113    **"not intend to preside":** Kabaservice, "The Birth of a New Institution."

113    **"an intellectual investment banker":** Kabaservice, "The Birth of a New Institution."

113    **on a meritocratic model:** Following his time at Yale, Clark served as headmaster of the Horace Mann School, including during a time at which, subsequent reports revealed, there was

widespread sexual abuse of students. For background into the allegations and Clark's role at the time, see Amos Kamil, "Prep School Predators," *New York Times*, June 6, 2012, accessed November 18, 2018, www.nytimes.com/2012/06/10/magazine /the-horace-mann-schools-secret-history-of-sexual-abuse.html.

113 **ability and achievement:** Kabaservice, "The Birth of a New Institution."

113 **the ability to pay:** Kabaservice, "The Birth of a New Institution."

113 **"who will benefit most":** Kabaservice, "The Birth of a New Institution."

113 **turned their graduates away:** Kabaservice, "The Birth of a New Institution." Kabaservice cites an article from the *Yale Daily News*. See Tom Herman, "New Concept of Yale Admissions," *Yale Daily News*, December 16, 1965. That article, however, does not use the term "ingrown."

113 **in 1968, for example:** Kabaservice, "The Birth of a New Institution."

113 **Yale's biggest donor:** Daniel Golden, *The Price of Admission: How America's Ruling Class Buys Its Way into Elite Colleges— and Who Gets Left Outside the Gates* (New York: Three Rivers Press, 2007), 129.

113 **its median student's SATs:** Kabaservice, "The Birth of a New Institution." Another report of Yale's SAT revolution appears in Murray, *Coming Apart*, 54.

114 **set a school record:** Kabaservice, "The Birth of a New Institution."

114 **"a statement, really":** Kabaservice, "The Birth of a New Institution"; R. Inslee Clark, interview with Geoffery Kabaservice, Yale Manuscripts and Archives Library, May 13, 1993.

114 **"a Mexican-American from El Paso":** Kabaservice, "The Birth of a New Institution"; William F. Buckley Jr., "What Makes Bill Buckley Run," *Atlantic Monthly*, April 1968, 68.

114 **"You're talking about Jews":** Kabaservice, "The Birth of a New Institution."

114 **the privileged took pride":** Kabaservice, "The Birth of a New Institution."

114 **some admit fewer than 5 percent:** U.S. Department of Education College Scorecard Database, last updated September 28, 2018, https://collegescorecard.ed.gov/data; Richard Pérez-Peña, "Best, Brightest and Rejected: Elite Colleges Turn Away up to 95%," *New York Times*, April 18, 2014, https://www.nytimes .com/2014/04/09/us/led-by-stanfords-5-top-colleges -acceptance-rates-hit-new-lows.html. The "top-ten" for these purposes are the eleven universities that dominate the top spots of the strikingly stable *U.S. News & World Report* rankings: Princeton, Harvard, Yale, Columbia, Stanford, the University of Chicago, Duke, MIT, the University of Pennsylvania, the California Institute of Technology, and Dartmouth.

114 **have improved as well:** Kabaservice, "The Birth of a New Institution." Kabaservice notes that the Yale faculty, particularly the science professors, were struck by the quality of students. The chairman of the chemistry department penned a letter to Brewster noting that "all of our staff who have had any contact with this year's freshmen agree that someone has done a spectacular job of recruiting. We are accustomed to meeting excellent students in introductory courses but never in such numbers."

114 **above the 99th percentile:** These are necessarily estimates, because the colleges do not all publicly report medians or composite scores, rather than scores for each section of the test. For Yale, see "What Yale Looks For," Yale University, https://admissions .yale.edu/what-yale-looks-for; for Harvard, see "Applying to Harvard," Harvard University, https://college.harvard.edu/fre quently-asked-questions; for Princeton, see "Admission Statistics," Princeton University, updated July 15, 2018, https:// admission.princeton.edu/how-apply/admission-statistics; for Stanford, see "Our Selection Process," Stanford University, updated July 2018, http://admission.stanford.edu/basics/selec tion/profile.html.

115 **between its most and least skilled citizens:** OECD, *OECD Skills Outlook 2013: First Results from the Survey of Adult Skills*, OECD Publishing (2013), http://dx.doi.org/10.1787/9789 264204256-en, 118. Hereafter cited as OECD, *OECD Skills Outlook 2013*.

115 **"stands out as having":** OECD, *OECD Skills Outlook 2013*, 118.

115 **validate its inputs:** The difference in skills between citizens with a BA or more and citizens with less than a high school education in the United States is a quarter greater than the OECD average and fully a third greater than in Australia, Austria, Estonia, Finland, Italy, Japan, Norway, and the Slovak Republic. OECD, *OECD Skills Outlook 2013*, 117.

115 **"Whosoever hath":** Holy Bible, King James Version, Matthew 13:12. Note that the Gospel is at this point expressly addressing knowledge and wisdom, and the uptake of Jesus's teachings.

115 **"Matthew Effect":** The name comes from Robert Merton, "The Matthew Effect in Science," *Science* 159 (January 5, 1968): 56–63. See also Annie Murphy Paul, "Educational Technology Isn't Leveling the Playing Field," *Slate*, June 25, 2014, accessed November 18, 2018, https://slate.com/technology/2014/06 /neuman-celano-library-study-educational-technology -worsens-achievement-gaps.html.

115 **"revolution in family wealth transmission":** Langbein, "Twentieth-Century Revolution," 722.

116 **The elite increasingly:** See Robert D. Mare, "Educational Homogamy in Two Gilded Ages: Evidence from Inter-generational Social Mobility Data," *Annals of American Academy of Political and Social Science* 663 (January 2016): 117–39, and Robert D. Mare, "Educational Assortative Mating in Two Generations: Trends and Patterns Across Two Gilded Ages," California Center for Population Research On-Line Working Paper Series, January 12, 2013, http://papers.ccpr.ucla.edu/papers/PWP -CCPR-2014-015/PWP-CCPR-2014-015.pdf.

116 **two college graduates:** See Murray, *Coming Apart*, 62. For further reference, see Christine Schwartz and Robert Mare, "Trends in Educational Assortative Marriage from 1940 to 2003," *Demography* 42 (2005): 621–46, reporting that both partners had sixteen or more years of schooling in 3.95 percent of married couples in 1960 and in 27.7 percent of married couples in 2000.

116 **over 5 percent in 2005:** Jeremy Greenwood et al., "Marry Your Like: Assortative Mating and Income Inequality," *American Economic Review (Papers and Proceedings)* 104 (May 2014): 348, 350. Hereafter cited as Greenwood et al., "Marry Your Like." More generally, a regression that assesses the additional impact of the husband's education on the wife's, relative to the baseline year 1960, shows a steadily and substantially rising coefficient on the impact term; and the ratio of the actual shares of couples whose members possess identical education levels to the shares that would arise if marriage partners were randomly matched by education has dramatically increased.

117 **evenly balanced by gender:** Princeton first admitted women in 1969, and Yale in 1969. Judith Schiff, "Resources on Yale History: A Brief History of Yale," Yale University Library, http:// guides.library.yale.edu/yalehistory; "Yale Will Admit Women in 1969; May Have Coeducational Housing," *Harvard Crimson*, November 15, 1968, www.thecrimson.com/article/1968/11 /15/yale-will-admit-women-in-1969/. It is hard to put a date on when Harvard College admitted women because of the existence of Radcliffe College, which admitted only women. Radcliffe College was opened as an annex to Harvard College in 1879. In 1963, Harvard degrees were awarded to Radcliffe students for the first time. In 1975, the two colleges merged their admissions. In 1977, "a critical date," Harvard's ratio of four men to one woman ended with "sex-blind admissions." In 1999, Radcliffe officially merged with Harvard, and created the Radcliffe Institute for Advanced Study. Colleen Walsh, "Hard-Earned Gains for Women at Harvard," *Harvard Gazette*, April 26, 2012.

Before those years, these colleges graduated literally zero women. Today, women make up almost precisely 50 percent of the undergraduate student bodies at Harvard, Yale, and Princeton, and the top ten undergraduate colleges are 54 percent male and 46 percent female (or 51 percent male and 49 percent female, if West Point is excluded). For example, for 2015, Yale has a 51:49 male-to-female ratio; for 2014, the ratio was 48:52. David Burt and Emily Wanger, "Gender Ratio Flips for 2015," *Yale News*, September 5, 2015; "Yale University Undergraduate Information—Student Life," *U.S. News & World Report*, http://colleges.usnews.rankingsandreviews.com/best-colleges /yale-university-1426.

Professional schools tell a similar, although slightly less stark, tale. Women constituted only about 3 percent in each

Harvard Law School class between 1951 and 1965, for example. Today, the student bodies at the top ten law schools are 50 percent male and 50 percent female, the student bodies at the top ten business schools are 58 percent male and 42 percent female, and the student bodies at the top ten medical schools are 49 percent male and 51 percent female. These calculations are based on the *U.S. News & World Report* 2019 rankings: "Best Law Schools," www.usnews.com/best-graduate-schools/top -law-schools; "Best Business Schools," www.usnews.com/best -graduate-schools/top-business-schools; "Best Medical Schools," www.usnews.com/best-graduate-schools/top-medical-schools /research-rankings.

117 **a fifth or more:** Greenwood et al., "Marry Your Like," 352. This effect operates, in significant part, through rising female labor force participation, especially among better-educated women. As educated women increasingly work, assortative mating increasingly compounds household income inequality, and random mating would increasingly reduce household income inequality.

117 **less educated counterparts:** They also bear children later in life: mothers' mean age at their first birth is roughly 23 for women without a bachelor's degree, 29.5 for women with a BA only, and 31.1 for women with at least some graduate education. Murray, *Coming Apart*, 40. An alternative study that uses less fine-grained categories confirms the basic story told by these numbers. In 2010, mean age at first birth for women college graduates was roughly 30, for women with high school diplomas or some college it was roughly 24, and for women with less than a high school education it was roughly 20. Kay Hymowitz et al., *Knot Yet: The Benefits and Costs of Delayed Marriage in America,* National Marriage Project (2013), 8, http://nationalmarriageproject.org /wp-content/uploads/2013/03/KnotYet-FinalForWeb.pdf. Hereafter cited as Hymowitz et al., *Knot Yet.*

117 **across all education levels:** In 1970, out-of-marriage births accounted for 10.7 percent of all births. Stephanie J. Ventura and Christine A. Bachrach, Nonmarital Childbearing in the United States, 1940–99, National Center for Health Statistics, Division of Vital Statistics (October 18, 2000), 17, www.cdc.gov /nchs/data/nvsr/nvsr48/nvs48_16.pdf. An alternative report finds a slightly larger share—nearer to 15 percent than to 10 percent. Hymowitz et al., *Knot Yet,* 7; Murray, *Coming Apart,* 161. According to Sara McLanahan and Christine Percheski, "Family Structure and the Reproduction of Inequalities," *Annual Review of Sociology* 34 (2008): 257–76, the share was one in twenty.

117 **born outside of marriage:** Moreover, only about 10 percent of college-educated women and 5 percent of women with post -college educations bear children before marriage. Hymowitz et al., *Knot Yet,* 8, reports that as of the 2010 census, 12 percent of women with college degrees are unmarried at first birth; it was 8 percent as of the 2000 census. The cited figure for mothers with post-college degrees is calculated from CDC VitalStats data on 2010 Births. For more information, see Jennifer Silva, "The 1 Percent Ruined Love: Marriage Is for the Rich," *Salon,* July 27, 2013, accessed November 18, 2018, www.salon.com/2013/07 /27/the_1_percent_ruined_love_marriage_is_for_the_rich/, hereafter cited as Silva, "The 1 Percent Ruined Love"; Galena K. Rhoades and Scott M. Stanley, "Before I Do: What Do Premarital Experiences Have to Do with Marital Quality Among Today's Young Adults?," National Marriage Project at the University of Virginia, 11, http://nationalmarriageproject.org /wordpress/wp-content/uploads/2014/08/NMP -BeforeIDoReport-Final.pdf; Murray, *Coming Apart,* 161; Jason DeParle, "Two Classes Divided by 'I Do,'" *New York Times,* July 14, 2012, accessed November 18, 2018, www.nytimes.com /2012/07/15/us/two-classes-in-america-divided-by-i-do.html, hereafter cited as DeParle, "Two Classes"; Robert D. Putnam, Carl B. Frederick, and Kaisa Snellman, "Growing Class Gaps in Social Connectedness Among American Youth," Harvard Kennedy School of Government, The Saguaro Seminar: Civic Engagement in America, July 12, 2012, Figure 1, accessed January 12, 2019, https://hceconomics.uchicago.edu/sites/default/files /file_uploads/Putnam-etal_2012_Growing-Class-Gaps.pdf, hereafter cited as Putnam, Frederick, and Snellman, "Growing Class Gaps."

This difference feeds back into income inequality. Depending on how one measures, between 14 and 40 percent of household income inequality's overall growth in recent years may be attributed to the increasingly different rates of single parenthood among lower-middle- and upper-middle-income families. See DeParle, "Two Classes." See also Bruce Western, Deirdre Bloom, and Christine Percheski, "Inequality Among American Families with Children, 1975–2005," *American Sociological Review* 73, no. 6 (2008): 903–20, hereafter cited as Western, Bloom, and Percheski, "Inequality Among American Families"; Gary Burtless, "Effects of Growing Wage Disparities and Changing Family Composition on the U.S. Income Distribution," Center on Social and Economic Dynamics, Working Paper No. 4 (July 1999), 12, hereafter cited as Burtless, "Effects of Growing Wage Disparities"; Robert I. Lerman, "The Impact of the Changing U.S. Family Structure on Child Poverty and Income Inequality," *Economica* 63, no. 250 (1996): S122, hereafter cited as Lerman, "The Impact of the Changing U.S. Family Structure."

117 **nearly 60 percent of all children are born outside of marriage:** Moreover, 40 percent of these mothers have children before marrying. See "Vital Stats Data," Centers for Disease Control (2010), www.cdc.gov/nchs/data_access/vitalstats/Vi talStats_Births.htm. Jennifer Silva points out in "The 1 Percent Ruined Love" that "while nine out of ten college-educated women wait to have children until after they get married, only six out of ten with a high school degree postpone childbearing until after marriage." See also DeParle, "Two Classes"; Western, Bloom, and Percheski, "Inequality Among American Families"; Burtless, "Effects of Growing Wage Disparities"; Lerman, "The Impact of the Changing U.S. Family Structure."

Even new mothers who possess some college education remain five times as likely to have given birth outside of marriage as new mothers who have completed a college degree. Data from the 2010 American Community Survey show that among women who gave birth to a child during the year prior to the survey, 31 percent of those with some college were unmarried, while 6 percent of those with a BA or more were unmarried. See DeParle, "Two Classes." See Jank and Owens, "Inequality in the United States," slide 24, for data from the June 2008 Current Population Survey, showing that for mothers between fifteen and twenty-nine years old, 47.6 percent of those with some college who had a child in the past year did so outside of marriage, while only 18.2 percent of those with at least a bachelor's degree did so. For mothers between thirty and forty-four, the shares were 20.8 percent and 7.1 percent respectively.

117 **two years after marriage:** See Hymowitz et al., *Knot Yet,* reporting that for mothers with a high school diploma or some college, the mean age at first birth is twenty-four and the median age at first marriage is twenty-six, while for mothers with a college degree, the mean age at first birth is thirty while the median age at first marriage is twenty-eight. The same information may be found in the project's full report at http://nationalmarriage project.org/wordpress/wp-content/uploads/2013/04 /KnotYet-FinalForWeb-041413.pdf, 18, Figures 10A–10C.

118 **back to 1960 levels:** Murray, *Coming Apart,* 353.

118 **35 percent versus roughly 15 percent:** Jank and Owens, "Inequality in the United States," slide 25. See Steven P. Martin, "Trends in Marital Dissolution by Women's Education in the United States," *Demographic Research* 15 (2006): 537, 546, Table 1 for a report of Survey of Income and Program Participation (SIPP) data showing that, for women first married in 1990–94, 46.3 percent of those with no high school degree are divorced within ten years of married, as compared to 37.9 percent with a high school diploma, 36 percent with some college, 16.5 percent with a four-year degree, and 14.4 percent with a master's or professional degree. Jennifer Silva similarly writes that "women with a four-year college degree are half as likely as other women to experience marital dissolution in the first ten years of a marriage." See Silva, "The 1 Percent Ruined Love."

Divorce rates are typically expressed in terms of the odds of divorce within some number of years of marriage, and so their calculation depends on the choice of the number of years. An alternative tabulation concludes that divorce rates roughly tripled for all Americans between 1960 and 1980 and then doubled again between 1980 and 2010 for Americans without college degrees (both for those with high school educations only and for those with some college but no BA), but remained effectively flat for Americans with a college education or more. Ben Casselman, "Marriage Isn't Dead—Yet," FiveThirtyEight, September 29, 2014, accessed November 18, 2018, https://fivethirtyeight .com/features/marriage-isnt-dead-yet/. Casselman uses data from the U.S. Census to compute the percentage of once married Americans aged thirty-five to forty-four who had been divorced. Between 1960 and 1980, this percentage rose nearly identically—from roughly 3.5 percent to roughly 11.5 percent— for those with high school educations only, with some college but no degree, and with a BA. Between 1980 and 2010, the share rose again, roughly in tandem, for the first two groups, reaching about 20 percent. For Americans with a BA, it stayed between 10 and 12 percent.

118 **high school educations only:** D'Vera Cohn et al., "Barely Half of U.S. Adults Are Married—a Record Low," Pew Research Center, December 14, 2011, http://www.pewsocialtrends.org /2011/12/14/barely-half-of-u-s-adults-are-married-a-record -low/; Jank and Owens, "Inequality in the United States," slide 23.

118 **a rich person's affair:** This is literally true. Enduring marriages correlate with income growth and high incomes: median incomes in households with unmarried heads (both male and female) grew steadily from 1950 to 1970 but have been effectively flat ever since; median household incomes for married couples, by contrast, have grown almost without interruption through the present day. See Jank and Owens, "Inequality in the United States," slide 26, using data from www.recessiontrends.org updated with 2010 census data and data from the census historical income tables. For the original data used in creating the graph, see U.S. Census Bureau, "Historical Income Tables: Families," last revised August 28, 2018, www.census.gov/data/tables /time-series/demo/income-poverty/historical-income-families .html.

118 **households in the top third:** The share of the top third grew from 5 percent to 12 percent; the share of the middle third grew from 5 percent to 29 percent. DeParle, "Two Classes." Between the 1964 and 1994 birth cohorts of non-Hispanic whites, the percentage of high school sophomores living with a single parent nearly doubled among the lowest socioeconomic status quartile even as it declined (very) slightly among the highest quartile. See Putnam, Frederick, and Snellman, "Growing Class Gaps," Figure 2.

118 **The size of the differences:** These shares are calculated using data collected by the Census Bureau for the 2018 Current Population Survey. See U.S. Census Bureau, "Current Population Survey (CPS)," www.census.gov/programs-surveys/cps/data -detail.html.

118 **both their biological parents:** Murray, *Coming Apart,* 269. Murray uses data from the National Longitudinal Surveys of Mature Women, Young Women, and Youth for children whose mothers turned forty between 1997 and 2004. To identify the richest and best-educated zip codes, Murray used the shares of adults with a college education and median family incomes, which he standardized and ranked. Murray, *Coming Apart,* Appendix C.

119 **money troubles strain marriages:** Sarah Stuchell and Ruth Houston Barrett, "Clinical Update: Financial Strain on Families," *American Association for Marriage and Family Therapy Magazine* (May 2010).

119 **especially for women:** Karen C. Holden and Pamela J. Smock, "The Economic Costs of Marital Dissolution: Why Do Women Bear a Disproportionate Cost?," *Annual Review of Sociology* 17 (August 1991): 51–78.

119 **more volatile:** Tom Hertz, *Understanding Mobility in America,* Center for American Progress (April 26, 2006), 29, https://cdn .americanprogress.org/wp-content/uploads/issues/2006 /04/Hertz_MobilityAnalysis.pdf. Hertz found that "income security is rising for households in the top decile. For the middle class, however, an increase in income volatility has led to an increase in the frequency of large negative income shocks." For a visual representation of this reality, see Peter Gosselin and Seth Zimmerman, "Trends in Income Volatility and Risk, 1970–2004," Urban Institute Working Paper (2008), 27, Figure 3. However, see also Peter Gottschalk and Robert Moffitt, "The Rising Instability of US Earnings," *Journal of Economic Perspectives* 23, no. 4 (Fall 2019): Figure 2, for a chart showing volatility

increasing for the bottom quartile, the middle 50 percent, and the top quartile, but at a much higher rate for the bottom quartile.

119 **doubled between 1970 and 2000:** On the probability of an average person experiencing an income drop of 50 percent or more, see Karen Dynan, Douglas Elmendorf, and Daniel Sichel, "The Evolution of Household Income Volatility," *B.E. Journal of Economic Analysis & Policy* 12, no. 2 (2012): 17, Figure 3, showing that the probability of an income decline of greater than 50 percent increased from 7 percent in 1971 to 13 percent in 2005, before dropping to around 10 percent in 2008. On the prevalence of a 50 percent or greater drop in family income, see Jacob S. Hacker and Elisabeth Jacobs, "The Rising Instability of American Family Incomes, 1969–2004: Evidence from the Panel Study of Income Dynamics," Economic Policy Institute, EPI Briefing Paper No. 213 (2008), Figure C. For an analysis of the data from the Panel Study of Income Dynamics, see Hacker, *The Great Risk Shift,* 31–32, Figure 1.4. Hacker deduced that an average's person's chance of experiencing an income drop of 50 percent or more increased from around 7 percent in 1970 to 17 percent in 2002.

119 **stress impedes children's development:** W. Jean Yeung, Miriam R. Linver, and Jeanne Brooks-Gunn, "How Money Matters for Young Children's Development: Parental Investment and Family Processes," *Child Development,* 73, no. 6 (December 2002): 1872, Figure 2. Yeung, Linver, and Brooks-Gunn demonstrate that a decrease in family income affects child cognitive ability through many different pathways—economic pressures, changing the physical home environment, reducing the number of cognitively stimulating materials available, and making the cost of childcare unaffordable. For a discussion about the impact of a familial job or income loss on a child's mental health, see Vonnie C. McLoyd, "Socialization and Development in a Changing Economy: The Effects of Paternal Job and Income Loss on Children," *American Psychologist* 44, no. 2 (1989): 298–99. McLoyd concludes that while these factors can negatively impact a child's mental health and ability to interact normally with peers, the effects are not necessarily long-lasting.

119 **than their unexposed siblings:** Anna Aizer, Laura Stroud, and Stephen Buka, "Maternal Stress and Child Outcomes: Evidence from Siblings," *Journal of Human Resources* 51, no. 3 (August 2016): 353. Hereafter cited as Aizer, Stroud, and Buka, "Maternal Stress." The children also suffered 48 percent more chronic illnesses. This paper carries out robustness checks to rule out other explanations, involving causes correlated with in utero stress but that don't operate through prenatal development. "We include the following controls: maternal race (indicator for black), maternal education, marital status at birth, maternal age at birth, family income during pregnancy, offspring gender, number of siblings at age 7, birth order, whether the husband lives at home with the mother, and the number of times the family moved between birth and age 7 (a measure of instability), as well as the week of gestation that the cortisol was measured. We also include an indicator for whether the mother worked during pregnancy (a potential source of stress) and whether there was any pregnancy complication to control for the possibility that the increase in maternal cortisol observed simply reflects maternal anxiety over the health of the fetus."

Another study surveyed pregnant women who were exposed to grave danger—in a massive earthquake—but ended up unharmed in order to isolate the independent effects of stress in itself, and again found "much lower levels of cognitive ability" in children exposed to gestational stress than in unexposed control groups. Florencia Torche, "Prenatal Exposure to an Acute Stressor and Children's Cognitive Outcomes," *Demography* 55, no. 5 (October 2018): 1617–18. Hereafter cited as Torche, "Prenatal Exposure."

As research mounts, concern about prenatal stress is entering the broader public arena. See Annie Murphy Paul, *Origins: How the Nine Months Before Birth Shape the Rest of Our Lives* (New York: Free Press, 2011). A recently released film, *In Utero,* also explores our time in the womb and its impact on human health and society. See Kathleen Man Gyllenhaal, *In Utero,* filmstrip, 85 mins. (2015).

119 **befalls non-elite mothers:** See Aizer, Stroud, and Buka, "Maternal Stress," Table 8; Torche, "Prenatal Exposure."

120 **among the youngest children:** In a study of mothers with small children conducted over the period between 2003 and 2010, mothers with a high school education or less (roughly the bottom two-thirds of the distribution) spent about forty-five minutes in developmental childcare, while mothers with a BA or more (roughly the top third) spent over an hour. Putnam, Frederick, and Snellman, "Growing Class Gaps," 10–11.

120 **their children's development:** Mothers with high school degrees only devoted a few more minutes per day than college-educated mothers, while high-school-only fathers spent less time than fathers with college degrees, so that overall parental investment was roughly equal across children of educated and uneducated parents. June Carbone and Naomi Cahn, *Marriage Markets: How Inequality Is Remaking the American Family* (New York: Oxford University Press, 2014), 85–86. Hereafter cited as Carbone and Cahn, *Marriage Markets.*

120 **increased their investments more rapidly:** Carbone and Cahn, *Marriage Markets,* 85–86.

120 **twice as rapidly, according to one study:** Reardon, "No Rich Child Left Behind." Reardon refers to Meredith Phillips, "Parenting, Time Use, and Disparities in Academic Outcomes," in *Whither Opportunity? Rising Inequality, Schools, and Children's Life Chances,* ed. Greg J. Duncan and Richard J. Munane (New York: Russell Sage Foundation, 2011), 210–11. Hereafter cited as Phillips, "Parenting, Time Use, and Disparities in Academic Outcomes."

120 **high-school-only parents:** Garey Ramey and Valerie A. Ramey, "The Rug Rat Race," *Brookings Papers on Economic Activity* (Spring 2010): 134–37. Mothers with college degrees spend perhaps six more hours each week with their children than do their less educated counterparts. On top of the six additional hours per week spent by mothers, college-educated fathers spend three additional hours per week educating their children. Ramey and Ramey narrow their focus to parents aged twenty-five to thirty-four, and define childcare as "care of infants, care of older children, medical care of children, playing with children, helping with homework, reading to and talking with children, dealing with childcare providers, and travel related to childcare" (133). This definition emphasizes immediate interactions with children and excludes any number of activities—shopping, cleaning, preparing food, keeping watch, and maintaining a safe house—that might also be classed as childcare more broadly understood. The narrow definition thus focuses on activities that contribute directly to children's emotional development and intellectual education.

120 **in order to care for their children:** "Life and Leadership After HBS: Findings from Harvard Business School's Alumni Survey on the Experiences of Its Alumni Across Career, Family, and Life Paths," Harvard Business School (2015), 8, www.hbs.edu/women50/docs/L_and_L_Survey_2Findings_13final.pdf. Twenty-one percent of female Harvard Business School graduates aged thirty-one to sixty-six with two or more children care for their children full time, and 20 percent work only part-time. For data on women with MBAs from the University of Chicago, see Marianne Bertrand, Claudia Goldin, and Lawrence F. Katz, "Dynamics of the Gender Gap for Young Professionals in the Corporate and Financial Sectors," NBER Working Paper 14681 (January 2009), www.nber.org/papers/w14681.pdf. Fully 50 percent of female Chicago MBAs with two or more children (and 48 percent with at least one child) no longer work full time ten years after getting their degrees. Anne Alstott and Emily Bazelon provided helpful discussion and references on this point.

120 **a "flight risk":** Williams, *White Working Class,* 55. See also Lauren Rivera and Andreas Tilcsik, "Research: How Subtle Class Cues Can Backfire on Your Resume," *Harvard Business Review,* December 21, 2016.

121 **much less match:** The phrase comes from Annette Lareau, who observes, "Middle-class parents who comply with current professional standards and engage in a pattern of concerted cultivation deliberately try to stimulate their children's development.... The commitment among working-class and poor families to provide comfort, food, shelter, and other basic support . . . stops short of the deliberate cultivation of children and their leisure activities that occurs in middle-class families." Annette Lareau, *Unequal Childhoods: Class, Race, and Family Life* (Los Angeles: University of California Press, 2011), 5.

121 **read to their children:** See Pew Research Center, "Parenting in America," December 17, 2015, http://www.pewsocialtrends.org/2015/12/17/parenting-in-america. Hereafter cited as Pew Research Center, "Parenting in America." For more information, see Claire Cain Miller, "Class Differences in Child-Rearing are on the Rise," *New York Times,* December 17, 2015, accessed November 18, 2018, www.nytimes.com/2015/12/18/upshot/rich-children-and-poor-ones-are-raised-very-differently.html. Hereafter cited as Miller, "Class Differences in Child-Rearing."

121 **take their children to art galleries:** When asked whether they had taken their children to an art gallery, museum, or historical site in the past month, 15 percent of high-school-only parents, 25 percent of parents with a BA, and 30 percent of parents with a graduate or professional degree answered that they had. Amber Noel, Patrick Stark, Jeremy Redford, and Andrew Zukerberg, *Parent and Family Involvement in Education, from the National Household Education Surveys Program of 2012,* U.S. Department of Education, National Center for Education Statistics (June 2016), Table 6, https://nces.ed.gov/pubs2013/2013028rev.pdf.

121 **enroll them in arts classes:** Miller, "Class Differences in Child-Rearing"; Pew Research Center, "Parenting in America."

121 **speak to their children more:** Betty Hart and Todd R. Risley, "The Early Catastrophe: The Thirty Million Word Gap," *Education Review* 17, no. 1 (2003): 116. Hereafter cited as Hart and Risley, "The Early Catastrophe." Hart and Risley analyzed data gathered in observations of forty-two families for one hour per month for thirty months and concluded that the average child in a family on welfare heard 616 words per hour, the average working-class child heard 1,251 words per hour, and the average child in a professional family heard 2,153 words per hour, extrapolating based on a fourteen-hour waking day over four years to thirteen million words heard by the average child in a family on welfare, twenty-six million by the average child in a working-class family, and forty-five million by the average child in a professional family. On the connection between early language exposure and wealth, see Kirp, *The Sandbox Investment,* 127–28.

121 **The rich also speak:** Kathy Hirsh-Pasek et al., "The Contribution of Early Communication Quality to Low-Income Children's Language Success," *Psychological Science* 26 (June 25, 2015); Douglas Quenqua, "Quality of Words, Not Quantity, Is Crucial to Language Skills, Study Finds," *New York Times,* October 16, 2014, accessed November 18, 2018, www.nytimes.com/2014/10/17/us/quality-of-words-not-quantity-is-crucial-to-language-skills-study-finds.html?_r=2.

121 **Three-year-old children:** Hart and Risley, "The Early Catastrophe," 113. Hart and Risley report the following average recorded vocabularies at three years: 1,116 words for a child in a professional family, 749 words for a child in a working-class family, and 525 words for a child in a family on welfare. Differences in vocabulary by socioeconomic status have been observed in children as young as eighteen months. Similarly, other researchers report that at eighteen months, children in lower-SES families had a mean vocabulary of 114 words, while children in higher-SES families had a mean vocabulary of 174 words; at twenty-four months, it was 288 words and 442 words. See Anne Fernald, Virginia A. Marchman, and Adriana Weisleder, "SES Differences in Language Processing Skill and Vocabulary Are Evident at 18 Months," *Developmental Science* 16 (December 8, 2012): 240, Table 3.

121 **more quickly than the poor ones:** John K. Niparko et al., "Spoken Language Development in Children Following Cochlear Implantation," *Journal of the American Medical Association* 303 (April 21, 2010): 1505, Table 2; Ann E. Geers, "Predictors of Reading Skill Development in Children with Early Cochlear Implantation," *Ear and Hearing* 24 (2003): 64S, Table 6; Sara Neufeld, "Baby Talk Bonanza," *Slate,* September 27, 2013, accessed November 18, 2018, https://slate.com/technology/2013/09/childrens-language-development-talk-and-listen-to-them-from-birth.html.

121 **half as likely to spank:** Pew Research Center, "Parenting in America"; Miller, "Class Differences in Child-Rearing."

121 **more open affection:** P. Lindsay Chase-Landsdale and Laura D. Pittman, "Welfare Reform and Parenting: Reasonable

Expectations," *The Future of Children* 12 (2002): 168–71. The article surveys research showing that six "dimensions of parenting" affect child outcomes: (1) warmth and responsiveness; (2) control and discipline; (3) cognitive stimulation; (4) modeling of attitudes, values, and behaviors; (5) gatekeeping; (6) family routines and traditions. It concludes that "low-income parents have been found to use less effective parenting strategies, including less warmth, harsher discipline, and less stimulating home environments." For further discussion and analysis, see Stacey Aronson and Aletha Houston, "The Mother-Infant Relationship in Single, Cohabiting, and Married Families: A Case for Marriage?," *Journal of Family Psychology* 18 (2004): 5–18; Vonnie McLoyd, "Socioeconomic Disadvantage and Child Development," *American Psychologist* 53 (1998): 185–204; Toby Parcel and Elizabeth Menaghan, "Determining Children's Home Environments: The Impact of Maternal Characteristics and Current Occupational and Family Conditions," *Journal of Marriage and Family* 53, no. 2 (1991); Julia B. Isaacs, *Starting School at a Disadvantage: The School Readiness of Poor Children*, Center on Children and Families (Brookings Institution, 2012), www.brookings.edu/wp-content/uploads/2016/06/0319_school_disadvantage_isaacs.pdf.

122 **long-term academic achievement:** See Paul Tough, *How Children Succeed: Grit, Curiosity, and the Hidden Power of Character* (Boston: Houghton Mifflin Harcourt, 2012), xviii, reporting on Heckman's work that GED recipients look like high school dropouts when measured by income, unemployment, divorce, drug use, and low college enrollment. For a more detailed analysis of Heckman's study, see James J. Heckman, "The Economic and Social Benefits of GED Certification," in *The Myth of Achievements: The GED and the Role of Character in American Life*, ed. James J. Heckman, John Eric Humphries, and Tim Kautz (Chicago: University of Chicago Press, 2014). Other researchers found that "observed levels of affection between mothers and their 8-month infants are associated with fewer symptoms of distress 30 years later among the offspring." J. Maselko et al., "Mother's Affection at 8 Months Predicts Emotional Distress in Adulthood," *Journal of Epidemiology and Community Health* 65 (2001): 625–26. This is a new line of research, however, and at present "the link between [socioeconomic status] and emotional well-being is not as consistent as the link with cognitive attainment." Robert H. Bradley and Robert F. Corwyn, "Socioeconomic Status and Child Development," *Annual Review of Psychology* 53 (2002): 371, 377.

122 **attend preschool at twice the rate:** W. Steven Barnett and Donald J. Yarosz, "Who Goes to Preschool and Why Does It Matter?," *National Institute for Early Education Research* 15 (2007): 7, Figure 6. In 2005, the data were as follows. For children age three, around 35 percent of those with family incomes (FI) of less than $60,000 participated in preschool, 44 percent of those with FI between $60,000 and $75,000 did so, 52 percent of those with FI between $75,000 and $100,000 did so, and 71 percent of those with FI of $100,000 or greater did so. For children age four, around 60 percent of those with family incomes of less than $60,000 participated in preschool, 77 percent of those with FI between $60,000 and $75,000 did so, 84 percent of those with FI between $75,000 and $100,000 did so, and 89 percent of those with FI of $100,000 or greater did so. Compare Robert J. Gordon, "The Great Stagnation of American Education," *New York Times*, September 7, 2013, accessed November 18, 2018, http://opinionator.blogs.nytimes.com/2013/09/07/the-great-stagnation-of-american-education, and Timothy Noah, "The 1 Percent Are Only Half the Problem," *New York Times*, May 18, 2013, accessed November 18, 2018, https://opinionator.blogs.nytimes.com/2013/05/18/the-1-percent-are-only-half-the-problem.

122 **$50,000 per year:** Ethical Culture Fieldston School, "Tuition and Financial Aid," October 30, 2018, https://www.ecfs.org/en/tuition-and-financial-aid/.

122 **pay the full price:** Michael Hwang and Taisha Thompson, "Financial Aid Task Force Report," Ethical Culture Fieldston School (2015) (unpublished document on file with author), 6. Hereafter cited as Hwang and Thompson, "Financial Aid Task Force Report."

122 **between $100,000 and $149,000:** Hwang and Thompson, "Financial Aid Task Force Report," 8. The school reports that among the 21 percent of students who receive financial aid, 35 percent come from families with household incomes below $75,000. Hwang and Thompson, "Financial Aid Task Force Report," 8. Assuming that all students with low household incomes get financial aid, this entails that only about 7 percent of students at Fieldston come from families with annual incomes below $75,000, which is still nearly one and a half times the national median.

Fieldston is not more expensive or exclusive than other elite private schools. Indeed, Fieldston claims that "among the peer schools in New York, we rank second in percent of students on financial aid and percent of dollars allocated to financial aid relative to gross tuition." Hwang and Thompson, "Financial Aid Task Force Report," 6. Fees at Bank Street School were $48,444 for preschool in 2018–19. "Tuition & Financial Aid," Bank Street School, https://school.bankstreet.edu/admissions/tuition-financial-aid/. Over 60 percent of students paid full tuition. Riverdale Country School costs $54,150 for preschool (2018–19). "Tuition and Fees," Riverdale Country School, www.riverdale.edu/page.cfm?p=786. Approximately 80 percent of students pay full tuition. "Fast Facts: Financial Aid," Riverdale Country School, www.riverdale.edu/page.cfm?p=521. And Avenues World School costs $54,000 for preschool (2018–19), and financial aid is not available for nursery or pre-kindergarten. "Tuition and Financial Aid," Avenues World School, www.avenues.org/en/nyc/tuition-and-financial-aid.

122 **harder to get into than Harvard and Yale:** For reports of admissions rates at elite preschools, see LearnVest, "Confessions of a Preschool Admissions Coach," *Huffington Post*, June, 24, 2013, accessed November 18, 2018, www.huffingtonpost.com/learnvest/confessions-of-a-preschool-admissions-coach_b_3461110.html, and Emily Jane Fox, "How New York's 1% Get Kids into Preschool," CNN Money, June 19, 2014, accessed November 18, 2018, http://money.cnn.com/2014/06/10/luxury/preschool-new-york-city. The acceptance rates at Harvard and Yale were 5.4 and 6.3 percent respectively. "Admissions Statistics," Harvard College, https://college.harvard.edu/admissions/admissions-statistics; Jon Victor, "Yale Admits 6.27 Percent of Applicants," *Yale Daily News*, March 31, 2016.

123 **might reach $6,000:** This is the fee charged by Manhattan Private School Advisors. Andrew Marks, "Cracking the Kindergarten Code," *New York Magazine*, accessed November 18, 2018, http://nymag.com/nymetro/urban/education/features/15141/.

123 **in order to impress on school visits:** For a description of an educational consultancy practice, see "An Hereditary Meritocracy," *The Economist*, January 22, 2015, www.economist.com/briefing/2015/01/22/an-hereditary-meritocracy. For more information, see also Kirp, *The Sandbox Investment*, and Liz Moyer, "The Most Expensive Preschools," *Forbes*, September 17, 2007, accessed November 18, 2018, www.forbes.com/2007/09/18/education-preschool-kindergarten-biz-cx_lm_0919preschool.html#43c4e100763d.

123 **is largely fixed by age ten:** James Heckman, "Schools, Skills, and Synapses," *Economic Inquiry* 46, no. 3 (2008): 305–7. Heckman summarizes research showing that IQ scores become stable by age ten, that ability gaps between socioeconomic groups appear at a young age, and that interventions to correct them are more effective at a young age. For further analysis of fixed IQ scores, see James Heckman, "Lessons from the Bell Curve," *Journal of Political Economy* 103, no. 5 (October 1995). Heckman writes, "The available evidence suggests that ability—or IQ—is not a fixed trait for the young. Sustained high-intensity investments in the education of young children, including parental activities such as reading and responding to children, stimulate learning and promote education, although they do not necessarily boost IQ by very much. The available evidence suggests that such interventions stimulate motivation and social performance in the early adult years even if they do not raise IQ" (1112).

123 **when children enter kindergarten:** Sean F. Reardon, "The Widening Income Achievement Gap," *Educational Leadership* 70, no. 8 (May 2013): 10–16. Reardon similarly writes that "children from rich and poor families score very differently on school readiness tests when they enter kindergarten, and this gap grows

by less than 10 percent between kindergarten and high school." Reardon, "No Rich Child Left Behind."

123 **that their alumni eventually attend:** For example, see "Fast Facts: Most Frequently Attended College/Universities by Recent Alumni," Riverdale Country School, www.riverdale.edu /page.cfm?p=521.

123 **perfect practice makes perfect:** The phrase is commonly attributed to the football coach Vince Lombardi. For example, see David A. Sousa, *How the Brain Learns* (Thousand Oaks, CA: Corwin, 2011), 105.

123 **roughly twenty-one, nineteen, and twenty-three months:** The test score gaps between median children in the most and least elite deciles in mathematics, reading, and science literacy were 125, 116, and 132 points respectively. The test score gaps between the median children in most elite and middle-class groups in mathematics, reading, and science literacy were 69, 63, and 76 points respectively. OECD, *PISA Codebook*, PISA 2015 Database, www.oecd.org/pisa/data/2015database/Codebook _CMB.xlsx. Twenty points on the test amounts to a half year of schooling. See also Niall Ferguson, "The End of the American Dream? How Rising Inequality and Social Stagnation Are Reshaping Us for the Worse," *Newsweek*, June 28, 2013, accessed November 18, 2018, www.newsweek.com/2013/06/26/niall -ferguson-end-american-dream-237614.html.

124 **already locked in:** Julia B. Isaacs, "Starting School at a Disadvantage: The School Readiness of Poor Children," Center on Children and Families at Brookings (March 2012), 3, Figures 1, 2. Isaacs reports that 52 percent of poor children score very low on one of five measures of school readiness, while only 25 percent of moderate- or high-income children do so; this includes 26 percent of poor children scoring very low on math skills and 30 percent scoring very low on reading skills, while only 7 percent of moderate- or high-income children score very low in either of those areas. She also shows that low maternal supportiveness has a significant negative effect on school readiness (Figure 7).

124 **active leisure:** Richard V. Reeves, *Dream Hoarders: How the American Upper Middle Class Is Leaving Everyone Else in the Dust, Why That Is a Problem, and What to Do About It* (Washington, DC: Brookings Institution, 2017), 42. Hereafter cited as Reeves, *Dream Hoarders*. Reeves cites Phillips, "Parenting, Time Use, and Disparities in Academic Outcomes."

124 **By the time she is eighteen:** Rich children spend nearly thirteen hundred more hours in novel places between birth and age six than poor children do, they spend a total of perhaps eighteen hundred more hours in novel places over the course of their school-aged years than poor children do, and they spend a total of perhaps eighteen hundred more hours speaking to their parents over the course of their school-aged years than poor children do. See Phillips, "Parenting, Time Use, and Disparities in Academic Outcomes," 217–21. Rich children of course also take more arts and music lessons, receive more coaching at sports, and so on.

124 **hours of screen time:** Rich children (aged zero to eight), for example, spend nearly two and a half fewer hours per week watching television and playing video games than poor children and nearly one and a half fewer hours per week than middle-class children. Among zero- to eight-year-old children, those with a parental income of less than $30,000 spend one hour and seven minutes per day watching TV, those with a parental income of between $30,000 and $75,000 spend fifty-eight minutes per day watching TV, and those with greater than $75,000 spend forty-six minutes per day watching TV. "Zero to Eight: Children's Media Use in America 2013," Common Sense Media (October 2013), Table 8, www.commonsensemedia.org/research/zero-to -eight-childrens-media-use-in-america-2013.

The differences grow as the children get older: among eight- to twelve-year-olds, rich children spend roughly twelve and a half fewer hours per week using screen media than poor children and roughly seven fewer hours per week than middle-class children, and for thirteen- to eighteen-year-olds, the rich /poor and rich/middle-class differences rise to seventeen and eleven hours respectively. Among eight- to twelve-year-olds, those with a parental income of less than $35,000 spend five hours and thirty-two minutes per day using screen media, those with a parental income between $35,000 and $99,999 spend four hours and thirty-two minutes per day using screen media, and those with a parental income greater than $100,000 spend three hours and forty-six minutes per day using screen media. For students ages thirteen to eighteen, those numbers rise to eight hours and seven minutes, six hours and thirty-one minutes, and five hours and forty-two minutes respectively. "Fact Sheet: Digital Equity Gaps—The Common Sense Census: Media Use by Tweens and Teens," Common Sense Media (2015), Table 2, www.commonsensemedia.org/research/the-common-sense -census-media-use-by-tweens-and-teens.

This comes as no surprise, as rich adults watch nearly four fewer hours each week than poor adults. For adults, daily television viewing for those in middle socioeconomic positions ranged from 170 to 200 minutes per day, while for those in the highest socioeconomic position, it ranged from 140 to 160 minutes per day. E. Stamatakis et al., "Television Viewing and Other Screen-Based Entertainment in Relation to Multiple Socioeconomic Status Indicators and Area Deprivation: The Scottish Health Survey 2003," *Journal of Epidemiology and Community Health* 60 (2009): 737, Figure 2. Murray reports that the average American watches 35 hours of TV per week, while elites barely watch at all. Murray, *Coming Apart*, 27. Murray cites Nielsen data for average TV viewing, "State of the Media TV Usage Trends, Q2 2010," Nielsen, November 18, 2010, www.nielsen.com/us/en /insights/news/2010/state-of-the-media-tv-usage-trends-q2 -2010.html, and Trish Gorely, Simon Marshall, and Stuart Biddle, "Couch Kids: Correlates of Television Viewing Among Youth," *International Journal of Behavioral Medicine* 11, no. 3 (2004): 152–56, for elite viewing.

124 **professional chefs to tutor him:** See Katy McLaughlin, "Haute Home Schools Designed to Give Kids a Bespoke Education," *Wall Street Journal*, February 18, 2016, accessed November 18, 2018, www.wsj.com/articles/haute-home-schools-designed-to -give-kids-a-bespoke-education-1455807796. Hereafter cited as McLaughlin, "Haute Home Schools Designed to Give Kids a Bespoke Education."

125 **his own catering business:** McLaughlin, "Haute Home Schools Designed to Give Kids a Bespoke Education."

125 **341,300 students in 1965:** Allan C. Ornstein, "The Growing Popularity of Private Schools," *The Clearing House* 63, no. 5 (January 1990): 210.

125 **1.4 million today:** "Private School Enrollment," National Center for Education Statistics (May 2016), https://nces.ed.gov /programs/coe/indicator_cgc.asp. The upward trend, moreover, continues. Enrollment increased by more than 15 percent between just the 1995–96 and 2011–12 school years. Enrollment statistics for 2011–12 are available at "Private School Universe Survey 2011–2012," National Center for Education Statistics (2012), https://nces.ed.gov/surveys/pss/tables/table _2011_02.asp; the 1995–96 statistics are available at "Private School Universe Survey 1995–1996," National Center for Education Statistics (1998), https://nces.ed.gov/pubsearch/pub sinfo.asp?pubid=98229.

The general population, by contrast, grew by a factor of just 1.66. The U.S. population has grown from 194.3 million in 1965 to 323 million in 2016. "Annual Estimates of the Resident Population: April 1, 2010 to July 1, 2016," American Fact Finder: United States Census Bureau (2016), https://factfinder .census.gov/faces/tableservices/jsf/pages/productview.xhtml; "Population in the U.S.," Google: Public Data, www.google .com/publicdata/explore?ds=kf7tgg1uo9ude_&met_y=popu lation&idim=country:US.

125 **$50,000 per child:** As recently as 2000, so few rich students were homeschooled that the Department of Education did not even collect data on them. By 2012, 1.6 percent of homeschooled students came from households with annual incomes above $100,000. McLaughlin, "Haute Home Schools Designed to Give Kids a Bespoke Education."

125 **make less than $50,000:** The precise rates are 26 percent and 6 percent respectively. Jed Kolko, "Where Private School Enrollment Is Highest and Lowest Across the U.S.," City Lab, August 13, 2014, www.citylab.com/housing/2014/08/where -private-school-enrollment-is-highest-and-lowest-across-the-us /375993/. Another study reports that 18 percent of children from the richest fifth of households attend private schools,

compared to 9 percent of children from the next two-fifths and just 4 percent of children from the bottom two-fifths. Reeves, *Dream Hoarders*, 47. For the purposes of this study, private schools included parochial schools, and data came from the Educational Longitudinal Study of 2002 Senior Class of 2004 First Follow-Up survey, National Center for Education Statistics.

125 **only 7 percent from the bottom half:** For a compilation of these data, see Michael T. Owyang and E. Katarina Vermann, "Measuring the Effect of School Choice on Economic Outcomes," *Regional Economist*, Federal Reserve Bank of St. Louis (October 2012). The study bases its calculations on data from the National Center for Education Statistics.

125 **from the top 4 percent of the income distribution:** Ruben A. Gaztambide-Fernandez, *The Best of the Best: Becoming Elite at an American Boarding School* (Cambridge, MA: Harvard University Press, 2009), 35. The author cites a now-defunct blog article at Patrick F. Bassett, "Bassett Blog: Affordability and the Family Ford," *NAIS eBulletin*, April 2006, www.nais.org /about/article.cfm?ItemNumber=148304&sn.ItemNumber =4181&tn.ItemNumber=147271. Hereafter cited as Bassett, "Affordability and the Family Ford."

Only 30 percent of the students at the schools conventionally thought of as "elite boarding schools"—a group of twenty-eight schools that collectively enroll over fifteen thousand students—get any financial aid. Ruben Gaztambide-Fernandez, "What Is an Elite Boarding School?," *Review of Educational Research* 79, no. 3 (September 2009): 1098–99, Table 1. And even financial aid recipients are overwhelmingly rich: the National Association of Independent Schools' *Trendbook* reports that "there are nearly five times more families in the top 20 percent of family incomes who received need-based aid in 2015–16 than there were families in the bottom 20 percent." Mark Mitchell, "Are Low-Income Families Being Squeezed Out of Independent Schools?," *The Independent School Magazine Blog*, September 28, 2015, accessed November 18, 2018, www.nais.org/learn/in dependent-ideas/september-2015/are-low-income-families -being-squeezed-out-of-inde/. The association estimates that a family needs an annual household income greater than $200,000 to afford its schools without support. Bassett, "Affordability and the Family Ford." Indeed, financial aid sometimes goes to students from households with incomes as high as $300,000. Paul Sullivan, "For Boarding Schools, an Evolving Financial Aid Philosophy," *New York Times*, March 14, 2014, accessed November 18, 2018, www.nytimes.com/2014/03/15 /your-money/for-boarding-schools-an-evolving-financial-aid -philosophy.html. See "Who Gets Financial Aid," Groton School, www.groton.org/page/admission/who-gets-financial -aid, for an example of an independent school in which families with incomes above $300,000 are eligible to receive financial aid based on a combination of income, assets, debt, and other expenses.

125 **Small student/teacher ratios—7:1:** Even as enrollments at nonsectarian private schools grew, for example, student/teacher ratios at these schools declined between 1995 and 2012, from 9:1 to 7:1. See "Private School Universe Survey 1995–96," and "Private School Universe Survey 2011–2012."

125 **16:1 in public schools:** The average student/teacher ratio at public schools nationwide, by contrast, is 16:1, and average class sizes are 21 in elementary schools and 27 in secondary schools. The reported ratios are for 2013 and the reported class sizes are for the 2011–12 academic year. "Fast Facts," National Center for Education Statistics, https://nces.ed.gov/fastfacts/display.asp ?id=28.

125 **A student tour guide:** Conversation with author.

126 **for 90,000 more:** "About," Phillips Exeter Academy, www.exe ter.edu/academics/library/about; "An Open Book," *The Exeter Bulletin*, Winter 2016, www.exeter.edu/documents/Exeter _Bulletin/An_Open_Book.pdf.

126 **private day schools:** For rankings, see "America's Best Prep Schools," *Forbes*, April 29, 2010, accessed November 18, 2018, http://www.forbes.com/2010/04/29/best-prep-schools -2010-opinions-private-education.html. For rankings that contain tuition data, see "2019 Best Schools in America," *Niche*, accessed November 18, 2018, http://k12.niche.com. Even less elite private schooling is expensive, with average annual tuition across all private day schools in the Northeast and New England

reaching nearly $35,000. Tuition varies by geographic region, and schools in other parts of the country cost less, although they remain expensive. The comparatively cheapest private schools are in the Southeast, where average annual tuition at private day schools is slightly less than $20,000. Alia Wong, "When Private School Tuition Costs More Than College," *Atlantic*, November 21, 2014, accessed November 18, www.theatlantic.com/educa tion/archive/2014/11/when-private-school-tuition-costs -more-than-college/383003/.

126 **$700,000 per student:** The average endowment across the whole list exceeds $250 million, or over $350,000 per student. The average endowment of the day schools is nearly $100 million, or over $100,000 per student. These figures reflect data gathered at the schools' websites or, where websites did not report data, from the Form 990s that the schools, as tax-exempt 501(c)(3) organizations, were required to file with the Internal Revenue Service in 2015, for the 2014 tax year. For a summary of this data, see "Largest Endowments," Boarding School Review, www.boardingschoolreview.com/top-twenty-schools-listing /largest-endowments.

Endowments among a slightly broader elite of private schools remain enormous: the average endowment of the twenty-eight boarding schools mentioned earlier is about $225 million. Gaztambide-Fernandez, "What Is an Elite Boarding School?," Table 1.

126 **between $15,000 and $25,000 per student:** For example, on their website, the Roxbury Latin School states, "In fact, for this 2018–2019 school year, tuition accounts for about 41 percent of the School's budget, with the remainder provided through income from contributions to the Annual Fund (22 percent) and from the endowment (37 percent). This year, the total budgeted cost per student . . . is almost $25,000 more than RL's tuition . . . ; so essentially every boy at RL receives a scholarship." "Annual Fund," Roxbury Latin School, www.roxburylatin.org/page/sup porting-rl/annual-fund.

126 **every year of her education:** The sum reflects tuition charges between $35,000 and $55,000 per year and subsidies between $15,000 and $25,000 per year. Again, some schools report expenditures per student, and the reports confirm this calculation. Roxbury Latin says that it spends $55,264 annually on each student. "Annual Fund." The Collegiate School says that it spends roughly $56,000. "Why Give?," The Collegiate School, https:// www.collegiateschool.org/page/support/why-give. The Lawrenceville School reports expenditures per student of nearly $90,000. "The Lawrenceville Fund," Lawrenceville School, www.lawrenceville.org/page/giving/the-lawrenceville-fund. And Deerfield Academy reports that the cost of its education runs to roughly $84,000 per student per year. "Support," Deerfield Academy, https://deerfield.edu/dpn/parent-support/. These numbers were calculated by using the percentage of expenditure covered by tuition, which is reported on each school's relevant "giving" page, to calculate total expenditure per student.

126 **just over $12,000:** According to the National Center for Education Statistics (housed in the United States Department of Education), the national average per-pupil expenditure at public schools, for the 2012–13 school year, was $12,296. "Public School Expenditures," National Center for Education Statistics, May 2016, https://nces.ed.gov/programs/coe/pdf/Indicator _CMB/coe_cmb_2016_05.pdf.

126 **public school funding in the United States:** Stephen Q. Cornman, *Revenues and Expenditures for Public Elementary and Secondary School Districts: School Year 2011–2012 (Fiscal Year 2012)*, U.S. Department of Education, National Center for Education Statistics (2015), https://nces.ed.gov/pubs2014 /2014303.pdf. State governments contribute 45.1 percent of funding and local governments contribute 44.8 percent. The federal government contributes 10.1 percent.

126 **spends barely $8,000:** U.S. Census Bureau, "Per Pupil Amounts for Current Spending of Public Elementary -Secondary School Systems by State: Fiscal Year 2014," Annual Survey of School System Finances, June 10, 2016, https://fact finder.census.gov/faces/tableservices/jsf/pages/productview .xhtml?pid=SSF_2014_00A08&prodType=table. Connecticut has in the recent past spent still more—$18,512—and Mississippi still less—$7,928. Reid Wilson, "Best State in America:

Connecticut, for Its Teachers," *Washington Post*, September 5, 2015, accessed November 18, 2018, www.washingtonpost.com /opinions/best-state-in-america-connecticut-for-its-teachers /2014/09/05/8e11ac88-3457-11e4-8f02-03c644b2d7d0 _story.html?utm_term=.5cd4ba377ed5; Lyndsey Layton, "Study: Poor Children Are Now the Majority in American Public Schools in South, West," *Washington Post*, October 16, 2013, accessed November 18, 2018, www.washingtonpost .com/local/education/2013/10/16/34eb4984-35bb -11e3-8a0e-4e2cf80831fc_story.html?utm_term=.a7ff 5647e08a.

The richest five states today (Connecticut, Maryland, Massachusetts, New Jersey, and New Hampshire) spend an average of $15,815 per public school student per year, while the middle six (Nebraska, Kansas, Oregon, Maine, Texas, and Ohio) spend $10,716, and the poorest five (New Mexico, West Virginia, Idaho, Arkansas, and Mississippi) spend on average only $9,099. U.S. Census Bureau, "Per Capita Income in the Past 12 Months (in 2015 Inflation-Adjusted Dollars)," 2011–2015 American Community Survey 5-Year Estimates, https://fact finder.census.gov/faces/tableservices/jsf/pages/productview .xhtml?pid=ACS_15_5YR_B19301&prodType=table. For purposes of identifying the poorest states, I do not include Puerto Rico and the District of Columbia.

The gaps between average school expenditures in rich, middling, and poor states have grown over time—in parallel, incidentally, with gaps between incomes in rich, middling, and poor states.

126   **more per student than others do:** In Pennsylvania, for example, per-student public expenditures in low-poverty districts are nearly 33 percent higher than in high-poverty districts ($12,529 versus $9,387). U.S. Department of Education, National Center for Education Statistics, Education Finance Statistics Center, "School District Current Expenditures Per Pupil with and Without Adjustments for Federal Revenues by Poverty and Race/Ethnicity Characteristics," 2015, Table A-1.

In Connecticut, in spite of an aggressive litigation campaign aimed at school finance equalization, the difference remains nearly 10 percent. U.S. Department of Education, National Center for Education Statistics, Education Finance Statistics Center, "School District Current Expenditures Per Pupil with and Without Adjustments for Federal Revenues by Poverty and Race/Ethnicity Characteristics," 2015, Table A-1. A Connecticut court recently held that the inequities in school funding among districts violated the right to public education guaranteed by the state's constitution. The court ordered the state to develop a funding system that would be influenced only by school needs and good practices." *Connecticut Coal. for Justice in Educ., Inc. v. Rell*, No. X07HHDCV145037565S, 2016 WL 4922730, at *33 (Conn. Super. Ct. Sept. 7, 2016), *aff'd in part, rev'd in part and remanded sub nom. Connecticut Coal. for Justice in Educ. Funding, Inc. v. Rell*, 327 Conn. 650, 176 A.3d 28 (2018).

127   **spent only about $8,000:** The data for Scarsdale and Barbourville follow Michael B. Sauter et al., "The 10 Richest—and Poorest—School Districts in America," Alternet, June 11 2012, accessed November 18, 2018, www.alternet.org/story/155824 /the_10_richest_—_and_poorest_—_school_districts_in _america, and Douglas A. McIntyre, "America's Richest School Districts," *24/7 Wall Street*, June 6, 2012, accessed November 18, 2018, http://247wallst.com/special-report/2012/06/06 /americas-richest-school-districts/. Sauter and his coauthors chose Scarsdale and Barbourville and derived their numbers from data in the U.S. Census and the American Community Survey, 2006–10. They studied only the 9,627 districts that served 250 or more students in the relevant school year, whereas the census reports data for over 13,000 districts.

Note also that the full ranges of household incomes in the districts reinforce the economic segregation of their schools. Sixty-four percent of households in Scarsdale earned more than $200,000 annually, and 0 percent earned less than $10,000. By contrast, 0 percent of households in Barbourville earned over $200,000 annually, and 7 percent earned less than $10,000.

The precise numbers have, unsurprisingly, changed since Sauter and his coauthors complied their data. In 2012–13, Scarsdale spent $28,204 and Barbourville spent $8,993. Scarsdale's

median household income had increased to $238,478. (The 2012–13 data report one district that is richer still—the Hillsborough City Elementary School District in Northern California, with median household income above $250,000—but this is a K–8 district only and thus not a good candidate for the comparisons made here.) Barbourville's median income had grown to $19,760. Census data from 2014 show many—presumably small—school districts with median household incomes in the range of $14,000 to $16,000.

127   **a few dollars per pupil:** The Junipero Serra PTA, in the Bernal Heights neighborhood of San Francisco, for example, raised just $25 per student in a recent year. Jeremy Adam Smith, "How Budget Cuts and PTA Fundraising Undermined Equity in San Francisco Public Schools," *San Francisco Public Press*, February 3, 2014, accessed November 18, 2018, https://sfpublicpress.org /news/2014-02/how-budget-cuts-and-PTA-fundraising -undermined-equity-in-san-francisco-public-schools. Hereafter cited as Smith, "How Budget Cuts and PTA Fundraising Undermined Equity in San Francisco Public Schools."

127   **figure prominently in school funding overall:** Nationwide, roughly 3,500 private groups, serving 12 percent of school districts, raised $271 million to support public schools across the country in 1995; by 2010, roughly 11,500 such groups, serving 29 percent of districts, raised $957 million. Ashlyn Aiko Nelson and Beth Gazley, "The Rise of School-Supporting Nonprofits," *Education and Finance Policy* 9, no. 4 (February 2014): Table 4. These numbers come from annual tax reports that such groups are required to file with the IRS. Both sums set updates to constant (2015) dollars, using the Bureau of Labor Statistics' CPI calculator, available at "CPI Inflation Calculator," https://data .bls.gov/cgi-bin/cpicalc.pl. The nominal sums were $197 million for 1995 and $880 million for 2010. This is a natural and almost inevitable response to litigation aiming to distribute tax revenues more evenly across a state's rich and poor districts, as privately raised funds fall outside of the pool that must be spread in this way.

127   **at least $2,300 per child:** Robert Reich, "Not Very Giving," *New York Times*, September 4, 2013, accessed November 18, 2018, www.nytimes.com/2013/09/05/opinion/not-very-giving .html; Laura McKenna, "How Rich Parents Can Exacerbate School Inequality," *Atlantic*, January 28, 2016, accessed November 18, 2018, www.theatlantic.com/education/archive/2016 /01/rich-parents-school-inequality/431640/. Hereafter cited as McKenna, "How Rich Parents Can Exacerbate School Inequality."

127   **$400,000 in a single night:** McKenna, "How Rich Parents Can Exacerbate School Inequality."

127   **wealthy public schools:** Between 2005 and 2011, the total budget of elementary school PTAs in San Francisco increased by about 800 percent, and by 2011, ten rich schools raised more money than the remaining sixty-one schools combined. Smith, "How Budget Cuts and PTA Fundraising Undermined Equity in San Francisco Public Schools."

127   **"public privates":** Kyle Spencer, "Way Beyond Bake Sales: The $1 Million PTA," *New York Times*, June 1, 2012, accessed on November 18, 2018, www.nytimes.com/2012/06/03/nyregion /at-wealthy-schools-ptas-help-fill-budget-holes.html.

127   **in one recent year:** Smith, "How Budget Cuts and PTA Fundraising Undermined Equity in San Francisco Public Schools." More generally, recall that principals of schools with richer students possess a full year's more experience on average than principals of schools with poorer students; teachers possess two years' more experience on average and 25 percent more master's degrees; and first-year teachers, who commonly struggle as they learn their craft, are less than half as common. Tara Béteille, Demetra Kalogrides, and Susanna Loeb, "Stepping Stones: Principal Career Paths and School Outcomes," *Social Science Research* 41 (2012): 904–19.

127   **extravagant facilities:** See Reich, "Back to School"; Motoko Rich, "Nation's Wealthy Places Pour Private Money into Public Schools, Study Finds," *New York Times*, October 21, 2014, accessed November 18, 2018, www.nytimes.com/2014/10/22 /us/nations-wealthy-places-pour-private-money-into-public -schools-study-finds.html.

127   **While Barbourville receives:** "District Directory Information: Barbourville Independent," National Center for Education

Statistics, 2018, https://nces.ed.gov/ccd/districtsearch/district
_detail.asp?Search=2&ID2=2100240&DistrictID=21
00240&details=4. Nonlocal sources include 11 percent federal
revenue and 70 percent state.

127   **nearly $100,000 per year to own:** The median price in Scars-
dale is $1,059,700. "Scarsdale Home Prices & Values," Zillow,
October 2018, www.zillow.com/scarsdale-ny/home-values/.
The payments on a $1.2 million mortgage (required to finance a
$1.5 million home with a 20 percent down payment) amount to
roughly $70,000 per year at current interest rates, and median
real estate taxes in Scarsdale are $20,813. Based on $1.059 million estimate, 10583 Scarsdale zip code, and using calculator
from "New York Property Tax Calculator," SmartAsset, https://
smartasset.com/taxes/new-york-property-tax-calculator.

Rich residents of "Scarsdales" across the country ensure
that their communities remain exclusive by insisting on zoning
regulations that keep lots and houses large and rejecting efforts
to build affordable housing in their communities. Scarsdale itself has faced litigation and scandal concerning these practices.
For information on the scandal, see Kate Stone Lombardi,
"Home Sweet Affordable Home?," *Westchester Magazine*, April
1, 2016, accessed November 18, 2018, www.westchestermaga
zine.com/Westchester-Magazine/April-2016/Home-Sweet
-Affordable-Home/.

128   **that serve poor students:** OECD, *Education at a Glance 2013:
OECD Indicators*, OECD Publishing (2013), http://dx.doi
.org/10.1787/eag-2013-en; Reich, "Back to School"; Eduardo
Porter, "In Public Education, Edge Still Goes to Rich," *New York
Times*, November 5, 2013, accessed November 18, 2018, www
.nytimes.com/2013/11/06/business/a-rich-childs-edge-in
-public-education.html.

The unequal spending patterns, incidentally, almost certainly contribute to the striking inefficiency of public education
in the United States, which spends more per student than every
OECD nation save Luxembourg, Norway, Switzerland, and
Austria, but produces average academic achievement levels at the
middle of the OECD pack. OECD, *Country Note: Key Findings
from PISA 2015 for the United States*, OECD Publishing (2016),
7, 9, www.oecd.org/pisa/PISA-2015-United-States.pdf.

128   **multibillion-dollar industry today:** See, for example, Patrick
Clark, "The Test Prep Industry Is Booming," Bloomberg, October 8, 2014, accessed November 18, 2018, www.bloomberg
.com/news/articles/2014-10-08/sats-the-test-prep-business-is
-booming.

128   **skew overwhelmingly toward wealth:** *2013 College-Bound
Seniors: Total Group Profile Report*, College Board, 4, http://
media.collegeboard.com/digitalServices/pdf/research/2013
/TotalGroup-2013.pdf; Ezra Klein, "Wall Street Steps In When
Ivy League Fails," *Washington Post*, February 16, 2012, accessed
November 18, 2018, www.washingtonpost.com/business/econ
omy/wall-street-steps-in-when-ivy-league-fails/2012/02/16
/gIQAX2weIR_story.html; Daniel Pink, "How to Predict a
Student's SAT Score: Look at the Parents' Tax Return," *Dan
Pink*, www.danpink.com/archives/2012/02/how-to-predict-a
-students-sat-score-look-at-the-parents-tax-return, hereafter cited
as Pink, "How to Predict."

129   **as much as $100,000:** Emma Jacobs, "The $600-an-Hour
Private Tutor," *Financial Times*, December 12, 2013, accessed
November 18, 2018, www.ft.com/content/080d6cce-61aa-11e3
-aa02-00144feabdc0. Hereafter cited as Jacobs, "The $600-an-
Hour Private Tutor."

129   **$1,250 per hour:** Caroline Moss, "Meet the Guy Who Makes
$1,000 an Hour Tutoring Kids of Fortune 500 CEOs over
Skype," *Business Insider*, August 26, 2014, accessed November
18, 2018, www.businessinsider.com/anthony-green-tutoring
-2014-8. Hereafter cited as Moss, "Meet the Guy Who Makes
$1,000 an Hour Tutoring Kids of Fortune 500 CEOs over
Skype." Robert Frank, "Meet the $1,250-an-Hour Tutor,"
CNBC, December 12, 2013, accessed November 18, 2018, www
.cnbc.com/2013/12/12/meet-the-400000-a-year-tutor.html.
Hereafter cited as Frank, "Meet the $1,250-an-Hour Tutor."

129   **charging the students substantially more:** Email conversation
with author.

129   **accepted the arrangement:** Email conversation with author.

129   **In addition to earning:** Frank, "Meet the $1,250-an-Hour
Tutor."

129   **years in advance:** Moss, "Meet the Guy Who Makes $1,000 an
Hour Tutoring Kids of Fortune 500 CEOs over Skype."

129   **"If you've invested":** Jacobs, "The $600-an-Hour Private Tutor."

129   **have become national celebrities:** Simon Mundy, "South
Korea's Millionaire Tutors," *Financial Times*, June 16, 2014,
accessed November 18, 2018, www.ft.com/content/c0b611fc
-dab5-11e3-9a27-00144feabdc0.

129   **will soon surpass $100 billion:** "Private Tutoring," Global In-
dustry Analysts, Inc., September 2016, www.strategyr.com
/Private_Home_Tutor_Services_Market_Report.asp; James
Marshall Crotty, "Global Private Tutoring Market Will Surpass
$102.8 Billion By 2018," *Forbes*, November 12, 2012, accessed
November 18, 2018, www.forbes.com/sites/jamesmarshall
crotty/2012/10/30/global-private-tutoring-market-will
-surpass-102-billion-by-2018/#3820c5cd2ee0.

129   **roughly $5 billion:** Drew Gilpin Faust, "Financial Report, Fis-
cal Year 2017," Harvard University, October 26, 2017, 6, https://
finance.harvard.edu/files/fad/files/final_harvard_university
_financial_report_2017.pdf.

129   **highly educated mothers:** For more on the claim that maternal
education significantly influences children's participation in
extracurricular activities—especially those that require significant parental time investment—see Elliot Weininger, Annette
Lareau, and Dalton Conley, "What Money Doesn't Buy: Class
Resources and Children's Participation in Organized Extracurricular Activities," *Social Forces* 94, no. 2 (December 2015):
479.

130   **in the first place:** For example, 84 percent of children of high-
income parents participate in sports or athletic activities, compared with 69 percent of their middle-income peers and 59
percent of their low-income peers. Similarly, 64 percent of children of the rich do volunteer work, compared with just 49 percent and 37 percent of their middle-income and lower-income
counterparts, respectively. Children of rich parents are also
more likely to gain work experience, participate in peer organizations like the Scouts, and take lessons in music, dance, or art.
Pew Research Center, "Parenting in America"; Miller, "Class
Differences in Child-Rearing."

130   **Moreover, the gap:** Kaisa Snellman et al., "The Engagement
Gap: Social Mobility and Extracurricular Participation Among
American Youth," *Annals of the American Academy of Political
and Social Science* 657 (January 2015): 194–207; Robert Putnam, *Our Kids: The American Dream in Crisis* (New York: Simon & Schuster, 2015), 177. Hereafter cited as Putnam, *Our
Kids: The American Dream in Crisis.*

130   **$7,500 annually:** Greg J. Duncan and Richard J. Murnane, "In-
troduction: The American Dream, Then and Now," in *Whither
Opportunity? Rising Inequality, Schools, and Children's Life
Chances*, ed. Greg Duncan and Richard Murnane (New York:
Russell Sage Foundation, 2011), 11.

(The calculations are based on the U.S. Bureau of Labor
Statistics' Consumer Expenditure Survey and use 2008 dollars.
Adjusted to 2018 values, $75,000 in 2008 is equivalent in pur-
chasing power to $87,834.12 in 2018.) For further discussion,
see Miles Corak, "Income Inequality, Equality of Opportunity,
and Intergenerational Mobility," *Journal of Economic Perspectives* 27, no. 3 (Summer 2013): 79–102; Miller, "Class Differences in Child-Rearing"; and Pew Research Center, "Parenting
in America."

Ratios of expenditure also roughly tripled, from 3:1 in the
1970s to almost 8:1 today, so that rich parents' expenditures increased dramatically—by nearly $4,000 per child per year—
even as both poor and indeed middle-class parents' expenditures
remained effectively flat. See Carbone and Cahn, *Marriage
Markets*, 85–86. According to another study (again reporting
constant dollars), in 1972 the richest 10 percent of families spent
$2,832 per child, the middle tenth spent $1,143, and the bottom
spent $607. In 2006, the disparity grew substantially: $6,573
per child for the richest families, $1,421 for the middle tenth,
and $750 for bottom tenth. Sabino Kornrich and Frank Fursten-
berg, "Investing in Children: Changes in Parental Spending on
Children, 1972–2007," *Demography* 50, no. 1 (February 2013).
Hereafter cited as Kornrich and Furstenberg, "Investing in
Children."

130   **through the end of high school:** Abby Abrams, "Raising a Bal-
lerina Will Cost You $100,000," FiveThirtyEight, August 20,

2015, accessed November 18, 2018, https://fivethirtyeight.com /features/high-price-of-ballet-diversity-misty-copeland/.

130   **in lessons alone:** Though the prices of violin lessons vary, it is expected that for an experienced and well-qualified instructor, private lessons can cost around $100 per session. For a discussion of lesson costs, see "How Much Are Violin Lessons for Kids?" *Take Lessons,* January 25, 2015, https://takelessons.com/blog /violin-lesson-prices. Three half-hour lessons per week at $100 each amounts to $15,600 per year. This sum does not include other costs related to equipment, sheet music, and books.

130   **between the ages of six and ten:** Chris Taylor, "How Much Does It Cost to Raise a Child Prodigy?," Reuters, September 11, 2015, accessed November 18, 2018, http://time.com/money /4031222/child-prodigy-cost/.

130   **training their children:** Kornrich and Furstenberg, "Investing in Children."

130   **expenditure on education:** Mark Aguiar and Mark Bils, "Has Consumption Inequality Mirrored Income Inequality?," *American Economic Review* 105, no. 9 (September 2015): 2725–56, 2746, 2753. Hereafter cited as Aguiar and Bils, "Has Consumption Inequality Mirrored Income Inequality?" Aguiar and Bils study rising consumption inequality between 1980 and 2010 and report that over the course of these three decades, consumption inequality increased by a little more than 30 percent, a rise that roughly equaled the increase of income inequality over the same period. They also break down rising consumption inequality across categories of consumption and report that by 2008–10, education expenditures had become the single most income elastic expenditure category. These observations about consumption inequality benefited from discussions with Conor Clarke.

130   **produce higher-achieving students:** For a detailed discussion on the effects of better-equipped schools on education, see Jonathan Rothwell, "Housing Costs, Zoning, and Access to High -Scoring Schools," Brookings Institution, www.brookings.edu /research/housing-costs-zoning-and-access-to-high-scoring -schools/. Hereafter cited as Rothwell, "Housing Costs." Rothwell writes that "studies show important benefits from attending classes with higher scoring students and higher 'value-added' teachers. In addition to those factors, teacher experience is strongly related to student outcomes but experienced teachers are less likely to teach disadvantaged students. Furthermore, teacher experience is highly correlated with school test scores, even adjusting for other factors, and the average black, Hispanic, or low-income student attends a school with significantly less experienced teachers than white and Asian students." For causal effects of teacher quality on test scores for students in grades three through eight, see Raj Chetty, John N. Friedman, and Jonah E. Rockoff, "The Long-Term Impacts of Teachers: Teacher Value-Added and Student Outcomes in Adulthood," NBER Working Paper No. 17699 (issued December 2011, revised January 2012). For the effects of teacher quality and experience on standardized test scores in math and reading, see Jonah E. Rockoff, "The Impact of Individual Teachers on Student Achievement: Evidence from Panel Data," *American Economic Review* 94, no. 2 (May 2004): 247–52. Another study considered data from all North Carolina students and teachers over a ten-year period to demonstrate that teacher credentials have large effects on student achievement—particularly math achievement. Charles Clotfelter, Helen Ladd, and Jacob Vigdor, "How and Why Do Teacher Credentials Matter for Student Achievement?," Urban Institute National Center for Longitudinal Analysis of Education Research working paper no. 2 (2007).

130   **"better at what the test measures":** Jacobs, "The $600-an-Hour Private Tutor."

130   **retreat in reading and math:** Karl L. Alexander, Doris R. Entwisle, and Linda S. Olson, "Schools, Achievement, and Inequality: A Seasonal Perspective," *Educational Evaluation and Policy Analysis* 23, no. 2 (Summer 2001): 171, Table 2. Alexander, Entwisle, and Olson show summer gains on the CAT-V (Reading) and the CAT-V (Math) across four consecutive summers for high-SES students, while low-SES students experienced losses on both tests during the first two summers, small gains on the Reading test after the third summer, and small gains on both tests after the fourth summer. For a similar discussion, see

Alan B. Krueger, "Inequality, Too Much of a Good Thing," in *Inequality in America: What Role for Human Capital Policies?,* ed. Alan B. Kruger and Benjamin M. Friedman (Cambridge, MA: MIT Press, 2005), 1, 15, Table 2.

131   **for example, in Japan:** Raghuram G. Rajan, *Fault Lines: How Hidden Fractures Still Threaten the World Economy* (Princeton, NJ: Princeton University Press, 2010), 188. Hereafter cited as Rajan, *Fault Lines.* James J. Shields, *Japanese Schooling: Patterns of Socialization, Equality, and Political Control* (University Park: Pennsylvania State University Press, 1989), 82. For a sample calculation, see "Mathematics Teaching and Learning Strategies in PISA," OECD (2010), Table A.1. The 75th percentile of number of weeks of instruction in Japan is 43; multiplied by 5 days of instruction per week, that is roughly 215 days of instruction per year.

131   **do no such activities at all:** Putnam, *Our Kids: The American Dream in Crisis,* 175.

131   **adds the most value to her human capital:** One study found, "Low-income students perform better when their non-low -income schoolmates perform better. Low-income students who attend schools with the lowest-scoring middle/high-income students score 18.5 percentage points below the state average for their subject/grade, but those who attend schools with top -scoring middle/high-income peers score 2 percentage points above state averages. Further regression analysis finds that the proficiency rates of low-income students increase by 0.7 percentage points for every 1 percentage point increase in the proficiency rates of middle/high-income students in the same school, controlling for factors such as the school's racial diversity, enrollment, share of low-income students, pupil-teacher ratio, and location." Rothwell, "Housing Costs," 10.

131   **four grade levels ahead of those from poor ones:** Reardon, "The Widening Academic Achievement Gap," 94–97.

131   **three grade levels:** Reardon, "The Widening Academic Achievement Gap," 97–99; Reardon, "No Rich Child Left Behind."

131   **International comparisons:** Achievement in this comparison is measured by scores on the Programme for International Student Assessment (PISA) tests of academic skills. For an analysis of this data, see Reich, "Back to School."

131   **between the middle class and the poor:** The studies are rendered comparable in spite of measuring achievement on different scales by adjusting scores for the reliability of the tests and then expressing test score gaps in terms of standard deviations. This is, as Reardon says, "standard practice when comparing achievement gaps measured with different tests [citations omitted]. So long as the true variance of achievement remains constant over time, this allows valid comparisons in the size of the gaps across different studies using different tests." Reardon, "The Widening Academic Achievement Gap," 94. The basic result that 90/50 achievement gaps have been rising even as 50/10 gaps have fallen roughly steady—and in some cases even fallen— reappears across a range of estimation techniques. See Reardon, "The Widening Academic Achievement Gap," Online Appendix 5.A2, www.russellsage.org/sites/default/files/duncan _murnane_online_appendix.pdf.

132   **The income/achievement gaps on the SAT:** For a visualization of these data, see Zachary Goldfarb, "These Four Charts Show the SAT Favors Rich, Educated Families," *Washington Post,* March 5, 2014, accessed November 18, 2018, www.washington post.com/blogs/wonkblog/wp/2014/03/05/these-four-charts -show-how-the-sat-favors-the-rich-educated-families/. Hereafter cited as Goldfarb, "These Four Charts Show the SAT Favors Rich, Educated Families." See also Anthony P. Carnevale and Jeff Strohl, "How Increasing College Access Is Increasing Inequality, and What to Do About It," in *Rewarding Strivers: Helping Low-Income Students Succeed in College,* ed. Richard D. Kahlenberg (New York: Century Foundation Press, 2010). Hereafter cited as Carnevale and Strohl, "How Increasing College Access Is Increasing Inequality." The charts are constructed from the College Board's own data, located at "2013 College -Bound Seniors: Total Group Profile Report," College Board, http://media.collegeboard.com/digitalServices/pdf/research /2013/TotalGroup-2013.pdf.

        For the income percentiles, see Carmen DeNavas-Walt and Bernadette D. Proctor, *Income and Poverty in the United*

*States: 2013*, U.S. Census Bureau, Current Population Reports no. P60-249 (September 2014), 23, Table A-1, www2.census .gov/library/publications/2014/demographics/p60-249.pdf, and "Historical Income Tables: Households," U.S. Census Bureau, last revised August 28, 2018, Table H-1, www.census.gov /data/tables/time-series/demo/income-poverty/historical -income-households.html. For the education percentiles, see Camille L. Ryan and Julie Siebens, *Educational Attainment in the United States: 2009*, U.S. Census Bureau, Current Population Reports no. P60-566 (February 2012), 6, Table 1, accessed December 30, 2018, www.census.gov/prod/2012pubs/p20-566 .pdf.

132 **In each case, these gaps:** These are rough fractions only because eliteness combines parents' incomes and educations and because the College Board reports percentiles only for each section of the test and not for overall scores. To arrive at the top and bottom quarter claim, take mean scores for income and educational achievement in the highest and lowest categories that the College Board reports and calculate percentiles for each section of the test, and then average these percentiles.

132 **As recently as the late 1990s:** The College Board began reporting SAT scores specifically for students from narrowly elite households—with incomes exceeding $200,000—only in 2008, making precise comparisons between present-day and past data difficult. But rougher income categories remain revealing, and as recently as 1996 the gap between the SAT scores of children from households whose income exceeded $100,000 and the scores of children from households whose income fell between $40,000 and $60,000 was 104 points while the score gap between the middle-class children and children from households whose incomes were less than $20,000 was 121 points. These numbers are calculated using the College Board's Total Group Profile Reports, which list scores by family income for each year between 1996 and 2016. They 2016 gaps exclude the scores on the writing section, which was not included in the 1996 test, in order to render scores comparable across the two years. "1996 College-Bound Seniors: A Profile of SAT Program Test Takers," College Board, https://research.collegeboard.org/programs /sat/data/archived/cb-seniors-1996; "2016 College-Bound Seniors: Total Group Profile Report," College Board, https://se cure-media.collegeboard.org/digitalServices/pdf/sat /total-group-2016.pdf. For a visualization of similar data from 2011, see Pink, "How to Predict."

132 **fully 250 points less than rich students:** Goldfarb, "These Four Charts Show the SAT Favors Rich, Educated Families"; "2013 College-Bound Seniors: Total Group Profile Report." The middle-class students come from households with annual incomes between $40,000 and $60,000, the poor students from households with annual incomes below $20,000, and the rich students from households with annual incomes above $200,000.

Defining the rich, the middle-class, and the poor according to the categories used in the 1996 data, the 2016 gap between the rich and the middle class had grown to 116 points and the gap between middle-class and poor children had fallen to 95 points. The relationship between the rich/middle-class and the middle-class/poor gaps therefore reversed over the two decades.

132 **whose parents have completed graduate school:** Goldfarb, "These Four Charts Show the SAT Favors Rich, Educated Families"; "2013 College-Bound Seniors: Total Group Profile Report." See also Carnevale and Strohl, "How Increasing College Access Is Increasing Inequality."

133 **a parent with a graduate degree:** Murray, *Coming Apart*, 67. The data Murray reports are otherwise unpublished, though provided to him by the College Board. Children from households in the broader elite are similarly overrepresented among the larger class of high-achieving (but not exceptionally so) high school graduate. According to one recent study, households from the top quarter of the income distribution account for twice the share of high school graduates with SAT scores in the 90th percentile or higher and A-minus GPAs as households in the bottom quarter of the distribution, and nearly one and a half times the share of these high-achieving graduates as households in the middle two quarters. Caroline M. Hoxby and Christopher Avery, "The Missing 'One-Offs': The Hidden Supply of High-Achieving, Low Income Students," NBER Working Paper

No. 18586 (2012), www.nber.org/papers/w18586.pdf. Hereafter cited as Hoxby and Avery, "The Missing 'One-Offs.'"

The College Board has established its own benchmark for college readiness, by determining the lowest SAT score associated with a 65 percent or greater chance of earning a B-minus average or higher in the first year of college. Using this benchmark, the College Board determined that just 15 percent of students whose parents had less than a high school education and 27 percent of students whose parents had a high school education met the benchmark, compared with 33 percent of students whose parents held an associated degree, 52 percent of students whose parents had a bachelor's degree, and 68 percent of students whose parents held a graduate degree. Jeffrey Wyatt et al., *SAT Benchmarks: Development of a College Readiness Benchmark and Its Relationship to Secondary and Postsecondary School Performance*, College Board (2011), 22, Table 6, https://files. eric.ed.gov/fulltext/ED521173.pdf.

133 **97 percent of its graduates to college:** For income in Scarsdale, see "QuickFacts, Scarsdale Village, New York," U.S. Census Bureau, www.census.gov/quickfacts/table/RHI105210/3665431. For college attendance rate, see "Scarsdale High School, 2015–2016 Profile," Scarsdale Schools, www.scarsdaleschools.k12.ny .us/cms/lib/NY01001205/Centricity/Domain/89/2016%20 -%202017%20Profile.pdf.

Nor is Scarsdale High exceptional among rich schools. To pick another example, River High School in Clarksville, Maryland (median annual household income $120,000), sends 98 percent of its graduates to college. For a discussion of Clarksville's education statistics, see Ted Mellnik and Carol Morello, "Washington: A World Apart," *Washington Post*, November 9, 2013, accessed November 18, 2018, www.washingtonpost.com /sf/local/2013/11/09/washington-a-world-apart/. Hereafter cited as Mellnik and Morello, "Washington: A World Apart." For data on River High School, see "River High School: Profile," Howard County Public School System, 2017–2018, www.hcpss .org/f/schools/profiles/prof_hs_riverhill.pdf. The examples may be further multiplied. Weston High School in Connecticut, with median household income of $218,152, sends over 95 percent of its graduates to college. "Weston High School: 2016 Profile for College Applications," Weston Public Schools, www .westonps.org/uploaded/Color_print_-_WHS_2016_Profile .pdf; "QuickFacts: Weston town, Fairfield County, Connecticut," U.S. Census Bureau, 2016, www.census.gov/quickfacts /table/PST045216/0900183430,00. Darien High School, also in Connecticut, with median household income over $200,000, again sends roughly 95 percent of its graduates to college. "Darien High School: 2018–2019 Profile," Darien Public Schools, www.darienps.org/uploaded/content/schools/dhs /guidance/Profile_2018-19.pdf?1537444361189; "QuickFacts: Darien town, Fairfield County, Connecticut," U.S. Census Bureau, 2016, www.census.gov/quickfacts/table/PST045216/09 00118850,0900183430,00.

133 **The top twenty private high schools:** Raquel Laneri, "America's Best Prep Schools," *Forbes*, April 29, 2010, accessed November 18, 2018, www.forbes.com/2010/04/29/best-prep-schools -2010-opinions-private-education.html#4760df66 5027.

133 **These schools send:** Fieldston's class of 2013, for example, sent 40 (out of 150) graduates to the Ivy League alone and 104 (or 69 percent) to universities of colleges ranked in the top twenty-five in their categories by *U.S. News & World Report*. See www.ecfs .org/admissions/college-destination/index.aspx. Fieldston's class of 2014 sent 28 (out of 150) graduates to the Ivy League alone and roughly 100 to universities or colleges ranked in the top twenty-five in their categories by *U.S. News & World Report*. Ethical Cultural Fieldston School, "Build NYC Resource Corporation," Statement, April 30, 2015, www.nycedc.com/sites /default/files/filemanager/Official_Statements/Ethical_Cul ture_Fieldston_School_Project_Series_2015.pdf. Graduates of St. Paul's School are more likely to attend Harvard than any other college, and 80 percent attend a college ranked among the top thirty by *U.S. News & World Report*. Austin Bramwell, "Top of the Class," *American Conservative*, March 13, 2012, accessed November 18, 2018, www.theamericanconservative.com/arti cles/top-of-the-class/.

For further discussion, see David Chung, "Top High Schools Find Admissions Success," *Brown Daily Herald*, April 27 2011, accessed November 18, 2018, www.browndailyherald.com/2011/04/27/top-high-schools-find-admissions-success/. Chung reports that Harvard-Westlake School and Phillips Academy each sent more than 45 graduates to Brown from 2006 to 2010; the "Collegiate School in New York City has sent 39.6 percent of its graduates in the past five years to universities falling under the "Ivy Plus" umbrella—the eight Ivy League universities, as well as Stanford University and the Massachusetts Institute of Technology"; and Trinity School in Manhattan matriculated 37.3 percent to "Ivy Plus" universities between 2006 and 2010.

133 **Colleges overall are not:** Caroline M. Hoxby, "The Changing Selectivity of American Colleges," *Journal of Economic Perspectives* 23, no. 4 (Fall 2009). Hereafter cited as Hoxby, "Changing Selectivity."

134 **two generations ago:** See admissions rates reported in Chapter 2.

134 **at these elite colleges:** The *Harvard Crimson* notes that "one out of every 20 Harvard Freshmen attended one of the seven high schools most represented in the class of 2017—Boston Latin, Phillips Academy Andover, Stuyvesant High School, Nobel and Greenough School, Phillips Exeter Academy, Trinity School in New York City, and Lexington High School." More generally, 6 percent of students came from the ten most represented schools and 32 percent of students came from the 11 percent most represented schools. Meg P. Bernhard, "The Making of a Harvard Feeder School," *Harvard Crimson*, December 13, 2013, www.thecrimson.com/article/2013/12/13/making-harvard-feeder-schools/.

134 **the most prestigious colleges in the country:** At Yale, for example, 44 percent of students come from formally private high schools and hence from families with the incomes needed to support private schooling, Oriana Tang, "The Practical Path: Socioeconomic Class and Academics at Yale," *Yale Daily News*, April 29, 2016, https://yaledailynews.com/blog/2016/04/29/the-practical-path-socioeconomic-class-and-academics-at-yale/. Moreover, in a typical recent year, 197 high schools provided Yale with one-third of its class. Email communication from Yale Office of Admissions, on file with author.

134 **to 32 percent in 2011:** Suzanne Mettler, *Degrees of Inequality: How the Politics of Higher Education Sabotaged the American Dream* (New York: Basic Books, 2014), 21. For top-quartile families, in 1970, 40 percent of twenty-four-year-olds had college degrees; by 2011 that number was 71 percent. For bottom-quartile families, the shares went up much less, from 6 percent to 10 percent. Another similar visualization and discussion of this data can be found in Pell Institute for the Study of Opportunity in Higher Education, *Indicators of Higher Education Equity in the United States: 2018 Historical Trend Report* (2018), 99, http://pellinstitute.org/downloads/publications-Indicators_of_Higher_Education_Equity_in_the_US_2018_Trend_Report.pdf, and in Catherine Rampell, "Data Reveal a Rise in College Degrees Among Americans," *New York Times*, June 12, 2013, www.nytimes.com/2013/06/13/education/a-sharp-rise-in-americans-with-college-degrees.html.

134 **between 1980 and 2010:** Martha J. Bailey and Susan M. Dynarski, "Gains and Gaps: Changing Inequality in U.S. College Entry and Completion," NBER Working Paper No. 17633 (2011), 7, www.nber.org/papers/w17633.pdf.

134 **all the way up the income distribution:** Raj Chetty et al., "Is the United States Still a Land of Opportunity? Recent Trends in Intergenerational Mobility," *American Economic Review Papers and Proceedings* 104, no. 5 (2014): 141–47.

134 **The effect of parental income:** The most dramatic difference is reported by Suzanne Mettler, who claims that whereas in 1970, just 55 percent of enrolled students from the top income quartile completed their degrees by age twenty-four, fully 97 percent get BAs by age twenty-four today and adds, by contrast, that the completion rates for students from the next three quartiles—who generally come to college less well prepared, enjoy less family support while in college, and attend colleges that provide students with less institutional support—remain much lower, at 51, 26, and 23 percent respectively. Mettler, *Degrees of Inequal-*

*ity*, 25. Pell Institute for the Study of Opportunity in Higher Education, *Indicators of Higher Education Equity in the United States: 45 Year Trend Report* (2015), 33, https://files.eric.ed.gov/fulltext/ED555865.pdf, data showed that in 2015 the completion rates by income quartile (from top to bottom) are 99, 51, 29, and 21 percent respectively.

The fact that universities integrate and organize their training into a BA degree—which renders *completing* college distinctively more valuable than taking some classes and then dropping out—increases the cost of dropping out and further exacerbates the contribution that universities make to educational inequality. According to the Bureau of Labor Statistics, the income boost that a completed BA gives relative to having had "some college" education is 14.5 times the income boost that "some college" gives relative to having a high school education only. "Unemployment Rates and Earnings by Educational Attainment, 2017," Bureau of Labor Statistics, last modified March, 27, 2018, www.bls.gov/emp/chart-unemployment-earnings-education.htm.

135 **Taken together, these effects:** Pell Institute for the Study of Opportunity in Higher Education, *Indicators of Higher Education Equity in the United States: 2018 Historical Trend Report* (2018), 99. http://pellinstitute.org/downloads/publications-Indicators_of_Higher_Education_Equity_in_the_US_2018_Historical_Trend_Report.pdf.

135 **nearly double what it was in 1970:** In "Tearing Down the Gates: Confronting the Class Divide in American Education," *Liberal Education* 95, no. 3 (Summer 2009), Peter Sacks cites a paper published online in 2008 by Thomas G. Mortenson, in no. 143 of his newsletter *Postsecondary Education Opportunity*, which is no longer available. The article reports that in 1970, 40 percent of high school graduates from the top quartile received a BA by age twenty-four, compared to an average of about 13 percent from the middle two quartiles. By 2002, the share from the top quartile had risen to 51 percent, while the average share from the middle two quartiles had risen to about 20 percent. For further discussion, see Florencia Torche, "Is a College Degree Still the Great Equalizer? Intergeneration Mobility Across Levels of Schooling in the United States," *American Journal of Sociology* 117, no. 3 (2011): 763–807.

135 **approaches the 80th percentile:** Raj Chetty et al., "Where Is the Land of Opportunity? The Geography of Intergenerational Mobility in the United States," *Quarterly Journal of Economics* 129, no. 4 (2014): 1584.

135 **highly selective colleges:** Sean F. Reardon, Rachel Baker, and Daniel Klasik, *Race, Income, and Enrollment Patterns in Highly Selective Colleges: 1982–2004*, Center for Education and Policy Analysis (Stanford, CA: Stanford University, 2012), 8, Figure 3; Reardon, "No Rich Child Left Behind."

136 **from the bottom quarter:** These shares are for students entering college born in the years from 1979 to 1982. Martha J. Bailey and Susan M. Dynarski, "Inequality in Postsecondary Education," in *Whither Opportunity? Rising Inequality, Schools, and Children's Life Chances*, ed. Greg J. Duncan and Richard J. Murnane (New York: Russell Sage Foundation, 2011), 120, Figure 6.2.

Also available at www.russellsage.org/sites/default/files/Duncan_Murnane_Tables_Figures.pdf. Bailey and Dynarski report that among this birth cohort 80 percent of people from households in the top quarter, about 54 percent from the middle half, and 29 percent from the bottom quarter enroll in college. The shares of enrollees reported in the main text are computed using these numbers.

136 **meritocracy's early, democratic years:** The shares of people in the 1961 to 1964 birth cohorts to enroll in college, by household income quartile, were 58 percent, 38 percent, 32 percent, and 19 percent. Bailey and Dynarski, "Inequality in Postsecondary Education," 121. This means that for the later birth cohort, the top/bottom-quartile gap in college enrollment rates was 51 percent while for the earlier birth cohort it was just 39 percent.

136 **The shares of all bachelor's degrees:** Karin Fischer, "Engine of Inequality," *Chronicle of Higher Education*, January 17, 2017, https://studentsuccess.unc.edu/files/2016/01/Engine-of-Inequality-The-Chronicle-of-Higher-Education.pdf.

136 **At the roughly 150 most competitive:** For the fourteen-to-one number, see Carnevale and Strohl, "How Increasing College Access Is Increasing Inequality," 137, Figure 3.7.

For the twenty-four-to-one number, see Jennifer Giancola and Richard D. Kahlenberg, *True Merit: Ensuring Our Brightest Students Have Access to Our Best Colleges and Universities* (Lansdowne, VA: Jack Kent Cooke Foundation, 2016), 5, Figure 1, www.jkcf.org/assets/1/7/JKCF_True_Merit_Report.pdf.

These ratios are not outliers but rather typical. Another study of students (in 2004) at the most selective 5 percent of colleges finds 69 percent from the top quartile of the income distribution, 18.7 percent from the second, 8.1 percent from the third, and 4.1 percent from the fourth. For the next most selective 7 percent of colleges, these shares were 66.2 percent, 19.5 percent, 9.3 percent, and 5.0 percent, from the top to bottom quartiles. By contrast, at noncompetitive four-year colleges (which accounted for the bottom 7 percent in selectivity), the shares were 25.9 percent, 29.1 percent, 25.4 percent, and 19.6 percent. Finally, the shares of college-aged young adults to receive no postsecondary education, by household income quartile, were 7.7 percent, 19.1 percent, 31.2 percent, and 42 percent. Michael N. Bastedo and Ozan Jaquette, "Running in Place: Low Income Students and the Dynamics of Higher Education Stratification," *Educational Evaluation and Policy Analysis* 33, no. 3 (September 2011): Appendix, Table 6, www.personal.umich.edu/~bastedo/papers/EEPA-Appendix.pdf. Hereafter cited as Bastedo and Jaquette, "Running in Place."

Finally, Charles Murray, citing Joseph Soares, similarly reports that in the 1990s, 79 percent of students at "tier one" colleges came from the top quartile of the socioeconomic distribution and only 2 percent came from the bottom quartile. Murray, *Coming Apart*, 59; Joseph Soares, *The Power of Privilege: Yale and America's Elite Colleges* (Stanford, CA: Stanford University Press, 2007), 4, Table 1.1.

136 **most elite institutions:** It is worth noting that the exclusion has become more dramatic over recent decades: the share of Pell Grant recipients among the student bodies at both public and private four-year colleges fell by about a third between the early 1970s and the early 2000s. Bishop, *The Big Sort*, 31. Bishop cites U.S. Department of Education, National Center for Education Statistics, Thomas D. Snyder (Project Director), Alexandra G. Tan, and Charlene M. Hoffman, *Digest of Education Statistics 2003*, December 2004 (1999–2000 data), 379, Table 325, http://nces.ed.gov/pubs2005/2005025.pdf. The level has remained roughly steady between 2001 and the present. Giancola and Kahlenberg, *True Merit*, 6, Figure 2.

136 **between eight and four to one:** Carnevale and Strohl, "How Increasing College Access Is Increasing Inequality," 137, Figure 3.7.

136 **At elite colleges:** These patterns are no less striking when viewed from the perspective of children hoping to get to college. Students from rich families are three times more likely to attend highly competitive colleges than middle-class students and nearly eight times more likely than poor students. Bailey and Dynarski, "Inequality in Postsecondary Education," 120, Figure 6.2; Reardon, "No Rich Child Left Behind."

137 **the early 2000s:** Alexander W. Astin and Leticia Oseguera, "The Declining 'Equity' of American Higher Education," *Review of Higher Education* 27, no. 3 (Spring 2004): 329–30, Figure 1. In 1985, the top quartile of the income distribution filled 46 percent of the places at elite colleges (defined as the top tenth of all colleges), for an overrepresentation of 84 percent. In 2000, the top quartile filled 55 percent of the places, for an overrepresentation of 120 percent. Another study reports that the gap between the shares of rich and poor Americans to earn a BA grew by nearly half between the early 1980s and the early 2000s. See Martha J. Bailey and Susan M. Dynarski, "Gains and Gaps: Changing Inequality in U.S. College Entry and Completion," NBER Working Paper No. 17633 (December 2011), 26, Figure 3, www.nber.org/papers/w17633.pdf. For the 1961–64 birth cohort, the top quartile of the income distribution had a 36 percent college completion rate by age twenty-four and the bottom quartile had a 5 percent college completion rate, for a difference of 31 percentage points. For the 1979–82 birth cohort, the top quartile of the income distribution had a 54 percent college completion rate and the bottom quartile had a 9 percent college completion rate, for a difference of 45 percentage points.

137 **hourly workers, teachers, clergy, farmers, and soldiers combined:** David Leonhardt, "Top Colleges That Enroll Rich, Middle Class and Poor," *New York Times*, September 8, 2014, https://www.nytimes.com/2014/09/09/upshot/top-colleges-that-enroll-rich-middle-class-and-poor.html; David Leonhardt, "As Wealthy Fill Top Colleges, Concerns Grow over Fairness," *New York Times*, April 22, 2014, www.nytimes.com/2004/04/22/us/as-wealthy-fill-top-colleges-concerns-grow-over-fairness.html.

137 **a ratio of about three and a half to one:** David Freed and Idrees Kahloon, "Class of 2019 by the Numbers: Makeup of the Class," *Harvard Crimson*, http://features.thecrimson.com/2015/freshman-survey/; Laya Anasu and Michael D. Ledecky, "Freshman Survey Part II: An Uncommon App," *Harvard Crimson*, September 4, 2013, www.thecrimson.com/article/2013/9/4/freshman-survey-admissions-aid/; Stephanie Addenbrooke and Emma Platoff, "2019 by the Numbers: First Impressions," *Yale Daily News*, http://features.yaledailynews.com/blog/2015/08/28/2019-by-the-numbers-first-impressions/.

The Harvard survey data suggest that 53 percent of students entering into the class of 2017 had parents making more than $125,000 per year (just above the lower limit for the top quintile). Those from families making more than $250,000 per year (roughly the top 5 percent of income earners in the country) made up 29 percent. Those from families making less than $40,000 per year (roughly the bottom two quintiles) represented just 15 percent of the students.

The Yale survey data suggest that students from families in the top quintile (over $125,000) represented 56 percent of the class, while those from the bottom two quintiles (less than $40,000) represented 14 percent. Students from families in the top 5 percent of income earners (over $250,000) represented 35 percent of the class. The mismatch between the categories in the surveys and income quintiles requires some interpolation, which explains the "about" in the main text. Finally, both surveys rely on self-reporting and thus undoubtedly reflect both selection biases and student errors about parental incomes. But the patterns that they report are so stark that they are revelatory nevertheless.

137 **the entire bottom half:** See Raj Chetty et al., "Mobility Report Cards: The Role of Colleges in Intergenerational Mobility," NBER Working Paper No. 23618 (July 2017), 1, 14, Figure 1, www.nber.org/papers/w23618; Gregor Aisch et al., "Some Colleges Have More Students from the Top One Percent Than the Bottom 60," *New York Times*, January 18, 2017, www.nytimes.com/interactive/2017/01/18/upshot/some-colleges-have-more-students-from-the-top-1-percent-than-the-bottom-60.html. See also David Freed and Idrees Kahloon, "Class of 2019 by the Numbers: Makeup of the Class," *Harvard Crimson*, http://features.thecrimson.com/2015/freshman-survey/; Stephanie Addenbrooke and Emma Platoff, "2019 by the Numbers: First Impressions," *Yale Daily News*, http://features.yaledailynews.com/blog/2015/08/28/2019-by-the-numbers-first-impressions/.

Other studies produce compatible results, reporting, for example, that Harvard and Princeton Colleges admit perhaps twenty-five rich students for each poor one. Elizabeth Stoker and Matthew Bruenig, "The 1 Percent's Ivy League Loophole," *Salon*, September 9, 2013. To be sure, some elite colleges do better at enrolling students from poor families than others. Thus at Berkeley and UCLA, 34 and 36 percent of students get Pell Grants (this is roughly the same as the national average across all schools), whereas at Michigan, only 16 percent do. See Richard Pérez-Peña, "Income-Based Diversity Lags at Some Universities," *New York Times*, May 30, 2013 accessed November 20, 2018, www.nytimes.com/2013/05/31/education/college-slots-for-poorer-students-still-limited.html?pagewanted=all.

137 **substantially greater economic diversity than Harvard and Yale:** According to one study, children from the top quarter of the socioeconomic distribution in the United States fill 79 percent of Yale's slots; to fill 79 percent of Oxford's slots requires expanding to the top 40 percent of the United Kingdom's socioeconomic distribution. Joseph A. Soares, *The Power of Privilege: Yale and America's Elite Colleges* (Stanford, CA: Stanford University Press, 2007), 14. Oxford has established a scholarship fund expressly and exclusively for undergraduates from lower-income families. See Chris Cook, "Oxford Sets Up £300

Million Scholarship Fund," *Financial Times*, July 11, 2012, www.ft.com/cms/s/0/c5c7835e-cb55-11e1-916f-00144 feabdc0.html#axzz4G63MSRuk. Similarly, following transformations in admissions practices in the 1960s, Oxford has had four times Harvard's share of students from blue-collar families. See Joseph A. Soares, *The Decline of Privilege: The Modernization of Oxford University* (Stanford, CA: Stanford University Press, 1999), 4, Table 1.1.

137 **from an elite college:** This state of affairs, in which rich parents are an effectively necessary condition for acquiring an elite education without being in any way a sufficient condition, follows directly from the basic combinatorics of social stratification.

A thought experiment illustrates this logic. Suppose a society maintains a steady overall size, with 10,000 people in each generation, who all marry and stay married, with each of the 5,000 households constructed in this way including two children. If just under one-third of each generation graduates college, there will be about 3,000 places in the society's colleges, and about 30 places in the most competitive 1 percent of the society's colleges. Now imagine that just under one-sixth of the children from households in the top 1 percent by income graduate from the most competitive 1 percent of colleges and universities. The richest 1 percent of households, in this society, collectively include 100 children, so one-sixth of these children —or roughly 15 students—take up half the places at the most competitive 1 percent of colleges. The remaining half of the places—that is, 15 places—would be distributed among the 9,900 students raised in households from the remaining 99 percent of the income distribution. These non-one-percenter students would have only a fraction of a percent chance of making it to the most competitive colleges. And having elite parents would thus be an effectively necessary condition for getting an elite BA without being anywhere near a sufficient condition.

Something like this combinatoric pattern applies in the United States today.

138 **total educational expenditures in the United States:** The United States spends $336 billion annually on public universities, compared to $668 billion annually on public K–12 schools, and 336/(336 + 668) = 0.334. See National Center for Education Statistics, "Fast Facts: How Much Do Colleges and Universities Spend on Students?," https://nces.ed.gov/fastfacts /display.asp?id=75, and Center for Education Statistics, "Fast Facts: How Much Money Does the United States Spend on Public Elementary and Secondary Schools?," http://nces.ed.gov /fastfacts/display.asp?id=66.

The shares of total (public and private) expenditures devoted to postsecondary education were 39.8 percent in 1996–97, 39.7 percent in 2008, and 43.75 percent in 2012. Thomas D. Snyder, Charlene M. Hoffman, and Claire M. Geddes, *Digest of Education Statistics 1997*, U.S. Department of Education, National Center for Education Statistics (December 1997), 35, Table 32, www.finaid.org/educators/educstat.pdf; Susan Aud et al., *The Condition of Education 2012*, U.S. Department of Education, National Center for Education Statistics (May 2012), 200, Table A-22-1, https://nces.ed.gov/pubs2012/2012 045.pdf; Grace Kena et al., *The Condition of Education 2016*, U.S. Department of Education, National Center for Education Statistics (May 2016), 141, Figure 3, https://nces.ed.gov/pubs 2016/2016144.pdf.

138 **in 1970:** National Center for Education Statistics, "Expenditures of Educational Institutions Related to the Gross Domestic Product, by Level of Institution: Selected Years, 1929–30 through 2014–15," Table 106.10, https://nces.ed.gov/pro grams/digest/d15/tables/dt15_106.10.asp?referrer=report. In 1970, the amount expended for all degree-granting postsecondary institutions was $23 billion in current dollars, which is $142 billion when adjusted to constant dollars based on the 2014 CPI. The table cites the following sources: U.S. Department of Education, National Center for Education Statistics, *Biennial Survey of Education in the United States*, 1929–30 through 1949–50; *Statistics of State School Systems*, 1959–60 through 1969–70; *Revenues and Expenditures for Public Elementary and Secondary Education*, 1970–71 through 1986–87; Common Core of Data (CCD), "National Public Education Financial Survey," 1987–88 through 2012–13; Higher Education General Information Survey (HEGIS), *Financial Statistics*

*of Institutions of Higher Education*, 1965–66 through 1985–86; Integrated Postsecondary Education Data System (IPEDS), "Finance Survey" (IPEDS-F:FY87–99); and IPEDS Spring 2001 through Spring 2015, Finance component. U.S. Department of Commerce, Bureau of Economic Analysis, National Income and Product Accounts Tables, retrieved January 29, 2016, from http://www.bea.gov/iTable/index_nipa.cfm. All figures in current dollars. Table prepared January 2016.

138 **investment in nonresidential physical capital:** See George E. Johnson, "Investment in and Returns from Education," in *The Level and Composition of Household Saving*, ed. Patric H. Hendershott (Cambridge, MA: Ballinger, 1985). See also Langbein, "Twentieth-Century Revolution," 732.

138 **the entire nation's 1840 investment in education:** Yale's fiscal year 2018 budget was $3.765 billion. See Yale University Office of the Provost, "Data at a Glance," https://provost.yale.edu /budget/data-glance. Total investments in education in the United States in 1840 were $9.2 million (roughly $250 million in 2015 dollars). See Albert Fishlow, "Levels of Nineteenth-Century American Investment in Education," *Journal of Economic History* 26 (1966): 418, 420. See also Langbein, "Twentieth-Century Revolution," 730.

138 **on postsecondary education:** See Grace Kena et al., *The Condition of Education 2016*, U.S. Department of Education, National Center for Education Statistics (May 2016), 141, Figure 3, https://nces.ed.gov/pubs2016/2016144.pdf. "Direct expenditures on education as a percentage of gross domestic product (GDP) for Organization for Economic Cooperation and Development (OECD) countries with the highest percentages, by level of education: 2012," at p. 141, https://nces.ed.gov/pubs 2016/2016144.pdf

138 **more rapidly than enrollments since 1970:** Expenditures (in constant 2009–10 dollars) were $461 billion in 2010, compared to $120.7 billion in 1970, which yields a growth factor of 3.8 over forty years. Enrollments were 8,581,000 in 1970, compared to 20,583,000, which yields a growth factor of 2.4. U.S. Census Bureau, "Section 4: Education," Statistical Abstract of the United States no. 131, 2012, www.census.gov/library/publica tions/2011/compendia/statab/131ed/education.html (see files 219, "School Enrollment," and 220, "School Expenditure by Type of Control and Level of Instruction in Constant (2008–2009) Dollars"). (Note that the constant dollars referred to in the file name and within the file itself are different.) Similarly, the National Center for Education Statistics reports that total postsecondary enrollment was 20,453,000 in 2007 and 8,005,000 in 1969, for a ratio of 2.56. See *Digest of Education Statistics 2017*, U.S. Department of Education, National Center for Education Statistics (2017), Table 105.30, https://nces.ed .gov/programs/digest/d17/tables/dt17_105.30.asp.

138 **increased by nearly 60 percent:** 3.8 ÷ 2.4 = 1.58.

138 **between just 2001 and 2015:** Median fall enrollments at Ivy League universities grew from 12,230 in 2001 to 13,702 in 2015, a 12.04 percent increase, while median expenditures grew from $944,755,880 to $1,904,823,037 (in constant 2015 dollars), an increase of 101.62 percent. See U.S. Department of Education, National Center for Education Statistics, "Use the Data," https://nces.ed.gov/ipeds/Home/UseTheData. Real dollars calculated using BLS CPI GDP Deflator. "The CPI inflation calculator uses the Consumer Price Index for All Urban Consumers (CPI-U) U.S. city average series for all items, not seasonally adjusted. These data represent changes in the prices of all goods and services purchased for consumption by urban households." "CPI Inflation Calculator," https://data.bls.gov /cgi-bin/cpicalc.pl/.

138 **at the least selective ones:** Hoxby, "Changing Selectivity," Figure 2. Hoxby develops comparable numbers across time by ranking schools according to their selectivity in 1962. Since the identities of the very most selective schools, in particular, have not changed over the past fifty years, this technique captures the changing effects of selectivity and not just spending by contingently chosen named schools. See also Highlights from *Rewarding Strivers*, ed. Richard Kahlenberg (New York and Washington, DC: Century Foundation Press, 2010), 4, accessed November 18, 2018, http://www.tcf.org/assets/downloads/tcf _rewarding.pdf. Hereafter cited as Highlights from *Rewarding Strivers*.

The difference in per-student spending between competitive colleges and noncompetitive colleges partly reflects the fact that the increasingly rich students at competitive colleges demand increasingly luxurious living conditions. The former president of Macalester College—an elite, competitive liberal arts college—observes that in order to succeed as a college president, "you have to recruit some affluent students, and part of the way you recruit affluent students is by having symbols of excellence, like an up-to-date campus center and up-to-date athletic facilities. . . . It's a visible demonstration that you're not about to go broke. . . . A few years ago we started investing in athletic facilities because we were being told by parents that the facilities weren't as good as the facilities in their high schools, and enterprises." Dylan Matthews, "The Tuition Is Too Damn High, Part VIII: Is This All Rich Kids' Fault?," *Washington Post*, September 4, 2013, accessed November 18, 2018, www.washington post.com/news/wonk/wp/2013/09/04/the-tuition-is-too -damn-high-part-viii-is-this-all-rich-kids-fault/.

Note, relatedly, that "auxiliary spending" accounted for 41.2 percent of total increased costs in public research universities between 2000 and 2010. Matthews, "The Tuition Is Too Damn High, Part VIII." For more on college spending per student and revenues, go to the Delta Cost Project, www.deltacost project.org/. For a list of data sources on colleges, see also Stacy Berg Dale and Alan B. Kreuger, "Estimating the Payoff to Attending a More Selective College: An Estimation of Selection on Observables and Unobservables," NBER Working Paper No. 7322 (August 1999).

138    **in the 1960s:** In 1966, for example, the most selective colleges spent about $18,000 per student, while the least selective spent about $4,000. See Hoxby, "Changing Selectivity," Figure 2. The expenditure gap, in other words, has grown by a factor of over five in the past half century, from about $14,000 to about $80,000, per student per year. Note that these numbers report constant 2007 dollars.

Other studies, which focus more narrowly on shorter time horizons, confirm this basic trend. According to the *Washington Post* series "The Tuition Is Too Damn High," private research universities spent $12,435 more per student in 2010 than in 2000, whereas public research universities increased spending by only $3,917. Dylan Matthews, "Introducing 'The Tuition Is Too Damn High,'" *Washington Post*, August 26, 2013, accessed November 18, 2018, www.washingtonpost.com/news/wonk/wp /2013/08/26/introducing-the-tuition-is-too-damn-high/?utm _term=.98a625a37dc1. Another study reports that between 1999 and 2009, educational resource expenditures remained flat at community colleges, grew by about $1,500 at public research universities, and grew by about $10,000 at private research universities. See David Leonhardt, "Though Enrolling More Poor Students, 2-Year Colleges Get Less of the Federal Pie," *New York Times*, May 22, 2013, accessed October 24, 2018, www.nytimes .com/2013/05/23/education/2-year-colleges-getting-a-falling -share-of-spending.html. See also Josh Freedman, "Why American Colleges Are Becoming a Force for Inequality," *Atlantic*, May 16, 2013, accessed October 2018, www.theatlantic.com /business/archive/2013/05/why-american-colleges-are-becom ing-a-force-for-inequality/275923/.

138    **who attend elite colleges:** Rising top incomes make it natural for rich parents to give their college-aged children greater financial support than poor parents, as they indeed do: a parent from the top income quartile is 205 percent more likely to give her child tuition support than a parent from the bottom quartile, and a college-educated parent is 277 percent more likely to provide tuition support than a parent without a college degree. The sums involved are large, moreover, with a top/bottom-quartile difference of over $16,000 annually. Patrick Wightman, Robert Schoeni, and Keith Robinson, "Familial Financial Assistance to Young Adults," National Poverty Center Working Paper Series 12-10 (May 2012), http://npc.umich.edu/publications/u/2012 -10%20NPC%20Working%20Paper.pdf. The gap was $13,326 in 2005 dollars, which is $16,185 in CPI-adjusted 2015 dollars.

138    **pay 78 cents on the dollar:** See Highlights from *Rewarding Strivers*, 4.

139    **ballooned to about $75,000:** See Hoxby, "Changing Selectivity," Figure 3.

This shift may be captured in another way also. Overall, the effective cost of college varies by increasingly less than the incomes of the families who pay it. At private colleges, the shift in effective costs from rich to poor students has been stark. Whereas poor students at private colleges paid 49.5 percent of what rich students paid in 1999–2000, in 2011–12 they paid 55.4 percent. Over those twelve years, the net cost of attendance rose by 32 percent for poor students but only 17.5 percent for rich students. See College Board, "Net Price by Income over Time: Private Sector" (last revised December 2013), https:// trends.collegeboard.org/college-pricing/figures-tables/net -prices-income-over-time-private-sector. Note that public colleges experienced a reversed shift: in 2007–8 poor students paid 55.7 percent of rich students' tuition; in 1992–93 they paid 67.1 percent.

139    **hence the name of the ceremony:** Phyllis Vine, "The Social Function of Eighteenth-Century Higher Education," *History of Education Quarterly* 16, no. 4 (1976): 417. As Vine describes, "Educators gradually invested commencement ceremonies with a symbolic significance that told students and the community that they were 'now about to step into life.' In addition to marking an important rite-de-passage for a select group of young men, the commencement ceremonies denoted, as Samuel Johnson told King's College students, that they would hence be 'called to act a more important part of life.'"

140    **including in the professions:** The first American law school was founded as a freestanding proprietary academy in Litchfield, Connecticut, in 1784. See "Litchfield Law School History," Litchfield Historical Society (2010), http://litchfield historicalsociety.org/ledger/studies/history_school. The first university law school, variously claimed to be at Harvard and William and Mary, was not founded until the turn of the nineteenth century. See Henry D. Gabriel, "America's Oldest Law School," *Journal of Legal Education* 39, no. 2 (1989): 269–74. The first American medical school, at the University of Pennsylvania, was founded in 1765. See www.archives.upenn.edu/histy /features/1700s/medsch.html. And the first business school, the Wharton School (again at Pennsylvania), was founded in 1881. See "About Wharton," The Wharton School, www.whar ton.upenn.edu/about/wharton-history.cfm.

140    **until the early twentieth century:** The shift to a graduate school model of professional education was partly motivated by a desire to keep immigrants and members of the lower classes out of the professions by increasing the cost (in both time and money) involved in acquiring a professional degree, so that only children of the elite could afford to pay. The graduate school model concentrates training in the elite not just by happenstance, but partly on purpose. Daniel Markovits, *A Modern Legal Ethics: Adversary Advocacy in a Democratic Age* (Princeton, NJ: Princeton University Press, 2011).

140    **had completed college:** Anthony J. Mayo, Nitin Nohria, and Laura G. Singleton, *Paths to Power: How Insiders and Outsiders Shaped American Business Leadership* (Boston: Harvard Business Review Press, 2007), x. Hereafter cited as Mayo, Nohria, and Singleton, *Paths to Power*.

140    **midcentury American firms:** For more on workplace training at midcentury, see John W. Kendrick, *The Formation and Stocks of Total Capital* (New York: Columbia University for NBER, 1976).

140    **trained by his employer:** Cappelli, *The New Deal at Work*, 70–73.

140    **over age twenty-five:** Cappelli, *The New Deal at Work*, 199.

140    **lasted fully eighteen months:** Cappelli, *The New Deal at Work*, 65–66, citing William H. Whyte, *The Organization Man* (New York: Simon & Schuster, 1956).

141    **close their stores:** Cappelli, *The New Deal at Work*, 70–73. John Hoerr, "System Crash," *The American Prospect*, December 19, 2001, accessed February 24, 2020, https://protect-us .mimecast.com/s/T0yfCwpk5nh1MYZRfVgPsQ?domain =prospect.org.

141    **internally trained workers:** Cappelli, *The New Deal at Work*, 199.

141    **any training program at all:** Cappelli, *The New Deal at Work*, 200–201.

141    **less than 2 percent of its payroll budget on training:** Cappelli, *The New Deal at Work*, 200–201. This suggests that the transference of training from workplace to school applies to non-elite

as well as elite workers. Other evidence reinforces this conclusion. A full quarter of community college students already possess BAs, for example, and are returning to school to acquire specific workplace skills that their employers no longer teach. And the rate of capital infusion into private technical schools, which similarly substitute for training that was once provided by employers, in the workplace, more than tripled over the course of the 1990s alone.

141   **"from the mail room to the corner office":** Anthony P. Carnevale, Stephen J. Rose, and Ban Cheah, *The College Payoff: Education, Occupations, Lifetime Earnings,* Georgetown University Center on Education and the Workforce (2011), 2. Hereafter cited as Carnevale, Rose, and Cheah, *The College Payoff.*

141   **over two decades:** Reich, *Supercapitalism,* 38, citing *Fortune* magazine's book *The Executive Life* (Garden City, NY: Doubleday, 1956), 30.

141   **by firms or even industries:** Carnevale, Rose, and Cheah, *The College Payoff,* 2.

141   **"that is probably finite":** Cappelli, *The New Deal at Work,* 26.

141   **beyond the residency:** See American Board of Medical Specialties, *ABMS Guide to Medical Specialties,* 2018, accessed October 24, 2018, www.abms.org/media/176512/abms-guide-to-medical -specialties-2018.pdf.

141   **over the past two decades:** U.S. Census Bureau, "Section 4: Education," Statistical Abstract of the United States no. 131, 2012, www.census.gov/library/publications/2011/compendia /statab/131ed/education.html (see file 304, "First Professional Degrees Earned in Selected Professions").

142   **over one hundred thousand new MBAs each year:** U.S. Census Bureau, "Section 4: Education," Statistical Abstract of the United States no. 131, 2012, www.census.gov/library/publica tions/2011/compendia/statab/131ed/education.html (see file 304, "First Professional Degrees Earned in Selected Professions"). See also Jonathan P. O'Brien et al., "Does Business School Research Add Economic Value for Students?," *Academy of Management Learning and Education* 9, no. 4 (2010): 638–51, 638. On the massive increase in business education as the mirror image of the decline in workplace training, see P. Friga, R. Bettis, and R. Sullivan, "Changes in Graduate Management Education and New Business School Strategies for 21st Century," *Academy of Management Learning and Education* 2 (2003): 233–49, and F. P. Morgeson and J. D. Nahrgang, "Same as It Ever Was: Recognizing Stability in the Business Week Rankings," *Academy of Management Learning and Education* 7 (2008): 26–41.

142   **had not even attended college:** See F. W. Tausig and C. S. Joslyn, *American Business Leaders* (Oxford: Macmillan, 1932).

142   **have completed college today:** Mayo, Nohria, and Singleton, *Paths to Power,* x.

142   **hold MBAs or JDs:** See M. Useem and J. Karabel, "Pathways to Top Corporate Management," *American Sociological Review* 51 (1986): 184–200.

142   **have exceeded $350,000:** In 2015, Harvard Business School's expenditures amounted to $660 million, and its enrollment was 1,865 students, yielding expenditure per student of nearly $354,000. Harvard Business School, *FY15 Financial Report* (2015), 3, www.hbs.edu/about/financialreport/2015/Docu ments/HBS-Financial-2015.pdf.

142   **therefore from richer families:** Such employer-provided training as endures in the American economy is skewing further and further in favor of elite workers. In 1983, college graduates were roughly three times as likely to receive workplace training as workers without high school degrees. By 1991, the educated workers were nearly four times as likely to receive training as the uneducated ones. Daron Acemoglu, "Changes in Unemployment and Wage Inequality: An Alternative Theory and Some Evidence," *American Economic Review* 89, no. 5 (December 1999): 1259–78, 1275, https://doi.org/10.3386/w6658 (citing the 1983 and 1991 CPS supplements, which report on the shares of workers who received some kind of "training to improve skills on the current job"). Hereafter cited as Acemoglu, "Changes in Unemployment and Wage Inequality."

143   **in the 97th percentile:** Stanford's median MCAT score is 519. See Farran Powell, "10 Medical Schools with the Highest MCATS Scores," *U.S. News & World Report,* March 23, 2018, accessed November 18, 2018, www.usnews.com/education/best

-graduate-schools/top-medical-schools/slideshows/10-med -schools-with-the-highest-mcat-scores?slide=3; Association of American Medical Colleges, Percentile Ranks for the MCAT Exam, https://students-residents.aamc.org/advisors/article/per centile-ranks-for-the-mcat-exam/.

143   **attended Harvard, Princeton, or Yale:** See Helen Diagama and Alda Yuan, *2016 Class/Action Report: A Triennial Report on Socioeconomic Class as Experienced by Students at Yale Law School* (2017), 10.

143   **charges over $70,000:** For Yale Law School, see "Cost of Attendance," Yale Law School, https://law.yale.edu/admissions/cost -financial-aid/cost-attendance. For Harvard Business School, see "Annual Cost of Attendance," Harvard Business School, www.hbs.edu/mba/financial-aid/Pages/cost-summary.aspx. For business schools more generally, see "2014 Ranking of the Top MBA Programs & Best Business Schools," MBAPrograms .org (2014), www.mbaprograms.org/rankings. More generally, one year of law school tuition, after internal grants, scholarships, and other discounts, averages about $32,000 at private schools, and $28,000 for out-of-state students at $15,000 for in-state students at public schools. These figures suggest a 20 to 30 percent discount of list prices. See Michael Simkovic and Frank Mcintyre, "The Economic Value of a Law Degree," *Journal of Legal Studies* 43, no. 2 (June 2014): 249–89, 281n.43. Another report of specific numbers on law school tuition (in 2013) appears at "Law School Costs," Law School Transparency, www .lawschooltransparency.com/reform/projects/Tuition-Tracker / and "Cost Calculator: Estimate the Cost of Law School," AdmissionsDean, www.admissionsdean.com/paying_for_law_sc hool/law-school-cost-calculator.

143   **more than $105,000:** For Yale Law School, see "Cost of Attendance," Yale Law School, https://law.yale.edu/admissions/cost -financial-aid/cost-attendance. For Harvard Business School, see "Annual Cost of Attendance," Harvard Business School, www .hbs.edu/mba/financial-aid/Pages/cost-summary.aspx.

143   **networking benefits of student life:** See Jodi Kantor, "Class Is Seen Dividing Harvard Business School," *New York Times,* September 9, 2013, accessed November 18, 2018, www.nytimes .com/2013/09/10/education/harvard-business-students-see -class-as-divisive-an-issue-as-gender.html. Hereafter cited as Kantor, "Class Is Seen Dividing Harvard Business School."

143   **equal or even exceed the direct costs:** Elite professional school students overwhelmingly possess elite BAs (the professional schools select for this criterion, after all) and so enjoy the employment opportunities that this credential provides. When they go back to school, professional students forswear immediate income. This indirect cost should not be treated as an investment in professional students' human capital (that would be double counting). But it nevertheless contributes to the concentration of human capital in the rich, by causing professional schools to select directly for students who possess sufficient family wealth to be able to afford the delay to their own income that professional school involves.

143   **properly regard as embarrassing:** The administrations at graduate and professional schools, like college administrations, advertise that large shares of students are eligible to receive need-based financial aid: 50 percent at Harvard Business School, for example, and 73 percent at Yale Law School. See "Financial Aid: MBAid Journey: Fast Facts," Harvard Business School, www.hbs.edu/mba/financial-aid/Pages/fast-facts.aspx; "Cost & Financial Aid," Yale Law School, https://law.yale.edu /admissions/cost-financial-aid. But as with undergraduate financial aid, so in this case also, nominally "need-based" financial aid is rendered merit-based by the competitiveness of the application process and directed toward rich students on account of the correlation between family background and academic performance. And widespread aid, far from promoting economic equality, thus constitutes a massive subsidy in favor of the already wealthy and well educated.

143   **"only $20,000":** Kantor, "Class Is Seen Dividing Harvard Business School."

144   **in or near poverty:** See Sackett et al., *Class/Action: A Report on Socioeconomic Class as Experienced by Students at Yale Law School* (March 2013), accessed September 28, 2018, https://law .yale.edu/system/files/area/department/studentaffairs/docu ment/class_action_report.pdf. Hereafter cited as Sackett et al.,

*Class/Action*. Moreover, the Yale Law School study tabulated students' parents' educations as well as incomes (this lends credibility to the income data, as children might mistake their parents' incomes but surely do know what degrees their parents hold): the median Yale Law student has at least one parent with a professional degree or PhD (the top 3 percent of the education distribution), and only 8 percent of Yale Law students have two parents without a BA. See Sackett et al., *Class/Action*. The skew to wealth might have diminished slightly in subsequent classes, with roughly equal shares of students coming from the top 1 percent and the bottom half.

144 **that Harvard Business School and Yale Law School are outliers:** Moreover, there is good reason to believe that, as with colleges, the most elite professional schools show the greatest skew toward wealth. For example, the Texas Medical and Dental School Application Service processes all applications to state-supported medical schools in Texas and collects demographic data about applications and accepted students. A study of medical school applications and enrollments in Texas in 2005 and 2006 found that the most selective school received a substantially higher share of applicants and enrolled a substantially higher share of students from the most elite of four SES categories than the least selective school. See Michael Kennedy, "Medical School Admissions Across Socioeconomic Groups: An Analysis Across Race Neutral and Race Sensitive Admissions Cycles" (unpublished PhD dissertation).

144 **two professional parents:** Linda F. Wightman, *Legal Education at the Close of the Twentieth Century: Descriptions and Analyses of Students, Financing, and Professional Expectations and Attitudes* (Newtown, PA: Law School Admission Council, 1995), 30, Table 15.

147 **"revolution in family wealth transmission":** Langbein, "Twentieth-Century Revolution."

147 **more rapidly even than income inequality:** Consumption here is measured and classified by the categories in the Consumer Expenditure Survey. See Aguiar and Bils, "Has Consumption Inequality Mirrored Income Inequality?," 2753. Education expenditures have for three decades displayed one of the three highest income elasticities of the twenty expenditure categories studied by Aguiar and Bils. By 2008–10, education expenditures had become the single most income elastic expenditure category.

148 **that their earlier academic achievements qualify them for:** See Gordon C. Winston and Catharine B. Hill, "Access to the Most Selective Private Colleges by High-Ability, Low-Income Students: Are They Out There?," Williams Project on the Economics of Higher Education, Discussion Paper no. 69 (2005), https://files.eric.ed.gov/fulltext/ED499443.pdf. See also Lisa R. Pruitt, "The False Choice Between Race and Class and Other Affirmative Action Myths," *Buffalo Law Review* 63 (2015): 1030; Thomas J. Espenschade and Alexandria Walton Radford, *No Longer Separate, Not Yet Equal: Race and Class in Elite College Admission and Campus Life* (Princeton, NJ: Princeton University Press, 2009), 97–98. These authors observe that a child from the professional elite is many times more likely to be admitted to a selective private college than a less privileged white child with similar qualifications. This claim is not, however, incompatible with the main thrust of the argument here—namely, that the skew to wealth among elite student bodies is predominantly caused by merit, simply because there are so few high-achieving children from poor parents to whom the claim applies.

149 **at the most selective colleges:** The rise of elite elementary and high school education explains the seemingly contradictory patterns concerning high school achievement and college admissions together and at once: "although low-income students have shown strong gains in the indicators that lead to admission to highly selective schools . . . higher income students have simultaneously made even stronger gains on these same indicators. Thus, enrollment in selective colleges has become a horse race in which wealthier students always remain at the head of the pack. As a result, low-income students have failed to make substantial gains in college placement despite substantial increases in academic course achievement." Bastedo and Jaquette, "Running in Place," 319.

149 **any way except toward wealth:** This may be straightforwardly read off the face of the SAT: in 2013, the 95th-percentile SAT scores for test takers from households earning less than $20,000 per year and the 95th-percentile scores for test takers from households earning $20,000 to $40,000 all fell well below the 25th percentile of Yale College's entering class in that year. Indeed, the 99.7th-percentile scores for test takers from both groups of households (with the exception of math) fell at roughly Yale's medians. At the same time, there are plenty of high-achieving rich graduates. Among high school students from households with incomes above $200,000 per year, the 95th percentile scores above the Yale median, and the 99.7th percentile has a perfect score on every section of the test. All these claims are derived from data on incomes and scores released directly by the College Board, at College Board, "2013 College-Bound Seniors: Total Group Profile Report," http://media.collegeboard.com/digitalServices/pdf/research/2013/TotalGroup-2013.pdf. Slightly less demanding thresholds and broader conceptions of high school achievement replicate the pattern. For example, only 17 percent of students with SAT or ACT scores in the 90th percentile or higher and A-minus-or-better high school averages come from families in the bottom quintile of the income distribution. See Hoxby and Avery, "The Missing 'One-Offs.'"

149 **"about the world by watching 'Jeopardy'":** The student, Kashawn Campbell, attended high school where "long" writing assignments took a page and where just under 13 percent of students were proficient in English and less than 1 percent were proficient in math. Campbell's straight As in high school failed to translate into college success, and he struggled massively during his freshman year at Berkeley to get his GPA above 2.0. See Kurt Streeter, "South L.A. Student Finds a Different World at Cal," *Los Angeles Times*, August 16, 2013, accessed November 18, 2018, www.latimes.com/local/la-me-c1-cal-freshmen-20130816-dto-htmlstory.html.

149 **who hail from low-income households:** These conclusions follow from a careful and comprehensive historical study that combined several massive databases of high school students to construct a nationally representative sample that extends over three decades (including high school graduates from 1972, 1982, 1992, and 2004) and used this data to investigate interactions among household income, high school achievement, and college placement. See Bastedo and Jaquette, "Running in Place," 318–39.

149 **in a typical year:** See "2013 College-Bound Seniors: Total Group Profile Report," College Board, http://media.collegeboard.com/digitalServices/pdf/research/2013/TotalGroup-2013.pdf.

149 **fully a quarter of these:** This share is calculated using the college's own reports of SAT scores at the 25th percentiles of their student bodies, combined with the numbers of students that they enroll.

149 **in the 99th percentile:** This share is calculated by combining the Law School Admissions Council's *Current Volume Summaries* of LSAT scores, which report the number of law school applicants each year whose scores reach the 99th percentile, with the top five law schools' reports of their enrollments and the LSAT scores at the 25th, 50th, and 75th percentiles of their student bodies. The precise numbers unsurprisingly vary from year to year. The *Current Volume Summaries* are available at www.lsac.org/data-research/data?search=&page=1. The law school class data are available at https://law.yale.edu/admissions/profiles-statistics/entering-class-profile; https://law.stanford.edu/aba-required-disclosures/; https://hls.harvard.edu/dept/jdadmissions/apply-to-harvard-law-school/hls-profile-and-facts/; www.law.uchicago.edu/files/Std509InfoReport-50-50-12-06-2017%2013-38-43.pdf; www.law.columbia.edu/admissions/jd/experience/class-profile.

149 **dominate meritocratic competition:** The United States is exceptional in this respect also. The skills gap between offspring of at least one college-educated parent and offspring of two parents without high school degrees is 50 percent higher in the United States than the OECD average and at least as great as in any other OECD country. See OECD, *OECD Skills Outlook 2013*, 113, Figure 3.6(L), "Differences in literary proficiency, by socioeconomic background."

150 **meritocracy's triumph:** For a similar conclusion, see Reeves, *Dream Hoarders,* 87. Reeves cites Sigal Alon, "The Evolution of Class Inequality in Higher Education: Competition, Exclusion, and Adaptation," *American Sociological Review* 74, no. 5 (2009): 731–55.

150 **from shirtsleeves to shirtsleeves in three generations:** The American version of the adage is often attributed to Andrew Carnegie, a late nineteenth- and early-twentieth-century steel baron and philanthropist. But the adage exists in different versions in other parts of the world. The Chinese have the ancient proverb "rice paddy to rice paddy in three generations," and the British version is "clogs to clogs in three generations." Arianna Degan and Emmanuel Thibault, "Dynastic Accumulation of Wealth," *Mathematical Social Sciences* 81 (May 2016): 66.

150 **hereditary landedness:** The analogy even penetrates the legal doctrines that support the two regimes. Aristocratic dynasties were supported by legal practices such as the fee tail. Entailed land—land conveyed by deed or settlement to the tenant in possession as a fee tail—could not be sold, devised, mortgaged, or otherwise alienated by the generation that possessed it. Instead, the land passed, undivided and unencumbered, down from generation to generation. This prevented the living from squandering a family's aristocratic inheritance and so ensured that land would pass down through the family's generations, in perpetuity.

Meritocratic dynasties are similarly supported by legal rules that limit a person's power to sell his human capital, by selling himself into slavery or even just making very long-term labor contracts. This prevents a person from squandering his meritocratic inheritance and so increases the likelihood that human capital will be passed down through the generations.

151 **a stepping-stone on the path of progress:** A wider lens generalizes this insight. When meritocracy remakes the family as a site of production, it restores preindustrial arrangements, under which nonaristocratic families were sites of industry and aristocratic families produced breeding. The period from the Industrial Revolution through the mid-twentieth century is distinctive for *not* centering production in the family. This is yet another way in which meritocracy harkens back to aristocratic social and economic forms. I owe this formulation to Sarah Bilston.

151 **energy from the outside:** These points owe a great deal to a conversation with Joseph Fishkin, author of *Bottlenecks: A New Theory of Equal Opportunity* (New York: Oxford University Press, 2016).

151 **Yale's greatest president:** See Pat Barnes, "Ex-President of Yale Kingman Brewster Dies," *Washington Post,* November 9, 1988, accessed October 24, 2018, www.washingtonpost.com/archive/local/1988/11/09/ex-president-of-yale-kingman-brewster-dies/9edcd521-a603-4f98-b264-88c83568e4fa/?utm_term=.11f6fa327fd4.

151 **no end in sight:** Kabaservice, "The Birth of a New Institution."

151 **are admitted to Ivy League colleges:** Sharon Otterman, "Diversity Debate Convulses Elite High School," *New York Times,* August 4, 2010, accessed October 20, 2018, www.nytimes.com/2010/08/05/nyregion/05hunter.html. Hereafter cited as Otterman, "Diversity Debate."

151 **ten times more applicants than spaces:** In 2014, 2,268 students applied for 225 places. Derrell Bradford, *In Defense of New York City's Selective High Schools,* Report, Thomas B. Fordham Institute, February 2, 2015, accessed October 20, 2018, https://edexcellence.net/articles/in-defense-of-new-york-citys-selective-high-schools.

152 **the school's entrance exam:** Christopher Hayes, *Twilight of the Elites,* 39.

152 **the New York City public schools generally:** Hayes, *Twilight of the Elites,* 40. The $45,000 threshold is for a family of four. See Paula Tyner-Doyle, "2018–2019 Free and Reduced Price Income Eligibility and Policy Information," Memorandum from the State Education Department, Albany, NY, June 2018, accessed October 24, 2018, 34, www.cn.nysed.gov/common/cn/files/2018policybooklet.pdf.

152 **fell by factors of four and six:** "In 1995, the entering seventh-grade class was 12 percent black and 6 percent Hispanic, according to state data. This past year, it was 3 percent black and 1 percent Hispanic." Otterman, "Diversity Debate."

152 **its fourth new head in five years:** Otterman, "Diversity Debate."

152 **in order to relieve student stress:** Jenny Anderson, "At Elite Schools, Easing Up a Bit on Homework," *New York Times,* October 23, 2011, accessed October 20, 2018, www.nytimes.com/2011/10/24/education/24homework.html. The discussion of Hunter High in particular occurs in a correction posted at the end of the article.

152 **"The value to me of my education":** In his classic book *Social Limits to Growth,* Fred Hirsch called goods that have this character *positional goods.* People derive well-being from positional goods based not on their absolute holdings but rather on whether they have more or less than others do, and this entails that an incremental addition to a person's stock of a positional good that increases her holdings relative to others—that moves her up in the ownership rankings—adds the same amount to her well-being, no matter how little or much of the good she and others held before the increase. One might even say that the true good, in such cases, is rank or position, and that the nominal good whose ownership is ranked is just an input into the production of position. People do not tire of the positional goods as they do of others. And demand for positional goods rises, unfettered, together with rising incomes. The term *positional good* has been used capaciously, to cover an overlapping set of phenomena, rather than in a narrow, parsimonious, or technical precise way. The approach to the term taken here falls within conventional usage, although it does not—indeed, it could not possibly—coincide with every precedent. Fred Hirsch, *Social Limits to Growth* (Cambridge, MA: Harvard University Press, 1976).

153 **do not become sated on schooling:** The distinction between ordinary goods and positional goods does not present a binary so much as a continuum, with chocolate near one end and education near the other. Luxury goods—which produce well-being not directly by being consumed but rather by signaling wealth and thus constituting status—fall in between. When clothes, or watches, or cars are desired for being expensive, demand might remain steady in the face of increases in their extravagance and cost, rather than declining as on the model of ordinary consumption. Which goods are positional depends on contingent social and economic factors rather than on logic. A thought experiment proposed by Robert Frank illustrates this. When people are asked whether they would rather live in four-thousand-square-foot houses in a world in which others live in six-thousand-square-foot houses, or live in three-thousand-square-foot houses in a world in which others live in two-thousand-square-foot houses, they prefer the second world. But when people are asked whether they would rather have four weeks of annual vacation in a world in which others have six weeks, or have two weeks of vacation in a world in which others have one, they prefer the first world. In the frame of the experiments, housing is a positional good but vacation time is not. Robert H. Frank, "Positional Externalities Cause Large and Preventable Welfare Losses," *American Economic Review* 95, no. 2 (May 2005): 137, accessed October 20, 2018, doi:10.1257/0028280577460392.

154 **"turtleneck syndrome":** Simon Mundy, "South Korea's Millionaire Tutors," *Financial Times,* June 16, 2014, accessed October 20, 2018, www.ft.com/content/c0b611fc-dab5-11e3-9a27-00144feabdc0.

154 **"experienced mental health challenges":** Jessie Agatstein et al., *Falling Through the Cracks: A Report on Mental Health at Yale Law School,* Yale Law School Mental Health Alliance, Yale Law School (2014), 14. Hereafter cited as Agatstein et al., *Falling Through the Cracks.*

154 **form of nervous exhaustion:** Agatstein et al., *Falling Through the Cracks,* 15.

154 **"no idea what to do next":** Ezra Klein, "Ivy League's Failure Is Wall Street's Gain," Bloomberg Opinion, February 15, 2012, accessed October 20, 2018, www.bloomberg.com/view/articles/2012-02-16/harvard-liberal-arts-failure-is-wall-street-gain-commentary-by-ezra-klein.

154 **"zombies":** William Deresiewicz, "Don't Send Your Kid to the Ivy League," *New Republic,* July 21, 2014, accessed October 20, 2018, https://newrepublic.com/article/118747/ivy-league-schools-are-overrated-send-your-kids-elsewhere.

154 **"excellent sheep":** William Deresiewicz, *Excellent Sheep: The Miseducation of the American Elite and the Way to a Meaningful Life* (New York: Free Press, 2014). Hereafter cited as Deresiewicz, *Excellent Sheep.*

154 **expressed surprise at the question:** Personal conversation with the author.

155 **gutless, mercenary children:** Deresiewicz, *Excellent Sheep.*

155 **"that a self is something you just have":** David Foster Wallace, *Consider the Lobster and Other Essays* (New York: Little, Brown, 2007).

155 **alive and well today:** Samuel Bowles and Herbert Gintis, *Schooling in Capitalist America: Educational Reform and the Contradictions of Economic Life* (New York: Basic Books, 1976).

156 **down through the generations:** See Numbers 14:18.

## Chapter Six: Gloomy and Glossy Jobs

157 **"by choice or by chance":** The quote is reported in Ho, *Liquidated*, 59–60.

157 **at once seeking work:** The data come from Ho, *Liquidated*, 59.

157 **"depended more on the number of years":** Reich, *Supercapitalism*, 38.

157 **"CEO [of a midcentury firm]":** Reich, *Supercapitalism*, 109–10.

157 **insulation from adversaries:** See William H. Whyte, *The Organization Man* (New York: Simon & Schuster, 1956).

157 **"Rivals did not impinge":** Reich, *Supercapitalism*, 109–10.

158 *labor market polarization:* The term comes from Maarten Goos and Alan Manning, *Lousy and Lovely Jobs: The Rising Polarization of Work in Britain*, London School of Economics, Center for Economic Performance Discussion Paper No. DP0604 (December 2003), http://eprints.lse.ac.uk/20002/1/Lousy_and_Lovely_Jobs_the_Rising_Polarization_of_Work_in_Britain .pdf, eventually published as Maarten Goos and Alan Manning, "Lousy and Lovely Jobs: The Rising Polarization of Work in Britain," *Review of Economics and Statistics* 89, no. 1 (February 2007): 118–33, hereafter cited as Goos and Manning, "Lousy and Lovely Jobs." For other uses, see David H. Autor, Lawrence F. Katz, and Melissa S. Kearney, "The Polarization of the U.S. Labor Market," *AEA Papers and Proceedings* 96 (2006): 189–94, hereafter cited as Autor, Katz, and Kearney, "The Polarization of the U.S. Labor Market"; Christopher L. Foote and Richard W. Ryan, "Labor-Market Polarization over the Business Cycle," *NBER Macroeconomics Annual* 29 (2015): 371–413.

158 *skill-biased technological change:* David Card and John E. Di-Nardo, "Skill-Biased Technological Change and Rising Wage Inequality: Some Problems and Puzzles," *Journal of Labor Economics* 20, no. 4 (October 2002): 734 ("This hypothesis—that a burst of new technology caused a rise in the demand for highly skilled workers, which in turn led to a rise in earnings inequality—has become known as the Skill-Biased Technical Change (SBTC) hypothesis."); Eli Berman, John Bound, and Stephen Machin, "Implications of Skill-Biased Technological Change: International Evidence," *Quarterly Journal of Economics* 113, no. 4 (November 1998): 1245–79.

158 **interesting and complex work at high pay:** Goos and Manning, "Lousy and Lovely Jobs."

159 **"everything we made was by hand":** Lydia DePillis, "Minimum-Wage Offensive Could Speed Arrival of Robot-Powered Restaurants," *Washington Post*, August 16, 2015, accessed November 18, 2018, www.washingtonpost.com/business/capitalbusiness/minimum-wage-offensive-could-speed-arrival-of-robot-powered-restaurants/2015/08/16/35f284ea-3f6f-11e5-8d45-d815146 f81fa_story.html?utm_term=.5e63a0f1d21e. Hereafter cited as DePillis, "Minimum-Wage Offensive."

159 **open their own restaurants:** Jessica Wohl, "Hamburger University Grills Students on McDonald's Operations," *Chicago Tribune*, April 18, 2015, accessed November 18, 2018, www .chicagotribune.com/business/ct-mcdonalds-hamburger -university-0419-biz-20150407-story.html; John F. Love, *McDonald's: Behind the Arches* (New York: Bantam, 1986), 148–50.

159 **to become CEO in 1991:** "Executive Profile: Edward H. Rensi," Bloomberg, accessed October 22, 2018, www.bloomberg.com /research/stocks/private/person.asp?personId=6309648priv capId=1598870; Bio, "Ed Rensi," Premiere Speakers Bureau, https://premierespeakers.com/ed_rensi/bio.

159 **far from exceptional:** Fred Turner, who founded Hamburger University and served as McDonald's CEO from 1974 to 1987, also worked his way up through the firm's hierarchy, and many other early McDonald's executives began their careers in entry-level jobs at the firm. See Laurence Arnold and Leslie Patton, "Fred Turner, McDonald's 'Hamburger U.' Founder, Dies at 80," Bloomberg, January 8, 2013, accessed November 18, 2018, www.bloomberg.com/news/articles/2013-01-08/fred-l-turner -mcdonald-s-hamburger-u-founder-dies-at-80.

160 **the number has fallen by over half:** DePillis, "Minimum-Wage Offensive."

160 **in favor of robots:** The Fight for $15's efforts to raise street-level wages is bringing the issue to a head. See Julia Limitone, "Fmr. McDonald's USA CEO: $35K Robots Cheaper Than Hiring at $15 Per Hour," Fox Business, May 24, 2016, accessed November 18, 2018, www.foxbusiness.com/features/fmr-mcdonalds-usa -ceo-35k-robots-cheaper-than-hiring-at-15-per-hour.

160 **new franchise operators:** Geoff Williams, "Hamburger U: Behind the Arches," *Entrepreneur*, January 2006, accessed November 18, 2018, www.entrepreneur.com/article/81692.

160 **Indeed, the school increasingly focuses:** "McDonald's Celebrates 50 Years of Training and Developing Employees at Hamburger University," *Market Wired*, April 5, 2011, accessed November 18, 2018, www.marketwired.com/press-release/mc donalds-celebrates-50-years-training-developing-employees -hamburger-university-nyse-mcd-1422879.htm. Hereafter cited as "McDonald's Celebrates 50 Years."

160 **Even its U.S. campus:** "McDonald's Celebrates 50 Years."

160 **"More and more of the labor":** DePillis, "Minimum-Wage Offensive."

160 **Burger King and Wendy's:** Mona Chalabi, "What Do McDonald's Workers Really Make Per Hour?," FiveThirtyEight, May 22, 2014, accessed November 18, 2018, http://fivethirtyeight .com/datalab/what-do-mcdonalds-workers-really-make-per -hour/.

161 **dispense with the need for mid-skilled workers at street level:** The transformation even blocks street-level workers from making the leap into management not by rising through the ranks but by buying a franchise. Whereas a midcentury worker might open a franchise using loans, McDonald's now requires franchise applicants to verify a minimum of $750,000 of liquid assets. Other fast-food chains demand still greater wealth: Taco Bell, for example, requires new franchisees to possess a minimum net worth of $1.5 million. See National Employment Law Project, *Going Nowhere Fast: Limited Occupational Mobility in the Fast Food Industry* (July 2013), Figure 5, www.nelp.org /wp-content/uploads/2015/03/NELP-Fast-Food-Mobility -Report-Going-Nowhere-Fast.pdf.

161 **has never done full-time nonmanagerial work in the restaurant business:** Lara O'Reilly, "The New McDonald's CEO Is British—Here's Everything We Know About Him," *Business Insider*, January 29, 2015, accessed November 18, 2018, www .businessinsider.com/everything-you-need-to-know-about -mcdonalds-new-ceo-steve-easterbrook-2015-1.

161 **(about $1.2 million in 2018 dollars):** See McDonald's Corporation, "Notice of Annual Meeting of Stockholders," April 8, 1969.

161 **a full-time minimum-wage worker:** The federal minimum wage in 1965 was $1.25 per hour, which yields an annual income (based on working forty hours per week for all fifty-two weeks of the year) of $2,600 in 1965 dollars. "History of Federal Minimum Wage Rates Under the Fair Labor Standards Act, 1938–2009," Wage and Hours Division, U.S. Department of Labor, accessed October 22, 2018, www.dol.gov/whd/minwage/chart.htm.

161 **(about $4 million in 2018 dollars):** McDonald's Corporation, Form 14A: Proxy Statement (April 12, 1996), 26, accessed October 22, 2018, http://d1lge852tjjqow.cloudfront.net/CIK-000 0063908/805ecc39-014d-49f9-a69b-febfa96a6ab5.pdf.

161 **more than 250 times the current minimum-wage income:** The federal minimum wage in 1993–95 was $4.25 per hour, which yields an annual income (based on working forty hours per week for all fifty-two weeks of the year) of $8,840 in mid-1990s dollars. "History of Federal Minimum Wage Rates Under the Fair Labor Standards Act, 1938–2009," Wage and Hours Division, U.S. Department of Labor, accessed October 22, 2018, www.dol.gov/whd/minwage/chart.htm.

161  **makes roughly $8 million:** McDonald's Corporation, Form 14A: Information Required in Proxy Statement (April 15, 2016), 33, accessed October 22, 2018, http://d1lge852zjjqow .cloudfront.net/CIK-0000063908/3fb68a12-ebe5-47c5-bd39 -2f6e0b5fe9c0.pdf.

161  **more than 500 times the minimum wage:** The federal minimum wage is $7.25 per hour, which yields an annual income (based on working forty hours per week for all fifty-two weeks of the year) of $15,080. See U.S. Department of Labor, "History of Federal Minimum Wage Rates Under the Fair Labor Standards Act, 1938–2009," Wage and Hours Division, accessed October 22, 2018, www.dol.gov/whd/minwage/chart.htm. For a report of ratios of the CEO's income to the income of a full-time minimum-wage worker, see Leslie Patton, "McDonald's $8.25 Man and $8.75 Million CEO Shows Pay Gap," Bloomberg, December 12, 2012, accessed November 18, 2018, www.bloom berg.com/news/articles/2012-12-12/mcdonald-s-8-25-man -and-8-75-million-ceo-shows-pay-gap.

161  **account for the CEOs' enormous pay:** See the discussion of management below.

161  **the market for workers:** According to one estimate, increased intensity in research and development accounts for 49 percent of the rise in worker productivity in the United States between 1950 and 1993. See Charles I. Jones, "Sources of U.S. Growth in a World of Ideas," *American Economic Review* 92, no. 1 (March 2002): 230. See also Claudia Goldin and Lawrence Katz, *The Race Between Education and Technology* (Cambridge, MA: Harvard University Press, 2008), 41. Hereafter cited as Goldin and Katz, *The Race Between Education and Technology*.

162  **technology's divergent influences:** New technologies may actually be increasing the wages of the least skilled workers, and this effect might contribute, alongside the social welfare programs inaugurated in the Great Society, to the declining poverty rates observed earlier. (Note, however, that the bulk of innovation's upward pressure on low-skilled wages might well be indirect, as newly flush superordinate workers increase the demand for services—housekeeping, for example, or personal care—that the least skilled provide.) See David H. Autor and David Dorn, "The Growth of Low-Skill Service Jobs and the Polarization of the US Labor Market," *American Economic Review* 103, no. 5 (August 2013): 1559 ("If consumer preferences do not admit close substitutes for the tangible outputs of service occupations—such as restaurant meals, house-cleaning, security services, and home health assistance—non-neutral technological progress concentrated in goods production (by which we mean non-service occupation activities) has the potential to raise aggregate demand for service outputs and ultimately increase employment and wages in service occupations.").

163  **"the world's most respectable declining industry":** "Has Banking a Future?," *The Economist*, January 26, 1963, 331. The full quotation from that article is "Can the bankers, after complacently relying on inflation to expand their deposits for so long and having wearied more recently of initiatives inadequately followed through, rise to the occasion now? It needs faith to believe they will, even if some of them see danger in presiding over the world's most respectable declining industry." The 1963 story was referenced in a 2013 *Economist* story on banking called "Twilight of the Gods." See "Twilight of the Gods," *The Economist*, September 2, 2013, accessed November 18, 2018, www.economist.com/news/special-report/215771 89-investment-banking-faces-humbler-future-says -jonathan-rosenthal-though. Hereafter cited as "Twilight of the Gods."

163  **went to work on Wall Street:** Fraser, *Every Man a Speculator*, 473. The Great Depression had badly discredited finance, and the leisure-class bankers' near-uniform opposition to the New Deal and their eventual bitter defeat sealed Wall Street's fate for a generation. "White-shoe Wall Street," one commentator observed, "suddenly seemed no better than a gang of common criminals, skimmers, double-dealers, and confidence men." Fraser, *Every Man a Speculator*, 431. And financiers appeared "not only narrow-mindedly selfish, but foolish, frail, and inept," so that "they were made fun of and stripped of every last vestige of moral authority and heroic virility they once laid claim to." Fraser, *Every Man a Speculator*, 439 (first quotation), 431 (second quotation), xix–xx, 415, 439, 441, 474.

163  **the private-sector workforce:** Until 1980, finance workers were only 2.5 percent more likely to hold college degrees than other private-sector workers. These percentages are derived by calculating the share of work hours provided by college-educated workers in each sector. See Thomas Philippon and Ariell Reshef, "Skill Biased Financial Development: Education, Wages and Occupations in the U.S. Financial Sector," NBER Working Paper No. 13437 (2007), 7–8, www.nber.org/papers/w13437. Hereafter cited as Philippon and Reshef, "Skill Biased Financial Development." From 1960 to 1980, elite finance workers earned roughly the same amount as elite manufacturing workers, 25 to 50 percent more than elite health sector workers, and 20 percent less than elite legal sector workers. By 2000 and into 2010, they earned about 60 percent more than elite manufacturing workers, more than double elite health workers, and around the same amount as elite legal sector workers. See also Thomas Philippon and Ariell Reshef, "Wages and Human Capital in the U.S. Finance Industry: 1909–2006," *Quarterly Journal of Economics* 127, no. 4 (November 2012): 1563–64, Figure III. Hereafter cited as Philippon and Reshef, "Wages and Human Capital."

163  **exemplify meritocratic inequality:** Overall the real incomes of finance workers with more than a BA were 130 percent higher in 2005 than in 1970, and these data are top-coded and so ignore the highest incomes and underestimate true growth among the narrow elite. Private-sector workers generally top-coded at rate of 1 percent, banking workers at 2 percent, insurance workers at 2.5 percent, and other finance workers at 13 percent. See Philippon and Reshef, "Skill Biased Financial Development," 12, Figure 6.

164  **has grown roughly tenfold since the 1970s:** See Posner and Weyl, "Against Casino Finance." See also David A. Zalewski and Charles J. Whalen, "Financialization and Income Inequality," *Journal of Economic Issues* 44, no. 3 (2010): 757–77, focusing on the twenty-five highest-paid hedge fund managers and the CEOs of the S&P 500. Both articles cite a study by Steven N. Kaplan and Joshua Rauh on the composition of the top 0.01 percent, 0.001 percent, and 0.0001 percent of the income distribution. See Kaplan and Rauh, "Wall Street and Main Street."

164  **the fifty richest Americans:** According to *Forbes*, twelve of the fifty richest Americans in 2013 were financiers, asset managers, or investors. In 2018, thirteen of the fifty richest Americans in 2013 were financiers, asset managers, or investors. See Kroll and Dolan, "Forbes 400."

164  **About a fifth of all billionaires now work in finance:** In 2012, of the 1,226 people on *Forbes*'s billionaires list, 77 were financiers and 143 were investors. Cited in Freeland, *Plutocrats*.

164  **investable assets of more than $30 million:** Many of the numbers in this paragraph come from Freeland, *Plutocrats*, 120.

164  **might reach $425,000:** Ho, *Liquidated*, 262–63, citing Erica Copulsky, "Ka-Ching!," *New York Post*, December 11, 2006, which lists ranges of $600,000 to $1,300,000 for directors, $500,000 to $925,000 for vice presidents, $325,000 to $525,000 for third-year associates.

164  **$500,000 per professional employee:** Duff McDonald, "Please, Sir, I Want Some More. How Goldman Sachs Is Carving Up Its $11 Billion Money Pie," *New York Magazine*, December 5, 2005, accessed November 18, 2018, http://nymag.com/ nymetro/news/bizfinance/biz/features/15197/. Hereafter cited as McDonald, "Please, Sir, I Want Some More."

164  **$150,000 in a good year:** McDonald, "Please, Sir, I Want Some More."

164  **70 percent more income than other workers:** Philippon and Reshef, "Wages and Human Capital," 1605.

164  **rising wage inequality in the economy overall:** Philippon and Reshef, "Wages and Human Capital," 1552.

164  **have actually fallen recently:** See Nelson D. Schwartz, "Gap Widening as Top Workers Reap the Raises," *New York Times*, July 24, 2015, accessed November 18, 2018, www.nytimes .com/2015/07/25/business/economy/salary-gap-widens-as-top -workers-in-specialized-fields-reap-rewards.html (reporting data gathered by the payroll company ADP for the first quarter of 2015).

165  **character and standing in the community:** Rajan, *Fault Lines*, 128 ("These assessments were not just based on hard facts; they also included judgment calls such as whether the borrower seemed well mannered, cleanly attired, trustworthy, and capable of holding a job.").

165 **"guidelines for credit underwriting":** North Carolina Housing Finance Agency, *Loan Originator's Guide* (1977), section 502.

165 **"special consideration":** North Carolina Housing Finance Agency, *Loan Originator's Guide* (1977), section 502.

165 **solidly middle-class status:** Joseph Nocera, *A Piece of the Action: How the Middle Class Joined the Money Class* (New York: Simon & Schuster, 1994), 22 ("Every time a man came into the branch to get a loan . . . he had to sit down with the loan officer and fill out his family history, even if he'd just been there a few months before. The loan officer had to reevaluate the man's fitness to get a loan. The man had to return to the branch with his wife to sign a note. Only then would the loan officer transfer the funds to the man's account."). Norman J. Collins, "Credit Analysis: Concepts and Objectives," in *The Bankers' Handbook*, ed. William H. Baughn and Charles E. Walker (Homewood, IL: Dow Jones-Irwin, 1966), 279–89 (emphasizing the many questions that a loan officer must ask the potential borrower, from the "C's of Credit" of "character, capacity, capital, collateral, and conditions" to government legislation that could affect the success of the borrower's enterprise). Edward J. Palkot, "Personnel Administration," in *The Bankers' Handbook*, 81–97 (highlighting the importance of "strong relationships with high schools and colleges" to employee referrals—it would be quite rare to find a finance firm hiring at high schools these days). See also Robert A. W. Brauns, Jr. and Sarah Slater, *Bankers' Desk Reference* (Boston: Warren, Gorham & Lamont, 1978), 161–73, 278–87 (describing the intricate process loan officers should go through in evaluating the creditworthiness of borrowers, but also stressing the importance of "reliable financial data").

166 **process a given volume of loans:** For numbers of loan officers, see *Occupational Outlook Handbook*, 2016–17 edition, "Loan Officers," Bureau of Labor Statistics, December 17, 2015; Deniz O. Igan, IMF, Report on the United States, June 17, 2015. The BLS does not make it easy to calculate the number of loan officers, as the categories used to sort workers change over time. A reasonable guess concludes that there were roughly 170,000 loan officers in 1990, 213,000 in 1997, 237,000 in 2003, and 302,000 in 2013. In 1997, the average loan officer originated $3.8 million in loans. This number spiked to $16 million per officer in 2003 and fell back again to $6.6 million per officer in 2013.

A blunderbuss approach, which simply calculates the number of bank employees (of all sorts) per residential loan, validates this conclusion. In 1987, there were seven bank employees per residential loan; in the most recent decade, there has been just one. See Federal Deposit Insurance Corporation, *Balance Sheet*, Aggregate Time Series Data 1984–2017 (2017), www5 .fdic.gov/idasp/advSearch_warp_download_all.asp?intTab=4. The data are insufficiently fine-grained to give any independent meaning to these numbers, but they nevertheless serve as a confirmatory reality check on the earlier calculation.

166 **rote repetition rather than independent judgment:** Rajan, *Fault Lines*, 128 ("All that seemed to matter to the investment banks and the rating agencies were the numerical credit score of the borrower and the amount of the loan relative to house value. These were hard pieces of information that could be processed easily and that ostensibly summarized credit quality.").

166 **the accuracy of the loan decisions:** Second Amended Complaint at 4, *U.S. ex rel. Edward O'Donnell v. Countrywide Financial Corp.* (S.D.N.Y. 2012) ("To further ensure that loans would proceed as quickly as possible to closing, Countrywide revamped the compensation structure of those involved in loan origination, basing performance bonuses solely on volume.").

166 **the model of an assembly line:** Rajan, *Fault Lines*, 128 ("But as investment banks put together gigantic packages of mortgages, the judgment calls became less and less important in credit assessments: after all, there was no way to code the borrower's capacity to hold a job in an objective, machine-readable way. Indeed, recording judgment calls in a way that could not be supported by hard facts might have opened the mortgage lender to lawsuits alleging discrimination. All that seemed to matter to the investment banks and the rating agencies were the numerical credit score of the borrower and the amount of the loan relative to house value. These were hard pieces of information that could be processed easily and that ostensibly summarized credit

quality. Accordingly, the brokers who originated loans focused on nothing else.").

166 **made any other approach practically impossible:** Second Amended Complaint at 3, *U.S. ex rel. Edward O'Donnell v. Countrywide Financial Corp.*, 83 F.Supp.3d 528 (S.D.N.Y. 2015).

166 **"A loan officer at a bank":** Linda Fiorella, "Secrets of a Mortgage Loan Officer," *Forbes*, July 17, 2013, accessed November 18, 2018, www.forbes.com/sites/learnvest/2013/07/17/secrets -of-a-mortgage-loan-officer/.

166 **"previously considered unqualified":** See Complaint-in-Intervention, U.S. ex rel. O'Donnell v. Countrywide Financial Corp., 83 F.Supp.3d 528 (S.D.N.Y. 2015); *U.S. ex rel. O'Donnell v. Countrywide Financial Corp.*, 83 F.Supp.3d 528, 535 (S.D.N.Y. 2015), *rev'd*, 822 F.3d 650 (2d Cir. 2016) (describing how Countrywide, which Bank of America merged with in 2008, "replac[ed] trained underwriters with entry-level 'loan specialists'").

167 **to be constructed and traded:** Perhaps most important, the 1960s inaugurated regulatory innovations, for example the weakening and eventual repeal (in 1990) of the Glass-Steagall Act, which had since 1933 limited collaboration between commercial and investment banks. See, for example, David H. Carpenter, Edward V. Murphy, and M. Maureen Murphy, *The Glass-Steagall Act: A Legal Analysis* (Washington, DC: Congressional Research Service, January 19, 2016), https://fas.org /sgp/crs/misc/R44349.pdf.

167 **to value such securities:** The 1950s and 1960s witnessed fundamental theoretical advances in the construction and pricing of financial instruments—including the capital asset pricing model that grew out of Harry Markowitz's work on portfolio allocation and the Black-Scholes model for pricing options and other derivatives. See Mark Rubenstein, *A History of the Theory of Investments* (Hoboken, NJ: John Wiley & Sons, 2006), 167–75; Fischer Black and Myron Scholes, "The Pricing of Options and Corporate Liabilities," *Journal of Political Economy* 81, no. 3 (May–June 1973): 637–54.

167 **to trade complex varieties at scale:** The innovations in computing and information technology that make it possible to collect, store, analyze, and quickly communicate the vast quantities of data on which securitization depends are well known. Other innovations are less familiar, but no less important. It is less well appreciated that modern finance would be impossible without them. Indeed, a credible case can be made that the spreadsheet was an essential trigger for the financial revolution.

167 **that administer securitization:** These are, of course, the core innovations that built the meritocratic elite.

167 **down to the smallest details:** An insurance company intermediates among policyholders across risks, much as a bank intermediates between savers and borrowers. All policyholders pay premiums that supply the insurance company with capital, which it invests in order to pay out to the subset of policyholders for whom insured-against risks eventuate. Under the midcentury model, insurance claims would be reviewed by a claims representative, who would confirm coverage and then pass the claim on to an investigator. The investigator would use interviews and on-the-ground inspections to determine the validity of a claim and then pass valid claims on to adjusters, who would settle with policyholders. Claims adjusters, investigators, and even claims representatives were all mid-skilled workers, who (filling roles much like the loan officer's) exercised independent and responsible judgment to determine the validity of policyholders' claims to compensation for losses. Increasingly, however, traditional claims adjusters are being pushed out in favor of deskilled replacements, who feed machine-scorable data into algorithms, known in the industry as "management information systems," that use statistical methods to confirm coverage and even detect fraud. See Cappelli, *The New Deal at Work*, 90–91, 253n.52–53 (reporting on a "study of performance in the insurance industry at the Wharton School"). These systems entirely eliminate claims representatives and vastly reduce the number of investigators—since low-value claims that set off no flags are paid without further review. Super-skilled workers design the new systems, of course. And so insurance claims review has become skill polarized in much the same fashion as home mortgage loan origination.

168 **to the exclusion of simple ones:** See Philippon and Reshef, "Wages and Human Capital," 1571, Figure VI.

168 **than other sectors:** See Philippon and Reshef, "Wages and Human Capital," 1571, Figure VI.

168 **to 45 percent in 2005:** See Philippon and Reshef, "Skill Biased Financial Development," Figure 5. An analysis of workplace task intensity using data from the *Dictionary of Occupational Titles* similarly reveals that, beginning in the 1970s, the finance sector's increasingly educated workers have performed relatively more complex and nonroutine tasks. See Philippon and Reshef, "Wages and Human Capital," 1571.

168 **by a factor of seven since 1980:** Whereas in 1980, finance-sector labor was only 2.5 percent more likely to be college educated than its nonfarm private-sector counterpart, by 2005, the gap had grown to 17.5 percent. These percentages are derived by calculating the share of hours provided by college-educated workers in each sector. See Philippon and Reshef, "Skill Biased Financial Development," 8. Note that the precise numbers in the figures and the text of the draft do not agree, for the reason that new data led to some revisions in the text. See email communication of February 23, 2017, on file with author.

168 **by a factor of nearly thirty:** See Philippon and Reshef, "Skill Biased Financial Development," Figure 5.

168 **draw their workers overwhelmingly:** Ho, *Liquidated*, 11–12.

168 **"We hire only superstars":** Ho, *Liquidated*, 50 (first three quotes), 39 (last quote).

168 **actually go to work in finance:** Ho, *Liquidated*, 43–66.

Thirty-nine percent of the members of the class of 2016 at Harvard surveyed by the *Harvard Crimson* indicated that they would work in either consulting or finance, while the same figure for Yale was 28.2 percent. See Cordelia F. Mendez, "The Graduating Class of 2016 by the Numbers," *Harvard Crimson*, accessed November 18, 2018, http://features.thecrimson.com /2016/senior-survey/post-harvard/; Office of Career Strategy, *First Destination Report: Class of 2016* (2016), http://ocs.yale .edu/sites/default/files/files/OCS%20Stats%20pages/Public %20-%20Final%20Class%20of%202016%20Report%20(6 %20months).pdf. The most recent figures for Princeton, which are from the class of 2015, indicate that 32.6 percent of the class will go into finance, insurance, and "professional, scientific, and technical services," a category that includes consulting groups. See Career Services at Princeton University, *Annual Report: 2014–2015* (2015), https://careerservices.princeton.edu/sites /career/files/Career%20Services%20Annual%20Report %202014-15.pdf. See also Catherine Rampell, "Out of Harvard, and into Finance," *New York Times*, December 21, 2011, accessed November 18, 2018, https://economix.blogs.nytimes .com/2011/12/21/out-of-harvard-and-into-finance/?_r=1 (citing figures of 35.9 percent in 2010 and 46 percent in 2006 from the Princeton Office of Career Services data).

Astonishingly, these shares used, before the financial crisis, to be greater still. In 2007, 43 percent of Princeton's graduating class with full-time jobs entered finance. See Posner and Weyl, "Against Casino Finance."

168 **(more than goes to work in any other sector):** See Fraser, *Every Man a Speculator*, 552; Harvard Business School, "Recruiting: Data & Statistics," accessed October 22, 2018, www.hbs.edu /recruiting/data/Pages/detailed-charts.aspx.

169 **falling proportion of the overall workforce:** Between 1947 and 1977, finance's shares of GDP and total employment grew together, from 2.32 percent (GDP share) and 2.25 percent (employment share) to 4.55 percent (GDP share) and 4.12 percent (employment share). Then, from the 1980s onward, finance's share of GDP accelerated its growth, rising to 7.69 percent by 2005, even as finance's employment share flattened and indeed began gently to decline, peaking at 4.64 percent in 1987 and falling to 4.32 percent by 2005. These numbers include insurance in finance but exclude real estate. GDP share is computed as the ratio of nominal value added by the finance sector to the nominal GDP of the United States. These data are obtained from the Annual Industry Accounts, published by the Bureau of Economic Analysis. Relative education is computed as the share of hours worked by employees with at least a college degree in the financial sector minus the corresponding share of hours in the rest of the private sector. These data are obtained from the March Current Population Survey (CPS), which is published monthly by the Census Bureau.

See Philippon and Reshef, "Skill Biased Financial Development," 3–6 (pointing out that the changes that they document are driven by a rebalancing of the financial sector's various subsectors, so that traditional banking has declined relative to other aspects of finance and in particular investment). For a different view, see Thomas I. Palley, "Financialization: What It Is and Why It Matters," Levy Economics Institute Working Paper no. 525, December 2007, http://www.levyinstitute.org/pubs /wp_525.pdf (using data from the 2007 Economic Report of the President). For finance's share of employee compensation, see David A. Zalewski and Charles J. Whalen, "Financialization and Income Inequality," *Journal of Economic Issues* 44, no. 3 (2010), 767–77, reporting on Philippon and Reshef, "Skill Biased Financial Development."

169 **higher in finance than in any other sector:** Harvard Business School, "Recruiting: Data & Statistics," accessed October 22, 2018, www.hbs.edu/recruiting/data/Pages/detailed-charts .aspx.

169 **make literally billions of dollars a year:** Deirdre Bolton, "Hedge Fund Billionaires: Who's Making the Most?," Bloomberg via YouTube, April 15, 2013, accessed November 18, 2018, www.youtube.com/watch?v=gP5JU9ZKt-M.

169 **about 100 percent per year:** Cappelli, *The New Deal at Work*, 57, citing Sumner H. Slichter, *The Turnover of Factory Labor* (New York: D. Appleton & Co., 1919), 375.

169 **each individual rock face:** For support for these claims, see Cappelli, *The New Deal at Work*, 51–53.

170 **to be manufactured by others:** Cappelli, *The New Deal at Work*, 51.

170 **virtually no managers at all:** Alfred D. Chandler, Jr., *The Visible Hand: The Managerial Revolution in American Business* (Cambridge, MA: Belknap Press of Harvard University Press, 1977). Hereafter cited as Chandler, *The Visible Hand*.

170 **selling their labor power as employees:** This formulation loosely follows Cappelli, *The New Deal at Work*, 51–57.

170 **or quality control:** Cappelli, *The New Deal at Work*, 51–53, quoting Chandler, *The Visible Hand*, 3.

170 **had not yet been invented:** The telephone was invented in 1876. The vertical filing cabinet was invented in 1895. The modern computer was not invented until the middle of the twentieth century.

170 **the Singer sewing machine company:** Cappelli, *The New Deal at Work*, 56.

171 **that the firm sought:** Cappelli, *The New Deal at Work*, 56, citing Daniel Nelson, *Managers and Workers: Origins of the New Factory System in the United States, 1880–1920* (Madison: University of Wisconsin Press, 1975), 35.

171 **management of industrial firms:** Andrew Hill, "What Is a Manager's Role in a Human-Robot World?," *Financial Times*, May 5, 2016, accessed November 18, 2018, www.ft.com/con tent/f619036a-0612-11e6-9b51-0fb5e65703ce.

171 **a third of the U.S. private-sector workforce:** James T. Bennett and Bruce E. Kaufmann, *The Future of Private Sector Unionism in the United States* (London: Routledge, 2015), 4–5. Only a tenth of workers belong to unions today (2016 figures). The share of private-sector workers to belong to unions in 2016 was even lower—6.4 percent. See Bureau of Labor Statistics, "Union Membership Rate 10.7 Percent in 2016," February 9, 2017, accessed October 22, 2018, www.bls.gov/opub/ted/2017/union -membership-rate-10-point-7-percent-in-2016.htm.

171 **"industrial self-government":** *United Steelworkers of Am. v. Warrior & Gulf Navigation Co.*, 363 U.S. 574, 581 (1960).

172 **an alternative control center:** In 1947, 35 percent of U.S. private-sector workers belonged to unions; by 2006, only 7.4 percent did. See Barry Hirsch, "Sluggish Institutions in a Dynamic World: Can Unions and Industrial Competition Coexist?," *Journal of Economic Perspectives* 22, no. 1 (2008): 155.

172 **"what was good for the country":** Wilson had been nominated by President Dwight Eisenhower to serve as secretary of defense and made this remark in response to a question in his confirmation hearing about whether he would be able to put the interests of the United States before those of General Motors. See "Charles E. Wilson," Department of Defense Historical Office, accessed October 22, 2018, https://history.defense.gov /Multimedia/Biographies/Article-View/Article/571268 /charles-e-wilson/.

172 **"Great Ideas of Western Man":** The print series was inaugurated in 1950–51 and ran through 1975. Artists including Ben Shahn, Alvin Lustig, René Magritte, Lester Beall, and Saul Bass created original works representing ideas from Aristotle, Kant, Rousseau, and Freud, among others. See Neil Harris and Martina Roudabush Norelli, *Art, Design, and the Modern Corporation: The Collection of Container Corporation of America, a Gift to the National Museum of American Art* (Washington, DC: Smithsonian Institution Press, 1985).

172 **"the ads in this series convey":** Tom Wolfe, "Advertising's Secret Messages," *New York Magazine*, July 17, 1972, 23.

172 **only about sixteen thousand employees:** Douglas MacMillan and Telis Demos, "Uber Valued at More Than $50 Billion," *Wall Street Journal*, July 31, 2015, accessed November 18, 2018, www.wsj.com/articles/uber-valued-at-more-than-50-billion-1438367457; "Uber Newsroom, Company Info," Uber, accessed October 22, 2018, www.uber.com/newsroom/company-info/.

172 **never met middle management:** Min Kying Lee et al., "Working with Machines: The Impact of Algorithmic and Data-Driven Management on Human Workers," *Proceedings of the 33rd Annual ACM Conference on Human Factors in Computing Systems* (April 2015): 1603, www.cs.cmu.edu/~mklee/materials /Publication/2015-CHI_algorithmic_management.pdf.

173 **every assembly line:** For a broad overview of modern supply chain management, see generally Martin Christopher, *Logistics and Supply Chain Management*, 5th ed. (Harlow: Pearson, 2016), 35 (discussing how "just-in-time" strategy results in minimal inventory), 194 (the use of event management software to manage inventory levels), 225–26 (discussing the merits of Six Sigma management techniques), 289 (a change-embracing corporate culture). For in-depth case studies of Walmart's and Amazon's supply chains, see Colby Ronald Chiles and Marguarette Thi Dau, "An Analysis of Current Supply Chain Best Practices in the Retail Industry with Case Studies of Wal-Mart and Amazon.com" (master's thesis, Georgia Institute of Technology, 2005), 66, 70, 103–4 (discussing both companies' culture of innovation, including Walmart's "Everyday Low Prices" mentality and its managers' autonomy and incentives to keep costs low).

173 **before the mid-1980s:** Cappelli, *The New Deal at Work*, 115–16. Note that Cappelli excepts "reductions in force caused by technological developments" or "sharp decline[s] in business" from this rule.

173 **express "no layoff" policies:** According to "The 100 Best Companies to Work for in America," in 1993 ten had "no layoff" policies; by 1997 only two did, and only one of the two was a public company. See Cappelli, *The New Deal at Work*, 115.

173 **"layers of bureaucrats reporting to bureaucrats":** See Carl Icahn, "Leveraged Buyouts: America Pays the Price; The Case for Takeovers," *New York Times Magazine*, January 29, 1989 (quoted in Adam Goldstein, "Revenge of the Managers: Labor Cost-Cutting and the Paradoxical Resurgence of Managerialism in the Shareholder Value Era, 1984 to 2001," *American Sociological Review* 77, no. 2 (2012): 273, hereafter cited as Goldstein, "Revenge of the Managers"). Goldstein adds that Icahn attributed Japan's then-greater manufacturing productivity growth to "our lack of managerial talent and the strangling bureaucracy that exists in most of corporate America."

173 **from 1:5 to 1:30:** See Rosemary Batt, "From Bureaucracy to Enterprise? The Changing Jobs and Careers of Managers in Telecommunications Service," in *Broken Ladders: Managerial Careers in the New Economy*, ed. Paul Osterman (New York: Oxford University Press, 1996), 55–80; Goldstein, "Revenge of the Managers," 273.

173 **twice the rate of nonmanagerial workers:** Managerial displacement rates roughly doubled over these decades (even as displacement rates for nonmanagerial workers declined). See Jennifer Gardner, "Worker Displacement: A Decade of Change," *Monthly Labor Review* 118 (1995): 45–57; Goldstein, "Revenge of the Managers," 273. White-collar and management employees bore disproportionate shares of the displacements, accounting for only 40 percent of jobs but between 60 and 75 percent of jobs cut. See Cappelli, *The New Deal at Work*, 117–19, Figure 4-2; Goldstein, "Revenge of the Managers," 273. See also American Management Association, *1998 AMA Survey on Job Creation, Job Elimination, and Downsizing* (New York:

American Management Association, 1998) and American Management Association, *1994 AMA Survey on Downsizing: Summary of Key Findings* (New York: American Management Association, 1994), 2, which found that the hundred largest companies in the United States have seen 22 percent of their workforce laid off since 1978, with 77 percent of those cuts targeted at white-collar jobs.

173 **between 1987 and 2006:** Paul Osterman, *The Truth About Middle Managers: Who They Are, How They Work, Why They Matter* (Cambridge, MA: Harvard Business Press, 2009), 54, Table 3-3. Hereafter cited as Osterman, *The Truth About Middle Managers*.

173 **"not [to] automat[e]":** Sarah O'Connor, "When Your Boss Is an Algorithm," *Financial Times*, September 8, 2016, accessed November 18, 2018, www.ft.com/content/88fdc58e-754f-11e6-b60a-de4532d5ea35. Hereafter cited as O'Connor, "When Your Boss Is an Algorithm."

173 **unprofitable firms:** See Dirk Zorn et al., "Managing Investors: How Financial Markets Reshaped the American Firm," in *The Sociology of Financial Markets*, ed. Karin Knorr Cetina and Alex Preda (New York: Oxford University Press, 2005), 269–89; Goldstein, "Revenge of the Managers," 271.

Managers were more likely to be downsized in heavily unionized firms (where the management function spread deeper into the nominally production workforce). See William Baumol, Alan Blinder, and Edward Wolf, *Downsizing in America: Reality, Causes, and Consequences* (New York: Russell Sage Foundation, 2003); Goldstein, "Revenge of the Managers," 271.

174 **booms as well as busts:** Bureau of Labor Statistics, "Industrial Production Managers," Occupation Outlook Handbook, 2016–17 Edition, December 17, 2015. The BLS statistics show the number of industrial production managers falling more or less consistently from 208,000 in 1997 to 183,050 in 2001 to 143,310 in 2010. While there has been a slight resurgence since then to 168,400 in 2016, the BLS projects a 4 percent decline in the occupation over the next ten years.

174 **in the 1990s:** Lori Kletzer, "Job Displacement," *Journal of Economic Perspectives* 12, no. 1 (Winter 1998): 118; Peter Cappelli, "Examining the Incidence of Downsizing and Its Effect on Organizational Performance," in *On the Job: Is Long-Term Employment a Thing of the Past?*, ed. David Neumark (New York: Russell Sage Foundation, 2000), 463–516; Goldstein, "Revenge of the Managers," 271.

The share of layoffs caused by corporate restructurings as opposed to economic losses nearly tripled. See Osterman, *The Truth About Middle Managers*, 45, citing Kevin Hallock, "A Descriptive Analysis of Layoffs in Large U.S. Firms Using Archival Data over Three Decades and Interviews with Senior Managers," working paper, Cornell Industrial and Labor Relations School, Ithaca, NY, August 2005, https://digitalcommons .ilr.cornell.edu/cgi/viewcontent.cgi?referer=&httpsredir=1 &article=1238&context=articles. According to the American Management Association, *1994 AMA Survey on Downsizing: Summary of Key Findings* (New York: American Management Association, 1994), 2, 66 percent of job cuts were due to restructuring (as compared to just 23 percent due to outsourcing). See also Cappelli, *The New Deal at Work*, 116–17.

174 **to under one-sixteenth today:** See Bureau of Labor Statistics, "Union Membership Rate 10.7 Percent in 2016," February 9, 2017, accessed October 22, 2018, www.bls.gov/opub/ted/2017 /union-membership-rate-10-point-7-percent-in-2016.htm.

174 **advanced inside the company:** Cappelli, *The New Deal at Work*, 140; Aaron Bernstein, "At UPS, Part-Time Work Is a Full-Time Issue," *Business Week*, June 16, 1997, 88–90.

174 **under ever more tightly controlled contracts:** Short-term contracts subject the jobs to market forces, which set and revise the terms of employment from outside the firm. Cappelli, *The New Deal at Work*, 28, 33, 41.

174 **even specified outputs:** Cappelli, *The New Deal at Work*, 28.

174 **returned to work for the firm as consultants:** Cappelli, *The New Deal at Work*, 74 (citing Dean Minderman, "Big Blues," *Credit Union Management* (February 1995): 15–17). IBM's practice, moreover, is typical rather than exceptional. According to the U.S. Department of Labor, 17 percent of temporary workers had a "previous, different relationship" with their current

employers, and an American Management Association survey found that 30 percent of employers surveyed had brought back downsized employees as contractors or otherwise temporary workers. See Cappelli, *The New Deal at Work*, 137.

Temporary or contract workers do necessarily cost employers less than the permanent workers that they replace. Temporary workers are paid 14 percent less in wages than permanent employees, on average, and are half as likely to receive health care benefits. But these savings must be set against the fees charged by the agencies that provide temporary workers, which amount to roughly 40 percent of temporary workers' wages. Indeed, only 20 percent of employers report that total hourly costs are lower for temporary, part-time, or contract workers than for permanent employees. The principal benefit firms receive from replacing permanent with temporary workers concerns not direct costs but rather flexibility. Temporary workers can be hired and fired as permanent workers cannot be. Cappelli, *The New Deal at Work*, 140. See also Susan N. Houseman, "Temporary, Part-Time, and Contract Employment in the United States," Department of Labor, November 1996, http://citeseerx.ist.psu.edu /viewdoc/download?doi=10.1.1.210.2922&rep=rep1&type =pdf.

The vast structural shift away from permanent employees and toward subcontractors is driven less by savings on direct compensation and more by managerial efficiencies, associated with the flatter hierarchies and rising elite powers of command that the main text elaborates.

174 **for each ride that they complete:** O'Connor, "When Your Boss Is an Algorithm."

174 **subcontractors who employ twenty-five thousand:** Cappelli, *The New Deal at Work*, 103.

174 **literally no employees at all:** Cappelli, *The New Deal at Work*, 51, 101.

174 **workers of its subcontractors:** Cappelli, *The New Deal at Work*, 104.

175 **put them into boxes:** Amazon does this using highly skilled production process engineers, including some hired as consultants from industrial firms such as Toyota. See Simon Head, *Mindless: Why Smarter Machines Are Making Dumber Humans* (New York: Basic Books, 2014), 29–46, hereafter cited as Head, *Mindless*; Niv Dror, "A Fireside Chat with Jeff Bezos: Innovation & All Things Amazon," *Data Fox*, accessed October 22, 2018, https://blog.datafox.com/jeff-bezos-fireside-chat/; Marc Onetto, "When Toyota Met E-commerce: Lean at Amazon," *McKinsey Quarterly* (February 2014), www.mckinsey.com/busi ness-functions/operations/our-insights/when-toyota-met-e-co mmerce-lean-at-amazon.

175 **buys each part individually:** See Head, *Mindless*, 29–46; Simon Head, "Worse Than Walmart: Amazon's Sick Brutality and Secret History of Ruthlessly Intimidating Workers," *Salon*, February 23, 2014, accessed November 18, 2018, www.salon .com/2014/02/23/worse_than_wal_mart_amazons_sick_bru tality_and_secret_history_of_ruthlessly_intimidating_work ers/.

175 **Kiva Systems:** Nick Wingfield, "As Amazon Pushes Forward with Robots, Workers Find New Roles," *New York Times*, September 10, 2017, accessed November 18, 2018, www.nytimes .com/2017/09/10/technology/amazon-robots-workers .html.

175 **only four human workers:** Danielle Paquette, "He's One of the Only Humans at Work—and He Loves It," *Washington Post*, September 10, 2018, accessed October 24, 2018, www.washing tonpost.com/world/asia_pacific/hes-one-of-the-only -humans-at-work—and-he-loves-it/2018/09/09/71392542 -9541-11e8-8ffb-5de6d5e49ada_story.html?utm_term=.9be 29f5cc435.

175 **differences of kind rather than degree:** Firms have reduced the number of positions between CEOs and division heads, increased the number of managers directly reporting to the CEO, and increased the size of executive teams. See Raghuram G. Rajan and Julie Wulf, "The Flattening Firm: Evidence from Panel Data on the Changing Nature of Corporate Hierarchies," *Review of Economics and Statistics* 88, no. 4 (November 2006): 759; Julie Wulf, "The Flattened Firm: Not as Advertised," *California Management Review* 55, no. 1 (Fall 2012): 5.

175 **(like McDonald's current CEO):** "Steve Easterbrook: President and Chief Executive Officer," McDonald's, accessed October 22, 2018, http://news.mcdonalds.com/executive-team/steve -easterbrook.

175 **have equivalent postgraduate training:** See Joe O'Mahoney, *Management Consultancy* (Oxford: Oxford University Press, (2010), 277. Hereafter cited as O'Mahoney, *Management Consultancy*.

176 **once performed internally:** Management consulting began, alongside industrialization, to provide advice to owners of newly large and elaborate factories. See O'Mahoney, *Management Consultancy*, 16. But it would be 1947 before the then-leading consultancy, Booz Allen, achieved revenues of $2 million. José de la Torre, Yves L. Doz, and Timothy Michael Devinney, *Managing the Global Corporation: Case Studies in Strategy and Management* (New York: McGraw-Hill, 2001). Throughout this period, virtually no elite college or business school graduates joined consulting firms. And as recently as 1980, management consulting remained an unusual—indeed rare—destination for MBAs at top schools such as Wharton. See Cappelli, *The New Deal at Work*, 143.

In the subsequent decades, however, consulting grew rapidly alongside middle management's decline. Between 1972 and 1997, employment in "business services," which includes strategy consulting, grew more than twice as fast as the rest of the economy. The sector has averaged 6.9 percent annual growth. Cappelli, *The New Deal at Work*, 143, citing Angela Clinton, "Flexible Labor: Restructuring and the American Work Force," *Monthly Labor Review* (August 1997): 3–17. And growth has been still more rapid in recent years, and especially at the top: for example, the big three strategy consulting firms (McKinsey & Company, Bain & Company, and the Boston Consulting Group) nowadays regularly boast double-digit revenue growth and today generate over $10 billion in revenues and employ over thirty thousand people. In 2018, Bain & Company had $3.4 billion in revenue and eight thousand employees, Boston Consulting Group had $6.3 billion in revenue and sixteen thousand employees, and McKinsey & Co. had $10 billion in revenue and twenty-seven thousand employees. See "America's Largest Private Companies 2016," *Forbes*, accessed October 22, 2018, www .forbes.com/largest-private-companies/list. See also "Management Consulting: To the Brainy, the Spoils," *The Economist*, May 11, 2013, accessed November 18, 2018, www.economist .com/business/2013/05/11/to-the-brainy-the-spoils. Hereafter cited as "To the Brainy, the Spoils."

Like the top banks, these firms self-consciously cast their consultants as not just elite but super-elite. Bob Bechek of Bain & Company insists that less elite business advisers, even though they might excel at "heavy lift, repeatable work," cannot do the work of management consultants, who "concoct novel solutions to unique problems, which is hard." See "To the Brainy, the Spoils." (The quoted words are *The Economist*'s paraphrase of Bechek's thoughts.) By the early 1990s, roughly a quarter of elite MBAs joined consulting firms, and by 2000 nearly half did. Cappelli, *The New Deal at Work*, 143, reporting that 26 percent of Wharton graduates went into consulting in 1990 and that 46 percent did in 1996.

176 **"with the push of a button":** "To the Brainy, the Spoils."

176 **In typical recent years:** These numbers come from data compiled by the research firm Equilar in conjunction with the *New York Times*, based on a systematic survey of all publicly traded, U.S.-based or -listed companies with annual revenues greater than $1 billion. See "Equilar 200: Ranking the Largest CEO Pay Packages," *Equilar*, May 25, 2017, accessed October 22, 2018, www.equilar.com/reports/49-equilar-200-ranking-the-largest -ceo-pay-packages-2017.html; "200 Highest-Paid CEOs 2016," *Equilar*, May 27, 2016, accessed October 22, 2018, www.equilar .com/reports/38-new-york-times-200-highest-paid-ceos-2016 .html.

176 **The three-hundred-times-median-work incomes:** Lawrence Mishel and Alyssa Davis, "CEO Pay Has Grown 90 Times Faster than Typical Worker Pay Since 1978," Economic Policy Institute, July 1, 2015, accessed October 22, 2018, www.epi.org /publication/ceo-pay-has-grown-90-times-faster-than-typical -worker-pay-since-1978/; Lawrence Mishel and Alyssa Davis,

"Top CEOs Make 300 Times More Than Typical Workers: Pay Growth Surpasses Stock Gains and Wage Growth of Top 0.1 Percent," Economic Policy Institute, June 21, 2015, accessed October 22, 2018, www.epi.org/publication/top-ceos-make-300-times-more-than-workers-pay-growth-surpasses-market-gains-and-the-rest-of-the-0-1-percent/.

176 **the entire S&P 1500's profits:** A 2005 analysis of compensation for the top five highest-paid officers in the ExecuComp database (which includes "all the S&P 500, Mid-Cap 400, and Small-Cap 600 companies . . . also known as the S&P 1,500") found that, between 2001 and 2003, the "ratio of aggregate [top-five] executive compensation to aggregate [S&P 1500] earnings" was 9.8 percent. See Lucian Bebchuk and Yaniv Grinstein, "The Growth of Executive Pay," *Oxford Review of Economic Policy* 21, no. 2 (2005): 283, 284, 297.

176 **fat and mean:** The phrase comes from David Gordon, *Fat and Mean: The Corporate Squeeze of Working Americans and the Myth of Managerial Downsizing* (New York: Free Press, 1996). A more recent and very careful study of managerial workers confirms Gordon's thesis, revealing that even as managers have become more elevated, with supervisory incomes growing faster than nonsupervisory incomes, supervisory jobs also account for an increasing share of the overall private-sector labor market. See Goldstein, "Revenge of the Managers."

176 **a set of tasks and skills:** Cappelli, *The New Deal at Work*, 159–60. Cappelli adds that on the midcentury model, the high/low-status fault line in the workplace lay between exempt and nonexempt workers under the Fair Labor Standards Act. Today, the fault line lies between top managers and everyone else. Cappelli, *The New Deal at Work*, 236–37.

177 **determine status and pay:** See generally Cappelli, *The New Deal at Work*, 163. See also Stephen R. Barley, "The Turn to a Horizontal Division of Labor: On the Occupationalization of Educational Research and Improvement, ES," paper prepared for the U.S. Department of Education, January 1994.

177 **a bright and glossy sheen:** Even the glossy jobs have become fewer as their shine has grown. There were, for example, nearly four hundred fewer corporate officer positions across Fortune 500 firms in 2005 than there had been a decade earlier, even though the economy was nearly 40 percent bigger. Hewlett and Luce, "Extreme Jobs," 52. The World Bank, "World Development Indicators," http://databank.worldbank.org/data/source/world-development-indicators.

177 **In 1967, single-store firms:** In 1948, single-location firms (some incorporated, some not) still made 70.4 percent of all retail sales, while large chains accounted for only 12.3 percent. Large chains, for purposes of these shares, are firms with more than one hundred retail locations. Ronald S. Jarmin et al., "The Role of Retail Chains: National, Regional, and Industry Results," in *Producer Dynamics: New Evidence from the Micro Data*, ed. Timothy Dunne, J. Bradford Jensen, and Mark J. Roberts (Chicago: University of Chicago Press, 2009), 237–38.

177 **"In the small independent establishment":** Herbert Koshetz, "The Merchant's View: An Examination of Retailing Discovers Few in Field Receive Proper Training," *New York Times*, March 18, 1962, accessed November 18, 2018, https://timesmachine.nytimes.com/timesmachine/1962/03/18/89502586.html?action=click&contentCollection=Archives&module=LedeAsset&region=ArchiveBody&pgtype=article&pageNumber=155. Hereafter cited as Koshetz, "Merchant's View."

177 **"In the larger establishments":** Koshetz, "Merchant's View."

177 **Today, retail is dominated:** See National Retail Federation, "Top 100 Retailers," *Stores*, June 26, 2017, https://stores.org/2017/06/26/top-100-retailers/.
These and other massive chains—over forty in total—all have over one hundred stores and, moreover, now dominate the market: by 2010, the ten largest grocery chains accounted for 70 percent of sales, for example. This is startlingly new. As recently as 2000, for example, the ten largest grocery chains made up 30 percent of the market. See Niraj Dawar and Jason Stornelli, "Rebuilding the Relationship Between Manufacturers and Retailers," *MIT Sloan Management Review* (Winter 2013). Chains also now account for over two-thirds of retail employment overall. Chains already accounted for a larger share of overall retail employment than single-store firms in 1980. See Ronald S.

Jarmin et al., "The Role of Retail Chains: National, Regional, and Industry Results," in *Producer Dynamics: New Evidence from the Micro Data*, ed. Timothy Dunne, J. Bradford Jensen, and Mark J. Roberts (Chicago: University of Chicago Press, 2009), 240.
As Amazon and other online retailers blossom, stores (now virtual) only get bigger. Between 2007 and 2012, for example, total online sales grew almost three times as fast as the number of online stores. Ominously, employment in online retail decreased slightly. The number of brick-and-mortar stores and total employment in such stores both declined by slightly over 5 percent over this period. See Robin Harding, "Technology Shakes Up US Economy," *Financial Times*, March 26, 2014, www.ft.com/cms/s/0/f8a95502-b502-11e3-af92-00144feabdc0.html#axzz4JxZMpgp9. Hereafter cited as Harding, "Technology Shakes Up US Economy." U.S. Census Bureau, "Economic Census: Tables: 2012," www.census.gov/programs-surveys/economic-census/data/tables.2012.html.html.

177 **according to another:** See Reich, *Supercapitalism*, 89–90; Sarah Nassauer, "At Walmart, the CEO Makes 1,188 Times as Much as the Median Worker," *Wall Street Journal*, April 20, 2018, accessed October 24 2018, www.wsj.com/articles/at-walmart-the-ceo-makes-1-188-times-as-much-as-the-median-worker-1524261608. Note that Walmart's profits on sales are roughly 3.5 percent, or about $6,000 per employee (reported for 2005). Hereafter cited as Nassauer, "At Walmart, the CEO Makes 1,188 Times as Much." This entails that although Walmart might pay its workers appreciably more and still generate profits for its shareholders, it would not afford to pay anything approaching GM's old wages. Once again, rising economic inequality more significantly reflects deep structural shifts in both production technologies and returns to skill than new exploitation or advantage taking by capital over labor.

178 **hosted, ironically, by Walmart's stores:** The poverty threshold for a family of four including two children is $24,339. U.S. Census Bureau, "Poverty Thresholds," 2017, www.census.gov/data/tables/time-series/demo/income-poverty/historical-poverty-thresholds.html. For food drives at Walmart, see Hayley Peterson, "Wal-Mart Asks Workers to Donate Food to Its Needy Employees," *Business Insider*, November 20, 2014, accessed November 18, 2018, www.businessinsider.com/walmart-employee-food-drive-2014-11.

178 **"let's succeed":** Krystina Gustafson, "Wal-Mart Defends Employee Food Drive," CNBC, November 20, 2014, accessed October 26 2018, www.cnbc.com/2014/11/20/wal-mart-defends-employee-food-drive.html.

178 **the firm's median worker:** Nassauer, "At Walmart, the CEO Makes 1,188 Times as Much."

178 **Percolata of Silicon Valley:** Percolata measures the effects of traffic, wealth, online browsing, and many other factors on customer behavior and installs sensors in stores to monitor customer flow, worker activity, and the interactions between them to measure and rank street-level workers for "true productivity" or "shopper yield," measures of how much revenue each generates. The firm then determines which workers are most productive in which circumstances and in what combinations and adjusts work schedules in fifteen-minute intervals to optimize selling efficiency, which it claims to boost by up to 30 percent. See O'Connor, "When Your Boss Is an Algorithm."

178 **hike prices where they do not:** Tim Adams, "Surge Pricing Comes to the Supermarket," *Guardian*, June 4, 2017, www.theguardian.com/technology/2017/jun/04/surge-pricing-comes-to-the-supermarket-dynamic-personal-data.

178 **without in-store assistance:** Manufacturers' applications for trademarks nearly tripled between 1968 and 1989. David W. Boyd, "From 'Mom and Pop' to Wal-Mart: The Impact of the Consumer Goods Pricing Act of 1975 on the Retail Sector in the United States," *Journal of Economic Issues* 31, no. 1 (1997): 226. And advertising's share of GDP, which had fallen throughout the Great Compression, began a steady climb in 1975. Douglas A. Galbi, "Some Economics of Personal Activity and Implications for the Digital Economy," August 6, 2001, 7, https://papers.ssrn.com/sol3/papers.cfm?abstract_id=275346.

178 **richest person in modern history:** See Robert Frank, "Jeff Bezos Is Now the Richest Man in Modern History," CNBC, July 18, 2018, accessed November 18, 2018, www.cnbc.com

/2018/07/16/jeff-bezos-is-now-the-richest-man-in-modern
-history.html.

178  **Rhodes Scholars studying at Oxford:** Tom Robinson, *Jeff Bezos: Amazon.com Architect* (Minneapolis: ABDO Publishing, 2010), 26. Jillian D'Onfro, "What Happened to 7 of the Earliest Employees Who Launched Amazon," *Business Insider*, April 18, 2014, accessed November 18, 2018, www.businessinsider.com /amazons-earliest-employees-2014-4.

178  **data entry workers:** The Department of Labor reports that over the first decade of the new millennium, the United States lost more than 1.1 million specifically secretarial jobs. The same decade also saw steep declines in other clerical jobs: employment for telephone operators, typists and word processors, travel agents, and bookkeepers fell by 64, 63, 46, and 26 percent respectively. See Andrew Leonard, "The Internet's Greatest Disruptive Innovation: Inequality," *Salon*, July 19, 2013, accessed November 18, 2018, www.salon.com/2013/07/19/the_inter nets_greatest_disruptive_innovation_inequality/. These job losses add up, so that since 2007, the United States has lost more than two million clerical jobs in total. Quoted in Robin Harding, "US Has Lost 2m Clerical Jobs Since 2007," *Financial Times*, April 1, 2013, accessed November 18, 2018, www .ft.com/content/37666e6c-9ae5-11e2-b982-00144feabdc0.

178  **workers with JDs and BAs:** See Michael Simkovic, "In Law Firms, Lawyers and Paralegals Prosper While Secretarial Jobs Disappear," *Brian Leiter's Law School Reports*, April 1, 2016, accessed November 18, 2018, http://taxprof.typepad.com/tax prof_blog/2016/04/simkovich-law-firms-lawyers-and-para legals-prosper-while-secretarial-jobs-disappear.html. As automation moves up the skill hierarchy, the least elaborately trained lawyers will also come increasingly under pressure.

178  **more intricate and inventive designs:** See Richard Sennett, *The Corrosion of Character: The Personal Consequences of Work in the New Capitalism* (New York: W. W. Norton, 2011), 73. See also Stanley Aronowitz and Willia DiFaxio, *The Jobless Future: Sci-Tech and the Dogma of Work* (Minneapolis: University of Minnesota Press, 1995), 110.

178  **within traveling range:** See Sherwin Rosen, "The Economics of Superstars," *American Economic Review* 71, no. 5 (December 1981): 845–58; and Frank and Cook, *The Winner-Take-All Society*.

178  **made nearly $100 million:** See "The World's Highest Paid Celebrities 2017," *Forbes*, June 12, 2017, accessed November 18, 2018, www.forbes.com/celebrities/list/#tab:overall.

178  **more than their midcentury counterparts:** Mickey Mantle, for example, made less than $1 million (2015 dollars) per year at midcentury. Michael Haupert, "MLB's Annual Salary Leaders Since 1874," Society for American Baseball Research, December 1, 2016.

178  **more than backup singers:** Pam McCallum, "The Average Salary of a Back-Up Singer," *Sapling*, June 17, 2011.

178  **the NBA's development league:** Michael McCann, "The G-League: 12 Takeaways on NBA's New Deal," *Sports Illustrated*, February 14, 2017, accessed November 18, 2018, www .si.com/nba/2017/02/14/nba-gatorade-g-league-deal-adam -silver-takeaways.

178  **television scriptwriters:** "How Much Does a Television Writer Make in the United States?," Sokanu, accessed October 10, 2018, www.sokanu.com/careers/television-writer/salary/.

178  **make today:** More generally, between 1982 and 2003, the share of total industry revenues captured by the top 1 percent of pop stars more than doubled. See Victor Ginsburgh and David Throsby, eds., *Handbook of the Economics of Art and Culture, Volume 1* (Amsterdam: Elsevier, 2006), 684. The ratios of CEO pay to the pay of the next highly paid employees of a firm, and the ratio of the highest-paid 10 percent of CEOs to the median CEOs, have similarly increased. See Carola Frydman and Raven E. Saks, "Executive Compensation: A New View from a Long-Term Perspective, 1936–2005," *Review of Financial Studies* 23, no. 5 (February 2010), http://web.mit.edu/frydman/www/trends _rfs2010.pdf.

179  **plus substantial benefits:** See Reich, *Supercapitalism*, 89–90. Note that Walmart's profits on sales are roughly 3.5 percent, or about $6,000 per employee (reported for 2005). This entails that although Walmart might pay its workers appreciably more and still generate profits for its shareholders, it would not afford

to pay anything approaching GM's old wages. Once again, rising economic inequality more significantly reflects deep structural shifts in both production technologies and returns to skill than new exploitation or advantages taking by capital over labor.

179  **trend toward robot production is accelerating:** U.S. investment in robotics more than doubled from 2014 to 2015. See Richard Waters and Kana Inagaki, "Investment Surge Gives US the Early Lead in Rise of the Robots," *Financial Times*, May 3, 2016, accessed November 18, 2018, www.ft.com/content /87f44872-1080-11e6-91da-096d89bd2173, reporting study by venture capital research group CB Insights. Hereafter cited as Waters and Inagaki, "Investment Surge." See also Research Brief, "Robots R' Us: Funding and Deal Activity to Robotics See New Highs in 2015," CB Insights, March 23, 2016, accessed November 18, 2018, www.cbinsights.com/research/robotics-start ups-funding/. And the worldwide market for production robots alone is growing at a compound annual rate of 17 percent, while annual patent filings related to robotics have tripled in the past decade. Richard Waters and Tim Bradshaw, "Rise of the Robots Is Sparking an Investment Boom," *Financial Times*, May 3, 2016, accessed November 18, 2018, www.ft.com/content/5a 352264-0e26-11e6-ad80-67655613c2d6. See also Waters and Inagaki, "Investment Surge," reporting study by economic research group IDC.

179  **in Europe and Asia:** See International Federation of Robotics, *World Robotics Report 2016*, September 29, 2016, Figure 2.9, https://ifr.org/ifr-press-releases/news/world-robotics-report -2016, and James Carroll, "Industrial Robots in the United States on the Rise," Vision Systems Design, September 6, 2016, www.vision-systems.com/articles/2016/12/industrial-robots -in-the-united-states-on-the-rise.html.

179  **since the late 1970s:** Total manufacturing employment peaked in the late 1970s, when roughly 19.5 million Americans held manufacturing jobs. See, e.g., Martin Neil Baily and Barry P. Bosworth, "U.S. Manufacturing: Understanding Its Past and Its Potential Future," *Journal of Economic Perspectives* 28, no. 1 (Winter 2004): 3–26, 12, Figure 2. Hereafter cited as Baily and Bosworth, "U.S. Manufacturing."

  Since then, domestic manufacturing employment has fallen steadily. By 1992 the sector sustained only 16.5 million jobs, and by 2012, manufacturing employment had fallen to below 12 million, although it would subsequently recover to just over 12 million. See also Bureau of Labor Statistics, "Employment, Hours, and Earnings from the Current Employment Statistics Survey (National)," extracted June 22, 2017, https://data .bls.gov/timeseries/CES3000000001.

179  **than it currently provides:** In the late 1960s, manufacturing accounted for nearly 25 percent of all U.S. employment. See Baily and Bosworth, "U.S. Manufacturing," 4, Figure 1. Today, the U.S. civilian labor force comprises roughly 160 million persons, of which roughly 150 million are employed. See Bureau of Labor Statistics, *The Employment Situation—May 2017*, Summary Table A, https://www.bls.gov/news.release/archives/emp sit_06022017.pdf. Twenty-five percent of 150 million is 37.5 million. On the other hand, total manufacturing today employs perhaps 12 million persons. See Baily and Bosworth, "U.S. Manufacturing," 12, Figure 2.

179  **increased by 44 percent:** This entails that more than 100 percent of the overall decline in manufacturing employment comes from the mid-skilled, non-college-educated segment of the industrial workforce. See Robert Shapiro, "Robotic Technologies Could Aggravate the U.S. Problem of Slow Jobs Growth," *Daily Beast*, July 19, 2013, accessed November 18, 2018, www.thedai lybeast.com/articles/2013/07/19/robotic-technologies-could -aggravate-the-u-s-problem-of-slow-jobs-growth.html. See also Manufacturing Institute, "Percent of Manufacturing Workforce by Education Level," April 2014, www.themanufactur inginstitute.org/Research/Facts-About-Manufacturing /Workforce-and-Compensation/Workforce-by-Education /Workforce-by-Education.aspx, and Elka Torpey, "Got Skills? Think Manufacturing," Bureau of Labor Statistics, June 2014, www.bls.gov/careeroutlook/2014/article/manufacturing.htm.

  The United States is not exceptional in this regard. In each of the seven largest advanced economies—Canada, France, Germany, Italy, Japan, the United Kingdom, and the United States—the share of manufacturing jobs held by white- rather than blue-collar workers increased in both the 1980s and the 1990s. See Mariacristina Piva, Enrico Santarelli, and Marco Vivarelli, "The Skill Bias Effect of Technological and Organizational Change: Evidence and Policy Implications," *Research Policy* 34 (2005): 141–57, 143.

179    **even as its share of employment declined:** Baily and Bosworth, "U.S. Manufacturing," 4, Figure 1. See also YiLi Chien and Paul Morris, "Is U.S. Manufacturing Really Declining?," Federal Reserve Bank of St. Louis On the Economy Blog, April 11, 2017, accessed January 28, 2019, www.stlouisfed.org/on-the-economy/2017/april/us-manufacturing-really-declining; Peter Wehner and Robert Beschel Jr., "How to Think About Inequality," *National Affairs* 11 (Spring 2012), accessed November 18, 2018, www.nationalaffairs.com/publications/detail/how-to-think-about-inequality; Rex Nutting, "Think Nothing Is Made in America? Output Has Doubled in Three Decades," MarketWatch, March 28, 2016, www.marketwatch.com/story/us-manufacturing-dead-output-has-doubled-in-three-decades-2016-03-28; Harding, "Technology Shakes Up US Economy."

Manufacturing has sustained its output share almost entirely on account of massive increases in productivity and output in the computer and electronics industry, which hires disproportionately high-skilled workers, increasingly to design and implement robotic production. See Baily and Bosworth, "U.S. Manufacturing," 3–26. For example, a computer's most valuable component, the motherboard, is today largely robot-made. See Catherine Rampell, "When Cheap Foreign Labor Gets Less Cheap," *New York Times*, December 7, 2012, accessed November 18, 2018, https://economix.blogs.nytimes.com/2012/12/07/when-cheap-foreign-labor-gets-less-cheap/?partner=rss&emc=rss&_r=0.

179    **increased by over 15 percent:** See Harding, "Technology Shakes Up US Economy."

179    **it was sold to Facebook for $1 billion:** On Kodak, see Susan Christopherson and Jennifer Clark, *Remaking Regional Economies: Power, Labor, and Firm Strategies in the Knowledge Economy* (New York: Routledge, 2007), 57–84.

On Instagram, see Scott Timberg, "Jaron Lanier: The Internet Destroyed the Middle Class," *Salon*, May 12, 2013, accessed November 18, 2018, www.salon.com/2013/05/12/jaron_lanier_the_internet_destroyed_the_middle_class/. Hereafter cited as Timberg, "Internet Destroyed."

Instagram's tiny super-skilled workforce can meet the firm's staffing needs only because it works alongside the mass of people who use its technology to stage, capture, process, and print images and thus constitute, in structure, a low-skilled labor force, even as they conceive of themselves not as producers but rather consumers. Jaron Lanier thus observes that lots of people—the site's users who contribute content and even formatting—"work" at Instagram, in a sense. See Timberg, "Internet Destroyed."

This pattern, incidentally, is far from unique. It has occurred before, including in connection with image production: photography, as Lanier also notes, itself enabled a mass of low-skilled snapshot takers to displace mid-skilled painters and illustrators. See Timberg, "Internet Destroyed." The same pattern arises in other sectors also: to name but one example, Ikea's customers also function, structurally speaking, as a mass of unskilled furniture assembly labor.

179    **fabulously wealthy, of course:** Facebook itself employs far fewer people than Kodak ever did, and several of them have become far richer than Kodak's founder, George Eastman, ever was.

180    **mostly since 2000:** The share of nonroutine cognitive jobs in the labor market overall grew by 8.2 percent between 1982 and 1992, 10.6 percent between 1992 and 2002, and 14.9 percent between 2002 and 2017. The share of nonroutine manual jobs grew by 0.8, 1.3, and 9.4 percent in each of these decades. And the share of routine jobs fell by 4.5, 6.7, and 13.7 percent. These data come from Nir Jaimovich and Henry E. Siu, "Job Polarization and Jobless Recoveries," 8, Figure 3, forthcoming in *Review of Economics and Statistics*, accessed November 18, 2018, http://faculty.arts.ubc.ca/hsiu/pubs/polar20180903.pdf. Hereafter cited as Jaimovich and Siu, "Job Polarization and Jobless Recoveries."

180    **increased by more than a third:** Nonroutine cognitive jobs have increased from 29 to 40 percent of all jobs, routine jobs have fallen from 56 to 42 percent, and nonroutine manual jobs have increased from 15 to 18 percent. These conclusions simply cumulate the decadal shifts reported in the prior note.

180    **is today nearly 20 percent:** Cappelli, *The New Deal at Work*, 159–60. Cappelli adds that on the midcentury model, the high/low-status fault line in the workplace lay between exempt and nonexempt workers under the Fair Labor Standards Act. See Cappelli, *The New Deal at Work*, 236–37. Today, the fault line lies between top managers and everyone else.

181    **falling middle-class incomes:** See Jeffrey P. Thompson and Elias Leight, "Do Rising Top Income Shares Affect the Incomes or Earnings of Low and Middle-Income Families," *B.E. Journal of Economic Analysis & Policy* 12, no. 1 (2012): 26. Thompson and Leight deploy cross-state comparisons, which reveal that states with more rapidly rising top income shares experience greater declines in middle incomes. The preferred specification associates a 3.5 percent increase in the top 1 percent's income share between 1979 and 2005, with a statistically significant 3.5 percent reduction over the same period in incomes of families between the 35th and 70th percentiles of the overall distribution. (The study also interestingly suggests, in line with the by now familiar pattern, that rising top incomes have only a smaller and less statistically significant negative impact on incomes at the bottom of the distribution, in families between the 5th and 30th percentiles.)

181    **throughout the world's rich societies:** One study found significant hollowing out of mid-skilled jobs in every European country but Portugal. And another study, compiled by the OECD using data aggregated across twenty-four countries, found that from 1998 to 2009, occupations in the highest and lowest quartiles by average skill scores experienced employment growth (of nearly 25 and 2 percent respectively), while occupations with the two middle skill quartiles experienced employment declines (of 1 percent for the second-highest skill quartile and 15 percent for the second-lowest skill quartile). Indeed, according to the OECD, "In half the OECD countries for which data are available, the loss of jobs associated with a medium level of education was greater than the loss of jobs associated with a low level of education." See Marten Goos et al., "Explaining Job Polarization in Europe: The Roles of Technology, Globalization and Institutions," Centre for Economic Performance Discussion Paper No. 1026 (November 2010); Daniel Oesch and Jorge Rodriguez Menes, "Upgrading or Polarization? Occupational Change in Britain, Germany, Spain, and Switzerland, 1990–2008," MPRA Paper No. 21040 (January 2010); but see Enrique Fernandez-Macias, "Job Polarization in Europe? Changes in the Employment Structure and Job Quality, 1995–2007," *Work and Occupations* 39, no. 2 (2012); Rachel E. Dwyer and Erik Olin Wright, "Job Growth and Job Polarization in the United States and Europe, 1995–2007," in *Transformation of the Employment Structures in the EU and USA*, ed. Enrique Fernandez-Macias, Donald Storrie, and John Hurley (Basingstoke: Palgrave Macmillan, 2012), 49, Appendix B, Table B1.6; Alexandra Spitz-Oener, "Technical Change, Job Tasks, and Rising Educational Demands: Looking Outside the Wage Structure," *Journal of Labor Economics* 24, no. 2 (April 2006): 235–70; Goos and Manning, "Lousy and Lovely Jobs."

181    **even as mid-wage employment declined:** See NELP, National Employment Law Project, *The Low-Wage Recovery and Growing Inequality* (New York: NELP, 2012).

181    **greater shares of gains than of losses:** Low-wage jobs accounted for 21 percent of job losses in the recession and 58 percent of job growth in the recovery, high-wage jobs accounted for 19 percent of losses and 20 percent of growth, and mid-wage jobs accounted for fully 60 percent of losses but just 22 percent of growth. See National Employment Law Project, *The Low-Wage Recovery*, 1. See also Robert Reich, "The Hidden Price of Your Amazon Shopping Spree: Skyrocketing Unemployment," *Salon*, December 4, 2013, accessed November 18, 2018, www.salon.com/2013/12/04/robert_reich_healthcare_gov_is_not_the_website_we_should_be_worrying_about_partner/.

181    **will all be either low- or super-skilled:** The fastest-shrinking job categories include mid-skill work such as apparel, leather, and allied manufacturing; tobacco manufacturing; the Postal

Service; other federal employment; and manufacturing and re-producing magnetic and optical media. The fastest-growing job categories include low-skill work such as home health care; outpatient health care; health office work; facilities support; and ambulatory care. They also included high-skill work such as management, scientific, and technical consulting; software publishing; computer systems design; and securities, commodity contracts, and financial investments. The only fast-growing mid-skill job categories are nursing and medical and diagnostic lab work. See also Max Nisen, "Ten American Industries That Are Going to Boom in the Next Decade," *Slate*, December 28, 2013, accessed November 18, 2018, https://slate.com/business /2013/12/booming-industries-for-the-next-decade.html.

Academic observers similarly predict that nearly half of jobs might be made redundant within twenty years. The jobs most likely to be displaced are routine or routinizable and therefore mid-skilled: loan officers, receptionists, paralegals, retail salespersons, and taxi drivers. The jobs least likely to be displaced are all fluid and require social perception and creative intelligence: reporters, physicians, lawyers, teachers, and doctors. Carl Benedikt Frey and Michael A. Osborne, "Job Automation May Threaten Half of U.S. Workforce," Bloomberg, March 12, 2014, accessed November 18, 2018, www.bloomberg.com/graphics /infographics/job-automation-threatens-workforce.html.

181 **displaced by automation by 2030:** James Manyika et al., "Jobs Lost, Jobs Gained: What the Future of Work Will Mean for Jobs, Skills, and Wages," McKinsey Global Institute, November 2017, accessed October 26 2018, www.mckinsey.com/featured -insights/future-of-work/jobs-lost-jobs-gained-what-the-future -of-work-will-mean-for-jobs-skills-and-wages.

181 **even a sea change:** Other explanations for labor market polar-ization that emphasize forces besides technological innovation of course also exist. Candidates include globalization, declining union membership, and changes in tax policy. All these causes certainly contribute to the demise of the middle class. But none has been as consequential as automation, some (most notably globalization) are themselves caused by automation, and all will have much small effects than automation on middle-class em-ployment going forward.

182 **isolates super-skilled workers from all others:** On the mid-century model, the high/low-status fault line in the workplace lay between exempt and nonexempt workers under the Fair La-bor Standards Act. Today, the fault line lies between top manag-ers and everyone else. Cappelli, *The New Deal at Work*, 236–37.

182 **provided in universities:** Workplace training makes sense where it can be delivered in small and regular increments, throughout a worker's career. The midcentury labor market sup-ported this model, by offering a many-tiered hierarchy of jobs, with each rung of the professional ladder in close proximity to the ones below and above it. University-taught and degree-based professional education, by contrast, must be delivered in large doses, and only irregularly, as workers interrupt their jobs to re-ceive extended spells of full-time education. Professional school makes sense where labor markets offer job hierarchies with fewer tiers, separated by wider gaps. The shift from workplace-centered to university-based professional training thus suggests that there has been a parallel and profound change in the labor market: a many-tiered hierarchy of jobs has had its middle rungs removed, leaving jobs at the bottom and jobs at the top, sepa-rated by a wide chasm.

182 **the right side of the meritocratic divide:** The returns to educa-tion have increased principally because education genuinely teaches real skills, and the transformation of the labor market has made the skills that education provides increasingly produc-tive. Superordinate workers, that is, get their enormous pay mostly in exchange for providing enormous economic value, rather than by theft, fraud, or other unmeritocratic means.

This is a controversial claim. Critics of inequality com-monly attribute rising top incomes to personal vices rather than to economic structures, and to too little meritocracy rather than too much, arguing that superordinate workers get their extrava-gant incomes through nepotism and class snobbery, rent seeking that exploits economic power, or even outright fraud. These ar-guments resemble suggestions, discussed earlier, that top in-comes must come from capital rather than labor.

Like those suggestions, these charges have a point. Merito-crats retain all the familiar vices, and class snobbery, rent seeking, and fraud contribute—including outrageously—to the advan-tages that superordinate workers enjoy. But once again, the scale of the moral vices does not match (or even approach) the scale of the rise in elite incomes. Structural arguments are needed to ac-count for rising inequality, and meritocracy provides the re-quired arguments.

182 **of the education distribution:** Reeves, *Dream Hoarders*, 61–64, using data from R. Chetty et al., "Where Is the Land of Op-portunity? The Geography of Intergenerational Mobility in the United States," *Quarterly Journal of Economics* 129, no. 4 (No-vember 2014): 1553–1623; Fabian T. Pfeffer and Alexandra Achen Killewald, "How Rigid Is the Wealth Structure and Why? Inter- and Multigenerational Associations in Family Wealth," PSC Research Report No. 15-845 (September 2015), 30; PSID data tabulated in Richard V. Reeves and Joanna Venator, "The Inheritance of Education," Brookings Institution, October 27, 2014, www.brookings.edu/blog/social-mobility-memos/2014 /10/27/the-inheritance-of-education/.

Fully one in three children from households in the top 1 percent of the income distribution captures an annual income of at least $100,000 by age thirty, compared to only one out of twenty-five children born into the bottom half of the distribu-tion. See Raj Chetty, John Friedman, and Nathaniel Hedren, "The Equality of Opportunity Project," www.equality-of-op portunity.org/documents/. See also David Leonhardt, "In Climbing Income Ladder, Location Matters," *New York Times*, July 22, 2013, accessed November 18, 2018, www.nytimes.com /2013/07/22/business/in-climbing-income-ladder-location -matters.html?pagewanted=all.

182 **one and the same:** Unemployment rates redouble the segmenta-tion of workers by wages, as college graduates (and especially graduate and professional degree holders) are only about half as likely to be unemployed as workers with just a high school educa-tion and only about a third as likely to be unemployed as workers without a high school degree. In 2016, the average unemploy-ment rate among workers aged twenty-five and older without a high school degree was 7.5 percent, the average for those with high school education only was 5.2 percent, the average for those with a BA only was 2.7 percent, and the average for those with a graduate or professional degree was 2.1 percent. Bureau of Labor Statistics, *Labor Force Statistics from the Current Population Survey*, Series LNU04027659Q, LNU04027660Q, LNU04-092221Q, LNU04091113Q, accessed April 10, 2017. The BLS has separated out workers with advanced degrees and with BAs only since 2014, and it has not released seasonally adjusted num-bers. Nevertheless, averaging quarterly data across 2016 pro-duces numbers that are roughly in line with the seasonally adjusted data presented by the BLS for its more traditional categories—less than high school, high school only, and BA and above. See Bureau of Labor Statistics, Labor Force Statistics from the Current Population Survey, Series LNU04027659Q, LNU04027660Q, LNU04092221Q, LNU04091113Q, ac-cessed April 10, 2017. See Bureau of Labor Statistics, "House-hold Data: Annual Averages," last modified January 18, 2019, www.bls.gov/cps/cpsaat07.htm.

Unemployment, moreover, understates the effects of edu-cation on work, as trends in the labor force participation rate re-veal that, on top of facing higher unemployment, less educated workers increasingly abandon the labor market entirely and, be-cause they no longer seek work, are not counted toward the un-employment rate. Uneducated and educated workers live in almost entirely separate worlds, which effectively never overlap. The least educated face a constant, demoralizing struggle to find work at all, while (contrary to popular stories of college gradu-ates living in their parents' basements) the most educated enjoy full employment. Changes in the labor force participation rate have many causes, including an aging population, changing gen-der norms, and the impacts of cyclical patterns in the business cycle. Nevertheless, the data clearly show a falling labor force participation rate even among prime-aged men and, more re-cently and after a decades-long rise, among prime-aged women also. The decline is especially prominent among less educated, lower-paid workers, and this reinforces the effects of education on work revealed in the unemployment statistics. The 2016 American Community Survey reports that just 78 percent of prime-aged men who have never attended college (roughly the bottom two-thirds of the educational distribution) were employed, compared to 90 percent of those with at least one year of college. In the 1950s, the two rates were virtually identical. See U.S. Census Bureau, "American Community Survey (ACS)," www.census.gov/programs-surveys/acs/.

Both trends are predicted to continue. See Bureau of Labor Statistics, "Labor Force Projections to 2022: The Labor Force Participation Rate Continues to Fall," *Monthly Labor Review* (December 2013), www.bls.gov/opub/mlr/2013/article /labor-force-projections-to-2022-the-labor-force-participation -rate-continues-to-fall.htm; Bureau of Labor Statistics, *The Recession of 2007–2009* (February 2012), www.bls.gov/spotlight /2012/recession/; and Executive Office of the President of the United States, *The Labor Force Participation Rate Since 2007: Causes and Policy Implications* (July 2014), https://scholar.har vard.edu/files/stock/files/labor_force_participation.pdf.

182 **with a BA only:** Carnevale, Rose, and Cheah, "The College Payoff," 6. Joan Williams, using less comprehensive data, reports slightly different shares: 19.4 percent of male college grads and 14 percent of female college grads earn less than the average high school grad. See Williams, *White Working Class*, 49. A few pages later, Williams reports that "a quarter of college grads and advanced degree holders will work for a lower median wage than associate degree holders." See Williams, *White Working Class*, 86. See also Rework America, *America's Moments: Creating Opportunity in a Connected Age* (New York: W. W. Norton, 2015), 200; John Schmitt and Heather Boushey, *The College Conundrum: Why the Benefits of a College Education May Not Be So Clear, Especially to Men* (Washington, DC: Center for American Progress, 2010), 3, 8, 9.

182 **from the top tenth:** Slightly under half of the U.S. population over twenty-five has no education at all beyond high school (roughly 70 percent do not have a BA), and slightly over 10 percent hold a post-BA degree. See Camille L. Ryan and Kurt Bauman, *Educational Attainment in the United States: 2015*, U.S. Census Bureau, Current Population Reports no. P20-578 (March 2016), www.census.gov/content/dam/Census/library /publications/2016/demo/p20-578.pdf. See also Carnevale, Rose, and Cheah, "The College Payoff," 6 (citing 2007–9 American Community Survey, U.S. Census Bureau, "American Community Survey (ACS)," www.census.gov/programs-surveys /acs/).

183 **over a lifetime:** See Carnevale, Rose, and Cheah, "The College Payoff," 10, Figure 5. Slightly different figures appear in Christopher R. Tamborini, Chang Hwan Kim, and Arthur Sakamoto, "Education and Lifetime Earnings in the United States," *Demography* 52, no. 4 (2015): 1383–1407.

183 **as it was in 1980:** See R. G. Valletta, "Recent Flattening in the Higher Education Wage Premium: Polarization, Skill Downgrading, or Both?," NBER Working Paper No. 22935 (2016), www.nber.org/papers/w22935 (using Current Population Survey data to estimate the returns to college graduates over the period 1980–2015. In 1980, a college graduate earned 34 percent more than a high school graduate. By 1990, this premium had increased to 57 percent, and by 2000 it had increased to 71 percent. After 2000, the premium slowed, and it hit a plateau of roughly 78 percent from 2010 through 2015); see also Goldin and Katz, *The Race Between Education and Technology* (noting that "starting in the early 1980s the labor market premium to skill rose sharply and by 2005 the college wage premium was back at its 1915 level," and using CPS data to estimate the college wage premium as 36 percent in 1980 and 60 percent in 2005); Philippon and Reshef, "Wages and Human Capital" (finding the college premium to increase from 38 percent in 1970 to 58 percent in 2005); David H. Autor, "Skills, Education, and the Rise of Earnings Inequality Among the 'Other 99 Percent,'" *Science* 344, no. 6186 (May 2014): 843–51 (finding a wage premium between college graduates and non–college graduates of roughly 46 percent in 1980 and 96 percent in 2012).

183 **than it was in 1965:** See Christopher Avery and Sarah Turner, "Student Loans: Do College Students Borrow Too Much—or Not Enough?," *Journal of Economic Perspectives* 26, no. 1 (2012): 175, www.jstor.org/stable/41348811. Avery and Turner use data

from the Bureau of Labor Statistics' March Current Population Survey files for "full-time, full-year workers using sample weights, assuming 42 years of work experience per person. Results for college-educated workers are net of four years of tuition and fees associated with appropriate year-specific values for public universities." While the study subtracts the cost of a public university education from overall earnings of BA holders, these earning reflect the average incomes of all BA holders, whether educated at public or private colleges.

183 **provided by the stock market:** Estimating the economic return of a college education requires judgment, and estimates unsurprisingly vary. See "Is College Worth It?," *The Economist*, April 5, 2014, accessed November 18, 2018, www.economist.com /news/united-states/21600131-too-many-degrees-are-waste -money-return-higher-education-would-be-much-better. The figures reported reflect the implicit twenty-year return on tuition net of financial aid, using data from PayScale. Rankings of colleges by implicit rate of return closely track rankings by academic reputation (with some additions for specialist technical colleges and unusually cheap state schools). See also Highlights from *Rewarding Strivers*. A more conservative estimate appears in Hoxby, "Changing Selectivity," 115. Even this estimate concludes that the returns on education match the returns on the stock market.

Note that most estimates understate the true earnings boost afforded by the most elite schools, both because their broad approach to selectivity dilutes the earnings boosts provided by the super-elite universities and because they suppress a substantial difference between graduation rates at elite (88 percent) and noncompetitive (35 percent) schools. See Stephanie Owen and Isabel Sawhill, *Should Everyone Go to College?*, Brookings Institution, CCF Brief no. 50 (May 2013): 1–9, 6, www.brookings.edu/wp-content/uploads/2016/06/08-should -everyone-go-to-college-owen-sawhill.pdf. Hereafter cited as Owen and Sawhill, *Should Everyone Go to College?*

The average rate of return of a diversified stock portfolio over the past decades is under 7 percent. The average annual return over the last ten years for the Vanguard Balanced Composite Index, for example, is 6.83 percent. See "Benchmark Returns," Vanguard, last modified September 30, 2018, https:// personal.vanguard.com/us/funds/tools/benchmarkreturns. See Goldin and Katz, *The Race Between Education and Technology*, 336. See also David Card, "The Causal Effect of Education on Earnings," in *Handbook of Labor Economics*, vol. 3A, ed. Orley C. Ashenfelter and David Card (Amsterdam: Elsevier, 1999): 1801–63; David Card, "Estimating the Return to Schooling: Progress on Some Persistent Econometric Problems," *Econometrica* 69 (September 2001): 1127–60.

183 **bigger than in Sweden:** U.S. college graduates make 68 percent more than workers with just a high school degree, compared to 48 percent more in Britain, 41 percent more in France, and just 23 more percent in Sweden. See OECD, "Education and Earnings, OECD Dataset," https://stats.oecd.org/Index.aspx?Data SetCode=EAG_EARNINGS (figures range from 2012 to 2014, and are the most recent figures as of April 2017). See also "Wealth by Degrees," *The Economist*, June 28, 2014, www.econ omist.com/finance-and-economics/2014/06/28/wealth-by -degrees, citing OECD data. See also "Healthy, Wealthy and Wise," *The Economist*, September 11, 2012, accessed November 18, 2018, www.economist.com/graphic-detail/2012/09/11 /healthy-wealthy-and-wise.

183 **amplifies this pattern:** The very weakest colleges, by contrast, generate no income boost at all, and a broad basket of nonselective colleges generates only one-third the lifetime earnings increase of a broad basket of selective schools. See Owen and Sawhill, *Should Everyone Go to College?* Study and statistic cited in Walter Hamilton, "College Is a Bad Financial Bet for Some, Study Says," *Los Angeles Times*, May 8, 2013, accessed November 18, 2018, http://articles.latimes.com/2013/may/08/business/la -fi-mo-college-is-a-bad-financial-bet-for-some-study-says -20130508. The same basic result, achieved through a slightly different calculation, appears in Mark Schneider, *How Much Is That Bachelor's Degree Really Worth? The Million Dollar Misunderstanding* (Washington, DC: American Enterprise Institute, 2009), Figure 1, www.aei.org/publication/how-much-is -that-bachelors-degree-really-worth/. The thirty-year return on

a degree at Valley Forge Christian College is $-148,000. "Wealth by Degrees," *The Economist*, June 28, 2014, www.econ omist.com/finance-and-economics/2014/06/28/wealth-by-de grees, reporting on data collected by PayScale.com.

183 **more than BAs from lower-ranked schools:** See, e.g., Jere R. Behrman, Mark R. Rosenzweig, and Paul Taubman, "College Choice and Wages: Estimates Using Data on Female Twins," *Review of Economics and Statistics* 78 (1996): 672–85. The re search shows that attending private, PhD-granting, smaller-enrollment, and higher-faculty-salary universities leads to 10–25 percent higher earnings. "The [statistically preferred] BRT estimates of the school characteristics effects indicate that, controlling for family and individual endowments, attendees at colleges that grant Ph.D.s, that are private, that have small en rollments, and that have well-paid professors earn significantly higher wages later in life." Jere R. Behrman, Mark R. Rosenz weig, and Paul Taubman, "College Choice and Wages: Estimates Using Data on Female Twins," *Review of Economics and Statis tics* 78 (1996), 681, 682, Table 4; Dominic Brewer, Eric Eide, and Ronald Ehrenberg, "Does It Pay to Attend an Elite Private Col lege? Cross-Cohort Evidence on the Effects of College Type on Earnings," *Journal of Human Resources* 34, no. 1 (Winter 1999): 114 (39 percent premium for attending elite schools versus low-ranked public schools ten years out for the 1982 cohort and 19 percent fourteen years out for the 1972 cohort; the study also compares 1980 and 1972 cohort premiums six years post–high school graduation, at 20 percent and 9 percent respectively; note that the premiums for the 1982 cohort are greater than for the 1972 cohort).

183 **double the rate of return on the tuition:** Selective private and selective public colleges produce 11 and 13 percent rates of re turn on tuition paid, while noncompetitive private and public colleges produce rates of return of 6 and 9 percent respectively. See Owen and Sawhill, *Should Everyone Go to College?* The study cites to another that uses PayScale return on investment data and Barron's index of school selectivity. The same basic re sult, achieved through a slightly different calculation, appears in Mark Schneider, *How Much Is That Bachelor's Degree Really Worth? The Million Dollar Misunderstanding* (Washington, DC: American Enterprise Institute, 2009), 1–7, 4, Figures 2 and 3, www.aei.org/publication/how-much-is-that-bachelors-degree -really-worth/.

183 **doubling the gains produced by an average BA:** A degree from MIT or Caltech, for example yields a thirty-year income increase of $2 million. See "Wealth by Degrees," *The Economist*, June 28, 2014, www.economist.com/finance-and-economics/2014/06 /28/wealth-by-degrees, reporting on data collected by PayScale .com.

183 **top earners with average BAs:** Ten years after getting to col lege, the highest-paid 10 percent of graduates of the ten colleges whose graduates are paid most had median salaries of $220,000, while the highest-paid 10 percent of graduates across all colleges had median salaries of $68,000. Note also that the highest-paid 10 percent from the next thirty highest-income colleges make $157,000. See Matthew Stewart, "The 9.9 Percent Is the New American Aristocracy," *Atlantic*, June 2018 accessed November 18, 2018, www.theatlantic.com/magazine/archive/2018/the -birth-of-a-new-american-aristocracy/559130/. Hereafter cited as Stewart, "The 9.9 Percent." Stewart cites data from the U.S. Department of Education, *College Scorecard Data*, last updated September 28, 2018, https://collegescorecard.ed.gov/data/.

183 **just six years after graduation:** See Stewart, "The 9.9 Percent."
183 **only twelve universities:** See Thomas R. Dye, *Who's Running America? The Obama Reign*, 8th ed. (New York: Routledge, 2014), 180 (48.5 percent "corporate," 60.6 percent "financial," 50 percent "government," and 66 percent "other," including me dia, law, civic organizations); Thomas R. Dye and John W. Pick ering, "Governmental and Corporate Elites: Convergence and Differentiation," *Journal of Politics* 36, no. 4 (November 1974), 914, Table 4 (55 percent "corporate," 43.9 percent "governmen tal," 78.8 percent "public interest"). Hereafter cited as Dye and Pickering, "Governmental and Corporate Elites." An excerpt from Thomas R. Dye, *Who's Running America? The Bush Resto ration*, 7th ed. (New York: Pearson, 2002), gives a brief overview of where the data originate: "Who's Running America? has not been supported by any grant or contract from any institution,

public or private. It grew out of a graduate seminar 'Research on Power and Elites' at Florida State University. Initially, biograph ical data for over 5,000 members of various institutional elites were collected and coded by students. These computerized biog raphies constituted the original database for the continuing project Who's Running America? The database has been revised periodically, and data on over 7,000 institutional elites have been collected and coded." See also Thomas R. Dye, Eugene R. DeGlercq, and John W. Pickering, "Concentration, Specializa tion and Interlocking Among Institutional Elites," *Social Sci ence Quarterly* 54, no. 1 (June 1973), 8–28; Dye and Pickering, "Governmental and Corporate Elites," 900–925. A report of the study appears also in Elizabeth Stoker and Matthew Bruenig, "The 1 Percent's Ivy League Loophole," *Salon*, September 9, 2013, accessed November 18, 2018, www.salon.com/2013/09 /09/the_1_percents_ivy_league_loophole/.

The pattern holds in academia also: in one study analyz ing business, computer science, and history departments, just a quarter of all universities accounted for the production of as much as 86 percent of tenure-track faculty; in some subjects, fewer than ten departments produce over half of all ladder fac ulty. See Joel Warner and Aaron Clauset, "The Academy's Dirty Secret: An Astonishingly Small Number of Elite Universities Produce an Overwhelming Number of America's Professors," *Slate*, February 23, 2015, accessed November 18, 2018, www .slate.com/articles/life/education/2015/02/university_hiring _if_you_didn_t_get_your_ph_d_at_an_elite_university _good.html, citing Aaron Clauset et al., "Systematic Inequality and Hierarchy in Faculty Hiring Networks," *Science Advances* 1, no. 1 (2015), http://advances.sciencemag.org/content/1/1/e14 00005/tab-pdf. See also Robert L. Oprisko, "Superpowers: The American Academic Elite," *Georgetown Policy Review*, Decem ber 3, 2012, gppreview.com/2012/12/03/superpowers-the-ame rican-academic-elite/.

183 **was effectively zero:** In 1965, even the Cravath firm, long the market leader in lawyer salaries, paid first-year associates just $7,500 (or roughly $55,000 in 2015 dollars). See Tamar Lewin, "At Cravath, $65,000 to Start," *New York Times*, April 18, 1986, accessed November 18, 2018, www.nytimes.com/1986/04/18 /business/at-cravath-65000-to-start.html ("Setting the pace in compensation is a tradition at Cravath. In 1968, when Cravath nearly doubled its starting salary, to $15,000, it began a pay spi ral that has raised the going rate at the fanciest Wall Street firms to more than $50,000."). Similarly, the median first-year salary for Harvard Business School graduates today is 50 percent more in real terms than the 1977 median. See Harvard Business School, "Recruiting: Data & Statistics," accessed October 13, 2018, www.hbs.edu/recruiting/data/pages/detailed-charts.aspx. And as recently as 1991, the average salary four years out from an elite MBA was just $63,000 (roughly $110,000 in 2015 dollars), while a study of MBA incomes discarded a salary of $450,000 (or about $800,000 in 2015 dollars) as an outlier so far from the pack that its inclusion would misleadingly skew averages. See Charles A. O'Reilly III and Jennifer A. Chatman, "Working Smarter and Harder: A Longitudinal Study of Managerial Suc cess," *Administrative Science Quarterly* 39, no. 4 (December 1994): 614.

For a more general report on the professional school pre mium at midcentury's close, see Michael Simkovic, "The Knowl edge Tax," *University of Chicago Law Review* 82 (2015), Hereafter cited as Simkovic, "The Knowledge Tax."

183 **is much greater still:** The postgraduate income premium rela tive to a high school education only is greater still and is now 70 percent higher for men and 90 percent higher for women than it was as recently as 1970. See Simkovic, "The Knowledge Tax," 2036–37, Tables 1 and 2. Simkovic used data from the Minne sota Population Center. Integrated Public Use Microdata Series, Current Population Survey, "Current Population Survey Data for Social, Economic and Health Research," https://cps.ipums .org/cps/.

Much of this increase has come since 2000. See "Wealth by Degrees," *The Economist*, June 28, 2014, www.economist .com/finance-and-economics/2014/06/28/wealth-by-degrees; David H. Autor, "Skills, Education, and the Rise of Earnings Inequality Among the 'Other 99 Percent,'" *Science* 344, no. 6186 (May 2014): 843–51, 849, Figure 6A. See also David H. Autor,

Lawrence F. Katz, and Melissa Schettini Kearney, "Trends in U.S. Wage Inequality: Revising the Revisionists," *Review of Economics and Statistics* 90, no. 2 (May 2008): 305, Table 1. Hereafter cited as Autor, Katz, and Kearney, "Trends in U.S. Wage Inequality."

183 **five times the median high-school-only graduate:** Carnevale, Rose, and Cheah, "The College Payoff," 3, 7. These are 2009 dollars. Similarly, by 2010, the average male worker with a graduate or professional degree earned $86,700 more annually than the average man with a high school education only, and the average woman earned $50,600 more. See Simkovic, "The Knowledge Tax," 2036–37, Tables 1 and 2.

184 **approaching $200,000:** Forty to 60 percent of the graduates of top-tier law schools take jobs as associates at large, prestigious firms. "The Top 50 Go-To Law Schools," *National Law Journal*, March 6, 2017, accessed November 18, 2018, www.nationallaw journal.com/id=1202780534815?slreturn=20170312154418. These firms paid first-year associates $180,000 in 2017, and several have increased this to $190,000 in 2018. Year-end bonuses raise incomes higher still.

These numbers understate the size of the long-term flow from elite law schools to elite firms, as many graduates of the most prestigious schools spend their first year or two after graduation in expressly short-term judicial clerkships and are thus reported in the data working outside of large firms. The clerkships, however, are widely understood as preliminary to large-firm employment; indeed, large signing bonuses for former law clerks mean that the clerks are even—indirectly—paid by the firms.

184 **nearly $400,000:** See David Wilkins, Bryon Fong, and Ronit Dinovitzer, *The Women and Law School: Preliminary Results from the HLS Career Study* (Cambridge, MA: Harvard Law School Center on the Legal Profession, 2015). The median was $370,000 in 2007 dollars. Female graduates had median incomes of $140,000, and their spouses had median incomes of $200,000, yielding a combined household income, at $340,000, just outside the top 1 percent. (Note that the study also surveyed graduates from decades earlier and later, who had lower median incomes. This is not surprising, as the earlier classes would have preceded the greatest rise in top incomes, and the later classes would still hold more junior jobs.)

184 **graduated from a top-tier school:** "Attorney Search," Wachtell, Lipton, Rosen & Katz, accessed July 25, 2018, www.wlrk.com /Attorneys/List.aspx?LastName=.

184 **schools ranked twenty-one to one hundred:** For the claim about starting salaries for top-ten law school graduates, see Susan Adams, "Law Schools Whose Grads Make the Highest Starting Salaries," *Forbes*, March 28, 2014, accessed November 18, 2018, www.forbes.com/sites/susanadams/2014/03/28/law -schools-whose-grads-make-the-highest-starting-salaries /#73a6c3389ec7, and Staci Zaretsky, "Salary Wars Scorecard: Which Firms Have Announced Raises?," *Above the Law*, June 13, 2016, accessed November 18, 2018, http://abovethelaw.com /2016/06/salary-wars-scorecard-which-firms-have-announced -raises/. (The figure does not reflect salaries at judicial clerkships, which are treated as nonpermanent jobs.) For the comparison between early career (second- and seventh-year) salaries for graduates of schools ranked in the top ten, eleven through twenty, and twenty-one through one hundred, see Paul Oyer and Scott Schaefer, "Welcome to the Club: The Returns to an Elite Degree for American Lawyers," Stanford GBS Working Paper no. 3044 (December 11, 2012). Hereafter cited as Oyer and Schaefer, "Welcome to the Club."

These income differences follow directly from differences in the kinds of jobs that graduates of super-elite and less elite law schools get. Graduates of top-ten law schools join the nation's largest and most lucrative law firms at nearly twice the rate of graduates of schools ranked eleven through twenty (46 percent versus 27 percent), and they eventually make partner at roughly one and a half times the rate of graduates of those schools and at quadruple the rate of graduates of schools ranked twenty-one through one hundred (as of the summer of 2007, for graduates between 1970 and 2005, 13.4 percent of graduates from schools in the top ten, 8.9 percent of graduates from schools ranked eleven to twenty, and 3.5 percent of graduates from schools ranked twenty-one to one hundred were partners at one of 285

of the 300 largest law firms in the United States). See Oyer and Schaefer, "Welcome to the Club," 9, 19.

184 **how much tuition assistance a law student receives:** The internal rate of return ranges between roughly 13.5 percent for those who pay tuition of $60,000 per year, to roughly 19 percent for those who pay $30,000 per year, to roughly 32 percent for those who attend law school on full scholarship. See Michael Simkovic and Frank McIntyre, "The Economic Value of a Law Degree," HLS Program on the Legal Profession Research Paper No. 2013-6 (last modified November 26, 2014), Table 10, https://papers.ssrn.com/sol3/papers.cfm?abstract_id=225 0585. Simkovic and McIntyre sort out the data by gender, and these rates of return reflect a rough average of the rates for the two genders. The rates of return reflect not just tuition but also other costs of attending law school, including forgone earnings. This is why the rate of return for those who pay no tuition is "only" about 30 percent.

184 **in excess of $1 million:** See "The Best Business Schools," *Forbes*, accessed October 13, 2018, www.forbes.com/business -schools/; Louis Lavelle, "MBA Pay: The Devil's in the Details," Bloomberg, November 19, 2012, www.bloomberg.com /news/articles/2012-11-19/mba-pay-the-devils-in-the-details. See also Jonathan Rodkin and Francesca Levy, "Best Business Schools 2015," Bloomberg, accessed November 18, 2018, www .bloomberg.com/features/2015-best-business-schools.

184 **the fiftieth-ranked program:** According to 2013 data gathered by PayScale, the twenty-year returns at Harvard were double the twenty-year returns at Texas A&M. See Anne VanderMey, "MBA Pay: Riches for Some, Not All," Bloomberg, September 28, 2009, accessed November 18, 2018, www.bloomberg.com /news/articles/2009-09-28/mba-pay-riches-for-some-not-all. And the *Forbes* data show that Stanford's five-year gains are triple the five-year gains produced by the fiftieth-ranked program. See "The Best Business Schools," *Forbes*, accessed October 13, 2018, www.forbes.com/business-schools/list/. The pay drop-off begins long before rank fifty, with Harvard's $250,000 incomes nearly 66 percent higher than number-ten-ranked Cornell's incomes of $150,000.

184 **25 percent joined consulting firms:** "Recruiting: MBA Students, Career Industry Statistics, Class of 2016," Harvard Business School, accessed October 13, 2018, www.hbs.edu/recru iting/data/Pages/industry.aspx?tab=career&year=2016.

184 **now exceeds $75,000:** See "The Best Business Schools," *Forbes*, accessed October 13, 2018, www.forbes.com/business -schools/list/. See also Peter Arcidiacono, Jane Cooley, and Andrew Hussey, "The Economic Returns to an MBA," *International Economic Review* 49, no. 3 (2008): 873–99. See also Jonathan P. O'Brien et al., "Does Business School Research Add Economic Value for Students?," *Academy of Management, Learning, and Education* 9, no. 4 (2010): 638–51.

184 **"The B.A. gets you in the door":** Quoted in Nelson D. Schwartz, "Gap Widening as Top Workers Reap the Raises," *New York Times*, July 24, 2015, accessed November 18, 2018, www.nytimes.com/2015/07/25/business/economy/salary-gap -widens-as-top-workers-in-specialized-fields-reap-rewards .html.

185 *The Right to Be Lazy:* Paul Lafargue, *The Right to Be Lazy, and Other Studies*, trans. Charles H. Kerr (Chicago: C. H. Kerr & Company, 1907).

185 **Calls for a thirty-hour week:** The Black-Connery bill nearly wrote a thirty-hour workweek into law. The bill, proposed in 1932 by then-senator Hugo Black, received support from both the AFL and the incoming Roosevelt administration and passed the Senate in early 1933, by a vote of 53–30, and Frances Perkins, the new secretary of labor, testified in favor of the bill before the House. Rising opposition from industry, and a change of heart at the AFL, caused President Roosevelt to pursue other New Deal programs rather than the bill, and it was eventually replaced by the Fair Labor Standards Act, which essentially enshrined the forty-hour work week into federal law. See Benjamin Hunnicut, *Free Time: The Forgotten American Dream* (Philadelphia: Temple University Press, 2013), 117–19.

185 **"four-day week, four-hour day":** See Nathan Schneider, "Who Stole the Four-Hour Workday," Vice News, December 30, 2014, accessed November 18, 2018, www.vice.com/read/who-stole -the-four-hour-workday-0000406-v21n8. See also Jon Bekken,

"Arguments for a Four-Hour Day," *Libertarian Labor Review* 1 (1986).

185 **might be possible within a century:** See John Maynard Keynes, "Economic Possibilities for Our Grandchildren" (1930), in *Essays in Persuasion* (New York: W. W. Norton, 1963). Keynes believed that technological progress, combined with the rapid growth produced by compound interest, entailed that "the *economic problem* may be solved, or at least within sight of solution, within a hundred years." It is worth nothing that Keynes's thought on this question was not simply utopian: he worried that mankind possesses an innate drive to work and that a "dread" would set in among people confronting a surfeit of leisure. Keynes couched these thoughts in terms of human nature, but they quite possibly reflect an early internalization of the end of Veblen's social world and the coming merger of status and extravagant industry. An excellent account of the essay appears in Elizabeth Kolbert, "No Time: How Did We Get So Busy," *New Yorker*, May 26, 2014, accessed November 18, 2018, www .newyorker.com/magazine/2014/05/26/no-time. A broader philosophical reflection on the perils of acquisitiveness appears in Skidelsky and Skidelsky, *How Much Is Enough?*

185 **captivated hopeful dreamers:** For an appealing introduction to this line of thought, see Thomas Frank, "David Graber: 'Spotlight on the Financial Sector Did Make Apparent Just How Bizarrely Skewed Our Economy Is in Terms Who Gets Rewarded,'" *Salon*, June 1, 2014, accessed November 18, 2018, www.salon.com/2014/06/01/help_us_thomas_piketty_the _ls_sick_and_twisted_new_scheme/.

185 **among adults of prime working age:** In 2012, 11 percent of prime-aged men and 26 percent of prime-aged women were not even seeking work. In 1992, these shares were 7 percent of men and 26 percent of women. In 1970, the shares were 4 percent of men and 50 percent of women. The Bureau of Labor Statistics predicts that both falling trends will continue. See Bureau of Labor Statistics, "Labor Force Projections to 2022: The Labor Force Participation Rate Continues to Fall," *Monthly Labor Review* (December 2013), www.bls.gov/opub/mlr/2013/article /labor-force-projections-to-2022-the-labor-force-participation -rate-continues-to-fall.htm. Melinda Pitts, John Robertson, and Ellyn Terry, "Reasons for the Decline in Prime-Age Labor Force Participation," Federal Reserve Bank of Atlanta Macroblog, April 10, 2014, http://macroblog.typepad.com/macroblog/2014/04 /reasons-for-the-decline-in-prime-age-labor-force-part icipation-.html. See also Martin Wolf, "America's Labor Market Is Not Working," *Financial Times*, November 3, 2015. The share of U.S. prime-aged adults to have left the labor force is large, compared to advanced economies. For men, the analogous shares today are 8 percent in the United Kingdom, 7 percent in Germany and France, and 4 percent in Japan; for women, only Italy has a lower labor force participation rate among the G-7. Finally, U.S. labor force participation rates are projected to continue to decline.

186 **less dangerous than it once was:** The Occupational Safety and Health Administration (OSHA) sets guidelines for heavy lifting and offers extensive guides detailing the proper way to lift heavy weights without leading to workplace injuries. "Materials Handling: Heavy Lifting," Occupational Safety and Health Administration, accessed October 13, 2018, www.osha.gov/SLTC /etools/electricalcontractors/materials/heavy.html. Meanwhile, in fiscal year 2016, the Bureau of Labor Statistics documented 5,090 workplace fatalities, while in 1913 it documented approximately 23,000 industrial deaths alone. See "Number of Fatal Work Injuries by Employee Status," Bureau of Labor Statistics, accessed October 13, 2018, www.bls.gov/charts/census-of-fatal -occupational-injuries/number-of-fatal-work-injuries -by-employee-status-self-employed-wage-salary.htm, and Centers for Disease Control and Prevention, "Achievements in Public Health, 1900–1999," *Morbidity and Mortality Weekly Report* 48, no. 22 (1999): 1.

186 **wealthier than ever before:** Median wages have stagnated, to be sure, but they have not fallen, and median consumption continues to rise. Carmen DeNavas-Walt, Bernadette Proctor, and Jessica C. Smith, *Income, Poverty, and Health Insurance Coverage in the United States: 2012*, U.S. Census Bureau, Current Population Reports no. P60-245 (September 2013), 5, www .census.gov/prod/2013pubs/p60-245.pdf. Meanwhile, wages at

the bottom of the labor market have in fact risen slightly in recent decades, and the social safety net (inadequate as it is) continues to meet basic material needs and to protect most households from the severest absolute deprivations. Autor, Katz, and Kearney, "Trends in U.S. Wage Inequality," 319. Once again, poverty today is between a quarter and a tenth as prevalent as it was in 1930 and between a half and a quarter as prevalent as it was in 1960. See Chapter 4.

187 **imposed on women at midcentury:** For prime-aged men, the labor force participation rate has fallen substantially, from roughly 96 percent in 1970 to roughly 88 percent today (the second-lowest rate of any advanced industrialized country, ahead only of Italy). See Melinda Pitts, John Robertson, and Ellyn Terry, "Reasons for the Decline in Prime-Age Labor Force Participation," Federal Reserve Bank of Atlanta Macroblog, April 10, 2014, http://macroblog.typepad.com/macroblog/2014 /04/reasons-for-the-decline-in-prime-age-labor-force-part icipation-.html; Nicholas Eberstadt, "Where Did All the Men Go?," *Milken Institute Review*, April 28, 2017, www.milkenre view.org/articles/where-did-all-the-men-go. Hereafter cited as Eberstadt, "Where Did All the Men Go?" For prime-aged women, by contrast, the labor force participation rate rose by an almost equal amount (although from a lower baseline) between 1970 and 2000, and has fallen slightly since. See Melinda Pitts, John Robertson, and Ellyn Terry, "Reasons for the Decline in Prime-Age Labor Force Participation," Federal Reserve Bank of Atlanta Macroblog, April 10, 2014, http://macroblog.typepad.com/macroblog /2014/04/reasons-for-the-decline-in-prime-age-labor-force -participation-.html.

Moreover, unemployment is increasingly further concentrated in the long-term unemployed: those who have unsuccessfully sought work for more than six months accounted for 8.6 percent of unemployment in 1979 and 26.1 percent today. See Peter Schuck, *One Nation Undecided: Clear Thinking About Five Hard Issues That Divide Us* (Princeton, NJ: Princeton University Press, 2017), 50, citing Bureau of Labor Statistics, "Economic News Release," Table A12, last modified October 5, 2018, www .bls.gov/news.release/empsit.t12.htm.

Taken together, these effects entail that the share of prime-aged men in paid work today is almost 10 percentage points lower Than it was at the start of the Great Compression and that the decline in work rates since 1965 represents the disappearance of roughly ten million overwhelmingly mid-skilled jobs. Indeed, the work rate for prime-aged men was slightly lower in 2015, when the unemployment rate fell to 5 percent, than it had been in 1940, when unemployment was at 14.6 percent. See Eberstadt, "Where Did All the Men Go?"

The Bureau of Labor Statistics projects that by 2050 the male labor force participation rate will be nearly 20 percentage points below its 1950 peak and the female labor force participation rate will be nearly 6 percentage points below its 2010 peak. See Mitra Toossi, "A Century of Change: The U.S. Labor Force, 1950–2050," *Monthly Labor Review* (May 2002): 22, Table 4. By comparison, the gaps between labor force participation rates for men and women were roughly 36 percentage points in 1970 and 26 percentage points in 1980. Data reported earlier revealed that prime-aged employed men in the bottom half of the income distribution work roughly 20 percent fewer weekly hours than they did in 1940. The combination of these two effects on average hours worked, across all working- and middle-class men, exceeds the male-female difference in labor force participation in 1980 and approaches the male-female difference in 1970.

187 **scratch themselves or fidget:** Ceylan Yeginsu, "If Workers Slack Off, the Wristband Will Know. (And Amazon Has a Patent for It.)," *New York Times*, February 1, 2018, accessed October 26, 2018, www.nytimes.com/2018/02/01/technology /amazon-wristband-tracking-privacy.html. See also U.S. Patent and Trademark Office, "Ultrasonic Bracelet and Receiver for Detecting Position in 2D Plan," Amazon Technologies, Inc., Applicant, Appl. No.: 15/083,083, March 28, 2016.

187 **within twenty seconds of receiving them:** See, e.g., O'Connor, "When Your Boss Is an Algorithm."

188 **with middle-class incomes but without college degrees:** Between 1998 and 2015, the rate of suicide, overdose, and alcohol-related deaths grew over three times faster for middle-aged white

men with a high school degree or less education than for men with a BA or more education, and this mortality rate grew over five times faster for uneducated than for educated middle-aged white women. See Case and Deaton, "Mortality and Morbidity," 415, using data from Centers for Disease Control and Prevention, *National Vital Statistics System*, 2018. The data collect suicide, overdose, and alcohol-related deaths per 100,000 persons for white, non-Hispanic fifty- to fifty-four-year-old men and women, by their level of education. For men with a high school degree or less, this rate increased by 130 percent between 1998 and 2015; for men with a BA or more, it increased by 44 percent. For women with a high school degree or less, this rate increased by 381 percent; for women with a BA or more, it increased by 70 percent. See Case and Deaton, "Mortality and Morbidity." See also Joel Achenbach and Dan Keating, "New Research Identifies a 'Sea of Despair' Among White, Working-Class Americans," *Washington Post*, March 23, 2017, accessed November 18, 2018, www.washingtonpost.com/national/health -science/new-research-identifies-a-sea-of-despair-among-white -working-class-americans/2017/03/22/c777ab6e-0da6-11e7 -9b0d-d27c98455440_story.html?utm_term=.3b4d0390d167.

And the core of Donald Trump's support comes from voters with middle-class incomes but no college degrees. See Thomas Edsall, "The Not-So-Silent White Majority," *New York Times*, November 17, 2016, accessed November 18, 2018, www .nytimes.com/2016/11/17/opinion/the-not-so-silent-white -majority.html; Jon Huang, Samuel Jacoby, Michael Strickland, and K. K. Rebecca Lai, "Election 2016: Exit Polls," *New York Times*, November 8, 2016, accessed November 18, 2018, www .nytimes.com/interactive/2016/11/08/us/politics/election -exit-polls.html. For a largely congruent analysis of the sources of Trump's support using a massive data set of preelection Gallup surveys, see Jonathan Rothwell and Pablo Diego-Rosell, "Explaining Nationalist Political Views: The Case of Donald Trump," SSRN working paper (November 2, 2016), https:// papers.ssrn.com/sol3/papers.cfm?abstract_id=2822059.

188 **"nonlinear relationship between earnings and hours":** June Carbone and Naomi Cahn, "Unequal Terms: Gender, Power, and the Recreation of Hierarchy," *Studies in Law, Politics, and Society* 69 (2016): 15199. Hereafter cited as Carbone and Cahn, "Unequal Terms."

188 **"a flexible schedule":** Claudia Goldin, "A Grand Gender Convergence: Its Last Chapter," *American Economic Review* 104, no. 4 (2014): 1117.

188 **A "winner take all" society therefore arises:** Frank and Cook, *The Winner-Take-All Society*.

188 **less to gain from clawing up one:** Throughout the Great Compression—in the three and a half decades between 1946 and 1980—average annual incomes grew most rapidly at the bottom of the income distribution and then grew steadily less rapidly as incomes increased, right up to and into the 99th percentile. The median worker enjoyed almost precisely the average rate of income growth. All these data come from Facundo Alvaredo et al., *World Inequality Report 2018* (World Inequality Lab, 2017), https://wir2018.wid.world/. They are elegantly organized by David Leonhardt (using figures by Jessica Ma and Stuart A. Thompson) in David Leonhardt, "Our Broken Economy, in One Simple Chart," *New York Times*, August 7, 2017, accessed November 18, 2018, www.nytimes.com/interactive/2017/08 /07/opinion/leonhardt-income-inequality.html. Hereafter cited as Leonhardt, "Our Broken Economy."

188 **at the very top rungs:** In the years since 1980, income growth has shifted up the distribution. Between 1979 and 2007, the only income group to capture a rising share of total national income was the top 1 percent (even the rest of the top quintile— the next 19 percent—suffered a declining income share). See Congressional Budget Office, "Trends in the Distribution of Household Income," Figure 2. By roughly 1990, incomes were growing fastest in the top 1 percent of the distribution, and by roughly 2000, incomes were growing steadily faster as incomes increased, fully inverting the midcentury pattern. (Today, the average income growth is not reached until nearly the 90th percentile of the income distribution.) Finally, in the three and a half decades between 1980 and 2014, incomes at the 99.999th percentile grew nearly three times as fast as incomes at the 99th percentile, and only the richest one-twentieth of 1 percent

enjoyed the same income growth that the poorest Americans experienced in the Great Compression.

All these data come from Facundo Alvaredo et al., *World Inequality Report 2018* (World Inequality Lab, 2017), https:// wir2018.wid.world/. See also Leonhardt, "Our Broken Economy."

189 **on his children:** I owe this formulation to Gemma Mortensen.
189 **rat-race equilibrium:** George Akerlof, "The Economics of Caste and of the Rat Race and Other Woeful Tales," *Quarterly Journal of Economics* 90, no. 4 (November 1976). See also Alan Day Haight, "Padded Prowess: A Veblenian Interpretation of the Long Hours of Salaried Workers," *Journal of Economic Issues* 31, no. 1 (March 1997): 33–34. Hereafter cited as Haight, "Padded Prowess."

189 **cannot be measured directly:** Haight, "Padded Prowess," 33–34.

189 **use long hours as a proxy:** See Golden, "A Brief History of Long Work Time," 221, citing James Rebitzer and Lowell J. Taylor, "The Consequences of Minimum Wage Laws: Some New Theoretical Ideas," *Journal of Public Economics* 56, no. 2 (1995); Linda Bell and Richard Freeman, "Why Do Americans and Germans Work Different Hours?," in *Institutional Frameworks and Labor Market Performance*, ed. Friedrich Buttler et al. (London: Routledge, 1995); Samuel Bowles and Yongjin Park, "Emulation, Inequality, and Work Hours: Was Thorsten Veblen Right?," University of Massachusetts Economics Department Working Paper no. 62 (2004), hereafter cited as Bowles and Park, "Emulation, Inequality, and Work Hours"; Robert Drago, Mark Wooden, and David Black, "Who Wants and Gets Flexibility? Changing Work Hours Preferences and Life Events," *ILR Review* 62, no. 3 (April 2009).

189 **less effortful or productive workers:** Golden, "A Brief History of Long Work Time," 221.

190 **a reduction in vacation actually taken:** See Jessica Stillman, "This U.K. Company Offered Its Employees Unlimited Vacation Time. It Was a Total Failure," *Slate*, June 14, 2015, accessed November 18, 2018, https://slate.com/business/2015/07/unli mited-vacation-time-this-company-tried-it-and-it-was-a-total -failure.html.

190 **countries with greater economic inequality:** See, e.g., Bowles and Park, "Emulation, Inequality, and Work Hours," 10–13.

190 **longer work hours in the United States:** See, e.g., Bowles and Park, "Emulation, Inequality, and Work Hours," 12–13. For purposes of this analysis, inequality in the two countries was measured by the ratio between the 90th and 50th percentiles in the income distributions.

190 **within-industry income inequality:** Kuhn and Lozano, "The Expanding Workweek?," 336. See also Daniel Hecker, "How Hours of Work Affect Occupational Earnings," *Monthly Labor Review* (October 1998); Linda Bell and Richard Freeman, "Why Do Americans and Germans Work Different Hours?," NBER Working Paper No. 4808 (July 1994), www.nber.org/papers /w4808. The same point is noted in Bowles and Park, "Emulation, Inequality, and Work Hours."

190 **these perverse incentives:** The precise estimate was 44.5 percent. Landers, Rebitzer, and Taylor, "Rat Race Redux."

Long work hours also correlate not just to within-industry wage inequality but also to across-industry wage inequality. This suggests a direct impact of competitive status seeking on work effort. Bowles and Park, "Emulation, Inequality, and Work Hours," 16.

190 **take delivery of furniture:** Hewlett and Luce, "Extreme Jobs," 52.

190 **"if someone sends you a message":** See Laura Noonan, "Goldman Sachs Attempts to Woo Junior Bankers with Swift Promotions," *Financial Times*, November 5, 2015, accessed November 18, 2018, www.ft.com/content/7af51792-83e4-11e5-8e80-157 4112844fd.

190 **"stories of lawyers":** Rhode, *Balanced Lives*, 17, citing Meredith Wadman, "Family and Work," *Washington Lawyer*, November/December 1998, 33; Deborah L. Rhode, "Gender and Professional Roles," *Fordham Law Review* 63 (1994); and Keith Cunningham, "Father Time: Flexible Work Arrangements and the Law Firm's Failure of the Family," *Stanford Law Review* 53 (2001): 987. Nearly three in four lawyers report that they cannot successfully balance the demands of their work with their personal lives. Rhode, *Balanced Lives*, 11, citing Deborah L. Rhode,

*In the Interests of Justice: Reforming the Legal Profession* (Oxford: Oxford University Press, 2000), 10; Cameron Stracher, "Show Me the Misery," *Wall Street Journal*, March 6, 2000, A31; Carl T. Bogus, "The Death of an Honorable Profession," *Indiana Law Review* 71 (1996): 926; and Catalyst, Women in Law: Making the Case (2001), 9, executive summary available at http://womenlaw.stanford.edu/pdf/law.inside.fixed.pdf.

191 **shifting family funerals to make meetings:** Hewlett and Luce, "Extreme Jobs," 49–50.

A financial services executive participating in a focus group on elite overwork reported that he had lost the trust of his wheelchair-bound father by breaking too many promises of weekend visits. In another focus group from the same study, the teenage daughter of a partner at a major accounting firm reported that her father, who had promised he would spend more time at home once he'd made partner, instead had only increased his work hours; he was, she said, "gone when I get up, and not back when I go to sleep." The daughter regarded this as normal, as all her friends' fathers worked similar hours. Hewlett and Luce, "Extreme Jobs," 53, 58. A senior banker at JPMorgan similarly refused to allow a vice president a few hours off to attend his daughter's first dance recital, saying simply, "Don't worry—I haven't been to any of my kid's baseball games." Kevin Roose, *Young Money: Inside the Hidden World of Wall Street's Post-Crash Recruits* (New York: Grand Central Publishing, 2014), Chapter 14.

Parents appear to try to compensate for such behavior by spending their income on their children. But it is not clear that the children even want all the gifts that they receive. According to work by one child psychologist, for example, preschool-aged children on average ask for 3.4 toys for Christmas but receive 11.6. The study was conducted by Marilyn Bradford and is cited in Hochschild, *The Time Bind*, 217.

191 **"happy guy in college":** Ho, *Liquidated*, 89–90.

191 **"eager and energetic":** Leslie Kwoh, "Hazard of the Trade: Bankers' Health," *Wall Street Journal*, February 15, 2012, accessed November 18, 2018, www.wsj.com/articles/SB10001424052970204062704577223623824944472, citing Alexandra Michel, *Transcending Socialization: A Nine-Year Ethnography of the Body's Role in Organizational Control and Knowledge Worker Transformation* (2011), http://alexandramichel.com/ASQ%2011-11.pdf. Another study reports that more than two-thirds of overworked professionals do not sleep enough. Hewlett and Luce, "Extreme Jobs," 54.

191 **just the first half of the 1980s:** Schor, *The Overworked American*, 11.

191 **260 annual days of sunshine:** Jeffrey M. O'Brien, "Is Silicon Valley Bad for Your Health?," *Fortune*, October 23, 2015, accessed November 18, 2018, http://fortune.com/2015/10/23/is-silicon-valley-bad-for-your-health/.

191 **"personal matters":** See Laura Noonan, "Morgan Stanley to Offer Paid Sabbaticals to Retain VPs," *Financial Times*, June 2, 2016, accessed November 18, 2018, www.ft.com/content/d316dc38-28d2-11e6-8ba3-cdd781d02d89. Hereafter cited as Noonan, "Paid Sabbaticals to Retain VPs."

191 **required analysts to take Saturdays off:** See Olivia Oran, "Goldman to Summer Interns: Don't Stay in the Office Overnight," Reuters, June 17, 2015 accessed November 18, 2018, www.reuters.com/article/us-goldmansachs-interns/goldman-to-summer-interns-dont-stay-in-the-office-overnight-idUSKBN0OX1LA20150617, and Andrew Ross Sorkin, "Reflections on Stress and Long Hours on Wall Street," *New York Times*, June 17, 2015, accessed November 18, 2018, www.nytimes.com/2015/06/02/business/dealbook/reflections-on-stress-and-long-hours-on-wall-street.html.

191 **not perceived as "weak" for taking time off:** See Noonan, "Paid Sabbaticals to Retain VPs."

191 **incrementally less and less well-being:** This is only more true when the extra income gets spent on superfluous extravagances, in mutually destructive status competition. In some instances—for example, housing in elite urban neighborhoods or art or antique furnishings—rising incomes and wealth among the rich principally drive up prices for a fixed supply of goods. Increased top incomes yield literally just paper gains, as the rich simply consume the same goods that they otherwise would, but at inflated prices. The top 1 percent of households today receive

roughly twice and the top one-tenth of 1 percent roughly four times the income (measured in constant dollars) that they received in 1970. See "Income Inequality, USA, 1970–2014," World Inequality Database, accessed October 16, 2018, http://wid.world/country/usa/. But one cannot credibly say that they enjoy twice or quadruple the material well-being overall on this account, or indeed that their greater incomes make them materially better off at all.

192 **experience of elite overwork:** Nor are these reports artifacts of an unreflective focus on hours at the cost of neglecting the fact that longer hours yield greater incomes. When elite law firm associates were given a hypothetical choice among decreasing hours at their current incomes, increasing incomes at their current hours, and increasing both incomes and hours, nearly two-thirds chose to decrease hours and only one in ten preferred to increase both hours and incomes. See Landers, Rebitzer, and Taylor, "Rat Race Redux," 338–39. Perhaps these preferences merely reflect the fact that the associates were working optimally so that their hours and incomes had just reached the point at which the diminishing marginal utility of income caused them to begin to prefer leisure over greater pay and more work. But the preference for reducing hours did not grow with the associates' incomes. This suggests that the associates in the study were overworked and in a rat race, rather than working precisely their preferred hours. See Landers, Rebitzer, and Taylor, "Rat Race Redux," 339. Notwithstanding their preferences for marginal leisure over marginal income, lawyers have seen a steady parallel rise in pay and hours. One further reason behind this trend bears mention. Between 1970 and 2000, "associate compensation [at large law firms] increased 1000% . . . while billing rates . . . increased only 400%." Law firms, it seems, "paid for the higher salaries by increasing billable hours rather than charging higher rates." Associate preferences for reducing hours even at the cost of lower salaries have not translated into law firm behavior. See Schiltz, "An Unhappy, Unhealthy, and Unethical Profession," 900, citing William G. Ross, *The Honest Hour: The Ethics of Time-Based Billing by Attorneys* (Durham, NC: Carolina Academic Press, 1996), 2, and North Carolina Bar Association, *Report of the Quality of Life Task Force and Recommendations* (1991), 11–12.

Other surveys replicate these results. According to the American Bar Association, "In recent surveys, most men as well as women indicate a willingness to take lower salaries in exchange for more time with their families." Deborah L. Rhode, "Balanced Lives for Lawyers," *Fordham Law Review* 70 (2002): 2212, citing Family and Work Institute, *National Study of the Changing Workplace*, a study involving some twenty-eight hundred workers that found that workplace flexibility and family support was the second-most-significant factor in job satisfaction, after job quality. Nearly two-thirds of all workers would reduce their workweek by an average of ten hours. Steven Ginsberg, "Raising Corporate Profits by Reaching Out to Families," *Washington Post*, April 19, 1998, H7; Sue Shellenbarger, "Study of U.S. Workers Finds Sharp Rise Since 1992 in Desire to Reduce Hours," *Wall Street Journal*, April 15, 1998, A10. For discussion of the generational shift in priorities within law and accounting firms as young men as well as women express greater desire for time with their families, see Douglas McCracken, "Winning the Talent War for Women: Sometimes It Takes a Revolution," *Harvard Business Review* (November–December 2000): 159, 161; Bruce Balestier, "'Mommy Track' No Career Derailment," *New York Law Journal*, June 9, 2000, 24; Terry Carter, "Your Time or Your Money," *ABA Journal* (February 2001): 26. One survey by Harris Interactive and the Radcliffe Public Policy Center found that almost three-quarters of men in their middle thirties, compared to only a quarter of men over sixty-five, would be willing to take lower salaries in exchange for more time available for their family. Kirsten Downey Grimsley, "Family a Priority for Young Workers: Survey Finds Changes in Men's Thinking," *Washington Post*, May 3, 2000, E1. See generally Bruce Tulgan, *The Manager's Pocket Guide to Generation X* (Amherst, MA: HRD Press, 1997).

192 **prefer to work fewer hours:** Jacobs and Gerson, *The Time Divide*, 65–66.

192 **nearly twelve hours of weekly overwork:** Jacobs and Gerson, *The Time Divide*, 68.

192 **thirteen weekly hours of overwork:** Jacobs and Gerson, *The Time Divide*, 68.

192 **five hours of overwork per week:** Jacobs and Gerson, *The Time Divide*, 68.

192 **fight Mike Tyson:** Will Meyerhofer, "Not Worth It," The People's Therapist, April 13, 2011, accessed November 18, 2018, https://thepeoplestherapist.com/2011/04/13/not-worth-it/#more-3292 (Meyerhofer worked at the law firm Sullivan and Cromwell).

192 **"sick and insane":** Ho, *Liquidated*, 115.

192 **"not a life":** Cynthia Fuchs Epstein et al., "Glass Ceilings and Open Doors: Women's Advancement in the Legal Profession," *Fordham Law Review* 46 (1995): 385.

192 **"no way to have a child":** Rhode, *Balanced Lives*, 14.

192 **to the Holocaust:** See Ho, *Liquidated*.

193 **"less smart":** The quotations come from Ho, *Liquidated*, 44, 56.

## Chapter Seven: A Comprehensive Divide

197 **the forty-second and forty-third presidents of the United States:** "Timeline Guide to the U.S. Presidents," Scholastic, accessed October 1, 2018, www.scholastic.com/teachers/articles/teaching-content/timeline-guide-us-presidents/.

197 **ran a small grocery store:** Bill Clinton, *My Life* (New York: Vintage, 2005), 4, 8–18.

197 **Brown Brothers Harriman & Co.:** Kitty Kelley, *The Family: The Real Story of the Bush Dynasty* (New York: Doubleday, 2004), 42, 80.

198 **whom he eventually married:** Russell L. Riley, "Bill Clinton: Life Before the Presidency," Miller Center at the University of Virginia, accessed October 6, 2018, https://millercenter.org/president/clinton/life-before-the-presidency.

198 **middle-class neighborhood:** "About the Project," George W. Bush Childhood Home, Inc., accessed October 1, 2018, www.bushchildhoodhome.org/about.

198 **Cozumel, Mexico:** Laura Bush, *Spoken from the Heart* (New York: Scribner, 2010), 94–96.

198 **a white-collar future:** Over 20 percent of veterans surveyed either would not or probably would not have gone to college but for the GI Bill, which provided a "ticket of admission to the middle class that quickly rivalled the union card as a significant economic lever of upward mobility." William G. Bowen, Martin A. Kurzweil, and Eugene M. Tobin, *Equity and Excellence in American Higher Education* (Charlottesville: University of Virginia Press, 2006), 31–32.

199 **one-twentieth of their present levels:** See Chapter 1.

199 **perhaps 40 percent today:** Thomas Piketty and Emmanuel Saez, "How Progressive Is the U.S. Federal Tax System? A Historical and International Perspective," *Journal of Economic Perspectives* 21, no. 1 (Winter 2007): 3.

199 **between 1950 and 1970:** Bishop, *The Big Sort*, 130. For further discussion, see Berry and Glaeser, "The Divergence of Human Capital."

199 **an ordinary car:** Murray, *Coming Apart*, 27–28. See also Kathleen Leonard Turner, "Commercial Food Venues," in *Material Culture in America: Understanding Everyday Life*, ed. Helen Sheumaker and Shirley Teresa Wajda (Santa Barbara, CA: ABC-CLIO), 112–13; "How Much Cars Cost in the 60s," The People History, accessed October 7, 2018, www.thepeoplehistory.com/60scars.html.

199 **a typical midcentury year:** Murray, *Coming Apart*, 26.

199 **including among elites:** Kristina Wilson, *Livable Modernism: Interior Decorating and Design During the Great Depression* (New Haven, CT: Yale University Art Gallery, 2004), 14–17.

199 **including into leadership positions:** Bishop, *The Big Sort*, 225. The place in civil society that these membership organizations once held is today roughly occupied by professionally run advocacy groups, whose supporters are often segregated by class and, in any event, do not interact much (and certainly not with their managers). For further discussion, see Theda Skocpol, *Diminished Democracy: From Membership to Management* (Norman: University of Oklahoma Press, 2004), 291.

200 **"lives on an economic scale":** Duncan Norton-Taylor, "How Top Executives Live (Fortune 1955)," *Fortune*, last modified May 6, 2012, accessed November 19, 2018, http://fortune.com/2012/05/06/how-top-executives-live-fortune-1955/#. Hereafter cited as Norton-Taylor, "How Top Executives Live."

200 **"live[d] in an unpretentious brick house":** Norton-Taylor, "How Top Executives Live."

200 **"bought a new Ford":** Norton-Taylor, "How Top Executives Live."

200 **"The executive's home today":** Norton-Taylor, "How Top Executives Live."

200 **"The executive who feels":** Norton-Taylor, "How Top Executives Live."

200 **"'Top executives . . . are not expected'":** Norton-Taylor, "How Top Executives Live."

201 **"no evidence of class effects":** William J. Wilson, *When Work Disappears* (New York: Vintage, 1997), 195. Hereafter cited as Wilson, *When Work Disappears*.

201 **which class cannot displace:** Powerful statements of the view that white supremacy remains the dominant ideology in American life include Ta-Nehisi Coates, *Between the World and Me* (New York: Spiegel & Grau, 2015), and Charles Mills, *The Racial Contract* (Ithaca, NY: Cornell University Press, 1997).

201 **(as Wilson himself has acknowledged):** Wilson observed, for example, that toward the end of the Great Compression, in the mid-1960s, "class began to affect career and generation mobility for Blacks as it has regularly done for whites." Wilson, *When Work Disappears*, 195.

201 **just one case in point among many:** For example, roughly 35 percent of African Americans owned their own homes in 1950; roughly 39 percent of Americans in the bottom income quartile do today. U.S. Census Bureau, Census of Housing, "Historical Census of Housing Tables: Ownership Rates," last modified October 31, 2011, www.census.gov/hhes/www/housing/census/historic/ownrate.html; "Data by Issue: Homeownership and Housing," Prosperity Now Scorecard, https://scorecard.prosperitynow.org/data-by-issue#housing/outcome/homeownership-by-income (2016 data). Similarly, in 1954 the unemployment rate among African Americans was roughly 10 percent; in 2009, the unemployment rates among the bottom four deciles of the income distribution were roughly 12, 15, 19, and 31 percent. Drew Desilver, "Black Unemployment Rate Is Consistently Twice That of Whites," Pew Research Center, August 21, 2013, www.pewresearch.org/fact-tank/2013/08/21/through-good-times-and-bad-black-unemployment-is-consistently-double-that-of-whites/.

   When class and race intersect, their cumulative effects become enormous. For example, among black men born in 1960, high school dropouts have a 59 percent chance of going to prison at some point in their lives, whereas college graduates have a 5 percent chance. See James Forman Jr., "Racial Critiques of Mass Incarceration: Beyond the New Jim Crow," 25 (on file with author). See also Bruce Western and Christopher Wildeman, "The Black Family and Mass Incarceration," *Annals of the American Academy of Political and Social Sciences* 621 (2009): 221–42.

202 **fallen by roughly a third:** The share of households has fallen from 61 percent to just under 50 percent, and the share of income has fallen from 62 percent to 43 percent. Pew Research Center, "The American Middle Class Is Losing Ground."

202 **no longer middle class:** Pew Research Center, "The American Middle Class Is Losing Ground." For further discussion, see Marilyn Geewax, "The Tipping Point: Most Americans No Longer Are Middle Class," National Public Radio, last modified December 9, 2015, www.npr.org/sections/thetwo-way/2015/12/09/459087477/the-tipping-point-most-americans-no-longer-are-middle-class.

202 **no longer stands out for its wealth:** Here see David Leonhardt and Kevin Quealy, "The American Middle Class Is No Longer the World's Richest," *New York Times*, April 22, 2014, accessed November 19, 2018, www.nytimes.com/2014/04/23/upshot/the-american-middle-class-is-no-longer-the-worlds-richest.html?_r=0. Leonhardt and Quealy use data from the Luxembourg Income Study to show that around 2010, median incomes in Canada and Norway overtook those in the United States and that median incomes in almost every other rich nation have been catching up rapidly over the past three decades.

202 **a kind of narcissism:** Marianne Cooper, "Being the 'Go-To Guy': Fatherhood, Masculinity, and the Organization of Work in Silicon Valley," in *Families at Work: Expanding the Bounds*, ed. Naomi Gerstel, Dan Clawson, and Robert Zussman

(Nashville: Vanderbilt University Press, 2002), 26; Williams, *White Working Class*, 37–38.

203 **"If we had a vacancy"**: Richard J. Murnane and Frank Levy, *Teaching the New Basic Skills: Principles for Educating Children to Thrive in a Changing Economy* (New York: Free Press, 1996), 19. See also Daron Acemoglu, "Technical Change, Inequality, and the Labor Market," *Journal of Economic Literature* 40, no. 1 (March 2002): 41, https://doi.org/10.1257/0022051026976. Hereafter cited as Acemoglu, "Technical Change."

203 **not appreciably more skilled, on average, than others**: See Chapter 6.

203 **even within cities**: Berry and Glaeser, "The Divergence of Human Capital," 415–16.

203 **separate physical spaces**: Moreover, the increases are greatest among high-wage, technology-intensive employers: a recent study of nearly three thousand firms found a robust correlation between the intensity of applicant screening on the one hand and, on the other, the levels of formal education, self-reported skills, and extent of computer use among a firm's employees. Steffanie L. Wilk and Peter Cappelli, "Understanding the Determinants of Employer Use of Selection Methods," *Personnel Psychology* 56, no. 1 (Spring 2003): 117–19, https://doi.org /10.1111/j.1744-6570.2003.tb00145.x. See also Acemoglu, "Technical Change," 41.

203 **hire casually**: For example, Sports Plus, which in the 1990s paid assemblers between $5.50 and $7.00 per hour, still hires in the casual fashion one employed by Ford. Richard J. Murnane and Frank Levy, *Teaching the New Basic Skills: Principles for Educating Children to Thrive in a Changing Economy* (New York: Free Press, 1996), 47. See also Acemoglu, "Changes in Unemployment and Wage Inequality," 1270.

203 **formal cognitive tests and lengthy interviews**: These innovations were introduced in the mid-1980s by firms such as Honda of America and Diamond Star Motors, and are now widely used by employers seeking mid-skilled workers. Acemoglu further discusses this in his work, saying, "These are high-wage employers, with somewhat higher real wages than Ford in the 1960's, and the first two are in the same industry as Ford. All three companies spend substantial resources on recruitment and hire only a fraction of those who apply. The first two use formal cognitive tests, including mathematics, aptitude, and English tests, as well as a series of lengthy interviews. The third company employs more intensive interviews but no formal tests. The interview process in all three companies is quite costly as it involves a large number of fellow employees and managers, but they view this as a worthwhile activity." Acemoglu, "Changes in Unemployment and Wage Inequality," 1270.

203 **lasting entire days**: Rivera, *Pedigree*, 31–34.

204 **steadily more precise over time**: The share of workers who possess precisely the education level required for their jobs increased between 1976 and 1985, for example, and the extent of the education gap for mismatched workers (the average excess years of schooling possessed by overeducated workers) declined. Acemoglu, "Changes in Unemployment and Wage Inequality," 1271–72, Table 1. Daron Acemoglu's work tests the robustness of this result against effects concerning the changing composition of the workforce, e.g., a rise of young workers who tend to be overeducated.

204 **entirely separate firms**: Acemoglu, "Technical Change," 7–72, 48–49.

204 **without college degrees**: Bishop, *The Big Sort*, 135.

204 **from the educated elite**: The pattern has become so extreme that the military itself now worries about the educational level of its recruits. The Pentagon has thus bemoaned that the "propensity to enlist is lower for high quality youth, youth with better educated parents, and youth planning to attend college." John T. Warner, Curtis J. Simon, and Deborah M. Payne, *Enlistment Supply in the 1990's: A Study of the Navy College Fund and Other Enlistment Incentive Programs* (Ft. Belvoir, VA: Defense Technical Information Center, 2001), 21–22. See also Bishop, *The Big Sort*, 137.

205 **more Yale students were murdered in New Haven than were killed in Iraq**: See John Nordheimer, "Son of Privilege, Son of Pain: Random Death at Yale's Gates," *New York Times*, June 28, 1992, accessed November 19, 2018, www.nytimes.com/1992 /06/28/nyregion/son-of-privilege-son-of-pain-random-death

-at-yale-s-gates.html; Paul Gunther, "The End of Shared Sacrifice Set in Stone: Yale as Metaphor," *Huffington Post*, December 6, 2017, accessed November 19, 2018, www.huffington post.com/paul-gunther/the-end-of-shared-sacrifi_b_6124098 .html.

205 **centered on the workplace**: Hochschild, *Strangers in Their Own Land*, 121. For further discussion, see also James B. Steward, "Looking for a Lesson in Google's Perks," *New York Times*, March 15, 2013, accessed November 19, 2018, www.nytimes .com/2013/03/16/business/at-google-a-place-to-work-and-play .html.

205 **"throwing on a goofy hat"**: Tan Chen, "The Spiritual Crisis of the Modern Economy."

206 **the association between work and honor**: Eberstadt, "Where Did All the Men Go?" According to one researcher's statistics, incarceration has quadrupled within the past forty years. Sarah Shannon et al., "The Growth, Scope, and Spatial Distribution of People with Felony Records in the United States, 1948–2010," *Demography* 54, no. 5 (October 2017): 1804–5, Table 1.

206 **the New Jim Crow**: Michelle Alexander, *The New Jim Crow: Mass Incarceration in the Age of Colorblindness* (New York: New Press, 2010).

207 **middle-class sexual habits**: In the late eighteenth century, aristocratic society began rejecting puritanism. See Faramerz Dabhoiwala, *The Origins of Sex: A History of the First Sexual Revolution* (Oxford: Oxford University Press, 2012).

207 **without her labor**: Veblen, *Theory of the Leisure Class*, 34.

208 **rarer among the rich than the rest**: See Chapter 5.

208 **almost unheard of**: See Chapter 5.

208 **middle-class households**: Annette Lareau, *Unequal Childhoods: Class, Race, and Life* (Berkeley: University of California Press, 2011), 45, 55–57, 76–77.

208 **remains where it was**: In 1970, 73 percent of educated and 67 percent of working-class white Americans reported "very happy" marriages; today the share among professionals remains roughly the same, while the share among the working class has fallen to roughly 50 percent. "Men Adrift: Badly Educated Men in Rich Countries Have Not Adapted Well to Trade, Technology or Feminism," *The Economist*, May 28, 2015, accessed November 19, 2018, www.economist.com/news/essays/21649050-badly -educated-men-rich-countries-have-not-adapted-well-trade -technology-or-feminism.

208 **fell by a quarter between 2002 and 2012**: The question was asked in the National Survey of Family Growth. Forty-two percent of college-educated women answered "yes" in 2002; just 31 percent did in 2012. Helaine Olen, "Think Divorce Is Miserable? Look How Bad Life Can Get When Divorcees Try to Retire. Especially When They're Women," *Slate*, March 18, 2016, accessed November 19, 2018, www.slate.com/articles/business /the_bills/2016/03/how_divorce_exacerbates_the_retire ment_crisis_especially_if_you_re_a_woman.html.

208 **nearly 20 percent among poor women**: "The Tissue Trade: Dislike of Abortion and Support for Planned Parenthood Should Go Together," *The Economist*, August 1, 2015, accessed November 19, 2018, www.economist.com/united-states/2015 /08/01/the-tissue-trade. See also Peter Schuck, *One Nation Undecided: Clear Thinking About Five Hard Issues That Divide Us* (Princeton, NJ: Princeton University Press, 2017), 110.

208 **"precisely . . . to teach"**: Putnam, Frederick, and Snellman, "Growing Class Gaps," 22.

208 **by 240, 40, and 130 percent respectively**: Putnam, Frederick, and Snellman, "Growing Class Gaps," 16–17, Tables 6–8.

209 **both roughly tripled**: Putnam, Frederick, and Snellman, "Growing Class Gaps," 17–18.

209 **"most people can be trusted"**: Putnam, Frederick, and Snellman, "Growing Class Gaps," 19.

209 **not at all for the bottom**: Putnam, Frederick, and Snellman, "Growing Class Gaps," 20.

209 **scorn the sexism of middle America**: Tan Chen, "The Spiritual Crisis of the Modern Economy."

209 **no women in top management**: Carbone and Cahn, "Unequal Terms." See also Rachel Soares et al., "2012 Catalyst Census: Fortune 500 Women Executive Officers and Top Earners," Catalyst, December 11, 2012, www.catalyst.org/knowledge/2012 -catalyst-census-fortune-500-women-executive-officers-and -top-earners.

209 **remains overwhelmingly male-dominated:** Alexander Eichler, "Gender Wage Gap Is Higher on Wall Street Than Anywhere Else," *Huffington Post*, March 19, 2012, accessed November 19, 2018, www.huffingtonpost.com/2012/03/19/gender-wage-gap -wall-street_n_1362878.html; William Alden, "Wall Street's Young Bankers Are Still Mostly White and Male, Report Says," *New York Times*, September 30, 2014, accessed November 19, 2018, https://dealbook.nytimes.com/2014/09/30/wall-streets -young-bankers-are-still-mostly-white-and-male; and Andy Kiersz and Portia Crowe, "These Charts Show Just How White and Male Wall Street Really Is," *Business Insider*, August 25, 2015, accessed November 19, 2018, www.businessinsider.com /wall-street-bank-diversity-2015-8.

209 **equity partners at American law firms:** American Bar Association Commission on Women in the Profession, *A Current Glance at Women in the Law: January 2017* (2017), www.amer icanbar.org/content/dam/aba/marketing/women/current _glance_statistics_january2017.authcheckdam.pdf.

209 **has widened in recent years:** A. T. Lo Sasso et al., "The $16,819 Pay Gap for Newly Trained Physicians: The Unexplained Trend of Men Earning More Than Women," *Health Affairs* 30, no. 2 (February 2018): 193–201.

209 **bearing (let alone raising) children:** Claudia Goldin, "A Grand Gender Convergence: Its Last Chapter," *American Economic Review* 104, no. 4 (2014): 1–30; and Carbone and Cahn, "Unequal Terms."

209 **delay childbirth and remain in the workforce:** Clare Cain Miller, "Freezing Eggs as Part of Employee Benefits: Some Women See Darker Message," *New York Times*, October 14, 2014, accessed November 19, 2018, www.nytimes.com/2014 /10/15/upshot/egg-freezing-as-a-work-benefit-some-women -see-darker-message.html.

210 **conventionally done by middle-class women:** Carbone and Cahn, "Unequal Terms"; and Michelle Rendall, "The Service Sector and Female Market Work: Europe vs. U.S.," working paper, University of Zurich, January 22, 2013, www.economicdy namics.org/meetpapers/2013/paper_1202.pdf.

210 **declining wages for men without a college degree:** Carbone and Cahn, "Unequal Terms," 191.

210 **with annual incomes below $30,000:** U.S. Department of Education, National Center for Education Statistics, National Postsecondary Student Aid Studies, 1995–96, 1999–2000, 2003–4. All incomes are in 1996 dollars. By contrast, men make up 49 percent of college students from households with incomes above $70,000. Carbone and Cahn, "Unequal Terms"; and Mary Beth Marklein, "College Gender Gap Widens: 57% Are Women," *USA Today*, October 19, 2005.

210 **the no-longer adequacy of the male wage:** Williams, *White Working Class*, 76.

210 **falling among the middle class and the poor:** Carbone and Cahn, "Unequal Terms."

210 **wives out-earn their husbands:** Carbone and Cahn, "Unequal Terms"; and Sarah Jane Glynn, "Breadwinning Mothers Are Increasingly the U.S. Norm," Center for American Progress, December 19, 2016, www.americanprogress.org/issues/women /reports/2016/12/19/295203/breadwinning-mothers-are -increasingly-the-u-s-norm.

210 **the bottom of the economic distribution:** Claire Cain Miller and Quoctrung Bui, "Equality in Marriages Grows, and So Does Class Divide," *New York Times*, February 27, 2016, accessed November 19, 2018, www.nytimes.com/2016/02/23/upshot /rise-in-marriages-of-equals-and-in-division-by-class.html; and Marianne Bertrand, Jessica Pan, and Emir Kamenica, "Gender Identity and Relative Income Within Households," NBER Working Paper No. 19023 (May 2013), www.nber.org/papers /w19023.

211 **feels distant and almost academic:** John Morley brought this difference to my attention.

211 **"love and work":** There is a controversy as to whether Freud ever actually said this quote that is so often attributed to him. The first recorded public attribution to Freud appeared in a book of psychoanalysis called *Childhood and Society* published by German-American psychoanalyst Erik Erikson in 1950. Even in its first appearance, the attribution is already secondhand. "Freud was once asked what he thought a normal person should be able to do well. . . . Freud, in the curt way of his old days, is reported to have said: 'Lieben und arbeiten' (to love and to work)."

Later in 1982, when asked in an interview, Erikson said of the quote, "I heard it in Vienna and it impressed me. I've never seen it in print. And some people now have said I made it up. If I did, I'm proud." Alan C. Elms, "Apocryphal Freud: Sigmund Freud's Most Famous 'Quotations' and Their Actual Sources," in *Annual of Psychoanalysis*, vol. 29: *Sigmund Freud and His Impact on the Modern World*, ed. Jerome A. Winer and James W. Anderson (Hillsdale, NJ: Analytic Press 2001).

211 **Anglicans/Episcopalians, Jews, and Hindus:** Murphy, "The Most and Least Educated U.S. Religious Groups"; Masci, "How Income Varies Among U.S. Religious Groups."

211 **By contrast, Jehovah's Witnesses:** Murphy, "The Most and Least Educated U.S. Religious Groups"; Masci, "How Income Varies Among U.S. Religious Groups."

211 **Interestingly, Catholics:** Murphy, "The Most and Least Educated U.S. Religious Groups"; Masci, "How Income Varies Among U.S. Religious Groups."

212 **"Morally, I'm a Democrat":** Thomas Edsall, "How the Other Fifth Lives," *New York Times*, April 27, 2016, accessed November 19, 2018, www.nytimes.com/2016/04/27/opinion/cam paign-stops/how-the-other-fifth-lives.html. Hereafter cited as Edsall, "How the Other Fifth Lives."

212 **Most broadly stated:** Andrew Gelman, *Red State, Blue State, Rich State, Poor State* (Princeton, NJ: Princeton University Press, 2008), 106; Benjamin Page, Larry Bartels, and Jason Seawright, "Democracy and the Policy Preferences of Wealthy Americans," *Perspectives on Politics* 1, no. 1 (March 2013): 52. Hereafter cited as Page, Bartels, and Seawright, "Democracy and the Policy Preferences of Wealthy Americans." See also Benjamin Page and Cari Hennessy, "What Affluent Americans Want from Politics," APSA annual meeting, Washington, DC, September 2–5, 2010 (Working Paper 11-08, Institute for Policy Research, Northwestern University). Hereafter cited as Page and Hennessy, "What Affluent Americans Want from Politics."

212 **A meta-study of hundreds:** Page, Bartels, and Seawright, "Democracy and the Policy Preferences of Wealthy Americans," 52, quoting Martin Gilens, "Preference Gaps and Inequality in Representation," *PS: Political Science and Politics* 42, no. 2 (April 2009): 335–41. Hereafter cited as Gilens, "Preference Gaps and Inequality in Representation." Gilens tested and found significant difference in opinion between the two groups on the following policy positions: "Approve the abortion pill RU-486; Federal funding for abortions (for low-income women); Require biological father's notification/approval for abortion; Legalize gay marriage; Teach creationism in publish schools; and Fund stem cell research from newly created embryos."

212 **hold "consistently liberal" views:** "A Wider Ideological Gap Between More and Less Educated Adults," Pew Research Center, April 26, 2016, www.people-press.org/2016/04/26/a -wider-ideological-gap-between-more-and-less-educated-adults; Neil Gross, "Why Are the Highly Educated So Liberal?," *New York Times*, May 13, 2016, accessed November 19, 2018, www .nytimes.com/2016/05/15/opinion/why-are-the-highly -educated-so-liberal.html.

212 **The Phillips Exeter survey:** Edsall, "How the Other Fifth Lives."

212 **Finally, a pilot study:** Page, Bartels, and Seawright, "Democracy and the Policy Preferences of Wealthy Americans," 53. Of the sample, 32.4 percent had incomes greater than $1 million, and the median wealth was $7.5 million.

Another careful study, this time of Americans in the top tenth of the income distribution, confirms that they are "more liberal [than less rich Americans] on issues like abortion, gay rights, and foreign aid." Gilens, *Affluence and Influence*, 5. More specifically, when compared to median Americans, rich Americans were substantially more likely to favor approving emergency contraception and to oppose banning abortions, substantially more likely to favor stem cell research, substantially more likely to favor same-sex marriage and permitting openly gay Americans to serve in the military, and substantially less likely to favor a constitutional amendment permitting school prayer or (in the 1980s) mandatory AIDS testing of all citizens. Yet another study exploited transitory idiosyncrasies in certain administrations of the General Social Survey to identify a similarly distinctive social liberality among Americans in the top 4 percent of the income distribution. According to this study, the top 4 percent were much more likely to support abortion, allowing atheists and communists to "make a speech in public" and teach and write books, and, interestingly, funding for space exploration. Page and Hennessy, "What Affluent Americans Want from Politics," 16.

213 **social welfare spending:** For example, wealthier Americans are more likely to support time limits on welfare receipt, to support cutting the top marginal tax rate as well as the capital gains and estate taxes, and to disfavor a universal health care plan. Page, Bartels, and Seawright, "Democracy and the Policy Preferences of Wealthy Americans," 52, quoting Gilens, "Preference Gaps and Inequality in Representation."

213 **government regulation of corporations and industry:** Gilens, *Affluence and Influence*, 114.

213 **as on social ones:** Edsall, "How the Other Fifth Lives."

213 **the most pressing issue:** Page, Bartels, and Seawright, "Democracy and the Policy Preferences of Wealthy Americans," 55–56, 59–60, 64.

213 **in particular Social Security:** Page, Bartels, and Seawright, "Democracy and the Policy Preferences of Wealthy Ameri-cans," 65.

213 **$180,000 at the time of the study:** See Chapter 6.

213 **less equality-minded than typical Americans:** Ray Fisman, Shachar Kariv, and Daniel Markovits, "The Distributional Preferences of an Elite," *Science* 349, no. 6254 (September 2015).

214 **professed motivations to make money or to gain knowledge:** The one exception to this rule is that being African American more powerfully predicts rejecting economic conservatism than attending a school with a poorer student body. Tali Mendelberg et al., "College Socialization and the Economic Views of Affluent Americans," *American Journal of Political Science* 61, no. 3 (July 2017): 606–23.

214 **progressive views on social questions:** The locus classicus is Theodore M. Newcomb, *Personality and Social Change: Attitude Formation in a Student Community* (New York: Dryden, 1943).

214 **"greater attraction of the free market to the affluent":** Gilens, *Affluence and Influence*, 116.

214 **"Silicon Valley is a meritocracy":** Andy Reinhardt, "How It Really Works," *Business Week*, August 25, 1997. The article goes on to quote Jobs as saying, "It doesn't matter what you wear. It doesn't matter how old you are. What matters is how smart you are."

214 **its aggressive pursuit of wealth:** Charles D. Ellis, "Goldman Sachs' Secret to Success Under Siege," *Institutional Investor*, August 8, 2013, accessed November 19, 2018, www.institutionalinvestor.com/article/b14zb9rlghm8l7/goldman-sachs-secret-to-success-under-siege. Ellis describes an "impatient" shift in the culture in the 1980s to make Goldman Sachs the premier leader in global finance: "In the past it was all about clients; now it was about accounts and counterparties, and terminology turned toward locker-room crudeness. . . . The securities business was changing rapidly, and Goldman Sachs was changing even more rapidly so its skillful, driven people could stay ahead of the curve of change and excel at making money."

214 **oppose unions among its staff and graduate students:** Peter Salovey, *Promoting Diversity and Equal Opportunity at Yale University: 2016–2017*, Yale University, 2, https://student-dhr.yale.edu/sites/default/files/files/YEO.pdf; Yuki Noguchi, "At Yale, Protests Mark a Fight to Recognize Union for Grad Students," National Public Radio, June 16, 2017, www.npr.org/sections/ed/2017/06/16/532774267/at-yale-protests-mark-a-fight-to-recognize-union-for-grad-students; and Markeshia Ricks, "Yale Cops Threaten Strike," *New Haven Independent*, September 6, 2018, accessed November 19, 2018, https://www.newhavenindependent.org/index.php/archives/entry/yale_police_union_threatens_strike.

215 **whose incomes fall below $20,000:** "Nice Work If You Can Get Out," *The Economist*, April 19, 2014, accessed November 19, 2018, www.economist.com/news/finance-and-economics/21600989-why-rich-now-have-less-leisure-poor-nice-work-if-you-can-get-out?fsrc=scn/tw/te/bl/ed/nicework.

215 **more educated men:** Mark Aguiar and Erik Hurst, *The Increase in Leisure Inequality: 1965–2005* (Washington, DC: AEI Press, 2009), 46, www.aei.org/wp-content/uploads/2014/03/-increase-in-leisure-inequality_095714451042.pdf.

215 **fitness has become a status symbol:** "Spin to Separate," *The Economist*, August 1, 2015, accessed November 19, 2018, www.economist.com/news/united-states/21660170-sweating-purpose-becoming-elite-phenomenon-spin-separate.

215 **than in the top:** Emily C. Bianchi and Kathleen D. Vohs, "Social Class and Social Worlds: Income Predicts the Frequency and Nature of Social Contact," *Social Psychology and Personality Science* 7, no. 5 (2016): 479–86; and Christopher Ingraham, "The Social Lives of Rich People, Explained," *Washington Post*, May 12, 2016, accessed November 19, 2018, www.washingtonpost.com/news/wonk/wp/2016/05/12/how-money-changes-everything-even-your-friendships/?utm_term=.5475a807dc28.

215 **"rooted self":** The quoted language comes from Hochschild, *Strangers in Their Own Land*, 166. See also "Why the White Working Class Voted for Trump," interview with Joan C. Williams.

215 **family and long-standing friends:** See Joan C. Williams, *Reshaping the Work-Family Debate: Why Men and Class Matter* (Cambridge, MA: Harvard University Press, 2012), 171–73. Williams cites Marjorie L. Devault, *Feeding the Family: The Social Organization of Caring as Gendered Work* (Chicago: University of Chicago Press, 1991), 208–12. See also Williams, *White Working Class*.

215 **straightforward and direct:** "Why the White Working Class Voted for Trump," interview with Joan C. Williams.

215 **chronic ailments, guns, and religion:** See David Leonhardt, "In One America, Guns and Diet. In the Other, Cameras and 'Zoolander'," *New York Times*, August 18, 2014, accessed July 19, 2018, www.nytimes.com/2014/08/19/upshot/inequality-and-web-search-trends.html. See also Chapter 3.

216 **the Wargaming and Roleplaying Society:** Hochschild, *Strangers in Their Own Land*, 19.

216 **from which they buy all these things:** These categories closely track the classification that *Consumer Reports* uses to organize its product reviews. "Products A–Z," *Consumer Reports*, accessed October 7, 2018, www.consumerreports.org/cro/a-to-z-index/products/index.htm.

216 **nearly 70 percent of GDP:** Maggie C. Woodward, "The U.S. Economy to 2022: Settling into a New Normal," *Monthly Labor Review*, December 2013, https://doi.org/10.21916/mlr.2013.43.

216 **now reveal more about her income than about her race:** Marianne Bertrand and Emir Kamenica, "Coming Apart? Cultural Distances in the United States over Time," NBER Working Paper No. 24771 (2018), www.nber.org/papers/w24771. Hereafter cited as Bertrand and Kamenica, "Coming Apart? Cultural Distances in the United States over Time." See also Andrew Van Dam, "What We Buy Can Be Used to Predict Our Politics, Race or Education—Sometimes with More Than 90 Percent Accuracy," *Washington Post*, July 9, 2018, accessed November 19, 2018, www.washingtonpost.com/business/2018/07/10/rich-people-prefer-grey-poupon-white-people-own-pets-data-behind-cultural-divide/?utm_term=.75e85beb6d56.

Interpreting the study is a complicated matter. The authors conclude that "our headline result is that for all other demographic divisions and cultural dimensions [besides political ideology], cultural distance has been broadly constant over time." Bertrand and Kamenica, "Coming Apart? Cultural Distances in the United States over Time." But neither the paper's data nor its methods really support this conclusion, at least in an interesting way. First, the data series does not go back far enough. The consumption data, for example, begins in the mid-1990s. The interesting comparison, however, is between the present day and the 1950s. Second, the paper's analytic method does not allow for a scalar measure of cultural distance. The authors ask only whether machine learning can use consumer data inputs to predict income. They do not ask how great the differences between consumption patterns are, nor do they even propose a way to measure these differences.

216 **the pinnacle of the elite:** All others held land not directly as sovereigns but rather through the legal fiction of an "estate in land," which conveyed rights to occupy, use, and profit from land even as the land itself remained formally under the sovereign's ultimate control. The fiction remains in place to this day, and the power of eminent domain may be formalized as the sovereign's right to reoccupy its land, while compensating the owner for the value of the "estate" of which the sovereign deprives him. S. F. C. Milson, "Proprietary Ideas," in *The Legal Framework of English Feudalism* (Cambridge: Cambridge University Press, 1976), 36–64.

216 **eating opulent foods:** N. B. Harte, "State Control of Dress and Social Change in Pre-Industrial England," in *Trade, Government,*

*and Economy in Pre-industrial England,* ed. D. C. Coleman and A. H. John (London: Weidenfeld & Nicolson, 1976), 132–65.

216   **commercial rather than aristocratic wealth:** Herman Freudenberger, "Fashion, Sumptuary Laws, and Business," *Business History Review* 37, no. 1–2 (1963): 39–41.

216   **from 44 percent in 1940 to 63 percent by 1970:** U.S. Census Bureau, Census of Housing, "Historical Census of Housing Tables: Homeownership," last modified October 31, 2011, www .census.gov/hhes/www/housing/census/historic/owner.html.

216   **no further substantial increase since then:** U.S. Census Bureau, Census of Housing, "Historical Census of Housing Tables: Homeownership," last modified October 31, 2011, www.census .gov/hhes/www/housing/census/historic/owner.html.

217   **widely dispersed throughout the middle class:** See Chapter 1.

217   **a proprietary Sears credit card:** "Sears, Roebuck & Co.," *AdAge Encyclopedia,* September 15, 2003, accessed November 19, 2018, https://adage.com/article/adage-encyclopedia/sears-roebuck /98873; and Gordon L. Weil, *Sears, Roebuck, U.S.A.* (New York: Stein & Day, 1977), 146.

217   **able to afford them:** Henry Ford, *Today and Tomorrow* (London: William Heinemann 1926), 152. Hereafter cited as Ford, *Today and Tomorrow.*

217   **at the very top of the distribution:** Aguiar and Bils, "Has Consumption Inequality Mirrored Income Inequality?"

218   **revenue growth in recent years:** See Dollar General Corporation, "DG's Revenue Growth by Quarter and Year," CSIMarket .com, accessed November 19, 2018, http://csimarket.com /single_growth_rates.php?code=DG&rev, and Family Dollar Stores, Inc., "FDO's Revenue Growth by Quarter and Year," CSIMarket.com, accessed November 19, 2018, http://csimarket .com/stocks/single_growth_rates.php?code=FDO&rev.

218   **less downmarket big-box stores like Target:** These relationships are calculated using data on incomes for shoppers at Family Dollar, Dollar General, Walmart, and Target, reported in Hayley Petersen, "Meet the Average Walmart Shopper," *Business Insider,* September 18, 2004, accessed November 19, 2018, www .businessinsider.com/meet-the-average-wal-mart-shopper -2014-9.

218   **epitomizes today's unequal economy:** Ford tied his workers' wages expressly to this logic. "Wages," he observed, "is more of a question for business than it is for labor. It is more important to business than it is to labor. Low wages will break business far more quickly than it will labor." Ford, *Today and Tomorrow,* 151. A legend involving Ford's son, Henry Ford II, illustrates the same lesson with respect to automation. While showing union leader Walter Reuther around a mechanized factory in the 1960s, Ford reportedly joked, "Walter, how are you going to get those robots to pay your union dues?" Reuther reportedly answered, "Henry, how are you going to get them to buy your cars?" Rutger Bregman, "Free Money Might Be the Best Way to End Poverty," *Washington Post,* December 29, 2013, accessed November 19, 2018, www.washingtonpost.com/opinions/free-mo ney-might-be-the-best-way-to-end-poverty/2013/12/29/679c 8344-5ec8-11e3-95c2-13623eb2b0e1_story.html?utm_term =.065017746030.

218   **even week to week:** The average payday borrower's annual household income is just $30,000. This number is calculated using data compiled in Pew Charitable Trusts, *Payday Lending in America: Who Borrows, Where They Borrow, and Why* (July 2012), 35, www.pewtrusts.org/~/media/legacy/%20uploaded files/pcs_assets/2012/pewpaydaylendingreportpdf.pdf.

218   **to twenty-two thousand by 2016:** See Federal Deposit Insurance Corporation, "For Your Information: An Update on Emerging Issues in Banking, Payday Lending," January 29, 2003, www.fdic.gov/bank/analytical/fyi/2003/012903fyi .html; Stephen J. Dubner, "Are Payday Loans Really as Evil as People Say?," *Freakonomics,* April 6, 2016, accessed November 19, 2018, http://freakonomics.com/podcast/payday-loans.

218   **McDonald's and Starbucks franchises combined:** Bethany McLean, "Payday Lending: Will Anything Better Replace It?," *Atlantic,* May 2016, accessed November 19, 2018, www.theat lantic.com/magazine/archive/2016/05/payday-lending /476403. McLean attributes the claim about McDonald's and Starbucks to Dartmouth economist Jonathan Zinman.

218   **$7.4 billion on payday loans:** Pew Charitable Trusts, *Payday Lending in America: Who Borrows, Where They Borrow, and*

*Why* (July 2012), 35, www.pewtrusts.org/~/media/legacy /%20uploadedfiles/pcs_assets/2012/pewpaydaylendingreport pdf.pdf.

218   **between 5 and 10 percent:** See Saez and Zucman, "Wealth Inequality in the United States," 563.

218   **funding for rising consumption:** For a more detailed discussion, backed by data, see Chapter 8.

218   **between the 50th and 75th percentiles:** Drennan, *Income Inequality,* 41; Bricker et al., "Changes in U.S. Family Finances from 2007 to 2010: Evidence from the Survey of Consumer Finances," *Federal Reserve Bulletin* 98, no. 2 (June 2012): 55, http://federalreserve.gov/pubs/bulletin/2012/PDF/scf12.pdf. See also Robert Hockett and Daniel Dillon, "Income Inequality and Market Fragility: Some Empirics in the Political Economy of Finance" (unpublished manuscript, January 21, 2013), https://papers.ssrn.com/sol3/papers.cfm?abstract_id =2204710. Hereafter cited as Hockett and Dillon, "Income Inequality and Market Fragility."

Debt payments unsurprisingly rose alongside debt for the middle class, reaching roughly a fifth of income for the bottom 90 percent by 2010. Jank and Owens, "Inequality in the United States"; Nicolas P. Retsinas and Eric S. Belsky, eds., *Borrowing to Live: Consumer and Mortgage Credit Revisited* (Washington, DC: Brookings Institution, 2008); Hockett and Dillon, "Income Inequality and Market Fragility," Figure 11.

These trends continue. The bottom 90 percent have saved effectively not at all since the turn of the millennium, and the bottom 80 percent have had negative net savings since the mid-1980s. Saez and Zucman, "Wealth Inequality in the United States"; David Bunting, "The Saving Decline: Macro-Facts, Micro-Behavior," *Journal of Economic Behavior and Organization* 70, no. 1–2 (2009): 293; Drennan, *Income Inequality.*

218   **mid-skilled labor can command:** Elizabeth Warren and Amelia Warren Tyagi, *The Two Income Trap* (New York: Basic Books, 2003), 15–54. Hereafter cited as Warren and Warren Tyagi, *The Two-Income Trap.*

219   **medical expenses and car and house repairs:** Center for Responsible Lending, *The Plastic Safety Net: The Reality Behind Debt in America* (October 2005), 4–5, www.responsiblelend ing.org/credit-cards/research-analysis/DEMOS-101205.pdf. See also Anika Singh Lemar, *Debt Weight: The Consumer Credit Crisis in New York City and Its Impact on the Working Poor,* Urban Justice Center (2007), 3, https://papers.ssrn.com /sol3/papers.cfm?abstract_id=3160600. Hereafter cited as Lemar, *Debt Weight.* Christian E. Weller, *Pushing the Limit: Credit Card Debt Burdens American Families,* Center for American Progress (2006), https://cdn.americanprogress.org /wp-content/uploads/kf/CREDITCARDDEBTREPORT _PDF.PDF; Brian K. Bucks, Arthur B. Kennickell, and Kevin B. Moore, "Recent Changes in U.S. Family Finances: Evidence from the 2001 and 2004 Survey of Consumer Finances," *Federal Reserve Bulletin* (2006): 92.

219   **increasingly insecure earnings:** The odds that a middle-class family would suffer an income decline of $20,000 or more grew by roughly a quarter between 1990 and 2003, and the odds of suffering a 50 percent or greater income drop doubled between 1970 and 2000. Tom Hertz, *Understanding Mobility in America,* Center for American Progress (April 26, 2006), 22, www .americanprogress.org/issues/economy/news/2006/04/26 /1917/understanding-mobility-in-america; and Hacker, *The Great Risk Shift,* 31–32, Figure 1.4. More generally, between 1991 and 2009, a composite index of economic insecurity grew by two and a half times as much for the middle three income quintiles as for the top and bottom quintiles. Insecurity increased by 14 percent for the richest quintile and 12 percent for the poorest, but by an average of 30 percent across the middle three quintiles. Drennan, *Income Inequality,* 53. Drennan bases his calculations on Jacob Hacker's Economic Security Index, www.economicsecurityindex.org/?p=home.

219   **"Annual income twenty pounds":** Charles Dickens, *David Copperfield* (Oxford: Oxford University Press, 1973 [1850]), 141.

219   **Dickens's own father:** Jerry White, *Mansions of Misery: A Biography of the Marshalsea Debtors' Prison* (London: Penguin Random House, 2016), 179–219.

219   **wave of foreclosures and bankruptcies:** Warren and Warren Tyagi, *The Two-Income Trap,* 20.

219  **in all federal courts that year:** Lemar, *Debt Weight*, 3.

219  **the *precariat*:** Guy Standing, *The Precariat: The New Dangerous Class* (London: Bloomsbury, 2011).

219  **social and economic caste:** A related argument appears in Bowles and Park, "Emulation, Inequality, and Work Hours."

220  **in every major city today:** "Super luxury" cars such as the Mercedes-Benz S-Class and the BMW 7 Series can range anywhere from the low $90,000s range to $250,000. "Best Super Luxury Cars," *U.S. News & World Report*, accessed October 7, 2018, https://cars.usnews.com/cars-trucks/rankings/super-luxury-cars. Extremely high-end household appliances are common as well, such as the Wolf and Thermador dual fuel ranges; the top high-end ranges recommended by the product review website owned by the *New York Times*, which start retailing at $9,200 and $14,700 respectively. Tyler Wells Lynch, "The Best High-End Ranges," *Wirecutter*, January 24, 2017, accessed November 19, 2018, https://thewirecutter.com/reviews/best-high-end-ranges.

220  **the entire automotive industry did in 2000:** "That's Two Million Dollars, Please," *The Economist*, January 20, 2015, accessed November 19, 2018, www.economist.com/news/business-and-finance/21640081-carmakers-are-targeting-wealthier-motorists-boost-sales-and-profits-thats-two-million.

220  **the world's "most powerful" brand:** Jerry Garrett, "Echoes of the '30s, Inflation-Adjusted," *New York Times*, March 8, 2013, accessed November 19, 2018 www.nytimes.com/2013/03/10/automobiles/autoshow/echoes-of-the-30s-inflation-adjusted.html.

220  **tens of thousands of dollars:** The "quintessential banker watch" is allegedly the Rolex Daytona, which retails for approximately $12,500, although "higher level employees such as managing directors" favor more expensive models such as the Patek Philippe chronograph, which costs upward of $40,000. Leslie Albrecht, "Wear This to Feel Dominant During Business Negotiations," MarketWatch, August 31, 2017, accessed November 19, 2018, www.marketwatch.com/story/this-accessory-makes-people-feel-dominant-in-business-negotiations-2017-08-30.

220  **from its cellars:** See "About/Restaurant," The French Laundry, accessed January 27, 2019, www.thomaskeller.com/yountville-california/french-laundry/restaurant. See also "What Is the Price Range for a Meal at the French Laundry?," *Forbes Travel Guide*, May 21, 2017, accessed November 19, 2018, https://stories.forbestravelguide.com/what-is-the-price-range-for-a-meal-at-the-french-laundry. The French Laundry serves scores of bottles that cost tens of thousands of dollars, including a 2009 Domaine de la Romanée-Conti bottle that sells for $25,000. "Wine Selection," The French Laundry, accessed October 7, 2018, https://hub.binwise.com/winelists/french-laundry-wine-list.html.

220  **more than 10 percent annually since 1990:** Naomi Barr, "Treasure, What's Your Pleasure?," *Slate*, November 19, 2013, accessed November 19, 2018, www.slate.com/articles/business/billion_to_one/2013/11/the_next_fashion_billionaire_michael_kors_marc_jacobs_and_others_on_the.html. Hereafter cited as Barr, "Treasure, What's Your Pleasure?" See also Bartels, *Unequal Democracy*, 14. Bartels cites Anna Bernasek, "The Rich Spend Just Like You and Me," *New York Times*, August 6, 2006, accessed November 19, 2018, www.nytimes.com/2006/08/06/business/yourmoney/06view.html, and Yacine Ait-Sahalia, Jonathan A. Parker, and Motohiro Yogo, "Luxury Goods and the Equity Premium," *Journal of Finance* 59, no. 6 (2004).
    The economy as a whole grew at an average annual rate of just under 2.5 percent between 1990 and 2016, and average annual economic growth is forecast to be just 2 percent in the coming decade. Kevin Dubina, "Projections of the U.S. Economy, 2016–26: Slow Growth Continues," *Career Outlook*, U.S. Bureau of Labor Statistics, November 2017, www.bls.gov/career outlook/2017/data-on-display/economic-growth.htm?view_full; and "GDP Growth (Annual %): United States," World Bank Open Data, World Bank, https://data.worldbank.org/indicator/NY.GDP.MKTP.KD.ZG?locations=US.

220  **doubling in the next decade:** Dominique Muret, "Luxury Goods: Goldman Sachs Forecasts 4% Average Growth for Next 10 Years," *Fashion Network*, September 30, 2016, accessed November 19, 2018, https://us.fashionnetwork.com/news/Luxury-goods-Goldman-Sachs-forecasts-4-average-growth-for

-next-10-years,737938.html. For an even more extravagant prediction of growth, see Barr, "Treasure, What's Your Pleasure?"

220  **trade in his Chevy for a Cadillac:** Billy Joel, "Movin' Out," *The Stranger* (Columbia Records, 1977).

221  **exceeded $350:** Emma Gaedeke, "Beyonce Extends the Formation World Tour 2016; Tickets Most Expensive in Recent History," *Music Times*, February 19 2016, accessed November 19, 2018, www.musictimes.com/articles/65535/20160219/beyonce-extends-formation-world-tour-tickets-expensive-recent-history.htm.

221  **easily cost over $200:** See "Los Angeles Lakers: 2018–19 Regular Season (All Times Pacific)," NBA.com (2019), www.nba.com/lakers/tickets/individual; "Dallas Cowboys Tickets," Ticketmaster, www.ticketmaster.com/artist/805931; "New York Yankees Tickets," MLB.com (2019), https://www.mlb.com/yankees/tickets.

221  **(not even by using points from loyalty programs):** Nelson D. Schwartz, "In an Age of Privilege, Not Everyone Is in the Same Boat," *New York Times*, April 23, 2016, accessed November 19, 2018, www.nytimes.com/2016/04/24/business/economy/velvet-rope-economy.html. Hereafter cited as Schwartz, "In an Age of Privilege."

221  **an ordinary entrance ticket:** Schwartz, "In an Age of Privilege."

221  **for these travelers:** Schwartz, "In an Age of Privilege."

221  **those rich enough to pay:** Andrew Leonard, "The 1 Percent's Loathsome Libertarian Scheme," *Salon*, July 11, 2014, accessed November 19, 2018, www.salon.com/2014/07/11/the_1_per cents_loathsome_libertarian_scheme_why_we_despise_the_new_scalping_economy.

221  **the equivalent of a fifteen-hour delay:** Katherine A. DeCelles and Michael I. Norton, "Physical and Situational Inequality on Airplanes Predicts Air Rage," *Proceedings of the National Academy of Sciences* 113, no. 20 (2016): 5588–91; Deborah Netburn, "First-Class Cabin Fuels 'Air Rage' Among Passengers Flying Coach," *Los Angeles Times*, May 3, 2016, accessed November 19, 2018, www.latimes.com/science/sciencenow/la-sci-sn-air-rage-first-class-20160502-story.html.

221  **provide luxury medical care:** Julie Connelly, "Doctors Are Opting Out of Medicare," *New York Times*, April 1, 2009, accessed November 19, 2018, www.nytimes.com/2009/04/02/business/retirementspecial/02health.html.
    These unconventional luxury businesses are indeed all expanding. One recent study reported a 30 percent increase in the number of concierge doctors in a single year (a shift that deprived nearly 2.5 million insurance-dependent patients of their doctors); and another found that one in fifteen conventional doctors plans to abandon insured patients in favor of concierge care within the coming three years. A. C. Shilton, "The Doctor Won't See You Now," *Slate*, May 4, 2015, accessed November 19, 2018, www.slate.com/articles/health_and_science/medical_examiner/2015/05/concierge_medicine_only_rich_people_can_find_a_doctor_in_naples_florida.html. Hereafter cited as Shilton, "The Doctor Won't See You Now." To arrive at the 2.5 million number, take the roughly 1,015 new concierge doctors reported in the study and multiply it by the 2,303 patients that the average family practice doctor keeps on. G. Caleb Alexander, Jacob Krulander, and Matthew K. Wynia, "Physicians in Retainer ('Concierge') Practice," *Journal of General Internal Medicine* 20, no. 12 (2005): 1079–83; and The Physicians Foundation by Merritt Hawkins, *2016 Survey of America's Physicians: Practice Patterns & Perspectives* (September 2016), www.merritthawkins.com/uploadedFiles/Physicians%20Foundation%202016%20Survey%20of%20Americas%20Physicians.pdf.

221  **median patient visit length:** Ming Tai-Seale, Thomas G. McGuire, and Weimin Zhang, "Time Allocation in Primary Care Office Visits," *Health Services Research* 42, no. 5 (2007): 1871–94, www.ncbi.nlm.nih.gov/pmc/articles/PMC2254573/pdf/hesr0042-1871.pdf.

221  **including on weekends:** Robert M. Portman, "Concierge Care: Back to the Future of Medicine?," *The Health Lawyer* 15, no. 1 (2002); Shilton, "The Doctor Won't See You Now"; Pauline W. Chen, "Can Concierge Medicine for the Few Benefit the Many?," *New York Times*, August 26, 2010, accessed November 19, 2018, www.nytimes.com/2010/08/26/health/26pauline-chen.html.

221 **on top of medical bills:** Nina Bernstein, "Chefs, Butlers, Marble Baths: Hospitals Vie for the Affluent," *New York Times*, January 21, 2012, accessed November 19, 2018, www.nytimes .com/2012/01/22/nyregion/chefs-butlers-and-marble-baths -not-your-average-hospital-room.html.

222 **two dresses at her boutique instead:** Freeland, *Plutocrats*, 107; Joan Juliet Buck, "Drill Bébé Drill," *T Magazine*, August 10, 2011, accessed November 19, 2018, http://tmagazine.blogs.ny times.com/2011/08/10/drill-bebe-drill; Hilary Rose, "Meet the Super-Dentists," *Times of London Magazine*, November 26, 2011, accessed November 19, 2018, www.thetimes.co.uk/tto /magazine/article3233551.ece.

222 **on the concierge model:** Concierge billing (as opposed to public provision or private legal or financial insurance) is so dominant in these areas that the lack of mass, middle-class provision of the services goes almost unnoticed.

222 **to rich clients:** The term "income defense" comes from Winters, *Oligarchy*, 217.

222 **the gap between the middle and the bottom:** The class gap, moreover, far exceeds the racial gap; indeed, once adjustments for class are made, race appears to have virtually no independent effect. Dong D. Wang et al., "Trends in Dietary Quality Among Adults in the United States, 1999 Through 2010," *JAMA Internal Medicine* 174, no. 10 (2014): 1587–95; and Tom Philpott, "The Rich Are Eating Richer, the Poor Are Eating Poorer," *Mother Jones*, September 11, 2014, accessed November 19, 2018, www.motherjones.com/food/2014/09/food-inequality.

222 **both thrive:** Publicly held, midpriced restaurant chains, known in the industry as "casual dining" enterprises, have experienced a decline in sales despite a fairly even level of American restaurant spending overall. Elizabeth G. Dunn, "As Goes the Middle Class, So Goes TGI Fridays," *Eater*, October 3, 2017, accessed November 19, 2018, www.eater.com/2017/10/3/16395490/tgi-fridays -death-of-middle-class; James F. Peltz, "Americans Still Love Eating Out. So Why Are Restaurants Like Chili's, BJ's and Cheesecake Factory Struggling?," *Los Angeles Times*, September 18, 2017, accessed November 19, 2018, www.latimes.com/busi ness/la-fi-agenda-casual-dining-20170918-story.html; and Kate Taylor, "Applebee's, TGI Fridays, and Chili's Are Trying to Claw Their Way Out of a Restaurant Death Trap," *Business Insider*, March 7, 2017, accessed November 19, 2018, www.busines sinsider.sg/can-chains-survive-death-of-casual-dining-2017-2/.

222 **iconic Chelsea storefront:** Nelson D. Schwartz, "The Middle Class Is Steadily Eroding. Just Ask the Business World," *New York Times*, February 2, 2014, accessed November 19, 2018, www.nytimes.com/2014/02/03/business/the-middle -class-is-steadily-eroding-just-ask-the-business-world.html.

222 **a third of their incomes:** Saez and Zucman, "Wealth Inequality in the United States." The top 1 percent by income saves 20 to 25 percent of its income. Saez and Zucman, "Wealth Inequality in the United States," 563.

223 **a single common designer:** Family Dollar sells clothing made by "Pro Player" and "Modessa" only, and these are not among the designers carried by Neiman Marcus. Casey Graetz, Memo to Daniel Markovits, Word file, on file with author; "Designers by Category: Women's Clothing," Neiman Marcus, accessed October 9, 2018, www.neimanmarcus.com/Womens-Clothing/All -Designers/cat000009_cat000001_cat000000/c.cat.

223 **not even salt:** The French Laundry gets its salt exclusively from Le Sanctuaire, which was "conceived from the desire to provide only the rarest choice ingredients and tools to passionate home cooks with the most discriminating appetite for culinary excellence . . . [and] now caters to fine dining restaurants and professional chefs." See Le Sanctuaire, "About Us," accessed October 26, 2018, www.le-sanctuaire.mybigcommerce.com/about -us. Taco Bell does not.

223 **"safe and approved by the FDA":** Susanna Kim, "Taco Bell Reveals Its Mystery Beef Ingredients," ABC News, April 29, 2014, https://abcnews.go.com/Business/taco-bell-reveals-mystery -beef-ingredients/story?id=23514878; and "Ingredient Statements," Taco Bell, accessed October 9, 2018, www.tacobell.com /food/nutrition/ingredients.

223 **"To make butter":** The French Laundry, *Farmers and Foragers*. See also Tanya Gold, "A Goose in a Dress," *Harper's Magazine*, September 2015, 75, accessed November 19, 2018, https://harp ers.org/archive/2015/09/a-goose-in-a-dress/3/.

223 **class-segregated airplane cabins:** See generally Richard Sennett, *Building and Dwelling* (London: Penguin Press, 2018).

223 **In Sigmona Park:** See Mellnik and Morello, "Washington: A World Apart."

224 **over those years:** Peter Ganong and Daniel Shoag, "Why Has Regional Income Convergence in the U.S. Declined," *Journal of Urban Economics* 102 (November 2017): 79; and Phillip Longman, "Bloom and Bust: Regional Inequality Is Out of Control. Here's How to Reverse It," *Washington Monthly*, November/ December 2015, accessed November 19, 2018, http://washing tonmonthly.com/magazine/novdec-2015/bloom-and-bust. Hereafter cited as Longman, "Bloom and Bust."

224 **between 1945 and 1979:** Longman, "Bloom and Bust."

224 **the country's twenty-five richest metro areas included:** Longman, "Bloom and Bust."

224 **relatively evenly across cities:** Bishop, *The Big Sort*, 130.

224 **a "single American standard of living" emerged:** Longman, "Bloom and Bust."

224 **knowledge spillovers:** See Enrico Moretti, *The New Geography of Jobs* (New York: Houghton Mifflin Harcourt, 2012), 138– 44. Hereafter cited as Moretti, *The New Geography of Jobs*. Edward Glaeser, *The Triumph of the City: How Our Greatest Invention Makes Us Richer, Smarter, Greener, Healthier, and Happier* (New York: Penguin, 2012).

225 **resegregating by income:** See Matthew P. Drennan, Jose Lobo, and Deborah Strumsky, "Unit Root Tests of Sigma Income Convergence Across US Metropolitan Areas," *Journal of Economic Geography* 4, no. 5 (2004): 583–95.

225 **moving itself now marks eliteness:** Between 1980 and 1999, nearly half (45 percent) of all young college graduates moved between states, with the vast majority of these (80 percent in the 1990s) moving to the twenty-one cities with the highest levels of technology and patent production. By contrast, merely 19 percent of young people with only high school degrees moved between states. Bishop, *The Big Sort*, 130–33. For further discussion, see Costa and Kahn, "Power Couples," 1287–1315.

225 **living in the average city:** U.S. Agriculture Economic Research Service, *Rural Education at a Glance: 2017 Edition*, Economic Information Bulletin 171, April 2017, 2, www.ers.usda.gov /webdocs/publications/83078/eib-171.pdf?v=0.

225 **in the years since:** U.S. Agriculture Economic Research Service, *Rural Education at a Glance: 2017 Edition*, Economic Information Bulletin 171, April 2017, 2, www.ers.usda.gov /webdocs/publications/83078/eib-171.pdf?v=0.

225 **in many poor countries:** For more information on brain drain's economic effects, see Jagdish Bhagwati's work exploring brain drain in various developing countries. Jagdish Bhagwati and Carlos Rodriguez, "Welfare-Theoretical Analyses of the Brain Drain," *Journal of Development Economics* 2, no. 3 (1975): 195– 221.

225 **certain cities and not others:** Between 2000 and 2014, the share of middle-class households fell in 203 of 229 metropolitan areas considered in a recent study, even as the shares of lower- and upper-income households grew in 160 and 172 of the cities. See "America's Shrinking Middle Class: A Close Look at Changes Within Metropolitan Areas," Pew Research Center, May 11, 2016, www.pewsocialtrends.org/2016/05/11/americas -shrinking-middle-class-a-close-look-at-changes-within-metro politan-areas/.

225 **more than 34 percent were college graduates:** Bishop, *The Big Sort*, 131. For more information, see Berry and Glaeser, "The Divergence of Human Capital," 417.

225 **have college degrees:** "Educational Attainment of Population Ages 25 to 34," Kids Count Data Center, last modified October 2017, https://datacenter.kidscount.org/data/tables/6294-edu cational-attainment-of-population-ages-25-to-34#detailed/3 /10,55-56,58-61,64-77,79-84,86,88-94,96-109,9428-9429 /false/870,573,869,36,868,867,133,38,35,18/5924,1265,1309, 1304,1311/13091,13090.

225 **all average nearly 50 percent:** See Paul A. Jargowsky, "Take the Money and Run: Economic Segregation in U.S. Metropolitan Areas," *American Sociological Review* 61, no. 6 (1996): 984–98. Hereafter cited as Jargowsky, "Take the Money and Run." Bishop, *The Big Sort*, 131. Richard Florida, "More Losers Than Winners in America's New Economic Geography," CityLab, January 30, 2013, accessed November 19, 2018, http://www

.citylab.com/work/2013/01/more-losers-winners-americas
-new-economic-geography/4465/.

225 **fell by 15 percent:** See Catherine Rampell, "Who Says New
York Is Not Affordable?," *New York Times Magazine*, April 23,
2013, accessed November 19, 2018, www.nytimes.com/2013
/04/28/magazine/who-says-new-york-is-not-affordable.html.

225 **a handful of large cities:** See Bishop, *The Big Sort*, 132. See also
Costa and Kahn, "Power Couples," 1287–1315. Similar trends
arise internationally. Across the planet, roughly a quarter of all
people with a two-year college education or more live in the
world's one hundred largest cities. And the share of residents of
those cities with this much education doubles that of the population worldwide and grew by a sixth (from 18 to 21 percent) in just
the decade between 2005 and 2014. See Emily Badger, "A Quarter
of the World's Most Educated People Live in the 100 Largest Cities," *Washington Post*, July 18, 2014, accessed November 19, 2018,
www.washingtonpost.com/news/wonk/wp/2014/07/18
/a-quarter-of-the-worlds-most-educated-people-live-in-the
-100-largest-cities/?utm_term=.2e8e2e0ce30c.

225 **variation in wages across regions:** Bishop, *The Big Sort*, 134.
See also Michael Porter, "The Economic Performance of Regions," *Regional Studies* 37, no. 6 (2003): 549–78, 550, 551.

225 **nearly 30 percent for San Francisco:** See Longman, "Bloom
and Bust," Figure 2.

225 **the ten worst-educated metro areas:** Bishop, *The Big Sort*,
131–32.

225 **the least educated cities:** See Moretti, *The New Geography of
Jobs*, 107–11. See also Enrico Moretti, "America's Great Diver-
gence: The New Innovation Economy Is Making Some Cities
Richer, Many Cities Poorer—and It's Transforming Our Coun-
try," *Salon*, May 12, 2012. Hereafter cited as Moretti, "America's
Great Divergence."

225 **House prices and rents follow suit:** Indeed, the ratios between
per capita incomes in the tenth and ninetieth most expensive
housing markets, after hitting a low of 1.36, have grown steeply
since, to reach 1.61 in 2013. The relevant cities in 1976 were San
Francisco and El Paso; in 2013 they were Boston and Cincinnati.
See Anjli Raval, "Record Income Gap Fuels U.S. Housing
Weakness," *Financial Times*, August 12, 2014, accessed November 19, 2018, www.ft.com/content/1b294ed0-222b-11e4-9d4a
-00144feabdc0.

226 **as recently as 2000:** These figures combine data from two studies. See Laura Kusisto, "Renters Spent a Record-High Share of
Income on Rent This Spring," *Wall Street Journal*, August 13,
2015, accessed November 19, 2018, https://blogs.wsj.com/eco
nomics/2015/08/13/renters-spent-a-record-high-share-of
-income-on-rent-this-spring/. See also Shaila Dewan, "In Many
Cities, Rent Is Rising Out of Reach of Middle Class," *New York
Times*, April 14, 2014, accessed November 19, 2018, www.ny
times.com/2014/04/15/business/more-renters-find-30
-affordability-ratio-unattainable.html. The Dewan study finds
slightly lower income shares for contemporary rents than the
Kusisto study, presumably because it was done roughly a year
earlier.

226 **rents increase by 0.6 percent:** See Emily Badger, "A 'Nationwide Gentrification Effect' Is Segregating Us by Education,"
*Washington Post*, July 11, 2014, accessed November 19, 2018,
www.washingtonpost.com/news/wonk/wp/2014/07/11/col
lege-graduates-are-sorting-themselves-into-cities-increasingly
-out-of-reach-of-everyone-else/?utm_term=.4629fe194009.
Badger cites work by the economist Rebecca Diamond.

226 **today, only two-fifths do:** See Mellnik and Morello, "Washington: A World Apart." See also Sean Reardon and Kendra Fischoff,
"Income Segregation in the United States' Largest Metropolitan
Areas: The Disappearance of Middle Class Neighborhoods,"
Stanford Center on Poverty and Inequality, http://inequality
.stanford.edu/income-segregation-maps. Hereafter cited as Reardon and Fischoff, "Income Segregation."

226 **in rich and poor neighborhoods both doubled:** See Mellnik
and Morello, "Washington: A World Apart." See also Reardon
and Fischoff, "Income Segregation"; Richard Fry and Paul Taylor, "The Rise of Residential Segregation by Income," Pew Research Center, August 1, 2012, www.pewsocialtrends.org/20
12/08/01/the-rise-of-residential-segregation-by-income/; Carol
Morello, "Study: Rich, Poor Americans Increasingly Likely to
Live in Separate Neighborhoods," *Washington Post*, August 1,

2012, accessed November 19, 2018, www.washingtonpost.com
/local/rich-and-poor-grow-more-isolated-from-each-other-stu
dy-finds/2012/08/01/gJQABC5QPX_story.html?utm_term
=.54bf100b47a6.

226 **over the past forty years:** Between 1970 and 2000, the high
school/college dissimilarity index rose from 0.16 to 0.24 by
county and from 0.21 to 0.34 by census tract. See Douglas S.
Massey, Jonathan Rothwell, and Thurston Domina, "The
Changing Bases of Segregation in the U.S.," *Annals of the American Academy of Political and Social Science* 626, no. 1 (2009):
74–90, Figures 5 and 8. Hereafter cited as Massey, Rothwell, and
Domina, "The Changing Bases of Segregation."

226 **respectively since 1970:** The average poor family lived in census tracts that were 14 percent poor in 1970 and 28 percent poor
in 1990, and the average rich family lived in tracts that were 31
percent rich in 1970 and 36 percent rich in 1990. The neighborhood sorting index of class segregation rose roughly 25 percent
between 1970 and 1990 (from .34 to .42); the geographic isolation index for college graduates doubled between 1970 and 2000
(rising from .13 to .28 at the county level and from .19 to .36 at
the level of the census tract). See Murray, *Coming Apart*, 69. See
also Massey, Rothwell, and Domina, "The Changing Bases of
Segregation," Figures 5 and 8. Massey also reports that the high
school/college dissimilarity index rose 50 percent between 1970
and 2000 (from .16 to .24) at the county level and from .21 to .34
by census tract. Another prominent measure of neighborhood
economic segregation experienced a similar 20 percent rise over
the 1970s and 80s. For further discussion, see Jargowsky, "Take
the Money and Run."

226 **doubled and increased by one-fifth, respectively:** The average poor family lived in census tracts that were 14 percent poor
in 1970 and 28 percent poor in 1990; and the average rich family
lived in tracts that were 31 percent rich in 1970 and 36 percent
rich in 1990. See Massey, Rothwell, and Domina, "The Changing Bases of Segregation," Figures 5 and 8.

226 **reaching 74 percent:** See New York City Department of Mental Health and Hygiene, *Upper East Side Community Health
Profile 2006*, www.nyc.gov/html/doh/downloads/pdf/data
/2006chp-305.pdf.

226 **by income and education:** See Murray, *Coming Apart*, 72–73.

226 **most educated 5 percent of zip codes:** See Chapter 3.

226 **Elite professional school graduates:** See Murray, *Coming
Apart*, 78, 82, 8, 315–20. See also Charles Murray, "Charles
Murray, Author of *Coming Apart*, Examines Demographic
Shifts in This New Decade," Debate This Book, April 25, 2013,
http://debatethisbook.com/2013/04/25/charles-murray
-author-of-coming-apart-examines-demographic-shifts-in-this
-new-decade/.

227 **more political clout:** See Moretti, *The New Geography of Jobs*.
See also Moretti, "America's Great Divergence."

227 **inequality of dollar income:** See Rebecca Diamond, "The Determinants and Welfare-Implications of U.S. Workers' Divergent Location Choices by Skill: 1980–2000," *American
Economic Review* 106, no. 3 (2016): 479–524.

227 **others like themselves:** See Bishop, *The Big Sort*, 130. See also
Arlie Russel Hochschild, "I Spent 5 Years with Some of Trump's
Biggest Fans. Here's What They Won't Tell You," *Mother Jones*,
October 2016, accessed November 19, 2018, www.motherjones
.com/politics/2016/08/trump-white-blue-collar-supporters/,
adapted from Hochschild, *Strangers in Their Own Land*.

227 **are generally disappearing:** An experimental study that gave
some families a voucher to move from higher- to lower-poverty
areas found that children who moved before they turned thirteen had annual incomes in their twenties that were 31 percent
higher than the incomes of a control group. See Raj Chetty, Nathaniel Hendren, and Lawrence F. Katz, "The Effects of Exposure to Better Neighborhoods on Children: New Evidence from
the Moving to Opportunity Experiment," NBER Working Paper No. 21156 (May 2015). See also David Leonhardt, "In
Climbing the Income Ladder, Location Matters," *New York
Times*, July 22, 2013, accessed November 19, 2018, www.ny
times.com/2013/07/22/business/in-climbing-income-ladder
-location-matters.html?pagewanted=all&_r=0. See also Raj
Chetty, John Friedman, and Nathaniel Hendren, "The Equality
of Opportunity Project," accessed October 17, 2018, https:
//opportunityinsights.org/.

228 **elite government workers:** See Mellnik and Morello, "Washington: A World Apart."

228 **Stanford, Columbia, and Oxford Universities:** Alia Wong, "A Public-School Paradox," *Atlantic,* August 10, 2016, accessed November 19, 2018, www.theatlantic.com/education/archive /2016/08/a-public-school-paradox/495227/. See also Michelle Cottle, "Being Chelsea Clinton," *Atlantic,* July 2016, accessed November 19, 2018, www.theatlantic.com/magazine/archive /2016/07/being-chelsea-clinton/485627/.

228 **Avenue Capital Group:** "Avenue Capital and the Clintons: A Two-Way Street," *New York Times,* November 3, 2006, accessed November 19, 2018, https://dealbook.nytimes.com/2006/11 /03/avenue-capital-and-the-clintons-a-two-way-street/.

228 **his own hedge fund:** "Hedge Fund Rising Stars: Mark Mezvinsky," *Institutional Investor,* accessed October 28, 2018, www .institutionalinvestor.com/article/b14zb9g44397wg/hedge -fund-rising-stars-marc-mezvinsky; Matthew Goldstein and Steve Eder, "For Clintons, a Hedge Fund in the Family," *New York Times,* March 22, 2015, accessed November 19, 2018, www.nytimes.com/2015/03/23/business/dealbook/for -clintons-a-hedge-fund-in-the-family.html?_r=1; Sheryl Gay Stolberg and Nate Schweber, "State Secret: Chelsea Clinton's Wedding Plans," *New York Times,* July 16, 2010, accessed November 19, 2018, www.nytimes.com/2010/07/18/fashion /18CHELSEA.html, hereafter cited as Stolberg and Schweber, "Chelsea Clinton's Wedding."

229 **(unsurprisingly, in Manhattan):** Stolberg and Schweber, "Chelsea Clinton's Wedding"; Michael W. Savage, "Chelsea Clinton Marries Marc Mezvinsky in Rhinebeck, N.Y.," *Washington Post,* August 1, 2010, accessed November 19, 2018, www.washington post.com/wp-dyn/content/article/2010/07/31/AR 2010073103041.html; Cathy Horyn, "Chelsea Clinton's Gown Spoke Beyond the Silence," *New York Times,* August 1, 2010, accessed November 19, 2018, www.nytimes.com/2010 /08/02/fashion/02dress.html; "Chelsea Clinton Is Buying a $10.5M 4BR in NoMad," Curbed New York, accessed October 28, 2018, https://ny.curbed.com/2013/3/14/10264238/chel sea-clinton-is-buying-a-10-5m-4br-in-nomad.

229 **specially commissioned for the occasion:** "Jenna Bush Wedding Kept Low-Key," *Denver Post* via Associated Press, May 9, 2008, accessed November 19, 2018, www.denverpost.com /2008/05/09/jenna-bush-wedding-kept-low-key/.

229 **not in any way exceptional:** Even the private security that follows them as children of presidents is just an extreme case of private security—in the form of doormen, office guards, university policy systems, and gated communities—that protects the elite quite generally. The private security industry is growing at a rapid rate, with security systems integration and consulting growing the fastest. "Gains in Security Service Demand Will Be Supported by the Real and Perceived Risk of Crime and by Accelerating Economic Activity," Freedonia Group, accessed October 20, 2018, www.freedoniagroup.com/industry-study/private -security-services-3268.htm

229 **other advanced economies:** See OECD, *OECD Skills Outlook 2013,* 235, Figure 6.9; 238, Figure 6.10; 240, Figure 6.12; 241, Figure 6.13. With respect to pessimism, for example, college graduates are less than one-third as likely as nongraduates to believe that robots and computers will eliminate their jobs within the next five years. See Frank Newport, "One in Four U.S. Workers Say Technology Will Eliminate Job," Gallup, May 17, 2017, www .gallup.com/poll/210728/one-four-workers-say-technology -eliminate-job.aspx.

229 **than students from richer ones, for example:** See Kevin Carey, "The Ivy League Students Least Likely to Get Married," *New York Times,* March 29, 2018, accessed November 19, 2018, www .nytimes.com/interactive/2018/03/29/upshot/college -marriage-class-differences.html.

230 **past experience of class:** See Chapter 5.

230 **"Yale has the ability":** Jon Victor, "New Website Bolsters Financial Aid Protests," *Yale Daily News,* March 8, 2016, accessed November 19, 2018, http://yaledailynews.com/blog /2016/03/08/new-website-bolsters-financial-aid-protests/.

230 **absorb the strains of this dilemma:** A growing ecosystem of nonprofits seeks to support first-generation and low-income students through college graduation, responding not only to financial but also to cultural threats to college persistence. The Posse Foundation, for example, creates "posses," or cohorts of their peers, to offer social/emotional support to one another at elite colleges. The KIPP charter school network now also runs a KIPP Through College program, in response to finding that many of its high-achieving graduates were dropping out, partially for cultural reasons. See Posse Foundation, "About Posse," www.possefoundation.org/about-posse; "KIPP Through College," Knowledge Is Power Program, www.kipp.org/approach /kipp-through-college/.

230 **is their core mission:** Lani Guinier discusses these questions by elaborating the tensions among "sponsored mobility" (working within the meritocratic system to boost a few low-income students), "contest mobility" (typical meritocratic admissions with no boost), and "structural mobility" (disrupting the admissions system more severely in ways you might propose). See Lani Guinier, "Admissions Rituals as Political Acts: Guardians at the Gates of Our Democratic Ideals," *Harvard Law Review* 117 (2003): 113–224.

230 **"I feel like I have changed sides":** John Somes, "Working It Out," in *This Fine Place So Far from Home: Voices of Academics from the Working Class,* ed. Barney Drews and Carolyn Leste Law (Philadelphia: Temple University Press, 1995), 304.

230 **"a good general indicator of accumulated advantage":** Reeves, *Dream Hoarders,* 33.

231 **the middle-class/poor gaps:** See Lindsay Owens, "Inequality in the United States: Understanding Inequality with Data," presentation at Stanford Center on Poverty and Inequality, https://inequality.stanford.edu/sites/default/files/Inequality_Slide Deck.pdf. See also Centers for Disease Control and Prevention, *Health, United States, 2010;* Centers for Disease Control and Prevention, "Inadequate and Unhealthy Housing, 2007 and 2009," *Morbidity and Mortality Weekly Report* 60 (Suppl.) (2011): 21–27; J. S. Schiller et al., "Summary Health Statistics for U.S. Adults: National Health Interview Survey, 2010," *Vital and Health Statistics* 10, no. 252 (2012).

231 **the last two percentages are virtually identical:** Of Americans with any college education, only 14.5 percent smoke, compared to 26.1 percent of Americans with a high school degree only and 25.1 percent of high school dropouts. See J. S. Schiller et al., "Summary Health Statistics for U.S. Adults: National Health Interview Survey, 2010," *Vital and Health Statistics* 10, no. 252 (2012).

231 **also from the middle class:** See Chapter 4.

231 **"telltale, visible sign of wealth":** See Mary Jordan and Kevin Sullivan, "The Painful Truth About Teeth: You Can Work Full Time but Not Have the Money to Fix Your Teeth—Visible Reminders of the Divide Between Rich and Poor," *Washington Post,* May 13, 2017, accessed November 19, 2018, www .washingtonpost.com/sf/national/2017/05/13/the-painful -truth-about-teeth/?utm_term=.912ae5db0e89.

231 **continued to fall:** See Case and Deaton, "Rising Morbidity," 15078, 15080, Table 1.

231 **annual mortality declines:** See Case and Deaton, "Rising Morbidity," 15078, 15080, Table 1.

231 **for both men and women:** Alan Smith and Federica Cocco, "The Huge Disparities in U.S. Life Expectancy in Five Charts," *Financial Times,* January 27, 2017, accessed November 19, 2018, www.ft.com/content/80a76f38-e3be-11e6-8405 -9e5580d6e5fb. Hereafter cited as Smith and Cocco, "The Huge Disparities."

231 **(from four years to thirteen years):** Smith and Cocco, "The Huge Disparities."

232 **a high school degree only:** For men, life expectancy at twenty-five is: BA or more—54.7 years; some college but no BA—52.2 years; high school degree only—50.6 years; no high school degree—47.9 years. For women, life expectancy at twenty-five is: BA or more—58.5 years; some college but no BA—57.4 years; high school degree only—56.4 years; no high school degree—53.4 years. *More Education, Longer Life* (Princeton, NJ: Robert Wood Johnson Foundation: Commission to Build a Healthier America, 2008).

232 **among the top 10 percent:** See Saez and Zucman, "Wealth Inequality in the United States," Appendix, Figures C11, C12.

232 **between the early 1980s and the mid-2000s:** See Saez and Zucman, "Wealth Inequality in the United States," Appendix, Figures C11, C12.

232 **now nearly six years:** *The Measure of America: HD Index and Supplemental Indicators by State,* 2013–14 Dataset (Brooklyn, NY: Measure of America, 2014).

232 **between 2007 and 2011:** See Sarah Jones and J. D. Vance, "The False Prophet of Blue America," *New Republic,* November 17, 2016, accessed November 19, 2018, https://newrepublic.com /article/138717/jd-vance-false-prophet-blue-america.

232 **about four years:** Hochschild, *Strangers in Their Own Land,* 8.

232 **by only the same amount:** See Summers, "The Rich Have Advantages."

232 **the flesh surrounds us with its own decisions:** Philip Larkin, "Ignorance," in *The Whitsun Weddings* (London: Faber & Faber, 1964).

## Chapter Eight: Snowball Inequality

233 **employment and growth in a consumer economy depend:** The rich will never consume sufficiently to sustain demand, no matter how rich they are. As Keynes recognized long ago, the diminishing marginal utility of consumption entails that a person's propensity to consume her income falls as her income rises. See generally John Maynard Keynes, *The General Theory of Employment, Interest, and Money* (London: Macmillan, 1936).

234 **expanding private borrowing:** Economic modeling formalizes these intuitive connections. Models show that inequality increases the demand for credit and that loose credit can substitute for redistribution in stimulating aggregate demand and thus supporting employment and growth. See Christopher Brown, "Does Income Distribution Matter for Effective Demand? Evidence from the United States," *Review of Political Economy* 163 (2004): 291–307, https://doi.org/10.1080/095382504200022 5607.

The rising volatility of middle-class households' incomes (recall that even as median incomes stagnated, the odds that middle-class families would face significant financial reversals as much as doubled; see Chapter 5) further induced borrowing. See Tom Hertz, *Understanding Mobility in America,* Center for American Progress (April 26, 2006), 29, https://cdn.american progress.org/wpcontent/uploads/issues/2006/04/Hertz_Mobi lityAnalysis.pdf ("Income security is rising for households in the top decile. For the middle class, however, an increase in income volatility has led to an increase in the frequency of large negative income shocks.").

As the year-by-year variation of a household's income about its long-term average grows, the household will be increasingly attracted to debt. On the one hand, borrowed funds provide a rational mechanism for smoothing out the fluctuations in income and thus consumption. On the other, the financial strains associated with fluctuating incomes and financial reversals produce irrational borrowing, as any number of experimental studies associating scarcity and self-destructive borrowing reveal. See Benedict Carey, "Life in the Red," *New York Times,* January 14, 2013, accessed November 19, 2018, www.nytimes.com/2013 /01/15/science/in-debt-and-digging-deeper-to-find-relief.html; and Sendhil Mullainathan and Eldar Shafir, *Scarcity: Why Having Too Little Means So Little* (London: Allen Lane, 2013).

234 **ideologically opposed to outright redistribution:** See Rajan, *Fault Lines.* This phenomenon also had an international and macroeconomic dimension. On the global savings glut, see Martin Wolf, *The Shifts and the Shocks: What We've Learned—and Have Still to Learn—from the Financial Crisis* (London: Allen Lane, 2014).

234 **an almost actuarial logic:** These observations attribute debt and financialization to deep structural—and in this sense necessary—features of social and economic arrangements. But contingency of course also played a role. For example, it mattered to the inflation of the housing bubble that it is not practicable to make money off falling house prices by selling short individual houses. It also mattered that the credit rating agencies failed remarkably to identify and publicize mortgage default risk: whereas fewer than 1 percent of all corporate bonds are typically rated AAA, at the height of the mortgage lending and securitization boom, roughly two-thirds of asset-backed securities achieved this rating. See Rajan, *Fault Lines,* 134.

234 **alongside other causes:** Others included a change in how American companies paid for new ventures (shifting from using retained earnings to seeking outside capital) and a series of

geopolitical developments (for example, the 1973 OPEC oil embargo and its effects on inflation and interest rates).

Midcentury firms funded over 90 percent of their business investments from internal resources rather than new money raised on the capital markets. Fraser, *Every Man a Speculator,* 488. Today, by contrast, publicly traded firms retain only about 12 percent of their earnings and fund only 60 percent of their new expenditures and only 27 percent of "major" expenditures from past profits, a share that falls to just 15 percent when acquisitions are included. The retained earnings figure reflects retained earnings over net income. Data is for the S&P 500 for the period between 2005 and 2014. See Ralf Elsas, Mark J. Flannery, and Jon A. Garfinkel, "Financing Major Investments: Information About Capital Structure Decisions," *Review of Finance* 18, no. 4 (July 2014): 1341–86. Prior eras of intensive financialization produced similar patterns, so that, for example, U.S. firms reinvested only 30 percent of their profits in 1929. See Fraser, *Every Man a Speculator,* 488.

234 **debt-financed middle-class consumption:** This was the point of the famous "Greenspan put," first issued in the late 1990s in the context of the dot-com bubble and then effectively renewed with respect to the housing bubble in the early 2000s and then again by the new Federal Reserve chair Ben Bernanke in the aftermath of the Great Recession. See Rajan, *Fault Lines,* 112–15.

Even most conservative commentators object to this pattern, for example, calling it a "bailout arbitrage," which constituted "an implicit tax imposed by the predations of politically connected financial institutions." The put, incidentally, kept paying out, as sophisticated financial institutions, having bet rightly that the public would socialize the losses from the housing crash, once again reaped private gains during the nascent housing recovery. Private investors have taken substantial stakes in distressed housing—in April 2013, for example, 68 percent of sales of distressed homes involved investor buyers (the private equity firm Blackstone, for example, owns twenty-six thousand homes in nine states) and only 19 percent involved first-time buyers seeking to occupy their own homes. For conservative commentators' condemnations of the bailouts, see generally Posner and Weyl, "Against Casino Finance," 68 (bailout arbitrage), 76 (implicit tax), and John O. McGinnis, "Innovation and Inequality," *National Affairs,* no. 14 (Winter 2003): 135–48, 147 ("The too-big-to-fail regime that shields the financial sector has unfairly increased the incomes of some Americans by allowing them to ride to riches on a federal guarantee."). For investor purchases of distressed homes, see Nathaniel Popper, "Behind the Rise in House Prices, Wall Street Buyers," *New York Times,* June 3, 2013, accessed November 19, 2018, https://dealbook.ny times.com/2013/06/03/behind-the-rise-in-house-prices-wall -street-buyers/.

234 **"financing strategies fueled by":** See Rajan, *Fault Lines,* 36. The quoted text comes from U.S. Department of Housing and Urban Development, The National Homeownership Strategy: Partners in the American Dream (May 1995), www.globalur ban.org/National_Homeownership_Strategy.pdf.

234 **"address . . . financial barriers to homeownership":** See Rajan, *Fault Lines,* 36. The quoted text comes from U.S. Department of Housing and Urban Development, *The National Homeownership Strategy: Partners in the American Dream* (May 1995), www .globalurban.org/National_Homeownership_Strategy .pdf.

234 **"lack . . . cash available":** See Rajan, *Fault Lines,* 3. The quoted text comes from U.S. Department of Housing and Urban Development, *The National Homeownership Strategy: Partners in the American Dream* (May 1995), https://www.globalurban.org /National_Homeownership_Strategy.pdf.

234 **housing price appreciation:** See Atif Mian and Amir Sufi, "House Prices, Home Equity-Based Borrowing, and the United States Household Leverage Crisis," NBER Working Paper No. 15283 (August 2009), 1–2. See also Drennan, *Income Inequality,* 56.

235 **shift in wages from the middle to the top:** See Michael Kumhof and Romain Rancière, "Inequality, Leverage and Crises," IMF Working Paper no. 10/268 (2011); Robert Hockett and Daniel Dillon, "Income Inequality and Market Fragility: Some Empirics in the Political Economy of Finance," *North Carolina Banking Law Journal* 18 (2013): Anant Thaker and Elizabeth

Williamson, "Unequal and Unstable: The Relationship between Inequality and Financial Crises," New America Foundation, Next Social Contract Initiative Policy Brief, January 2012; Fadhel Kaboub, Zdravka Todorova, and Luisa Fernandez, "Inequality-Led Financial Instability," *International Journal of Political Economy* 39, no. 1 (2010): 3; Photis Lysandrou, "Global Inequality as One of the Root Causes of the Financial Crisis: A Suggested Explanation," *Economy and Society* 40, no. 3 (2011): 323–44; and James Galbraith, *Inequality and Instability: A Study of the World Economy Just Before the Great Crisis* (Oxford: Oxford University Press, 2012).

This effect is so powerful that it even operates between the several American states. A statistical analysis shows that each 1 percent fall in the share of total income captured by the bottom 80 percent of earners in a state is associated with a 0.2 percent increase in that state's per capital household debt three years later. See Drennan, *Income Inequality*, 47.

235 **"The negative impact":** See Joseph Stiglitz, *The Stiglitz Report: Reforming the International Monetary and Financial Systems in the Wake of the Global Crisis* (New York: New Press, 2010), 24.

235 **roughly doubled since 1970:** The financial sector accounted for 2.8 percent of GDP in 1950 and 8.3 percent at its peak, in 2006. See Philippon and Reshef, "Skill Biased Financial Development"; Greenwood and Sharfstein, "The Growth of Finance," 3.

235 **attributable to manufacturing:** Manufacturing now accounts for roughly 12 percent of GDP. See Yi Li Chien and Paul Morris, "Is U.S. Manufacturing Really Declining?," *On the Economy* (blog), St. Louis Fed, April 11, 2017.

235 **became relatively more important:** See *Gross Domestic Product by Industry: First Quarter 2018*, Bureau of Economic Analysis (2018), www.bea.gov/system/files/2018-07/gdpind118_3 .pdf.

235 **its financing subsidiary, GMAC:** See Steven Davidoff Solomon, "Profits in G.M.A.C. Bailout to Benefit Financiers, Not U.S.," *New York Times*, August 21, 2012, accessed November 19, 2018. https://dealbook.nytimes.com/2012/08/21/profits-in-g -m-a-c-bailout-to-benefit-financiers-not-u-s/?_r=0. In 2010, GMAC rebranded itself as Ally Financial. See Ally, "History," accessed January 27, 2019, www.ally.com/about/history/.

235 **swamped Main Street's industrial production:** Similarly, GE Capital came to control nearly three-quarters of General Electric's assets. It grew so large that it was designated a systemically important financial institution and was spun off in 2015. See Ted Mann, "How Big Is GE Capital? It Depends," *Wall Street Journal*, June 9, 2015, accessed November 19, 2018, www.wsj .com/articles/ge-uses-own-metric-to-value-its-finance-arms -assets-1433842205.

236 **contributed substantially to this facet of finance:** See Greenwood and Sharfstein, "The Growth of Finance," 17.

236 **output of the securities industry:** See Greenwood and Sharfstein, "The Growth of Finance," 7.

236 **between 2000 and 2008:** Once again, mortgage securitization was so profitable that some Wall Street banks acquired lending institutions in order to secure for themselves a steady supply of new mortgages to securitize and trade. See Michael A. Santoro and Ronald J. Strauss, *Wall Street Values: Business Ethics and the Global Financial Crisis* (Cambridge: Cambridge University Press, 2012), 109–10.

236 **rising household borrowing:** See Greenwood and Sharfstein, "The Growth of Finance," 12.

236 **over this period:** See Greenwood and Sharfstein, "The Growth of Finance," 7.

236 **"rested on the housing market":** Rajan, *Fault Lines*, 6. Rajan continues to say that "new housing construction and existing housing sales provided jobs in construction, real estate brokerage, and finance, while rising house prices provided the home equity to refinance old loans and finance new consumption."

236 **rested on economic inequality:** International comparisons reinforce this domestic story. Economies that suffer from great economic inequality also display greater financialization. See David A. Zalewski and Charles J. Whalen, "Financialization and Economic Inequality," *Journal of Economic Issues* 44, no. 3 (2010): 764–75.

236 **through the 1950s and 1960s:** See David Kaiser, *American Physics and the Cold War Bubble* (Chicago: University of Chicago Press, in preparation). See more at http://web.mit.edu /dikaiser/www/CWB.html#CWBChapters.

237 **"science in the service of war":** Emanuel Derman, *My Life as a Quant: Reflections on Physics and Finance* (Hoboken, NJ: John Wiley & Sons, 2004), 4. Hereafter cited as Derman, *My Life as a Quant*.

237 **research dried up:** Derman, *My Life as a Quant*, 4.

237 **found themselves without academic jobs:** The number of physics PhDs produced by American universities, for example, surged in the 1950s and 1960s, peaked in 1970, and then collapsed, falling by over 40 percent by the early 1980s. It would not recover its 1970 level until roughly 2010. See Patrick Mulvey and Star Nicholson, "Trends in Physics PhDs," American Institute of Physics, Focus On, February 2014, www.aip.org/sites/default/files/sta tistics/graduate/trendsphds-p-12.2.pdf. Fewer PhD students meant smaller physics departments, and this meant fewer openings for new professors.

237 **absorbed the new super-skilled workforce:** Derman, *My Life as a Quant*, 92.

237 **"that paid $150,000":** Derman, *My Life as a Quant*, 119.

237 **and then move on:** Derman, *My Life as a Quant*, 123.

237 **"skilled mathematicians, modelers":** Derman, *My Life as a Quant*, 5.

237 **by implementing them:** See William F. Sharpe, "Capital Asset Prices: A Theory of Market Equilibrium Under Conditions of Risk," *Journal of Finance* 19, no. 3 (September 1964): 425–42, and Fischer Black and Myron Scholes, "The Pricing of Options and Corporate Liabilities," *Journal of Political Economy* 81, no. 3 (1973): 637–54.

238 **measure and manipulate the odds in their wagers:** F. N. David, *Games, Gods and Gambling* (Mineola, NY: Dover, 1998).

238 **the services they made possible:** See generally Dan Awrey, "Toward a Supply-Side Theory of Financial Innovation," *Journal of Comparative Economics* 41, no. 2 (2013): 401, and Donald MacKenzie, "Is Economics Performative? Option Theory and the Construction of Derivatives Markets," paper presented in Tacoma, WA, June 25, 2005, who argues that financial models, and in particular Black-Scholes option pricing, shape financial markets.

238 **between just 1970 and 1982:** For a list, see William L. Silber, "The Process of Financial Innovation," *American Economic Review* 73, no. 2 (1983): 89 (listing thirty-eight innovative financial products developed from 1970 to 1982, ranging from "Debit Cards" and ATMs to "Interest Rate Futures").

For more on financial innovation in the period, see Merton Miller, "Financial Innovation: The Last Twenty Years and the Next," *Journal of Financial and Quantitative Analysis* 21, no. 4 (December 1986): 459 (describing the financial "revolution" of the previous twenty years as having occurred largely due to reactions to regulation and taxes), and Peter Tufano, "Financial Innovation," in *The Handbook of Economics of Finance*, ed. George Constantinides, Milton Harris, and René Stulz (Amsterdam: North Holland, 2003), 307 (exploring the history of financial innovation and the explanations given for the extensive amount of innovation seen in both the past and the present). The number of financial patents awarded annually has also increased starkly since midcentury, although changes in patent law confound efforts to read innovation directly off patent numbers. Financial patents remained relatively unused until the *State Street* decision in 1998. *State Street Bank & Trust Co. v. Signature Financial Group, Inc.*, 149 F.3d 1368 (Fed. Cir. 1998). (For instance, Bob Merton and Paul Samuelson did not patent their work on infinitely lived options in the 1960s.) After that, financial patents rose markedly until 2014, when the Supreme Court narrowed the availability of patents for such financial products in its *Alice* decision. *Alice Corp. v. CLS Bank International*, 134 S.Ct. 2347 (2014). See Adam B. Jaffe and Josh Lerner, *Innovation and Its Discontents: How Our Broken Patent System Is Endangering Innovation and Progress, and What to Do About It* (Princeton, NJ: Princeton University Press, 2011), 147.

238 **immensely profitable:** "Twilight of the Gods," *The Economist*.

238 **so profitable today:** See Michael Lewis, *Flash Boys* (New York: W. W. Norton, 2014).

238 **less valuable:** Gerald F. Davis, *Managed by the Markets: How Finance Reshaped America* (New York: Oxford University Press, 2009), 37–38, and Greta Krippner, *Capitalizing on Crisis: The*

*Political Origins of the Rise of Finance* (Cambridge, MA: Harvard University Press, 2011), who document the shift from originate and hold to originate and distribute. See also Mark S. Mizruchi, "The American Corporate Elite and the Historical Roots of the Financial Crisis of 2008," in *Markets on Trial: The Economic Sociology of the U.S. Financial Crisis: Part B*, ed. Michael Lounsbury and Paul M. Hirsch (Bingley: Emerald Group Publishing, 2010), 103–39, 122–23; and Andrew Leyshon and Nigel Thrift, "The Capitalization of Almost Everything," *Theory, Culture, and Society* 24 (2007): 100. The first to do this was Fannie Mae. Guy Stuart, *Discriminating Risk: The U.S. Mortgage Lending Industry in the Twentieth Century* (Ithaca, NY: Cornell University Press, 2003), 21–22, 68.

238 **shadow banks and other investors:** See Greenwood and Sharfstein, "The Growth of Finance," 7.

239 **many with PhDs:** The Financial Strategies Group at the Fixed Income Division of Goldman Sachs is a prime example. See Derman, *My Life as a Quant*, 123.

239 **"talent is the most precious commodity":** Duff McDonald, "Please, Sir, I Want Some More. How Goldman Sachs Is Carving Up Its $11 Billion Money Pie," *New York Magazine*, December 5, 2005.

239 **a typical Wall Street firm's net revenue:** "The standard portion of net revenue (total revenue minus interest expense) earmarked for compensation at Wall Street firms stands at a staggering 50 percent." Ho, *Liquidated*, 255 (quoting Duff McDonald, "Please, Sir, I Want Some More. How Goldman Sachs Is Carving Up Its $11 Billion Money Pie," *New York Magazine*, December 5, 2005). In 2011, 42 percent of Goldman Sachs's revenues were paid to its employees (who received, on average, $367,057); in 2010, compensation accounted for 51 percent of revenues at Morgan Stanley, 34 percent at Barclays, and 44 percent at Credit Suisse. See Freeland, *Plutocrats*, 122.

239 **for other workers:** See Philippon and Reshef, "Wages and Human Capital." In another paper, Philippon and Reshef estimate the premium at nearer 50 percent. See Philippon and Reshef, "Skill Biased Financial Development." Although college graduates in certain technical fields enjoy a wage premium similar to that received by college graduates in finance, finance workers with postgraduate degrees increasingly out-earn even postgraduates in these technical fields. See Rajan, *Fault Lines*, 142.

239 **down through the generations:** On the feedback loop between returns to elite education and educational investments by elite parents, see Frank and Cook, *The Winner-Take-All Society*, 148.

240 **"research and development sector":** See Goldin and Katz, *The Race Between Education and Technology*, 40 ("Finally, education contributes to innovation and technological advance because scientists, engineers, and other highly educated workers are instrumental to the research and development (R&D) sector as well as to the creation and application of new ideas."). The effect becomes especially large when elite education reaches a critical mass, so that innovators do not work severally or in isolation but instead come together and support one another. See Oded Galor and Omer Moav, "Ability-Biased Technological Transition, Wage Inequality, and Economic Growth," *Quarterly Journal of Economics* 115, no. 2 (May 2000): 469–97, https://doi.org/10.11 62/003355300554827.

240 **household debt and dependency:** See Safeway Stores, Incorporated, *1975 Annual Report*, 2.

240 **"In 1919 I had never seen":** See Safeway Stores, Incorporated, *1970 Annual Report*, 9.

240 **"Drive the Safeway; Buy the Safeway":** See Olive Gray, "Seelig's Chain Is Now Safeway," *Los Angeles Times*, March 15, 1925, B8 ("The adopted slogan of the old-new organization—old in fact and in tested operation but new in name—is an admonition and an invitation: 'Drive the Safeway; Buy the Safeway.'").

240 **"Safeway Offers Security":** See Susan Faludi, "The Reckoning: Safeway LBO Yields Vast Profits but Exacts a Heavy Human Toll," *Wall Street Journal*, May 16, 1990. Hereafter cited as Faludi, "The Reckoning." The firm had other mottos also. Annual reports indicate that at least from 1929 to 1932 the motto was "Distribution Without Waste." See Safeway Stores, Incorporated, *1929 Annual Report*, 1; Safeway Stores, Incorporated, *1930 Annual Report*, 1; Safeway Stores, Incorporated, *1931 Annual Report*, 1; Safeway Stores, Incorporated, *1932 Annual Report*, 1.

241 **"a simple formula for success":** "Safeway Stores, Inc.," *Fortune*, vol. 26, October 1940, 60. Hereafter cited as "Safeway Stores, Inc.," *Fortune*.

241 **to fire any of its employees:** See Safeway Stores, Incorporated, *1939 Annual Report*, "Personnel," 5; Safeway Stores, Incorporated, *1940 Annual Report*, "Personnel," 5; Safeway Stores, Incorporated, *1941 Annual Report*, "Personnel," 5. Such attitudes persisted. The *1955 Annual Report*, for example, declared that Safeway "desires to be a part of each community in which it does business. It strives to carry its share of community charity and welfare costs and to pay its fair share of local and state taxes." Safeway Stores, Incorporated, *1955 Annual Report*, 9.

241 **In 1968, Safeway worked:** See Safeway Stores, Incorporated, *1975 Annual Report*, 13, and Safeway Stores, Incorporated, *1968 Annual Report*, 16–17. Asked why a business should be interested in helping to solve the problems of society,' the *1968 Annual Report* observes, "We have answered that in our opinion it is not only good citizenship, but is necessary for a good business environment and perhaps even for the survival of private enterprise itself." Safeway Stores, Incorporated, *1968 Annual Report*, 17.

241 **"social responsiveness and accountability":** See "How Consumer Organizations Rate Corporations," *Business and Society Review*, no. 3 (September 1972): 94.

241 **underprivileged minority workers:** Safeway Stores, Incorporated, *1975 Annual Report*, 13.

241 **working his way up to lead the firm:** See Safeway Stores, Incorporated, *1965 Annual Report*, 8.

241 **"We live and preach people development":** See Safeway Stores, Incorporated, *1972 Annual Report*, "Young Managers Move Up," 4.

241 **as a bakery helper:** See "Safeway Stores, Inc.," *Fortune*, 128.

241 **half the pay of the CEO:** See "Safeway Stores, Inc.," *Fortune*, 128.

241 **roughly $1.2 million in 2018 dollars:** See Safeway Stores, Incorporated, 1965 Proxy Statement (Form DEF 14A), 9.

241 **"Safeway has rationalized":** See "Safeway Stores, Inc.," *Fortune*, 134.

242 **performing basic management tasks:** See Goldin and Katz, *The Race Between Education and Technology*, 19–22.

242 **returning them to shareholders or creditors:** Roughly 70 percent. See Fraser, *Every Man a Speculator*, 488.

242 **raised on the capital markets:** Over 90 percent. See Fraser, *Every Man a Speculator*, 488.

242 **raise operating capital by borrowing:** Indeed, U.S. nonfinancial corporations have, in aggregate, issued negative net equity since 1980, devoting some of the funds raised by issuing new debt to buying back old equity. Net equity was negative not just over the longer period but also in almost every individual year, with only a few exceptions in the early 1990s. See Board of Governors of the Federal Reserve System, "Flow of Funds Accounts of the United States, Annual Flows and Outstanding," Tables F2 and F4, 1985–1994, 1995–2004, 2005–2010. See also Thomas I. Palley, "Financialization: What It Is and Why It Matters," Levy Economics Institute Working Paper no. 525, December 2007, 19–20, Figure 4, "Nonfinancial corporation net equity issuance and new borrowing, 1959–2006."

Corporate filings made in relation to share buybacks display the connection between repurchasing and new borrowing. For a sample of filings from 1994 to 2012, for example, in close to 40 percent of the cases in which the source of financing was disclosed, the firm said it expected to use some form of debt to fund the share repurchases. See Zicheng Lei and Chendi Zhang, "Leveraged Buybacks," *Journal of Corporate Finance* 39 (2016): 244.

242 **from past profits:** They retain just about 12 percent of earnings and fund only 60 percent of their new expenditures and only 27 percent of "major" expenditures from past profits, a share that falls to just 15 percent when acquisitions are included.

The retained earnings figure reflects retained earnings over net income. Data are for the S&P 500 for the period between 2005 and 2014: William Lazonick, "How Stock Buybacks Make Americans Vulnerable to Globalization," Institute for New Economic Thinking, Working Paper 8 (March 1, 2016). Prior eras of intensive financialization produced similar patterns, so that, for example, U.S. firms reinvested only 30 percent of their profits in 1929. See Fraser, *Every Man a Speculator*, 488.

The data on financing new investments come from Ralf Elsas, Mark J. Flannery, and Jon A. Garfinkel, "Financing Major Investments: Information About Capital Structure Decisions," *Review of Finance* 18, no. 4 (2014).

242 **prefer owners over other stakeholders:** See Michael C. Jensen, "Agency Cost of Free Cash Flow, Corporate Finance and Take-overs," *American Economic Review* 76, no. 2 (May 1986): 323–29. A review of the many complementary factors that favor debt-financed buybacks (including the connections to share-holder activism on managerial inclinations to serve other stakeholders) appears in Joan Farre-Mensa, Roni Michaely, and Martin C. Schmalz, "Financing Payouts," Ross School of Business Paper No. 1263 (December 2016), 31–37.

243 **"separation of ownership and control":** See Adolph Berle and Gardiner Means, *The Modern Corporation and Private Property* (New York: Macmillan, 1932).

243 **maximize shareholder value:** The term "shareholder value" was introduced by the lawyer-economist Henry Manne in his classic article "Mergers and the Market for Corporate Control." See Henry Manne, "Mergers and the Market for Corporate Control," *Journal of Political Economy* 73, no. 2 (April 1965): 110. Note that the date of publication comes at the twilight of the Great Compression.

243 **incumbent managers:** As with the purely financial innovations discussed earlier, the leveraged buyout was conceived in the 1950s but did not become practically consequential until the 1980s, when a sufficient supply of super-skilled labor capable of deploying the innovation at scale first became available. The first leveraged buyout may have been the purchase of Waterman Steamship Corporation in 1955 by McLean Industries, Inc. McLean issued $7 million in preferred stock and took out $42 million in bank loans to purchase Waterman. Marc Levinson, *The Box: How the Shipping Container Made the World Smaller and the World Economy Bigger* (Princeton, NJ: Princeton University Press, 2016), 49.

243 **activist investing on a massive scale:** See Robert Teitelman, *Bloodsport: When Ruthless Dealmakers, Shrewd Ideologues, and Brawling Lawyers Toppled the Corporate Establishment* (New York: Perseus, 2016), 66–72; Moira Johnston, *Takeover: The New Wall Street Warriors; The Men, the Money, the Impact* (New York: Arbor House, 1986), 34. Hereafter cited as Johnston, *Takeover*; and Bruce Wasserstein, *Big Deal: Mergers and Acquisitions in the Digital Age* (New York: Warner Business Books, 2001), 548. Hereafter cited as Wasserstein, *Big Deal*. Wachtell is also famous for helping firms resist takeovers, including on account of having invented the poison-pill defense. See Johnston, *Takeover*, 36; Wasserstein, *Big Deal*, 552.

243 **(similar years in the business cycle):** See IDD Enterprises, *M&A Almanac* (May–June 1992); Houlihan Lokey Howard & Zukin, *Mergerstat Review* (Los Angeles: Mergerstat, 1988), 1.

243 **between 1988 and 1999:** See W. T. Grimm & Co., *Mergerstat Review* (Schaumburg, IL: Merrill Lynch Business Brokerage and Valuation, 1988), 3; Houlihan Lokey Howard & Zukin, *Mergerstat Review* (Los Angeles: Mergerstat, 1999), 1.

243 **implement anti-takeover defenses:** See Ho, *Liquidated*, 133; Marina Whitman, *New World, New Rules: The Changing Role of the American Corporation* (Boston: Harvard Business School Press, 1999), 9; and Michael Useem, *Investor Capitalism: How Money Managers Are Changing the Face of Corporate America* (New York: Basic Books, 1996), 2.

Private equity firms, for their part, today hold over $2.4 trillion in capital at the ready to target firms that they regard as badly run and to replace inefficient managers, a threat that disciplines management even where no takeover materializes. See Preqin, *2016 Preqin Global Private Equity & Venture Capital Report*, www.preqin.com/docs/samples/2016-Preqin-Global-Private-Equity-and-Venture-Capital-Report-Sample_Pages.pdf.

243 **change in the corporate workplace:** The new ideology also produced changes adjacent to the corporation. Managers at mid-century served many stakeholders—including the local communities in which a firm did business, the firm's customers, and (especially importantly) its employees. Moreover, midcentury managers often literally lived with a corporation's workforce, and this gave them an incentive to support local employment and civic life and to pay their neighbors good wages.

243 **rather than being managers themselves:** Top managers might monitor lower-level workers, but the distance between the tasks that these workers perform and the firm's share price makes it difficult to incentivize them directly to promote shareholder value.

244 **(stock- and option-based pay packages):** Rising CEO compensation has been accompanied by a shift away from fixed pay to compensation packages that tie pay to stock performance. Indeed, between 1990 and 2015, the non-equity component of income among CEOs of the S&P 1500 barely increased (from roughly $1.2 million to roughly $1.5 million, on average), even as the equity component more than tripled (from $800,000 to over $2.5 million, on average). See Cremers, Masconale, and Sepe, "CEO Pay Redux," 240. The authors exclude from their data set on CEO pay managers of firms that have dual-class stock and firms in regulated industries. These comprise a little less than 10 percent of all firms in the S&P 1500.

244 **(the threat of being ousted):** By the turn of the twenty-first century, a downgrade in stock analysts' investment recommendations—from "buy" to "hold" or from "hold" to "sell"—increased by half the chance that the downgraded firm's CEO would be fired within six months. Indeed, performance-related firings of the CEOs of the world's twenty-five hundred largest firms quadrupled between just 1995 and 2005. See Reich, *Supercapitalism*, 76, citing Chuck Lucier, Paul Kocourek, and Rolf Habbel, *The Crest of the Wave* (New York: Booz Allen Hamilton, 2006).

244 **if properly incentivized, as a benefit:** See Charles J. Whalen, "Money-Manager Capitalism and the End of Shared Prosperity," *Journal of Economic Issues* 31, no. 2 (June 1997): 522; and David A. Zalewski and Charles J. Whalen, "Financialization and Income Inequality," *Journal of Economic Issues* 44, no. 3 (2010): 762. Employers, moreover, increasingly oppose unionization and prosecute their opposition increasingly aggressively: the share of union elections to receive employer consent fell by four-fifths between 1962 and 1977, and according to the National Labor Relations Board, the rate at which employers used illegal firings to try to deter unionization increased fivefold between the early 1950s and 1990. Reich, *Supercapitalism*, 80–81.

244 **in favor of meritocratic hierarchy:** They also—because managers are socially isolated not just from communities and employees but also from shareholders—empowered managers to bargain hard to capture from shareholders whatever incomes their skills can sustain.

244 **management has itself become financialized:** See David Carey and John E. Morris, *King of Capital: The Remarkable Rise, Fall, and Rise Again of Steve Schwarzman and Blackstone* (New York: Random House, 2012), 100. See also Gerald Davis, *Managed by the Markets: How Finance Reshaped America* (Oxford: Oxford University Press, 2009).

244 **incumbent firms then still deployed:** The connections between meritocracy and mergers-and-acquisitions practice run very deep: the overwhelmingly Protestant white-shoe firms that dominated midcentury legal practice shunned litigation, bankruptcy, and takeover law, on the grounds that these were unseemly practice areas and became necessary only where a lawyer had failed in his primary role. Wachtell and Skadden were both open to Jews who had been excluded from Protestant firms—indeed, Wachtell's founders were all Jewish—and made their businesses in areas that white-shoe firms avoided. Wachtell's success, and older firms' imitative aspirations, testify to meritocracy's rising dominance in elite legal practice. See Eli Wald, "The Rise and Fall of the WASP and Jewish Law Firms," *Stanford Law Review* 60 (April 2008): 1803–66.

245 **very top graduates from the very best schools:** The cutoffs are chosen because these are the numbers of schools that, with ties, regularly appear in the *U.S. News & World Report* rankings of top-ten and top-five schools.

245 **the same legal talent:** In 2016, the top tier of M&A firms (besides Wachtell and Skadden) were Cravath Swaine & Moore; Kirkland & Ellis; Paul, Weiss, Latham & Watkins; Simpson Thacher & Bartlett; Sullivan & Cromwell; and Weil, Gotshal. Each hires not just principally but overwhelmingly from the very most elite law schools. See "The Legal 500 Rankings of M&A Litigation," The Legal 500, www.legal500.com/c/united-states/dispute-resolution/manda-litigation-defense.

245　inside their firms: See Dirk Zorn, "Here a Chief, There a Chief: The Rise of the CFO in the American Firm," *American Sociological Review* 69 (June 2004): 345–64.

245　"fledgling at best": Matthias Kipping and Lars Engwall, *Management Consulting: Emergence and Dynamics of a Knowledge Industry* (New York: Oxford University Press, 2002), 71.

245　the leisured norms of the aristocratic elite: The industry, moreover, devoted itself less to management and more to technical problems in production processes—to increasing the efficiency of "line workers at the bottom of the organizational chart." The first "management consultant" was, after all, Frederick Taylor. See Duff McDonald, *The Firm: The Story of McKinsey and Its Secret Influence on American Business* (New York: Simon & Schuster, 2013), 26–28. Hereafter cited as McDonald, *The Firm.* See generally Walter Kiechel, *The Lords of Strategy: The Secret Intellectual History of the New Corporate World* (Cambridge, MA: Harvard Business Press, 2010). Hereafter cited as Kiechel, *The Lords of Strategy.* See also Terrence Deal and Allan A. Kennedy, *The New Corporate Cultures: Revitalizing the Workplace After Downsizing, Mergers, and Reengineering* (Reading, MA: Perseus, 1999), 64.

245　until President Kennedy stopped: See David Burkus, *Under New Management: How Leading Organizations Are Upending Business as Usual* (New York: Houghton Mifflin Harcourt, 2016), 194.

245　applicants who might be turned down: McDonald, *The Firm,* 94.

245　to its own business: McDonald, *The Firm,* 113.

246　(the top 5 percent of the class): Kiechel, *The Lords of Strategy,* 9.

246　join elite consulting firms: See, e.g., Harvard Business School, "Recruiting: Data & Statistics," www.hbs.edu/recruiting/data/Pages/detailed-charts.aspx.

246　"Investment Banking vs. Consulting": See Ho, *Liquidated,* 332–33.

246　"foment a stratification within companies and society": Kiechel, *The Lords of Strategy,* 9.

246　"silver-haired industry experience": Kiechel, *The Lords of Strategy,* 9.

246　"break an organization down": John Micklethwait and Adrian Wooldridge, *The Witch Doctors: Making Sense of the Management Gurus* (New York: Random House, 1996), 26. Hereafter cited as Micklethwait and Wooldridge, *The Witch Doctors.*

246　responsible for their downsizings: See Micklethwait and Wooldridge, *The Witch Doctors,* 29–31; Thomas Davenport, "The Fad That Forgot People," *Fast Company,* October 31, 1995, accessed November 19, 2018, www.fastcompany.com/26310/fad-forgot-people.

246　"Overhead Value Analysis": Terrence Deal and Allan A. Kennedy, *The New Corporate Cultures* (New York: Perseus, 1999), 64.

246　excessive embrace of middle management: McKinsey argued that the midcentury approach had allowed "the number of nonproduction employees in manufacturing industry, for example, [to] increase six times as fast as that of production workers [between 1950 and 1970]." See John L. Neuman, "Make Overhead Cuts That Last," *Harvard Business Review,* May 1975, https://hbr.org/1975/05/make-overhead-cuts-that-last. Hereafter cited as Neuman, "Make Overhead Cuts That Last."

246　"process, though swift": The firm insisted, however, that its approach could cut overhead costs by 15 to 30 percent swiftly (within four months). See Neuman, "Make Overhead Cuts That Last."

　　　Often, the consultants shifted these "wrenching" decisions to the managers themselves, who were "expected . . . to identify ways in which they and lower-level managers [could] be eliminated in order to purge the corporation of 'managerial bloat.'" Randy Hodson, "3 Reviews: The Many Faces of Organizational Control," *Administrative Science Quarterly* 36, no. 3 (1991): 490, reviewing Vicki Smith, *Managing in the Corporate Interest: Control and Resistance in an American Bank* (Berkeley: University of California Press, 1990), http://ark.cdlib.org/ark:/13030/ft267nb1gt/.

246　"we are all in this together": Kiechel, *The Lords of Strategy,* 9.

246　"contributed to the fiercer feel": Kiechel, *The Lords of Strategy,* 9.

246　the skill profile of American executives: It does not help, as commentators sometimes try to do, to derive changes to managerial styles directly from the complexity of production. It is true that twentieth-century firms—recall the story of the Singer sewing machine company—brought production inside the firm in order to secure uniformity and compatibility among increasingly complex machine parts. But explaining why management rather than contract better secures these ends requires a further argument, and that argument must sound in the relative cost and effectiveness of the technologies that each approach to coordination deploys.

　　　The transformation from twentieth- to twenty-first-century management styles drives this point home. Production today is surely still more complicated than it was at the middle of the last century, and yet managerial hierarchies have become not more layered but flatter. Increasing production complexity thus favored more elaborate management at midcentury and favors less elaborate management today. The difference comes down to changing managerial technologies and, ultimately, to the changing work ethic and skill of the managerial class.

247　concentrate them in top executives: CEOs now make roughly three hundred times the median income. See Lawrence Mishel and Alyssa Davis, "Top CEOs Make 300 Times More Than Typical Workers," Economic Policy Institute, June 2015, www.epi.org/publication/top-ceos-make-300-times-more-than-workers-pay-growth-surpasses-market-gains-and-the-rest-of-the-0-1-percent/. In 2010, the top 1 percent by income captured roughly 20 percent of all income but owned approximately 35 percent of all publicly traded shares owned by U.S. households. The bottom 90 percent owned only 19.2 percent. Edward N. Wolff, "The Asset Price Meltdown and the Wealth of the Middle Class," NBER Working Paper No. 18559 (November 2012), www.nber.org/papers/w18559.

247　succumbed to a leveraged buyout: See Faludi, "The Reckoning."

247　"Targeted Returns on Current Investment": See Faludi, "The Reckoning" ("Not long after [Mr. Magowan began firing Safeway employees following the LBO], Safeway replaced its longtime motto, 'Safeway Offers Security.' The new corporate statement, displayed on a plaque in the lobby at the corporate headquarters, reads in part: 'Targeted Returns on Current Investment.'").

247　costing jobs: See Faludi, "The Reckoning." See also Mord Bogie, *Churchill's Horses and the Myths of American Corporations* (London: Quorum Books, 1998), 168–69.

247　were fired: See Faludi, "The Reckoning," 2, col. 4.

247　wrongful termination suits: See Faludi, "The Reckoning," 2, col. 4.

247　acquired Safeway through a merger: See Christine Wilcox, "Bob Miller Assumes Role of Chairman & CEO of Albertsons, NAI & Safeway." *Market Mixx* (blog), *Albertsons,* www.albertsons.com/bob-miller-assumes-role-of-chairman-ceo-of-albertsons-nai-safeway/, and "Executive Profile of Robert G. Miller," Bloomberg, accessed October 9, 2018, www.bloomberg.com/research/stocks/private/person.asp?personId=23462422&privcapId=25591240.

247　transportation and energy industries: See "Steven A. Burd, 1949–," Reference for Business, www.referenceforbusiness.com/biography/A-E/Burd-Steven-A-1949.html.

247　from 40 to 110 percent of base pay: See Faludi, "The Reckoning." Faludi reports the potential bonus set by the CEO's compensation plan and observes that he earned the highest possible bonus in each of the initial years following the buyout. These increases came atop a salary that had already grown by the 1980s. In 1986, just before the buyout, CEO Peter Magowan (Robert Magowan's son) earned $925,000 (roughly $2 million in 2015 dollars). See Jonathan Greenberg, "Sold Short," *Mother Jones,* May 1988, 39.

247　only increased over time: See, e.g., Safeway, Inc. U.S. SEC Filings, Form DEF 14A, March 25, 1994, 8; Safeway, Inc., U.S. SEC Filings, Form DEF 14A, March 22, 1996, 11.

247　his predecessor in the 1960s was paid: Safeway, Inc., U.S. SEC Filings, Form 10-K, January 3, 2015, 117.

248　riots against the machine looms: See J. F. C. Harrison, *Society and Politics in England, 1780–1960* (London: Harper & Row, 1965), 70–72. See also Paul Halsall, "Leeds Woollen Workers

Petition, 1786," Fordham University, Modern History Sourcebook, August 1997, https://sourcebooks.fordham.edu/mod/1786machines.asp.

248 **"many of the major technological advances":** See Goldin and Katz, *The Race Between Education and Technology*, 122.

Conclusive evidence that the Industrial Revolution biased the labor market systematically against skill remains elusive. And industrial innovations did not bias the labor market against *all* skills, to be sure. Demand increased for engineers, for example, and eventually also for managers. See Goldin and Katz, *The Race Between Education and Technology*, 265. But evidence to generalize the example in the main text does exist. John James and Jonathan Skinner use the 1850 census of manufacturers to show that capital replaced skilled workers more rapidly than unskilled workers at the height of industrialization and that the replaced workers had previously enjoyed substantial (more than 60 percent) wage premiums over unskilled laborers. John A. James and Jonathan S. Skinner, "The Resolution of the Labor-Scarcity Paradox," *Journal of Economic History* 45, no. 3 (September 1985): 513–40.

248 **mass production using prefabricated parts:** See Goldin and Katz, *The Race Between Education and Technology*, 122.

248 **"The butcher, baker, glassblower":** See Goldin and Katz, *The Race Between Education and Technology*, 122.

248 **had previously dominated production:** In 1910, two-thirds of Ford's workers were skilled mechanics. By 1914, over half were unskilled recent immigrants without any mechanical experience. See Cappelli, *The New Deal at Work*, 58; Stephen Meyer, *The Five Dollar Day: Labor Management and Social Control in the Ford Motor Company* (Albany: State University of New York Press, 1981). See also Goldin and Katz, *The Race Between Education and Technology*, 123; Harry Braverman, *Labor and Monopoly Capital: The Degradation of Work in the Twentieth Century* (New York: Monthly Review Press, 1974), 146; and David Hounshell, *From the American System to Mass Production* (Baltimore: Johns Hopkins University Press, 1984).

Note the contrast to technology's effect on carmaking later in the twentieth century, when robotic assembly displaced less skilled line workers with more skilled machinists. See Goldin and Katz, *The Race Between Education and Technology*, 123. Goldin and Katz summarize the contrasting eras: "The movement from artisanal production to factories in the nineteenth century involved the substitution of capital and unskilled labor for skilled (artisanal) labor, while the adoption of continuous-process and unit drive methods in the twentieth century involved the substitution of capital and skilled (educated) labor for unskilled labor." Goldin and Katz, *The Race Between Education and Technology*, 125.

248 **"a decrease in the fraction":** See Joseph J. Spengler, "Changes in Income Distribution and Social Stratification: A Note," *American Journal of Sociology* 59, no. 3 (November 1953): 247. Simon Kuznets famously held a similar view. Simon Kuznets, "Economic Growth and Income Inequality," *American Economic Review* 45, no. 1 (March 1955): 1. See also Jeffrey Winters and Benjamin Page, "Oligarchy in the United States?," *Perspectives on Politics* 7, no. 4 (December 2009): 731.

248 **now opposes economic equality:** A common view treats technology's forward march as a brute fact to which social and economic life must adjust, but that society cannot aspire to control, and for which society cannot be held to account. The dominant metaphor for innovation's interactions with the labor market and its impact on economic inequality imagines, in the words of the title to a prominent book, a "race between education and technology," in which growing inequality arises because the social institutions that produce and distribute education cannot keep up with technology's growing demands for skill. See Goldin and Katz, *The Race Between Education and Technology*. Other expressions of the dominant view include Alan B. Krueger, "How Computers Have Changed the Wage Structure," *Quarterly Journal of Economics* 108, no. 1 (February 1993): 33; Eli Berman, John Bound, and Zvi Griliches, "Changes in Demand for Skilled Labor Within U.S. Manufacturing," *Quarterly Journal of Economics* 109, no. 2 (May 1994): 367; David H. Autor, Lawrence F. Katz, and Alan B. Krueger, "Computing Inequality: Have Computers Changed the Labor Market?," *Quarterly Journal of Economics* 113, no. 3 (November 1998):

1169. The metaphor treats innovation's skill bias as inevitable, and certainly as independent of the institutions and practices that dispense education: for a race to make sense, the competitors must each run under separate power. The assumption behind this metaphor—that innovation necessarily favors skill—is so powerful and so pervasive that it resembles the air that we breathe, being almost entirely unnoticed even as everything else depends on it. Even when they describe technological innovation's skill bias and its consequences for rising economic inequality in elaborate detail, conventional views never even ask *why* technology works in just *this* way, just *now*.

249 **to develop and implement:** See, e.g., Herbert Marcuse, *One Dimensional Man* (Boston: Beacon, 1964), 154 (describing how "'man-made creations' issue from and re-enter a societal ensemble"); Frederick Ferré, *Philosophy of Technology* (Athens: University of Georgia Press, 1995), 38–42 (differentiating between theoretical and practical intelligence while connecting both back to the society in which they are formed).

Economists sometimes distinguish between an economy's meta-production function, which consists of all technologies that are theoretically discoverable (or the "envelope of all known and potentially discoverable activities"), and its actual production function, which involves only the technologies that innovators, given the social and economic forces that they face, have actually discovered. See Yujiro Hayami and V. W. Ruttan, "Agricultural Productivity Differences Among Countries," *American Economic Review* 60 no. 5 (December 1970): 898. Hereafter cited as Hayami and Ruttan, "Agricultural Productivity."

249 **opportunities for profit:** Here see Acemoglu, "Technical Change," 37, and Daron Acemoglu, "Why Do New Technologies Complement Skills? Directed Technical Change and Wage Inequality," *Quarterly Journal of Economics* 113, no. 4 (November 1998): 1055. Hereafter cited as Acemoglu, "Why Do New Technologies Complement Skills?"

249 **in productive engines:** See, e.g., Aldo Schiavone, *The End of the Past* (Cambridge, MA: Harvard University Press, 2002), 136, hereafter cited as Schiavone, *The End of the Past*; James E. McClellan III and Harold Dorn, *Science and Technology in World History* (Baltimore: Johns Hopkins University Press, 2006), 103–4. Aristotle observed—and Cicero repeated the observation—that "only in a fantastic world where shuttles were capable of weaving by themselves could the institution of slavery be dispensed with." See Schiavone, *The End of the Past*, 135. The availability of slave labor (with slaves themselves being expressly conceived of as what Aristotle called "animate instruments" or human production machines) rendered industrial machines economically unnecessary. See Schiavone, *The End of the Past*, 132, 136.

Social norms that elevated theoretical (and especially philosophical) learning and belittled applied and practical sciences present another much-cited reason why ancient Greece and Rome (and also ancient China) never industrialized. See Schiavone, *The End of the Past*, 136–53; Justin Yifu Lin, *Demystifying the Chinese Economy* (Cambridge: Cambridge University Press, 2012), 48–51.

249 **(such as Japan):** See Hayami and Ruttan, "Agricultural Productivity," 898.

Even among otherwise similarly situated societies, such as the European colonies in the New World, the choice of crops, size of farms, nature of labor (whether indigenous or immigrant, free or slave), and other technologies of production all varied depending on soil and climate. See, e.g., Stanley L. Engerman and Kenneth L. Sokoloff, "History Lessons: Institutions, Factor Endowments, and the Path of Development in the New World," *Journal of Economic Perspectives* 14, no. 3 (Summer 2000): 217.

Similar effects, moreover, govern the more recent history of technological innovation, including through the present. The rapid growth and contours of industrial production in the nineteenth and twentieth centuries were fundamentally shaped by the availability of ready and abundant sources of fossil fuels and also of ready and capacious sinks for the by-products of burning them. And twenty-first-century industrial technologies, it is already clear, will be powerfully influenced by the draining of the sources and especially the overflow of the sinks. These influences penetrate the details of the technologies developed in each era, contributing, for example, to the dominance of the internal combustion engine over electric alternatives in the twentieth century and the comeback of electric engines in the twenty-first. See Rebecca Matulka, "The History of the Electric Car," Department of Energy, September 2014, www.energy.gov/articles /history-electric-car.

249 **dominated by industrial machines:** For an effort to identify the sources of wealth in several countries over the past three centuries, see Thomas Piketty and Gabriel Zucman, "Wealth-Income Ratios in Rich Countries 1700–2010," 6, Figures 9–12, Figure 15, www.parisschoolofeconomics.com/zucman-gabriel /capitalisback/PikettyZucman2013WP.pdf. Piketty and Zucman count slaves as capital—in effect as complements to land—but expressly decline to include the human capital of free workers in their calculations. Their data, however, support the view that the share of total wealth attributable to this human capital has grown in the past two centuries: human capital is in effect the present discounted value of future labor income, and Piketty and Zucman report that between 1820 and 2010, both UK and French national incomes slowly and occasionally unsteadily, but nevertheless distinctly, shifted away from capital and toward labor.

250 **Between 1811 and 1911:** This work is based on data provided through www.VisionofBritain.org.uk and uses statistical material which is copyright of the Great Britain Historical GIS Project, Humphrey Southall, and the University of Portsmouth.

The London figures report the numbers for the London Government Office Region, Current Total Population. The Manchester figures report the numbers for Greater Manchester, Total Population, Now. The Birmingham figures report the numbers for the West Midlands, Total Population, Now. And the Liverpool figures report the numbers for Merseyside, Total Population, Now. The data are available at www.visionofbrit ain.org.uk.

250 **who once deployed them:** See Acemoglu, "Technical Change," 37, 39.

250 **tasks of unprecedented complexity:** Some of these newly minted super-skilled workers took jobs in the public rather than the private sector, as regulators in the increasingly intricate administrative regime that the state adopted in the years following World War II. The rising complexity of government regulation exerted an additional force in favor of super-skilled private-sector labor, by increasing the analytic and managerial skills private firms needed to deploy in order to navigate regulations and comply with the law. More recently, the rise of a global administrative order—associated, for example, with the World Trade Organization or the European Union—added a further layer of complexity to commercial affairs, and this imposes a further increase on the skills that private enterprise must deploy in order to achieve commercial success within the law.

250 **with intense industry:** Law embraced and even mandated the new norms' inversion of the old order: even as low- and mid-skilled workers became subject to labor law regimes that limited weekly hours, elite workers—managers and professionals—insistently exempted themselves from labor regulation, including on dignitary grounds that presaged the Stakhanovite norms that now govern the superordinate working class. See, e.g., Fair Labor Standards Act of 1938, 29 U.S.C. §§ 206, 207 & 213 (1938) (putting in place a minimum hourly wage, limiting the maximum hours in a workweek without overtime pay, and exempting from these requirements those employees "employed in a bona fide executive, administrative, or professional capacity"); National Labor Relations Act, 29 U.S.C. § 152(3) (1935) (defining employees covered by the act broadly, but explicitly excluding "any individual employed as a supervisor").

250 **to build on one another:** Inventions interact to make the product of skill-biased innovation, taken all together, exceed the sum of its several parts. Abraham Wickelgren emphasized the importance of this point.

251 **had previously relied:** Acemoglu, "Technical Change," 37. See also Anthony B. Atkinson and Joseph E. Stiglitz, "A New View of Technological Change," *Economic Journal* 79, no. 315 (September 1969): 573–78.

251 **funded the innovations:** It is hard to miss the irony that this process follows Marx's logic of proletarian exploitation almost perfectly, now applied to the elite. Even rising elite labor incomes and rising elite training investments are connected by a

Marxist logic, namely the thought that the present wage includes the cost of reproducing the next generation of workers. An exchange with David Grewal contributed substantially to my thinking on this point.

251 **"highly skilled men":** See David Montgomery, *Workers' Control in America: Studies in the History of Work, Technology, and Labor Struggles* (Cambridge: Cambridge University Press, 1979), 188, quoting S. H. Bunnell, "Jigs and Fixtures as Substitutes for Skill," *Iron Age* (March 1914): 610–11.

251 **invent jigs that make other workers cheap:** A theoretical account of the mechanism appears in Acemoglu, "Technical Change," 7. The theory stresses that induced-innovation-driven demand for super-skills can (at least in the short to medium term) even outstrip the supply of super-skilled workers, causing elite wages to rise still further. See Acemoglu, "Technical Change," 7, 37–38 ("The endogenous response of firms to the increase in supply will raise the demand for skills. In fact, supply may not simply create its own demand, but the response of firms could be so pronounced that demand could *overshoot* the supply. In this theory, therefore, the increased supply may be the cause of the increase in the skill premium [see Acemoglu 1998, and also Michael Kiley 1999].")

251 **unprecedentedly large cohort of college graduates:** The data behind these claims come from Daron Acemoglu and David Autor, "Skills, Tasks, and Technologies: Implications for Employment and Earnings," in *Handbook of Labor Economic Economics*, vol. 4b, ed. David Card and Orley Ashenfelter (Amsterdam: Elsevier, 2011). Acemoglu and Autor use raw data from the Census Bureau's March CPS. See also Acemoglu, "Technical Change," 37.

According to another estimate, the relative supply of college-educated workers grew nearly twice as fast in the 1970s as over the previous three decades. According to this estimate, the relative supply of college-educated workers (measured as 100 times annual log changes) grew by a factor of 2.35 in the 1940s, 2.91 in the 1950s, 2.55 in the 1960s, and 4.99 in the 1970s. See Goldin and Katz, *The Race Between Education and Technology*, 297, Table 8.1. Goldin and Katz note elsewhere that the supply of skilled workers measured more broadly—by the mean years of education of the American workforce—also increased more rapidly between 1960 and 1980 than in the decades either before or afterward. Between 1940 and 1960, the mean worker's education increased by 1.52 years; between 1960 and 1980, the increase was 1.93 years; and between 1980 and 2005, the increase was 1.08 years. See Goldin and Katz, *The Race Between Education and Technology*, 39, Table 1.3.

251 **than over the previous four decades:** According this estimate, the relative demand of college-educated workers (measured as 100 times annual log changes) grew by a factor of −0.69 in the 1940s, 4.28 in the 1950s, 3.69 in the 1960s, 3.77 in the 1970s, and 5.01 in the 1980s. See Goldin and Katz, *The Race Between Education and Technology*, 297, Table 8.1 (these numbers come from the column that uses the preferred estimate for the elasticity of substitution between skilled and unskilled labor, 1.64).

252 **the wage premium that they enjoy:** An alternative explanation proposes that the demand for college skills grew more or less steadily over this period and that the wage premium increased when the growth in the supply of college skills began to slow. See, e.g., Goldin and Katz, *The Race Between Education and Technology*. The two explanations use the same raw data but classify and interpret it differently.

252 **elite BAs or professional degrees:** Data concerning these workers is too thin and journalistic for the argument here to proceed through anything other than speculative inferences.

252 **to 10.4 percent in 1976:** See World Top Incomes Database, United States / Pre-tax national income / P99-P100 / Share, 29 October 2018, https://wid.world/data/#countrytimeseries/spt inc_p0p50_992_j;sptinc_p99p100_992_j/US/1970/2014/eu /k/p/yearly/s.

252 **continuing to rise into the new millennium:** See World Top Incomes Database, United States / Pre-tax national income / P99-P100 / Share, 29 October 2018, https://wid.world/data /#countrytimeseries/sptinc_p0p50_992_j;sptinc_p99p100 _992_j/US/1970/2014/eu/k/p/yearly/s. Recall, moreover, that these incomes increasingly came from labor rather than capital,

which is to say that they took the form of an economic return to super-skill.

252 **that the meritocratic revolution in elite education created:** Acemoglu, who aspires to a general theory of induced innovation—a general account of the relationship between the skill distribution of the labor pool and the skill bias of new technologies—proposes that the pattern also arose, in an earlier era, nearer the bottom of the skill distribution. Acemoglu thus suggests that the returns to a high school education, after declining in response to rising supply during the first years of the high school boom in the earlier part of the twentieth century, then rose rapidly as the new supply of high-school-educated workers induced innovations that increased the demand for high school skills. Acemoglu, "Technical Change." The labor economist and later senator Paul Douglas embraced a similar explanation when he suggested that newly invented office machinery reduced the demand for high school clerical skills over the first decades of the twentieth century (although he did not claim that the rise of high school education induced these innovations). See Goldin and Katz, *The Race Between Education and Technology,* 288. Goldin and Katz, by contrast, claim that the return to high school fell for much longer in response to rising supply, falling steadily from 1915 right through 1945—probably too long a period for the induced innovation theory to explain its path. See Goldin and Katz, *The Race Between Education and Technology,* 82, 85, Figure 2.9, 288–89. One possible account for this disagreement about the facts is that Acemoglu reports the return to a high school degree while Goldin and Katz emphasize the return to an additional year of post-elementary schooling. It is not immediately obvious whose analysis this difference favors.

252 **the rise of a super-skilled workforce:** Other factors besides the feedback loop between education and work of course also contribute to the exceptional concentration of industry and income in the elite in the United States. But often these mechanisms complement rather than substitute for the mechanism emphasized here.

252 **GDP per capita of about $50,000:** See World Bank, World Economic Outlook Database, October 2018 Edition, accessed March 11, 2019, www.imf.org/external/pubs/ft/weo/2018/02/weodata/index.aspx. These data measure GDP per capita not in terms of purchasing power parity but rather in nominal dollars. The data therefore adjust for exchange rates, differences in inflation, and differences in cost of living, in order to produce an international measure of the material standards of living in different countries.

252 **per capita GDPs greater than $50,000:** See World Bank, World Economic Outlook Database, October 2018 Edition, accessed March 11, 2019, www.imf.org/external/pubs/ft/weo/2018/02/weodata/index.aspx.

253 **a larger and larger segment of its population:** Between 1970 and 2015, Germany increased the share of students who attend academic high schools (called *Gymnasia*) that qualify graduates for university places and the professions from under a tenth to over a third. See "Abitur Für Alle," *Welt am Sonntag,* June 15, 2014, www.welt.de/print/wams/article129082343/Abitur-fuer-alle.html. German universities naturally experienced parallel increases in enrollments: while roughly 5 percent of German adults had university degrees in 1970, roughly half of Germans enroll in and roughly a third of Germans graduate from university today. See OECD, *Education at a Glance: OECD Indicators—Germany,* www.oecd.org/edu/Germany-EAG2014-Country-Note.pdf.

253 **outside of the university-educated elite:** German firms, supported by the German state, have embraced a massive program of vocational education, with over 70 percent of young German workers receiving formal workplace training (as compared to only 10 percent in the United States). See Daron Acemoglu and Jörn-Steffen Pischke, "The Structure of Wages and Investment in General Training," *Journal of Political Economy* 107, no. 3 (June 1999): 542 (citing an OECD report that 71.5 percent of young workers receive formal training in Germany while only 10.2 percent of U.S. workers receive any formal training during their first seven years of work [the shares in Japan and France are 67.1 and 23.6 percent respectively]). Hereafter cited as Acemoglu and Pischke, "The Structure of Wages." The training, moreover, can be intensive, as German firms commonly offer young

workers apprenticeships that cost employers as much as $10,000 per apprentice per year. See Acemoglu and Pischke, "The Structure of Wages," 540. Workplace training binds workers to firms, and so worker turnover rates convey the extent of training, and conspicuously reveal the size of the difference between the United States and Germany: while the median male U.S. worker holds six jobs in his first decade in the labor market, the median German holds between one and two. See Acemoglu and Pischke, "The Structure of Wages," 549. See also Daron Acemoglu and Jörn-Steffen Pischke, "Why Do Firms Train? Theory and Evidence," *Quarterly Journal of Economics* 113 (February 1998): 79–119 (who estimate one), and Christian Dustmann and Costas Meghir, "Wages, Experience and Seniority," manuscript, London: University College London, Economics Department, 1997 (who estimate two).

253 **90 euros a month:** See "Gesetz über die Beteiligung an den Kosten der Betreuung von Kindern in Tageseinrichtungen und in Kindertagespflege sowie in außerunterrichtlichen schulischen Betreuungsangeboten (Tagesbetreuungskostenbeteiligungsgesetz—TKBG) in der Fassung vom 23. April 2010, "Berliner Vorschrifteninformationssystem," http://gesetze.berlin.de/jportal/?quelle=jlink&query=TagEinrKostBetG+BE&psml=bsbeprod.psml&max=true. See also Senatsverwaltung für Bildung, Jugend und Familie, "Kostenbeteiligung und Zuzahlungen," www.berlin.de/sen/jugend/familie-und-kinder/kindertagesbetreuung/kostenbeteiligung/.

253 **disproportionately to complement high-skilled workers:** Increases in the capital-to-labor ratio in the U.S. economy have quite generally been heavily concentrated in skill-intensive industries. See Winfried Koeniger and Marco Leonardi, "Capital Deepening and Wage Differentials: Germany Versus the U.S.," *Economic Policy* 22, no. 49 (January 2007): 74. See also Daron Acemoglu, "Cross-Country Inequality Trends," *Economic Journal* 113, no. 485 (February 2003): 121–49; Daron Acemoglu and Jörn-Steffen Pischke, "Worker Well-Being and Public Policy," *Research in Labor Economics* 22 (2003): 159–202; Acemoglu, "Changes in Unemployment and Wage Inequality," 1259.

This result holds even within industries. For example, beginning in the 1970s manufacturing firms that employed more skilled workers began to invest more heavily in equipment than those that employed less skilled workers. See Acemoglu, "Changes in Unemployment and Wage Inequality," 1259, 1275–76. Acemoglu cites Franceso Caselli, "Technological Revolutions," *American Economic Review* 89, no. 1 (March 1999): 78–102.

Moreover, the rush toward investing in capital that complements specifically high-skilled labor encompasses not just investment in existing technology but also research and development into new ones. For example, in 1960, only 3 percent of privately funded research and development expenditures promoted innovations in office computing; by 1987, the share had risen fourfold, to 13 percent. See Acemoglu, "Why Do New Technologies Complement Skills?," 1083. College graduates are twice as likely to use computers in their jobs as are workers with only a high school education. See Acemoglu, "Why Do New Technologies Complement Skills?" Acemoglu cites to David Autor, Alan Krueger, and Lawrence Katz, "Computing Inequality: Have Computers Changed the Labor Market?," *Quarterly Journal of Economics* 113 (1998): 1169–1213.

253 **unskilled or mid-skilled labor dominates production:** Winfried Koeniger and Marco Leonardi, "Capital Deepening and Wage Differentials: Germany Versus the U.S.," *Economic Policy* 22, no. 49 (January 2007): 72–116; Daron Acemoglu, "Cross-Country Inequality Trends," *Economic Journal* 113, no. 485 (February 2003): 121–49; Daron Acemoglu and Jörn-Steffen Pischke, "Worker Well-Being and Public Policy," *Research in Labor Economics* 22 (2003): 159–202; Acemoglu, "Changes in Unemployment and Wage Inequality," 1275–76.

254 **decreased wage inequality in that sector by fully a third:** Winfried Koeniger and Marco Leonardi, "Capital Deepening and Wage Differentials: Germany Versus the U.S.," *Economic Policy* 22, no. 49 (January 2007): 72–116. Note that Koeniger and Leonardi test this conclusion against alternative explanations that emphasize other general differences between the U.S. and German labor markets, including generally higher German unemployment over the period and greater skill specificity in European production.

254 **rise and fall in tandem:** The OECD directly measures the returns to skill across its member states. See OECD, *OECD Skills Outlook 2013*, Table A4.13. No direct measure of the gap between elite and middle-class investments in education across countries exists. But good proxies do exist. Most notably, the OECD measures the effects of parents' income and education on children's skills. These differences in outputs are a reasonable proxy for differences in inputs—which is to say in parental investment in their children's education. See, e.g., OECD, *OECD Skills Outlook 2013*, Table A3.1.

254 **meritocratic developments in elite education:** I borrow the term *designed* from Daron Acemoglu, "Why Do New Technologies Complement Skills?," 1055, 1056 ("new technologies are not complementary to skills by nature, but by design").

254 **"the Vietnam War draft laws":** Acemoglu, "Technical Change," 7. On pp. 37–38, Acemoglu notes that "such an interpretation is not literal."

256 **pulling the ladder of opportunity up behind them:** See, e.g., Reeves, *Dream Hoarders*. See also Chrystia Freeland, "When Supercitizens Pull Up the Opportunity Ladder," *New York Times*, February 28, 2013, accessed November 19, 2018, www .nytimes.com/2013/03/01/us/when-supercitizens-pull-up-the -opportunity-ladder.html.

257 **resource curse:** See Jeffrey A. Frankel, "The Natural Resource Curse: A Survey," NBER Working Paper No. 15836 (March 2010), www.nber.org/papers/w15836.pdf. See also Stanley Engerman and Kenneth Sokoloff, "Factor Endowments, Institutions, and Differential Paths of Growth Among New World Economies: A View from Economic Historians of the United States," in *How Latin America Fell Behind*, ed. Stephen Haber (Stanford, CA: Stanford University Press, 1997), 260–304; Stanley Engerman and Kenneth Sokoloff, "Institutions, Factor Endowments, and Paths of Development in the New World," *Journal of Economic Perspectives* 14 (2000): 217–32; Stanley Engerman and Kenneth Sokoloff, "Factor Endowments, Inequality, and Paths of Development Among New World Economies," NBER Working Paper No. 9259 (October 2002); Jeffrey D. Sachs and Andrew M. Warner, "Natural Resource Abundance and Economic Growth," NBER Working Paper No. 5398 (December 1995).

## Chapter Nine: The Myth of Merit

258 **The word meritocracy:** *Oxford Etymology Dictionary*, s.v., "Meritocracy," accessed October 2, 2018, www.etymonline.com /word/meritocracy#etymonline_v_31201.

258 *The Rise of the Meritocracy:* Young, *The Rise of the Meritocracy*.

259 **even into the new millennium:** Michael Young, "Comment: Down with Meritocracy," *Guardian*, June 29, 2001, accessed September 28, 2018, www.theguardian.com/politics/2001 /jun/29/comment.

259 **by deploying the norms of the old regime:** The rise of mass democracy, for example, cannot be assessed according to earlier political principles concerning lineage and the authority of a sovereign over her subjects. Rather, democracy requires a new politics, constructed to be sensitive to the new relation between a republic and citizens who themselves, collectively, constitute the sovereign. The invention of companionate marriage similarly ushered in a new complex of values concerning intimacy, transforming domestic life from a tool for pooling resources and asserting governance into an institution that corrals sexuality into a site of communication, understanding, and recognition. Even the discovery of analgesics fundamentally transformed the ethics of self-control and self-possession, to demote stoic determination in the face of pain from its earlier high perch among the virtues.

260 **coined his term:** *Oxford Etymology Dictionary*, s.v., "aristo-," accessed October 2, 2018, www.etymonline.com/word/aristo -?ref=etymonline_crossreference; *Oxford Dictionaries*, s.v., "Merit," accessed September 28, 2018, https://en.oxforddiction aries.com/definition/merit.

260 **"aristocratic democracy" or "democratic aristocracy":** The phrases are spoken by Lord Summerhays in Shaw's play *Misalliance*. George Bernard Shaw, *Misalliance, The Dark Lady of the Sonnets, and Fanny's First Play* (London: Constable, 1934).

260 **six of the past seven French presidents:** "Alumni," Portail Sciences Po, accessed September 28, 2018, www.sciencespo.fr

/international/en/content/alumni. Nicolas Sarkozy attended but did not graduate from Sciences Po. Renaud Février, "Nicolas Sarkozy, diplômé 'avec distinction' de Sciences Po?," *L'Obs*, April 12, 2013, accessed October 19, 2018, www.nouvelobs .com/politique/20130412.OBS7758/nicolas-sarkozy-diplome -avec-distinction-de-sciences-po.html. Charles de Gaulle helped establish the École nationale d'administration (ENA), an elite postgraduate training ground for civil servants. Peter Allen, "France Demands That Its Future Leaders Must Speak English," *Telegraph*, February 15, 2015, accessed October 19, 2018, www .telegraph.co.uk/news/worldnews/europe/france/11414245 /France-demands-that-its-future-leaders-must-speak-English .html. Those who wish to enter the ENA strive to graduate from Sciences Po, the feeder university for the ENA. Mary Elizabeth Devine and Carol Summerfield, *International Dictionary of University Histories* (Chicago: Fitzroy Dearborn Publishers, 1998), 147.

260 **"upper classes [could] preserve their political hegemony":** Emile Boutmy, *Quelques idée sur la création d'une Faculté libre d'enseignement supérieur* (Paris, 1871), quoted in Piketty, *Capital*, 487. Paul Segal emphasized this historical background to me.

260 **Fabian English mind:** See "Famous Fabians," Fabian Society, accessed September 28, 2018, www.fabians.org.uk/about /famous-fabians.

260 **"virtue and talent":** "Thomas Jefferson to John Adams, 28 October 1813," *The Papers of Thomas Jefferson*, Retirement Series, vol. 6, *11 March to 27 November 1813*, ed. J. Jefferson Looney (Princeton, NJ: Princeton University Press, 2009), 562–68.

261 **endured across generations:** Land was unquestionably the dominant source of wealth in Europe throughout the ancien régime, and it remained so in the New World through the early years of the American republic. Land (and, in the South, slaves, who were economic complements to land) constituted between two-thirds and four-fifths of American wealth at the time of the Revolution and still composed roughly half of American wealth at the start of the Civil War. See, for example, Piketty, *Capital*, 141–42, 150–51.

At the time of the American Revolution, land constituted 81.1 percent of wealth in New England, 68.5 percent in the mid-Atlantic region, and 48.6 percent in the South (with slaves constituting 35.6 percent). Alice Hanson Jones, *Wealth of a Nation to Be: The American Colonies on the Eve of the Revolution* (New York: Columbia University Press, 1980), 98, Table 4.5. See also Marc Egnal, *A Mighty Empire: The Origins of the American Revolution* (Ithaca, NY: Cornell University Press, 1988), 14, Table 1.2. See also Thomas Piketty and Gabriel Zucman, *Capital Is Back: Wealth-Income Ratios in Rich Countries 1700–2010*, Paris School of Economics, July 26, 2013, accessed September 28, 2018, www.parisschoolofeconomics.com/zucman-gabriel/capi talisback/PikettyZucman2013WP.pdf (estimating that land and slaves constituted roughly two-thirds of American wealth in 1770 and half in 1850). Similarly, a study of inheritances in Bucks County, Pennsylvania, reveals that realty constituted more than half of the wealth in probated estates in the seventeenth and eighteenth centuries. See Carole Shammas, Marylynn Salmon, and Michel Dahlin, *Inheritance in America: From Colonial Times to the Present* (Long Beach, CA: Frontier Press, 1987), 19; Langbein, "Twentieth-Century Revolution," 722, 723n.4.

261 **"Wealth, in a commercial age":** Roscoe Pound, *An Introduction to the Philosophy of Law* (New Haven, CT: Yale University Press, 1922), 236.

261 **to husband its caste:** These are new behaviors, as older elites did not invest in human capital with anything close to the same rigor or effectiveness. The winners of the early-nineteenth-century Georgia Cherokee Land Lottery, for example, who acquired the median wealth as a windfall, did not invest in schooling for their children, who did not enjoy greater literacy, income, or wealth than the children of non-winners. See Hoyt Bleakley and Joseph P. Ferrie, "Shocking Behavior: Random Wealth in Antebellum Georgia and Human Capital Across Generations," NBER Working Paper No. 19348 (August 2013), www.nber.org/pa pers/w19348. More recently, the advent of meritocratic admissions could transform student bodies at elite universities so quickly because the incumbent elite lacked the capacity and inclination to train its children to succeed under the new regime,

261 **kept aristocratic lands in the family:** Even the inheritance tax favors meritocratic succession. Because such a large part of the education expenditures that constitute the meritocratic inheritance are paid while rich children are still minors, they are exempted from the estate and gift tax. This literally exempts the meritocratic inheritance from the taxes that help to dissipate aristocratic fortunes.

262 **rendered the aristocratic version unsustainable:** Meritocracy resembles aristocracy in one other way as well. The aristocracy of the ancien régime united economics, politics, and culture around a single organizing ideal: hereditary landedness sustained material production, underwrote political power, and constituted moral and social virtue, all through a single, integrated mechanism.

The Industrial Revolution and then the rise of the knowledge economy shattered this unity, producing, for perhaps two centuries, separate, distinct, and competing sources of (and sometimes even freestanding) economic, political, and cultural power. Land remained a significant source of wealth, and breeding remained a significant source of cultural status, well into the twentieth century. In the meantime, industrialization created immense fortunes based on physical capital, and these fortunes came in time to assert themselves politically and culturally as well. Finally, in the twentieth century, a professional class, including on account of administering both private and public bureaucracies, also began to assert itself, especially culturally and politically. Competition among hierarchies tends to flatten the gradient of each, and it is therefore no coincidence that the relative equality of the Great Compression came at a time when all three hierarchies—of land, of machines, and of skill—retained some power.

The rise of the superordinate working class reunifies these hierarchies through the reciprocal mechanisms of training concentration and skill fetishism. These mechanisms are beginning to re-create the formal unity and cohesion of value and life achieved by the ancien régime, only now organized around a new substance—skill and labor rather than breeding and land. Super-skilled labor thus increasingly dominates not just income and wealth, but also politics (especially the politics of private influence) and culture.

As it vanquishes competing hierarchies, meritocracy inevitably steepens its own.

262 **possessed the greatest virtue:** Aristotle, *Aristotle's Politics*, trans. Benjamin Jowett (Oxford: Clarendon Press, 1905). Aristotle reserved the term *aristocracy* for government by the virtuous few. Where a ruling elite lacked the virtue that it claimed, Aristotle called the government an *oligarchy*, which is a pejorative term. Dieter Rucht, "Oligarchy and Organization," in *The Blackwell Encyclopedia of Sociology*, ed. George Ritzer (Malden, MA: Blackwell, 2008).

262 **(which was nearly zero-sum):** See John Plender, *Capitalism: Money, Morals and Markets* (London: Biteback Publishing, 2015), 135. Hereafter cited as Plender, *Capitalism*. John Plender, "Capitalism: Morality and the Money Motive," *Financial Times*, July 17, 2015, accessed September 28, 2018, www.ft.com/content/33d82de6-2bc3-11e5-8613-e7aedbb7bdb7?mhq5j=e1.

262 **"the interests of posterity":** See Young, *The Rise of the Meritocracy*, 20. See also M. L. Bush, *The English Aristocracy: A Comparative Synthesis* (Manchester: Manchester University Press, 1984).

263 **both household and national affairs:** This theme comes out, for example, in Montesquieu's *The Spirit of the Laws*. Charles de Secondat, baron de Montesquieu, *The Spirit of the Laws*, trans. Thomas Nugent (New York: Hafner Publishing Company, 1949). See also Jonathan Powis, *Aristocracy* (Malden: Blackwell, 1984), 80.

263 **did not yet exist:** See, generally, Baldassarre Castiglione, *The Book of the Courtier*, trans. Thomas Hoby (London: Dent, 1974).

263 **cast chivalry as ridiculous:** Plender, *Capitalism*, 137.

263 **skewer aristocratic vanity and greed:** Plender, *Capitalism*, 137.

263 **"third-generation Yale man":** See Chapter 4.

263 **aristocratic prep schools:** See Chapter 5.

264 **an already completed revolution:** Kabaservice, "The Birth of a New Institution."

264 **artifact of the game that frames it:** Pitching is nevertheless an immensely valuable skill within this frame. More than forty-seven active pitchers boast career wages (directly for playing baseball and without counting payments received for making advertising endorsements) exceeding $50 million. See SPO-TRAC, accessed September 28, 2018, www.spotrac.com/mlb/rankings/earnings/pitching/.

264 **disappears altogether:** Perhaps there exist skills that are sufficiently broad or generic that they avoid or at least hedge their dependence on a particular frame. When the American Jim Thorpe won the decathlon at the 1912 Stockholm Olympics, King Gustav V of Sweden told him, "You, sir, are the world's greatest athlete." Juliet Macur, "Decathletes Struggle for Any Recognition," *New York Times*, September 2, 2007, accessed September 28, 2018, www.nytimes.com/2007/09/02/sports/othersports/02decathlon.html. The informal title has been acknowledged ever since, probably on account of the variety and hence generality of the athleticism that the decathlon's ten disciplines demand. The competition is constructed to pick a winner who would thrive in almost any athletic competition. Meritocracy, by contrast, has developed to suit a very particular, highly peculiar set of economic and social conditions.

264 **Certainly, the training and capacities:** A friend who saw a Harvard professor throw a boomerang once observed, "In a society of hunter-gatherers, you would be a gatherer."

264 **artifacts of baseball:** A frame-dependent virtue might receive a sort of noncontingent justification in terms of the goodness of the frame itself. And a grand folk tradition, extending from Walt Whitman through John Rawls, proclaims baseball's intrinsic moral worth. Even in this case, there are reasons to treat the tradition as a conceit that should not be taken at face value. In any event, no analogous tradition proclaims economic inequality's intrinsic moral worth.

265 **reorganize production optimally in her absence:** A version of this measure has been proposed by John Roemer. See John E. Roemer, *A General Theory of Exploitation and Class* (Cambridge, MA: Harvard University Press, 1982). A similar idea also appears in Kenneth J. Arrow, "Political and Economic Evaluation of Social Effects and Externalities," in *The Analysis of Public Output*, ed. Julius Margolis (Cambridge, MA: NBER, 1970), 1–30.

266 **(as they could do without her):** This formulation masks substantial complexities, which are not essential to the larger argument and may be set aside. The root of the complexity is that the ability of other workers to pick up the slack when one worker withdraws her labor varies across contexts, for reasons that have nothing to do with meritocracy or snowball inequality.

267 **by the median household, for example:** Philippon and Reshef, "Skill Biased Financial Development," Figure 11.

267 **accelerating economic growth or increasing productivity:** Per capita gross domestic product actually grew more quickly at midcentury than in recent decades of rising inequality: between 1950 and 1973, real GDP per capita grew by an average of 2.5 percent per year; between 1973 and 2007, real GDP per capita grew by just 1.93 percent per year. See Charles I. Jones, "The Facts of Economic Growth," in *Handbook of Macroeconomics*, vol. 2, ed. John B. Taylor and Harald Uhlig (Amsterdam: North Holland, 2016), 3–69, Table 1.

Similarly, the productivity of labor grew at an annual rate of 2.4 percent between 1950 and 1969, compared to annual growth of 2.0 percent between 1980 and 2009 (growth rates calculated using data from the Bureau of Labor Statistics, Major Sector Productivity and Costs, Nonfarm Business Labor Productivity (output per hour) series PRS85006092). And no decade since 1970 has produced increases in the productivity of labor as great as the 1960s. The productivity of labor grew by nearly 30 percent in the 1960s, and then by just 19 percent, 16 percent, 20 percent, and 25 percent in the 1970s, 1980s, 1990s, and 2000s respectively (growth rates calculated using data form the Bureau of Labor Statistics, Major Sector Productivity and Costs, Nonfarm Business Labor Productivity (output per hour) series PRS85006092).

Most significantly, total factor productivity—the portion of output not accounted for by conventional inputs (of capital and labor)—has again grown more slowly during the recent decades of rising economic inequality than it did during the relatively more egalitarian decades at midcentury: growing by just 0.9 percent annually between 1980 and 2009, compared to 1.0 percent between 1950 and 1969. (The dividing decade between the two eras, the 1970s, showed truly anemic growth.) See "Total Factor Productivity at Constant National Prices for the United States," St. Louis Fed FRED, accessed September 28, 2018, https://fred.stlouisfed.org/series/RTFPNAUSA632N RUG. This observation borrows from Acemoglu, "Technical Change."

All these data suggest that meritocratic skills, for all the returns that they yield superordinate workers, yield little or no net social product, or boost in total output as compared to a world that had carried midcentury America's democratic regimes of training and work forward into the present. As the economist Robert Solow, whose work on economic growth won him the Nobel Prize, once wryly admitted, it is "somewhat embarrass[ing] . . . that what everyone feels to have been a technological revolution, a drastic change in our productive lives, has been accompanied everywhere . . . by a slowing-down of productivity growth, not by a step up. We can see the computer age everywhere but in the productivity statistics." Robert Solow, "We'd Better Watch Out," *New York Times*, July 12, 1987 (reviewing Stephen S. Cohen and John Zysman, *Manufacturing Matters: The Myth of the Post-Industrial Economy*).

## Conclusion: What Should We Do?

271  **"a thousand years of successful German history"**: The phrase comes from Alexander Gauland, the head of the populist Alternativ für Deutschland. See Guy Chazan, "Germany's Increasingly Bold Nationalists Spark a New Culture War," *Financial Times*, July 29, 2018, accessed September 28, 2018, www .ft.com/content/348a1bce-9000-11e8-b639-7680cedcc421.

271  **on-site gyms and nap rooms**: See Tony Schwartz and Christine Porath, "Why You Hate Work," *New York Times*, May 30, 2014, accessed September 28, 2018, www.nytimes.com/2014/06/01 /opinion/sunday/why-you-hate-work.html?mcubz=0 &_r=0.

272  **extend fertility later into life**: See Anne Weisberg, "The Workplace Culture That Flying Nannies Won't Fix," *New York Times*, August 24, 2015, accessed September 28, 2018, www .nytimes.com/2015/08/24/opinion/the-workplace-culture -that-flying-nannies-wont-fix.html?mcubz=0.

272  **caring and communal engagement**: Nearly a hundred presidents and chancellors of selective universities and liberal arts colleges have now signed letters disapproving college rankings and pledging to develop alternative (nonhierarchical) ways of communicating quality to students. The participation rate for *U.S. News & World Report*'s annual reputational survey of college leaders has fallen from 67 percent in 2002 to 46 percent in 2008. Similarly, a consortium of elite educators (including from Harvard's Graduate School of Education) has recently released a report on college admissions—*Turning the Tide*—that aims to reduce pressure on applicants. Driven by what one observer calls the "competitive frenzy" surrounding admissions and the threat that the competition poses to applicants' "mental health," the report recommends dramatic changes. As one of its authors says, meritocratic university admissions have reached a "pivot point," so that "it's really time to say 'enough,' to stop wringing our hands and figure out some collective action." More concretely, *Turning the Tide* encourages admissions committees to deemphasize the quantity of applicants' achievements—AP tests, extracurricular activities—in favor of quality. It also aims to refocus attention away from SAT scores and other competitive achievements in favor of ethical and cooperative accomplishments such as caring and communal engagement. Making Caring Common, *Turning the Tide: Inspiring Concern for Others and the Common Good Through College Admissions*, Harvard Graduate School of Education (2016). See Presidents' Letter, The Education Conservancy, May 10, 2007, www.educa tionconservancy.org/presidents_letter.html. See Frank Bruni, "Rethinking College Admissions," *New York Times*, January 19, 2016, accessed September 28, 2018, www.nytimes.com/2016 /01/20/opinion/rethinking-college-admissions.html?mcubz =0. The words come from Richard Weissbourd, the faculty director of the group at Harvard's Graduate School of Education that contributed most substantially to *Turning the Tide*.

272  **cut down on long hours rather than alcohol**: On living in the present, see Eckhart Tolle, *The Power of Now* (Vancouver, BC: Namaste Publishing, 2004). On New Year's resolutions to reduce work, see, e.g., Lucy Kellaway, "January Is for Cutting Down on Long Hours, Not Alcohol," *Financial Times*, January 24, 2016, accessed September 28, 2018, www.ft.com/content /916fa2b0-c059-11e5-846f-79b0e3d20eaf; John Gapper, "Resolve to Kick the Addiction to Work Email," *Financial Times*, January 4, 2017, accessed September 28, 2018, www.ft.com /content/6a4ec5c2-d1d7-11e6-b06b-680c49b4b4c0.

272  **disdained his hard sell**: Anonymous resident in conversation with the author, St. Clair Shores, Michigan, May 2, 2018.

272  **would stay the same or get worse**: See "Nearly One in Five Female Clinton Voters Say Husband or Partner Didn't Vote," *PRRI/The Atlantic Post-election Survey*, December 1, 2016, accessed September 28, 2018, www.prri.org/research/prri -atlantic-poll-post-election-white-working-class.

272  **"an unwavering commitment"**: See Julie Coffman and Bill Neuenfeldt, "Everyday Moments of Truth: Frontline Managers Are Key to Women's Career Aspirations," Bain & Company Insights, June 17, 2014, accessed September 28, 2018, www.bain .com/publications/articles/everyday-moments-of-truth.aspx.

273  **"from the rich to the poor"**: See Arthur Okun, *Equality and Efficiency: The Big Tradeoff* (Washington, DC: Brookings Institution, 1975), 91. Hereafter cited as Okun, *Equality and Efficiency*.

273  **"will simply disappear in transit"**: See Okun, *Equality and Efficiency*.

274  **"large-scale redistribution of income"**: Robert M. Solow, "Stray Thoughts on How It Might Go," in *100 Years: Leading Economists Predict the Future*, ed. Ignacio Palacios-Huerta (Cambridge, MA: MIT Press, 2013), 142.

274  **"those who are doing well"**: Angus Deaton, "Through the Darkness to a Brighter Future," in *100 Years: Leading Economists Predict the Future*, ed. Ignacio Palacios-Huerta (Cambridge, MA: MIT Press, 2013), 38.

274  **losing a war or succumbing to a revolution**: This conclusion follows from Winters, *Oligarchy*. Winters himself is too circumspect a scholar to assert the conclusion outright, although his book as a whole suggests that he recognizes what his study reveals.

274  **"only [an] all-out thermonuclear war"**: See Walter Scheidel, *The Great Leveler: Violence and the History of Inequality from the Stone Age to the Twenty-First Century* (Princeton, NJ: Princeton University Press, 2017), 438. The quotation is reported in Eduardo Porter, "A Dilemma for Humanity: Stark Inequality or Total War," *New York Times*, December 6, 2016, accessed September 28, 2018, www.nytimes.com/2016/12/06/business /economy/a-dilemma-for-humanity-stark-inequality-or-total -war.html.

Scheidel is not alone in his view. At least two other comprehensive studies conclude that orderly corrections of concentrated income and wealth are immensely rare and that the principal historical mode of unwinding extreme wealth has been large-scale violence. See Kenneth Scheve and David Stasavage, *Taxing the Rich: A History of Fiscal Fairness in the United States and Europe* (Princeton, NJ: Princeton University Press, 2016); Winters, *Oligarchy*.

274  **build the midcentury middle class**: See Winters, *Oligarchy*, 232. Britain in the twentieth century might present a second instance, if Britain is treated as winning the two world wars and decolonization is treated as different from revolution. But both these characterizations capture just the formal rather than the substantial truth of the matters that they address. Britain won the First World War only in the narrowly legal sense that Germany surrendered: the British "victory" achieved no significant objective, and Britain suffered devastating losses in blood and treasure (with an entire generation destroyed by the war). And decolonization deprived the British of an empire and converted Britain from a global hegemon to a minor power. The redistribution that remedied inequality within British society was thus accompanied by a reduction in Britain's overall wealth and power, of thus the sort associated with internal revolution or external military defeat.

274  **what's past need not be prologue**: See William Shakespeare, *The Tempest* (Cambridge, MA: Harvard University Press, 1958), Act II, scene i.

275 **abolitionists and civil rights campaigners emphasized:** "Many of our white brothers, as evidenced by their presence here today, have come to realize that their destiny is tied up with our destiny. And they have come to realize that their freedom is inextricably bound to our freedom." Martin Luther King Jr., "I Have a Dream" (speech), March on Washington for Jobs and Freedom, Washington, DC, August 1968, accessed October 19, 2018, http://avalon.law.yale.edu/20th_century/mlk01.asp.

275 **"the work of a civilization":** The phrase comes from Michael Gerson, "Our Disconnected Working Class," *Washington Post*, May 15, 2014, accessed September 28, 2018, www.washingtonpost.com/opinions/michael-gerson-our-disconnected-working-class/2014/05/15/f02fdac8-dc52-11e3-8009-71de85b9c527_story.html?utm_term=.706543dfd8e6.

276 **to attack meritocratic inequality head-on:** This agenda represents a revolution in education reform. Education reformers of all stripes conventionally focus their efforts on the lowest-performing schools, whose students typically hail from the poorest families. Charter schools gravitate toward inner cities, and school finance equalization litigation seeks to close the funding shortfall suffered by the poorest school districts. Generalist policymakers who turn to education typically follow suit, as when Federal Reserve chair Janet Yellen, in a recent speech on "Perspectives on Inequality and Opportunity," devoted the portion of her remarks that took up education to promoting prekindergarten education for the poor and increased spending in low-income schools. See Janet Yellen, "Perspectives on Inequality and Opportunity from the Survey of Consumer Finances," *Conference on Opportunity and Equality, Federal Reserve Bank of Boston*, October 17, 2014, accessed September 28, 2018, www.federalreserve.gov/newsevents/speech/yellen20141017a.htm.

But while the undereducated poor may present economic inequality's most heartrending face, the overeducated rich present its most consequential one. Even narrowly within education, the gaps between investments made in poor and middle-class students are perhaps a fifth as large as the gaps between investments made in middle-class students and rich ones. Moreover, the overeducated rich rather than the undereducated poor drive meritocratic inequality's broader systemic failures. They concentrate industry, income, and status. They condemn middle-class workers to hopeless idleness and superordinate workers to alienated overwork. They isolate themselves comprehensively from the rest of society. And they corrupt democratic politics.

Achieving equality requires closing the educational gap between the middle class and the rich. And this requires massively expanding access to education not at the bottom, but at the top. The conventional approach to education reform is simply mismatched to meritocratic inequality's distinctive profile.

276 **not included in their estates:** The estate and gift tax applies to estates greater than $11.2 million for individuals and $22.4 million for married couples and imposes a top rate of 40 percent. Brian J. O'Connor, "Heirs Inherit Uncertainty with New Estate Tax," *New York Times*, February 23, 2018, accessed September 28, 2018, www.nytimes.com/2018/02/23/business/estate-tax-uncertainty.html. At present, money that rich parents spend on their children's educations is not included in their estates, for purposes of computing the tax. But these meritocratic inheritances have become essential to the dynastic transmission of privilege, and the sums involved are enormous. The present tax regime amounts, in effect, to a massive tax shelter for rich families that prefer meritocratic over aristocratic mechanisms for securing their dynasties. Inheritance taxes played a central role in the reforms that reined in the aristocracy. Including a rich child's meritocratic inheritance in her parents' estate would play a similar role in reining in the meritocracy today.

276 **devoted to the public interest:** A public charity is, in effect, a tax-exempt organization that is not a private foundation. IRC [26 U.S.C.] §§ 501(c)(3), 509(a)(1)–(a)(4).

277 **Essex County College in Newark:** These numbers reflect 2013 budgets. The average implicit public subsidy at the ten most highly endowed colleges in that year was $41,000. See Kellie Woodhouse, "The Widening Wealth Gap," *Inside Higher Ed*, May 21, 2015, accessed September 28, 2018, www.insidehighered.com/news/2015/05/21/rich-universities-get-richer-are-poor-students-being-left-behind. *Rich Schools, Poor Students: Tapping Large University Endowments to Improve Student*

*Outcomes*, 7, Table 1, Nexus Research & Policy Center, accessed September 28, 2018, http://nexusresearch.org/wp-content/uploads/2015/06/Rich_Schools_Poor_Students.pdf.

277 **"hedge funds with universities attached":** See, e.g., Astra Taylor, "Universities Are Becoming Billion-Dollar Hedge Funds with Schools Attached," *The Nation*, March 8, 2016, accessed September 28, 2018, www.thenation.com/article/universities-are-becoming-billion-dollar-hedge-funds-with-schools-attached.

277 **U.S. households generally:** The 7 percent figure reflects the past twenty years. See NACUBO-Commonfund, "U.S. and Canadian Institutions Listed by Fiscal Year (FY) 2017 Endowment Market Value and Change in Endowment Market Value from FY2016 to FY2017," accessed September 29, 2018, www.nacubo.org/-/media/Nacubo/Documents/EndowmentFiles/2017-Endowment-Market-Values.ashx?la=en&hash=E71088CDC05C76FCA30072DA109F91BBC10B0290; IPEDS, U.S. Department of Education, National Center for Educational Statistics, Integrated Postsecondary Education Data System (IPEDS), Table 333.90, "Endowment funds of the 120 degree-granting postsecondary institutions with the largest endowments, by rank order: Fiscal year 2015," accessed September 29, 2018, https://nces.ed.gov/programs/digest/d16/tables/dt16_333.90.asp. Note that all private university endowments add up to about $550 billion but also that the smaller endowments grow at slower rates than the larger ones. Rick Seltzer, "Endowments Rebound, but Is It Enough?," *Inside Higher Ed*, January 25, 2018, accessed October 11, 2018, www.insidehighered.com/news/2018/01/25/college-endowments-rise-122-percent-2017-experts-worry-about-long-term-trends. Robert Reich, "Why the Government Spends More Per Pupil at Elite Private Universities Than at Public Universities," *Business Insider*, October 14, 2014, accessed September 28, 2018, www.businessinsider.com/government-spends-more-per-pupil-at-private-universities-than-at-public-niversities-2014-10.

277 **designed the new buildings to last forever:** Telephone conversation between Eric Veenstra of the Yale Office of General Counsel and Yicong (George) Shen, reported by email from Shen on September 14, 2017.

277 **from these sources:** See *Report of the Treasurer 2015–2016*, Princeton University, Princeton University Highlights (2015), accessed October 11, 2018, https://finance.princeton.edu/princeton-financial-overv/report-of-the-treasurer/2015-2016.pdf; *U.S. News & World Report*, "National University Rankings" (top twenty private universities selected), accessed September 29, 2018, www.usnews.com/best-colleges/rankings/national-universities.

277 **bottom two-thirds of the income distribution:** The policy should also apply to private educational endowments, including those that support rich but nominally public schools. In addition, elite but nominally public school districts—such as Scarsdale's—might be assessed luxury taxes even on their public budgets, based on the differences between their per-student spending and state medians, unless they admit more working- and middle-class students.

277 **by expanding enrollments:** Colleges might construct their newly economically diverse student bodies by giving an admissions preference to graduates of high schools whose student bodies skew away from wealth. This would connect reforms to schools and colleges, so that changes at each level support changes at the other.

A crude version of this approach already exists, although in a narrow context, in the University of Texas's commitment to admitting all applicants who graduate in the top 10 percent of their high school classes. A more sophisticated version, which takes into account the incentives that the college admissions preference would give to economic integration in high school, is developed by Thomas Scott-Railton in "Shifting the Scope: How Taking School Demographics into Account in University Admissions Could Improve Education and Reduce Inequality Nationwide," *Yale Law and Policy Review* (2017). Scott-Railton also helpfully assesses the legality of the preference that he proposes.

It would help if the publications that rank colleges and universities, which at present reward increased selectivity with higher rankings, recalibrated their methods to reward inclusive admissions practices. For accounts of the tension between open admissions and rankings competition that university presidents now feel, see The Education Conservancy, *Financial Aid: Examining the Thinking Behind the Policy* (2015), http://education conservancy.org/PresidentialThinking.pdf. See also Wendy Espeland and Michael Sauder, *Engines of Anxiety: Academic Rankings, Reputation, and Accountability* (New York: Russell Sage Foundation, 2016).

278 **can afford to grow:** Some universities are demonstrating that high-quality education can be delivered to large numbers of students at much lower costs still. Arizona State, for example, has dramatically opened its student body over the last decade, with its president Michael Crow going so far as to partner with Starbucks CEO Howard Schultz to make tuition support into a widely available employee benefit. Joe Nocera, "A New College Model: Arizona State Matches Starbucks in Its Trailblazing Ways," *New York Times*, June 16, 2014, accessed September 28, 2018, www.nytimes.com/2014/06/17/opinion/joe-nocera -starbucks-and-arizona-state-add-an-education-to-benefit-pack age.html?mcubz=3. See also Starbucks, "Starbucks College Achievement Plan," accessed September 29, 2018, www.star bucks.com/careers/college-plan.

278 **as it did in 2000:** See Chapter 5.
The new students would have to skew less to wealth than the old. At Princeton, for example, slightly more than 15 percent of the present class come from the bottom two-thirds of the income distribution. See Benjamin Wermund, "How U.S. News College Rankings Promote Economic Inequality on Campus," *Politico*, accessed September 28, 2018, www.politico.com/inter actives/2017/top-college-rankings-list-2017-us-news-investiga tion. If Princeton composed a doubled class using all the students that it presently admits plus additional students drawn evenly from households across the income distribution, then almost exactly half of the total class would come from the bottom two-thirds of the income distribution.

278 **as they did in 1970:** See Chapter 5.
278 **than their public counterparts:** See Chapter 5.
278 **may be transformed again:** If elite universities expand and open their student bodies at the same moment as elite schools, they will not yet have a larger and more inclusive pipeline from which to admit their classes, and they might lack qualified applicants. For this reason, it may be best to make education more inclusive from the bottom up, as it were, beginning with kindergarten and then moving through the grades.

278 **the most recent tax reform:** The Tax Cuts and Jobs Act of 2017 imposes a 1.4 percent excise tax on the endowment incomes of universities with endowments larger than $500,000 per full-time student and enrollments greater than five hundred students. Richard Rubin and Andrea Fuller, "Which Colleges Will Have to Pay Taxes on Their Endowment? Your Guess Might Not Be Right," *Wall Street Journal*, accessed September 28, 2018, www.wsj.com/articles/which-colleges-will-have-to-pay -taxes-on-their-endowment-your-guess-might-not-be-right -1516271400. Roughly twenty-seven universities will be affected. Ben Myers and Brock Read, "If Republicans Get Their Way, These Colleges Would See Their Endowments Taxed," *Chronicle of Higher Education*, accessed September 28, 2018, www.chronicle.com/article/If-Republicans-Get-Their-Way /241659; "Tax Reform," National Association of Independent Colleges and Universities, accessed September 28, 2018, www .naicu.edu/policy-advocacy/issue-brief-index/tax-policy/tax -reform.
The new tax follows a long line of unsuccessful prior efforts. In 2007 a Republican member of the Senate Finance Committee proposed that university endowments should be required to disburse 5 percent of their value each year, under the same rule that governs tax-exempt foundations. See, e.g., Janet Lorin, "Universities Seek to Defend Endowments from Republican Tax Plan," Bloomberg, April 18, 2017, accessed September 28, 2018, www.bloomberg.com/news/articles/2017-04-18/univer sities-seek-to-defend-endowments-from-republican-tax-plan. More recently, a Republican congressperson proposed requiring colleges with endowments greater than $1 billion to devote at least a quarter of their earnings to tuition assistance. See Stephanie Saul, "How Some Would Level the Playing Field: Free Harvard Degrees," *New York Times*, January 14, 2016, accessed

September 28, 2018, www.nytimes.com/2016/01/15/us /a-push-to-make-harvard-free-also-questions-the-role-of -race-in-admissions.html?mcubz=3&_r=0. Some state lawmakers are embracing similar proposals. A recent Connecticut proposal, for example, sought to subject profits on university endowments greater than $10 billion (which is to say, Yale University) to a tax, unless the university reinvested the profits in its educational mission or in the local economy. See Connecticut General Assembly Raised Bill No. 413, February Session 2016. See also Timothy W. Martin, "One New Fix for Connecticut's Budget Crunch: Yale University," *Wall Street Journal*, March 24, 2016, accessed September 28, 2018, www.wsj.com/articles /one-new-fix-for-connecticuts-budget-crunch-yale-university -1458853613.

278 **narrowly political motives:** See "Sharp Partisan Divisions in Views of National Institutions," Pew Research Center, July 10, 2017, accessed September 28, 2018, www.people-press.org /2017/07/10/sharp-partisan-divisions-in-views-of-national -institutions. See also Sofia Tesfaye, "America Hits Peak Anti-intellectualism: Majority of Republicans Now Think College Is Bad," *Salon*, July 11, 2017, accessed September 28, 2018, www .salon.com/2017/07/11/america-hits-peak-anti-intellectualism -majority-of-republicans-now-think-college-is-bad.

279 **did not require excluding men:** When Yale College first admitted women, in 1969, it made this logic distressingly explicit. Yale had long advertised a commitment to training a thousand American leaders each year. The college observed that by growing its class, rather than displacing men with women, Yale could honor this commitment even as it embraced coeducation. Linda Greenhouse, "How Smart Women Got the Chance," *New York Review of Books*, April 6, 2017, accessed October 10, 2018, www .nybooks.com/articles/2017/04/06/coeducation-how-smart -women-got-chance/. See also Nancy Weiss Malkiel, *Keep the Damned Women Out: The Struggle for Coeducation* (Princeton, NJ: Princeton University Press, 2016).

279 **relax competition among rich applicants:** The combinatorics of stratification ensures this. As where only a small slice of all applicants are competitive to begin with, a small increase in available places dramatically increases admissions chances within this competitive slice. Moreover, fixed absolute changes in acceptance rates have greater effects on the intensity of admissions competition at low rates than at high rates: raising the acceptance rate from 10 to 20 percent transforms admissions competition, even as raising the acceptance rate from 60 to 70 percent would not.

279 **the most modest incursions:** Yale University, for example, aggressively resisted not just the Connecticut endowment tax but also a recent proposal to subject just some of its buildings to local real estate taxes, even though the sums at stake in that proposal had only symbolic significance. See Connecticut General Assembly SB 414 (2016). See also Christine Stuart, "Bill Allowing New Haven to Tax Yale Moves Forward," *New Haven Register*, April 7, 2016, accessed September 28, 2018, www.nhregister .com/colleges/article/Bill-allowing-New-Haven-to-tax-Yale -moves-forward-11336701.php; "Yale Decries Tax Bill as Unconstitutional," *YaleNews*, April 11, 2016, accessed September 28, 2018, https://news.yale.edu/2016/04/11/yale-decries-tax-bill -unconstitutional.

280 **finance for nearly one-tenth:** See "Historical," Centers for Medicare & Medicaid Services, accessed September 28, 2018, www.cms.gov/Research-Statistics-Data-and-Systems/Statis tics-Trends-and-Reports/NationalHealthExpendData/Na tionalHealthAccountsHistorical.html.

280 **perhaps half of the richest 1 percent of workers:** See Chapter 4.
280 **emphasizes nurse-practitioners rather than doctors:** Assembly Bill-1810 (Cal. 2017–2018), http://leginfo.legislature .ca.gov/faces/billTextClient.xhtml?bill_id=201720 180AB1810.

280 **ordinarily diagnosed by doctors:** See, e.g., Nisarg A. Patel, "Could Your Next Doctor Be Your Dentist?," *Slate*, August 28, 2017, accessed September 28, 2018, www.slate.com/articles /health_and_science/medical_examiner/2017/08/why_your _next_doctor_could_be_your_dentist.html.

280 **routine legal services:** See Washington State Bar Association, Legal Technician Program, "Become a Legal Technician," ac-

cessed September 29, 2018, www.wsba.org/for-legal-profes
sionals/join-the-legal-profession-in-wa/limited-license-legal
-technicians/become-a-legal-technician. Substantive law might
also be changed to encourage mid-skilled legal labor. Larry Lessig, for example, proposes a copyright registration scheme that
would reduce the complexity of intellectual property rights creation and registration and dramatically reduce skill fetishism in
intellectual property law. See Lawrence Lessig, *Free Culture:
How Big Media Uses Technology and the Law to Lock Down Culture and Control Creativity* (New York: Penguin Press, 2004),
287–93.

280  **a cost/benefit analysis:** This requirement traces back to the
Reagan administration. See Executive Order 12291, 46 Fed.
Reg. 13193 (1981).

281  **outcomes that the procedures produce:** See Kevin M. Stack,
"The Paradox of Process in Administrative Rulemaking," University of Cambridge, Conference Panel, Faculty of Law, Public
Law Conference Presentation, Cambridge, England, September
17, 2014.

281  **to which it applies:** "Policy Basics: Federal Payroll Taxes," Center on Budget and Policy Priorities, March 23, 2016, accessed
October 11, 2018, www.cbpp.org/research/federal-tax/policy
-basics-federal-payroll-taxes. For 2018, the Social Security tax
applied to only the first $128,400 of income, and only the Medi-
care tax applied after that. For 2019, the threshold is $132,900.
This means that the tax imposes rates of 15.3 percent on the first
$132,900 of individual income but just 2.9 percent on income
between $132,900 and $200,000 and 3.8 percent on all income
above $200,000. See IRS, *Tax Topics*, "Topic Number: 751—
Social Security and Medicare Withholding Rates," www
.irs.gov/taxtopics/tc751. For employed workers, both taxes are
charged half to the employee and half to the employer. But regardless of who must pay the payroll tax, it amounts economically to a burden on labor understood as a factor of production.

The cap reflects historical contingencies rather than any
deeper logic. Franklin Roosevelt's Committee on Economic Security introduced Social Security as an antipoverty measure and so
proposed to exempt high-earning nonmanual workers from the
program altogether, but Congress instead included all workers,
while capping the earnings subject to the tax that funded the program. See Congressional Research Service, *Social Security: Raising
or Eliminating the Taxable Earnings Base*, CRS Report no.
RL32896 (2017), 3, 4, https://fas.org/sgp/crs/misc/RL32896
.pdf. Quite possibly, Congress took this route in order to frame
Social Security as a pension program rather than as poverty relief:
as the House Ways and Means Committee observed in recom-
mending the Social Security Act, the program "is not class legislation, but a measure which will benefit the entire public." H.R.
Rep. No. 74-615 (1935), 16.

In any event, the original arguments for capping the Social
Security payroll tax cannot justify the cap today. For one thing,
the cap has moved down the income scale, and the share of total
payroll earnings that are taxable for Social Security is substantially lower today than it was at the program's inception. In 1937,
92 percent of payroll income was subject to Social Security taxation; today, just 83 percent is. Social Security Administration,
*Fast Facts and Figures About Social Security, 2017*, SSA Publication No. 13-11785 (September 2017), accessed October 11, 2018,
www.ssa.gov/policy/docs/chartbooks/fast_facts/2017
/fast_facts17.pdf.

Moreover, by suppressing mid-skilled and encouraging
superordinate labor, the cap itself gives Social Security a class
profile. Pure social insurance is a myth, and payroll taxes inevitably influence labor markets against or for democratic models of
work. The status quo is not neutral but rather affirmatively sides
with meritocratic inequality. Moreover, Social Security no longer requires the cap on the payroll tax in order to survive politically. The Medicare payroll taxes that fund Social Security's
sister program were originally subject to the same cap as Social
Security payroll taxes, but the Medicare income cap was raised in
1990 and repealed entirely in 1993. See Omnibus Budget Reconciliation Act of 1990, Pub. L. 101-508, 104 Stat. 1388, and Omnibus Budget Reconciliation Act of 1993, Pub. L. 103-66, 107
Stat. 312. Some legislators did object that removing the cap adul-
terated the program's tradition of pure social insurance, but
Medicare survives and even expands. See, e.g., U.S. Congress,

Senate, Committee on Finance, *Administration's Tax Proposals:
Hearings Before the S. Comm. on Finance*, 103rd Cong., 1st sess.,
1993, 169 (statement of Sen. Harvey Coustan).

281  **of the income tax:** Today, for example, a married couple filing
jointly pays income tax at a rate of 15 percent on its first $36,900 of
taxable income, 28 percent on taxable income between $36,900
and $89,150, 31 percent on taxable income between $89,150 and
$140,000, 36 percent on taxable income between $140,000 and
$250,000, and 39.6 percent on taxable income above $250,000.
See 26 U.S.C. § 1 (2018).

People whose incomes exceed the Social Security contribution cap must pay, on the margin, only income taxes. Others
must pay both income and wage taxes.

Together, these rate structures entail that a person with an
annual income of $1 million pays a marginal income tax rate just
8.6 percent higher than a person with an annual income of
$90,000 but pays a wage tax rate 12.4 percent lower.

281  **highest aggregate marginal federal tax rate:** Since 1982, the
top marginal federal income tax rate has never exceeded 50 percent. "U.S. Federal Individual Income Tax Rates History, 1862–
2013 (Nominal and Inflation-Adjusted Brackets)," Tax
Foundation, October 17, 2013, accessed October 19, 2018,
https://files.taxfoundation.org/legacy/docs/fed_individual
_rate_history_nominal.pdf. The Social Security wage tax has
over this period risen from 10.8 percent in 1982 to 12.4 percent
beginning in 1990 and has held steady ever since. See www.ssa
.gov/oact/progdata/taxRates.html.

Combining the two rates reveals the distinctive burden
on middle- and upper-middle-class labor. In 1990, for example, a
married couple filing jointly in which each partner earned the
equivalent of $100,000 (in current dollars) faced a total mar-
ginal tax rate of 45.4 percent, while someone whose income was
$1 million faced a rate of just 28 percent. In 2000, the upper-
middle-class coupled faced a total marginal tax rate of 42.9 percent, while the millionaire faced a rate of 39.1 percent. And in
2010, the upper-middle-class couple faced a total marginal tax
rate of 40.4 percent while the millionaire faced a rate of 35 percent. The effect is still larger for households with a single earner
only, because the payroll tax, being assessed on individual wages
rather than household incomes, does not decrease to reflect a
spouse's lack of income, whereas the income tax does.

Moreover, many superordinate workers (hedge fund managers paid in "carried interest," entrepreneurs paid in "founder's
shares," and elite executives paid in appreciated stock) can effectively avoid the progressive income tax, arranging to receive income in ways that are taxed at the lower rates imposed on "capital
gains." Income from capital also faces much, much lower marginal tax rates. Taxes on capital income can often be delayed
(which is economically equivalent to lowering tax rates) and also
often face only the lower capital gains rates.

The Trump tax reforms, although broadly regressive, have
actually helped relieve the relative overtaxation of specifically
middle-class labor income, as whatever wage tax relief they provide is in fact concentrated on middle-class labor. See Rob
Berger, "The New 2018 Federal Income Tax Brackets Rates,"
*Forbes*, December 17, 2017, accessed October 11, 2018, www
.forbes.com/sites/robertberger/2017/12/17/the-new-2018
-federal-income-tax-brackets-rates/#15ef3d52292a.

281  **only half as high:** See Tax Policy Center, Historical Capital
Gains and Taxes, 1954–2014, May 4, 2017, https://www.tax
policycenter.org/statistics/historical-capital-gains-and-taxes.

281  **only about $90,000:** 100,000 × 15.3/100 × 20 = 306,000;
(132,900 × 15.3/100) + (67,100 × 2.9/100) + (1,800,000 × 3.8/
100) = 90,679.6.

282  **by 1.1 percent of GDP:** See "Social Security Policy Options,
2015," Congressional Budget Office, December 2015, accessed
September 29, 2018, www.cbo.gov/sites/default/files/114th
-congress-2015-2016/reports/51011-SSOptions_OneCol-2
.pdf; "Single-Year Tables Consistent with 2016 OASDI Trustees
Report," Social Security Administration, accessed September
29, 2018, www.ssa.gov/oact/tr/2016/lrIndex.html; "Increase
the Maximum Taxable Earnings for the Social Security Payroll
Tax," Congressional Budget Office, December 8, 2016, accessed
September 29, 2018, www.cbo.gov/budget-options/2016
/52266; Jeffrey Liebman and Emmanuel Saez, "Earnings Responses to Increases in Payroll Taxes," September 2006, accessed

September 29, 2018, https://eml.berkeley.edu/~saez/liebman
-saezSSA06.pdf. Expanding the tax base to include non-payroll
labor income would plausibly double the new revenues raised.
See "Publication 15-B (2017), Employer's Tax Guide to Fringe
Benefits," Internal Revenue Service, accessed September 29,
2018, www.irs.gov/publications/p15b/ar02.html; "Relative
Standard Errors for Estimates Published in Employer Costs for
Employee Compensation—News Release Tables," Bureau of
Labor Statistics, June 2018, Table 1, accessed September 29,
2018, www.bls.gov/web/ecec/ececrse.pdf; "Reduce Tax Prefer-
ences for Employment-Based Health Insurance," Congressional
Budget Office, December 8, 2016, accessed September 29, 2018,
www.cbo.gov/budget-options/2016/52246.

282 **its 2018 budget:** See "Fiscal Year 2018 Budget in Brief," Department of Labor, 7, accessed September 29, 2018, www.dol.gov
/sites/default/files/FY2018BIB_0.pdf.

282 **U.S. colleges and universities:** See "Expenditures of Educational Institutions Related to the Gross Domestic Product, by
Level of Institution: Selected Years, 1929–30 Through 2014–
15," National Center for Education Statistics, accessed September 29, 2018, https://nces.ed.gov/programs/digest/d15/tables
/dt15_106.10.asp?referrer=report. The table cites the following
sources: U.S. Department of Education, National Center for
Education Statistics; Biennial Survey of Education in the
United States, 1929–30 Through 1949–50; Statistics of State
School Systems, 1959–60 Through 1969–70; Revenues and Expenditures for Public Elementary and Secondary Education,
1970–71 Through 1986–87; Common Core of Data (CCD),
"National Public Education Financial Survey," 1987–88
through 2012–13; Higher Education General Information Survey (HEGIS), Financial Statistics of Institutions of Higher Education, 1965–66 Through 1985–86; Integrated Postsecondary
Education Data System (IPEDS), "Finance Survey"
(IPEDS-F:FY87–99); and IPEDS Spring 2001 Through Spring
2015, Finance Component. "Selected National Income and
Product Accounts Tables," U.S. Department of Commerce, Bureau of Economic Analysis, retrieved January 29, 2016, https:
//apps.bea.gov/scb/pdf/2016/01%20January/0116_selected
_nipa_tables.pdf (table prepared January 2016; all figures in
current dollars).

282 **mid-skilled, middle-class workers:** Paying the subsidies to
employers will drive up pretax wages and emphasize middle-
class industry and the dignity of mid-skilled work (whereas paying subsidies to employees would drive down pretax wages and
establish an atmosphere of condescension). This point is also
made by Zachary Liscow, "A Plan for America's Dispossessed"
(manuscript, November 2016).

283 **from capturing the subsidies:** See, e.g., Matthew Dimick,
"Should the Law Do Anything About Economic Inequality?,"
*Cornell Journal of Law and Public Policy* 26, no. 1 (2016); Jesse
Rothstein, "Is the EITC as Good as an NIT? Conditional Cash
Transfers and Incidence," *American Economic Journal: Eco-
nomic Policy* 2 (2010): 177–79; David Lee and Emmanuel Saez,
"Optimal Minimum Wage Policy in Competitive Labor Mar-
kets," *Journal of Public Economics* 96 (2012): 739 ("With a bind-
ing minimum wage . . . an EITC expansion would increase
after-tax incomes of low-skilled workers dollar for dollar.").

283 **support middle-class jobs and wages:** "Sens. Warner, Casey,
and Stabenow Introduce Proposal to Encourage Employers to
Provide Job Training That Moves Workers up the Economic
Ladder," Mark R. Warner, U.S. Senator from the Common-
wealth of Virginia, October 31, 2017, www.warner.senate.gov
/public/index.cfm/pressreleases?ID=F440D3FD-3C49-4111
-8C7C-61CA0B0C3D05.

283 **roughly $150 billion per year:** See Neera Tanden et al.,
"Toward a Marshall Plan for America," Center for American
Progress, May 16, 2017, www.americanprogress.org/issues
/economy/reports/2017/05/16/432499/toward-marshall-plan
-america.

283 **backs federal wage subsidies:** See Peter Georgescu, *Capitalists
Arise! End Economic Inequality, Grow the Middle Class, Heal the
Nation* (Oakland, CA: Berrett-Koehler, 2017); Peter Georgescu,
"Capitalists, Arise: We Need to Deal with Income Inequality,"
*New York Times*, August 7, 2015, accessed September 29, 2018,
www.nytimes.com/2015/08/09/opinion/sunday/cap
italists-arise-we-need-to-deal-with-income-inequality.html

?mcubz=3. In the 2016 cycle, Langone contributed $535,700 to
support exclusively Republican candidates. See "Kenneth Langone Political Campaign Contributions—2016 Election Cycle,"
Campaignmoney.com, www.campaignmoney.com/political
/contributions/kenneth-langone.asp?cycle=16.

283 **for middle-class labor in its stead:** See Lawrence L. Katz,
"Wage Subsidies for the Disadvantaged," in *Generating Jobs*, ed.
Richard B. Freeman and Peter Gottschalk (New York: Russell
Sage Foundation, 1998), 21–53; Timothy J. Bartik, *Jobs for the
Poor: Can Labor Demand Policies Help?* (New York: Russell
Sage Foundation, 2001). See also Zachary Liscow, "A Plan for
America's Dispossessed" (manuscript, November 2016). Liscow
would concentrate the wage subsidies geographically, in counties
with low ratios of employment to population.

284 **"Same Bosses, Same Fight":** See "Same Bosses, Same Fight,"
Poster Workshop, www.posterworkshop.co.uk/students/page
_14.html.

285 **the grand alliance that the poster championed:** The diagnosis
of meritocratic inequality invites a new politics of redistribution
in another sense also. The case for democratic equality suits a
broad range of incumbent political ideologies. Progressives
straightforwardly embrace democratic equality because it un-
does the massive social and economic stratification that meritocracy has produced. Conservatives can also embrace democratic
equality, although this affinity takes a little more explaining.
Insofar as meritocratic inequality reflects distortions in training
and labor markets, democratic reforms would perfect rather
than obstruct free markets. Democratic equality sets aside redistribution in favor of achieving a more equal market distribution;
it aspires not to constrain but rather to perfect labor markets
(freeing markets from the hyper-meritocratic distortions). By
marrying markets and equality, the democratic project brings
free-market conservatives and egalitarian progressives together.

286 **only by working together:** This coalition is no more fanciful
than the coalitions that the Enlightenment ideal of universal
humanity created when it allowed people to look past clan, religion, and race to see one other as free and equal citizens. Most
recently, this ideal has enabled the civil rights movement, from
midcentury through the present day, to appreciate the harms
that racial discrimination imposes on everyone whom it affects,
across the racial divide.

The diagnosis of meritocratic inequality offers a similar
promise for economic life. The diagnosis invites, for the first
time in human history, a cooperative politics of economic redistribution. It replaces the zero-sum competition between the rich
and the rest and between capital and labor that has dominated
redistribution from time immemorial with a positive-sum collaboration to restore industry, income, and honor to middle-
class workers and to restore freedom and authenticity to
superordinate ones.

286 **they have reason to join:** These formulations apply the old
Fabian slogan—"Educate, Agitate, Organize." "Our History,"
Fabian Society, accessed September 29, 2018, https://fabians
.org.uk/about-us/our-history.

286 **a whole world to win:** See Karl Marx and Friedrich Engels, *The
Communist Manifesto* (New York: Simon & Schuster, 1988).

## Figures and Tables

292 **Average Hours Worked per Week by Income Rank:** Systematic data on the work habits of the top 1 percent are difficult to
come by. Many of the most prominent data sets on wages and
hours top-code. This means that they decline to separate out the
most elite slices of their populations, but rather merge these
(without identification) into larger, less select groups. Moreover,
the elite (including because they work such long hours) are reluctant to participate in time-consuming and intrusive surveys.

The data in the figure come from the Integrated Public
Use Microdata Series (funded by the National Institute of Child
Health and Human Development), which includes information
about incomes and usual hours worked from the Federal Census
and the American Community Survey. Data for 1940, 1950,
1960, 1970, 1980, 1990, and 2000 come from the census. Annual data from 2001 onward come from the American Community Survey. All observations in the sample used to construct
this figure are (1) full-time employed, (2) not self-employed, (3)
male, and (4) age 25–64.

The data set, which is based on survey responses, collected 340,000 observations in 1950 and has expanded, after 1970, to include between two and eleven million valid observations per year. See IPUMS-USA Table 2, "Valid Income Observations." For each person, the data set reports both income and, for persons who worked in the previous year, the average number of hours usually worked per week. (For 1940, 1950, 1980, and 1990, the data reports "Hours worked last week"—HRSWORK1—and beginning in 1980 the data reports "Usual hours worked per week"—UHRSWORK. The data also include an income variable, INCWAGE, which includes wages, salaries, commissions, cash bonuses, tips, and other money income received from an employer but does not include payments in kind or reimbursements for business expenses. See IPUMS USA, "INCWAGE: Wage and Salary Income: Description," https://usa.ipums.org /usa-action/variables/INCWAGE#description_section. The income variable is top-coded, but in a way that makes it possible to identify the very top earners, by coding U.S. state means above the top-coding threshold until 2002 and coding at the 99.5th percentile for each state from 2003 onward. See IPUMS USA, "INCWAGE: Wage and Salary Income: Codes," https://usa.ip ums.org/usa-action/variables/INCWAGE#codes_section. The top 1 percent in the figure may thus depart from the true top 1 percent, but not by much and in either direction.

The data make it possible to depict the evolving relationship between the income and usual hours, as in the figure in the text. The patchwork character of the data behind the figure counsels against reading a false precision into the levels that it reports. But the trends are robust enough to remain persuasive even if necessarily imprecise. Moreover, the figure's basic lesson—of a rising time divide between elite and non-elite work hours—is confirmed by any number of other studies, which gather data on work hours using a wide variety of methods, ranging from surveys like those that underlie the figure to time diaries to buzzers that are worn by subjects and solicit contemporaneous responses stating whether or not the subject is working at random times throughout the day.

293 **Income Poverty, Consumption Poverty, and the Income Share of the Top 1 Percent:** The data behind the figure may be found in the following sources: The World Wealth and Income Database, Top 1% Income Share—Including Capital Gains; U.S. Census Bruse, "Historical Poverty Tables: People and Families—1959 to 2017," Current Population Survey, Table 2, last modified August 28, 2018, www.census.gov/data/tables /time-series/demo/income-poverty/historical-poverty-people .html; Bruce Meyer and James X. Sullivan, "Winning the War: Poverty from the Great Society to the Great Recession," *Brookings Papers on Economic Activity* (Fall 2012): 133–200, Table 1.

It would be instructive to construct a series for the top 1 percent's consumption share, but existing data do not allow this. The Consumer Expenditure Survey tracks expenditure shares by quintiles of pretax income, and (beginning more recently) by deciles of pretax income. See, e.g., Bureau of Labor Statistics, Consumer Expenditure Survey (2015), Table 1101, www.bls .gov/cex/2015/combined/quintile.pdf, and Bureau of Labor Statistics, Consumer Expenditure Survey (2015), Table 1110, www.bls.gov/cex/2015/combined/decile.pdf. The survey also currently tracks consumption by income buckets that range from "less than $15,000" to "$200,000 or more" (which represents roughly the top 5 percent in 2015). See Bureau of Labor Statistics, Consumer Expenditure Survey (2015), Table 1203, www.bls.gov/cex/2015/combined/income.pdf. But decile tracking began only recently and the income buckets used by the survey have changed over time, so that no good time series for top/bottom ratios can be constructed using these categories. Moreover, the survey still does not track consumption in still narrower economic elites. Time trends in consumption by quintile are summarized over 1984–2010 by Kevin A. Hassett and Aparna Mathur, "A New Measure of Consumption Inequality," American Enterprise Institute Economic Studies Series, June 25, 2012, 5 and Figure 1, www.aei.org/publication/a-new-measure-of-consumption-inequality/. Hassett and Mathur find only a modest increase in the top/bottom quintile consumption ratios over the period of their study.

294 **Ratios of Representative High, Middle, and Low Incomes over Time:** Data from the World Top Incomes Database,

Post-tax national income / equal-split adults / Average / Adults / constant 2015 local currency, https://wid.world/country/usa/.

295 **key points in the overall income distribution:** The figure uses post-tax-and-transfer rather than market incomes in order to avoid repeating the errors made in computing the official poverty statistics. The true conditions of the rich, middle class, and poor in the United States today reflect the circumstances that they each enjoy after the state—with both its taxes and its social welfare programs—has intervened in their lives.

296 **U.S. Top-End, Bottom-End, and Full Gini Coefficients over Time:** Data from the World Top Incomes Database, Post-tax national income / equal-split adults / Average / Adults / constant 2015 local currency, https://wid.world/country/usa/.

297 **calculated in three ways:** The figures again calculate the Gini coefficients using post-tax-and-transfer incomes, in order to capture the true circumstances of the various segments of the economy that the coefficients describe.

297 **bottom seven-tenths of the U.S. income distribution:** Some studies go even further and question whether there has been any steady or even significant rise in economic inequality across the bottom 99 percent of the distribution. For a review, see Robert J. Gordon, "Misperceptions About the Magnitude and Timing of Changes in American Income Inequality," NBER Working Paper No. 15351 (September 2009), www.nber.org/papers/w15351.

298 **Ratios of Education Expenditures by Income and Education:** The data used to construct the ratios of education expenditures present two complexities. First, the most comprehensive data on education expenditures, produced by the Bureau of Labor Statistics, distinguish incomes by quintiles only rather than by any finer slices. So the rich are thus represented, in the education expenditure series, by the top quintile rather than by the average of the top 1 percent (as they are in Figure 1.3). Second, the BLS data independently measure education expenditures of many households composed of students and allocate these to the bottom quintile by income, which introduces a dramatic and misleading upward distortion into the education expenditure series for the poor. The figure therefore takes the second rather than the bottom quintile as its representative of education expenditures by the poor.

Both these decisions are validated by the third, shorter data series also represented in the figure. This series reports the ratios of elite/median and median/bottom expenditures on education, measuring eliteness not by income but rather by the highest degree held by the most educated household member. The BLS's education categories separate out both households without anyone who holds even a high school degree and households with members who hold post-BA degrees. These are truer measures of low and high socioeconomic status than the income categories that the BLS makes available. The series constructed in this way are shorter than the others (the BLS data do not go as far back in time). But they align nicely with the ratios reported using the longer if less precise income series.

300 **90/50 and 50/10 Income Achievement Gaps for Reading and Math:** See Reardon, "The Widening Academic Achievement Gap," 102, 103, Figures 5.7, 5.8. See also Reardon, "No Rich Child Left Behind."

Reardon observes that the timing of divergence in the achievement and income gaps does not quite match up, although efforts to make the association are complicated by the fact that a family's annual and lifetime incomes do not necessarily move together. Setting these complications aside, it remains true that a dollar of income appears to buy more academic achievement today than it did in past decades (100–104).

301 **constructed by the sociologist Sean Reardon:** Reardon aggregates the results of many achievement tests, administered in overlapping series over many years, and this aggregation requires him to make adjustments that render individual test results comparable and to fit a line over many data points. Studies are rendered comparable in spite of measuring achievement on different scales by adjusting scores for the reliability of the tests and then expressing test score gaps in terms of standard deviations. This is, as Reardon says, "standard practice when comparing achievement gaps measured with different tests (see, for example, Clotfelter, Ladd, and Vigdor 2006; Fryer and Levitt 2004, 2006; Grissmer, Flanagan, and Williamson 1998; Hedges and Nowell 1999; Neal 2006; Phillips et al. 1998; Reardon and

Galindo 2009). So long as the true variance of achievement remains constant over time, this allows valid comparisons in the size of the gaps across different studies using different tests." See Reardon, "The Widening Academic Achievement Gap," 94. The basic result that 90/50 achievement gaps have been rising even as 50/10 gaps have held roughly steady and in some cases even fallen reappears across a range of estimation techniques. See Charles A. Nelson and Margaret A. Sheridan, "Online Appendices and Glossary" to "Lessons from Neuroscience Research for Understanding Causal Links Between Family and Neighborhood Characteristics and Educational Outcomes," in *Whither Opportunity? Rising Inequality, Schools, and Children's Life Chances*, ed. Richard Murnane and Greg Duncan (New York: Russell Sage Foundation, 2011), section 5.A2, www .russellsage.org/sites/default/files/duncan_murnane_online _appendix.pdf.

The precise contours in the figure therefore reflect Reardon's considered judgments about the data and should be read to illuminate trends rather than for actuarial precision. The basic trends that the figure reports are robust.

302    **GDP Share, Employment Share, and Relative Income and Education for Finance, 1947–2005:** The figure is inspired by Philippon and Reshef, "Wages and Human Capital," 1558, Figure 1, and 1561, Figure 2. Finance includes insurance but excludes real estate. GDP share is computed as the ratio of nominal value added by the finance sector to the nominal GDP of the United States. Data from Annual Industrial Accounts, Bureau of Economic Analysis. Relative education is computed as the share of hours worked by employees with at least a college degree in the financial sector minus the corresponding share of hours in the rest of the private sector. Data from March CPS.

303    **relative income and education:** Relative income is the fraction of annual income per financial employee in excess of annual income per nonfinancial employee. Relative education is the difference between the fraction of financial employees with college degrees and the fraction of non-financial employees with college degrees. The relative education series is plotted as a linear transformation of the underlying values to allow for visual comparison of the series. While the correlation between the two series is unaffected by this transformation, their similar levels are an artifact of scaling.

303    **their private-sector counterparts:** See Philippon and Reshef, "Skill Biased Financial Development," 8. These percentages are derived by calculating the share of work hours provided by college-educated workers in each sector.

303    **began gently to decline:** See Philippon and Reshef, "Skill Biased Financial Development," 5. Philippon and Reshef point out that the changes that they document are driven by a rebalancing of the financial sector's various subsectors, so that traditional banking has declined relative to other aspects of finance and in particular investment (p. 6). For another view, see Thomas I. Palley, "Financialization: What It Is and Why It Matters," Levy Economics Institute Working Paper no. 525, December 2007 (using data from the Economic Report of the President [from 2007]).

For finance's share of employee compensation, see David A. Zalewski and Charles J. Whalen, "Financialization and Economic Inequality," *Journal of Economic Issues* 44, no. 3 (2010): 757–77, reporting on Philippon and Reshef, "Skill Biased Financial Development."

303    **increasing education and relative income:** See Philippon and Reshef, "Skill Biased Financial Development," 8. These percentages are derived by calculating the share of work hours provided by college-educated workers in each sector.

303    **fewer increasingly elite workers:** To be sure, deregulation changed the structure of finance just as elite finance-sector wages began to rise. Indeed, deregulation enabled the creation and adoption of the financial techniques that make super-skilled financial labor so highly paid today. But it is a mistake to leap from these uncontested facts to the conclusion that deregulated elite finance workers' immense incomes arise from exploitation or rent seeking. If the techniques employed by deregulated finance make super-skilled finance workers especially productive, then no increase in rent seeking is required to explain the increase in finance-sector wages. The figures, which show that relatively fewer, relatively more-skilled workers are taking the

same cut from a relatively rising share of GDP explain rising finance-sector wages in this way, without needing to resort to rising rent seeking.

None of this demonstrates, nor does it even assert, that finance workers extract no rents. They surely do, and the rents may even have increased in recent decades. But the greater part of rising finance-sector incomes neither requires nor in fact involves increased rent seeking.

Philippon and Reshef, who have made the most careful study of finance sector rents, conclude that nonmeritocratic causes contributed little to rising finance-sector incomes from the 1970s through the early 1990s and that, since the 1990s, between 20 and 30 percent of finance's risk-adjusted wages stems from sources besides skill. See Philippon and Reshef, "Wages and Human Capital," 1553, 1603, 1605. The report of a recent and substantial increase in finance-sector rents rightly received attention; but the study is most notable for the converse of this result, namely that even in recent decades, between 70 and 80 percent of the finance sector's rising wages stems from its workers' rising skill. Probably this underestimates the true share, as the study measures finance workers' skill by counting their number of years at school, and this single-minded focus on quantity neglects distinctive increases in the quality and intensiveness of elite finance workers' educations. Elite finance workers increasingly and now overwhelmingly graduate from the very most august and intensive colleges and universities, and these schools spend much, much more per student per year than their competitors today or than they themselves used to do.

304    **Percent Changes in Employment Shares for Routine and Fluid Skills:** The figure comes from Jaimovich and Siu, "Job Polarization and Jobless Recoveries."

305    **Earnings Segmentation by Education Level:** The data for the figure come from Carnevale, Rose, and Cheah, "The College Payoff."

305    **the median worker from the top twentieth:** Slightly under half of the U.S. population over twenty-five has no education at all beyond high school (roughly 70 percent do not have a BA), slightly over 10 percent hold a post-BA degree, and a little under 5 percent hold a doctorate or a professional degree. See Camille L. Ryan and Kurt Bauman, *Educational Attainment in the United States: 2015*, U.S. Census Bureau, Current Population Reports no. P20-578 (March 2016), accessed November 19, 2018, www .census.gov/content/dam/Census/library/publications/2016 /demo/p20-578.pdf. See also Carnevale, Rose, and Cheah, "The College Payoff," 6, and Sandy Baum and Patricia Steele, "Who Goes to Graduate School and Who Succeeds?," the Urban Institute (January 2017), accessed April 9, 2019, www.urban.org /sites/default/files/publication/86981/who_goes_to_gradu ate_school_and_who_succeeds_1.pdf.

306    **Incomes of the Bottom 90 Percent and Per Capita Consumption and Debt over Time:** The figure is inspired by Robert Hockett and Daniel Dillon, "Income Inequality and Market Fragility," Figure 8. Hockett and Dillon in fact find an even steeper increase in household debt. The data behind the figure come from: Federal Reserve Board, Flow of Funds—Households and Nonprofit Organizations, Total Liabilities; Bureau of Economic Analysis, Personal Consumption Expenditures (PCE) and PCE Price Index; The World Top Incomes Database, Bottom 90% Average Income Including Capital Gains; U.S. Census Bureau Population Estimates.

306    **but rather through debt:** The debt invites a hidden form of redistribution that lurks in the background of American policy as a kind of safety net below the social safety net of the conventional welfare state. Personal bankruptcy protection for insolvent debtors—the middle-class version of the Greenspan put—amounts to an implicit tax on all lenders and borrowers used to establish a social safety net for those borrowers who cannot sustain their consumption, even through ready credit. And bankruptcies have famously skyrocketed in recent years, effectively increasing the implicit tax rate, although tightening bankruptcy laws increasingly withdraw even the failsafe net and reduced even this highly attenuated form of economic redistribution. For more on bankruptcy and its connections to economic inequality and the welfare state, see, e.g., Karen Dynan, "The Income Rollercoaster: Rising Income Volatility and Its Implications," *Pathways* (Spring 2010): 3–6.

306   **as income fell short:** Others who have made similar observations
      include: Drennan, *Income Inequality*, 62 ("Money taken out from
      appreciating housing was *not* used to pay down debt because in-
      debtedness rose. Rather, it was used to support consumption in
      the face of stagnant income."); Edward Wolff, "Recent Trends in
      Household Wealth in the United States: Rising Debt and the
      Middle-Class Squeeze—An Update to 2007," Levy Economics
      Institute, Working Paper No. 589 ("Where did the borrowing
      go? . . . Middle class households experiencing stagnating incomes,
      expanded their debt almost exclusively in order to finance con-
      sumption expenditures."); Hockett and Dillon, "Income In-
      equality and Market Fragility" ("As the wealthy amass more of
      the aggregate income, the average household ramps up its borrow-
      ing to maintain accustomed living standards."). See also Atif
      Mian and Amir Sufi, "The Consequences of Mortgage Credit
      Expansion: Evidence from the U.S. Mortgage Default Crisis,"
      *Quarterly Journal of Economics* 24, no. 4 (November 2009):
      1449–96; Atif Mian and Amir Sufi, "House Prices, Home
      Equity–Based Borrowing, and the United States Household
      Leverage Crisis," NBER Working Paper No. 15283 (2009); and
      Atif Mian and Amir Sufi, "Household Leverage and the Reces-
      sion of 2007 to 2009," NBER Working Paper No. 15896 (2010).

306   **the same basic model as payday lending:** International compar-
      isons further emphasize the astonishing scale of debt-financed
      consumption in the United States. Americans financed their
      spending, in 2006, by borrowing roughly 70 percent of the entire
      world's excess savings (so that Americans became, in effect, the
      consumer of last resort sustaining demand across the entire global
      economic order). Rajan, *Fault Lines*, 203. Net exporting econo-
      mies, including most notably China, generated massive savings
      where—in stark contrast to the United States—social and politi-
      cal orders managed to restrain the consumption expectations of
      ordinary citizens. By loaning their savings to the United States,
      these economies artificially depress their own currencies, and fur-
      ther boost their exports and hence savings. Accordingly, insofar
      as U.S. policy that stimulates domestic debt-financed consump-
      tion also stimulates foreign export-financed savings, the U.S.
      stimulus supports employment overseas rather than at home. For
      a similar observation, see Rajan, *Fault Lines*, 106.
           Moreover, Americans consume staggeringly more than
      their counterparts in other rich nations. Broadly comparable

measures that aggregate an individual's personal consumption
      are difficult to construct. But because almost all consumption
      requires energy somewhere along the way, oil use is a good proxy
      for consumption. And the average American consumes roughly
      twice the oil of the average citizen of Germany, France, or
      Japan—even though the United States and these countries have
      roughly equivalent per capita GDPs. Rajan, *Fault Lines*, 203.
      The extra 100 percent of the average German's consumption
      that the average American consumes must, over the long run, be
      debt financed.

307   **The Returns to Skill and Unequal Investments in Education:**
      The data for the figure come from OECD, *OECD Skills Outlook
      2013*, "Difference between adults with at least one parent who
      attained tertiary and neither parent who attained upper second-
      ary," Table A3.1; "Tertiary gap in wages and in the use of skills at
      work," Table A4.13.

307   **"participate in society":** See OECD, *PISA 2012 Assessment
      and Analytic Framework* (2013), 60, www.oecd.org/pisa/pisap
      roducts/PISA%202012%20framework%20e-book_final.pdf.
      The figure uses literacy rather than mathematics skills because
      the OECD has not published data reporting the effect of par-
      ents' incomes on children's mathematics skills. Nevertheless,
      literacy and mathematics skills are highly correlated throughout
      the OECD's data.

308   **Children's Changing Odds of Earning More Than Their
      Parents:** The figure follows Raj Chetty et al., "The Fading
      American Dream: Trends in Absolute Income Mobility Since
      1940," *Science* 356, no. 6336 (April 2017): 398–406, Figure 1.

312   **The average age at first birth:** Hymowitz et al., *Knot Yet*, 8,
      Figures IIA–IIC.

312   **the average life expectancy:** Raj Chetty et al., "The Associa-
      tion Between Income and Life Expectancy in the United States,
      2001–2014," *Journal of the American Medical Association* 315,
      no. 16 (2016): 1750–66, 1753.

312   **the average annual . . . return for the S&P 500:** See "Online
      Data Robert Shiller," Yale University Department of Econom-
      ics, http://www.econ.yale.edu/~shiller/data.htm.

312   **the average annual real rate of return for the entire U.S.
      stock market:** Personal communication from Eric Haas, who
      derived the rates using index data from Dimensional Fund
      Advisors.

# INDEX

abortion, 208

Acemoglu, Daron, 359*n*(142), 379*nn*(203–204), 392*n*(249), 393*nn*(250–51), 394*nn*(252–53), 395*nn*(254), 397*n*(267)

achievement gaps
income-based, 26, 41, 131–33, 300fig, 301
race-based, 26, 50, 99, 131

*Affluent Society, The* (Galbraith), 21, 99

Afghanistan war, 205

alcohol abuse. *See* drug/alcohol abuse

alienation, 37–38, 39–40, 192–93

altruism. *See* elite service promise

Alvaredo, Facundo, 316*n*(13), 319*n*(23), 335*n*(87), 337*n*(91), 376*nn*(188)

Amazon
elite work intensity, 43, 44, 82–83
labor market polarization, 177, 178, 187
management innovations, 172–73, 175
workplace subordination, 173, 206

ancien régime. *See* aristocracy

anti-immigrant policies, 271

anti-intellectualism. *See* populism

Apple Computer, 83, 141, 246

aristocracy
capital dominance under, 92
class divide under, 46
consumption under, 216
economic justice arguments on, 15, 106, 109
elite education under, 6, 7, 17, 111–12, 114
elite leisure under, 3–4, 77, 79–80, 86–87, 95–96, 193–94, 207

and elite rituals, xii
elite work under, 8–9, 11
families under, 207
industry/income opposition under, 3–4
and inheritance, xiv–xv, 4, 89, 94, 115, 145–46, 150–51, 261
meritocracy as positive alternative to, ix, xi, 14, 263–64
meritocracy as return to, 15, 47, 260–62, 268–69
nature of elite wealth under, 3–4, 35–36, 262
1960s rebellion against, 284–85
as virtuous, 262–64, 268
wealth as emancipatory under, 36, 37, 41, 193–94

Aristotle, 262, 263

asset management services, 236
*See also* finance industry

assortative mating, 116–17

athletes, 43, 84

AT&T, 173

auto industry, 20–21, 22, 23

bankers' hours, 10, 81, 82

banking. *See* finance industry

Bell Labs, 237

Bender, Wilbur J., 112

Bentley Motors, 220

Beyoncé, 178, 221

Bezos, Jeff, 9, 82, 178

Biden, Joe, xii

and leisure, 215–16

and marriage, 48, 116–17, 207–8, 210–11

and meritocratic inequality, xvi, 201–2

midcentury dampening of, 46–47, 199–201, 217, 223–24

and middle-class resentment, xvi–xvii

and middle-class workplace subordination, 205–6

and military, 204–5

and nativism, 60

and politics, 211–14

and populism, 60, 64–65, 211

and private vs. public sector work, 56–57

and religion, 48, 208–9, 211

and shared dissatisfaction, xxii, xxiii, 274–75, 285

and shrinking of middle class, 201–2

and social connectedness, 51, 208–9

and Trump presidency, xvii, xviii, 69, 214

and valorization of industry, 202, 206

clerical jobs, 178

Clinton, Bill, xii, 197–98, 199, 224, 228, 234

Clinton, Chelsea, 228–29

Clinton, Hillary, 61, 69, 70, 198

Cohn, Gary, 58

collective anxiety, xvi, xviii, xix

college wage premium, 239, 251–52, 307fig

competition

and admissions, 6–7, 17, 33, 34, 122–23, 133–34, 142–43, 151–52

and burdens on elites, xvi, xvii–xviii, 33, 34–35, 37, 153–54, 155

and elite education, xvii–xviii, 8, 35, 153–54

and elite work, 33–34, 35, 82–83, 158, 188–89, 190

and human capital, 37, 154

and precarious dynastic succession, xv, 35, 115–16, 262

and valorization of industry, 157–58

Conant, James Bryant, 6, 112

Congress, 57

consulting industry, 90, 97, 174, 176, 245–46

*See also* management

consumption

and class divide, 216–21, 224–25

and debt, 233–35, 306fig

and poverty rates, 102–4, 293fig

Container Corporation of America, 172

corporate control, market for, 243–44, 280

corporate reengineering, 246

corporate restructuring, 83, 173–74, 176, 243, 244–45, 246

critiques of meritocracy, xx

and aristocracy, 15

and burdens on elites, 78, 273

and capital dominance, 13, 15, 88–89, 92–94

early, 258–59

and individual morality, x, 16–17, 18, 154–55, 268, 269

and meritocratic inequality as justified, 106–7, 109–10

unhelpfulness of, 16, 79, 272–73

culture, and class divide, 48, 202, 208–9, 211–16

cycle of meritocracy, 12–13, 27, 71–72

and competition, 34

and definition of merit, 264–67, 268

and elite dynastic inheritance, 71–73

and farmer/warrior parable, 267–68

and inequality of opportunity, 254–55

and innovation-based labor market polarization, 239–40, 254, 267–68

instability of, 264–65

and labor market polarization, 255

and reform agenda, 283–84

and resource curse, 256–57

and return to aristocracy, 261

Dahl, Robert, 51, 52

debt, 218–19, 222–23, 233–36, 306fig

debt financing, 242–43

democracy, suppression of, 71

and elite political power, 51–54

and government responsiveness, 52

and income defense industry, 54–58

democratic culture

midcentury society, 29, 47, 170, 197–201

in middle-class cities, 28–29

democratic equality, 70–71, 285–86

depression, 42

derivatives, 53–54, 167

*See also* finance industry

Dickens, Charles, 219

Dimon, Jamie, 18

Disraeli, Benjamin, 50

diversity. *See* identity politics